Edge-Cloud Computing and Federated-Split Learning in the Internet of Things

Edge-Cloud Computing and Federated-Split Learning in the Internet of Things

Editors

Qiang Duan
Zhihui Lu

Basel • Beijing • Wuhan • Barcelona • Belgrade • Novi Sad • Cluj • Manchester

Editors
Qiang Duan
Information Sciences &
Technology
Pennsylvania State University
Abington
USA

Zhihui Lu
School of Computer Science
Fudan University
Shanghai
China

Editorial Office
MDPI AG
Grosspeteranlage 5
4052 Basel, Switzerland

This is a reprint of articles from the Special Issue published online in the open access journal *Future Internet* (ISSN 1999-5903) (available at: https://www.mdpi.com/journal/futureinternet/special_issues/M1736LO4CB).

For citation purposes, cite each article independently as indicated on the article page online and as indicated below:

Lastname, A.A.; Lastname, B.B. Article Title. *Journal Name* **Year**, *Volume Number*, Page Range.

ISBN 978-3-7258-1994-2 (Hbk)
ISBN 978-3-7258-1993-5 (PDF)
doi.org/10.3390/books978-3-7258-1993-5

© 2024 by the authors. Articles in this book are Open Access and distributed under the Creative Commons Attribution (CC BY) license. The book as a whole is distributed by MDPI under the terms and conditions of the Creative Commons Attribution-NonCommercial-NoDerivs (CC BY-NC-ND) license.

Contents

About the Editors vii

Qiang Duan and Zhihui Lu
Edge Cloud Computing and Federated–Split Learning in Internet of Things
Reprinted from: *Future Internet* **2024**, *16*, 227, doi:10.3390/fi16070227 1

Fotis Nikolaidis, Moysis Symeonides and Demetris Trihinas
Towards Efficient Resource Allocation for Federated Learning in Virtualized Managed Environments
Reprinted from: *Future Internet* **2023**, *15*, 261, doi:10.3390/fi15080261 5

Weihong Cai and Fengxi Duan
Task Scheduling for Federated Learning in Edge Cloud Computing Environments by Using Adaptive-Greedy Dingo Optimization Algorithm and Binary Salp Swarm Algorithm
Reprinted from: *Future Internet* **2023**, *15*, 357, doi:10.3390/fi15110357 31

Lorenzo Ridolfi, David Naseh, Swapnil Sadashiv Shinde and Daniele Tarchi
Implementation and Evaluation of a Federated Learning Framework on Raspberry PI Platforms for IoT 6G Applications
Reprinted from: *Future Internet* **2023**, *15*, 358, doi:10.3390/fi15110358 54

Ahmed A. Al-Saedi, Veselka Boeva and Emiliano Casalicchio
FedCO: Communication-Efficient Federated Learning via Clustering Optimization
Reprinted from: *Future Internet* **2022**, *14*, 377, doi:10.3390/fi14120377 77

Liangkun Yu, Xiang Sun, Rana Albelaihi and Chen Yi
Latency-Aware Semi-Synchronous Client Selection and Model Aggregation for Wireless Federated Learning
Reprinted from: *Future Internet* **2023**, *1*, 352, doi:10.3390/fi15110352 104

Rezak Aziz, Soumya Banerjee, Samia Bouzefrane and Thinh Le Vinh
Exploring Homomorphic Encryption and Differential Privacy Techniques towards Secure Federated Learning Paradigm
Reprinted from: *Future Internet* **2023**, *15*, 310, doi:10.3390/fi15090310 119

Bowen Liu and Qiang Tang
Secure Data Sharing in Federated Learning through Blockchain-Based Aggregation
Reprinted from: *Future Internet* **2024**, *16*, 133, doi:10.3390/fi16040133 144

Hanyue Xu, Kah Phooi Seng, Jeremy Smith and Li Minn Ang
Multi-Level Split Federated Learning for Large-Scale AIoT System Based on Smart Cities
Reprinted from: *Future Internet* **2024**, *16*, 82, doi:10.3390/fi16030082 157

Feng Zhou, Shijing Hu, Xin Du, Xiaoli Wan and Jie Wu
A Lightweight Neural Network Model for Disease Risk Prediction in Edge Intelligent Computing Architecture
Reprinted from: *Future Internet* **2024**, *16*, 75, doi:10.3390/fi16030075 176

Lijun Zu, Wenyu Qi, Hongyi Li, Xiaohua Men, Zhihui Lu, Jiawei Ye and Liang Zhang
UP-SDCG: A Method of Sensitive Data Classification for Collaborative Edge Computing in Financial Cloud Environment
Reprinted from: *Future Internet* **2024**, *16*, 102, doi:10.3390/fi16030102 191

LiJun zu, Hongyi Li, Liang Zhang, Zhihui Lu, Jiawei Ye, Xiaoxia Zhao and Shijing Hu
E-SAWM: A Semantic Analysis-Based ODF Watermarking Algorithm for Edge Cloud Scenarios
Reprinted from: *Future Internet* **2023**, *15*, 283, doi:10.3390/fi15090283 . . . . **215**

Jadil Alsamiri and Khalid Alsubhi
Federated Learning for Intrusion Detection Systems in Internet of Vehicles: A General Taxonomy, Applications, and Future Directions
Reprinted from: *Future Internet* **2023**, *15*, 403, doi:10.3390/fi15120403 . . . . **232**

About the Editors

Qiang Duan

Qiang Duan is a professor at the College of Information Sciences and Technology, Pennsylvania State University Abington College. His current research interests include network virtualization and softwarization, cognitive and autonomous networking, and edge-computing-based ubiquitous intelligence. He has published three books and more than 100 research papers in these areas. He is a senior member of the IEEE.

Zhihui Lu

Zhihui Lu is a professor at the School of Computer Science at Fudan University. He received a Ph.D. computer science degree from Fudan University in 2004, and is a member of the IEEE and China Computer Federation's service computing specialized committee. His research interests include cloud computing and service computing technology, big data architecture, edge computing and IoT-distributed systems. He has (co-)authored two books and more than 100 journal articles and conference papers in these areas.

Editorial

Edge Cloud Computing and Federated–Split Learning in Internet of Things

Qiang Duan [1,*] and Zhihui Lu [2]

[1] Information Sciences and Technology Department, Pennsylvania State University, Abington, PA 19001, USA
[2] School of Computer Science, Fudan University, Shanghai 200437, China; lzh@fudan.edu.cn
* Correspondence: qduan@psu.edu

Citation: Duan, Q.; Lu Z. Edge Cloud Computing and Federated–Split Learning in Internet of Things. *Future Internet* **2024**, *16*, 227. https://doi.org/10.3390/fi16070227

Received: 12 June 2024
Accepted: 19 June 2024
Published: 28 June 2024

Copyright: © 2024 by the authors. Licensee MDPI, Basel, Switzerland. This article is an open access article distributed under the terms and conditions of the Creative Commons Attribution (CC BY) license (https:// creativecommons.org/licenses/by/ 4.0/).

The wide deployment of the Internet of Things (IoT) necessitates new machine learning (ML) methods and distributed computing paradigms to enable various ML-based IoT applications to effectively process huge amounts of data. Federated Learning (FL) is a new collaborative learning method that allows multiple data owners to cooperate in ML model training without exposing private data. Split Learning (SL) is an emerging collaborative learning method that splits an ML model into multiple portions that are then trained collaboratively by different entities. FL and SL each have unique advantages and limitations and may complement each other in facilitating effective collaborative learning in an IoT environment. On the other hand, the rapid development of edge cloud computing technologies enables a distributed computing platform in IoT upon which FL and SL frameworks can be deployed. Therefore, the deployment of FL and SL in an edge cloud platform in an IoT environment has become an active area of research, attracting interest from both academia and industry. This Special Issue aims to present the latest research advances in this interdisciplinary field of edge cloud computing and federated–split learning.

This Special Issue includes twelve research articles addressing various aspects of edge cloud computing and federated–split learning, including technologies for improving the performance and efficiency of both FL and SL in edge cloud computing environments, mechanisms for protecting data privacy and enhancing system security in FL and SL frameworks, and ways to exploit FL-/SL-based ML methods and edge cloud computing technologies in order to support various IoT applications.

The constrained computing and communication resources available in IoT constitute the main challenge to high-performance federated and split learning. Therefore, technologies for computation and communication efficiency play a crucial role in the effective deployment of FL/SL frameworks in IoT. In [1], Nikolaidis et al. investigate the resource allocation problem in virtualization-based edge cloud computing systems in order to maximize the efficiency of the FL process. The authors consider factors such as computational and network capabilities, the complexity of datasets, and the specific characteristics of the FL workflow. They explore two scenarios: (i) running FL over a finite number of nodes and (ii) hosting multiple parallel FL workflows on the same set of nodes. The research findings indicate that the default configurations of state-of-the-art cloud orchestrators are sub-optimal when orchestrating FL workflows, demonstrating that different libraries and ML models exhibit diverse computational footprints. Building upon these insights, the authors discuss methods to mitigate computational interference and enhance the overall performance of the FL pipeline's execution.

Task scheduling is another key technology that has been explored to enhance FL efficiency and performance. In [2], Cai et al. study two problems of task scheduling for FL in edge computing: (1) transmission power allocation (PA) and (2) the dual decision-making problems of joint request offloading and computational resource scheduling (JRORS). The authors propose an adaptive greedy dingo optimization algorithm (AGDOA) based on greedy policies and parameter adaptation in order to solve the PA problem. They also construct a binary salp swarm algorithm (BSSA) that introduces binary coding to solve the discrete JRORS problem. Their simulation results verify that the proposed algorithms improve FL convergence speed, shorten the system response time, and reduce energy consumption.

Future networking technologies such as the 6G network may greatly enhance edge-based IoT; however, they also introduce diverse and heterogeneous devices that present new challenges for FL and SL. In [3], Ridolfi and co-authors analyze FL processes tailored for 6G standards, implementing a practical FL platform that employs Raspberry Pi devices and virtual machines as client nodes and hosts the FL server on a Windows PC. Their analysis delves into the impact of computational resources, data availability, and heating issues across heterogeneous device sets.

The limited bandwidth for data transmission in edge-based IoT makes communication efficiency a critical aspect of deploying FL and SL in this domain. Optimal client selection and model aggregation offer promising approaches to achieving communication-efficient FL. In [4], the authors propose a Federated Learning via Clustering Optimization (FedCO) scheme to optimize model aggregation and reduce communication costs. In FedCo, participating clients are clustered based on the similarity of their model parameters; the best-performing client is selected from each group as a representative to communicate with the central server. The proposed FedCO approach updates clusters by repeatedly evaluating and splitting them, improving worker partitioning. The experimental results indicate that the FedCO approach is effective in reducing communication costs and improving model accuracy.

Client selection and model aggregation technologies have also been leveraged in [5] for reducing model training time while improving model accuracy in FL. The authors of this paper introduce the Latency-awarE Semi-synchronous client Selection and mOdel aggregation for federated learNing (LESSON) method, which allows clients to participate at different frequencies, thus mitigating straggler issues and expediting model convergence. Their simulation results show that LESSON outperforms two baseline methods, FedAvg and FedCS, in terms of convergence speed and maintains a higher model accuracy than FedCS.

Although FL is seen as a privacy-preserving distributed machine learning method, recent research has shown it to be vulnerable to some privacy attacks. Homomorphic Encryption (HE) and Differential Privacy (DP) are two promising techniques for privacy protection in FL. In [6], Aziz et al. first present consistent attacks on privacy in FL and then provide an overview of HE and DP techniques for securing FL in next-generation internet applications. This paper discusses the strengths and weaknesses of these techniques in different settings, as described in the literature, with a particular focus on the trade-off between privacy and convergence, as well as the computation overheads involved.

Blockchain technologies have been employed as an effective approach to improving FL performance in a variety of ways, including protecting data privacy and system security. In [7], Liu et al. examine the EIFFeL framework, a protocol for decentralized real-time messaging in continuous integration and delivery pipelines. The authors introduce an enhanced scheme that leverages the trustworthy nature of blockchain technology. The proposed scheme eliminates the need for a central server and any other third party, thereby mitigating the risks associated with any potential breach.

Combining federated and split learning may aid in fully exploiting the advantages of both while mitigating their respective shortcomings. Thus, this matter has recently become an active research topic attracting extensive interest. In [8], the authors propose a multi-level split–federated learning (multi-level SFL) framework that merges the benefits of both SL and FL. This framework leverages the Message Queuing Telemetry Transport (MQTT) protocol to geographically cluster IoT devices, employing edge and fog computing layers for the initial model parameter aggregation. Their simulation experiments verify that the multi-level SFL framework outperforms traditional SFL by improving the model accuracy and convergence speed in large-scale IoT environments.

The aforementioned research primarily focuses on addressing the challenges of deploying FL/SL frameworks in edge cloud computing-based IoT environments. Another active theme of research is employing FL-/SL-based machine learning techniques together with edge cloud computing technologies to solve various problems in a broad range of IoT applications.

In [9], Zhou and co-authors design an image pre-processing method and propose a lightweight neural network model called LINGE (Lightweight Neural Network Models for the Edge). This paper proposes an FL-based distributed intelligent edge computing technology for disease risk prediction. The proposed scheme performs prediction model training and inference at the edge without increasing storage space, reduces communication load on the network, and releases computing pressure on the server.

The authors of [10] present a edge cloud collaborative banking data open application scenario, focusing on the critical need for an accurate and automated sensitive data classification and categorization method. In this paper, the authors propose a scheme, UP-SDCG, for automatically classifying and grading financial data and develop a financial data hierarchical classification library. The results of their experimental analysis indicate that UP-SDCG achieves a precision of over 95%, outperforming the baseline models.

In [11], the authors propose a dynamic watermarking service framework, E-SAWM, designed for edge cloud scenarios. This framework incorporates dynamic watermark information at the edge, allowing for the precise tracking of leakage throughout the data-sharing process. E-SAWM utilizes semantic analysis to generate highly realistic pseudo statements that ensure resistance to removal or destruction. Their experimental results demonstrate the effectiveness and efficiency of the proposed scheme.

Various FL-based methods have been proposed for security protection in edge-based IoTs, including intrusion detection systems (IDSs) in Internet of Vehicles (IoVs). In [12], Alsamir et al. present a comprehensive review of FL-based IDSs in an IoV environment. Their paper introduces a general taxonomy to describe FL systems in order to ensure a coherent structure and guide future research. Then, the authors identify the relevant state of the art in FL-based IDS technologies in the IoV domain, covering the years from FL's inception in 2016 through to 2023, discussing challenges and future research directions based on the existing literature.

As Guest Editors, we would like to take this opportunity to thank all the authors who submitted their manuscripts to this Special Issue. Furthermore, we would like to acknowledge all the reviewers whose thorough reviews have helped improve the quality of the manuscripts in this Special Issue. Last but not least, we would like to express our appreciation to the MDPI Editorial Team, who have provided unwavering support throughout this project.

Conflicts of Interest: The authors declare no conflicts of interest.

References

1. Nikolaidis, F.; Symeonides, M.; Trihinas, D. Towards Efficient Resource Allocation for Federated Learning in Virtualized Managed Environments. *Future Internet* **2023**, *15*, 261. [CrossRef]
2. Cai, W.; Duan, F. Task Scheduling for Federated Learning in Edge Cloud Computing Environments by Using Adaptive-Greedy Dingo Optimization Algorithm and Binary Salp Swarm Algorithm. *Future Internet* **2023**, *15*, 357. [CrossRef]
3. Ridolfi, L.; Naseh, D.; Shinde, S.S.; Tarchi, D. Implementation and Evaluation of a Federated Learning Framework on Raspberry PI Platforms for IoT 6G Applications. *Future Internet* **2023**, *15*, 358. [CrossRef]
4. Al-Saedi, A.A.; Boeva, V.; Casalicchio, E. FedCO: Communication-efficient federated learning via clustering optimization. *Future Internet* **2022**, *14*, 377. [CrossRef]
5. Yu, L.; Sun, X.; Albelaihi, R.; Yi, C. Latency-Aware Semi-Synchronous Client Selection and Model Aggregation for Wireless Federated Learning. *Future Internet* **2023**, *15*, 352. [CrossRef]
6. Aziz, R.; Banerjee, S.; Bouzefrane, S.; Le Vinh, T. Exploring homomorphic encryption and differential privacy techniques towards secure federated learning paradigm. *Future Internet* **2023**, *15*, 310. [CrossRef]
7. Liu, B.; Tang, Q. Secure Data Sharing in Federated Learning through Blockchain-Based Aggregation. *Future Internet* **2024**, *16*, 133. [CrossRef]

8. Xu, H.; Seng, K.P.; Smith, J.; Ang, L.M. Multi-Level Split Federated Learning for Large-Scale AIoT System Based on Smart Cities. *Future Internet* **2024**, *16*, 82. [CrossRef]
9. Zhou, F.; Hu, S.; Du, X.; Wan, X.; Wu, J. A Lightweight Neural Network Model for Disease Risk Prediction in Edge Intelligent Computing Architecture. *Future Internet* **2024**, *16*, 75. [CrossRef]
10. Zu, L.; Qi, W.; Li, H.; Men, X.; Lu, Z.; Ye, J.; Zhang, L. UP-SDCG: A Method of Sensitive Data Classification for Collaborative Edge Computing in Financial Cloud Environment. *Future Internet* **2024**, *16*, 102. [CrossRef]
11. Zu, L.; Li, H.; Zhang, L.; Lu, Z.; Ye, J.; Zhao, X.; Hu, S. E-SAWM: A Semantic Analysis-Based ODF Watermarking Algorithm for Edge Cloud Scenarios. *Future Internet* **2023**, *15*, 283. [CrossRef]
12. Alsamiri, J.; Alsubhi, K. Federated Learning for Intrusion Detection Systems in Internet of Vehicles: A General Taxonomy, Applications, and Future Directions. *Future Internet* **2023**, *15*, 403. [CrossRef]

Disclaimer/Publisher's Note: The statements, opinions and data contained in all publications are solely those of the individual author(s) and contributor(s) and not of MDPI and/or the editor(s). MDPI and/or the editor(s) disclaim responsibility for any injury to people or property resulting from any ideas, methods, instructions or products referred to in the content.

Article

Towards Efficient Resource Allocation for Federated Learning in Virtualized Managed Environments

Fotis Nikolaidis [1,*], Moysis Symeonides [2] and Demetris Trihinas [3]

[1] Institute of Computer Science, Foundation for Research and Technology Hellas, 70013 Heraklion, Greece
[2] Department of Computer Science, University of Cyprus, 1678 Nicosia, Cyprus; symeonidis.moysis@ucy.ac.cy
[3] Department of Computer Science, School of Sciences and Engineering, University of Nicosia, 2417 Nicosia, Cyprus; trihinas.d@unic.ac.cy
* Correspondence: fnikol@ics.forth.gr

Citation: Nikolaidis, F.; Symeonides, M.; Trihinas, D. Towards Efficient Resource Allocation for Federated Learning in Virtualized Managed Environments. *Future Internet* 2023, 15, 261. https://doi.org/10.3390/fi15080261

Academic Editors: Qiang Duan and Zhihu Lu

Received: 3 July 2023
Revised: 19 July 2023
Accepted: 25 July 2023
Published: 31 July 2023

Copyright: © 2023 by the authors. Licensee MDPI, Basel, Switzerland. This article is an open access article distributed under the terms and conditions of the Creative Commons Attribution (CC BY) license (https://creativecommons.org/licenses/by/4.0/).

Abstract: Federated learning (FL) is a transformative approach to Machine Learning that enables the training of a shared model without transferring private data to a central location. This decentralized training paradigm has found particular applicability in edge computing, where IoT devices and edge nodes often possess limited computational power, network bandwidth, and energy resources. While various techniques have been developed to optimize the FL training process, an important question remains unanswered: how should resources be allocated in the training workflow? To address this question, it is crucial to understand the nature of these resources. In physical environments, the allocation is typically performed at the node level, with the entire node dedicated to executing a single workload. In contrast, virtualized environments allow for the dynamic partitioning of a node into containerized units that can adapt to changing workloads. Consequently, the new question that arises is: how can a physical node be partitioned into virtual resources to maximize the efficiency of the FL process? To answer this, we investigate various resource allocation methods that consider factors such as computational and network capabilities, the complexity of datasets, as well as the specific characteristics of the FL workflow and ML backend. We explore two scenarios: (i) running FL over a finite number of testbed nodes and (ii) hosting multiple parallel FL workflows on the same set of testbed nodes. Our findings reveal that the default configurations of state-of-the-art cloud orchestrators are sub-optimal when orchestrating FL workflows. Additionally, we demonstrate that different libraries and ML models exhibit diverse computational footprints. Building upon these insights, we discuss methods to mitigate computational interferences and enhance the overall performance of the FL pipeline execution.

Keywords: federated learning; machine learning; edge computing; Internet of Things

1. Introduction

Federated Learning (FL) is transforming the field of Artificial Intelligence (AI) by allowing collaborative training of statistical models in decentralized environments [1]. It enables multiple devices or entities to contribute their local data for training a shared model without requiring the raw data to be transferred to a central server [2]. Instead, the models are trained locally on each device, and only the model updates, which are lightweight and privacy-preserving, are exchanged with a central server or coordinator [3]. This approach ensures data privacy, as sensitive information remains on the local devices, and it also addresses challenges associated with data silos and data transmission costs. FL is particularly useful for organizations operating in collaborative and cross-border settings, such as health and financial institutions, as they are subject to regulatory and legal frameworks like the EU's General Data Protection Regulation (GDPR) [4]. These frameworks mandate strict data governance policies for managing, processing, and exchanging data among different administrative sites [5].

Federated learning workloads, which involve communication, synchronization, and aggregation of model updates, are typically implemented using specialized frameworks like Flower [6]. These frameworks not only handle the complexities of the FL process but also establish standardized APIs, protocols, and conventions, promoting interoperability and compatibility among different components of the FL ecosystem. However, migrating ML training from centralized cloud data centers to distributed environments presents significant challenges that frameworks alone cannot easily address [7]. In these distributed settings, heterogeneity is common, with federated clients run on hardware with varying levels of capabilities and availability [8]. Additionally, clients may differ in network capabilities and geographic distance from the server [9], which can cause bottlenecks that affect the overall duration of the FL training process [10].

Moreover, as deployments scale up and organizations add more clients and administrative sites, managing the system becomes increasingly complex. This can become a nightmare for organizations. Cloud-native technologies such as Docker (a virtualized container execution runtime) and Kubernetes [11] (a cluster management service) are frequently considered to tackle these challenges [12]. Virtualization offers two main benefits: (i) it abstracts physical resources like compute, memory, and storage, allowing them to be shaped according to deployment needs; and (ii) it provides essential isolation when multiple models are trained simultaneously on the same set of nodes. The cluster management service, also known as the cluster orchestrator, automates the deployment of FL clients on the available compute nodes and provides a global view of the deployment's operating conditions [13,14].

However, the different objectives and requirements between cluster orchestrators and FL frameworks can lead to conflicting resource management schemes. Cluster orchestrators rely on predefined specifications for resource requests and limits, prioritizing fairness and fault tolerance in their task-scheduling algorithms. Their aim is to minimize resource wastage and enhance the Quality Of Service (QoS) [15]. In contrast, FL frameworks have their own scheduling mechanisms for distributed model training, considering factors like dataset size, data freshness, and model synchronization requirements. Typically, their goal is to minimize model loss and achieve convergence in fewer training rounds [3]. This misalignment between cluster orchestrators and FL frameworks can lead to inefficient resource allocation, impacting the timely execution and convergence of FL workflows.

Despite the existence of several FL frameworks (i.e., Flower, FATE) and plethora of studies in relevance to FL performance [16,17], the impact of the underlying computing system to FL deployments is significantly overlooked. Our work fills this gap by providing a comprehensive overview of the impact of resource allocation schemes on FL deployments. The focus is on a single organization that manages multiple administrative sites through a shared control plane. For this scenario, we investigate two challenge vectors related to the Quality of Service (QoS) of FL deployments: *"resource fitting"* and *"multi-tenancy"*. Resource fitting involves aligning available resources with the specific requirements of FL clients, while multi-tenancy focuses on running multiple FL workloads concurrently on a shared cluster of resources. To study the scenario in real-world settings, we utilize two widely used open-source frameworks: Kubernetes for cluster orchestration and Flower for FL execution. For the observability of experiments, we extend Flower's codebase by introducing a monitoring module that captures performance metrics from physical clients, containerized services, and FL workloads. To enhance reproducibility and streamline experimentation, we containerize Flower and provide abstractions for configuring FL deployments, eliminating the need for rebuilding containers.

Towards this, the main contributions of our work are as follows:

- We present an FL use-case for a healthcare provider with geographically distributed branches, highlighting the challenge vectors of resource fitting and deploying multiple FL workflows. These challenges are fundamental and remain relevant across numerous other applications considering FL adoption.
- We document the experimental setup designed for rapid and reproducible benchmarking of the FL infrastructure and deployment configuration. This includes con-

tainerizing the FL framework (Flower), using Kubernetes as the cluster orchestrator, employing a testing toolkit (Frisbee) to adjust Kubernetes' placement policies, and extensively monitoring infrastructure, virtual, and FL execution metrics.
- We conduct a comprehensive experimentation study, systematically analyzing performance, scalability, and resource efficiency. We evaluate different combinations of orchestrator policies and FL configurations using popular ML/FL datasets (MNIST [18] and CIFAR [19]) and frameworks (PyTorch [20] and TensorFlow [21]). We explore various resource configurations, server/client co-location, pod placement policies, and investigate the effects of running multiple FL training workloads simultaneously.

The remainder of this paper is organized as follows: In Section 2, we provide a short introduction to Federated Learning. In Section 3, we describe a high-level problem statement, including a critical evaluation of the associated challenges that exist nowadays. In Section 4, we provide an overview of our testing infrastructure, tools, and experiment methodology. In Section 5 we provide an in-depth performance analysis for a single workflow, whereas in Section 6 we provide an analysis for two concurrently executed workflows. Section 7 presents a literature review including a critical evaluation of the strengths and limitations of existing approaches. Finally, in Section 8, we summarize the key findings of our experiments, discuss their implications on Federated Learning deployments, and suggest future research directions.

2. Background

2.1. Federated Learning Applicability

The origins of Federated Learning date back to a set of seminal papers in 2015–2016 [22,23] with Google's GBoard (Android keyboard) one of the early and prominent production systems that FL was tested and still in use today [24]. There are several real-world cases where FL is an appealing setting. First, as the premises of FL is to avoid overwhelming, and often sensitive, volumes of data moving from the edge to the cloud for training, organisations such as hospitals and financial institutes can take advantage of distributed learning without sharing patient (i.e., bio-signals, imaging) and customer data (i.e., credit scores) with other branches and third-party organisations [9]. Second, model training is feasible on data collected from geo-distributed devices (i.e., smart phones, IoTs, wearable, voice assistants) where the generation rate and high communication cost makes it impractical to send data to centralized data centers for processing [16]. Third, it allows for the training of models to be achieved on larger datasets (the "big data multiplier"), since the data from multiple parties are aggregated and used to achieve intelligence far greater than what a single entity could achieve [25]. Fourth, the central server does not exercise control over the clients and hence, clients can go offline willingly or due to unreliable network links, and participate in the model training process only if they desire with the server selecting clients based on availability and resource capacity criteria.

2.2. The Federated Learning Process

Figure 1 depicts a typical FL training flow where a FL central server obtains a set of available clients ($c_1, c_2, \ldots, c_k$) that meet certain criteria (i.e., availability) and subsequently broadcasts to the clients the training program and an initial model parameterization $\mathbf{W}_{t_0}$ with t_0 denoting the initial training round. At this point, the clients update the model locally $\mathbf{w}_{c_i,t_1}$, based on their data and current knowledge without exchanging (sensitive) data among themselves. The local data of each client and the number of samples $s_k \in S$ used during local training can differ per client. When finished, the server collects an aggregate of the client updates, creating a new global model $\mathbf{W}_{t_1}$. This process is repeated for several rounds until it reaches a max number of rounds or the convergence exceeds a certain accuracy/loss for early termination.

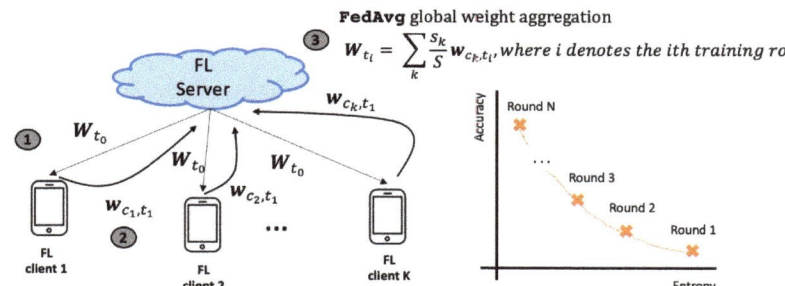

Figure 1. FL example where initial model W_{t_0} is disseminated to clients for round t_0 (step 1), clients update their local model state at t_1 (step 2) and afterward the central FL server employs a global aggregation to infer a new model state W_{t_1} (step 3) where in this case a weighted average is used.

2.3. Federated Learning Algorithms

Algorithm 1 provides an overview of FL, where at a high level, FL boils down to the coordination process overseeing the distributed training of a model on data that never leaves its origins. That said, both the aggregation function applied by the server and the client selection can take many forms.

Algorithm 1 High-Level Federated Learning Process

Input: Training rounds T, Clients K, local training epochs E, public dataset D for initial training
Output: Trained model W_T
Ensure: Central Server is running
1: $W_0 \leftarrow$ initialize(D)
2: **for** each training round t in T **do**
3:     **for** each c_k in K **in parallel do**
4:         $w_{t,c_k} \leftarrow$ ClientUpdate(W_{t-1}, E)
5:     **end for**
6:     $W_t \leftarrow$ Aggregate($w_{t,c_1}, \ldots, w_{t,c_K}$)
7: **end for**
8: **return** W_T

As an example, one may consider FedAvg [1], the most well-known FL algorithm and often considered the baseline for FL. After model initialization, FedAvg embraces local training where each client employs, in parallel, E epochs of Stochastic Gradient Descent (SGD), where the weights of the local model are updated to optimize the model loss based on the local data. At the end of the round, the central server collects the derived model weights per client. Aggregation is then performed using a weighted average where s_k is the number of samples used by each client during local training and $S = \sum_k s_k$:

$$W_t = \sum_k \frac{s_k}{S} w_{t,c_k} \quad (1)$$

With this, clients that have used more samples have a larger influence on the new state of the model. Hence, despite the simplicity of FedAvg, the literature has shown that for non-IID data, there are no convergence guarantees [26]. To compensate, FedProx [3] has been proposed as a generalization of FedAvg where the clients extend the SGD process so that clients optimize a regulated loss with a proximal term that enforces the local optimization of the loss in the vicinity of the global model per training round. Similarly, SCAFFOLD is a FL algorithm that attempts to optimize the training process for non-IID data by providing a "correction" mechanism for the client-drift problem during local training [27]. In brief, SCAFFOLD estimates the update direction for the global model at the FL server and the update direction for each client with the difference used to correct the local model versions.

To reduce the significant communication overhead imposed by FL, FedDyn is an algorithm that "pushes" to the client level more processing and optimization to reduce the overall communication burden and the number of training rounds [28]. For this, FedDyn adopts a regularization optimizer per round that dynamically modifies the client side objective with a penalty term so that, in the limit, when model parameters converge, they do so to stationary points of the global empirical loss.

In terms of client selection, the aforementioned algorithms employ a common strategy where the FL server opts for a random selection from the pool of available clients via a uniform distribution. On the other hand, two notable studies show that performing a biased selection of clients can yield faster global model convergence and reduce communication overhead. For example, after a few initial training rounds, the Power-of-Choice [29] opts for a biased selection towards clients with higher local loss. This way, the algorithm achieves faster error convergence by $3\times$ and 10% higher test performance. In turn, FedCS [30] requires clients to send updates of their resource availability (i.e., computational power, network bandwidth) to estimate the time required to complete a training round that fits a large sample of clients. Subsequently, it only considers local model updates from those that actually meet the estimated deadline, penalizing the stragglers.

3. Motivation

This section introduces a use case and challenges that motivate the experimentation part of this article. The use case involves a large-scale Healthcare Provider with multiple branches (such as hospitals and clinics) spread across an association of countries (i.e., the European Union). Each branch of the Healthcare Provider is the bearer of its patients' data, with data governance obeying regional legislation. The goal is to develop medical AI applications trained on the available data. Researchers focus on various areas like cancer tumor detection in MRIs and abnormalities detection in patient electrocardiograms (ECGs). Although each branch can initiate ML model training using its own data, training complex medical models requires abundant data and computational resources. While computational resources can be shared among branches, data are unshareable due to regulatory restrictions.

Therefore, federated learning (FL) is the preferred training paradigm, where models are trained collaboratively on distributed data without sharing it. To facilitate FL implementation, the healthcare provider's IT team adopts a Kubernetes cluster management service. This service manages the diverse computational resources available at each branch, linking them through a common control plane (Figure 2). Kubernetes enables provisioning of the FL workflow by containerizing Flower server and client instances for distributed training. By establishing a single administrative domain, the healthcare provider can effectively offer an FL system to multiple researchers, providing them with sufficient computational resources to train complex models on their localized data. However, as more researchers adopt FL and resources are divided among them, resource allocation and workload distribution become critical challenges. Hence, from the Healthcare Provider's perspective, the interest is in reducing the FL model training time when utilizing a fixed set of (computational) resources. Subsequently, the throughput for multiple FL workloads will increase by reducing the training completion time.

Next, we highlight two main challenges faced in this deployment:resource fitting and parallel FL workflow execution.

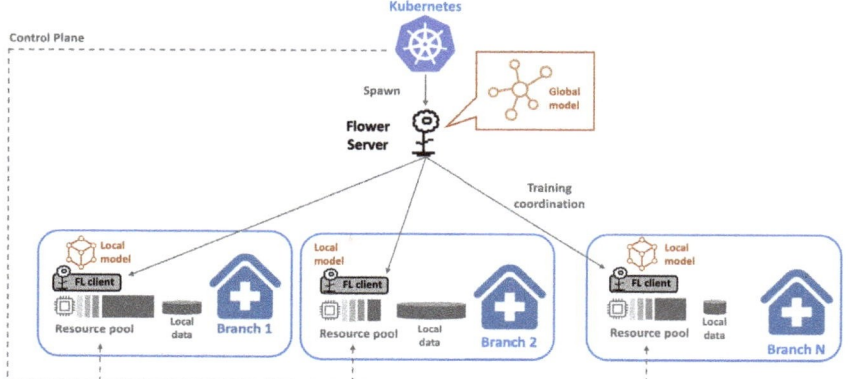

Figure 2. Healthcare provider use-case with containerized FL (Flower server and clients) employed over Kubernetes managed cluster administering common control plane and resource pool.

3.1. Challenge 1: Resource Fitting

Resource fitting refers to the process of mapping the available resource pool to the application services so that the use of the available resources meets the specific application demands as expressed by the user requirements. This process requires evaluating resource characteristics, capabilities, and availability, and assigning them to appropriate tasks [31]. To achieve effective resource fitting in FL, users must undergo an extensive and rigorous process that includes training with different properties, evaluating their impact on resource utilization and training performance, and revealing the inter-component dependencies.

Defining Application Requirements. While orchestrators like Kubernetes can automate the deployment of containerized FL workflows, they are generally agnostic to the specific requirements of each application. Users are responsible for specifying the desired amount of resources for their application to run smoothly. However, different FL workflows have varying computational requirements. For example, a time series prediction model may require significant memory but fewer computations, while a cancer image detection model relies heavily on computational power. Furthermore, ML models can have diverse parameters, structures, and libraries such as TensorFlow [21] and PyTorch [20]. To finely tune the resource requests, researchers need to extensively profile each component of the FL workflows and identify the application's actual needs.

Increasing Resource Utilization And Minimizing Wastage. Even when users understand the workflow profile and resource requirements, they may face limitations in allocating the desired resources due to quotas or allocation requests from other users in a multi-tenant environment. It is therefore important to consider the effects of resource saturation and starvation on submitted FL workflows. Such effects may also be caused by opportunistic schedulers who allocate fewer resources than is necessary, thus causing bottlenecks. Oppositely, conservative schedulers tend to allocate more resources than is necessary (over-provision), thus wasting precious resources and minimizing the potential for multi-tenancy.

Revealing Inter-Component Dependencies. Despite the decentralized nature of FL, the training is still a synchronous process that requires all clients to synchronize with the server at the end of each training round. This synchronization introduces a dependency among participating clusters, as rigorous clients have to wait for latent ones, introducing straggling task effects. To address this, users need to consider the computation- and network-aware placement of FL clients across managed nodes. By optimizing the placement of clients, the system can mitigate the impact of stragglers and improve overall efficiency, even with varying numbers of clients and data sizes.

3.2. Challenge 2: Parallel Workflows

Multi-tenancy and the implications of parallel FL workflow execution on a single administrative domain is another point of consideration for our healthcare provider use case. When users opt to run parallel FL workflows on the same physical resource pool, complexities arise that can impact the convergence speed and overall efficiency of the FL process or even cause unexpected system failures. To alleviate these threats, users need to consider the Resource Contention of parallel workloads, the Communication overhead that may be caused due to the repeatable patterns of FL workloads, and possible optimization opportunities for Workflows Synchronization.

Resource Contention. When multiple users choose to run parallel FL workflows on the same physical resource pool, resource contention issues arise. In limited resources, lightweight virtualization technologies like containers are used to share the resource pool among multiple users. However, when multiple FL workflows run simultaneously, the capacity of the nodes to handle the resource requirements becomes a bottleneck. If multiple workflows request the same constrained resources, they face resource starvation and contention problems. This conflict over shared resources (i.e., CPU, memory) hampers performance, impacts training efficiency, and hinders convergence rates.

Communication Overhead Or Synchronization. FL involves frequent communication between the central server and the distributed client services. This interaction becomes critical when training models with a large number of parameters. Communication overhead and contention must be carefully examined to identify potential bottlenecks during FL cycles. For example, in a scenario where FL clients from different workloads attempt to update the global model simultaneously, the network remains idle while the clients are training the model locally, with network spikes occurring at the end of the round, during which the clients submit the training results to the central server. This strain on the network impacts overall performance and saturates the network bandwidth. By analyzing the communication overhead, optimization opportunities can be identified. For instance, shifting the starting point of one FL workflow or isolating FL servers and clients on different nodes may help avoid bandwidth congestion and minimize peak network traffic.

4. Testbed Design

FL experiments face challenges due to their distributed nature and reliance on multiple components and backend systems. These challenges hinder experiment reproducibility, making it difficult to evaluate performance under different configurations, assess scalability, and capture the dynamic behavior of FL algorithms. To address these issues, a testbed is necessary. This testbed should allow experiment replication, facilitate the comparison of approaches, and streamline the identification of performance bottlenecks and issues. In this section, we present the design of a Kubernetes-based testbed that provides a controlled environment for researchers and developers to conduct reproducible FL experiments with consistent settings, configurations, and data.

4.1. Building Parameterizable Containers for Federated Learning

Containers have proven to be effective in providing lightweight and isolated environments for testing distributed applications [12,32]. However, incorporating FL workflow components into containers presents challenges due to the need for dynamic parameterization, dependency injection, and complex networking requirements between clients and a central server, which can be difficult to manage within the scope of the containerized environment. These obstacles hinder the direct usability of FL frameworks within containerized environments, limiting their portability and scalability benefits. Therefore, there is a need for an FL framework able to interact with an external cluster orchestrator responsible for managing the execution order, network connectivity, and resource allocation to ensure the effective management of the distributed training process while maintaining the portability and scalability benefits offered by containerization in a cloud-edge continuum.

To address these challenges, we built a tool based on the Flower FL execution framework to interact with an external cluster orchestration system, out-of-the-box models, parametrizable configurations, and fine-grained monitoring. Our approach wraps Flower's configuration into a generic frontend script. This script serves two purposes: (i) defining the container's runtime environment, including model type, number of rounds, aggregation algorithm, etc., and (ii) configuring Flower's parameters accordingly and invoking the appropriate backend implementation. Currently, we support two deep-learning backends, PyTorch and TensorFlow, and two dataset types, MNIST and CIFAR-10. More information about the ML datasets and backends can be found in Sections 4.5 and 4.6, respectively. We also introduced code breakpoints for measuring the execution duration of ML training, evaluation, round duration, and code for capturing overall accuracy and loss of the FL pipeline. For building the containers, we utilized Dockerfiles [33]. These Dockerfiles include the code of the Flower FL framework and provide all the necessary instructions and environment variables for running the FL services. The resulting Docker image contains the required service codes, dependencies, and files and is uploaded to a private Docker repository. This allows us to download the image at runtime on the compute node, which can function as either an FL client or server.

4.2. Multi-Node Container Orchestration

Kubernetes is an open-source platform that streamlines the deployment, scaling, and management of containerized applications, relieving users from infrastructure concerns. It comprises two main components: the centralized control plane (Kubernetes master) and the decentralized data plane. The control plane consists of modular services like the K8s API, scheduler, and controller. The data plane is made up of distributed node agents called Kubelets [34], which act as local executors following commands from the master, such as starting or stopping containers. This separation allows users to define their desired application state, with Kubernetes striving to maintain that state. Figure 3 provides a high-level overview of our Kubernetes-enabled testing environment.

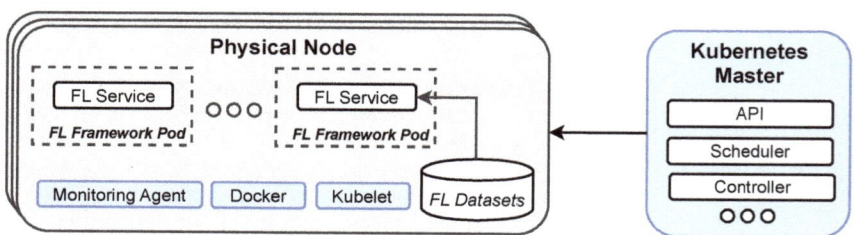

Figure 3. High-level overview of multi-host Kubernetes deployment.

A notable feature of Kubernetes is its ability to schedule the deployment and execution of containers across a node cluster using a scheduling algorithm. However, the default scheduler is designed to optimize node utilization and remain application-agnostic. For example, it may not consider data locality in scenarios like federated learning, where training data are distributed across edge devices or clusters. This can increase network traffic and latency due to unnecessary data movement. Moreover, federated learning requires frequent communication between edge devices/clusters and the central server for model updates. The default scheduler does not optimize scheduling decisions with regard to communication overhead, potentially increasing latency and impacting the training process. Additionally, each edge device or cluster in federated learning has its own resource constraints, such as limited computation power, memory, and network bandwidth.

In our analysis, we examine the default policies of Kubernetes for federated learning applications. We specifically assess the performance of the default scheduler under two scenarios: one with user-defined constraints that cater to the application's specific requirements, and another without any user-defined constraints. Our analysis revolves around three key user-based constraints:

- *Placement constraints:* dictate the selection of nodes for scheduling FL clients, specifying which nodes should be chosen.
- *Resource constraints:* determine the minimum and maximum amount of resources, such as CPU and memory, that an FL client can consume.
- *Timing constraints:* define when a new training workflow will be instantiated.

Our analysis aims to deliver insights into the impact of user-defined constraints and the potential for automatically inferring these constraints, rather than proposing a new scheduling algorithm.

4.3. Testing Workflows in Kubernetes

Kubernetes is a powerful platform, but it has a steep learning curve. Testers need to acquire knowledge of its concepts, configuration, and management, which can be challenging. Moreover, the dynamic nature of Kubernetes deployments can pose challenges when executing specific testing scenarios, especially those involving conditional executions.

To simplify testing on Kubernetes, we utilized the Frisbee platform, a Kubernetes-native framework specifically designed for testing distributed systems [35,36]. Frisbee offers several advantages over vanilla Kubernetes, such as orchestrating the testing actions and providing abstractions for managing containers as logical groups (e.g., servers, clients). This way, we can easily create complex placement schemes, as shown in Listing 1. Additionally, we take advantage of Frisbee's volume-sharing feature to enhance dataset acquisition from clients. Instead of each client downloading the dataset locally, we create a virtual shareable folder and pass it to the virtualized environment. FL clients are then programmed to read the datasets from this shared folder, reducing network pressure as the number of clients increases. Furthermore, to ensure reproducibility and flexibility for future experiments, we have incorporated the testing patterns for Federated Learning into the GitHub repository of the Frisbee platform [37]. This allows researchers to easily repeat and configure the experiments for different frameworks and datasets.

4.4. Monitoring Stack

Our testing environment incorporates a transparent monitoring stack (Figure 4) capable of extracting various utilization metrics from the system under test. These metrics encompass CPU, memory, network utilization, and FL-level metrics, including model accuracy/loss and training time per round (Table 1). To achieve this, we deploy a containerized monitoring agent on each node that follows a probe-based multi-threaded paradigm [38]. The agent, namely cAdvisor [39], collects performance metrics by initiating different probes for each sub-component, such as the cgroup probe and OS probe. It then exposes an http endpoint for Prometheus [40] to periodically retrieve and store the metrics in its embedded timeseries databases. Prometheus is integrated with Grafana [41] to provide real-time inspection of our experiments through its dashboard-as-a-service software.

As for the performance and FL monitoring metrics, the challenging part is to expose fine-grained metrics from the running FL workloads. To do that, we enhance the existing codebase of Flower to record accuracy, loss, and duration data into well-organized files, which are stored locally on each client. To capture performance metrics, we employ timers that intersect with the existing methods to extract the duration of training time. As for accuracy and loss, we extract these metrics from the FL master. At the end of the experiment, these files are automatically transferred into a central repository and combined with the performance metrics collected by Prometheus.

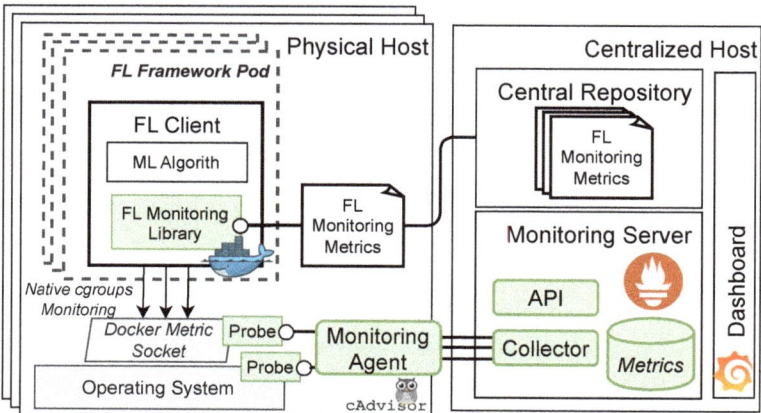

Figure 4. Monitoring stack for repeatable FL experimentation.

Listing 1. Snippet of a Frisbee scenario showing placement policies for groups of clients.

```yaml
---
apiVersion: frisbee.dev/v1alpha1
kind: Scenario
metadata:
  name: node-placement
spec:
  actions:
    # Step 1: Create FedBed server
    - action: Service
      name: server
      service:
        templateRef: frisbee.apps.fedbed.server
        inputs:
          - { min_fit_clients: 20, min_available_clients: 20 }

    # Step 2: Place clients[0,4] to Node-1
    - action: Cluster
      name: group-a
      depends: { running: [ server ] }
      cluster:
        placement:
          nodes: [ k8s-node1 ]   # Change values here
        templateRef: frisbee.apps.fedbed.client
        inputs:
          - { fl_server: server, total_nodes: 20, node_id: 0 }
          - { fl_server: server, total_nodes: 20, node_id: 1 }
          - { fl_server: server, total_nodes: 20, node_id: 2 }
          - { fl_server: server, total_nodes: 20, node_id: 3 }
          - { fl_server: server, total_nodes: 20, node_id: 4 }

    # Step 2: Place clients[5,9] to Node-2
    - action: Cluster
      name: group-b
      depends: { running: [ server ] }
      cluster:
        placement:
          nodes: [ k8s-node2 ]   # Change values here
        templateRef: frisbee.apps.fedbed.client
        inputs:
          - { fl_server: server, total_nodes: 20, node_id: 5 }
          - { fl_server: server, total_nodes: 20, node_id: 6 }
          - { fl_server: server, total_nodes: 20, node_id: 7 }
          - { fl_server: server, total_nodes: 20, node_id: 8 }
          - { fl_server: server, total_nodes: 20, node_id: 9 }
```

Table 1. Experimental Testbed Metric Description.

Metric	Category	Description
Accuracy	FL/ML	The model accuracy per round
Loss	FL/ML	The model loss per round
Round Duration	Performance	The overall round duration
Overall Duration	Performance	The overall FL duration
CPU Utilization	Utilization	The CPU utilization of FL client or server
Memory Utilization	Utilization	The memory utilization of FL client or server
Network I/O	Utilization	The network data (both incoming and outgoing) of FL client or server in bytes
Disk I/O	Utilization	Disk I/O of FL client or server in bytes

4.5. ML Datasets for Experimentation

Driven by our motivating example of a healthcare provider in the field of imaging diagnostics (i.e., MRI-based research), we have based our evaluation on two widely recognized databases in computer vision: MNIST [18] and CIFAR-10 [19].

The fundamental difference between them lies in the complexity and characteristics of the images they contain. MNIST is a simple database that consists of grayscale images of handwritten digits. It includes 60,000 training images and 10,000 test images, each measuring 28×28 pixels. The dataset is divided into 10 different classes representing digits from 0 to 9. CIFAR10 is more complex and contains colored images of everyday objects like airplanes, cars, and animals. These images are larger, measuring 32×32 pixels, and contain three color channels (RGB). CIFAR-10 consists of 50,000 training images and 10,000 test images, spanning 10 distinct object classes.

Albeit both databases are common in the benchmarking of computer vision algorithms, the choice between MNIST and CIFAR-10 depends on the complexity of the task and the specific application scope. MNIST, with its simplicity and small image size, serves as a foundational dataset for evaluating and prototyping machine learning algorithms. It is commonly used to explore different classification techniques and benchmark the performance of new models. On the other hand, CIFAR-10 presents a more challenging task for algorithms due to its higher complexity and inclusion of color images. It serves as a stepping stone to more advanced computer vision tasks and is often used to assess the performance of deep learning architectures. Working with CIFAR-10 allows researchers to tackle the challenges posed by color information and gain insights into developing more robust and accurate models for image classification.

4.6. ML Backends and Models

PyTorch and TensorFlow are popular deep learning frameworks with distinct features capable of serving as the ML backend for FL deployments. Both libraries are open-source and utilize data flow graphs, where nodes represent mathematical operations and edges represent tensors (multi-dimensional arrays) carrying data. However, they differ in their programming interfaces. TensorFlow, developed by Google, initially adopted a declarative programming model with a static computational graph. On the other hand, PyTorch follows an imperative programming model, allowing computations to be defined and executed dynamically. Despite this distinction, both frameworks enable the seamless deployment of models on CPUs or GPUs without needing code modification.

To assess their performance on the MNIST dataset, we construct a Convolutional Neural Network (CNN) with connected layers using both PyTorch and TensorFlow. The network architecture includes multiple layers, with six trainable layers: two 2D convolutional layers, two 2D dropout layers, and two linear layers. Additionally, there are non-trainable layers for activation and transformation operations, such as a ReLU activation layer after the first and second convolutional layers, a MaxPool2D layer following the second ReLU layer, and a Log-Softmax activation function for generating the final output. For CIFAR datasets, we implement the well-known MobileNetV2 model architecture in both TensorFlow and PyTorch. In brief, MobileNetV2 adopts a CNN model commonly used for image classification, comprising 53 layers. More details about the MobileNetV2 architecture can be found in [42].

4.7. Experimental Testbed

For the experimentation, we consider a bare-metal Kubernetes cluster with four server-grade physical nodes, each equipped with 24 cores over 2 Intel Xeon E5-2630v3 processors, 128 GB of DDR3 ECC main memory, and 250 GB of locally attached NVMe storage. The four nodes are connected via 1Gbps links to the top-of-rack switch. On top of the physical infrastructure, we deploy the rest of our end-to-end evaluation software stack, which operates as our main evaluation tool and automates the submission of FL systems, algorithms and ML models.

5. Case-Study: Resource Fitting

5.1. Experiment 1: Comparison of Native Performance of ML Backends

This experiment compares the performance and resource utilization of different machine learning (ML) libraries and models within a Federated Learning (FL) pipeline. We focus on TensorFlow and PyTorch as ML backends and evaluate their performance using the MNIST and CIFAR-10 datasets. We consider various factors such as model accuracy, completion time per training round, and resource utilization, including CPUs, memory, and network traffic. The FL workloads are executed for five rounds, utilizing an FL client and server with unrestricted resources. We determine the round duration by measuring the average duration of the last five rounds, while the accuracy of the fifth round serves as the representative value. To calculate CPU utilization we average the rate of change of cumulative CPU time consumed over a sampling window. Equally, we use the same formula for calculating the network throughput. In this case, the cumulative count of bytes that is transmitted and received. The term "window" refers to a specific time interval or data range over which the rate of change is calculated. To minimize the impact of monitoring on actual performance, we set the sampling interval to 15 s.

5.1.1. Training Round Duration and Model Accuracy

Firstly, we investigate if there is a significant variance in the duration of training rounds and the accuracy of the ML model, depending only on the dataset and ML backend. Figure 5a shows that both TensorFlow and PyTorch have comparable accuracy on the MNIST dataset, while PyTorch outperforms TensorFlow by 5% on the CIFAR-10 dataset. However, the average round duration varies significantly between the two ML backends and is an aspect for consideration (Figure 5b). Despite the 5% accuracy gain, training the MobileNetV2 model on PyTorch has a round duration of slightly over 5 min, while TensorFlow takes up to 140 s. Similarly, TensorFlow outperforms PyTorch, in terms of training round completion, by a large margin (around 60 s) for the CNN model on the MNIST dataset. Hence, *the absence of a dominant implementation across all cases, highlights the need to finely tune the ML backend and model architecture on a per-case basis, in order to improve the duration and accuracy of the FL pipeline.*

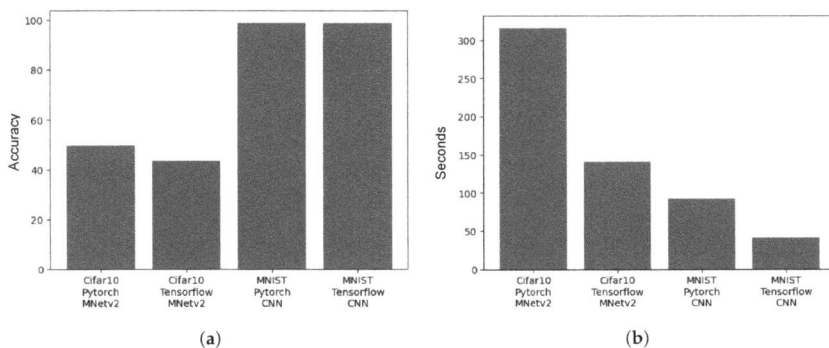

Figure 5. FL-level performance overview for different ML backends and datasets. (**a**) Model accuracy after 5 training rounds. (**b**) Mean training round duration after the completion of 5 rounds.

5.1.2. Resource Utilization for FL Clients and Server

Next, we elaborate on the reasons for the differences in the per-round time duration by analyzing the resource utilization of FL clients and servers for each ML backend. In Figure 6a, we compare the CPU utilization, memory allocation, and network traffic for different models, frameworks, and datasets on the client services. For clarity, we note that for the network, we account only for the outgoing traffic from the clients to filter noise, such as downloading the dataset. Interestingly, all examples utilize a comparable number of CPUs, with the only exception being the TensorFlow CNN model for the MNIST dataset. We attribute this behavior to the simple data layout of MNIST and the asynchronous capabilities of TensorFlow, which aims to load up the CPUs with as much work as possible and process a larger number of images in a parallel and vectorized fashion.

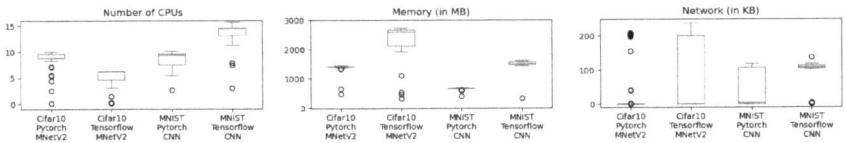

(**a**) Resource reservation as requested by PyTorch and TensorFlow clients.

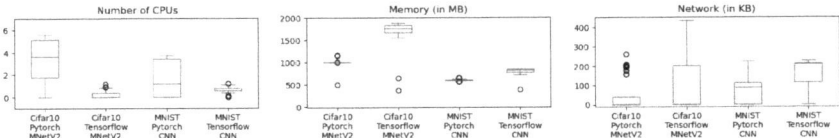

(**b**) Resource reservation as requested by PyTorch and TensorFlow server.

Figure 6. Resource reservation for different Datasets/Framework/Models.

Moving now to the FL server resource consumption (Figure 6b), we first observe that PyTorch features a slightly higher CPU utilization than TensorFlow. Another observation is that TensorFlow consistently requires more memory and network bandwidth than PyTorch. This suggests that TensorFlow may not be suitable for FL training on extremely constrained IoT or edge devices. Additionally, the TensorFlow deployment exhibits higher memory utilization and network traffic on the server side than PyTorch, as shown in Figure 6b. These findings indicate that *TensorFlow-based FL pipelines are memory- and network-intensive, while PyTorch-based FL servers require more processing power.*

5.1.3. FL Network Usage Pattern

Although the previous remark effectively highlights the divergence in performance profiles between ML implementations, an important question arises regarding the dominance of recurrent or episodic events in these profiles. The network traffic patterns depicted in Figure 7a reveal that both ML backends exhibit recurring patterns, characterized by alternating periods of (a) relative inactivity, attributed to the initiation of local training on clients; and (b) high activity, attributed to the communication among clients and the server for the exchange of model updates and parameterization between rounds.

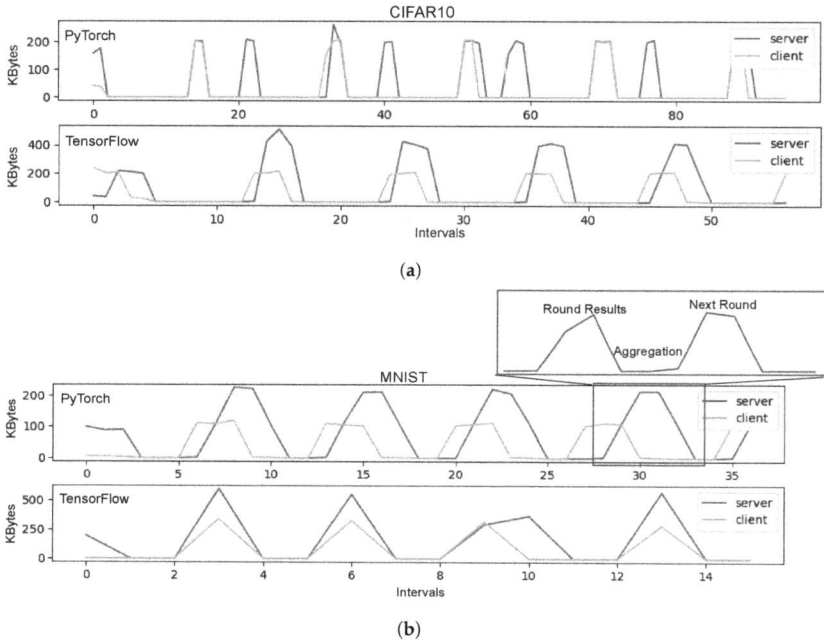

Figure 7. Network profiles profile for different framework/datasets/models. (**a**) Outbound Network Traffic for the CIFAR10 dataset. (**b**) Outbound Network Traffic for the MNIST dataset. The ratio between the sampling interval and the local processing can affect the visualization.

Specifically, after the initial model dissemination, the communication among clients and the server unfolds in three distinct steps. In the first step, the client transmits the local training results (model weights) to the server. In the second step, the server aggregates the outcomes from all clients and computes performance metrics (i.e., entropy) to assess if additional rounds are required. Finally, in the third step, the server sends the updated weights back to the clients to initiate a new round of local training.

As illustrated in the PyTorch plot of Figure 7b and in the zoom box of Figure 7b, the interval between the two peaks depends on the duration required for the server to aggregate and evaluate the results. A shorter duration results in the peaks appearing closer to each other. If the distance between peaks is less than twice the sampling interval, the synchronization step exhibits a "rectangular" shape. If the distance is less than one sampling interval, the peaks are calculated within the same interval, creating a "triangle" shape (as observed in TensorFlow-MNIST). In addition to the visualization artifacts, it is worth noting that *TensorFlow demonstrates steeper peaks and valleys compared to PyTorch, indicating larger communication messages and consequently higher demands for network bandwidth.*

5.2. Experiment 2: FL Clients' and Server Collocated vs. Isolated

In this experiment, we investigate the performance implications when collocating the FL server with the client services. For this, we explore two configurations: (i) the client and server share the same physical node and resources; and (ii) the client and server run on separate nodes. The purpose of this experiment is to establish a baseline for subsequent experiments that involve multiple clients. Our goal is to determine whether it is feasible to schedule the server on the same testbed node as the clients without affecting their performance, or if a dedicated physical node for the server is necessary.

5.2.1. Collocation Impact on Training Round Duration

We found that the difference in per-round duration between the co-located and isolated configurations was negligible. For TensorFlow, the co-located execution took about 40.7 s per round, while the isolated execution took 41.4 s per round, resulting in a mere 1.6% difference. Similarly, for PyTorch, the co-located execution took 90.8 s per round, and the isolated execution took 92.4 s per round, resulting in a 1.7% difference. Hence, *the duration of a training round is not impacted by the collocation of the FL server and clients.*

5.2.2. Collocation Impact on Resource Utilization

We also examined the resource utilization for the two setups. The results in Figure 8a present a similar negligible difference in compute and memory footprint. However, we observed a significant difference in network traffic for the TensorFlow framework. When the clients and server are deployed on different machines, the network throughput is higher and more stable than the collocated configuration. At the same time, we can notice a relationship between memory and network. The faster the network, the less the allocated memory. This relation can be attributed to buffering effects on the clients, who need to store packets locally before sending them to the server. Additionally, this observation suggests a correlation between TensorFlow as a network-intensive framework and the overhead of network virtualization in Kubernetes. In summary, our findings indicate that *the co-location and isolation of client and server do not significantly impact the deployment's performance or resource utilization metrics, except for the network traffic of network-intensive ML models/backends like TensorFlow.*

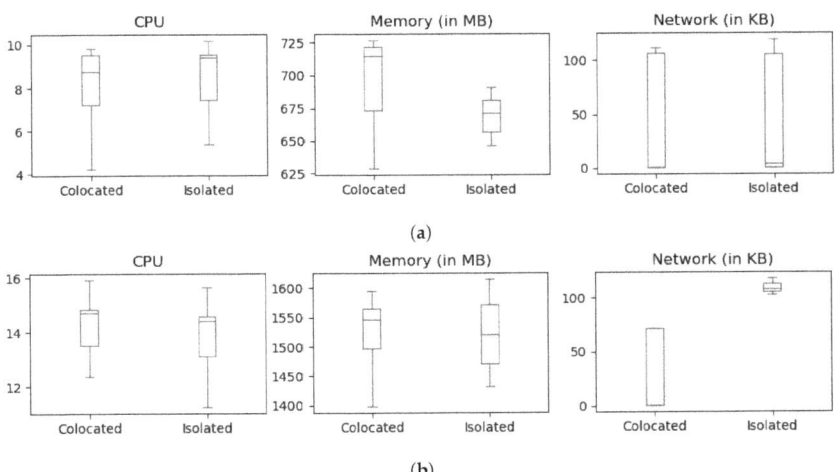

Figure 8. Analysis of collocations effects for PyTorch and TensorFlow. (**a**) Resource utilization for PyTorch client, in collocated and isolated setups. No apparent variation between the two setups. (**b**) Resource utilization for TensorFlow client, in collocated and isolated setups. Insignificant variation between the two setups.

5.3. Experiment 3: Performance of ML Backends under Constrained Resources

In previous experiments, we assessed the performance of FL deployments on fully allocated "server-grade" machines. In such a configuration, the containerized FL clients can use all of the CPU resources available on the node where the container is running. However, this scenario is uncommon at the edge, where devices have limited resources or share them among multiple applications. To understand how resource allocation can affect FL performance, we now focus on investigating FL deployments under different CPU allocation policies.

While resource management (reservation or limitation) can apply to other resources like memory and network, there are some distinctions. Memory management requires a static definition of the desired capacity, as dynamically shrinking or expanding memory can lead to application crashes (due to invalid memory addresses causing segmentation faults) or frequent swapping to disk, which harms overall performance. Network bandwidth can be limited, but end-to-end reservation is impossible without complete access to the network's switches and routers. Therefore, our investigation focuses solely on CPU adjustments, which can be made without affecting the application's correctness. For our FL deployment, we specifically consider the PyTorch CNN model applied to the MNIST dataset, and study the effects CPU policies may have on the training performance and the utilization of memory and network resources.

5.3.1. Resource Configurations for Containerized Services

Figure 9 presents the results of studying the round duration and average CPU utilization for different resource reservation policies. These policies represent various scenarios that a user may encounter in an FL deployment:

- *Native:* This configuration serves as the baseline, where no resource capping policies are applied. Because this represents what a non-expert user might consider first, we use it interchangeably with the term "Native performance".
- *Extreme over-provisioning:* Users aim for optimal training time without much concern for resource spending. This involves reserving more CPUs than what the ML frameworks require. For our setup, this configuration entails reserving 16 CPUs.
- *Best Resource Fitting:* This configuration reserves the number of CPUs that the ML framework can fully utilize without significantly extending the training time. In our setup, this is eight CPUs.
- *Resource Constrained Environments:* This configuration examines how FL frameworks perform in execution environments with limited resources. This can be motivated by cost reduction or resource-constrained edge devices (like single-board computers). The available CPUs for the client are limited to four or two.

We note that in all configurations, the accuracy remains consistent (as shown in Figure 5a) and thus, we omit the respective plots.

Starting from the Native and Extreme Over-Provisioning configurations, we observe that the FL workflow only utilizes nine CPUs, demonstrating that the training time matches the native performance in both cases (left plot). However, for Extreme Over-Provisioning, six CPUs remain unused (right plot). This highlights that FL/ML systems may not fully utilize available resources, leading to unnecessary resource spending. Next, we examine the Best Resource Fitting scenario. Compared to Extreme Over-Provisioning, this configuration reduces the number of required resources by 50% (from 16 to 8) but with a modest 22% increase in training time. Therefore, *it becomes crucial to develop a Kubernetes scheduling mechanism that dynamically adjusts the capping to match the native value of ML frameworks.*

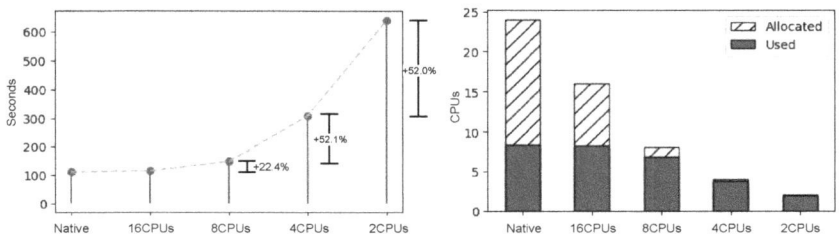

Figure 9. Correlation between training time (**left**) and resource allocation strategies (**right**).

Now, for Resource Constrained environments, there is a trade-off between increased training time and reduced processing power. Reserving four CPUs increases the training time by a factor of three (from 100 s to 300 s) but reduces the CPU allocation by a factor of eight compared to the native performance (from 24 to 4). In the extreme case of two CPUs, the training duration is doubled compared to four CPUs and is six times higher than the native performance. This indicates that *the training time increases inversely exponential to the available processing power*.

5.3.2. Inter-Winded resources

Figure 10 examines the impact of capped CPUs on memory and network metrics. In terms of memory, we observe minimal impact as the used memory remains unchanged. However, the network is significantly affected. While the total number of transferred bytes remains the same, the transmission of can vary significantly. In particular, the outliers are caused by the fewer reserved CPUs (four CPUs and two CPUs), resulting in increased per-round training time as now the processor becomes more strained due to handling both the computations and the network I/O coordination. We also observe a significant reduction in the number of transmitted packets when reservation (capping) policies are applied. In conclusion, *CPU capping can influence resource utilization of other uncapped resources, such as network traffic or packets*.

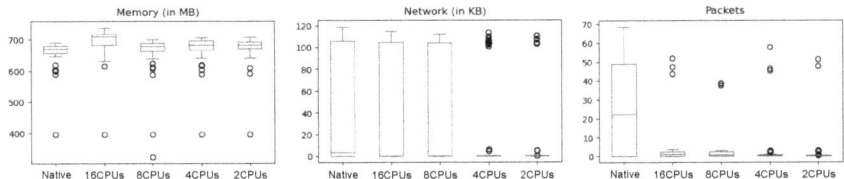

Figure 10. Correlation between CPU allocation strategies (x-axis) and utilization of memory and network resources (y-axis).

5.4. Experiment 4: Service Placement for Multi-Client Deployments

In this experiment, we build upon the previous experiment and investigate the FL performance using a single server and multiple clients. We employ 20 clients with no resource capping and evaluate how the distribution of clients across physical nodes can affect the performance of an FL deployment. As a baseline, we employ the default placement policy of Kubernetes, and compare it against a manual placement, where five client containers are fairly distributed to each physical node. For thoroughness, we repeat this experiment three times to assess the determinism of the Kubernetes placement strategy along with its impact to the predictability of the FL training time.

Default Placement Is Unbalanced and Unpredictable

Figure 11a depicts the distribution of client containers across the physical nodes of the Kubernetes cluster when adopting a manual placement compared to the default placement strategy employed by Kubernetes. From this, we immediately observe that the default Kubernetes placement strategy exhibits two undesirable characteristics. First, it results in an uneven load distribution among nodes. Second, the distribution is unpredictable because clients may be assigned to different physical nodes during each execution. In contrast, the manual strategy ensures an equal and deterministic distribution of client containers among the physical nodes. It is important to note that with 20 clients and 4 physical nodes, one would expect the manual distribution to be split, with each node hosting 25% of the total clients. However, we see a <23.8%, 23.8%, 23.8%, 28.6%> split. The difference is attributed to the fact that 1 physical node must also run the FL server, effectively deploying 21 containers. As demonstrated in the experiment referenced in Section 5.2, the collocation of clients and the server does not impact overall performance.

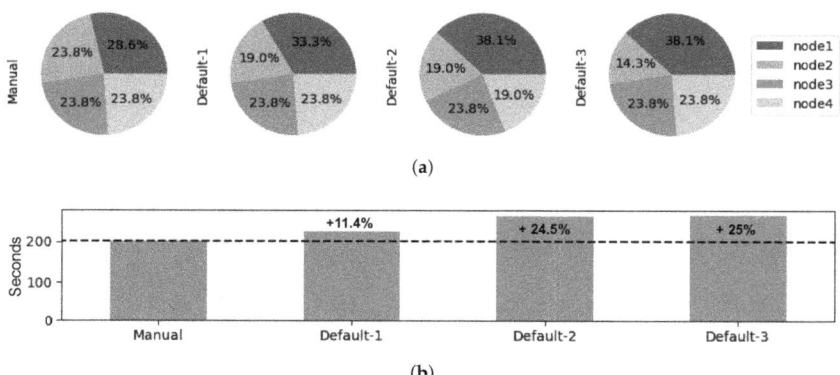

Figure 11. Training performance for different placement strategies. (**a**) Pod Placement strategies. The default strategy causes an unbalanced load among nodes. (**b**) FL round duration for different FL clients' placement strategies. The default strategy is non-deterministic and less performant than the manual strategy.

To assess the impact of the placement strategies on the FL training performance, we measure the duration of the FL rounds for each strategy, as depicted in Figure 11b. The manual strategy achieves the best performance, with a round duration of approximately 200 s. The default strategy performs worse than the manual strategy and is less deterministic. The first trial of the default strategy exhibits an 11.4% longer duration, while the subsequent trials (Default-2 and 3) with more uneven distributions increase the training time by about 25%. We observe that over-provisioned nodes, where multiple clients share limited resources, resulting in each client receiving fewer resources compared to clients on under-provisioned nodes. To further investigate this issue, we analyze the CPU profiles of the clients in Figure 12. The clients assigned through the manual strategy consume roughly the same CPU resources. In contrast, the default placement strategy of Kubernetes creates imbalances among the clients, which leads to straggling nodes [43] that become bottlenecks and prolong the training time. Examples of straggling clients are c1, c9, and c18 of the Default-3 run.

Based on our analysis, we draw two key takeaways: *(i) Evenly distributed FL clients contribute to improved performance (reduced training time) and predictable resource profiles of FL clients; (ii) the default Kubernetes scheduler creates an unbalanced FL deployment and may potentially introduce stragglers.*

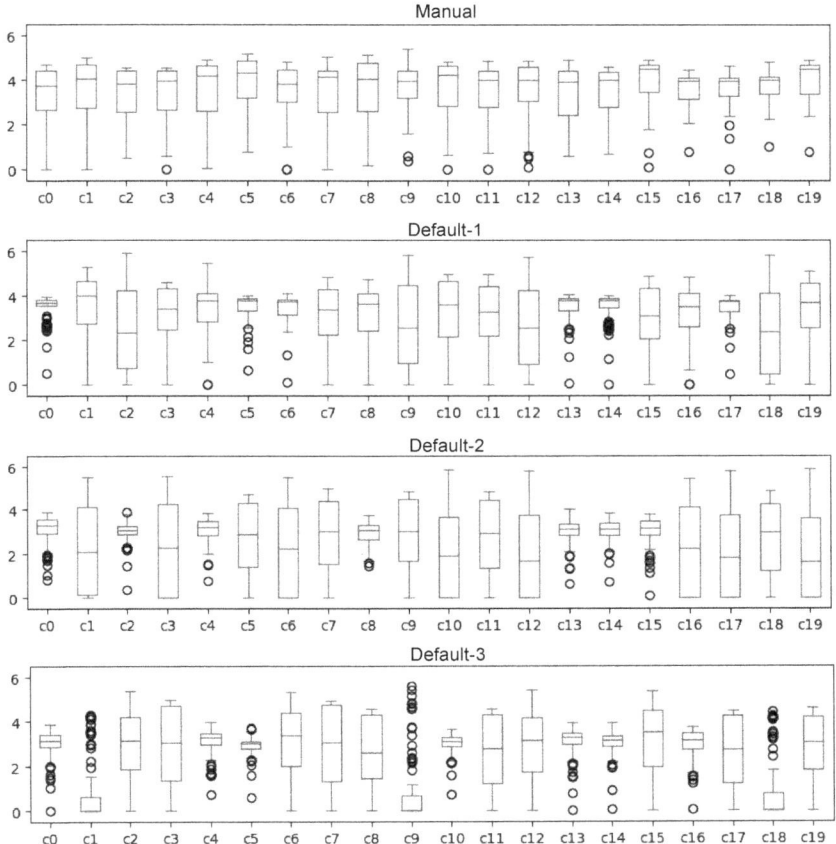

Figure 12. CPU utilization for different FL clients' (c0–c19) placement strategies. The default strategy is non-deterministic (different CPU per execution) and with significant variation among clients.

6. Case-Study: Parallel Workflows

6.1. Experiment 1: Evaluating Performance of Parallel Workflows

This experiment evaluates the overall performance when employing two FL workflows in parallel, meaning both are scheduled for execution concurrently on the same physical resources. By studying multiple parallel workflows instead of just one, we can differentiate factors specific to individual workflows from those with broader implications. Two different configurations are employed to conduct this experiment. At first, the workflows run unrestricted, allowing them to utilize their full native performance capacity. Next, each client is limited to two CPUs, thus enabling workflows with a larger number of clients while maintaining the training time within a reasonable timespan (as seen in Figure 6).

6.1.1. Enhanced Performance Stability with Capping

In the absence of resource capping, clients consume resources on a physical node arbitrarily, resulting in undesirable consequences. Firstly, the chaotic CPU usage (see Figure 13) leads to frequent context switching and cache invalidation at the operating system level, resulting in increased overheads and longer training times. Secondly, without explicit placement or resource requirement hints, the Kubernetes scheduler tries to maximize CPU utilization by fitting as many containers as possible onto a single physical machine.

However, as demonstrated in previous experiments, this approach creates a significantly imbalanced load among nodes. As a result, the performance profile becomes highly unstable (see Figure 14), making it challenging to differentiate between different training phases (e.g., local training and client-to-server communication) within the same workflow. On the other hand, *enforcing resource-capping policies brings about several benefits. It leads to more regular CPU utilization and improves the placement of containers on nodes, thereby enhancing the stability and performance of workflows.*

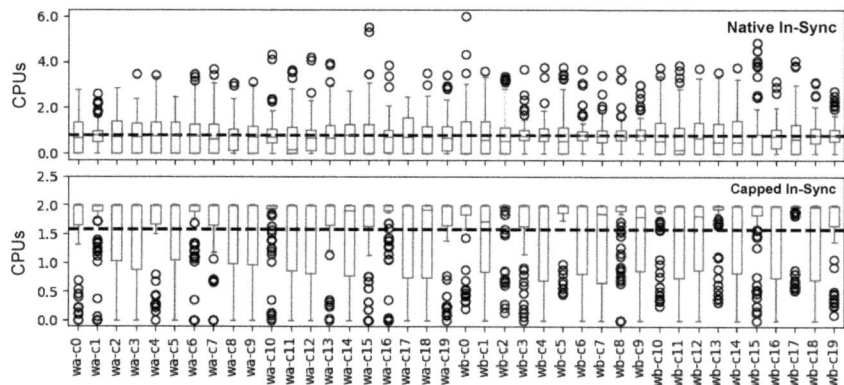

Figure 13. Average CPU utilization across all clients of parallel workloads. Properly capping the CPU can yield more predictable and stable utilization profiles.

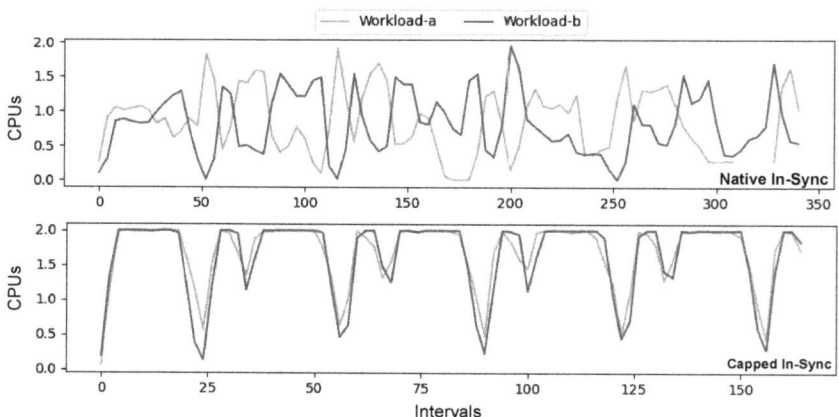

Figure 14. Per-client CPU utilization for parallel workloads.

6.1.2. Potential Deadlocks Caused by Capping

While resource capping offers benefits, there is a potential drawback in the context of Federated Learning: the possibility of deadlocks. This arises from the combination of three factors. First, training rounds commence only when all clients have joined the server. Second, resource reservation employs "thick-provisioning", allocating the full requested resources upon creation. Third, each workflow requires the total available resources from the node. The problem occurs when the shared physical resources become insufficient to serve both workflows simultaneously. If a node from workflow B interferes with the scheduling of workflow A, the resources on the node may deplete before all clients of workflow A are scheduled. Consequently, *the federated learning server will not dispatch jobs to the scheduled clients, rendering them idle or wasting resources, and mitigation of the deadlock risks needs careful resource management and allocation strategies.*

6.2. Experiment 2: Analyzing Network Behavior of Parallel Workflows

In Figure 14 we observe that, when two capped workflows are started simultaneously, their performance patterns align perfectly, resulting in synchronized peaks and valleys. However, the synchronization of communication phases (valleys) doubles the requirements for network bandwidth, which is ironic given that the network remains largely idle for most of the training time. Unfortunately, dividing network bandwidth is more challenging than dividing CPUs or memory because network operations are influenced by external factors such as congestion and latency.

In this experiment, we investigate the possibility of reducing peak demand for bandwidth by spreading out the network operations over time. To do so, we examine the behavior of parallel workflows in two scenarios: (i) simultaneous execution, denoted as *in-sync*; and (ii) the execution with a time offset, denoted as *shifted*. These scenarios are compared against a baseline where workflows are started simultaneously without any capping (*native*). We note that to determine an optimal time offset, we leverage the predictable performance profile of capped workflows and attempt to find an offset that minimizes overlap during communication phases. In our setup, a time offset of 3 min proved to be near-optimal.

Predicting Workload Shifts for Reduced Bandwidth

Figure 15 demonstrates the highly predictable performance profiles of capped workflows, with actual CPU utilization closely matching the theoretical estimation. Furthermore, Figure 16 reveals that by carefully scheduling the start times of workflows, we can achieve the same training time while utilizing only half of the network bandwidth compared to the in-sync execution. Though somewhat arbitrary, the 3 min offset between workflows effectively reduces bandwidth requirements by minimizing overlap during communication phases. Consequently, *an important area for future investigation involves exploring techniques to determine the optimal shift between workflows, aiming to further minimize communication phase overlaps.*

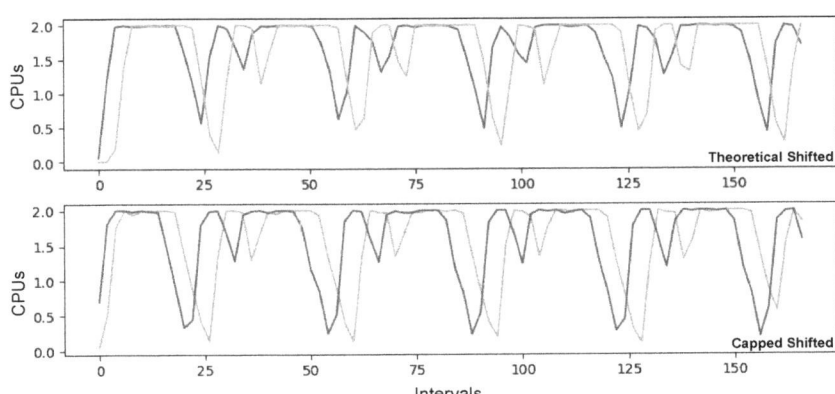

Figure 15. Performance prediction and performance upon actual deployments. Federated learning workloads can be highly predictable.

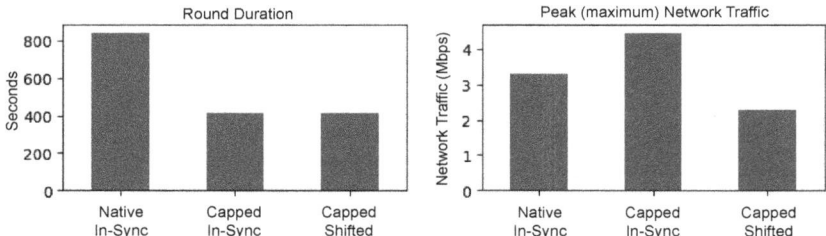

Figure 16. Duration per round and Peak network traffic of FL Servers. Capped and Shifted workloads have smaller round duration, with shifted workloads needing less bandwidth to be optimal.

7. Related Work

Due to its large-scale distributed nature, Federated learning (FL) presents unique challenges in creating FL orchestration systems including the minimization of communication cost, node heterogeneity, and unreliable network links [2,9]. Evaluating FL system performance requires stress testing the infrastructure with representative workloads and analyzing a wide range of quantitative and qualitative performance metrics [44].

Several FL frameworks exist in the ML community. LEAF offers FL training workloads and datasets [45], while FedML [46] and Flower [47] provide interoperability and extensibility across ML models. However, these frameworks often overlook the implications related to computing systems. Simulation-based studies like FedScale [17] examine the system-based performance of FL at scale by simulating realistic data partitioning approaches, network delays, and resource constraints. This approach, however, is only effective for theoretical estimations rather than benchmarking actual implementations. Oppositely, studies like EdgeTB [16] combine distributed learning techniques with virtualized testbed but do not explore the full range of implications related to FL and ML frameworks, such as resource fitting or parallel FL workflow execution. As a result, no evaluation framework currently examines resource fitting and co-location of FL workloads in cloud and edge environments while providing configurable workloads and datasets.

Performance profiling on cloud-based environments with virtualized resources has been explored from various perspectives, such as resource allocation, workload co-location, and interference analysis in cloud data centers [48–50]. Existing efforts often extract traces from entire data centers without considering the performance of specific applications. PANIC focuses on extracting insights from complex applications and creating their resource profiles [51]. BenchPilot [44] automates the deployment and evaluation of big data streaming analytics frameworks on edge data centers, aiming for repeatability and reproducibility. Unfortunately, these frameworks do not provide specialized functionalities for FL workloads and primarily focus on general-purpose applications running on virtualized cloud or edge resources.

Another aspect of research involves extracting performance insights from co-located FL workloads and analyzing how native cloud-based orchestrators place FL services in virtualized environments. Chen et al. [52] analyze interference impact on hardware and application-level behaviors in co-located online and offline workloads on the cloud. Researchers also try to exploit this information to create more efficient workload schedulers. Frameworks like Perph [53] and Perphon [54] employ ML-based methods for performance prediction and resource inference, while CTCL scheduler [55] aims to improve resource utilization and minimize task evictions in containerized cloud computing environments. While these papers contribute to resource allocation, workload co-location, and interference analysis in cloud data centers, they lack a specific focus on FL pipelines.

8. Key Takeaways and Future Work

The article presented a comprehensive and reproducible experimentation process that aimed to understand the relationship between deployment configurations and the performance of Federated Learning workflows. The study integrated Kubernetes for cluster orchestration and Flower for distributed training, both of which are widely used open-source frameworks. The benchmarking analysis focused on assessing the performance of the default scheduler with and without user hints regarding the specific requirements of a Federated Learning deployment. We experimented using two popular ML/FL datasets (MNIST, CIFAR10) and two ML backends (PyTorch, TensorFlow).

Our experiments provided many takeaways that we divide into three classes:

1. Native Performance of ML Frameworks:
   - TensorFlow requires more memory and network resources per FL training round, but demands less computational processing power compared to PyTorch.
   - The performance and accuracy of these frameworks can vary depending on the model architecture and dataset.
2. Performance over Constrained Resources:
   - Training time increases exponentially as processing power decreases.
   - Implementing resource-capping policies can improve workflow stability, but CPU capping may impact the utilization metrics of other uncapped resources like network traffic.
   - Resource homogeneity leads to faster training times and more predictable resource utilization.
3. Scheduling across Multiple Nodes:
   - Using the default Kubernetes scheduler without user hints can result in imbalanced deployment and introduce stragglers in a Federated Learning deployment.
   - Deadlocks can occur when multiple concurrent training workflows have resource-capping constraints.
   - Introducing time skew among concurrent workflows can significantly reduce network bandwidth requirements.
   - Co-locating clients and servers does not affect performance and resource utilization.

Based on the aforementioned findings, it is clear that local optimization alone, whether at the FL framework or orchestrator level, is insufficient. To achieve globally optimal decision-making, information exchange across layers is necessary. For example, FL framework client-selection algorithms should consider Kubernetes information, while Kubernetes should incorporate FL-level metrics like entropy loss and completion time. Furthermore, since FL involves geo-distributed deployments with unpredictable runtime conditions, continuous updating of information is crucial. Fortunately, FL exhibits highly predictable performance patterns that can reduce the need for continuous profiling and enhance deployment performance.

Building upon these insights, our future work focuses on two main objectives. Firstly, we aim to develop a recommendation service that provides (near-) optimal scheduling policies and configurations for federated learning. This service will be particularly valuable for novice users, offering a solid starting point to minimize resource wastage and prevent resource starvation and contention in the presence of multiple workloads. Additionally, our second goal is to create a runtime module specifically designed for profiling the current state of a dedicated FL cluster. This module will dynamically adjust configurations based on current demand and user-defined policies. By leveraging data from ongoing runs, we can fine-tune the selected parameterization to ensure efficient resource allocation and meet the evolving requirements of the FL environment. We aspire that such an adaptive approach will ultimately lower the adoption barrier for FL by reducing the time and monetary efforts involved in the design, testing, and runtime management.

Author Contributions: All three authors contributed equally towards the Conceptualization and Methodology. The Experimentation and Validation was lead by F.N., Software design was lead equally by F.N. and M.S., while the Project Management was conducted by D.T. All authors have read and agreed to the published version of the manuscript.

Funding: This research received no external funding.

Data Availability Statement: In order to foster reproducibility and enhance flexibility for upcoming experiments, we have openly shared the testing patterns we devised for this paper on the GitHub repository of Frisbee [37]. This ensures that researchers and practitioners can access and utilize these patterns to replicate our results and explore further variations in their own work.

Conflicts of Interest: The authors declare no conflict of interest.

References

1. McMahan, B.; Moore, E.; Ramage, D.; Hampson, S.; y Arcas, B.A. Communication-efficient learning of deep networks from decentralized data. In Proceedings of the 20th International Conference on Artificial Intelligence and Statistics (AISTATS) 2017, Fort Lauderdale, FL, USA, 20–22 April 2017; pp. 1273–1282.
2. Zhang, C.; Xie, Y.; Bai, H.; Yu, B.; Li, W.; Gao, Y. A survey on federated learning. *Knowl. Based Syst.* **2021**, *216*, 106775. [CrossRef]
3. Li, L.; Fan, Y.; Tse, M.; Lin, K.Y. A review of applications in federated learning. *Comput. Ind. Eng.* **2020**, *149*, 106854. [CrossRef]
4. The European General Data Protection Regulation (EU 2016/67). *Off. J. Eur. Union* **2016**, *L 119*, 1–88.
5. Truong, N.; Sun, K.; Wang, S.; Guitton, F.; Guo, Y. Privacy preservation in federated learning: An insightful survey from the GDPR perspective. *Comput. Secur.* **2021**, *110*, 102402. [CrossRef]
6. Flower: A Friendly Federated Learning Framework. Available online: https://flower.dev/ (accessed on 24 July 2023).
7. Bonawitz, K.A.; Eichner, H.; Grieskamp, W.; Huba, D.; Ingerman, A.; Ivanov, V.; Kiddon, C.; Konečný, J.; Mazzocchi, S.; McMahan, H.B.; et al. Towards Federated Learning at Scale: System Design. *arXiv* **2019**, arXiv:1902.01046.
8. Liu, R.; Wu, F.; Wu, C.; Wang, Y.; Lyu, L.; Chen, H.; Xie, X. No one left behind: Inclusive federated learning over heterogeneous devices. In Proceedings of the 28th ACM SIGKDD Conference on Knowledge Discovery and Data Mining, Washington, DC, USA, 14–18 August 2022; pp. 3398–3406.
9. Xia, Q.; Ye, W.; Tao, Z.; Wu, J.; Li, Q. A survey of federated learning for edge computing: Research problems and solutions. *High Confid. Comput.* **2021**, *1*, 100008. [CrossRef]
10. Symeonides, M.; Trihinas, D.; Georgiou, Z.; Pallis, G.; Dikaiakos, M. Query-driven descriptive analytics for IoT and edge computing. In Proceedings of the 2019 IEEE International Conference on Cloud Engineering (IC2E), Prague, Czech Republic, 24–27 June 2019; pp. 1–11.
11. Production-Grade Container Orchestration. Available online: https://kubernetes.io/ (accessed on 24 July 2023).
12. Nikolaidis, F.; Marazakis, M.; Bilas, A. IOTier: A Virtual Testbed to evaluate systems for IoT environments. In Proceedings of the 2021 IEEE/ACM 21st International Symposium on Cluster, Cloud and Internet Computing (CCGrid), Melbourne, Australia, 10–13 May 2021; pp. 676–683.
13. Brewer, E.A. Kubernetes and the path to cloud native. In Proceedings of the Sixth ACM Symposium on Cloud Computing, Kohala Coast, HI, USA, 27–29 August 2015; p. 167.
14. Al-Dhuraibi, Y.; Paraiso, F.; Djarallah, N.; Merle, P. Autonomic vertical elasticity of docker containers with elasticdocker. In Proceedings of the 2017 IEEE 10th International Conference on Cloud Computing (CLOUD), Honolulu, HI, USA, 25–30 June 2017; pp. 472–479.
15. Arunarani, A.; Manjula, D.; Sugumaran, V. Task scheduling techniques in cloud computing: A literature survey. *Future Gener. Comput. Syst.* **2019**, *91*, 407–415. [CrossRef]
16. Yang, L.; Wen, F.; Cao, J.; Wang, Z. EdgeTB: A Hybrid Testbed for Distributed Machine Learning at the Edge with High Fidelity. *IEEE Trans. Parallel Distrib. Syst.* **2022**, *33*, 2540–2553. [CrossRef]
17. Lai, F.; Dai, Y.; Singapuram, S.; Liu, J.; Zhu, X.; Madhyastha, H.; Chowdhury, M. FedScale: Benchmarking Model and System Performance of Federated Learning at Scale. In Proceedings of the 39th International Conference on Machine Learning, Baltimore, MD, USA, 17–23 July 2022; Volume 162, pp. 11814–11827.
18. THE MNIST DATABASE of Handwritten Digits. Available online: http://yann.lecun.com/exdb/mnist/ (accessed on 24 July 2023).
19. The CIFAR-10 Dataset. Available online: https://www.cs.toronto.edu/~kriz/cifar.html (accessed on 24 July 2023).
20. PyTorch. Available online: https://pytorch.org/ (accessed on 24 July 2023).
21. TensorFlow: An End-to-End Machine Learning Platform. Available online: https://www.tensorflow.org/ (accessed on 24 July 2023).
22. Konečný, J.; McMahan, B.; Ramage, D. Federated optimization: Distributed optimization beyond the datacenter. *arXiv* **2015**, arXiv:1511.03575.
23. Konečný, J.; McMahan, H.B.; Ramage, D.; Richtárik, P. Federated optimization: Distributed machine learning for on-device intelligence. *arXiv* **2016**, arXiv:1610.02527.
24. McMahan, B.; Ramage, D. Federated Learning: Collaborative Machine Learning without Centralized Training Data. 2017. Available online: https://ai.googleblog.com/2017/04/federated-learning-collaborative.html (accessed on 24 July 2023).
25. Gadekallu, T.R.; Pham, Q.V.; Huynh-The, T.; Bhattacharya, S.; Maddikunta, P.K.R.; Liyanage, M. Federated Learning for Big Data: A Survey on Opportunities, Applications, and Future Directions. *arXiv* **2021**, arXiv:2110.04160.
26. Li, T.; Sahu, A.K.; Talwalkar, A.; Smith, V. Federated Learning: Challenges, Methods, and Future Directions. *IEEE Signal Process. Mag.* **2020**, *37*, 50–60. [CrossRef]

27. Karimireddy, S.P.; Kale, S.; Mohri, M.; Reddi, S.J.; Stich, S.U.; Suresh, A.T. SCAFFOLD: Stochastic Controlled Averaging for Federated Learning. *arXiv* **2021**, arXiv:1910.06378.
28. Acar, D.A.E.; Zhao, Y.; Navarro, R.M.; Mattina, M.; Whatmough, P.N.; Saligrama, V. Federated Learning Based on Dynamic Regularization. *arXiv* **2021**, arXiv:2111.04263.
29. Cho, Y.J.; Wang, J.; Joshi, G. Client Selection in Federated Learning: Convergence Analysis and Power-of-Choice Selection Strategies. *arXiv* **2020**, arXiv:2010.01243.
30. Nishio, T.; Yonetani, R. Client Selection for Federated Learning with Heterogeneous Resources in Mobile Edge. In Proceedings of the ICC 2019—2019 IEEE International Conference on Communications (ICC), Shanghai, China, 20–24 May 2019.
31. Li, T.; Sanjabi, M.; Beirami, A.; Smith, V. Fair resource allocation in federated learning. *arXiv* **2019**, arXiv:1905.10497.
32. Symeonides, M.; Georgiou, Z.; Trihinas, D.; Pallis, G.; Dikaiakos, M.D. Fogify: A fog computing emulation framework. In Proceedings of the 2020 IEEE/ACM Symposium on Edge Computing (SEC), San Jose, CA, USA, 12–14 November 2020; pp. 42–54.
33. Dockerfile Reference. Available online: https://docs.docker.com/engine/reference/builder/ (accessed on 24 July 2023).
34. Kubernetes Components. Available online: https://kubernetes.io/docs/concepts/overview/components/ (accessed on 24 July 2023).
35. Nikolaidis, F.; Chazapis, A.; Marazakis, M.; Bilas, A. Frisbee: Automated testing of Cloud-native applications in Kubernetes. *arXiv* **2021**, arXiv:2109.10727.
36. Nikolaidis, F.; Chazapis, A.; Marazakis, M.; Bilas, A. Event-Driven Testing For Edge Applications. *arXiv* **2022**, arXiv:2212.12370.
37. Testing Patterns for Federated Learning Deployments. Available online: https://github.com/CARV-ICS-FORTH/frisbee/tree/main/examples/patterns/federated-learning (accessed on 24 July 2023).
38. Trihinas, D.; Pallis, G.; Dikaiakos, M.D. Monitoring Elastically Adaptive Multi-Cloud Services. *IEEE Trans. Cloud Comput.* **2018**, 6, 800–814. [CrossRef]
39. cadvisor: Analyzes Resource Usage and Performance Characteristics of Running Containers. Available online: https://github.com/google/cadvisor (accessed on 24 July 2023).
40. Prometheus: From Metrics to Insight. Available online: https://prometheus.io (accessed on 24 July 2023).
41. Grafana: Compose and Scale Observability with One or All Pieces of the Stack. Available online: https://grafana.com/ (accessed on 24 July 2023).
42. Sandler, M.; Howard, A.; Zhu, M.; Zhmoginov, A.; Chen, L.C. MobileNetV2: Inverted Residuals and Linear Bottlenecks. *arXiv* **2019**, arXiv:1801.04381.
43. Ananthanarayanan, G.; Ghodsi, A.; Shenker, S.; Stoica, I. Effective Straggler Mitigation: Attack of the Clones. In Proceedings of the 10th USENIX Symposium on Networked Systems Design and Implementation (NSDI 13), Lombard, IL, USA, 2–5 April 2013; pp. 185–198.
44. Georgiou, J.; Symeonides, M.; Kasioulis, M.; Trihinas, D.; Pallis, G.; Dikaiakos, M.D. BenchPilot: Repeatable & Reproducible Benchmarking for Edge Micro-DCs. In Proceedings of the 2022 IEEE Symposium on Computers and Communications (ISCC), Rhodes, Greece, 30 June–3 July 2022; pp. 1–6. [CrossRef]
45. Caldas, S.; Duddu, S.M.K.; Wu, P.; Li, T.; Konečný, J.; McMahan, H.B.; Smith, V.; Talwalkar, A. LEAF: A Benchmark for Federated Settings. *arXiv* **2018**, arXiv:1812.01097. [CrossRef]
46. He, C.; Li, S.; So, J.; Zeng, X.; Zhang, M.; Wang, H.; Wang, X.; Vepakomma, P.; Singh, A.; Qiu, H.; et al. FedML: A Research Library and Benchmark for Federated Machine Learning. *arXiv* **2020**, arXiv:2007.13518. [CrossRef]
47. Beutel, D.J.; Topal, T.; Mathur, A.; Qiu, X.; Parcollet, T.; Lane, N.D. Flower: A Friendly Federated Learning Research Framework. *arXiv* **2020**, arXiv:2007.14390.
48. Sharma, P.; Chaufournier, L.; Shenoy, P.; Tay, Y.C. Containers and Virtual Machines at Scale: A Comparative Study. In Proceedings of the 17th International Middleware Conference, New York, NY, USA, 12–16 December 2016. [CrossRef]
49. Jiang, C.; Qiu, Y.; Shi, W.; Ge, Z.; Wang, J.; Chen, S.; Cérin, C.; Ren, Z.; Xu, G.; Lin, J. Characterizing Co-Located Workloads in Alibaba Cloud Datacenters. *IEEE Trans. Cloud Comput.* **2022**, 10, 2381–2397. [CrossRef]
50. Gao, J.; Wang, H.; Shen, H. Machine Learning Based Workload Prediction in Cloud Computing. In Proceedings of the 2020 29th International Conference on Computer Communications and Networks (ICCCN), Honolulu, HI, USA, 3–6 August 2020; pp. 1–9. [CrossRef]
51. Giannakopoulos, I.; Tsoumakos, D.; Papailiou, N.; Koziris, N. PANIC: Modeling Application Performance over Virtualized Resources. In Proceedings of the 2015 IEEE International Conference on Cloud Engineering, Tempe, AZ, USA, 9–13 March 2015; pp. 213–218. [CrossRef]
52. Chen, W.; Ye, K.; Xu, C.Z. Co-Locating Online Workload and Offline Workload in the Cloud: An Interference Analysis. In Proceedings of the 2019 IEEE 21st International Conference on High Performance Computing and Communications; IEEE 17th International Conference on Smart City; IEEE 5th International Conference on Data Science and Systems (HPCC/SmartCity/DSS), Zhangjiajie, China, 10–12 August 2019; pp. 2278–2283. [CrossRef]
53. Zhu, J.; Yang, R.; Hu, C.; Wo, T.; Xue, S.; Ouyang, J.; Xu, J. Perph: A Workload Co-location Agent with Online Performance Prediction and Resource Inference. In Proceedings of the 2021 IEEE/ACM 21st International Symposium on Cluster, Cloud and Internet Computing (CCGrid), Melbourne, Australia, 10–13 May 2021; pp. 176–185. [CrossRef]

54. Zhu, J.; Yang, R.; Hu, C.; Wo, T.; Xue, S.; Ouyang, J.; Xu, J. Perphon: A ML-Based Agent for Workload Co-Location via Performance Prediction and Resource Inference. In Proceedings of the SoCC '19 ACM Symposium on Cloud Computing, New York, NY, USA, 20–23 November 2019; p. 478. [CrossRef]
55. Zhong, Z.; He, J.; Rodriguez, M.A.; Erfani, S.; Kotagiri, R.; Buyya, R. Heterogeneous Task Co-location in Containerized Cloud Computing Environments. In Proceedings of the 2020 IEEE 23rd International Symposium on Real-Time Distributed Computing (ISORC), Nashville, TN, USA, 19–21 May 2020; pp. 79–88. [CrossRef]

Disclaimer/Publisher's Note: The statements, opinions and data contained in all publications are solely those of the individual author(s) and contributor(s) and not of MDPI and/or the editor(s). MDPI and/or the editor(s) disclaim responsibility for any injury to people or property resulting from any ideas, methods, instructions or products referred to in the content.

Article

Task Scheduling for Federated Learning in Edge Cloud Computing Environments by Using Adaptive-Greedy Dingo Optimization Algorithm and Binary Salp Swarm Algorithm

Weihong Cai * and Fengxi Duan

Department of Computer, Shantou University, Shantou 515063, China; 22fxduan1@stu.edu.cn
* Correspondence: whcai@stu.edu.cn

Abstract: With the development of computationally intensive applications, the demand for edge cloud computing systems has increased, creating significant challenges for edge cloud computing networks. In this paper, we consider a simple three-tier computational model for multiuser mobile edge computing (MEC) and introduce two major problems of task scheduling for federated learning in MEC environments: (1) the transmission power allocation (PA) problem, and (2) the dual decision-making problems of joint request offloading and computational resource scheduling (JRORS). At the same time, we factor in server pricing and task completion, in order to improve the user-friendliness and fairness in scheduling decisions. The solving of these problems simultaneously ensures both scheduling efficiency and system quality of service (QoS), to achieve a balance between efficiency and user satisfaction. Then, we propose an adaptive greedy dingo optimization algorithm (AGDOA) based on greedy policies and parameter adaptation to solve the PA problem and construct a binary salp swarm algorithm (BSSA) that introduces binary coding to solve the discrete JRORS problem. Finally, simulations were conducted to verify the better performance compared to the traditional algorithms. The proposed algorithm improved the convergence speed of the algorithm in terms of scheduling efficiency, improved the system response rate, and found solutions with a lower energy consumption. In addition, the search results had a higher fairness and system welfare in terms of system quality of service.

Keywords: edge cloud computing; Internet of things; dingo optimization algorithm; salp swarm algorithm; federated learning

Citation: Cai, W.; Duan, F. Task Scheduling for Federated Learning in Edge Cloud Computing Environments by Using Adaptive-Greedy Dingo Optimization Algorithm and Binary Salp Swarm Algorithm. *Future Internet* **2023**, *15*, 357. https:// doi.org/10.3390/fi15110357

Academic Editors: Qiang Duan and Zhihui Lu

Received: 28 September 2023
Revised: 23 October 2023
Accepted: 27 October 2023
Published: 30 October 2023

Copyright: © 2023 by the authors. Licensee MDPI, Basel, Switzerland. This article is an open access article distributed under the terms and conditions of the Creative Commons Attribution (CC BY) license (https:// creativecommons.org/licenses/by/ 4.0/).

1. Introduction

With the arrival of the era of the Internet of things (IoT), there is an emerging demand for various types of portable smart devices and IoT services. In modern society, IoT technology has greatly facilitated the development of healthcare, autonomous driving, social entertainment, etc. and has become a necessity in people's lives, which has gradually transformed traditional cities into smart cities [1–3]. Federated learning (FL) has received attention recently for its cutting-edge uses in industries like health, finance, and Industry 4.0. FL makes it possible for numerous mobile devices to work together in training machine learning models without transferring raw data, safeguarding the privacy of users. FL is limited, though, because it must rely on mobile devices having the appropriate CPU power to solve the challenges faced by the millions of parameters in machine learning models in real applications [4]. FL has a substantial number of client nodes—possibly millions—each with a significantly varied data distribution. High communication latency and instability between the client and the central server are present at the same time [5].

Currently, mobile devices produce a lot of data every day, and the available local computation and storage resources are scarce. There are numerous IoT applications that simultaneously have strong criteria for high accuracy and low latency. Utilizing remote clouds with high-speed processing and abundant storage resources to offload activities and data from compute-intensive applications, the potential of mobile devices can be more fully exploited [6]. Data storage and compute demands are growing rapidly as a result of people's growing reliance on IoT. The conventional approach of directly offloading to the cloud may result in network congestion, accompanied by unavoidable response delays, and a lower overall quality of service (QoS) [7]. In addition, these resource-intensive computing and storage tasks come at a significant cost.

Distributed edge computing makes full use of distributed resources at the edge of the network, including routers, network gateways, and base stations, to provide real-time and context-aware services, which perform better when processing tasks with low latency or complex computation. The application of edge computing can effectively alleviate the problem of network delays, share the load of local devices, and improve the overall performance. However, it is important to point out that edge computing has some limitations in terms of resource and functional scalability compared to cloud computing [8].

Therefore, edge cloud computing was introduced to solve latency-sensitive computing tasks, in place of cloud computing [9]. Edge cloud computing shows a better balance between overcoming the limited computational speed of mobile devices on the one hand and reducing the too-long computational latency when offloading to remote clouds on the other hand [10,11]. However, determining which tasks are suitable for running locally or offloading to a node is a very challenging NP-hard dilemma [12].

To solve this problem, Hu and Li [13] used a subgradient-based non-cooperative game model to solve the transmission power allocation problem and the MO-NSGA algorithm to solve the joint request offloading and computational resource scheduling problems. However, the non-cooperative game model usually lacks global coordination, and each device only focuses on maximizing its own interests, resulting in insufficient overall system performance. Meanwhile, the system involves the edge system cost when considering the JRORS problem, but does not take into account the cost of cloud servers, which affects the overall cost of the system operation. In this study, when we study the task scheduling of a federated mobile edge computing (MEC) three-layer computing model, we not only consider the decisions regarding request offloading and computational resource scheduling, but also incorporate the budget constraints of the users, to improve the QoS. In addition, we consider the degree of completion of the computational request offloading task, which makes the system network fairer, and introduce a scheduling dominance degree to determine the fairness metrics. Such improvements can simultaneously improve user-friendliness and fairness.

The main contributions of this paper are as follows:

- We propose an adaptive dingo optimization algorithm (DOA) based on greedy strategies to search for the optimal solution to the PA problem, called AGDOA. The DOA incorporates a greedy algorithm, to optimize the initial value of the DOA, which improves the convergence speed. It also makes its parameters adaptively adjusted according to the convergence speed of the algorithm, to prevent it from falling into a local optimum;
- We advocate utilizing a binary salp swarm algorithm (SSA) method, known as BSSA, for the JRORS problem. We can use our approach for federated learning tasks in edge cloud computing environments;
- Simulations showed that the individual improvements of AGDOA significantly improved on the original algorithm, in terms of optimization results and convergence speed, while the search results outperformed the traditional algorithm. BSSA had a superior performance compared to the conventional algorithm for different numbers of mobile users, different workloads, and different configurations.

The rest of this study is organized as follows: Section 2 reviews related work on task allocation in edge cloud computing. Section 3 introduces the network architecture and problem analysis. Section 4 describes the original structure and construction process of the BSSA algorithm and the AGDOA algorithm. Section 5 details the configuration of the experiment, and Section 6 presents the results and a discussion of the experiment. Finally, Section 7 presents our conclusions and makes recommendations for future research.

2. Related Work

In this section, we summarize the latest research related to our proposed algorithm. The International Data Corporation (IDC) predicts that spending within the IoT ecosystem will exceed USD 1 trillion in 2060, with an expected compound annual growth rate (CAGR) of 10.4% from 2023 to 2027 [14]. One of the key elements determining the price of mobile computing in FL is communication overheads. Therefore, a major concern when implementing joint learning for IoT and mobile computing scenarios is how to lower the computation, storage, and communication costs of joint learning privacy protection approaches and how to improve the efficiency of joint learning [15]. In order to reduce the cost of the IoT ecosystem, the key issue is how to optimize the task computation strategy based on the specific user requirements of mobile devices. Based on the process of task allocation, we can categorize most of the existing research on edge cloud computing scheduling problems into two groups. In one category, we need to consider the decision problem for joint request offloading and resource scheduling (JRORS) before task execution, and in the other category, we need to consider the transmission power allocation problem (PA) during task communication.

The rational allocation of computational resources prior to the start of a task, in order to achieve optimal performance or efficiency during execution, is the focus of JRORS. This involves the task scheduling arrangement, resource allocation, offloading strategy, etc. Tran and Pompili [16] integrated the problems of co-optimizing the task offloading strategy, transmission capacity of mobile users, and resource allocation of edge servers into two separate problems of joint task offloading (TO) and resource allocation (RA), which they solved using convex and quasi-convex optimization techniques. However, making the entire system bandwidth available to a mobile device to transmit data may lead to network congestion and increase the energy consumption of the mobile device. Du and Tang [17] constructed a data placement model that dynamically allocates newly generated datasets to appropriate data centers and removed exhausted datasets during workflow execution. Ra [18] proposed a greedy staged offloading algorithm to solve the problem of task offloading. Although Odessa is fast, its offloading strategy is not optimal. Chen [19] developed a simple architecture for offloading information-centric IoT applications based on task classification and computation functions. However, the architecture does not consider communication latency. Chang and Niu [20] provided a task offloading approach using power as a constraint, emphasizing the energy consumption and measurement latency factors in the optimization problem. Alazab et al. [21] proposed an optimal routing algorithm that determines the optimal route by modifying Dijkstra's algorithm under real-time dynamic traffic flow conditions, allowing the users to interactively determine the optimal path and identify destinations efficiently. Pham et al. [22] proposed a method for allocating resources in wireless networks using the whale optimization algorithm (WOA) and improving it as a binary version based on specific scenarios. ABdi et al. [23] proposed a modified particle swarm optimization algorithm (MPSO) for task scheduling, in order to achieve the goal of shortening the completion time of a task in cloud computing. Mao et al. [24] and Shojafar et al. [25] studied the joint computation offloading and resource scheduling (RS) problem; however, they only considered a base station (BS), to accomplish the computational tasks in IoT systems.

During the task of carrying out the communication process, PA mainly solves the problem of how to allocate the transmission power appropriately to optimize the communication quality, energy consumption, and other factors during the communication process.

Haxhibeqiri [26] reported a study of LoRaWAN uplink traffic, in which the packet delivery rate decreased exponentially with the increase in the number of end nodes in the network. Mikhaylov et al. [27] presented an estimation of the throughput of the

LoRa technology taking into account the broadcast time of the packet transmission. As a result, the maximum number of end nodes that could communicate with the gateway could be determined. Tang et al. [28] proposed an efficient coordinate-based indexing mechanism to solve the fast lookup problem, using a superposition jump to minimize the index lookup delay. Rajab et al. [29] considered a dense network deployment of IoT devices and propose a time scheduling algorithm and a distance spreading factor algorithm to reduce the probability of collisions, thus achieving higher throughput and lower transmission power. Rodrigues et al. [30] proposed a deployment strategy for 6 G IoT environments utilizing the machine learning algorithms particle swarm optimization (PSO) and k-means clustering (KMC), and considering processing, transmission, and backhaul communication to improve the transmission power. All of the above studies considered the system operational efficiency without taking into account factors such as fairness, user friendliness, and user budget related to QoS.

Hu and Li [13] considered a system with one macro BS and several micro BSs and solved the transmission power allocation problem using a subgradient-based non-cooperative game model and solved the dual decision-making problem of request offloading and computational resource scheduling using MO-NSGA. The system operation cost was minimized and QoS improved by solving both PA and JRORS in the same network system. However, a non-cooperative game model usually lacks global coordination, and each device only focuses on maximizing its own interest, which may lead to the degradation of the overall system performance. Meanwhile, the system involves the edge system cost when considering the JRORS problem but does not consider the cost of cloud servers, and the overall cost of system operation is not sufficiently involved.

Many heuristic algorithms are suitable for solving the edge cloud computing scheduling problem. Kishor [3] proposed a nature-inspired meta-heuristic scheduler smart ant colony optimization (SACO) task offloading algorithm for offloading IoT sensor application tasks in a foggy environment. Vispute et al. [31] proposed particle swarm optimization (EETSPSO) for fog computing for energy efficient task scheduling. Xia et al. [32] used ant colony optimization (ACO) and the genetic algorithm (GA) to maximize the system utility and to meet various quality requirements of latency sensitive and computationally intensive applications for mobile users.

Referring to the above related works, in this paper, we focus on taking into account the whole process of task scheduling when solving PA and JRORS problems. In order to improve QoS, the pricing and task completion of cloud servers are added to the JRORS problem, which ensure the system efficiency and consider the budget constraints and fairness of users. Meanwhile, we propose AGDOA and BSSA to better solve the PA and JRORS problems, respectively. In addition, we introduce a scheduling dominance degree (SDD) to measure the fairness of the algorithm.

3. Preliminaries and Definitions

This section introduces the network structure and related definitions, and describes the specific construction of the JRORS problem and the PA problem.

3.1. Network Architecture

In this paper, we consider a simple three-layer edge cloud computing model for multi-user MEC, as shown in Figure 1. The first layer is the IoT layer, which consists of a set of mobile devices. After the user decides the request offloading and computational resource scheduling, the IoT layer sends the request from mobile devices to the second edge layer or the third cloud layer. The edge layer is closer to the IoT layer and consists of a set of miniature base stations with edge servers. The cloud layer is further away from the IoT layer and consists of a macro base station with one deep cloud for processing large amounts of data and storing them for future use.

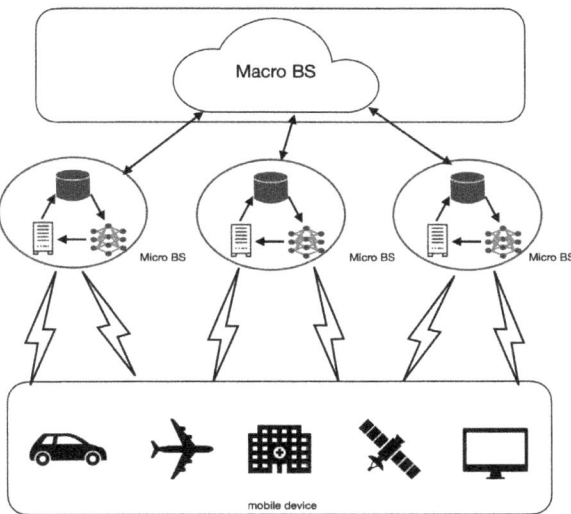

Figure 1. A three-layer edge cloud computing model.

We assume that there is one macro base station with a cloud server, n micro base stations (BSs) with edge servers, and that the total number of mobile users is n. The locations and heights of all BSs are fixed. The average power consumption Pma and computational power Rma of the macro base station are two times the average power consumption Pmi and computational power Rmi of the micro base station, respectively. The maximum transmission power of a mobile user is Pmax. Each mobile user u generates one computational request at a time, and the request includes Qu = <Wq, Sg, Prg, Tgq, Tbq>, where Wq represents the workload of request q, i.e., the amount of computation required to fulfill the request, and Sg represents the size of the request input data. We use Prg to denote the request priority that represents the importance of different requests. Tgq and Tbq are the desirable latency threshold and tolerable latency threshold, respectively. The average delay Tavg = (Tgq − Tbq)/2 for request q. The location of the mobile user is denoted by put and the location of the base station is denoted by pnt.

3.2. Definition of JRORS

The JRORS problem is integrated as a system welfare maximization problem, and the goodness of solutions to the resource offloading and computational resource scheduling problems is summarized as the system welfare (W). In order to optimize the system efficiency, W takes into account the request response time, edge system utility, edge system cost, and extra cost. Moreover, to improve QoS, we add application completion and cloud server pricing to the considerations. We formulate the PA problem as in Equations (1) and (2). Request q is obtained from all request queues Q, and the base station n belongs to all BSs. Where x_{qn} denotes an indication whether request q is assigned to the base station or not, where 0 denotes assignment to a macro base station and 1 denotes assignment to a micro base station. R_n represents the computing power of base station n, and R_{qn} represents the computing resources allocated by base station n to request q, k_q denotes the edge system utility, c_q denotes the edge system cost of processing request q, and e_q denotes the additional cost of offloading request q to the macro base station. In Equation (3), c_r denotes the computation of the application completion rate, and in Equation (4), $cost$ denotes the server pricing, which consists of the edge server pricing $cost_{Mi}$ and the cloud server pricing $cost_{Ma}$. λ_1 and λ_2 are the weights of the program completion rate and the server pricing.

$$\begin{aligned} &\text{max} W \\ \text{s.t.} \quad &\sum_{n \in N} x_{qn} \leq 1, \forall q \in Q \\ &x_{qn} \in \{0,1\} \ \forall q \in Q, n \in N \\ &\sum_{q \in Q} R_{qn} \leq R_n \ \forall n \in N \\ &R_{qn} > 0, \ \forall q \in Q, n \in N. \end{aligned} \quad (1)$$

$$W = \sum_n^N \sum_q^Q [x_{qn}(k_q - c_q) - (1 - x_{qn})e_q] + \lambda_1 \times c\_r - \lambda_2 \times cost \quad (2)$$

$$c\_r = \frac{\sum_{n \in N} x_{qn}}{cost} \quad (3)$$

$$cost = cost_{Ma} + cost_{Mi} \quad (4)$$

3.3. Definition of PA

The PA problem is a key issue in IoT that involves rationally distributing the limited transmission power to different users to maximize the system performance. To minimize the energy E consumed by the entire system in transmitting data, we formulate the PA problem as Equation (5). Where, $p_{un}(t)$ represents the transmission power from mobile user u to base station n, and this is limited by the upper power limit p_{max}.

$$\text{min} E = \sum_n^N \sum_u^U E_u^{tra}(t) \quad (5)$$

$$\begin{aligned} E_u^{tra}(t) &= p_{un}(t) \cdot t_{up}^q \\ \text{s.t.} \ 0 &\leq p_{un}(t) \leq p_{max} \ \forall n \in N, \forall u \in U \end{aligned} \quad (6)$$

where $E_u^{tra}(t)$ is the transmission energy consumption for each data offload from mobile user u to the BS n, described by Equation (6). The constraint on $p_{un}(t)$ guarantees the transmission power of each mobile user. t_{up}^q represents the uplink transmission time from request q to base station n.

The solution of the power allocation problem can help optimize network performance and improve communication quality and energy efficiency. However, due to the complex channel characteristics, interference, and power constraints involved, the problem is a nonconvex, nonlinear, and multidimensional optimization problem that requires the use of appropriate optimization algorithms to find the optimal solution.

4. Proposed Approach

This section describes the detailed construction process of the two proposed algorithms AGDOA and BSSA.

4.1. BSSA Algorithm

4.1.1. SSA Model

SSA is an optimization algorithm inspired by the migratory and collaborative behaviors of a salp swarm in nature, and solves optimization problems by simulating these behaviors. After initializing the population, each bottlenose sea squirt is evaluated for fitness and ranked in the chain according to its fitness value. The top ranked bottlenose sea squirts in the chain are called leaders, and the remaining part are called followers [33].

They update their positions according to different principles, and the position x^i_j of the leader is updated using Equation (7).

$$x^i_j = \begin{cases} F_j + c_1((ub_j - lb_j) \cdot c_2 + lb_j) & c_3 \geq 0 \\ F_j - c_1((ub_j - lb_j) \cdot c_2 + lb_j) & c_3 < 0 \end{cases} \quad (7)$$

where F_j is the position of the food source in the jth dimension; ub_j is the upper bound of the jth dimension; lb_j is the lower bound of the jth dimension; and c_1, c_2, and c_3 are random numbers.

The updating of the follower's position is borrowed from the idea of Newtonian motion and is represented by Equation (8).

$$\begin{aligned} x^i_j &= \tfrac{1}{2}at^2 + v_0 t, \\ a &= \tfrac{v_{\text{final}}}{v_0}, \\ v &= \tfrac{x - x_0}{t}. \end{aligned} \quad (8)$$

where $i \geq 2$ denotes the position of the ith follower bottle sea squirt in the jth dimension, and t is the time. v stands for velocity, where v_0 is the initial velocity, v_{final} is the final velocity, x and x_0 represent the current and initial locations, respectively. The pseudo-code for SSA is shown in Algorithm 1.

Algorithm 1: Salp Swarm Algorithm (SSA)

Input: ub, lb
Output: fitness
1: $x_i \leftarrow$ initial salp population considering ub and lb
2: **function** SSA()
3:    **while** end condition is not satisfied **do**
4:       Calculate the fitness of each search agent (salp)
5:       Set F as the food source
6:       **for** each salp (x_i) **do**
7:          **if** The salp population is in the top half **then**
8:             Update the position of the leading salp using Equation (7)
9:          **else**
10:             Update the position of the follower salp using Equation (8)
11:          **end if**
12:       **end for**
13:    **end while**
14:    return F
15: **end function**

The movement and interaction of virtual sheaths in the search space give SSA a strong global search capability; meanwhile, the diversity characteristics of SSA make it perform well in dealing with multi-peak optimization problems, which is suitable for searching for the optimal workload allocation scheme.

4.1.2. Proposed BSSA Algorithm

SSA has wide applicability and can solve continuous or discrete optimization problems. The load allocation problem we are going to solve is also a discrete optimization problem, this problem requires finding a set of binary schemes for power allocation that maximizes the fairness of the whole system. When we decide to allocate or not to allocate a certain workload to a particular base station, this is represented by 1 or 0. If this decision variable is represented using binary, it can be better adapted to the characteristics of the problem and the problem complexity can be reduced, to improve the performance of the algorithm. Therefore, we introduce binary coding into SSA, as in BSSA.

The pseudo-code for the key parts of the BSSA algorithm is reported in Algorithm 2. The fval_BSSA is the optimal fitness value, i.e., the maximum welfare value for searching for load assignments using BSSA. BSSA uses the pseudo-code of the binary modified procedure for Algorithm 2.

Algorithm 2: BSSA

Input: user_profile , na_min, na_max, max_lter, N
Output: fval_BSSA
Initialize parameters
1: $lb \leftarrow 0$
2: $ub \leftarrow 1$
3: $thres \leftarrow 0.5$
4: $max\_lter \leftarrow 600$
5: $convlter \leftarrow 0$
6: $dim \leftarrow$ length(user_profile)
7: $Q \leftarrow 0.7$
8: $beta1 \leftarrow -2 + 4 \times$ rand()
9: $beta2 \leftarrow -1 + 2 \times$ rand()
10: $nalni \leftarrow 2$
11: $na \leftarrow$ round(na_min + (na_max − na_min) × rand())
12: **while** t <= max_lter **do**
13:     **for** i ← 1 to N **do**
14:         Calculate fitness fit(i) using JRORS function
15:         Negate fit(i)
16:         **if** fit(i) > fitF **then**
17:             Set Xf = X(i,:) and fitF = fit(i)
18:         **End if**
19:     **End for**
20:     Update X as Leader Salp or Follower Salp
21:     Set curve(t) ← fitF
22:     Increment t
23: **End while**
24: Convert binary positions to feature subsets
25: Determine Sf, Nf based on Xf
26: Calculate sFeat from user_profile and Sf
27: **return fval_BSSA** ← fitF

According to Algorithm 2, the detailed steps of BSSA are as follows:

1. Initialize the population. Within the upper bound 1 and lower bound 0 of the search space, a salp swarm of size N × D whose position is binary is randomly initialized;
2. Calculate the initial fitness. According to Equation (1), the fitness values of N salps in the JRORS problem are calculated;
3. Choose food. The salp swarm is sorted according to the fitness value, and the position of the salp swarm with the best fitness in the first place is set as the current food position;
4. Choose leaders and followers. After the food location is selected, there are N − 1 remaining salps in the group, and according to the ranking of the salp groups, the salps in the first half are regarded as leaders and the rest as followers;
5. Location update. First, the position of the leader is updated according to Equation (7), and then the position of the follower is updated according to Equation (8);
6. Calculate the fitness. Compute the fitness of the updated population. The updated fitness value of each individual salp sheath is compared with the fitness value of the current food. If the fitness value of the updated salp sheath is higher than that of the food, the salp sheath position with the higher fitness value is taken as the new food position;

7. Repeat steps 4–6 until a certain number of iterations is reached, and the current food position is output as the estimated position of the target.

4.2. AGDOA Algorithm

4.2.1. DOA Model

The DOA is a group intelligence optimization algorithm inspired by the hunting strategy of the Australian dingo, and the algorithm implements three strategies based on the dingo's social behaviors, which are group hunting, individual attack, and scavenging behavior. Meanwhile, considering the species endangerment of the Australian dingo, a survival probability strategy is added to this algorithm [34].

The trajectory of the group hunting is modeled by Equation (9):

$$\vec{x}_i(t+1) = \beta_1 \sum_{k=1}^{na} \frac{\left[\vec{\varphi}_k(t) - \vec{x}_i(t)\right]}{na} - \vec{x}_*(t), \qquad (9)$$

The trajectories of individual attacks are modeled by Equation (10):

$$\vec{x}_i(t+1) = \vec{x}_*(t) + \beta_1 * e^{\beta_2} * \left[\vec{x}_{r_1}(t) - \vec{x}_i(t)\right], \qquad (10)$$

The trajectory of the sweeping behavior is simulated by Equation (11):

$$\vec{x}_i(t+1) = \frac{1}{2}\left[e^{\beta_2} * \vec{x}_{r_1}(t) - (-1)^\sigma * \vec{x}_i(t)\right], \qquad (11)$$

When in low survival, Equation (12) will be used to update the position:

$$\vec{x}_i(t) = \vec{x}_*(t) + \frac{1}{2}\left[\vec{x}_{r_1}(t) - (-1)^\sigma * \vec{x}_{r_2}(t)\right], \qquad (12)$$

Table 1 summarizes the key notations of DOA. The dingo in the algorithm chooses the strategy for updating the position based on a specific probability. The DOA relies on its strategy for updating the diversity of strategies to have an advantage in solving NP-hard puzzles to find a globally optimal solution.

Table 1. Key Notations of DOA.

Symbol	Description
$\vec{x}_i(t+1)$	New location for dingoes
$\vec{\varphi}_k(t)$	Subset of search agents
$\vec{x}_i(t)$	Current search agent, i.e., subset of wild dogs being attacked
$\vec{x}_*(t)$	Iteration of the best subset of dingoes so far
$\vec{x}_{r_1}(t), \vec{x}_{r_2}(t)$	Randomly selected r_1, r_2 search agent, i.e., subset of dingoes, where $r_1 \neq i$
SizePop	Total size of the dingo population
σ	Randomly generated binary numbers, $\sigma \epsilon \{0, 1\}$
β_1, β_2	Randomly generated scale factor
r_1, r_2	Random numbers generated from [1, maximum search agent size] with $r_1 \neq r_2$; $\vec{x}_{r_1}(t)$

4.2.2. DOA Considering Greedy Strategies

A population intelligence optimization algorithm's optimization performance is, in part, determined by how well it is initialized. The initialization of the population position of the DOA is generated in a random way. It is quite challenging to find the optimal solution around the feasible solution when the objective value is modest in relation to the data and the first solution chosen at random is considerably far from the ideal solution. The usual methods of optimization initialization are greedy algorithm initialization [35], sampling initialization [36], and heuristic rules initialization [37]. In practice, sampling initialization and heuristic rules initialization are often used in combination. Sampling initialization can provide diversity and help the algorithm better explore the search space, while heuristic rules initialization can provide better quality initial solutions, which helps accelerate the convergence of the algorithm and improves the quality of the final solution. The greedy algorithm constructs the solution step by step in a locally optimal way and tries to satisfy the constraints as much as possible. This method can obtain a better initial solution. We will use the greedy principle to optimize the initialization process of DOA. The pseudocode for the greedy strategy is shown in Algorithm 3.

Algorithm 3: Greedy Initialization

Input: alloted_bs, U, punt
Output: initial_profile
Initialize parameters:
1: initial_profile ← Create a matrix of size (|U| × |n|) with initial values as pmax
2: **function** greedy_initialization(alloted_bs, U, punt)
3:    **for** each user u in U **do**
4:       Get the current allocated base station index n for user u
5:       Set initial_profile[u,n] to punt[u,n]
6:    **end for**
7:    **return** initial_profile
8: **end function**

This greedy initialization procedure receives some input parameters: alloted_bs, gunt, U, punt, and pmax. These parameters denote the assigned base station for each user, the channel power gain, the set of mobile users, the transmission power, and the maximum transmission power, respectively. The allocation assigns the user power allocation scheme to the nearest base station, while the initial power of the other base stations remains unchanged. Finally, the initial power allocation scheme for each user to each base station is returned.

The greedy algorithm, as a concise method for optimizing the initial value, can provide an initial solution closer to the global optimal solution for the PA problem, reduce the number of iterations of the DOA, speed up the convergence of the algorithm, and improve the search performance of the DOA on the PA problem.

4.2.3. Proposed AGDOA Algorithm

The PA problem is a complex non-convex problem, and as it requires nonlinear computation, taking into account the data demand, channel gain, noise level, etc., this optimization method is more likely to find a local optimum. Therefore, in order to reduce the possibility of DOA falling into local optimality, we introduce the convergence speed adaptive adjustment mechanism.

We judge the convergence speed of the algorithm by monitoring the change in the optimal fitness, and then dynamically adjust the parameter na of the number of wild dogs involved in the attack strategy in DOA to balance the exploration and exploitation strategies of the algorithm. When the continuous change in the optimal fitness is small, this indicates that the algorithm may be converging, at which time, na is multiplied by 0.9 to reduce the number of dingoes participating in the attack, thus slowing down the search speed, with a view to better converging in the local search space; when the continuous change of the optimal fitness is large, na is multiplied by 1.1 to increase the number of dingoes participating in the attack, thus speeding up the search speed, with a view to better search the global space.

The pseudo-code for the adaptive tuning scheme is reported in Algorithm 4. Where tol is the convergence criterion, max_counter is the maximum number of convergence counts, and na_min and na_max are the minimum and maximum values of na, respectively. In each iteration, the optimal fitness change diff_vMin is computed, based on which the value of na is adaptively adjusted.

Algorithm 4: Adjust Parameters Adaptively

Input: Max_iter, Curve, tol, max_counter, vMin
Output: Adjusted value of **na** based on adaptive mechanism
1: tol_counter ← 0
2: **for** t ← 1 to Max_iter **do**
3:     Calculate vMin for current iteration
4:     **if** t > 1 **then**
5:         Calculate diff_vMin = abs(Curve(t) − Curve(t + 1))
6:         **if** diff_vMin < tol **then**
7:             Increase tol_counter by 1
8:         **else**
9:             Reset tol_counter to 0
10:        **if** tol_counter >= max_counter **then**
11:            Decrease na
12:        **else**
13:            Increase na
14: **end for**
15: **return** na

The pseudo-code for the key parts of the AGDOA algorithm is reported in Algorithm 5. SearchAgents_no is the number of search agents, Max_iter is the maximum number of iterations, fobj is the fitness function, positions is the initial individual position matrix, ub and lb are the upper and lower bounds of the solution space, and vMin is the optimal fitness value. In order to facilitate an intuitive understanding, Figure 2 shows an algorithm flow chart. Figure 2 shows the process of the DOA algorithm integrating the greedy strategy to obtain the initial solution and dynamically changing the parameter adaptive strategy according to the degree of convergence, thus forming the operation flow of the AGDOA algorithm.

According to Algorithm 5 and Figure 2, the specific steps of AGDOA are as follows:

1. Use Algorithm 3 to initialize the dingo population position through the greedy strategy;
2. Calculate the survival probability;
3. If the survival probability is greater than the set point, jump to step 4, otherwise jump to step 9;
4. If the random value is less than P, jump to step 5, otherwise jump to step 8;
5. If the random value is less than Q, jump to step 6, otherwise jump to step 7;
6. Perform a group attack according to Equation (9) to update the agent location;
7. Perform individual persecution according to Equation (10) to update the agent location;
8. Perform the clearance strategy according to Equation (11) to update the agent location;
9. Update the position of the group with low survival rate according to Equation (12);
10. Update the fitness value and the agent location;
11. If the maximum number of iterations is not reached, update the adaptive parameters according to Algorithm 4 and repeat steps 2–10, otherwise output the optimal fitness;

Algorithm 5: AGDOA

Input: Max_iter, Curve, conver_tol, conver_counter, na_min, na_max
Output: vMin
Initialize parameters
    1: threshold ← 0.005
    2: converged ← false
    3: consecutive_iterations ← 10
    4: iteration_count ← 0
    5: convIter ← 0
    6: P ← 0.5
    7: Q ← 0.7
    8: beta1 ← −2 + 4 × rand()
    9: beta2 ← −1 + 2 × rand()
    10: nalni ← 2
    11: na ← round(na_min + (na_max − na_min) × rand())
    12: Positions ← initialize from **Algorithm 3**
    13: **for** each position i in Positions **do**
    14:    Calculate Fitness(i)
    15: **end for**
    16: **for** each iteration t from 1 to Max_iter **do**
    17:    **for** each agent r from 1 to SearchAgent_no **do**
    18:        sumatory ← 0
    19:        **if** random number() < P **then**
    20:            Calculate sumatory using Attack function
    21:            **if** random number() < Q **then**
    22:                Update Agent position using strategy for group attack by Equation (9)
    23:            **else**
    24:                Update agent position using strategy for persecution by Equation (10)
    25:            **end if**
    26:        **else**
    27:            Update agent position using strategy for scavenging by Equation (11)
    28:        **end if**
    29:        **if** survival rate is below 0.3 **then**
    30:            Execute survival process to update agent position by Equation (12)
    31:        **end if**
    32:        Calculate Fnew
    33:        **if** Fnew <= Fitness(r) **then**
    34:            Update agent position and fitness value
    35:        **end if**
    36:        **if** Fnew <= vMin **then**
    37:            Count and update convIter
    38:            Update theBestVct and vMin
    39:        **end if**
    40:    **end for**
    41:    Update na by **Algorithm 4**
    42: **end for**
    43: **return** vMin

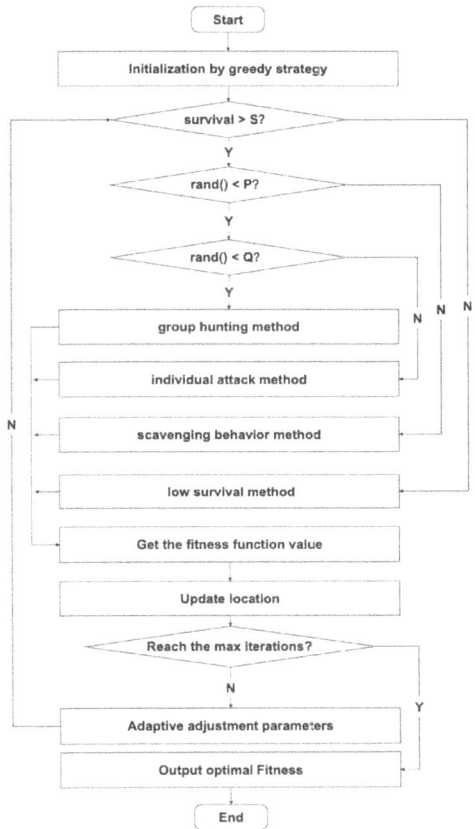

Figure 2. AGDOA algorithm flow chart.

5. Experimental Setup

In this section, computer simulations were used to evaluate the performance of the proposed AGDOA algorithm and BSSA algorithm. The performance of the proposed algorithms was evaluated under different system parameters in comparison with the existing schemes.

5.1. Simulation Settings

To evaluate the performance of the algorithms, we ran the AGDOA algorithm and the BSSA algorithm using MATLAB R-2021a. The simulation device PC was configured with 16 GB of memory, and a 2.6 GHz Intel Core i7. The simulation parameters are shown in Table 2.

Table 2. Simulation Parameters.

Parameter	Value
Number of Mobile Users u	{12,20,32,40,52,60,72,80,92,100}
Number of Micro-BSs n	{3,5,8,10,13,15,18,20,23,25}
The fixed bandwidth B	20 (MHz)
The fixed height of BSs H	10 (m)
Workload of request wq	600–1000 (MHz)
Input data of request lq	300–1500 (KB)
Ideal delay of request q Tgq	0.5 ± 0.1 (s)
Tolerable delay of request q Tbq	Tgq + [0.1, 0.15] (s)
Maximum transmission power for mobile users Pmax	5 (w)
Background Gaussian noise power Sig	-100 (dBm)
Average power consumption of microbase station Pmi	7500 (w)
Average power consumption of macrobase station Pma	15,000 (w)
The computing power of edge servers Rmi	70 (GHz)
Computing power of the cloud server Rma	140 (GHz)

5.2. Comparative Experiments

5.2.1. Comparative Experiments of BSSA

We compared the performance of the BSSA algorithm with the following methods:

1. Northern Goshawk Algorithm (NGO): NGO is a relatively new algorithm that has the advantage of diverse search strategies that may help to better explore the solution space [13];
2. Genetic Algorithm (GA): The GA performs well in dealing with discrete problems and can effectively represent and manipulate discrete decision variables through the use of binary or integer coding [38].
3. Binary Particle Swarm Optimization Algorithm (BPSO): BPSO is suitable for discrete optimization problems and it can represent the decision variables of the problem in binary [39].

5.2.2. Comparative Experiments with AGDOA

We compared the performance of the AGDOA algorithm with the following methods:

1. Greedy Particle Swarm Optimization (GPSO): The PSO application has advantages for multivariate problems and is suitable for solving PA problems involving power allocation decisions among multiple mobile users and multiple base stations. Meanwhile, the initialization of the particle swarm was optimized using a greedy strategy to obtain GPSO [40];
2. Simulated Annealing PA: Simulated annealing (SA) is suitable for complex problems and can effectively solve discrete NP-hard problems [41];
3. Subgradient-based non-cooperative game model (NCGG): the NCGG algorithm is usually used to solve the problem of optimal decision making for multiple participants in a game, and is suitable for optimizing the multi-user PA problem [42].

5.3. Performance Metrics

5.3.1. Convergence Speed

To evaluate the convergence speed of the algorithm, we used the successive absolute change magnitude to determine whether the change in the objective function value was stabilizing or not. The absolute change in the objective function value between adjacent iterations was calculated, i.e., $r = |f(i) - f(i-1)|$, and the magnitude threshold e was set to 0.005. The algorithm was judged to have stabilized when the absolute change in the magnitude of r was less than the magnitude threshold e. The algorithm was also evaluated to prevent the algorithm from falling into a local optimum. At the same time, in order to prevent the algorithm from being misjudged as converging when it fell into a local optimum, when the algorithm's r was less than e for 10 consecutive iterations, we considered that the algorithm had reached convergence, and the mobile user was considered to have found the best solution.

5.3.2. System Response Rate

To evaluate the efficiency and performance of the system, we considered the number of tasks completed within a tolerable delay time for the request versus the total number of requested tasks, defined as the system response rate.

5.3.3. Scheduling Dominance Degree (SDD)

In order to evaluate the task completion degree, i.e., the fairness, we used SSD in the performance evaluation. SSD is a metric used to evaluate the fairness of a task resource allocation scheme, and there is an inverse relationship between it and the fairness metric. SSD is expressed by Equation (13). F is the fairness metric, and r_i indicates the resource allocation for user i. In general, a larger SSD value indicates better fairness, while a smaller SSD value indicates worse fairness. We calculated SSD based on the fairness indicator Jain's fairness index.

$$SSD = \frac{1}{F} \quad (13)$$

$$F = \frac{\left(\sum_{i=1}^{N} r_i\right)^2}{N \times \sum_{i=1}^{N} r_i^2}$$

$$\text{s.t.} \quad r_i \in \{0, 1\}$$

6. Performance Evaluation and Analysis

In this section, we performed a simulation and analyzed the results of the experiment.

6.1. Performance of BSSA

6.1.1. Impact of the Number of Mobile Users

In this section, we set the base station with the same computational power, i.e., Rn = 70 GHz, and all mobile user offloading tasks were configured with the same request conditions, wq = 1500 (Megacycles), lg = 700 KB, Tgq = 0.5 (s), Tbg = 0.65 (s). We output the welfare of the system after it had run, in order to assess the effectiveness of the solution to the resource offloading and computational resource scheduling problem; that is, the performance of the fitness function JRORS, under the influence of various numbers of mobile users. To assess the efficiency and performance of the system, we took into account the system response rate, and to assess the fairness of the system, we took into account the SSD. NGO, BPSO, GA, and BSSA are all suitable algorithms for solving discrete optimization problems.

From Figure 3a, we can observe that NGO and GA showed an overall increasing trend in welfare with the increase in the number of mobile users, but there was oscillating instability. BPSO and BSSA showed a flat increase in welfare with the increase in the number of mobile users. This was because, as the number of users increased, more requests may be generated in the system, and when these requests are reasonably handled and satisfied, the total utility of the system may increase. In terms of welfare performance, NGO performed poorly, which means that NGO cannot achieve good results for the JRORS problem. BSSA had a larger welfare with a different number of mobile users, which means that BSSA can obtain a better solution when multiple factors are considered for scheduling computational resources. Compared to GA, the proposed BSSA improved by about 100% for welfare when the number of mobile users was 12 and by about 20% when the number of mobile users was 100. The complexity of the problem grows exponentially as the number of users increases. Both BSSA and GA needed to search the large-scale solution space, and hence the size of the BSSA boost became smaller. However, due to the addition of binary, the complexity of BSSA decreased on the discrete problem JRORS, so it was easier to search for a better resource allocation scheme for welfare. Figure 3b illustrates that BPSO and BSSA had a larger system responsiveness, and BPSO's system responsiveness did not change much for different numbers of mobile users. Compared with BPSO, BSSA had almost a 1x improvement in the corresponding rate when the number of mobile users was 12. BSSA's response rate naturally decreased slightly with the increase in the number of mobile users, due to the consequent increase in the search space and the complexity of the problem, but it still managed to maintain a higher response rate, which also reflects the scalability of BSSA. Compared with BPSO, at a mobile user number of 100, BSSA improved in its response rate by about 40%, which was due to the fact that the search strategy of BSSA is more suitable for the JRORS problem. From Figure 3c, it can be seen that the SSD of BSSA and GA was larger in most of the cases in the comparison experiments, which proved that the fairness of BSSA was better. Moreover, the SSD of BSSA decreased smoothly with the increase in the number of mobile users, which proved that BSSA had the best fairness when the number of mobile users was small. This is due to the fact that competition among a large number of users may lead to more competitive resource allocation. This may result in certain users always having a dominant position, while other users are unable to obtain a fair share, thus reducing the fairness. At the same time, since the SSA algorithm has the unique advantage that the group tends to move in the direction of greater comfort, this leads to a smooth, progressive search process that avoids drastic fluctuations, and the experiments yielded smooth changes for each of the performance metrics as the number of mobile users was varied.

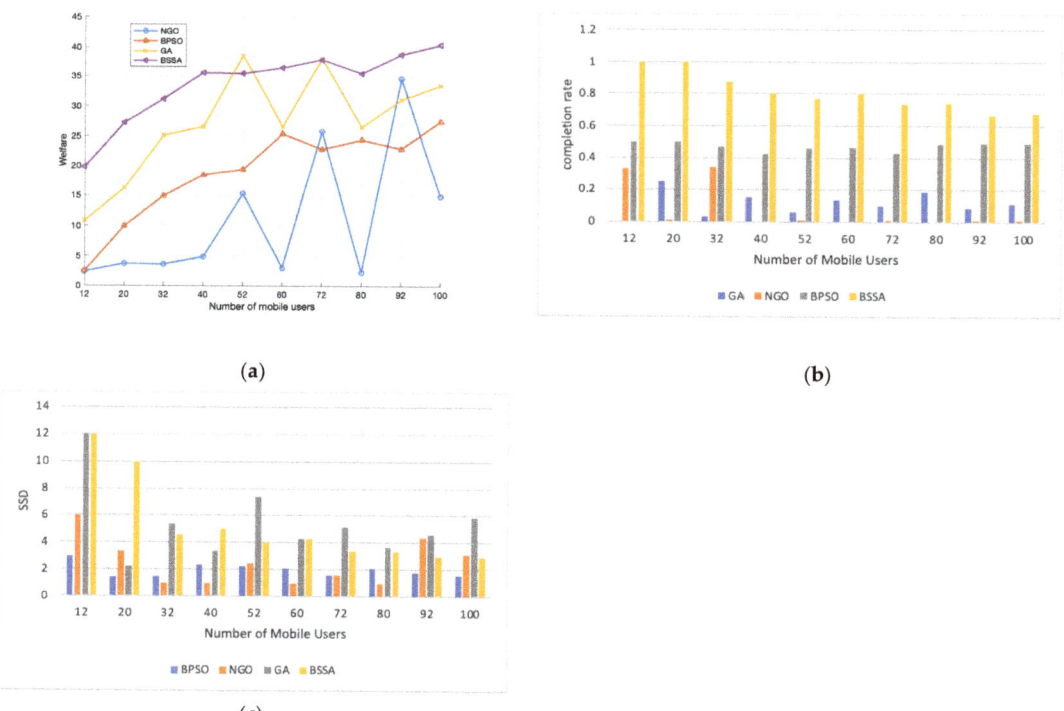

Figure 3. (a) The overall variation in the welfare of each algorithm with different numbers of mobile users; (b) the overall results of the system response rate of each algorithm with different numbers of mobile users; (c) the overall results of the SSD of each algorithm with different numbers of mobile users.

6.1.2. Impact of Request Workloads

In this section, we set the base station with the same computational power, i.e., Rn = 70 GHz, and all mobile users had offloading tasks configured with the same request conditions lg = 700 KB, Tgq = 0.5 (s), Tbg = 0.65 (s), except for the workload wq being set to a different request q. The performance of the BSSA was evaluated at wq = 1500, 2000, 2500.

From Figure 4a, it can be observed that the system welfare decreased as the request workload increased. When the workload increased from 1500 to 2000, welfare decreased by about 4% on average; when the workload increased from 2000 to 2500, the welfare decreased by about 2% on average. This is due to the fact that when the computational task requests from the BS exceed the scheduling load that the base station can handle, it becomes under-resourced and reduces the system welfare value. Figure 4b shows that when the number of mobile users is small, different request workloads have essentially no effect on the SSD. When the number of mobile users was high, the SSD decreased by 3% on average as the request workload increased; i.e., an appropriate request workload had a benign effect on the system fairness. At high loads, the system's resources became saturated and resource allocation delays increased, leading to a decrease in fairness when the system performed offloading tasks.

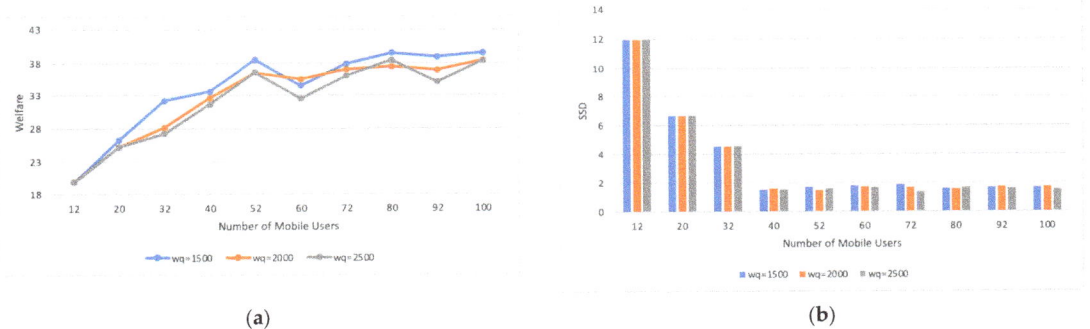

Figure 4. (**a**) The overall change in welfare for each algorithm when changing the request workload for different numbers of mobile users; (**b**) the overall results in SSD for each algorithm when changing the request workload for different numbers of mobile users.

6.1.3. Impact of Request Workload Configuration

In this section, different workload requests (wq) and different amounts of work input data requests (Iq) were configured, to evaluate the performance of the BSSA and compare the experiments with other optimization algorithms. The following figure shows the system welfare and SSD used for evaluating the system with different wq when the number of mobile users (u) was 40 and 100, respectively.

From Figure 5a,b, it can be observed that the welfare of the BSSA was consistently higher than other methods at different wq values when the number of mobile users was small. When the number of mobile users was 40, the proposed BSSA improved the welfare of GA by 36.2% on average. For SSD, the values of BSSA and GA were significantly larger than the other methods, and BSSA was inferior to GA for smaller wq. This implied that, at this point, BSSA sacrificed part of the system fairness to maintain a higher system welfare during the optimization process. From Figure 6a,b, it can be seen that the welfare of BSSA and GA became larger as the number of mobile users u increased, and the proposed BSSA improved the welfare of GA by only 29.4% on average, while at this time, the SSD of BSSA had a significant advantage at different wq. Meanwhile, the SSD of BSSA showed an overall decreasing trend with the increase in wq. Obviously, as the number of mobile users u increased with the increase in wq, more and more tasks could not be completed in time, resulting in a decrease in the fairness of the system. Similarly, as shown in Figure 7a,b, BSSA consistently performed the best in terms of system welfare for different amounts of Iq. The proposed BSSA's welfare improved by 35.7% and 16.0% on average under the conditions of 40 and 80 mobile subscribers, respectively. Thus, we can say that BSSA showed the best performance for the system welfare problem, even under different request work configurations.

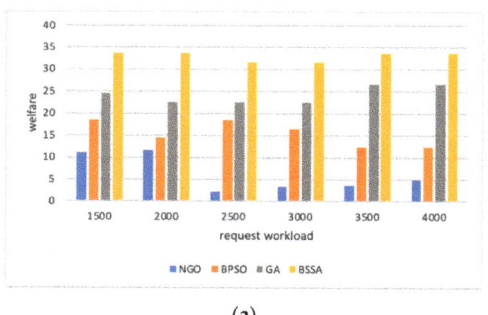
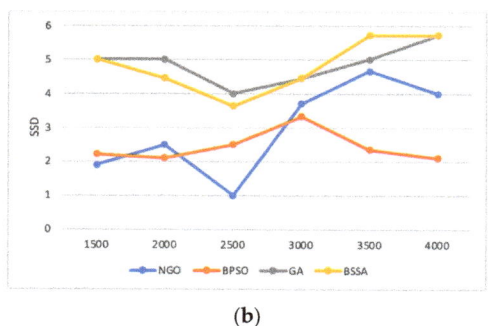

(a) (b)

Figure 5. The result of the experiment under u = 40. (**a**) The overall welfare results for each algorithm at different wq; (**b**) the variation in SDD for each algorithm at different wq.

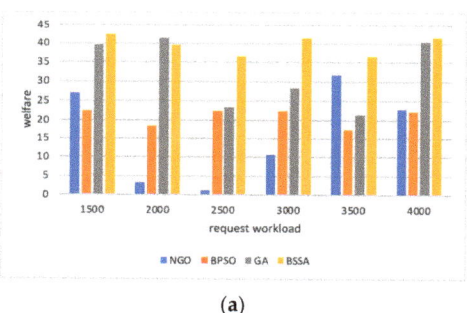
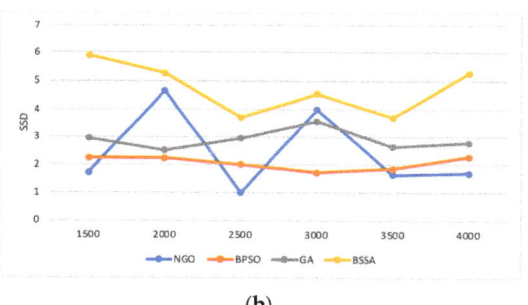

(a) (b)

Figure 6. The result of the experiment under u = 100. (**a**) The overall welfare results for each algorithm at different wq; (**b**) the variation in SDD for each algorithm at different wq.

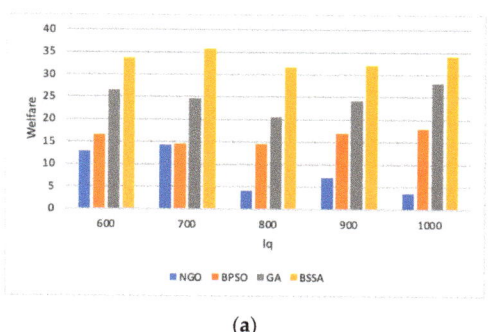
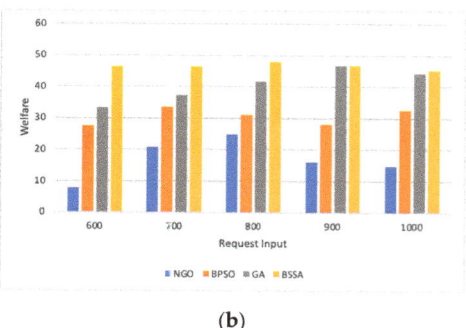

(a) (b)

Figure 7. (**a**) The overall welfare results for each algorithm with different Iq in the u = 40 condition; (**b**) the overall welfare results for each algorithm with different Iq in the u = 80 condition.

6.2. Performance of AGDOA

6.2.1. Ablation Experiments

The following figure shows a comparison of the energy consumption of DOA, GDOA, ADOA, and AGDOA for the same number of mobile users, number of server base stations, and maximum power. We can see from Figure 8a that a using greedy strategy to optimize the initial value of DOA, the initial energy consumption was significantly reduced, which was conducive to faster convergence. We can see from Figure 8b that after making the parameter na adaptive change, the iteration frequency was perturbed, and the speed of each descent became faster, which helped to prevent the DOA from falling into a local optimum. We can see from Figure 8c that after using the greedy strategy to optimize the initialization process of DOA and making the parameter na change adaptively, the optimized DOA algorithm obtained a better initial value, while descending faster. The overall ablation experiment results in Figure 8d showed that the greedy algorithm and the adaptive strategy improved the DOA significantly, bringing about a lower initial value, speeding up the iteration speed, and preventing from falling into a local optimum.

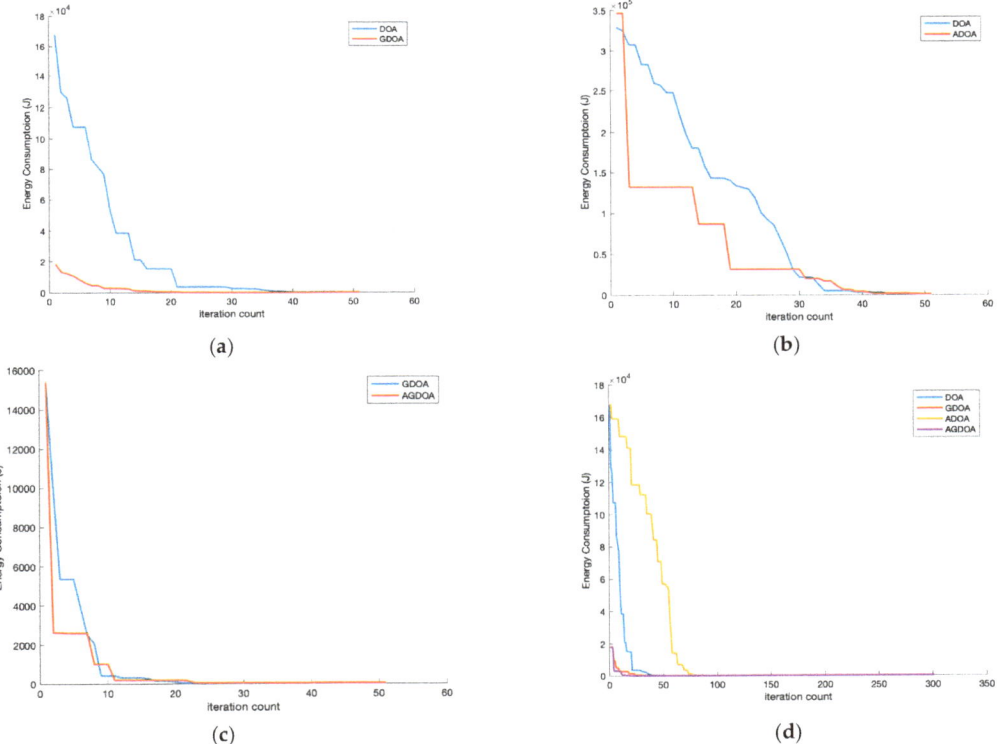

Figure 8. A direct comparison of the energy consumption results of the different algorithms as the number of iterations increased. (**a**) DOA versus GDOA; (**b**) DOA versus ADOA; (**c**) GDOA versus AGDOA; (**d**) DOA, GDOA, ADOA, AGDOA.

In order to assess the convergence properties of the AGDOA in the ablation experiments, we used the number of iterations required for the algorithm to reach the converged state as the convergence rate for comparison. The number of convergence iterations for the different numbers of mobile users in DOA, GDOA, ADOA, and AGDOA are listed in Table 3. As shown in Table 3, the greedy strategy contributed more to the convergence speed of DOA than parameter adaptation, and AGDOA exhibited the maximum convergence speed in the ablation experiments. In terms of the quantity of iterations required to obtain convergence, AGDOA was at least 11.2% faster than GDOA. This was the result of the joint involvement of the greedy strategy and the adaptive tuning parameter strategy.

Table 3. The converged iteration of each algorithm under different numbers of mobile users.

Algorithm	Number of Mobile Users									
	12	20	32	40	52	60	72	80	92	100
DOA	166	75	62	91	94	119	95	159	165	127
ADOA	125	69	97	69	76	111	90	110	142	142
GDOA	71	66	78	77	82	80	125	99	102	146
AGDOA	57	53	51	66	34	66	71	89	80	74

6.2.2. Energy Consumption vs. Number of Mobile Devices

We set the maximum transmission power Pmax for mobile users uniformly at 5 W. Figure 9 shows a comparison of the energy consumption of the proposed AGDOA compared to GPSO and NCGG for different numbers of mobile users. It is clear that the energy consumption increased as the number of mobile users increased. The energy consumption of AGDOA was always smaller than that of GPSO and NCGG for different numbers of mobile users, and the gap between the energy consumption of AGDOA and the comparison algorithms gradually increased as the number of mobile users increased. The proposed AGDOA increased the degree of improvement in energy consumption from 8.3% to 163.9% compared to the GPSO. This suggests that the AGDOA outperforms GPSO and NCGG in the PA problem and performs better when there are a lot of mobile users.

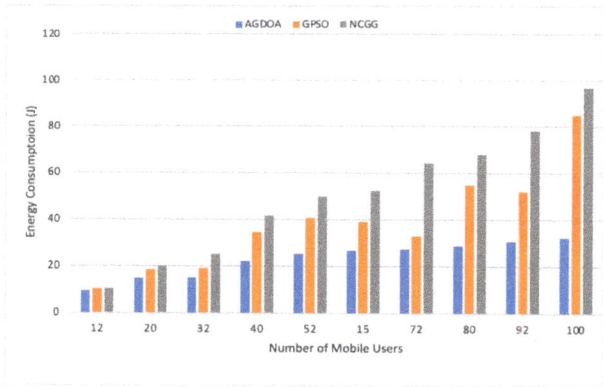

Figure 9. The energy consumption of different algorithms with different numbers of mobile users.

6.2.3. Convergence Properties of AGDOA

To determine the convergence characteristics of AGDOA, we similarly compared the number of iterations required for the algorithms to reach a converged state. The convergence characteristics of AGDOA were evaluated by setting the maximum transmission power Pmax of mobile users to 5 w with the same number of mobile users u and the number of base stations of edge servers n. The convergence characteristics of AGDOA were evaluated by setting the maximum transmission power Pmax of mobile users to 5 w. As shown in Figure 10a, when u was 12 and n was 3, AGDOA needed only 61 iterations to converge, while NCGG and GPSO needed 107 and 200 iterations, respectively; as shown in Figure 10b, when u was 40 and n is 10, AGDOA needed only 61 iterations to converge, while NCGG and GPSO needed 107 and 200 iterations, respectively; AGDOA required only 72 iterations to converge, while NCGG and GPSO required 168 and 229 iterations, respectively. As can be seen from Figure 10a,b below, AGDOA reached convergence in fewer iterations, even with larger initial values. This indicates that our proposed AGDOA has good convergence properties.

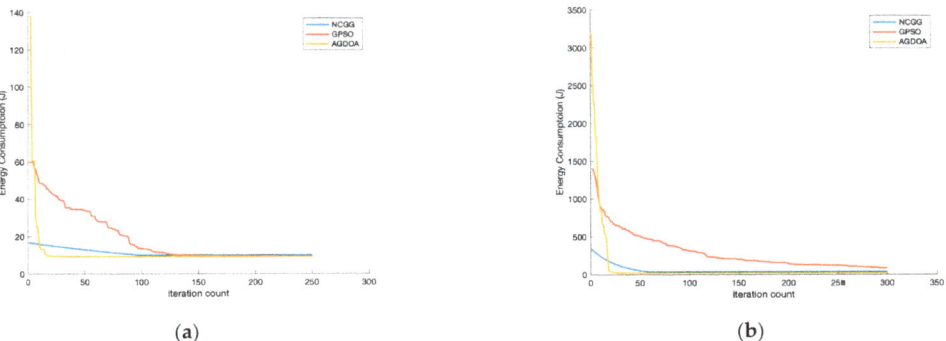

Figure 10. (**a**) Variation in energy consumption with the number of iterations when u = 12 and n = 3; (**b**) variation in energy consumption with the number of iterations when u = 40 and n = 10.

7. Conclusions

In this paper, we studied a MEC network consisting of a macro BS, a set of micro BSs, and a large number of mobile users, aiming to solve two main problems in task scheduling with federated learning in a network. For the JRORS dual decision problem, we incorporated the consideration of server pricing and task completion factors to improve user-friendliness and fairness. Meanwhile, a BSSA was proposed to solve this problem based on the discrete nature of JRORS, to reduce the problem complexity. Then, for the PA problem, an AGDOA was proposed to find the optimal power allocation scheme.

The simulation results validated the proposed algorithm, in which the BSSA maintained a good performance for welfare, response rate, and SSD for the JRORS problem. Compared with the heuristic algorithms NGO, BPSO, and GA, the proposed BSSA could find better solutions and obtained a higher welfare under different numbers of mobile users, workloads, and input data amounts. This was due to the addition of binaries, which reduced the complexity of the BSSA on discrete problems such as JRORS. In addition, the BSSA had a higher system response rate, and the number of tasks completed within a tolerable delay time of the request was more than the total number of requested tasks. Moreover, compared with the other heuristics compared, the BSSA paid more attention to fairness in task offloading.

In addition, compared with the other algorithms, on the PA problem, each improved module of AGDOA showed a significant improvement in convergence speed and initial performance over the DOA. Compared with the optimization algorithms GPSO and NCGG, the energy consumption of the AGDOA was significantly lower under different numbers of mobile users. At the same time, the AGDOA could reach a convergence state in fewer iterations for different numbers of mobile devices.

In the future, we will conduct experiments using real data, make improvements based on real applications, and apply the proposed algorithms to real applications to improve the MEC scheduling efficiency and the comprehensive level of QoS.

Author Contributions: Conceptualization, W.C.; methodology, W.C.; software, F.D.; validation, F.D.; formal analysis, F.D.; investigation, F.D.; resources, W.C.; data curation, W.C.; writing—original draft preparation, F.D. and W.C.; writing—review and editing, F.D. and W.C.; visualization, F.D.; supervision, W.C.; project administration, F.D. and W.C.; funding acquisition, W.C. All authors have read and agreed to the published version of the manuscript.

Funding: This research was funded by Science and Technology Planning Project of Guangdong Province, grant number (2019B010116001,2016B010124012).

Data Availability Statement: Not applicable.

Conflicts of Interest: The authors declare no conflict of interest.

References

1. Du, X.; Chen, X.; Lu, Z.; Duan, Q.; Wang, Y.; Wu, J.; Hung, P.C. A Blockchain-Assisted Intelligent Edge Cooperation System for IoT Environments with Multi-Infrastructure Providers. *IEEE Internet Things J.* **2023**, 1. [CrossRef]
2. Cao, X.W.; Wang, F.; Xu, J.; Zhang, R.; Cui, S. Joint computation and communication cooperation for energy-efficient mobile edge computing. *IEEE Internet Things J.* **2019**, *6*, 4188–4200. [CrossRef]
3. Kishor, A.; Chakarbarty, C. Task Offloading in Fog Computing for Using Smart Ant Colony Optimization. *Wirel. Pers. Commun.* **2022**, *127*, 1683–1704. [CrossRef]
4. Thapa, C.; Chamikara, M.A.P.; Camtepe, S.A. Advancements of federated learning towards privacy preservation: From federated learning to split learning. In *Federated Learning Systems: Towards Next-Generation AI*; Springer: Berlin/Heidelberg, Germany, 2021; pp. 79–109.
5. Ma, X.; Zhu, J.; Lin, Z.; Chen, S.; Qin, Y. A state-of-the-art survey on solving non-IID data in Federated Learning. *Future Gener. Comput. Syst.* **2022**, *135*, 244–258. [CrossRef]
6. Nadembega, A.; Taleb, T.; Hafid, A. A destination prediction model based on historical data contextual knowledge and spatial conceptual maps. In Proceedings of the 2012 IEEE International Conference on Communications (ICC), Ottawa, ON, Canada, 10–15 June 2012; pp. 1416–1420.
7. Hou, X.; Li, Y.; Chen, M.; Wu, D.; Jin, D.; Chen, S. Vehicular Fog Computing: A Viewpoint of Vehicles as the Infrastructures. *IEEE Trans. Veh. Technol.* **2016**, *65*, 3860–3873. [CrossRef]
8. Duan, S.; Wang, D.; Ren, J.; Lyu, F.; Zhang, Y.; Wu, H.; Shen, X. Distributed Artificial Intelligence Empowered by End-Edge-Cloud Computing: A Survey. *IEEE Commun. Surv. Tutorials* **2022**, *25*, 591–624. [CrossRef]
9. Du, X.; Tang, S.; Lu, Z.; Wet, J.; Gai, K.; Hung, P.C.K. A Novel Data Placement Strategy for Data-Sharing Scientific Workflows in Heterogeneous Edge-Cloud Computing Environments. In Proceedings of the 2020 IEEE International Conference on Web Services (ICWS), Beijing, China, 19–23 October 2020; pp. 498–507.
10. Chen, M.; Hao, Y.; Li, Y.; Lai, C.F.; Wu, D. On the Computation Offloading at Ad Hoc Cloudlet: Architecture and Service Modeo. *IEEE Commun. Mag.* **2015**, *53*, 18–24. [CrossRef]
11. Du, X.; Chen, X.; Lu, Z.; Duan, Q.; Wang, Y.; Wu, J. BIECS: A Blockchain-based Intelligent Edge Cooperation System for Latency-Sensitive Services. In Proceedings of the 2022 IEEE International Conference on Web Services (ICWS), Barcelona, Spain, 10–16 July 2022; pp. 367–372.
12. Krishnan, M.; Yun, S.; Jung, Y.M. Enhanced clustering and ACO-based multiple mobile sinks for efficiency improvement of wireless sensor networks. *Comput. Netw.* **2019**, *160*, 33–40. [CrossRef]
13. Hu, S.; Li, G. Dynamic Request Scheduling Optimization in Mobile Edge Computing for IoT Applications. *IEEE Internet Things J.* **2020**, *7*, 1426–1437. [CrossRef]
14. Market Research Report by International Data Corporation. Available online: https://www.idc.com/getdoc.jsp?containerId=prUS50936423 (accessed on 20 June 2023).
15. Yin, L.; Feng, J.; Xun, H.; Sun, Z.; Cheng, X. A Privacy-Preserving Federated Learning for Multiparty Data Sharing in Social IoTs. *IEEE Trans. Netw. Sci. Eng.* **2021**, *8*, 2706–2718. [CrossRef]
16. Tran, T.X.; Pompili, D. Joint task offloading and resource allocation for multi-server mobile-edge computing networks. *IEEE Trans. Veh. Technol.* **2019**, *68*, 856–868. [CrossRef]
17. Du, X.; Tang, S.; Lu, Z.; Gai, K.; Wu, J.; Hung, P.C. Scientific workflows in iot environments: A data placement strategy based on heterogeneous edge-cloud computing. *ACM Trans. Manag. Inf. Syst. (TMIS)* **2022**, *13*, 1–26. [CrossRef]
18. Ra, M.R.; Sheth, A.; Mummert, L.; Pillai, P.; Wetherall, D.; Govindan, R. Odessa: Enabling Interactive Perception Applications on Mobile Devices. In Proceedings of the 9th International Conference on Mobile Systems, Applications, and Services, Bethesda, MD, USA, 28 June–1 July 2011.
19. Chen, C.; Chang, Y.-C.; Chen, C.-H.; Lin, Y.-S.; Chen, J.-L.; Chang, Y.-Y. Cloud-fog computing for information-centric Internet-of-Things applications. In Proceedings of the 2017 International Conference on Applied System Innovation (ICASI), Sapporo, Japan, 13–17 May 2017; pp. 637–640.
20. Chang, Z.; Zhou, Z.; Ristaniemi, T.; Niu, Z. Energy efficient optimization for computation offloading in fog computing system. In Proceedings of the GLOBECOM 2017–2017 IEEE Global Communications Conference, Singapore, 4–8 December 2017; pp. 1–6.
21. Alazab, A.; Venkatraman, S.; Abawajy, J.; Alazab, M. An optimal transportation routing approach using GIS-based dynamic traffic flows. In *Proceedings of the ICMTA 2010, Proceedings of the International Conference on Management Technology and Applications, Singapore, 10 September 2010*; Research Publishing Services: Singapore, 2011; pp. 172–178.
22. Pham, Q.V.; Mirjalili, S.; Kumar, N.; Alazab, M.; Hwang, W.J. Whale optimization algorithm with applications to resource allocation in wireless networks. *IEEE Trans. Veh. Technol.* **2020**, *69*, 4285–4297. [CrossRef]

23. Abdi, S.; Motamedi, S.A.; Sharifian, S. Task scheduling using modified PSO algorithm in cloud computing environment. In Proceedings of the International Conference on Machine Learning, Electrical and Mechanical Engineering, Dubai, United Arab Emirates, 8–9 January 2014; Volume 4, pp. 8–12.
24. Mao, Y.; Zhang, J.; Letaief, K.B. Dynamic computation offloading for mobile-edge computing with energy harvesting devices. *IEEE J. Sel. Areas Commun.* **2016**, *34*, 3590–3605. [CrossRef]
25. Shojafar, M.; Cordeschi, N.; Baccarelli, E. Energy-efficient adaptive resource management for real-time vehicular cloud services. *IEEE Trans. Cloud Comput.* **2019**, *7*, 196–209. [CrossRef]
26. Haxhibeqiri, J.; Van den Abeele, F.; Moerman, I.; Hoebeke, J. LoRa scalability: A simulation model based on interference measurements. *Sensors* **2017**, *17*, 1193. [CrossRef]
27. Mikhaylov, K.; Petäjäjärvi, J.; Janhunen, J. On LoRaWAN scalability: Empirical evaluation of susceptibility to inter-network interference. In Proceedings of the 2017 European Conference on Networks and Communications (EuCNC), Oulu, Finland, 12–15 June 2017; pp. 1–6.
28. Tang, S.; Du, X.; Lu, Z.; Gai, K.; Wu, J.; Hung, P.C.; Choo, K.K.R. Coordinate-based efficient indexing mechanism for intelligent IoT systems in heterogeneous edge computing. *J. Parallel Distrib. Comput.* **2022**, *166*, 45–56. [CrossRef]
29. Rajab, H.; Cinkler, T.; Bouguera, T. IoT scheduling for higher throughput and lower transmission power. *Wirel. Netw.* **2021**, *27*, 1701–1714. [CrossRef]
30. Rodrigues, T.K.; Suto, K.; Kato, N. Edge cloud server deployment with transmission power control through machine learning for 6G Internet of Things. *IEEE Trans. Emerg. Top. Comput.* **2019**, *9*, 2099–2108. [CrossRef]
31. Vispute, S.D.; Vashisht, P. Energy-Efficient Task Scheduling in Fog Computing Based on Particle Swarm Optimization. *SN Comput. Sci.* **2023**, *4*, 391. [CrossRef]
32. Xia, W.; Shen, L. Joint Resource Allocation at Edge Cloud Based on Ant Colony Optimization and Genetic Algorithm. *Wirel. Pers. Commun.* **2021**, *117*, 355–386. [CrossRef]
33. Mirjalili, S.; Gandomi, A.H.; Mirjalili, S.Z.; Saremi, S.; Faris, H.; Mirjalili, S.M. Salp Swarm Algorithm: A bio-inspired optimizer for engineering design problems. *Adv. Eng. Softw.* **2017**, *114*, 163–191. [CrossRef]
34. Peraza-Vázquez, H.; Peña-Delgado, A.F.; Echavarría-Castillo, G.; Morales-Cepeda, A.B.; Velasco-Álvarez, J.; Ruiz-Perez, F. A bio-inspired method for engineering design optimization inspired by dingoes hunting strategies. *Math. Probl. Eng.* **2021**, *2021*, 9107547. [CrossRef]
35. Pan, G.; Li, K.; Ouyang, A.; Li, K. Hybrid immune algorithm based on greedy algorithm and delete-cross operator for solving TSP. *Soft Comput.* **2016**, *20*, 555–566. [CrossRef]
36. de Perthuis de Laillevault, A.; Doerr, B.; Doerr, C. Money for nothing: Speeding up evolutionary algorithms through better initialization. In Proceedings of the 2015 Annual Conference on Genetic and Evolutionary Computation, Yangon, Myanmar, 26–28 August 2015; pp. 815–822.
37. Guo, M.; Xin, B.; Chen, J.; Wang, Y. Multi-agent coalition formation by an efficient genetic algorithm with heuristic initialization and repair strategy. *Swarm Evol. Comput.* **2020**, *55*, 100686. [CrossRef]
38. Das, S.; Idicula, S.M. Greedy search-binary PSO hybrid for biclustering gene expression data. *Int. J. Comput. Appl.* **2010**, *2*, 1–5. [CrossRef]
39. Alrefaei, M.H.; Andradóttir, S. A simulated annealing algorithm with constant temperature for discrete stochastic optimization. *Manag. Sci.* **1999**, *45*, 748–764. [CrossRef]
40. Dehghani, M.; Hubálovský, Š.; Trojovský, P. Northern goshawk optimization: A new swarm-based algorithm for solving optimization problems. *IEEE Access* **2021**, *9*, 162059–162080. [CrossRef]
41. Mirjalili, S.; Mirjalili, S. Genetic algorithm. In *Evolutionary Algorithms and Neural Networks: Theory and Applications*; Springer: Berlin/Heidelberg, Germany, 2019; pp. 43–55.
42. El-Maleh, A.H.; Sheikh, A.T.; Sait, S.M. Binary particle swarm optimization (BPSO) based state assignment for area minimization of sequential circuits. *Appl. Soft Comput.* **2013**, *13*, 4832–4840. [CrossRef]

Disclaimer/Publisher's Note: The statements, opinions and data contained in all publications are solely those of the individual author(s) and contributor(s) and not of MDPI and/or the editor(s). MDPI and/or the editor(s) disclaim responsibility for any injury to people or property resulting from any ideas, methods, instructions or products referred to in the content.

Article

Implementation and Evaluation of a Federated Learning Framework on Raspberry PI Platforms for IoT 6G Applications

Lorenzo Ridolfi, David Naseh, Swapnil Sadashiv Shinde and Daniele Tarchi *

Department of Electrical, Electronic and Information Engineering "Guglielmo Marconi", University of Bologna, 40126 Bologna, Italy; lorenzo.ridolfi6@studio.unibo.it (L.R.); david.naseh2@unibo.it (D.N.); swapnil.shinde2@unibo.it (S.S.S.)
* Correspondence: daniele.tarchi@unibo.it

Abstract: With the advent of 6G technology, the proliferation of interconnected devices necessitates a robust, fully connected intelligence network. Federated Learning (FL) stands as a key distributed learning technique, showing promise in recent advancements. However, the integration of novel Internet of Things (IoT) applications and virtualization technologies has introduced diverse and heterogeneous devices into wireless networks. This diversity encompasses variations in computation, communication, storage resources, training data, and communication modes among connected nodes. In this context, our study presents a pivotal contribution by analyzing and implementing FL processes tailored for 6G standards. Our work defines a practical FL platform, employing Raspberry Pi devices and virtual machines as client nodes, with a Windows PC serving as a parameter server. We tackle the image classification challenge, implementing the FL model via PyTorch, augmented by the specialized FL library, Flower. Notably, our analysis delves into the impact of computational resources, data availability, and heating issues across heterogeneous device sets. Additionally, we address knowledge transfer and employ pre-trained networks in our FL performance evaluation. This research underscores the indispensable role of artificial intelligence in IoT scenarios within the 6G landscape, providing a comprehensive framework for FL implementation across diverse and heterogeneous devices.

Keywords: federated learning; transfer learning; virtual machines; raspberry PI; proof-of-concept

Citation: Ridolfi, L.; Naseh, D.; Shinde, S.S.; Tarchi, D. Implementation and Evaluation of a Federated Learning Framework on Raspberry PI Platforms for IoT 6G Applications. *Future Internet* **2023**, *15*, 358. https://doi.org/10.3390/fi15110358

Academic Editors: Qiang Duan and Zhihui Lu

Received: 28 September 2023
Revised: 27 October 2023
Accepted: 30 October 2023
Published: 31 October 2023

Copyright: © 2023 by the authors. Licensee MDPI, Basel, Switzerland. This article is an open access article distributed under the terms and conditions of the Creative Commons Attribution (CC BY) license (https://creativecommons.org/licenses/by/4.0/).

1. Introduction

The upcoming 6G technology is expected to create an intelligent, fully connected, and digitized society through large-scale deployments of distributed intelligent networks [1]. This is expected to create a plethora of new intelligent services and applications with specific demands. Internet of Things (IoT) technology has foreseen great success through enabling 5G solutions and is expected to play a key role in 6G society [2]. With the integration of IoT subcases into different wireless scenarios, many sensory nodes are expected to be deployed in the 6G world, with the ability to sense nearby environments and produce tons of high-quality data. This data can be extremely important to enable intelligent solutions in the 6G networks [3].

Machine Learning (ML) is another important technology that has acquired a central role in the 6G vision; in particular, to enable intelligent services [4,5]. Various ML methods are expected to be deployed in different wireless scenarios to enable intelligent solutions. ML can be extremely useful for analyzing the 6G network data and harnessing its intelligence. The Centralized Learning (CL) method is one of the most common approaches to generating AI algorithms in distributed communication scenarios. This involves concentrating all training data on a single server, which can complete the model's training individually due to its high computing power. However, this solution may not be particularly efficient when analyzed from a 6G perspective. Next-generation networks will need to handle large amounts of information, most of which will be produced by devices at the network's edge. In this scenario, moving data to a central server is expensive in terms of communication resources and represents a potential risk of network overload. It can induce large communication overheads and has limited applicability in the resource-constrained and time-critical 6G world. Furthermore, privacy and security restrictions can also limit the possibility of data transmissions to server nodes.

A more efficient alternative is offered by Distributed Learning (DL), which is based on decentralization of training [5]. In this approach, the training phase will be carried out directly on end devices or possibly on specific nodes located strategically on the edge of the network. DL allows for the training of models by processing the local data of each device directly within it. This approach enables the use of large amounts of heterogeneous data scattered throughout the vast network, involving a larger audience of users than the centralized variant. This approach also introduces additional advantages. First, it makes it possible to significantly reduce data flow, communication overhead, and network traffic. Second, there is greater protection for end-user privacy as data are processed directly on personal terminals. Finally, by distributing the computational load among the multitude of devices, it is also possible to obtain essential improvements in terms of energy management. Several forms of distributed learning, such as Federated Learning (FL), collaborative learning, split learning, and multi-agent reinforcement learning, are widely considered in wireless networks for enabling intelligence-at-the-edge. Among others, FL has achieved great success in building high-quality ML models based on dispersed wireless data [6,7]. FL is also a candidate for next-generation 6G communication standard allowing for setting up an intelligence-at-the-edge framework [8].

The traditional FL approach includes a set of devices with datasets and a server node [6]. The server node initiates the learning process by defining the learning task, and corresponding model, which is then transmitted to FL devices. With the help of received model parameters from the server node (also called the global model), their datasets, and onboard computation capabilities, each FL device is expected to train the ML model locally. Then, the updates to the ML model from each device are sent to the server. After receiving the updates from the devices, the server node can use the aggregation function (e.g., Federated Averaging (FedAvg)) to create a new global model. This aggregation phase allows devices to share their training knowledge. The devices then use the new global model in the next round of model local training. The process lasts for several rounds till some predefined stopping criteria are fulfilled. Though this approach has several advantages in terms of reduced data transmission costs, enhanced data privacy, etc., and several new challenges have emerged. One of the major challenges in the FL framework is the presence of heterogeneous nodes with different capabilities, in terms of available datasets, computation power, etc. The presence of heterogeneous nodes can be common in different 6G scenarios. Also, the amount of time required to achieve the convergence of the FL model can be unaccepted in latency-critical 6G use cases. Therefore, it is important to analyze the performance of the traditional FL approach in the presence of heterogeneous devices to have a common understanding of their behaviors and possible solutions to tackle the challenges.

1.1. Technological Background

ML technology has gained a lot of attention for enabling intelligent solutions in wireless networks including mobile communication networks [9], wireless sensor networks [10], transportation systems [6], non-terrestrial networks [11]. Complex wireless communication problems such as resource management [12], data offloading toward edge networks [13], spectrum management [14], routing [15], user-server allocation [7], etc., can effectively solve through different ML techniques. Among others, FL is widely considered a distributed learning approach to provide efficient learning solutions. In one paper [16], the authors proposed energy-efficient FL solutions in wireless communication environments. Work in [17] discusses the applicability of FL solutions in smart city environments. FL is also widely used to solve vehicular network problems, especially in edge computing environments [6].

FL solutions are also considered over different satellite networks [18]. However, these works have analyzed the performance of FL solutions in different wireless environments, without considering the practical implementations.

Recently, several authors considered a learning testbed implemented through different sensory nodes to measure the ML solution's performances. Raspberry Pi devices are commonly considered to analyze the performance of ML solutions proposed to solve different wireless networking problems. In [19], the authors proposed Reinforcement Learning (RL)-based solutions for efficient routing processes in software-defined wireless sensor networks. The testbed includes Raspberry Pi devices as sensor nodes to analyze the performance of RL solutions. In one paper [20], the proposed deep learning-based solutions for detecting a speed bump in an intelligent vehicular system to assist drivers are tested with the help of Raspberry Pi devices and associated camera modules. In one paper [21], an approach called Distributed Incremental Learning (DIL) was introduced to mitigate "Catastrophic Forgetting" in healthcare monitoring. However, the large model size (49 KB) poses challenges for Raspberry devices, and there is a lack of data batch quality details affecting convergence. In one paper [22], the proposed communication-efficient FL solutions are tested with the help of Raspberry Pi devices in edge computing environments. However, to the best of our knowledge, the most recent literature lacks the study associated with the analysis of FL performance in the presence of heterogeneous clients. Given the importance of different IoT subsystems with heterogeneous nodes, such studies can be extremely useful from the 6G network's perspectives. This is one of the main motivations behind this experimental analysis of the FL process in the presence of diverse sets of clients.

1.2. Contributions and Novelties

In this study, we present an in-depth exploration of Federated Learning (FL) methodology within the context of 6G technology, delving into its intricacies and challenges across heterogeneous nodes. Our work uniquely integrates hardware and software components, utilizing a distinctive combination of Raspberry Pi devices and virtual machines as FL clients, each equipped with diverse datasets sourced from the CIFAR10 dataset—a widely acknowledged benchmark in image classification. Our contributions and innovations can be outlined as follows:

- **Cooling Mechanism Impact (Section 4.1):** We meticulously investigate the influence of cooling mechanisms on training accuracy, underscoring their practical significance in accelerating model convergence, especially in resource-constrained environments. This detailed analysis, expounded on in Section 4.1, elucidates the pivotal role of cooling mechanisms, providing valuable insights into optimizing FL performance.
- **Heterogeneous Client Compensation (Section 4.2):** Through a thorough exploration of asymmetric data distribution scenarios, both with and without random selection, we dissect the intricate dynamics of FL performance. Our study highlights the delicate balance necessary in distributing training data among diverse nodes, revealing the complexities of FL dynamics in real-world scenarios. These findings, presented in Section 4.2, offer critical insights into the challenges and solutions concerning data heterogeneity in FL setups.
- **Overfitting Mitigation Strategies (Section 4.2):** We tackle the challenge of overfitting in FL by implementing meticulous strategies. By integrating random selection techniques, we effectively mitigate overfitting risks, optimizing model generalization and ensuring the resilience of FL outcomes. This contribution, outlined in Section 4.2, underscores our commitment to enhancing the robustness of FL models.
- **Scalability Analysis (Section 4.3):** Our study provides a comprehensive exploration of FL scalability, assessing its performance with an increasing number of users. This analysis, detailed in Section 4.3, offers crucial insights into FL's scalability potential, essential for its integration in large-scale, dynamic environments. It emphasizes the system's adaptability to diverse user configurations, laying the foundation for FL's applicability in real-world scenarios.

- **Pretraining Effectiveness (Section 4.4):** We delve into the effectiveness of pretraining techniques in enhancing accuracy rates. Pretraining emerges as a potent tool, significantly boosting the model's performance and showcasing its potential in optimizing FL outcomes. This contribution, discussed in Section 4.4, highlights the practical implications of pretraining in FL applications, providing actionable insights for future implementations.
- **Transfer Learning Impact (Section 4.5):** In Section 4.5, we investigate the potential of Transfer Learning, evaluating its impact under diverse client configurations. Our results underscore Transfer Learning's capacity to enhance FL model performance, especially in the face of varied client scenarios. This analysis showcases Transfer Learning's adaptability in real-world applications, emphasizing its role in improving FL outcomes across dynamic and heterogeneous environments.

These contributions collectively form a comprehensive and innovative exploration of FL dynamics, addressing key challenges and offering practical solutions essential for the advancement of Federated Learning technologies in complex, real-world settings.

1.3. Limitations

Despite these contributions, our study acknowledges certain limitations. While our findings offer valuable insights, the scope of this research is confined to specific FL configurations and dataset characteristics. Further exploration of different FL architectures, diverse datasets, and real-world deployment challenges remains an area ripe for future investigation. Additionally, the scalability analysis, while comprehensive, focuses on a limited range of users and could benefit from further exploration with more extensive user groups in practical scenarios.

2. Distributed Machine Learning

The traditional ML approach was based on the centralized structure, where distributed wireless nodes, a potential data source, were needed to transmit their data samples to the centralized, more powerful node with a large amount of storage and computation power. With growing interest in the 5G system and the upcoming 6G technology, the wireless world is filled with tiny devices capable of sensing the environment and generating tons of high-quality data. Such data can be extremely large, and if a traditional centralized approach is adopted, it can induce a huge communication overhead. On the other hand, with the presence of such a large number of devices, the global dataset generated at the centralized server node (i.e., through the accumulation of data from the distributed nodes) can be extremely large, inducing much higher training costs. In addition to this, novel intelligent services and applications are based upon stringent requirements in terms of latency, privacy, reliability, etc. This presents challenges when considering centralized ML model training for wireless scenarios. However, with recent innovations in hardware/software domains, the end devices' onboard capabilities have increased by several folds. With this new capability, these devices can train fairly complex ML models locally with their own datasets. This can omit the requirements for long-distance data communication and additional training overhead. In addition to this, devices can communicate with each other and server nodes to fine-tune the ML models with improved performances. This has opened a new trend of ML model training called distributed learning, for countering the drawbacks of traditional centralized methods. There are various forms of distributed learning methods considered in the recent past.

There are two main approaches available for performing distributed learning: with data in parallel or with models in parallel [23]. The former involves distributing training data on several servers, while the latter divides the model's parameters between different servers. However, implementing the parallel model approach is difficult due to the complexity of dividing machine learning models into distinct groups of parameters. Therefore, most distributed machine learning implementations work through data distribution. Federated Learning (FL), collaborative learning, Multi-agent Reinforcement

Learning (MARL), and split learning are some of the most important distributed learning methods. Among others, FL has been widely used in wireless networks to enable intelligent solutions efficiently.

FL is a framework for distributed machine learning that protects privacy by operating through decentralized learning directly on end devices. It involves a certain number of clients, distributed throughout the network, each of whom trains their local model using the data at their disposal. After training, the clients send their models to a central server, which aggregates them into a single neural network and then transmits it to the end devices. This is an iterative process, with each iteration called a federated round. The objective of federated learning is to minimize a function and ensure efficient FL, several variables must be considered [24].

For the efficient implementation of FL, it is imperative to take into account several variables, encompassing the following:

- Selection of devices for learning
- Disparities in performance levels among the clients in use
- Management of heterogeneous training data
- Potential algorithms for local models' aggregation
- Selection of a proper aggregation Strategy at the Parameter Server
- Resource allocation

Concerning the choice of devices, specific parameters, including the quality and quantity of local data, connection performance with the central server, and computational performance of the client, need to be evaluated.

In a heterogeneous environment that involves wireless nodes with various onboard capabilities, it is crucial to pay attention to differences in the computing capabilities of the devices. In fact, a client with reduced computational capabilities will require a longer time to train the model locally, thereby risking the deceleration of the entire learning process. The following two FL approaches are widely considered to enable distributed learning [25] and can be impacted by the heterogeneous nature of the computational capabilities of the devices:

- **Synchronous FL:** All devices participate in training the local models for a specific period, sending the parameters to the central server. In this case, the server receives the client models simultaneously and aggregates them with the certainty that it is using the contribution of all the devices. However, this approach poses some challenges, in the case of heterogeneous client nodes having different capabilities. In such cases, the less-performing clients are compelled to invest more resources to complete the training within the expected timeline. To match the latency performance of other, high-performing clients with more resources, devices can only use a subset of their data.
- **Asynchronous FL:** In this case, there are no time restrictions for local training operations, with each device training its model based on its own capabilities, after which it sends the parameters to the server that proceeds with aggregation. This approach is more appropriate even in the presence of unstable network connections, where a device without network access can continue to train its model until it reconnects. Such an asynchronous approach can potentially reduce the number of FL devices participating in the individual FL rounds. This also requires more complex server-side operations to manage the devices according to their needs.

In Section 4, we explore these FL approaches when evaluating the system performance; more specifically, we employ asynchronous FL in heterogeneous client compensation (Section 4.2), to tackle the challenge posed by the discrepancy between the relatively sluggish Raspberry PIs and the swift Virtual Machines, which ultimately leads to a decline in the overall accuracy of the aggregated data. This measure shall be taken to restore the balance between the two.

In another case, the presence of heterogeneous amounts of data on FL devices can also largely impact FL performance. In one paper [26], the authors propose federated continual learning to improve the performance of Non-IID data by introducing the knowledge of the other local models; however, the paper does not address the scalability of the proposed method for large-scale distributed learning systems. In such scenarios, locally generated models at different FL nodes may have distinct characteristics from each other and may not lead to proper convergence when aggregated into a single neural network. The convergence problem can directly impact the algorithm chosen for the aggregation. In particular, the traditional federated average (FedAvg) approach can have limited performance since it does not distinguish the model parameters from different devices (i.e., simple averaging) [25]. In another case, proper weights can be assigned to each device's models according to their quality (i.e., weighted average). In some cases, device selection policies can be adapted to avoid the participation of FL devices with imperfect models.

The use cases mentioned above indicate the importance of defining a proper FL framework in heterogeneous environments based on the properties of the FL device and the characteristics of the environment. A one-fit-all FL approach can have reduced performance in different cases. Therefore, it is vital to analyze the performance of FL models in various scenarios and to select a proper FL model.

3. Implementation of the System

The primary goal of this work is to design and analyze a comprehensive and well-structured FL framework to train machine learning algorithms using a federated approach involving heterogeneous FL clients. Here, we outline the important steps considered during the implementation of the FL process.

The considered FL system is based on a client-server architecture, with the server represented by a Windows PC and a set of Raspberry Pi devices acting as FL clients. In addition, a set of virtual clients are also considered, to build an FL framework with heterogeneous clients. Given the importance of network programmability and virtualization technologies in the 5G/6G networks, defining the FL framework with a set of hardware/software clients can have added advantages. Finally, inter-device communication is carried out through the local network, to which all hardware nodes are connected via Wi-Fi.

As mentioned above, the main objective is to evaluate the efficacy of FL in the context of devices with limited and heterogeneous resources.

We have considered a typical image classification problem and aim to build a proper Deep Neural Network (DNN) with the help of the considered FL framework. The well-known CIFAR10 dataset is considered during model training operations. It should be noted that to induce data heterogeneity over different FL clients, the original dataset is split into different datasets. Also, though the analysis is performed with a specific ML task with predefined datasets, this can be extended to any generic ML problem. The FL framework is built with the help of Python programming language. In particular, the PyTorch library is considered to train the neural network model, while Flower, a specialized library for federated machine learning, is considered to automate the client-server interactions more efficiently.

In the following, we describe in detail the various configurations used in client/server parts of the considered FL model. Figure 1, presents the basic elements of the considered FL framework that includes a set of Raspberry Pi devices, virtual machines, and an FL server.

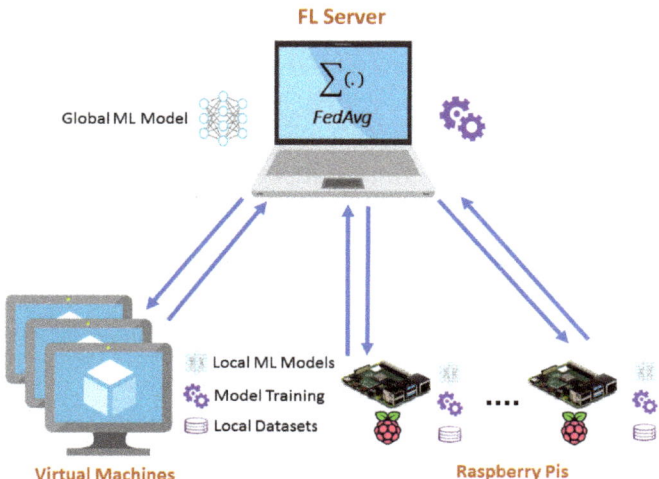

Figure 1. Considered FL Framework with Heterogeneous Clients.

3.1. Server Configurations and Functionalities

Here we introduce the main steps required to configure the server part of the FL system and the corresponding software employed. The FL server is installed on a Windows computer, which exhibits high-performance levels compared to the client devices. Specifically, the server is an Asus ROG Zephyrus S GX502GV with an Intel Core i7-9750H 6 x 2.6–4.5 GHz, Coffee Lake-H processor, NVIDIA GeForce RTX 2060 Mobile (6 GB VRAM, GDDR6 graphics card) and 16 GB DDR4–2666 Hz RAM. Furthermore, Wi-Fi connectivity is 802.11 a/b/g/n/ac with Intel Wireless-AC 9560.

We used the Anaconda platform, which allows the development of Python-based solutions with advanced package and library management. The current project was developed using the basic Anaconda environment, which includes Python 3.9.13. We downloaded and installed two further libraries, namely PyTorch version 2.0.0 and Flower version 1.3, through the integrated terminal. The framework is built around three Python scripts: one to run the server, another to run the client, and a third to define specific neural network training methods. It should be noted that the system can only communicate on the local network. Data are transmitted and received between the various devices using specific methods defined in the scripts.

The FL server needs to perform several functions to enable the FL. At first, the server establishes communication with a considered set of clients through the local network. Next, it initializes the global DNN model. DNN model can be initialized through random parameters or pre-trained models saved in memory based on the considered scenarios. After that, the network parameters are transmitted to all clients to have a common starting point for federated training.

Throughout the federated training process, clients train their models locally for a specified number of local rounds; then, they send the respective local model parameters to the server. The server then aggregates the parameters of all the models received from clients into a single neural network. For this implementation, the chosen algorithm for aggregating the parameters of all models received from clients into a single neural network is the federated average (FedAvg). FedAvg is an FL algorithm that enables collaborative model training across multiple devices or clients while preserving data privacy. It aggregates local model updates from individual clients to create a global model. Its procedure and formula are described in Algorithm 1.

Algorithm 1: Federated Averaging (FedAvg) Algorithm

Input: Global model parameters θ
Output: Updated global model parameters θ
Initialization: Initialize θ with random values;
while *not converged* **do**
　for *each client i in the federated network* **do**
　　Compute local model update w_i using client's local data;
　　Send w_i to the server;
　end
　Aggregation (FedAvg):
　　Compute updated global model parameters θ as the average of received local updates;
　$\theta = \frac{1}{N}\sum_{i=1}^{N} w_i$;
end

The performance of the aggregated model is then assessed in terms of accuracy and losses using a pre-loaded test data set on the server. The results of this assessment are then recorded in a CSV file. After that, the new aggregated model is returned to the clients to repeat the training procedure with the next federated round. The described process is reiterated until the designated number of iterations is reached. Each of these functions is important for enabling the FL process.

3.2. Client Configurations and Functionalities

Client devices include a set of Raspberry Pi devices along with the virtualized clients in the form of virtual machines. In particular, Raspberry Pi 3B+ is considered as a client during the experiments. The Raspberry Pi 3B+ is equipped with a Broadcom BCM2837B0 processor, Cortex-A53 (ARMv8) 64-bit SoC with a clock speed of 1.4 GHz, a 1GB LPDDR2 SDRAM, and 2.4 GHz and 5 GHz IEEE 802.11.b/g/n/ac wireless LAN. Moreover, it has Bluetooth 4.2, BLE, Gigabit Ethernet over USB 2.0 (max throughput 300 Mbps), a 40-pin GPIO header, Full-size HDMI, 4 x USB 2.0, DSI, a Micro SD slot, and a power supply of 5V/2.5A DC.

To facilitate the experiment, the Raspberry PI OS 64-bit operating system was installed on each Raspberries through the official imager. The 64-bit system is necessary for the proper functioning of PyTorch, which currently does not support 32-bit variants. Configuring the devices via SSH enabled the Virtual Network Computing (VNC) service, which uses the local network to transmit the Raspberry desktop to the connected Windows computer. The remote connection via the cloud could further extend the functionality of VNC. Such a procedure allowed interaction with the Raspberry desktop directly on the notebook that hosts the server, facilitating monitoring of the simulation's progress from a single screen.

The client-side code was executed in the Python environment pre-installed on the Raspberry Pis and updated to version 3.9.2. Moreover, the installation of the PyTorch and Flower libraries was necessary. The clients are based on the client.py script, which inherits all the contents of the file cifar.py. This file is essential for generating, training, and evaluating the neural network. Such a configuration allowed the devices to participate in the training process by sharing their computational power with the server. In this way, training time and computational costs can be reduced. The Raspberry Pi 3B+ devices were a suitable choice for this experiment due to their low cost and high customizability. They allow users to modify the hardware and software configurations, facilitating the implementation of ML models and algorithms. Raspberry Pi devices can also be used in various applications, such as robotics, automation, and the Internet of Things (IoT). The proposed setup could be replicated in various scenarios where training machine learning models on devices with limited resources could be beneficial.

In addition to the Raspberry devices, up to eight virtual clients are also considered during the experimentation. It should be noted that all the virtual clients were installed on the same PC. However, this can be easily extended to multi-PC scenarios to enable more diverse sets of clients. Such an approach is beyond the scope of this work. In general, virtual clients have more resources compared to hardware clients. The virtual clients are based on the same scripts used in the implementation of the physical clients, and their execution simultaneously is facilitated using multiple Python terminals open on different screens. A cooling fan was necessary to prevent excessive degradation of computational performance in the Raspberry devices due to overheating. The fan was operational during all the tests conducted to maintain the optimal performance of the devices, as indicated in Figure 2. Later, in the simulation and performance evaluation section, we explore the effect of cooling on accuracy and convergence rate.

Figure 2. Cooling Mechanism for Raspberry Pi Devices.

In the FL framework, client nodes are required to perform a distinctive set of functions. In the beginning, each client should establish a communication channel with the server through a local network. At the beginning of each FL round, the client should receive the updated global model parameters from the server machine. These parameters along with the local data should be used to update the ML model through local training operations. Client devices should train the neural network on local data, iterating for a certain number of periods, i.e., local epochs. Furthermore, it is important to evaluate the performance of the newly trained local model using a local test data set and send the obtained metrics to the server. Finally, the client should transmit the parameters of the trained model back to the server. Figure 3, provides a detailed experimental setup used during the implementation of FL with the help of Raspberry Pi nodes, a virtual machine, and an FL server installed on a Windows PC.

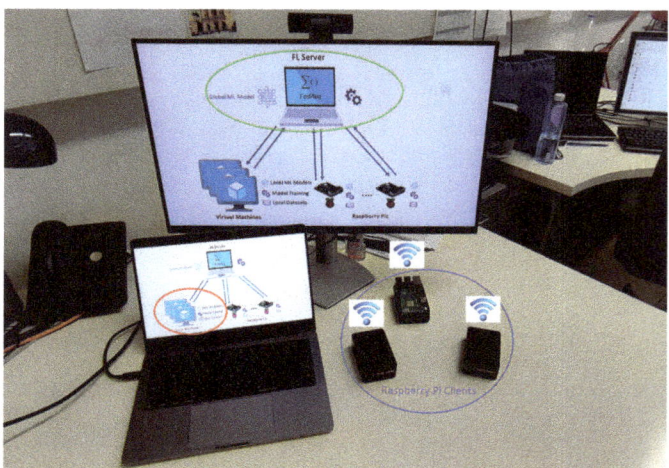

Figure 3. Experimental Setup Used During the FL Implementation.

4. Simulations and Performance Evaluations

In this section, with the help of the Python simulation environment, we analyze the performance of the FL framework proposed before. For a considered image classification problem, the CIFAR10 dataset is used. It contains 60,000 colorful pictures, with a resolution of 32×32 pixels, separated into 10 classifications with 6000 pictures in each category. The CIFAR10 incorporates 50,000 samples for training and the remaining 10,000 samples for verification. The images are randomly arranged while maintaining a perfectly uniform distribution of the classes. In the training set, each client has precisely 5000 images. In the experimental setup considered, two Raspberry Pi devices are considered as well as up to 8 virtual clients. In our setup, each virtual client was allocated an equal share of CPU resources on the 8-core host machine. This means that the CPU resources were evenly distributed among the virtual clients, ensuring a fair and consistent experimental environment. By allocating an equal portion of the available 8-core CPU to each virtual client, we maintained a balanced and representative simulation, allowing us to assess the FL framework's performance accurately. This approach ensures that the results obtained were not influenced by uneven resource distribution among the virtual clients, providing a reliable basis for our experimental findings. At first, the CIFAR10 training set was distributed among the clients. The 10 FL iterations are considered with 3 local training epochs. The server uses the test data of 10,000 CIFAR10 samples throughout the simulation. The accuracy of the model was determined using a metric that calculated the percentage of correct predictions among all predictions. The accuracy values presented in our figures are indeed normalized, ranging from 0 to 1, and not represented in percentages. For example, an accuracy value of 0.7 corresponds to 70 percent. Note that, to avoid the extensive training process we have limited the number of training iterations and the overall data size. However, this also upper-bounds the overall performance of DNN. In the experimental studies considered, DNN can only achieve an accuracy of up to 65%. However, the performance can be improved with additional resources, i.e., data samples, devices, training iterations, etc.

Figure 4, presents the performance of the FL framework considered in the basic settings, that is, a set of users having the same amount of data and onboard capabilities. This simulation is limited to Raspberry PI devices only. Both centralized and FL models are trained for 30 epochs. To have an adequate comparison over different training epochs, both models' performance in terms of accuracy is plotted with respect to the incremental values of the training epoch. It should be noted that in a considered simulation, the overall epochs represent the overall training process iterations, and therefore for the case of FL, the epochs are based on the number of FL iterations (rounds) times the local epoch performed. From Figure 4, it can be visualized that the FL framework can emulate the performance of a centralized approach in close proximity. Though FL can have a slightly reduced performance compared to the centralized case, the added advantage in terms of reduced communication overheads, and enhanced data privacy can be crucial advantages in the novel wireless scenarios. It also highlights that all the components of the proposed FL framework are configured properly and thus the platform is ready to perform the additional experimental steps.

In the next parts, to evaluate the performance of the models trained with FL, they are compared with a centralized learning benchmark with the same neural network. Some of the key variables considered during the experimentation are the number of clients participating in the simulation, the amount of data used for learning, and the selection and partitioning of the training data. Simulations are conducted to assess the impact of a single variable as well as different combinations. Additionally, performance differences between virtual clients implemented on Windows computers and hardware clients of Raspberry PI are carefully analyzed. The introduction of pre-trained models and alternative learning paradigms such as Transfer Learning (TL) are also considered.

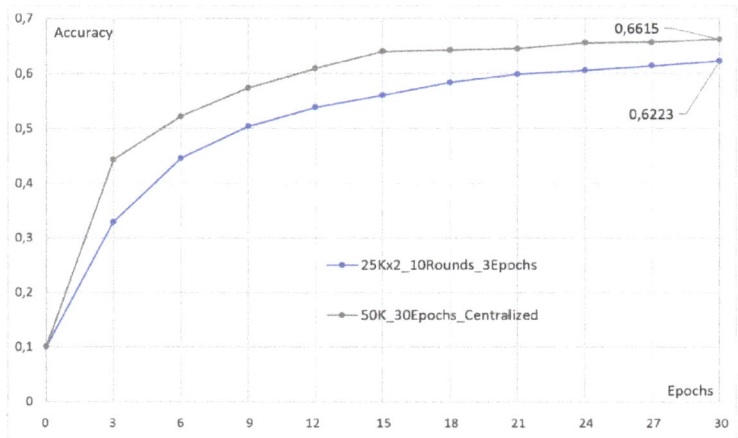

Figure 4. Accuracy of FL for 2 clients compared to the centralized benchmark vs. epochs.

4.1. Effect of a Cooling Mechanism

The excessive amount of heat generated by the computation hardware can have a severe impact on the environment and is underlined quite often. Such issues can also affect the performance of the device, which can impact the model training performance. For the case of FL, it is important to analyze the impact of such heating issues on the training performances given the involvement of a large number of sensory devices. Therefore, in Figure 5, we have presented the performance of two FL models with similar tasks and training environments. One of the FL studies involves the utilization of a cooling fan to reduce the heating issues of Raspberry Pi clients. As is evident from this figure, accuracy can be improved with the use of cooling devices, which can help to achieve model convergence rapidly. This highlights the importance of incorporating novel cooling mechanisms into end devices to enable efficient intelligent solutions in wireless networks. As such, all subsequent simulations were conducted in the presence of a cooling fan.

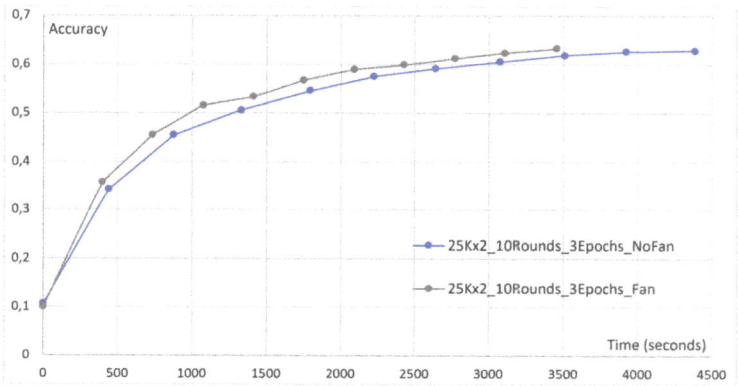

Figure 5. The effect of a cooling fan on the accuracy of training.

4.2. Heterogeneous Client Compensation

One of the significant challenges in implementing distributed learning techniques such as FL is the presence of heterogeneous client devices with different amounts of resources, i.e., computational capabilities, training data, etc. In a considered FL implementation two sets of clients are considered. While implementing the FL solutions, a significant disparity in performance was promptly observed between clients operating as virtual machines and those operating on Raspberry Pis. In the case of the traditional FL approach with heterogeneous sets of clients, the server node waits until it receives the updates from all the clients in question. In a considered FL setup, Specifically, it has been observed that the server waits until even the Raspberry Pi clients complete their training, even after the most powerful clients have finished their training. We have implemented two approaches to mitigate this waiting time and make the best use of the highest-performing clients. The first approach involves training the best devices for several rounds before transmitting the model to the server. In contrast, the second approach involves training all clients with the same number of periods but using more data for high-performance clients. Raspberry Pi devices with their limited capabilities often take longer duration to communicate their model updates adding a large amount of communication overhead. On the other hand, virtual clients with a significant amount of resources are able to conclude the learning process promptly, they suffer due to the poor behavior of hardware clients. To counter this issue, we have adopted two different strategies. In the first case, we have normalized the FL iteration time by inducing the harsh local training conditions over the virtual machine-based clients by increasing the number of local epochs performed. With this approach, instead of staying in an idle state and waiting for the parameter updates from the slow-performing clients, the virtual clients try to optimize the local model performance through more training. In the second approach, we have normalized the FL iteration time through different data splits. In this case, each node performs the same amount of training epoch; however, the number of data samples considered at a virtual machine is significantly higher than the Raspberry Pi clients.

The FL data split can be performed with different methods. In Figure 6, we have presented the FL model performance with asymmetric data split between heterogeneous clients. Each subfigure includes a centralized benchmark with 50 K samples, an FL approach with a 4:1 split, and another FL case with a 3:2 split. The subfigure on the left is based on the deterministic data split approach, where the repetition of data samples at different nodes is avoided. While in the subfigure on the right, a random data selection approach is adopted, without taking into account the repetitions of data samples at different devices. There is a significant gap between the performance of deterministic and random selection approaches. The deterministic approach can improve the accuracy of the FL model by up to 3.3% compared to the random case.

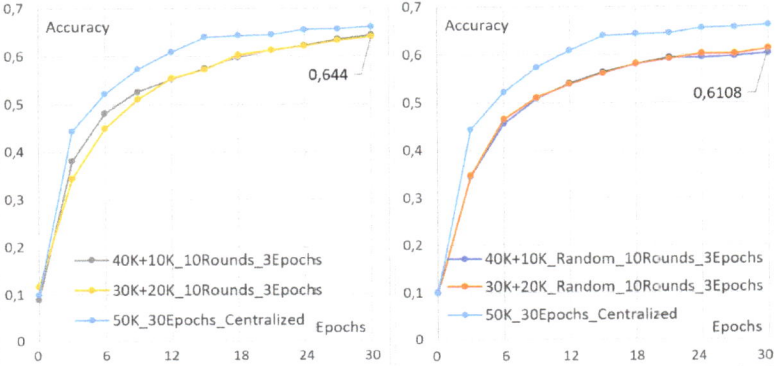

Figure 6. Simulations with asymmetric data distribution, without and with random selection compared to the Centralized Benchmark.

In the next case, we varied the local training epoch over different clients to analyze the performance. In this case, all devices use the same amount of training samples, while varying the nature of the local training process. In particular virtual machine-based clients perform more local epochs compared to the hardware nodes, before communicating their updates to the parameter server. Figure 7 compares the accuracy of different data split options along with the differing local training processes. In this case, asynchronous data split achieves higher accuracy, compared to the two FL cases where the same amount of data is used by the FL clients while normalizing the FL process time through the adaptive local training operations. To verify this trend and lend it further credence, it was deemed necessary to perform several similar tests. These tests were carefully arranged so that their execution times were identical, thus rendering it feasible to obtain a more precise comparison in the time domain. This is demonstrated in Figure 8, which compares the two aforementioned methods for distributing the workload between two heterogeneous clients through several simulations. These simulations entail the following conditions:

- Two clients, each with 25,000 images. The first client undergoes two local epochs, while the second undergoes eight.
- Two clients, each with five local epochs. The first client is assigned 10,000 images, while the second is assigned 40,000.
- Two clients, each with 25,000 images. The first client undergoes three local epochs, while the second undergoes twelve.
- Two clients, each with seven local epochs. The first client is assigned 10,000 images, while the second is assigned 40,000.

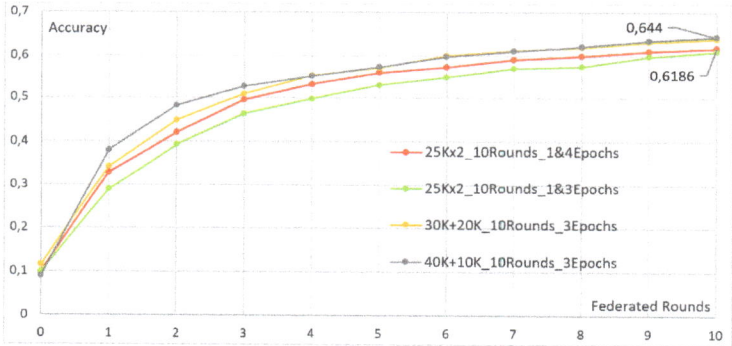

Figure 7. Accuracy with asymmetric distribution of data vs different numbers of local epochs.

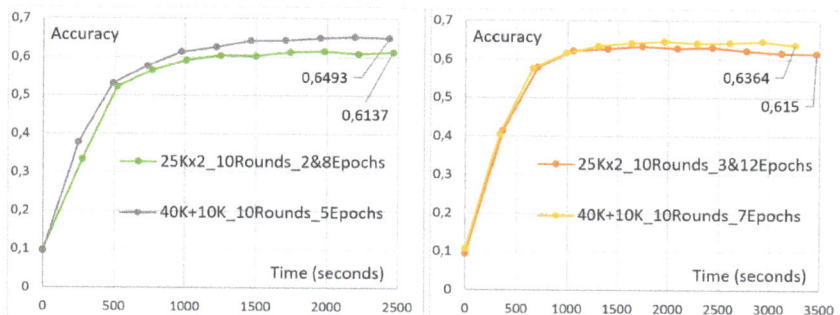

Figure 8. Accuracy for asymmetric data distribution vs. different numbers of local epochs, in time domain.

In our study, we intentionally introduced inhomogeneous and asymmetric data distribution to mimic real-world scenarios where data across users can vary significantly. Specifically in Figure 8, the yellow line corresponds to a balanced data distribution, where the dataset was evenly split between users (i.e., Raspberry Pis), with each user having 20,000 images. In contrast, the orange line illustrates an uneven data distribution. In this scenario, one user was allocated 10,000 images, while the other user had 40,000 images. This intentional variation allows us to evaluate the FL framework's ability to handle disparate data quantities among users. In all cases, the aforementioned trend is consistently observed. This underscores the efficiency of adapting asynchronous data splitting across heterogeneous FL clients, rather than modifying the overall training process to enforce synchronization of FL updates from diverse devices.

Another issue that frequently impacts the DNN performance is the concept of overfitting especially for the case of unbalanced datasets with a large number of local training epochs. While modifying the local training process for the case of FL with heterogeneous nodes, the data available at different nodes should be taken into account. When examining the final parts of the two simulations, in Figure 9, it is possible to observe the effect of overfitting. The accuracy has somewhat lessened due to excessive training of the model on a small amount of data, leading to a decrease in universality for examples that were not utilized for training.

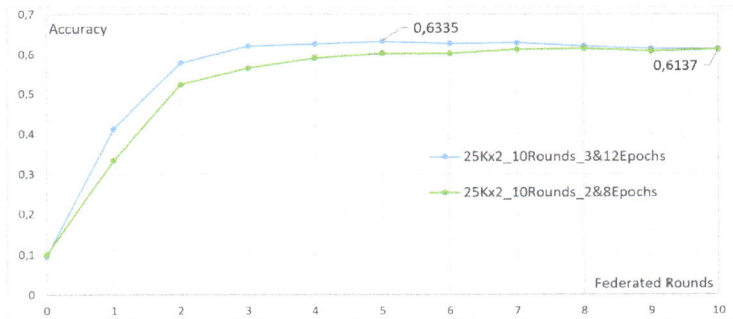

Figure 9. Overfitting for different numbers of local epochs.

It is worth mentioning that compensating for performance by distributing unequal amounts of data between devices is a challenging approach to implement. This is because it may not be possible to control the volumes of data collected by different clients. Conversely, increasing the workload of the highest-performing devices by increasing their local epochs can be easily achieved with communications from the server.

After defining the scenarios mentioned above, further exploration was conducted to determine the impact of a random selection of data compared to an ordered split without overlaps. It is important to note that the CIFAR10 dataset samples are inherently unordered, with images following one another irrespective of their class.

The initial approach involved dividing the dataset among multiple clients without repetition, resulting in a total of 50,000 samples between all clients, which is the complete training data. Imagine a circumstance where a pair of patrons are tasked with handling the preparation assortment of CIFAR10, with one individual managing the initial 25,000 samples and the other in command of the residual 25,000 samples. These two data groups do not overlap, thus utilizing the entire training set.

Expanding this approach to five clients would require dividing the data set into five categories, each with 10,000 samples, with no overlaps or sample duplications. The second approach, however, was based on the random selection of samples from the dataset, allowing for a single data piece to be chosen several times within the same client. Moreover, data could be common to different clients, even if the sum of the samples from both clients exceeds the total number of samples from the training set. Thus, this method may yield a generally substandard model performance that aligns more with actual situations.

It is essential to consider that performance may vary from simulation to simulation, even with the same conditions, due to the random variables of these tests. As a result, the tests involving random samples were repeated multiple times, and the results presented represent their average. The impact of random selection, with identical data amounts and epoch numbers, is evident in Figure 10, which compares two centralized learnings.

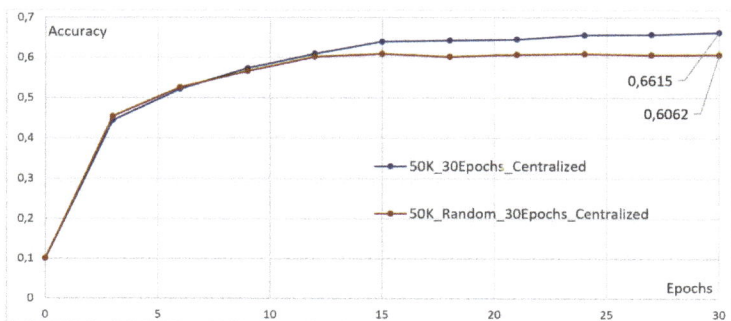

Figure 10. Centralized Learning with and without random data selection.

The aforementioned phenomenon is similarly observed in a federated scenario, as illustrated in Figure 11 by comparing two basic FLs involving two clients, each containing 25,000 images. The likelihood of encompassing a greater portion of the dataset and subsequently enhancing the ultimate accuracy increases as the number of randomly selected training samples increases.

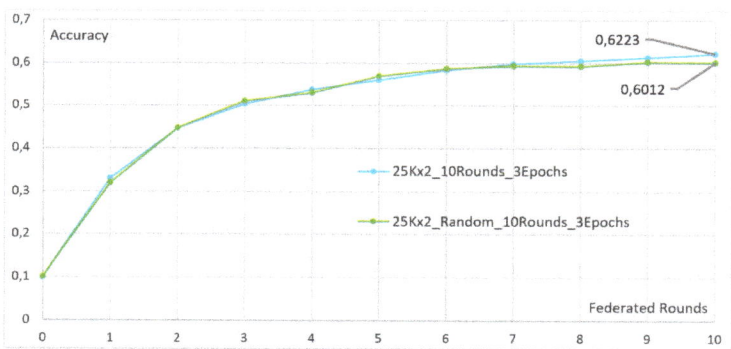

Figure 11. Federated Learning of 2 clients with and without random data selection.

As the quantity of randomly selected samples utilized for training increases, the probability of encompassing a more significant portion of the dataset also increases. This subsequently results in an enhancement of the final accuracy. This correlation is visually depicted in Figure 12, showcasing three FL evaluations conducted on two devices. The number of samples on each client has been progressively augmented from one simulation to the next, positively impacting the accuracy metric at the conclusion of each federated round.

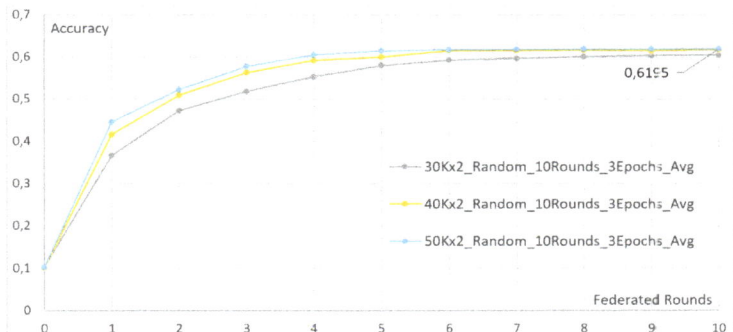

Figure 12. FL with different amounts of randomly chosen samples for two clients.

4.3. Increasing the Number of Clients

The subsequent phase, aimed at enhancing the observance of FL and its scalability, entailed increasing the number of clients participating in the simulation to a maximum of 10. Of these, 2 were Raspberry clients, and 8 were virtual clients, coexisting with the server on the computer. The 10-client threshold could not be exceeded due to the restricted RAM on the laptop and the considerable resources required to train neural networks. Nevertheless, this number of clients proved adequate in inducing a noteworthy decline in the model's performance as the number of devices involved escalated. In addition, it can be seen that the accuracy calculated by the server of the global model after each federated round is progressively sluggish as the number of clients used grows.

Figure 13 portrays the accuracy value for each federated round for five different simulations, each divided equally across all clients, using the internal training set (50,000 images). The specific parameters for each test are as follows: two clients with 25,000 samples each, four clients with 12,500 samples each, five clients with 10,000 samples each, eight clients with 6250 samples each, and ten clients with 5000 samples each. The simulation employing only two clients is the best, whereas the test with ten devices yields the worst performance, requiring 40 federated rounds before achieving accuracy comparable to the former. However, it should be noted that, in the first case, Raspberries must operate with 25,000 samples each, resulting in relatively slower local periods, while in the second case, each client uses only 5000 samples, thereby completing its local epochs much faster.

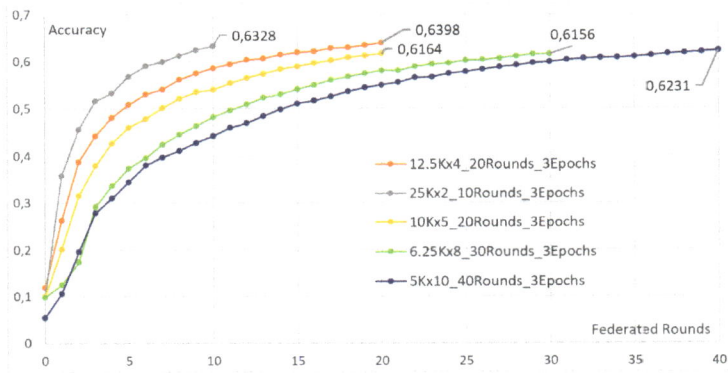

Figure 13. FL with different amounts of randomly distributed samples among different number of clients.

Examining Figure 14, representing the same performance while in the time domain, it is evident that the actual difference in performance between the simulations is much lower and sometimes even nonexistent. For instance, the test with ten clients completed its 40 rounds at a time, close to the tenth round of the test with only two clients. The same applies to the other curves, with the simulation involving four clients overlapping perfectly with that of two. This implies that, in the context of a system with limited computational capacity, as represented by the Raspberry Pi, a federated approach generates relatively similar performance to centralized ones.

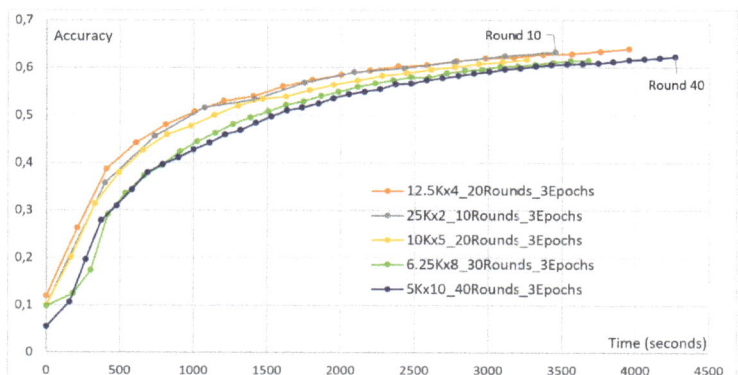

Figure 14. Accuracy vs. the number of rounds for different numbers of clients.

A similar pattern can be witnessed even with random samples, as illustrated in the two simulations depicted in Figure 15. The clients work with 30,000 and 12,000 images randomly selected from the dataset, and the algorithm trained with five clients obtains lower accuracy per round. However, since these simulations are completed twice as fast as the two-client simulation, the result is that the accuracy values are very similar moment by moment.

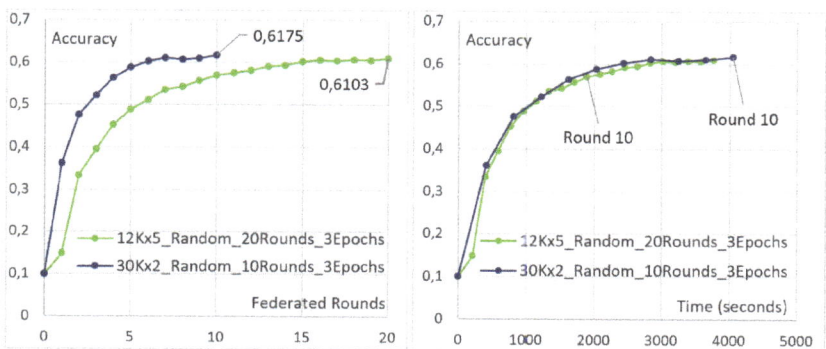

Figure 15. Accuracy with random samples and different numbers of clients.

4.4. Effect of Pretraining

Upon completion of the previous phase, the training framework was further explored, emphasizing the introduction of pre-trained models. In all tests conducted thus far, the initial accuracy starts at approximately 0.1 (i.e., 10%), which aligns with a randomly initialized model. In this FL implementation, at the beginning of each simulation, the server randomly selects a client to transmit its original model, a neural network with randomly assigned node weights, generating a very low accuracy of approximately 10%. This model is then disseminated from the server to all clients to establish a common starting point for training. Alternatively, it may be feasible to directly preserve a fundamental model on the server that is conveyed to all users during the initial stage. This method allows for using a pre-trained neural network already on the server, resulting in enhanced performance for FL.

For this specific scenario, the model pre-training was conducted centrally on 30,000 samples randomly selected by CIFAR10, with data processing for 3, 6, or 9 periods, leading to three pre-trained models with varying levels of accuracy. This approach observed how pretraining at different intensities contributes to FL's performance. As demonstrated in Figure 16, each test has a distinct initial accuracy value, followed by training through a straightforward implementation of federated learning with two clients, each with half a dataset and three local epochs per round. The impact of pretraining is discernible in the initial rounds, where trained simulations exhibit a significant advantage over cases without pretraining. This discrepancy weakens as the federated rounds continue until all curves converge around the tenth round, resulting in a final accuracy value that is relatively high, especially considering that the previous centralized benchmark on the internal training set had a score of 65%.

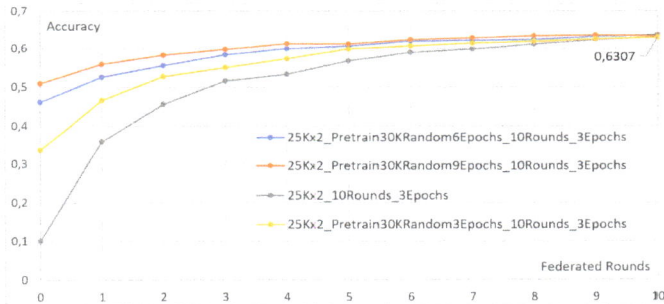

Figure 16. Accuracy with 2 clients and different pretraining levels.

Similar examinations were replicated in a federated context comprising five clients, each trained on a fifth of the dataset to extend the findings. Once again, as can be seen in Figure 17, a trend similar to the previous one is discernible, with a substantial effect of pretraining in the initial stages that diminishes until the curves converge. The incorporation of pre-trained models thus represents a commendable strategy to accelerate the federated learning of the network. This technique is particularly advantageous in situations with limited time available for training, as in this case, FL could be stopped before converging to maximum accuracy, and pretraining would bring significant benefits, as observed in the first part of the graph.

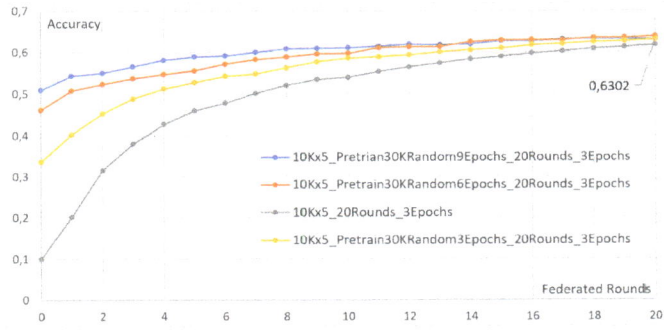

Figure 17. Simulations with 5 clients and different pretraining levels.

To further emphasize the impact of pretraining, FL was conducted again with 10 clients who had previously exhibited reduced performance compared to other simulations. However, this time a starting model already trained with 30,000 random samples for six periods was used. The outcome is shown in Figure 18, where the new simulation has substantially higher accuracy than the previous test with 10 clients and even surpasses the scenario with only two devices. This exemplifies how one can compensate for the decline in the accuracy of FL due to the increase in the number of devices involved by incorporating pretraining.

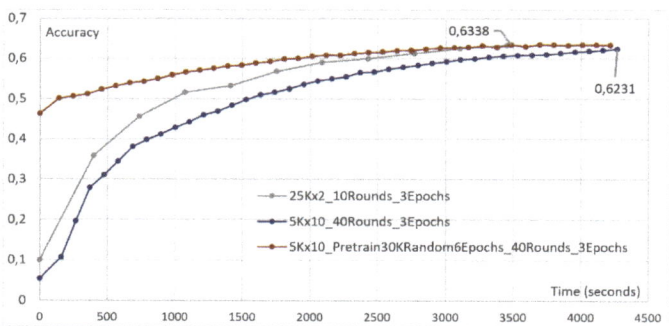

Figure 18. 2 simulations with 10 clients with or without pretraining vs. simulation with 2 clients without pretraining.

However, we must recognize the deficiencies of this approach. Pretraining a model demands time and energy. Ideally, the optimal solution would be to conduct the pretraining directly on the server in a centralized manner. In this case, the reduced number of periods required to obtain a good starting model and the high computing capacity of the server would render the pretraining time almost negligible compared to the duration of the subsequent federated training. Nonetheless, this solution may not be feasible in a practical scenario as it implies the presence of a certain amount of training data directly on the server when, in several cases, FL is chosen precisely to circumvent the transfer of the local data collected by the various devices. A possible alternative could be the utilization of a more generic dataset for pretraining, then leaving clients with the task of integrating the model's specific features with their local data, akin to what occurs for TL.

4.5. Transfer Learning

Drawing inspiration from the aforementioned analogy of TL, executing its functionality in the present framework has been feasible. However, it is imperative to specify that the measures implemented to achieve this outcome do not facilitate the attainment of the same level of automation as federated simulations. The practical principle is akin to pretraining, wherein an initial model is trained through centralized machine learning. Subsequently, this model is disseminated to various devices that conduct local training with their unique dataset.

In the first part of Figure 19, the fundamental model training is depicted, followed by the curves of multiple models obtained by the clients. The two models produced in the first scenario are almost identical, as both clients have 25,000 images of data and have been trained for the same number of epochs.

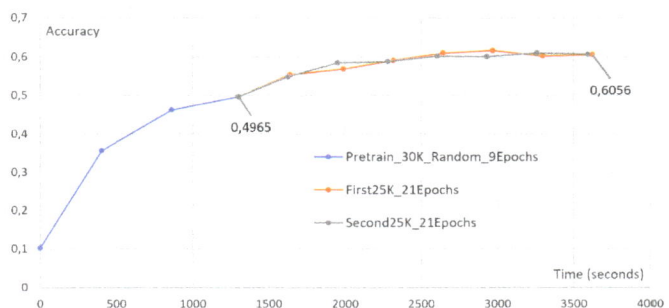

Figure 19. TL with 2 clients.

In contrast, in Figure 20, differences in terms of accuracy and training time between the three devices are apparent, which is expected since all the clients have trained for 21 periods. However, each client had varying sample sizes available, with the first client having 10,000, the second having 20,000, and the third having 30,000 elements of CIFAR10. Thus, clients with more data will exhibit slower periods that guarantee greater accuracy.

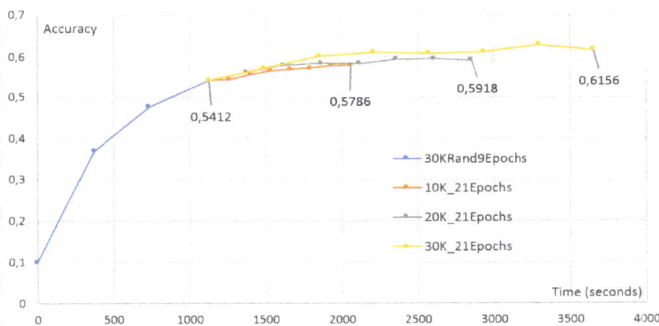

Figure 20. TL with 3 clients.

5. Discussion

In this study, we conducted an in-depth exploration of Federated Learning (FL) methodology across heterogeneous nodes, offering critical insights into its application within the context of 6G technology. Our investigation revolved around a hardware-software integrated FL model, ingeniously leveraging a combination of Raspberry Pi devices and virtual machines as FL clients, each equipped with unique datasets sourced from the CIFAR10 dataset, a widely accepted benchmark in image classification. The experiments were meticulously designed to mirror real-world scenarios, addressing multifaceted challenges including varying computation resources, uneven dataset distributions, and the heating issues inherent in wireless devices.

A pivotal aspect of our research involved examining the impact of cooling mechanisms on training accuracy, elucidated in detail in Section 4.1. The insights garnered from Figure 5 underscore the significance of cooling devices in expediting model convergence, highlighting their practical relevance, especially in resource-constrained environments. Additionally, we delved into the complexities of heterogeneous client compensation, meticulously examining asymmetric data distribution scenarios, both with and without random selection, compared to a Centralized Benchmark, as delineated in Section 4.2 (Figures 6–8). These analyses illuminated the nuanced dynamics of FL performance, emphasizing the intricate balance required in distributing training data among disparate nodes. Furthermore, our study probed the issue of overfitting in FL, a critical concern often encountered in decentralized learning paradigms. Through Figure 9, we identified the challenge and subsequently addressed it by incorporating random selection strategies, showcased in Figures 10–12, thereby mitigating overfitting risks while optimizing model generalization. A comprehensive exploration into the scalability of FL was presented in Section 4.3, analyzing the impact of increasing the number of users on the system's performance (Figures 13–15). This analysis provided valuable insights into FL's scalability potential, crucial for its adoption in large-scale, dynamic environments. The effectiveness of pretraining in enhancing accuracy rates was explored in Section 4.4, revealing significant improvements showcased in Figures 16–18. Pretraining emerged as a powerful technique, elevating the model's performance and showcasing its potential for optimizing FL outcomes. Finally, in Section 4.5, we delved into Transfer Learning's potential, evaluating its impact with varying numbers of clients (Figures 19 and 20). The results underscored Transfer Learning's capacity to enhance FL model performance, particularly when faced with diverse client configurations.

6. Conclusions

In this work, we have investigated the performance of the FL method including a group of heterogeneous nodes. In particular, a hardware-software integrated FL model is developed by using a set of Raspberry PI devices and virtual machines acting as an FL client with their datasets. Performance is analyzed for the case of an image classification problem with a widely known CIFAR10 dataset. Given the importance of distributed intelligence with heterogeneous wireless nodes in the upcoming 6G technology, a set of experiments are performed to analyze the FL performance in different cases. Main issues such as differing computation resources, uneven distributions of datasets, and heating issues of wireless devices were considered while performing the experiments. In addition, novel technologies such as the users of pre-trained networks for knowledge transfer, were also considered. A more pro-analysis and concluding remarks are also presented during the discussion of simulation results. This study can be highly useful when considering the deployments of FL methods over heterogeneous 6G environments to enable large-scale, connected, cost-efficient, and reliable distributed intelligence.

In conclusion, our study's multifaceted approach, spanning cooling mechanisms, heterogeneous compensation strategies, overfitting mitigation, scalability analyses, and the integration of pretraining and Transfer Learning, provides a holistic understanding of FL's dynamics across heterogeneous nodes. These nuanced findings not only contribute significantly to the academic discourse but also hold practical implications for real-world 6G deployments. By illuminating the complexities and offering viable solutions, our research empowers the seamless integration of FL in diverse, large-scale, connected, cost-efficient, and reliable distributed intelligence systems, laying the foundation for the future of intelligent wireless networks.

Author Contributions: Conceptualization, D.T. and S.S.S.; methodology, S.S.S.; software, L.R. and D.N.; validation, L.R., S.S.S. and D.N.; formal analysis, S.S.S. and D.N.; investigation, L.R.; resources, D.T.; data curation, L.R.; writing—original draft preparation, D.N.; writing—review and editing, D.T., D.N, and S.S.S.; visualization, L.R.; supervision, D.T.; project administration, D.T.; funding acquisition, D.T. All authors have read and agreed to the published version of the manuscript.

Funding: This work has been partially supported by the ECOSISTER project funded under the National Recovery and Resilience Plan (NRRP), Mission 04 Component 2 Investment 1.5—NextGenerationEU, Call for tender n. 3277 dated 30 December 2021, Award Number: 0001052 dated 23 June 2022 and by the European Union under the Italian National Recovery and Resilience Plan (NRRP) of NextGenerationEU, partnership on "Telecommunications of the Future" (PE00000001—program "RESTART").

Data Availability Statement: Data available on request due to restrictions e.g., privacy or ethical.

Conflicts of Interest: The authors declare no conflict of interest.

References

1. Letaief, K.B.; Shi, Y.; Lu, J.; Lu, J. Edge Artificial Intelligence for 6G: Vision, Enabling Technologies, and Applications. *IEEE J. Sel. Areas Commun.* **2022**, *40*, 5–36. [CrossRef]
2. Nguyen, D.C.; Ding, M.; Pathirana, P.N.; Seneviratne, A.; Li, J.; Niyato, D.; Dobre, O.; Poor, H.V. 6G Internet of Things: A Comprehensive Survey. *IEEE Internet Things J.* **2022**, *9*, 359–383. [CrossRef]
3. *6G Technology Overview*, 2nd ed.; one6G White Paper; 2022. Available online: https://one6g.org/download/2699/ (accessed on 27 September 2023).
4. Tang, F.; Mao, B.; Kawamoto, Y.; Kato, N. Survey on Machine Learning for Intelligent End-to-End Communication Toward 6G: From Network Access, Routing to Traffic Control and Streaming Adaption. *IEEE Commun. Surv. Tutor.* **2021**, *23*, 1578–1598. [CrossRef]
5. Muscinelli, E.; Shinde, S.S.; Tarchi, D. Overview of Distributed Machine Learning Techniques for 6G Networks. *Algorithms* **2022**, *15*, 210. [CrossRef]
6. Shinde, S.S.; Bozorgchenani, A.; Tarchi, D.; Ni, Q. On the Design of Federated Learning in Latency and Energy Constrained Computation Offloading Operations in Vehicular Edge Computing Systems. *IEEE Trans. Veh. Technol.* **2022**, *71*, 2041–2057. [CrossRef]
7. Shinde, S.S.; Tarchi, D. Joint Air-Ground Distributed Federated Learning for Intelligent Transportation Systems. *IEEE Trans. Intell. Transp. Syst.* **2023**, *24*, 9996–10011. [CrossRef]
8. Duan, Q.; Huang, J.; Hu, S.; Deng, R.; Lu, Z.; Yu, S. Combining Federated Learning and Edge Computing Toward Ubiquitous Intelligence in 6G Network: Challenges, Recent Advances, and Future Directions. *IEEE Commun. Surv. Tutor.* **2023**, in press. [CrossRef]
9. Morocho-Cayamcela, M.E.; Lee, H.; Lim, W. Machine Learning for 5G/B5G Mobile and Wireless Communications: Potential, Limitations, and Future Directions. *IEEE Access* **2019**, *7*, 137184–137206. [CrossRef]
10. Praveen Kumar, D.; Amgoth, T.; Annavarapu, C.S.R. Machine learning algorithms for wireless sensor networks: A survey. *Inf. Fusion* **2019**, *49*, 1–25. [CrossRef]
11. Fontanesi, G.; Ortíz, F.; Lagunas, E.; Baeza, V.M.; Vázquez, M.; Vásquez-Peralvo, J.; Minardi, M.; Vu, H.; Honnaiah, P.; Lacoste, C.; et al. Artificial Intelligence for Satellite Communication and Non-Terrestrial Networks: A Survey. *arXiv* **2023**, arXiv:2304.13008.
12. Lee, H.; Lee, S.H.; Quek, T.Q.S. Deep Learning for Distributed Optimization: Applications to Wireless Resource Management. *IEEE J. Sel. Areas Commun.* **2019**, *37*, 2251–2266. [CrossRef]
13. Huang, J.; Wan, J.; Lv, B.; Ye, Q.; Chen, Y. Joint Computation Offloading and Resource Allocation for Edge-Cloud Collaboration in Internet of Vehicles via Deep Reinforcement Learning. *IEEE Syst. J.* **2023**, *17*, 2500–2511. [CrossRef]
14. Song, H.; Liu, L.; Ashdown, J.; Yi, Y. A Deep Reinforcement Learning Framework for Spectrum Management in Dynamic Spectrum Access. *IEEE Internet Things J.* **2021**, *8*, 11208–11218. [CrossRef]
15. Nayak, P.; Swetha, G.; Gupta, S.; Madhavi, K. Routing in wireless sensor networks using machine learning techniques: Challenges and opportunities. *Measurement* **2021**, *178*, 108974. [CrossRef]
16. Yang, Z.; Chen, M.; Saad, W.; Hong, C.S.; Shikh-Bahaei, M. Energy Efficient Federated Learning Over Wireless Communication Networks. *IEEE Trans. Wirel. Commun.* **2021**, *20*, 1935–1949. [CrossRef]
17. Jiang, J.C.; Kantarci, B.; Oktug, S.; Soyata, T. Federated Learning in Smart City Sensing: Challenges and Opportunities. *Sensors* **2020**, *20*, 6230. [CrossRef] [PubMed]
18. Matthiesen, B.; Razmi, N.; Leyva-Mayorga, I.; Dekorsy, A.; Popovski, P. Federated Learning in Satellite Constellations. *IEEE Netw.* **2023**, 1–16. in press. [CrossRef]
19. Younus, M.U.; Khan, M.K.; Bhatti, A.R. Improving the Software-Defined Wireless Sensor Networks Routing Performance Using Reinforcement Learning. *IEEE Internet Things J.* **2022**, *9*, 3495–3508. [CrossRef]
20. Dewangan, D.K.; Sahu, S.P. Deep Learning-Based Speed Bump Detection Model for Intelligent Vehicle System Using Raspberry Pi. *IEEE Sens. J.* **2021**, *21*, 3570–3578. [CrossRef]
21. Cicceri, G.; Tricomi, G.; Benomar, Z.; Longo, F.; Puliafito, A.; Merlino, G. DILoCC: An approach for Distributed Incremental Learning across the Computing Continuum. In Proceedings of the 2021 IEEE International Conference on Smart Computing (SMARTCOMP), Irvine, CA, USA, 23–27 August 2021; pp. 113–120. [CrossRef]
22. Mills, J.; Hu, J.; Min, G. Communication-Efficient Federated Learning for Wireless Edge Intelligence in IoT. *IEEE Internet Things J.* **2020**, *7*, 5986–5994. [CrossRef]
23. Farkas, A.; Kertész, G.; Lovas, R. Parallel and Distributed Training of Deep Neural Networks: A brief overview. In Proceedings of the 2020 IEEE 24th International Conference on Intelligent Engineering Systems (INES), Reykjavík, Iceland, 8–10 July 2020; pp. 165–170. [CrossRef]
24. Li, T.; Sahu, A.K.; Talwalkar, A.; Smith, V. Federated Learning: Challenges, Methods, and Future Directions. *IEEE Signal Process. Mag.* **2020**, *37*, 50–60. [CrossRef]

25. Hong, C.S.; Khan, L.U.; Chen, M.; Chen, D.; Saad, W.; Han, Z. *Federated Learning for Wireless Networks*; Springer: Singapore, 2022.
26. Zhang, Z.; Zhang, Y.; Guo, D.; Zhao, S.; Zhu, X. Communication-efficient federated continual learning for distributed learning system with Non-IID data. *Sci. China Inf. Sci.* **2023**, *66*, 122102. [CrossRef]

Disclaimer/Publisher's Note: The statements, opinions and data contained in all publications are solely those of the individual author(s) and contributor(s) and not of MDPI and/or the editor(s). MDPI and/or the editor(s) disclaim responsibility for any injury to people or property resulting from any ideas, methods, instructions or products referred to in the content.

Article

FedCO: Communication-Efficient Federated Learning via Clustering Optimization [†]

Ahmed A. Al-Saedi [1,*], Veselka Boeva [1] and Emiliano Casalicchio [1,2,*]

[1] Department of Computer Science, Blekinge Institute of Technology, SE-371 79 Karlskrona, Sweden
[2] Department of Computer Science, Sapienza University of Rome, 00185 Rome, Italy
* Correspondence: ahmed.a.al-saedi@bth.se (A.A.A.-S.); emiliano.casalicchio@uniroma1.it (E.C.)
[†] This paper is an extended version of our paper "Reducing Communication Overhead of Federated Learning through Clustering Analysis" published in Processing of the 2021 IEEE Symposium on Computers and Communications (ISCC), Athens, Greece, 5–8 September 2021.

Abstract: Federated Learning (FL) provides a promising solution for preserving privacy in learning shared models on distributed devices without sharing local data on a central server. However, most existing work shows that FL incurs high communication costs. To address this challenge, we propose a clustering-based federated solution, entitled Federated Learning via Clustering Optimization (FedCO), which optimizes model aggregation and reduces communication costs. In order to reduce the communication costs, we first divide the participating workers into groups based on the similarity of their model parameters and then select only one representative, the best performing worker, from each group to communicate with the central server. Then, in each successive round, we apply the Silhouette validation technique to check whether each representative is still made tight with its current cluster. If not, the representative is either moved into a more appropriate cluster or forms a cluster singleton. Finally, we use split optimization to update and improve the whole clustering solution. The updated clustering is used to select new cluster representatives. In that way, the proposed FedCO approach updates clusters by repeatedly evaluating and splitting clusters if doing so is necessary to improve the workers' partitioning. The potential of the proposed method is demonstrated on publicly available datasets and LEAF datasets under the IID and Non-IID data distribution settings. The experimental results indicate that our proposed FedCO approach is superior to the state-of-the-art FL approaches, i.e., FedAvg, FedProx, and CMFL, in reducing communication costs and achieving a better accuracy in both the IID and Non-IID cases.

Keywords: federated learning; Internet of Things; clustering; communication efficiency; convolutional neural network

1. Introduction

With recent advances in Internet of Things (IoT) devices and the fast growth of high-speed networks, the need to collect and process vast amounts of distributed data generated by these devices is significantly increasing. Furthermore, Artificial Intelligence (AI) has concurrently transformed the discovery of knowledge methods with cutting-edge success in several applications, including text prediction, facial recognition, natural language processing, document identification, and other tasks [1,2]. However, those applications require IoT devices to send sensitive information to a remote cloud server for centralized model training, which raises data privacy concerns [3,4]. These privacy concerns of IoT devices are supposed to be reduced by introducing an alternative setting, i.e., Federated Learning (FL). The main idea of FL is to collaboratively train a shared machine learning model across distributed devices, where the data are stored locally on devices [5,6]. However, a naive implementation of the FL setting requires that each participant has to upload a full model update to a central server during each iteration. For large updates with millions of parameters for deep learning models and thousands of iterations [7], this step is likely to be a major hindrance in FL when the network bandwidth is limited. Thus, Federated Learning can become completely impractical [8].

Over the past few years, there has been a growing consensus that the more data that can be guaranteed, the better and higher accuracy that will be achieved. It should not be assumed, however, that blindly introducing more data into a model will improve its accuracy, but only that ensuring high-quality data will guarantee a higher degree of accuracy.

Our Contributions: In this paper, we propose a novel FL framework, entitled Federated Learning via Clustering Optimization (FedCO), to lessen the challenges described above during the training process. In particular, FedCO draws inspiration from our previous work, Cluster Analysis-Based Federated Learning (CA-FL), presented in [9]. In the CA-FL framework, the server only communicates with the representative who achieved a higher level of accuracy in each cluster. We implemented a regression model in machine learning and evaluated and compared the CA-FL model using only the federated average (FedAvg) [6] for human activity recognition (HAR) datasets. In the current work, we have enhanced the original CA-FL framework with a dynamic clustering scheme that reduces communication costs and more quickly ensures global model convergence. The result of the improvements is a new version of a deep learning-based framework called FedCO. In contrast to the original framework and compared to related work studies, discussed in Section 2, FedCO incorporates the following amendments.

- We propose a deep learning-based FL framework, FedCO for short, that employs a dynamic adaptation procedure to new data, which evaluates representatives tied to their clusters at each learning round and redistributes them among the clusters if necessary. In addition, the quality of the obtained adapted clustering is evaluated at each round, and over-represented clusters of workers undergo a splitting procedure if this improves the whole clustering (Section 4).
- We provide a convergence analysis for our proposed FedCO algorithm (Section 6.2).
- We initially evaluate the proposed FedCO by comparing its performance with that of three baseline FL methods—FedAvg [6], FedProx [10], and CMFL [11]—on MNIST, CIFAR-10, and Fashion-MNIST under two different data-distribution scenarios, Independent and Identically Distributed (IID), and Non-IID.
- In addition, since our proposed FedCO algorithm is intended as a communication-mitigated version of FedAvg, we further study and assess the robustness of the FedCO with respect to FedAvg on two LEAF datasets under IID and Non-IID data.
- The conducted experiments have demonstrated the efficiency of FedCO over the FedAvg, FedProx, and CMFL algorithms in terms of convergence rate and communication overhead (Section 6).

The rest of the paper is structured as follows. Section 2 reviews the previous studies related to our work. The methodology used in our paper is presented in Section 3. Section 4 is devoted to the proposed FedCO and its strategy. The practical applications of those experimental settings are discussed in Section 5. The conducted experiments and the obtained results are analyzed and discussed in Section 6. The conclusions of our study and potential future works are presented in Section 7.

2. Related Work

This section mainly reviews the published research works aimed at reducing communication overheads in FL. In general, Federated Learning requires massive communication between the central server and the workers to train a global model [6]. Such an overhead is imputed to the size of the model exchanged and to the number of rounds to converge. Many works aim at reducing communication costs; e.g., HeteroFL [12] utilizes models of different sizes to address heterogeneous clients equipped with different computation and communication capabilities, while the work in [13] uses decentralized collaborative learning in combination with the master–slave model.

Among many of the published FL solutions, there are few existing FL works that use clustering techniques [14–18]. For example, in [14] the study proposes clustering algorithms based on clients' similarities. The authors have tried to find a cluster structure of data to collect clients with similar data distributions and to perform baseline FedAvg training per cluster. In [15], the authors introduce clustering techniques to partition the clients with similar data distribution using a measure of distance between the weight updates of the clients. A dynamic clustering through generative adversarial network-based clustering (GAN) is designed to obtain a partition of the data distributed on FL clients in [16]. The authors in [17] introduced a new framework, namely the Iterative Federated Clustering Algorithm (IFCA), in which clusters of users also aggregate their data with others in the same cluster (the same learning task) and optimize model parameters for the user clusters via gradient descent. Finally, Ouyang et al. [18] present clustering algorithms to cluster the heterogeneous data across clients into various clusters to participate in global model learning. The authors grouped the data after reducing its dimensions using PCA, and they measured the similarity of local updates.

Although the studies discussed above [14–18] have applied clustering techniques to FL scenarios, all of them have clustered the clients based on the distribution of their own data, while our proposed technique partitions the clients based on their training model parameters, i.e., in a way that ensures that each cluster will contribute to the model by learning different aspects (different model parameters' values) of the studied phenomenon. Evidently, our solution for mitigating communication costs of FL is conceptually different from the approaches discussed above, despite it also being based on clustering.

The majority of the studies in the field of resource-aware FL can be distributed into two main categories: a reduction in the total number of bits transferred, and a reduction in the number of local updates. Table 1 summarizes the techniques proposed by the research community, classifying them according to the categorization mentioned above.

Table 1. Summary of recent studies to minimize communication overhead in FL.

Categories	Existing Studies	ML Model Used	Datasets
First category	Chen et al. [19]	CNN, LSTM	MNIST, HAR
	Fed-Dropout [20]	DNN	CIFAR-10, MNIST, EMNIST
	Lin et al. [21]	CNNs, RNNs	Cifar10, ImageNet, Penn Treebank
	STC [22]	VGG11, CNN	CIFAR-10, MNIST
	PowerSGD [23]	ResNet-18, LSTM	CIFAR10, WIKITEXT-2
	FedOpt [24]	NN, LM	CIFAR10, MNIST
	FEDZIP [25]	CNN, VGG16	MNIST, EMNIST
	FetchSGD [26]	NN	CIFAR-100, CIFAR-10, FEMNIST
	T-FedAvg [27]	MLP, ResNet-18	MNIST, CIFAR-10
	FedAT [28]	CNN, Logistic	CIFAR-10, Fashion-MNIST, Sentiment140, FEMNIST, Reddit

Table 1. *Cont.*

Categories	Existing Studies	ML Model Used	Datasets
Second category	CMFL [11]	CNN, LSTM	MNIST, NWP
	FedMed [29]	LSTM	PTB, WikiText-2, Yelp
	CEEP-FL [30]	CNN	MNIST, CIFAR-10
	FedCS [31]	NN	CIFAR-10, FashionMNIST
	FedPSO [32]	CNN	MNIST, CIFAR-10
	AdaFL [33]	MLP, CNN	MNIST, CIFAR-10
	MAB [34]	NN, CNN	MNIST, Video QoE
	FedAtt [35]	GRU	WikiText-2, PTB, Reddit
	FedPAQ [13]	CNN, Logistic	MNIST, CIFAR-10
	Ribero et al. [36]	CNN, Logistic, RNN	Synthetic, EMNIST, Shakespeare
	CA-FL [9]	SGD	mHealth, Pamap2
	Proposed (FedCO)	CNN	MNIST, Fashion-MNIST, CIFAR-10, FEMNIST, CelebA

2.1. Reduction of the Total Number of Bits

The first category incorporates works that reduce the total number of bits transferred for each local update through data compression. Chen et al. [19] propose an enhanced Federated Learning technique by introducing an asynchronous learning strategy on the clients and a temporally weighted aggregation of the local models on the server. Different layers of the deep neural networks are categorized into shallow and deep layers, and the parameters of the deep layers are updated less frequently than those of the shallow layers. In addition, a temporally weighted aggregation strategy is applied on the server to make use of the previously trained local models, thereby enhancing the accuracy and convergence of the central model. Caldas et al. [20] design two novel strategies to reduce communication costs. The first relies on lossy compression on the global model sent from the server to the client. The second strategy uses Federated Dropout, which allows users to efficiently train locally on smaller subsets of the global model and reduces client-to-server communication and local computation. Lin et al. [21] propose Deep Gradient Compression (DGC) to significantly reduce the communication bandwidth. Sattler et al. [22] introduce a new compression framework, entitled Sparse Ternary Compression, that is specifically designed to meet the requirements of the Federated Learning environment. Asad et al. [24] implement a Federated Optimization (FedOpt) approach by designing a novel compression algorithm, entitled Sparse Compression Algorithm (SCA), for efficient communication, and then they integrate the additively homomorphic encryption with differential privacy to prevent data from being leaked. Malekijoo et al. [25] develop a novel framework that significantly decreases the size of updates while transferring weights from the deep learning model between the clients and their servers. A novel algorithm, namely FetchSGD, that compresses model updates using a Count Sketch and takes advantage of the mergeability of sketches to combine model updates from many workers, is proposed in [26]. Xu et al. [27] present a federated trained ternary quantization (FTTQ) algorithm, which optimizes the quantized networks on the clients through a self-learning quantization factor. Vogel et al. [23] design a PowerSGD algorithm that computes a low-rank approximation of the gradient using a generalized power iteration. A novel Federated Learning method, entitled FedAT, with asynchronous tiers under Non-IID data, is presented in [28]. FedAT synergistically combines synchronous intra-tier training and asynchronous cross-tier training. By bridging the synchronous and asynchronous training through tiering, FedAT minimizes the straggler effect with improved convergence speed and test accuracy. Our research does not consider methods that leverage data compression techniques because of reduced scalability in scenarios such as edge and fog computing, and 5G networks, where hundreds of thousands of nodes cooperate in updating global models on the central server. Moreover, these approaches strictly depend on the application field.

2.2. Reduction of the Number of Local Updates

The second category includes studies that aim at reducing the number of local updates during the training process. For example, Wu et al. [29] have proposed a novel FedMed method with adaptive aggregation using the topK strategy to select the top workers who have lower losses to update the model parameters in each round. Likewise, Asad et al. [30] have provided a novel filtering procedure on each local update that allows transferring only the significant gradients to the server. The authors in [11] identify the relevant updates of the participants and upload only them to the server. In particular, at each round, the participants receive the global tendency and check the relevancy of their local updates with the global model, and only upload them if they align. Nishio and Yonetani in [31] propose an FL protocol of two-step client selection based on their resource constraints instead of the random client selection. In addition, a global model update algorithm, namely FedPSO, proposed transmitting the model weights only for the client that has provided the best score (such as accuracy or loss) to the cloud server [32].

Notice that our proposed FL model falls into the second category. We have been inspired by the studies discussed above, especially by CMFL [11] and FedProx [10], and we explored an approach that applies clustering optimization to bring efficiency and robustness in FL's communication. The most representative updates are uploaded only to the central server to reduce network communication costs.

The state-of-the-art solutions analyzed mainly conduct experiments considering a CNN model, except for FedMed, which uses an LSTM model, and FedCS, which uses an NN model (cf. Table 1, second category). Hence, we have chosen to assess the performance of our approach (FedCO) by using a CNN model. While there are many datasets used for the evaluation of FL solutions in the literature, the recurrent ones are MNIST, FashionMNIST, and CIFAR-10. Hence, we have evaluated the performance of FedCO training the FL model on the three datasets mentioned above. Additionally, we used datasets from the LEAF FL repository (FEMNIST and CelebA) to benchmark the performance of our FL algorithm against FedAvg [6] and FedProx [10].

3. Preliminaries and Definitions

In this section, we first briefly present the communication model and describe some preliminaries of a naive method of FL [37]. We then describe three state-of-the-art FL algorithms used for the comparison of our solution. Finally, we introduce the techniques used to conduct clustering optimization, i.e., the k-medoids clustering algorithm, and the Silhouette Index validation method. Table 2 summarizes the main notations used in the paper.

Table 2. Main notations.

Notation	Description
W	Set of available workers
W_t	Set of selected workers at tth communication round
w_i	A worker, i.e., $w_i \in W$
$\mathcal{D}_i$	The local data in worker w_i
n_i	The size of data in worker w_i
n	Total size of data
k_t	The number of clusters in round t

Table 2. *Cont.*

Notation	Description
$C = \{C_1, \ldots, C_{k_t}\}$	The clustering solution in round t
$\mathcal{M}$	The global model
$\mathcal{M}^*$	The optimal global model
$\mathcal{M}_t$	The global model at tth round
$\mathcal{M}_t^i$	The local model of worker w_i at round t
$F(.)$	The objective function of the global model
$F_i(.)$	The objective function of the local model of worker w_i
T	Maximal number of communication rounds
E	The number of local epochs
η	Learning rate
g_t^i	The gradients computed using back-propagation
$s(.)$	Silhouette Index score

3.1. Communication Model

In the proposed FL environment, FL is split into two major parts: workers and the central server. Our work aims to reduce communication overhead without sacrificing accuracy value during the training process. In this setting, the server coordinates a network of workers, controls the training progress of the model, broadcasts the original model to all participating workers, and then executes all the aggregation processes of the model updates. All workers are share model updates instead of sending their private data to a central server for global model aggregation. Figure 1 outlines the overall operations of the Federated Learning procedure.

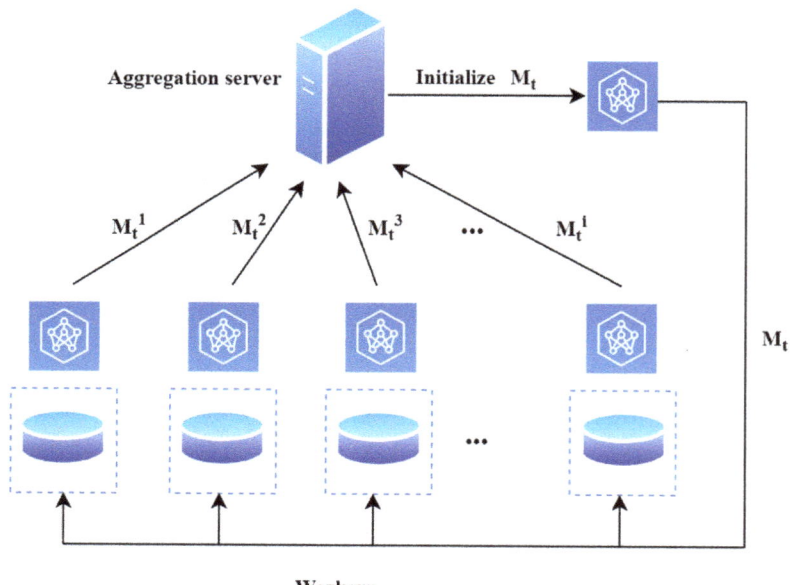

Figure 1. The general operations of the Federated Learning process.

Data are protected, with private access for each worker. Thus, model training occurs locally on each worker's side. In this context, we assume that each worker agrees on the same learning task and the model parameters throughout the training process. In particular, the proposed FL model updates the global model only with local model parameters from a few workers that are considered representative. Such workers are selected at each training round by identifying the highest quality of the local model produced of the worker. The selection policy is assumed to be implemented in a server, i.e., a central node selects a representative of the cluster with the highest accuracy. Furthermore, we assume that the server is always reachable by the workers. Finally, our proposed technique works by following this iterative collaboration between the central server and the workers.

3.2. Problem Description

In this work, we mainly concentrate on synchronous Federated Learning algorithms. A Federated Learning system consists of a global model $\mathcal{M}$ and a set of workers W. At each communication round t, the server deploys the current model $\mathcal{M}_t$ to a subset of workers $W_t \subset W$ that dynamically participate in the global aggregation at round t. Each worker $w_i \in W_t$ locally keeps its personal data $\mathcal{D}_i = \{x_{ij}\}_{j=1}^{n_i}$, ($j = 1, 2, \ldots, n_i$), where x_{ij} is the jth training sample in $\mathcal{D}_i$. The size of the local dataset $\mathcal{D}_i$ varies with different real-world applications.

In standard centralized Stochastic Gradient Descent (SGD), the local updates of each w_i are calculated according to Equation (1) to optimize $\mathcal{M}_t^i$, where η is the learning rate and g_t^i refers to the gradients computed:

$$\mathcal{M}_{t+1}^i = \mathcal{M}_t^i - \eta g_t^i. \tag{1}$$

Then, each worker w_i sends the local model changes $\mathcal{M}_{t+1}^i$ to the central server after the number of E local step, where p_i is the relative weight of worker w_i, and the global model is computed by applying Equation (2):

$$\mathcal{M}_{t+1} = \mathcal{M}_t + \frac{\sum_{w_i \in W_t} p_i \mathcal{M}_{t+1}^i}{\sum_{w_i \in W_t} p_i}. \tag{2}$$

These are iterated until a certain stop criterion is met.

The corresponding local loss function of $\mathcal{M}^i$ of each worker w_i is defined as

$$F_i(\mathcal{M}^i) = \frac{1}{|\mathcal{D}_i|} \sum_{x_{ij} \in \mathcal{D}_i} f(\mathcal{M}^i, x_{ij}), \tag{3}$$

where $f(\mathcal{M}^i, x_{ij})$ is the loss function for data point x_{ij} using (1). Each worker w_i independently updates the model over its own data $\mathcal{D}_i$ to optimize its local loss function $F_i(\mathcal{M}^i)$. The aim of improving the communication efficiency of Federated Learning is to minimize the cost of sending $\mathcal{M}_t^i$ to a central server while learning from the data distributed over a large number of decentralized edge devices. Similarly, the global loss function on all the distributed datasets is defined as:

$$F(\mathcal{M}) = \frac{1}{|W|} \sum_{w_i \in W_t} F_i(\mathcal{M}^i), \tag{4}$$

where $\mathcal{M}$ is the aggregated global model, and the overall goal is to decrease the global loss function $F(\mathcal{M})$, namely,

$$\mathcal{M}^* = \arg \min F(\mathcal{M}). \tag{5}$$

Other issues related to Federated Learning problems, such as system heterogeneity or privacy, are beyond the scope of this paper. Specifically, the proposed FedCO algorithm does not account for heterogeneity, which for example could affect the selection of workers that have enough power to transmit the model parameters. In the worst case, heterogeneity could increase the convergence time or reduce the accuracy, if for example, workers that achieve a higher accuracy cannot be selected because they have short battery lifetimes.

3.3. FL State-of-the-Art Algorithms

Most of the work on the convergence of compared FL algorithms such as FedAvg, CMFL, and FedProx centers around minimizing (4). We compare the proposed FedCO with the following state-of-the-art algorithms in the FL setting:

3.3.1. FedAvg

FedAvg, proposed by McMahan et al. in [6] can be viewed as a communication-light implementation of the standard centralized SGD, wherein the local updates are aggregated in the server after E local steps, where $E \geq 1$.

3.3.2. FedProx

FedProx [10] is a distributed algorithm, wherein a round-varying proximal term is introduced to control the deviation of the local updates from the most recent global model. A participating worker uses a proximal update that involves solving a minimization problem.

3.3.3. CMFL

Communication-Mitigated Federated Learning (CMFL) [11] improves the communication efficiency of Federated Learning while at the same time providing guaranteed learning convergence.

3.4. K-Medoids Clustering Algorithm

K-medoids is a robust clustering algorithm. It is used to partition a given set of data points into k disjoint clusters [38]. In contrast to the k-means, which use the mean value of the data points in each cluster as a cluster centroid, k-medoids chooses an actual data point, called a medoid. The medoid is the most centrally located point in a given cluster. Therefore, k-medoids are more robust to outliers and noise than other points. The algorithm works by arbitrarily choosing a set of k initial cluster medoids from a given set of data points, where k is preliminarily specified. Then, each data point is assigned to the cluster whose center is the nearest, and the cluster centers (medoids) are recomputed. This process is repeated until the points inside every cluster become as close to the center as possible, and no further item reassignments take place.

In our FedCO algorithm, we use k-medoids for partitioning the available workers into groups of similar workers with respect to their local updates. Furthermore, 2-medoids are used in the iteration phase of the algorithm for conducting cluster splitting.

3.5. Silhouette Index

The *Silhouette Index* (SI) is a widely used internal cluster validation technique, introduced in [39]. SI can be used to judge the quality of any clustering solution $C = \{C_1, C_2, \ldots, C_k\}$. It assesses the separation and compactness between the clusters. Suppose that a_i represents the average distance of item i from all the other items in the cluster to which item i is assigned, and b_i represents the minimum of the average distances of item i from the items of the other clusters. Then, the *Silhouette score* $s(i)$ of item i can be calculated as

$$s(i) = (b_i - a_i)/\max\{a_i, b_i\}. \tag{6}$$

$s(i)$ measures how well item i matches the clustering at hand. $s(i) \in [-1, 1]$, and if $s(i)$ is close to 1, this means that item i is assigned to a very appropriate cluster. The situation is different when $s(i)$ is near zero. Specifically, item i lies between two clusters. The worst case is when $s(i)$ is close to -1. Evidently, this item has been misclassified.

In addition, the overall Silhouette score for the whole clustering solution C of n items is determined as

$$s(C) = \frac{1}{n} \sum_{i=1}^{n} \frac{(b_i - a_i)}{\max\{a_i, b_i\}}. \tag{7}$$

The SI can also be calculated for each cluster C_j ($j = 1, 2, \ldots, k$) of n_j objects as follows:

$$s(C_j) = \frac{1}{n_j} \sum_{i=1}^{n_j} s(i). \tag{8}$$

The FedCO algorithm proposed in this study uses the Silhouette Index at each iteration round for assessing the current workers' partitioning and, based on this assessment, selects what optimizing actions to conduct. For example, we used SI to check whether a representative is still firmly tied to its current cluster of workers. It may happen that some representatives will change their clusters. If we have a worker that produces a negative SI value for all clusters, this means that this worker cannot be assigned to any of the existing clusters, and it will form a new singleton cluster; i.e., a new concept appears. In addition, SI is applied to assess whether an intended splitting of a cluster will improve the quality of the whole clustering solution, i.e., whether it should be conducted. For more details, see Section 4. Note also that in the implemented version of our FedCO algorithm, we use Euclidean distance to measure the similarity between each pair of workers. In particular, the Euclidean distance between the worker (the representative) and the cluster centers (medoids) has been computed.

4. Proposed Approach

Our proposed FedCO algorithm foresees two distinctive phases: *initialization* and *iteration*. These phases are described in what follows, along with cluster optimization algorithms. In addition, the algorithm pseudo-code is reported in Algorithms 1 and 2.

Let $W = \{w_1, w_2, \ldots, w_n\}$ be the set of all available workers, and W_t is a subset of W that contains the workers selected at round t. The workers in W_t can be the representatives of the clusters $C_t = \{C_{t1}, C_{t2}, \ldots, C_{tk_t}\}$ obtained by applying a clustering algorithm to W, or a set of randomly selected workers, and $|W_t| < n$.

Algorithm 1 Federated Learning Using Clustering Optimization (FedCO)

Output: The FEDCO procedure updates the global model $\mathcal{M}_t$ for T iterations

1: **procedure** FEDCO($\mathcal{M}_0, W_t \subseteq W, k_t, T$)
   Initialization Phase
2:     $t \leftarrow 0$
3:     $\forall\, w_i \in W_t$, SEND($w_i, \mathcal{M}_t$)
4:     **for** each worker $w_i \in W_t$ *in parallel* **do**
5:        $\mathcal{M}^i_{t+1} \leftarrow$ WORKERUPDATE($i, \mathcal{M}_t$)
6:     **end for**
7:     $\mathcal{M}_{t+1} = \sum_{w_i \in W_t} \frac{n_i}{n} \mathcal{M}^i_{t+1}$ following (2)
8:     $C_t \leftarrow$ KMEDOIDS($k_t, \{\mathcal{M}^i_{t+1} \mid w_i \in W_t\}, W_t$)
   Iteration Phase
9:     **while** $t \leq T$ **do**
10:       $t \leftarrow t + 1$
11:       $W_t \leftarrow$ SELECTTOPRANKED(p, C_t)
12:       $\forall\, w_i \in W_t$, SEND($w_i, \mathcal{M}_t$)
13:       **for** each worker $w_i \in W_t$ *in parallel* **do**
14:          $\mathcal{M}^i_{t+1} \leftarrow$ WORKERUPDATE($w_i, \mathcal{M}_t$)
15:       **end for**
16:       $\mathcal{M}_{t+1} = \sum_{w_i \in W_t} \frac{n_i}{n} \mathcal{M}^i_{t+1}$
17:       $C_{t+1} \leftarrow$ SILHOUETTE(k_t, C_t, W_t)
18:       **while** $\mid C_{t+1} \mid < \mid C_t \mid$ **do**
19:          $C_{t+1} \leftarrow$ CLUSTERINGOPTIMIZATION(k_{t+1}, C_{t+1})
20:       **end while**
21:     **end while**
22: **end procedure**

23: **function** SILHOUETTE((k_t, C_t, W_t))   ▷ *Check whether each cluster representative still belongs to its cluster*
24:     **for** $w_i \in W_t$ **do**
25:        **for** $j = 1, 2, \ldots, k$ **do**
26:           compute $s(w_i)$ ▷ *According to Equation (6)*
27:        **end for**
28:        **if** $s(w_i) < 0, \forall j \in \{1, 2, \ldots, k\}$ **then**
29:           $k_t \leftarrow k_t + 1$
30:           $C_{tk_t} \leftarrow w_i$
31:        **else**
32:           Assign w_i to the nearest cluster C_{tj}
33:        **end if**
34:     **end for**
35:     $\forall\, C_{tj}\,(j = 1, 2, \ldots, k)$ recompute the cluster center
36:     **return** C_{t+1} ▷ *The new set of clusters*
37: **end function**

38: **function** WORKERUPDATE($(w_i, \mathcal{M}_t)$)   ▷ *Local update*
39:     **while** True **do**
40:        RECEIVE($w_i, \mathcal{M}_t$)
41:        LOCALTRAINING($w_i, \mathcal{M}_t$)
42:        $\mathcal{M}^i_{t+1} \leftarrow \mathcal{M}^i_t - \eta g^i_t$ ▷ *Local update, (1)*
43:        SEND($i, \mathcal{M}^i_{t+1}$)
44:     **end while**
45: **end function**

Algorithm 2 ClusteringOptimization

Output: updated k_t and C_t

1: **procedure** CLUSTERINGOPTIMIZATION(k_t, C_t)
2:     $s(C_t) \leftarrow$ SILHOUETTESCORE(k_t, C_t, W_t)
3:     $C'_t \leftarrow \emptyset$
4:     **for** $C_{tj} \in C_t$ s.t. $|C_{tj}| > 1$ **do**
5:         $s(C_{tj}) \leftarrow$ SILHOUETTECLUSTER(C_{tj}, W_t)
6:         **while** $s(C_{tj}) < 0$ **do**
7:             $(C^1_{tj}, C^2_{tj}) \leftarrow$ KMEDOIDS($\{\mathcal{M}^i_{t+1} \mid w_i \in C_{tj}\}, k = 2$)   ▷ *run 2-medoids to generate two new clusters*
8:             $\tilde{C}_t \leftarrow \{C_t \setminus \{C_{tj}\}\} \cup \{C^1_{tj}, C^2_{tj}\}$
9:             $s(\tilde{C}_t) \leftarrow$ SILHOUETTESCORE(k_t, C_t, W_t)
10:            **if** $s(\tilde{C}_t) > s(C_t)$ **then**
11:                $C'_t \leftarrow C'_t \cup \tilde{C}_t$
12:                $k_t \leftarrow k_t + 1$
13:            **end if**
14:         **end while**
15:     **end for**
16:     **return** (C'_t, k_t)
17: **end procedure**

18: **function** SILHOUETTESCORE(k_t, C_t, W_t)   ▷ *Silhouette score of whole cluster solution C_t*
19:     Compute $s(w_i)$ between each $w_i \in W_t$ and each medoid $c_{tj} \in C_{tj}$ ($j = 1, 2, \ldots, k_t$) according to (6)
20:     Compute the average Silhouette score over all representatives $w_i \in W_t$ according to (7)
21:     **return** $s(C_t)$
22: **end function**

23: **function** SILHOUETTECLUSTER(C_{tj}, W_t)   ▷ *Silhouette Score of cluster $C_{tj} \in C_t$* ($j = 1, 2, \ldots, k$)
24:     Calculate Silhouette score $s(w_i)$ for each $w_i \in C_{tj}$ according to (6)
25:     Compute the mean over Silhouette scores of all cluster members $\{s(w_i) \mid w_i \in C_{tj}\}$ according to (8)
26:     **return** $s(C_{tj})$
27: **end function**

4.1. Initialization Phase

1. At time $t = 0$, the Server initializes the inputs for the FedCO algorithm (Algorithm 1). These are the model $\mathcal{M}_0$, the set of representative workers W_t, the number of clusters k_t, and the number of iterations T. $t = 0$ (line 1 in Algorithm 1).
2. A central Server transmits the initial global model $\mathcal{M}_t$ to a set of workers W_t ($W_t \subset W$). These are selected to be used for initial training in round $t = 0$ of Federated Learning (lines 3 in Algorithm 1).
3. Each worker $w_i \in W_t$ receives the global model $\mathcal{M}_t$ and optimizes its parameters locally; i.e., the $\mathcal{M}^i_t$ initial update is produced and sent back to the Server (Equation (1)) (lines 4–6 and lines 38–45 in Algorithm 1).
4. The Server aggregates the parameters $\{\mathcal{M}^i_t \mid w_i \in W_t\}$ uploaded by the selected workers W_t to update the global model $\mathcal{M}_t$ through the FedAvg algorithm (Equation (2)) (line 7 in Algorithm 1).
5. The local updates $\{\mathcal{M}^i_t \mid w_i \in W_t\}$ of the workers in W_t are analyzed by using the k-medoids clustering algorithm (function KMEDOIDS, line 8 in Algorithm 1)). As a result, k_t clusters of workers with similar updates are obtained; i.e., an initial clustering $C_t = \{C_{t1}, C_{t2}, \ldots, C_{tk_t}\}$ of the workers in W_t is produced.

4.2. Iteration Phase

1. At each iteration round t ($t \geq 0$), the Server evaluates each local update $\mathcal{M}_t^i$, $w_i \in W_t$ by using an evaluation measure that is suitable for the task under consideration. It ranks the workers in each cluster $C_{tj}, j = 1, 2, \ldots, k_t$ with respect to their evaluation scores and selects the top-ranked worker, i.e., the representative (function SELECT-TOPRANKED, line 11 in Algorithm 1). The selected representatives form a new set of workers W_{t+1}, where $|W_{t+1}| = k_t$ and $k_t << |W_0|$. Each selected worker $w_i \in W_{t+1}$ will check in with the Server.
2. The Server sends the global model $\mathcal{M}_t$ to each representative $w_i \in W_{t+1}$ (line 12 in Algorithm 1).
3. Each representative $w_i \in W_{t+1}$ receives the global model $\mathcal{M}_t$ and optimizes its parameters locally; i.e., the $\mathcal{M}_{t+1}^i$ update is produced (Equation 1) and sent back to the Server (lines 13 and 15 in Algorithm 1).
4. The Server aggregates the received local models $\{\mathcal{M}_{t+1}^i \mid w_i \in W_{t+1}\}$ uploaded by the representatives to update the global model through the FedAvg algorithm; i.e., an updated global model $\mathcal{M}_{t+1}$ is produced (Equation (2)) (line 16 in Algorithm 1).
5. The Server adapts C_t to the newly arrived local updates by conducting the following operations:

    (a) SI invokes the SILHOUTTE function (lines 17, 23–37 in Algorithm 1), which assesses whether each representative $w_i \in W_{t+1}$ is still adequately tight with its current cluster (Equation (6)). The updated clustering C_{t+1} of W_t is produced, and the clusters in C_{t+1} may contains a set of workers different from C_t. Note that $k_{(t+1)} \geq k_t$, where $k_{(t+1)} = |C_{t+1}|$, since new singleton clusters may appear due to the updating operation. This happens when the Silhouette coefficient $s(w_i)$ of a representative for all clusters gives a negative value (lines 28–30 in Algorithm 1), which means that this representative cannot be assigned to any existing cluster. Hence, this representative could be considered as a new cluster with a single item (singleton).

    (b) If there is a cluster $C_{(t+1)j} \in C_{t+1}$, such that $C_{(t+1)j} = \emptyset$, then $C_{t+1} = C_{t+1} \setminus \{C_{(t+1)j}\}$, and therefore, $|C_{t+1}| < |C_t|$. This condition/event triggers the optimization of the number of clusters by invoking the CLUSTEROPTIMIZATION function (lines 18–20 in Algorithm 1). This operation is repeated for each empty cluster of C_{t+1}.

A schematic illustration (flowchart) of the overall processes of the proposed FedCO algorithm is given in Figure 2.

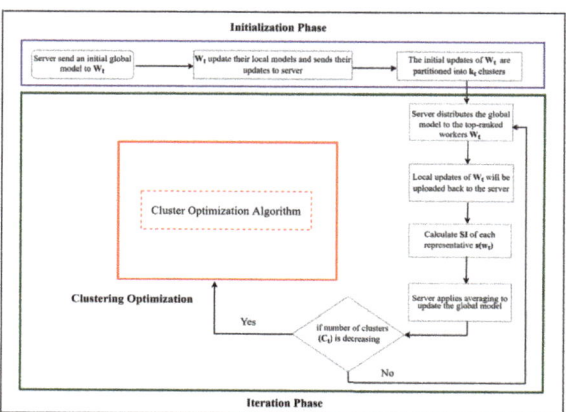

Figure 2. A schematic illustration of the entire process of the FedCO algorithm in two global communication rounds: Initialization Phase and Iteration Phase.

4.3. Cluster Optimization

The CLUSTEROPTIMIZATION algorithm works in what follows (cf. Algorithm 2):

1. Firstly, the SI score of the whole clustering solution C_{t+1} is computed. This score is used to check whether the splitting operation really improves the quality of the clustering solution (line 2 in Algorithm 2).
2. Then, the SI score is calculated for each cluster $C_{(t+1)j} \in C_{t+1}$, such that $|C_{(t+1)j}| > 1$ using Equation (8). If $s(C_{(t+1)j}) < 0$, then this cluster is a candidate to be split into two clusters, and the following operations are performed (lines 4–6 in Algorithm 2):

    (a) The two most distant points in the cluster $C_{(t+1)j}$ are found. They are used to seed 2-medoids clustering, which is applied to split the cluster $C_{(t+1)j}$ into two clusters (function KMEDOIDS at line 7 in Algorithm 2).
    (b) The clustering solution C_{t+1} is updated by replacing cluster $C_{(t+1)j}$ with the two clusters obtained due to the splitting operation (line 8 in Algorithm 2), and stored in the set $\tilde{C}_{t+1}$.
    (c) The SI score of the updated clustering solution $\tilde{C}_{t+1}$ is computed (line 9 in Algorithm 2 (7)).
    (d) If the SI score of the new clustering solution $\tilde{C}_{t+1}$ is higher than the one before splitting, the new clustering solution is adopted and stored in the set C'_{t+1}; otherwise, the clustering solution C_{t+1} is kept (lines 10–13 in Algorithm 2).

Steps 1–5 of the *iteration* phase are repeated until a certain number of training rounds T is reached. Figure 3 shows a flowchart depicting the cluster optimization algorithm in a single round of communication.

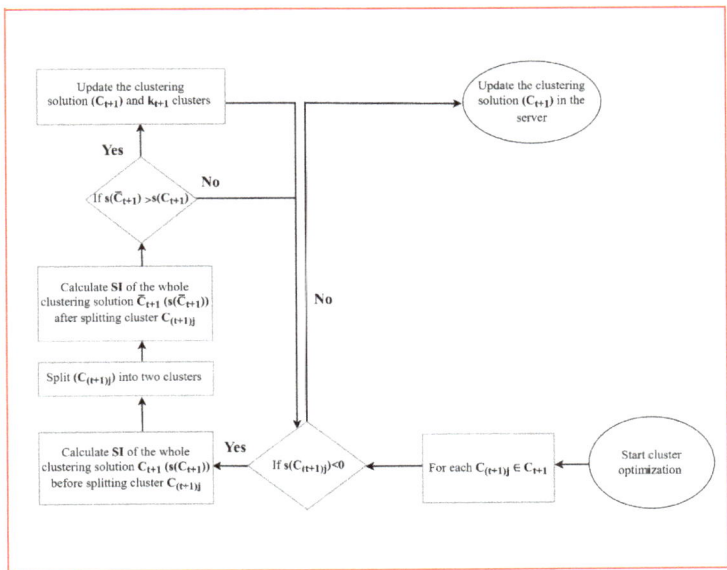

Figure 3. Flowchart depicting Cluster optimization algorithm.

The proposed FedCO implementation, at each training round, always selects the top performing representative; i.e., the size of the clusters is not reflected in the aggregated global model, and the size of the cluster does not impact the selection/importance of the representative. The FedCO design, however, allows from each cluster the selection of several top-ranked representatives, i.e., more than one, proportionally to the cluster size. In that way, the bigger clusters will have more weight in the building of the global model. It is also possible to assign explicit weights to the clusters representing their relative importance, and calculated based on their size. Our future plans include the investigation of an optimized version of the FedCO algorithm where the importance of clusters will be considered in the aggregated model.

5. Datasets and Experimental Setup

This section describes the datasets, the distribution of the data across the edge nodes, the model selected and related parameters, and the performance metrics used for evaluating FedCO.

5.1. Datasets

We conducted experiments using a wide range of datasets. Firstly, we selected three benchmark datasets widely used for image classification: MNIST [40], Fashion MNIST [41], and CIFAR-10 [42].

- The MNIST dataset contains a 60,000-point training set and a 10,000 point test set with 10 classes. Each sample is based on a grayscale image of handwritten digits with a size of 28×28 pixels.
- The Fashion MNIST dataset comprises a 60,000-point training set and a 10,000 point testing set of images of fashion items with 10 different classes. Each image has dimensions of 28×28 in grayscale.
- The CIFAR-10 dataset consists of a 50,000-point training set and a 10,000-point testing set with images of objects from frogs to planes, where each image is 32×32 pixels in 10 classes.

Secondly, we considered two LEAF datasets [43], an open-source benchmark for Federated Learning.

- FEMNIST for 62-class image classification, which serves as a more complex version of the popular MNIST dataset [44].
- CelebA for determining whether the celebrity in the image is smiling, which is based on the Large-scale CelebFaces Attributes Dataset.

5.2. Data Distribution

In an FL context, the performance is affected by the distribution of the training data stored on the various workers. Interestingly, unlike other FL studies using clustering techniques, different degrees of non-IID data do not affect the clustering results, as FedCO clustering occurs based on the model parameters and not on the data themselves. In order to assess the impact of different data distribution scenarios, we generated two experimental datasets for each dataset introduced above:

- The IID dataset: Each worker holds the local data equal in size and label distribution.
- The Non-IID dataset: Each worker holds different data distributions in size and label distribution compared to the global dataset.

5.3. Model Selection and Parameters

We have compared the proposed FedCO algorithm against the FedAvg, CMFL, and FedProx algorithms using the Convolutional Neural Network (CNN) classifier as a training model. The CNN model we used consists of two 5×5 convolution layers with a ReLU activation and a final softmax output layer.

The baseline configuration parameters' values listed in Table 3 are shared among the four compared algorithms.

Table 3. Hyper-parameter configuration.

Hyper-Parameter	Value
Workers	100
Optimizer	SGD
Classes	10
Batch Size	50
Learning rate	0.15
Local epochs	10
Global rounds	200
Clusters	8
Non-IID degree	0.5

5.4. Performance Metrics

FL typically relies on a large number of edge devices, sometimes in the magnitude of millions, and due to the limited computing capabilities of those devices, decreasing the communication rounds or communication overhead is crucial during the training process. Hence, the performance metrics selected are the *Number of Communication Rounds*, the *Communication Overhead*, and the model *Accuracy*. The *Communication Overhead* is defined in [9] as

$$(N \times |W_s|) \times (2 \times T + 1),$$

where N is the size of the trained model in bytes, $|W_s|$ is the number of selected workers, and T is the total number of training rounds. We assume the size of the model updates to be fixed. However, other communication costs are negligible.

It is worth mentioning that the total communication overhead of FedCO can be calculated as the summation of the communication costs of the initialization stage and the iteration stage together.

6. FedCO Performance Evaluation and Analysis

In this section, we first study the clustering optimization scheme used for the dynamic adaptation of partitioning of workers' updates at each communication round. This adaptive behavior contributes to achieving robust communication in FL. The performance of the proposed FedCO is then evaluated and compared to three other existing FL approaches (FedAvg, FedProx, and CMFL) in terms of accuracy, communication rounds, and communication overhead.

Our proposed FedCO algorithm is a communication-optimized version of FedAvg. Therefore, we further evaluate these two algorithms by benchmarking them on two datasets from the LEAF Federated Learning repository, namely FEMNIST and CelebA. In addition, we further study our FedCO algorithm for two different scenarios for selecting cluster representatives: a performance threshold-based worker selection versus the single (top-performer) cluster representative selection, explained in Algorithm 1.

6.1. Clustering Optimization Behavior

Our clustering optimization algorithm assesses the local updates of clusters' representatives at each communication round, and as a result, it assigns some workers to different clusters. An output of this cluster-updating procedure is that clusters may appear or disappear. Our solution is capable of catching and handling these scenarios. In addition, it implements a splitting procedure that performs a further fine calibration of the clustering for the newly uploaded updates.

In order to illustrate the properties of the clustering optimization scheme discussed above, we show in Figure 4 the clustering updates in the first five global communication rounds of the FedCO algorithm applied to the Non-IID FashionMNIST dataset. In the example, in round 2, cluster 5 has disappeared and cluster 3 is a singleton, i.e., it cannot be a candidate for splitting. Almost all of the remaining clusters (except cluster 6) have negative SI scores. The remaining clusters (0, 1, 2, 4, and 7) have been split into two new clusters and their cluster labels are replaced. Interestingly, in round 3, the unique number of clusters is 17. However, in round 4, five clusters have turned out empty and have disappeared (1, 4, 10, 13, and 16). Furthermore, eight clusters have positive SI scores (0, 2, 5, 6, 9, 12, 14, and 15), while four have negative SI scores (3, 7, 8, and 11). The algorithm did not split the clusters 7, 8, and 11 because this did not improve the quality of the clustering solution; i.e., it did not increase its SI score. Cluster 3 is still a singleton. The worker belonging to this cluster may be considered as one that provides unique model parameters due to its training data. Consequently, in round 5, we have only 12 clusters. Two clusters disappeared (2 and 14), and four new clusters appeared (1, 6, 12, and 17), while clusters 3 and 9 were singletons.

The cluster optimizations discussed above will continue in the same fashion for the upcoming communication rounds. The workers' partitioning is dynamically adapted at each communication round to reflect the new local updates of the representatives.

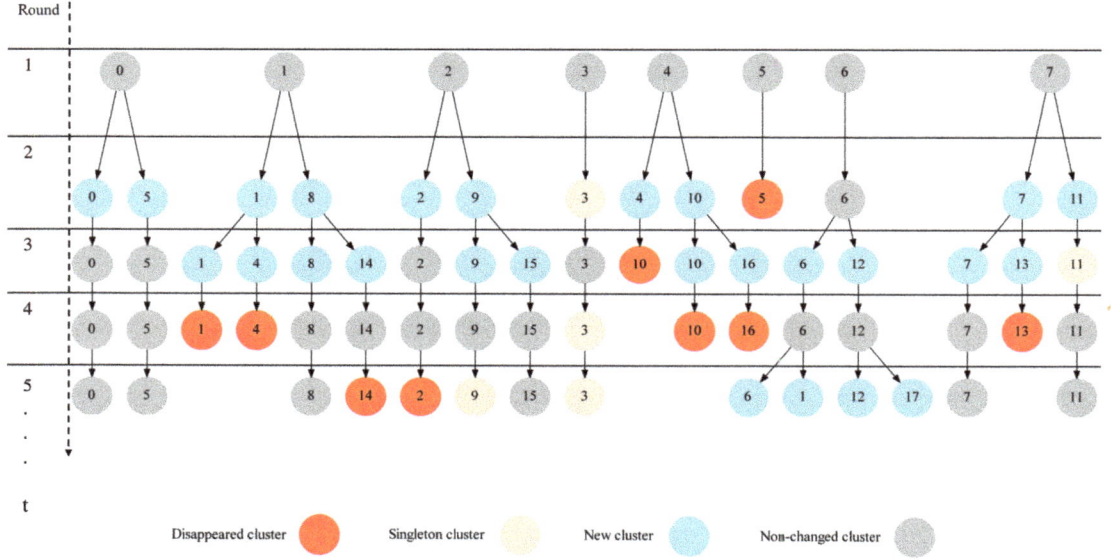

Figure 4. The clustering updates in the first five global communication rounds of the proposed FedCO algorithm applied on the Non-IID FashionMNIST dataset. Notice that the number in the circle represents the cluster label.

6.2. Convergence Analysis

In this section, we provide a convergence analysis of the proposed FedCO algorithm and theoretically show that it ensures a faster convergence than the baseline FedAvg algorithm.

Our analysis is based on two assumptions. The first one supposes that the data are non-IID. Secondly, we assume that there is a partial involvement of workers; this strategy is much more realistic as it does not require all of the worker output. Therefore, at each iteration, we can calculate the global update by aggregating the local updates by using those cluster representatives, which have reached a high accuracy level at this iteration phase. Two scenarios are considered to this end: (i) a global model is trained by FedAvg based on updates made by randomly selected workers, regardless of their accuracy value; (ii) a global model is trained by applying FedCO, and in that way, at each training round, only workers (cluster representatives) that have achieved the highest accuracy values are used.

Let us briefly summarize the working mechanism of the proposed FedCO algorithm. In the tth global training iteration, each worker involved ($w_i \in W_t$) calculates the average g_t^i gradients using the optimization algorithms in the local dataset in the current global model

$\mathcal{M}_t$. Note that according to Equation (5), high-quality data and a high accuracy of the workers' models can lead to a faster convergence of the local loss functions (Equation (3)) and the global loss function (Equation (4)) [45]. Both the local model update $\mathcal{M}_t^i$ of the worker in Equation (1) and the shared global model update $\mathcal{M}_{t+1}$ in Equation (5) can be more quick to converge to the target value with fewer iterations. Consequently, the training time of a worker in a global iteration is decreasing. Therefore, highly accurate workers' models can significantly improve the learning efficiency of Federated Learning; e.g., it can ensure less training time [31,46]. This process is iterative until a global accuracy ϵ ($0 \leq \epsilon \leq 1$) is achieved. Specifically, each update of the local model has a local accuracy w_i^ϵ that corresponds to the local quality of the worker w_i data. A higher local accuracy leads to fewer local and global iterations [46,47]. FedCO uses an iterative approach that requires a series of communication rounds to achieve a level of global accuracy ϵ. Server and representative communications occur during each global round of the iteration phase. Specifically, each representative minimizes its objective $F_i(\mathcal{M}^i)$ in Equation (3) using the local training data n_i. Minimizing $F(\mathcal{M})$ in Equation (4) also requires multiple local iterations up to a target accuracy. Then, the global rounds will be bounded as follows:

$$\frac{\mathcal{O}(\log(\frac{1}{\epsilon}))}{1 - w_i^\epsilon}$$

Thus, the global rounds are affected by both the global accuracy ϵ and the local accuracy w_i^ϵ. When ϵ and w_i^ϵ are high, FedCO needs to run a few global rounds. On the other hand, each global round consists of both computation and transmission time. Our primary motivation in this work is to consider the communication overhead, discussed and analyzed in detail in Section 6.3. The computation time (w_i^{cmp}), however, depends on the number of local iterations. When the global accuracy ϵ is fixed, the computation time is bound by $\log(\frac{1}{w_i^\epsilon})$ for an iterative algorithm to solve Equation 1; here, (SGD) is used [46]. Therefore, the total time of one global communication round for a set of representatives is denoted as

$$T^{com} = \sum_{w_i \in W_t} \log(\frac{1}{w_i^\epsilon}) w_i^{cmp} + w_i^{com},$$

where w_i^{com} represents the transmission time of a local model update. As a result, a high local accuracy value of w_i^ϵ leads to fewer local iterations w_i^{cmp} and eventually to lower global communication rounds T^{com}. Unlike FedCO's convergence rate, FedAvg does not necessarily guarantee a faster convergence speed. This is because FedAvg uses a much larger number of workers compared to the FedCO model. Therefore, if there are more workers with poor data quality, the convergence will be reached at a slower rate than when much fewer workers with high data quality are used. However, at each global round, FedCO may have selected a different set of workers. Those, however, are not selected randomly, but each one is a representative of a cluster of workers having modeled similar parameters, and in addition, it achieves the highest accuracy among the cluster members. Let T_{FedAvg} and T_{FedCO} represent the number of global rounds for which convergence has been reached by FedAvg and FedCO, respectively. Then, Tables 4 and 5 demonstrate that the inequality $T_{FedCO} < T_{FedAvg}$ is valid in the experiments aiming to reach the same accuracy using the two algorithms.

Table 4. The number of communication rounds to reach a target accuracy for the three compared FL algorithms.

	IID					
	MNIST		FashionMNIST		CIFAR-10	
	Rounds	Saving	Rounds	Saving	Rounds	Saving
FedAvg	190	(ref)	200	(ref)	200	(ref)
FedProx	185	26%	190	5%	188	6%
CMFL	50	73%	60	70%	80	60%
FedCO	25	86%	50	75%	30	85%
	Non-IID					
	MNIST		FashionMNIST		CIFAR-10	
	Rounds	Saving	Rounds	Saving	Rounds	Saving
FedAvg	170	(ref)	200	(ref)	200	(ref)
FedProx	167	17%	186	7%	>200	-
CMFL	60	64%	150	25%	160	20%
FedCO	30	82%	70	65%	60	70%

Table 5. The number of communication rounds to reach a certain accuracy level for the two compared FL algorithms on each LEAF dataset.

	IID			
	FEMNIST		CelebA	
	Rounds	Saving	Rounds	Saving
FedAvg	140	(ref)	110	(ref)
FedCO	12	91%	30	72%
	Non-IID			
	FEMNIST		CelebA	
	Rounds	Saving	Rounds	Saving
FedAvg	100	(ref)	150	(ref)
FedCO	14	86%	10	93%

6.3. Communication Rounds versus Accuracy

In this subsection, we present the results related to the evaluation of the accuracy of our distributed deep learning (DL) model. Figures 5–7 show how the compared FL (FedAvg, FedProx, CMFL, and FedCO) algorithms perform in terms of Accuracy versus the Number of Communication Rounds. For the MNIST dataset (see Figure 5), we can observe that the FedCO algorithm converges faster than with the state-of-the-art approaches. As is shown in Figure 5a (IID data distribution setting), FedAvg and FedProx use 100 rounds to obtain an accuracy of 85%. The CMFL reaches the same accuracy in 30 rounds, while our FedCO algorithm achieves this result with only 10 rounds. Furthermore, in Figure 5b, FedCO dramatically decreases the communication rounds with respect to FedAvg, FedProx, and CMFL. Indeed, in Non-IID data, a learning accuracy of 90% is achieved by FedCO in 40 rounds, FedAvg has conducted 160 rounds, FedProx requires 200 rounds, and CMFL needs 60.

In Figure 6a, we compare the accuracy of the four FL approaches in the case of the IID data distribution scenario of FashionMNIST. The FedCO outperforms FedAvg, FedProx, and CMFL in this experimental setting. Within 25 communication rounds, CMFL, FedAvg, and FedProx reach 81%, 69%, and 74% accuracy, respectively, while our FedCO algorithm achieves an accuracy of 90% with the same number of communication rounds. Notice that under the Non-IID data distribution setting, our FedCO algorithm outperforms the other, reaching an accuracy of nearly 79% with only 11 rounds; this costs 100 communication rounds for FedAvg and 80 rounds for FedProx. CMFL considerably minimizes this cost to 60; see Figure 6b.

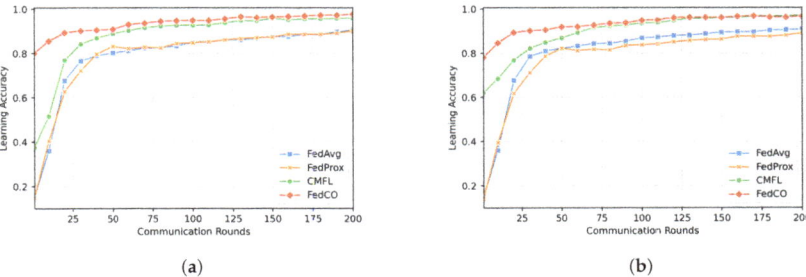

Figure 5. Learning accuracy versus the number of communication rounds for MNIST data. The top plot presents the results produced in the case of the IID data distribution scenario, while the bottom plot depicts the results generated in the case of the Non-IID data distribution scenario. (**a**) IID; (**b**) Non-IID.

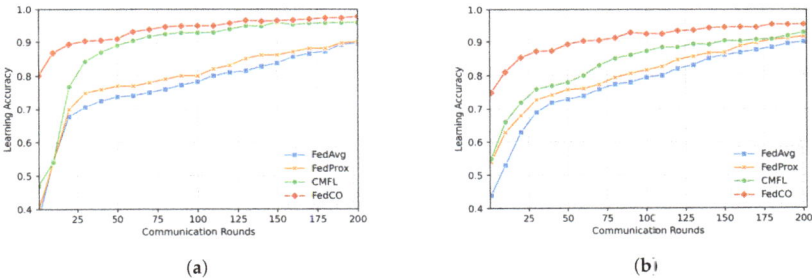

Figure 6. Learning accuracy versus communication rounds for FashionMNIST data. The top plot presents the results produced in the case of the IID data distribution scenario, while the bottom plot depicts the results generated in the case of the Non-IID data distribution scenario. (**a**) IID; (**b**) Non-IID.

Finally, for the CIFAR-10 IID data, the required communication costs of the FedAvg and FedProx to achieve 85% accuracy is 150 rounds, while CMFL obtains the same result for 75 rounds. Our FedCO algorithm outperforms the others, needing only nine rounds to reach this accuracy value (cf. Figure 7a). In the case of the CIFAR-10 Non-IID data (see Figure 7b), in 25 communication rounds, FedCO obtains an accuracy of 85%, while FedAvg and FedProx reach 79% and 80%, respectively. On the other hand, CMFL achieves a close result 82% of accuracy in the same number of rounds.

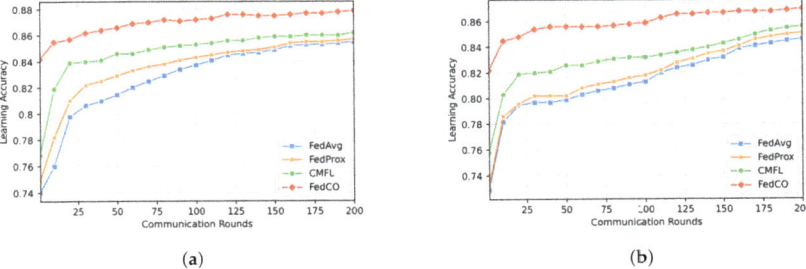

Figure 7. Learning accuracy versus communication rounds for the CIFAR-10 data. The top plot presents the results produced in the case of the IID data distribution scenario, while the bottom plot depicts the results generated in case of the Non-IID data distribution scenario. (**a**) IID; (**b**) Non-IID.

FedCO differs from the Federated Learning baseline FedAvg as follows: our algorithm uses a much smaller number of nodes while the aggregation procedure is the same. Thus, if we have a smaller number of workers, convergence is reached faster than in FedAvg, where all the available workers are used. At each round, FedCO selects and uses a different set of workers, and each worker is a representative that achieves the highest accuracy in each cluster. Hence, the accuracy is not sacrificed.

Table 4 shows the number of communication rounds to achieve the maximum model accuracy (i.e., to converge) for the datasets considered. Specifically, the target accuracy values are 90% for MNIST and FashionMNIST and 85% for CIFAR-10. FedAvg is the baseline benchmark, and the iterations saved for algorithm X (X = FedProx, CMFL, or FedCO) is computed as

$$1 - \frac{num\_of\_iteration\_X}{num\_of\_iteration\_FedAvg}.$$

FedCO saves from 75% to 86% of iterations to converge with respect to FedAvg for IID data distribution setting, and it saves from 65% to 82% iterations for the Non-IID data distribution scenario. Moreover, FedCO always converges with at least half of the iteration rounds needed by CMFL. In more detail, one can observe that the model on the MNIST IID data distribution setting converges to an accuracy of 90% in 190 rounds with the FedAvg algorithm, and in 25 rounds for our FedCO algorithm, providing savings of 86%, and in 185 rounds for FedProx, and in 50 rounds for CMFL, providing savings of 26% and 73%, respectively. The model trained on the FashionMNIST IID data distribution scenario converges to a target accuracy of 90% in 200 rounds for FedAvg, and in 50 rounds for FedCO, saving 75% of communication rounds, while it requires 190 and 60 rounds for FedProx (5% saving) and CMFL (70% saving), respectively. Furthermore, in the FashionMNIST Non-IID data distribution scenario, the model converges to an accuracy of 90% in 200 rounds for the FedAvg algorithm, and in 186 rounds for FedProx, saving only 7%. In contrast, it requires 70 and 150 communication rounds for FedCO and CMFL, with savings of 65% and 25%, respectively. The experimental results on the CIFAR-10 data show that the model trained in the IID and Non-IID data settings need 200 rounds for FedAvg to reach 85% of the accuracy, while it requires 188 rounds for FedProx to reach 85% in IID, and more than 200 rounds in Non-IID to obtain target accuracy. On the other hand, FedCO and CMFL require 30 and 80 rounds, respectively, to converge under the IID data distribution scenario. Furthermore, within the Non-IID data distribution setting, the model converges to an accuracy of 85% in 200 rounds for the FedAvg, while it requires 60 and 160 communication rounds for FedCO and CMFL, respectively. Similarly, in the Non-IID data distribution setting, the FedCO communication costs are reduced to 82% with the MNIST data, 65% with the FashionMNIST data, and up to 70% with the CIFAR-10 dataset, compared to the FedAvg.

Although FedProx is considered to be an optimized version of FedAvg, we can observe from the results discussed above that FedProx behaves very similarly to FedAvg and shows only a slightly better performance than FedAvg in the conducted experiments. In addition, as we mentioned earlier, our FedCO algorithm can also be interpreted as an optimized version of FedAvg. Therefore, we further study these two algorithms (FedCO and FedAvg) by conducting experiments and benchmarking their performance on two datasets from the LEAF repository, namely FEMNIST and CelebA. Figure 8 shows the final accuracy scores after several rounds of communication for the FEMNIST dataset. Comparing the results produced by the two methods, it is evident that FedCO performs significantly better than FedAvg, on both the IID and Non-IID data scenarios. Specifically, FedCO ensures a higher accuracy than that of FedAvg within a smaller number of communication rounds. For example, in Figure 8a, FedCO can reach 90% in only 110 iterations, while the FedAvg never reaches that level within 200 iterations.

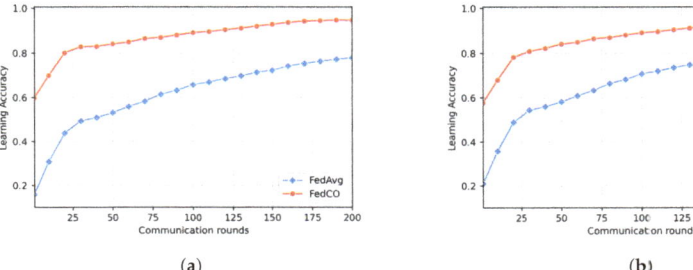

Figure 8. Learning accuracy versus number of communication rounds for FEMNIST data. The top plot presents the results produced in the case of the IID data distribution scenario, while the bottom plot depicts the results generated in the case of the Non-IID data distribution scenario. (**a**) IID; (**b**) Non-IID.

Analyzing the results in Figure 9, we can observe the following: (1) FedCO consistently outperforms FedAvg in both data distribution scenarios; (2) FedCO generally achieves better accuracies than FedAvg in most cases (see Figure 9b), considering that both of them have been trained with only 200 rounds.

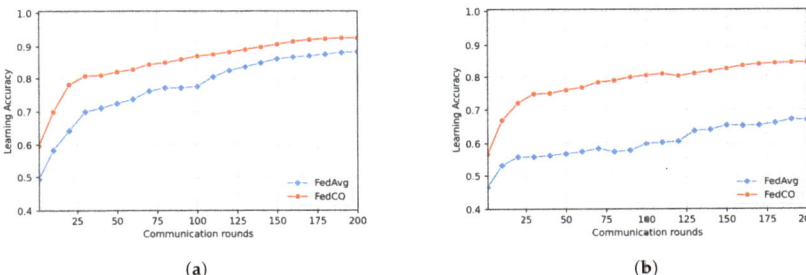

Figure 9. Learning accuracy versus number of communication rounds for CelebA data. The top plot presents the results produced in the case of the IID data distribution scenario, while the bottom plot depicts the results generated in case of the Non-IID data distribution scenario. (**a**) IID; (**b**) Non-IID.

Table 5 reports the number of communication rounds that the FedAvg and FedCO algorithms need in order to converge, for the considered datasets. Specifically, the target accuracy values are 70% for FEMNIST and 65% for CelebA, respectively. In addition, FedAvg is considered as the baseline.

Note that these results again verify the faster convergence of FedCO compared to that of FedAvg. Notice that we have also studied and compared FedProx and FedAvg on the same LEAF datasets, and they again have demonstrated very similar behaviors.

6.4. Communication Overhead Analysis

In this section, we compare the efficiencies of the two compared FL algorithms for 100 communication rounds with respect to different numbers of workers on the CIFAR-10 and the MNIST datasets, under the IID and Non-IID data distribution scenarios. The obtained results are reported in Figures 10 and 11, respectively. As one can notice, the FedCO algorithm has performed significantly better than the FedAvg, FedProx, and CMFL. The reader can also observe that the communication overhead increases linearly with the number of workers. Hence, to scale in a real scenario with thousands of workers, a FL algorithm should be capable of reducing the communication cost as much as possible, and reducing the number of rounds to converge, as with the proposed FedCO algorithm. Finally, the communication overhead in the IID and Non-IID cases is very close or identical. The results produced on the FashionMNIST dataset are similar to the other two datasets.

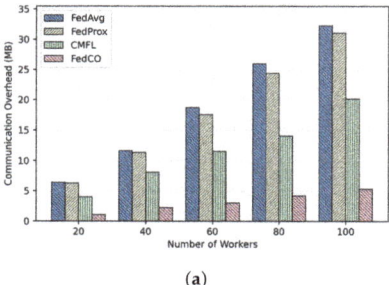 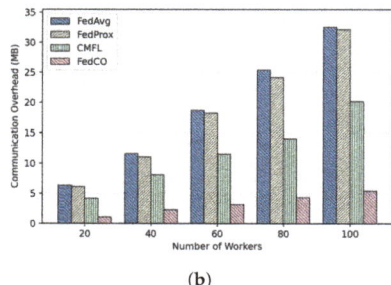

(a)   (b)

Figure 10. The communication overhead for 100 rounds for the CIFAR-10 data. The top plot presents the results produced in the case of the IID data distribution scenario, while the bottom plot depicts the results generated in the case of the Non-IID data distribution scenario. (**a**) IID. (**b**) Non-IID.

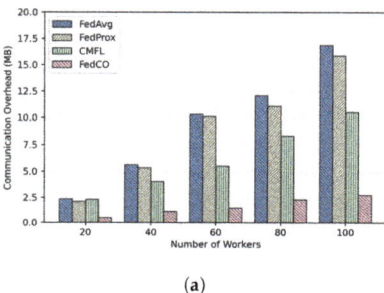 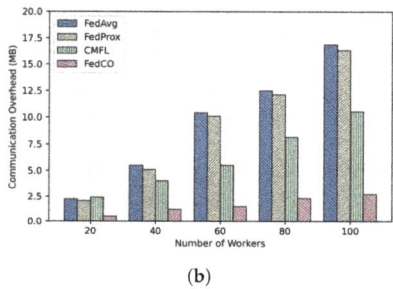

(a)   (b)

Figure 11. The communication overhead for 100 rounds for the MNIST data. The top plot presents the results produced in the case of the IID data distribution scenario, while the bottom plot depicts the results generated in the case of the Non-IID data distribution scenario. (**a**) IID. (**b**) Non-IID.

The communication cost savings for algorithm X (X = FedProx, CMFL, or FedCO) is computed as

$$1 - \frac{Communication\_overhead\_X}{Communication\_overhead\_FedAvg}.$$

As can be seen in Figure 10a,b, the FedCO costs on the CIFAR-10 IID data are 1 MB for 20 workers, which is a reduction in communication costs by 83% in comparison with FedAvg, while FedProx and CMFL are allowed to save only 12% and 36% in communication costs, respectively. In an experiment involving 100 workers on the CIFAR-10 dataset, FedAvg, FedProx, and CMFL exchange 32.5, 31.04, and 20 MB of data, while the proposed FedCO consumes only 5.4 MB, which means that FedCO reduces the communication overhead by 84% with respect to FedAvg, and CMFL reduces the communication overhead by 38%, while FedProx saves only 3% in communication costs.

Figure 11a,b report the communication costs under the MINIST IID and Non-IID data distribution scenarios, respectively. The trend is similar to the results of the CIFAR-10 data experiments. Both the IID and Non-IID data distribution settings confirm that our FedCO algorithm ensures a significantly smaller communication overhead in comparison with FedAvg, FedProx, and CMFL, by substantially reducing the required number of bytes exchanged. As can be noticed, FedCO allows a saving of between 80% and 85% with respect to FedAvg. In Figures 10 and 11, the communication costs increase linearly with the increasing number of workers for all of the compared algorithms. It is obvious that FedCO consistently outperforms FedAvg, FedProx, and CMFL in terms of reducing communication costs.

6.5. Threshold-Based Worker Selection

We also study scenarios in which we use an accuracy threshold to select the number of workers. The threshold is the specified cut-off of accuracy value for the selection of representatives of a cluster of workers. We select any worker where the local update ensures an accuracy of greater than or equal to the predefined threshold as a representative of a cluster. In this section, we report the results produced by testing four different threshold values for FedCO, namely 70%, 75%, 80%, and 85%. The network threshold for the selection of workers varies from bandwidth, transmission speed, or packet loss [48].

Table 6 reports the number of the top-ranked workers that the FedCO algorithm has selected to communicate with the server when the predefined threshold is met within 100 communication rounds.

Table 6. The number of selected representatives with respect to four different threshold values on the LEAF datasets CelebA (top) and FEMNIST (bottom) for 100 global rounds.

CelebA		
Threshold Accuracy	IID	Non-IID
≥70%	853	826
≥75%	673	515
≥80%	600	245
≥85%	257	226

FEMNIST		
Threshold Accuracy	IID	Non-IID
≥70%	912	844
≥75%	806	694
≥80%	730	604
≥85%	408	380

In the case of the CelebA data, the highest number of representatives has been selected when the accuracy of the local models is equal to or above 70%, namely 853 and 826 workers under IID and Non-IID, respectively. In the experiments conducted on the FEMNIST data, when the threshold of the local models was greater than or equal to 70%, 912 workers were selected as representatives for the IID scenario, and 844 workers for the Non-IID one. Similarly, these two values represent the highest numbers of selected workers. It is obvious from the number of representatives reported in Table 6 that the low threshold value implies the greater number of representatives to be selected for global training in FL and vice versa. Thus, we can observe that the proposed algorithm substantially reduces the accumulated communication overhead when FedCO selects only k representatives (i.e., one per cluster), rather than selecting a variable number of representatives based on a predefined threshold to train a global model.

Table 7 presents how many workers per round have been selected as representatives when various thresholds are applied for CelebA under the IID and Non-IID data scenarios, respectively.

We can see that until 10 communication rounds, the FedCO selects only k representatives, since there are no local models where the accuracy has reached 70% at 10 rounds. Thus, the number of representatives increases from 10 to 97 at round 12 due to the selection of all the clusters' workers, ensuring an accuracy that is equal to or above the given threshold. Notice that there are 97 workers of different clusters that reach the value of accuracy of their local models of 70% or above. We can see that FedCO needs 30 rounds to have a number of workers whose accuracy is greater than or equal to 80% and to meet this condition under IID data. Furthermore, to meet the threshold of 85%, FedCO requires 100 rounds to have a number of workers (98) such that their accuracy of the local models meets this condition under IID. On the other hand, for Non-IID, FedCO never meets this condition, since no local models have a accuracy value of higher than or equal to 85%; thus, FedCO selects only 36 workers to represent the different clusters.

Table 7. Total number of selected representatives when the given accuracy threshold is reached in CelebA dataset at different rounds.

Round	IID				Non-IID			
	$\geq$70%	$\geq$75%	$\geq$80%	$\geq$85%	$\geq$70%	$\geq$75%	$\geq$80%	$\geq$85%
1	10	10	10	10	10	10	10	10
10	10	12	16	14	14	16	18	16
12	97	13	16	16	14	18	22	18
20	102	103	20	20	104	26	25	24
30	105	104	95	18	104	30	28	24
40	102	108	98	20	110	32	30	26
50	106	108	100	22	112	96	32	28
60	106	110	104	24	114	99	34	28
70	107	111	106	26	116	102	36	32
80	108	114	108	22	120	104	38	35
90	110	116	110	26	118	106	38	34
100	112	116	112	98	122	108	97	36

Figure 12 provides communication overheads for various thresholds. It is obvious to the reader that a higher number of selected representatives implies a higher values of communication costs to the server.

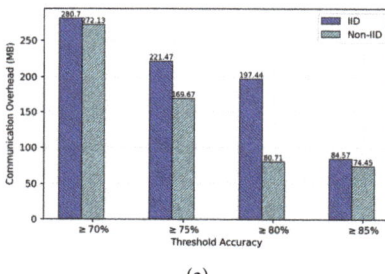 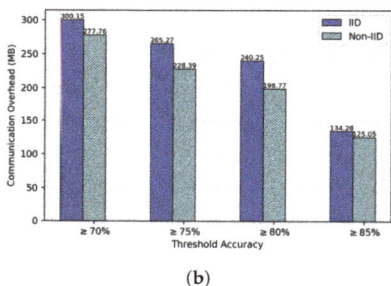

(a) (b)

Figure 12. The communication overhead for 100 rounds for the two LEAF datasets. The top plot presents the results produced for CelebA dataset, while the bottom plot depicts the results generated on FEMNIST dataset. (**a**) CelebA; (**b**) FEMNIST.

The above results suggest that our proposed FedCO algorithm can substantially reduce the communication overhead by using a higher accuracy threshold. In general, FedCO can be considered as being robust to different application scenarios by being able to tune its parameters (e.g., the accuracy threshold or the number of top-ranked representatives per cluster) to find a trade-off between the application-specific resource constraints and the accuracy requirements.

7. Conclusions

This paper proposes a clustering-based FL approach, entitled Federated Learning using Clustering Optimization (FedCO). The proposed FedCO approach partially builds upon our previous work and extending further towards proposing a dynamic clustering scheme that improves global accuracy and that reduces the communication overhead in a Federated Learning context. The proposed approach dynamically identifies worker participants in each communication round by initially clustering the workers' local updates and selecting a representative from each cluster to communicate with the central server, thus minimizing the communication cost. The proposed FedCO method is evaluated and benchmarked to three other state-of-the-art FL algorithms (FedAvg, FedProx, and CMFL) on five publicly available and widely exploited datasets for studying distributed ML algorithms. The experimental results have shown that the proposed FedCO algorithm significantly reduces communication rounds without sacrificing accuracy. In addition, the experimental evaluation has demonstrated that our FedCO algorithm outperforms the three other FL algorithms under the two studied data distribution scenarios. We have also shown that the FedCO algorithm can dynamically adapt the workers' partitioning at each communication round by relocating the representative workers and conducting the cluster splitting needed for the clustering improvement.

Our future plans include the enhancement of the FedCO approach through using other data distillation techniques; e.g., an interesting future direction could be made by applying computational topology methods for studying data topology and selecting representatives based on this. Another direction is the translation of the FedCO concept to unsupervised learning settings, i.e., developing a resource-efficient FL algorithm based on the unsupervised ML model.

Author Contributions: Conceptualization, A.A.A.-S., V.B. and E.C.; methodology, A.A.A.-S., V.B. and E.C.; software, A.A.A.-S.; validation, A.A.A.-S., V.B. and E.C.; formal analysis, A.A.A.-S. and V.B.; investigation, A.A.A.-S., V.B. and E.C.; data curation, A.A.A.-S.; writing—original draft preparation, A.A.A.-S., V.B. and E.C.; writing—review and editing, A.A.A.-S., V.B. and E.C.; visualization, A.A.A.-S.; supervision, V.B. and E.C. All authors have read and agreed to the published version of the manuscript.

Funding: This research received no external funding.

Institutional Review Board Statement: Not applicable.

Informed Consent Statement: Not applicable.

Data Availability Statement: Not applicable.

Acknowledgments: The first author is supported by an Iraq Ministry of Higher Education and Scientific Research PhD Scholarship.

Conflicts of Interest: The authors declare no conflict of interest.

References

1. Hatcher, W.G.; Yu, W. A Survey of Deep Learning: Platforms, Applications and Emerging Research Trends. *IEEE Access* **2018**, *6*, 24411–24432. [CrossRef]
2. Goodfellow, I.; Bengio, Y.; Courville, A. *Deep Learning*; The MIT Press: Cambridge, MA, USA, 2017.
3. Papernot, N.; McDaniel, P.; Sinha, A.; Wellman, M.P. Sok: Security and Privacy in Machine Learning. In Proceedings of the 2018 IEEE European Symposium on Security and Privacy (EuroS&P), London, UK, 24–26 April 2018. [CrossRef]
4. Liang, F.; Hatcher, W.G.; Liao, W.; Gao, W.; Yu, W. Machine Learning for Security and the Internet of Things: The Good, the Bad, and the Ugly. *IEEE Access* **2019**, *7*, 158126–158147. [CrossRef]
5. Li, T.; Sahu, A.K.; Talwalkar, A.; Smith, V. Federated Learning: Challenges, Methods, and Future Directions. *IEEE Signal Process. Mag.* **2020**, *37*, 50–60. [CrossRef]
6. McMahan, B.; Moore, E.; Ramage, D.; Hampson, S.; y Arcas, B.A. Communication-efficient learning of deep networks from decentralized data. *Artif. Intell. Stat.* **2017**, *54*, 1273–1282.
7. Huang, G.; Liu, Z.; Van Der Maaten, L.; Weinberger, K.Q. Densely Connected Convolutional Networks. In Proceedings of the 2017 IEEE Conference on Computer Vision and Pattern Recognition (CVPR), Honolulu, HI, USA, 21–26 July 2017. [CrossRef]
8. Sattler, F.; Wiedemann, S.; Muller, K.-R.; Samek, W. Sparse Binary Compression: Towards Distributed Deep Learning with Minimal Communication. In Proceedings of the 2019 International Joint Conference on Neural Networks (IJCNN), Budapest, Hungary, 14–19 July 2019. [CrossRef]
9. Al-Saedi, A.A.; Boeva, V.; Casalicchio, E. Reducing Communication Overhead of Federated Learning through Clustering Analysis. In Proceedings of the 2021 IEEE Symposium on Computers and Communications (ISCC), Athens, Greece, 5–8 September 2021. [CrossRef]
10. Li, T.; Sahu, A.K.; Zaheer, M.; Sanjabi, M.; Talwalkar, A.; Smith, V. Federated optimization in heterogeneous networks. *arXiv* **2021**, arXiv:1812.06127.
11. Wang, L.; Wang, W.; Li, B. CMFL: Mitigating Communication Overhead for Federated Learning. In Proceedings of the 2019 IEEE 39th International Conference on Distributed Computing Systems (ICDCS), Dallas, TX, USA, 7–9 July 2019. [CrossRef]

12. Diao, E.; Ding, J.; Tarokh, V. HeteroFL: Computation and Communication Efficient Federated Learning for Heterogeneous Clients. *arXiv* **2021**, arXiv:2010.01264.
13. Reisizadeh, A.; Mokhtari, A.; Hassani, H.; Jadbabaie, A.; Pedarsani, R. FedPAQ: A Communication-Efficient Federated Learning Method with Periodic Averaging and Quantization. *arXiv* **2020**, arXiv:1909.13014.
14. Sattler, F.; Muller, K.-R.; Samek, W. Clustered Federated Learning: Model-Agnostic Distributed Multitask Optimization under Privacy Constraints. *IEEE Trans. Neural Netw. Learn. Syst.* **2021**, *32*, 3710–3722. [CrossRef] [PubMed]
15. Shlezinger, N.; Rini, S.; Eldar, Y.C. The Communication-Aware Clustered Federated Learning Problem. In Proceedings of the 2020 IEEE International Symposium on Information Theory (ISIT), Los Angeles, CA, USA, 21–26 June 2020. [CrossRef]
16. Kim, Y.; Hakim, E.A.; Haraldson, J.; Eriksson, H.; da Silva, J.M.; Fischione, C. Dynamic Clustering in Federated Learning. In Proceedings of the ICC 2021—IEEE International Conference on Communications, Montreal, QC, Canada, 14–23 June 2021. [CrossRef]
17. Ghosh, A.; Chung, J.; Yin, D.; Ramchandran, K. An Efficient Framework for Clustered Federated Learning. *arXiv* **2020**, arXiv:2006.04088.
18. Ouyang, X.; Xie, Z.; Zhou, J.; Huang, J.; Xing, G. CLUSTERFL. In Proceedings of the 19th Annual International Conference on Mobile Systems, Applications, and Services, Virtual Event, WI, USA, 24 June–2 July 2021. [CrossRef]
19. Chen, Y.; Sun, X.; Jin, Y. Communication-Efficient Federated Deep Learning with Layerwise Asynchronous Model Update and Temporally Weighted Aggregation. *IEEE Trans. Neural Netw. Learn. Syst.* **2020**, *31*, 4229–4238. [CrossRef]
20. Caldas, S.; Konecný, J.; McMahan, H.B.; Talwalkar, A.S. Expanding the Reach of Federated Learning by Reducing Client Resource Requirements. *arXiv* **2018**, arXiv:1812.07210.
21. Lin, Y.; Han, S.; Mao, H.; Wang, Y.; Dally, W. Deep Gradient Compression: Reducing the Communication Bandwidth for Distributed Training. *arXiv* **2018**, arXiv:1712.01887.
22. Sattler, F.; Wiedemann, S.; Muller, K.-R.; Samek, W. Robust and Communication-Efficient Federated Learning from Non-I.i.d. Data. *IEEE Trans. Neural Netw. Learn. Syst.* **2020**, *31*, 3400–3413. [CrossRef]
23. Vogels, T.; Karimireddy, S.P.; Jaggi, M. PowerSGD: Practical Low-Rank Gradient Compression for Distributed Optimization. In Proceedings of the NeurIPS 2019—Advances in Neural Information Processing Systems, Vancouver, BC, Canada, 8–14 December 2019.
24. Asad, M.; Moustafa, A.; Ito, T. Fedopt: Towards Communication Efficiency and Privacy Preservation in Federated Learning. *Appl. Sci.* **2020**, *10*, 2864. [CrossRef]
25. Malekijoo, A.; Fadaeieslam, M.J.; Malekijou, H.; Homayounfar, M.; Alizadeh-Shabdiz, F.; Rawassizadeh, R. FEDZIP: A Compression Framework for Communication-Efficient Federated Learning. *arXiv* **2021**, arXiv:2102.01593.
26. Rothchild, D.; Panda, A.; Ullah, E.; Ivkin, N.; Stoica, I.; Braverman, V.; Gonzalez, J.E.; Arora, R. FetchSGD: Communication-Efficient Federated Learning with Sketching. *arXiv* **2020**, arXiv:2007.07682.
27. Xu, J.; Du, W.; Jin, Y.; He, W.; Cheng, R. Ternary Compression for Communication-Efficient Federated Learning. *IEEE Trans. Neural Netw. Learn. Syst.* **2022**, *33*, 1162–1176. [CrossRef]
28. Chai, Z.; Chen, Y.; Anwar, A.; Zhao, L.; Cheng, Y.; Rangwala, H. FedAT: A high-performance and communication-efficient federated learning system with asynchronous tiers. In Proceedings of the International Conference for High Performance Computing, Networking, Storage and Analysis, St. Louis, MI, USA, 14–19 November 2021. [CrossRef]
29. Wu, X.; Liang, Z.; Wang, J. FedMed: A Federated Learning Framework for Language Modeling. *Sensors* **2020**, *20*, 4048. [CrossRef] [PubMed]
30. Asad, M.; Moustafa, A.; Aslam, M. CEEP-FL: A Comprehensive Approach for Communication Efficiency and Enhanced Privacy in Federated Learning. *Appl. Soft Comput.* **2021**, *104*, 107235. [CrossRef]
31. Nishio, T.; Yonetani, R. Client Selection for Federated Learning with Heterogeneous Resources in Mobile Edge. In Proceedings of the ICC 2019—2019 IEEE International Conference on Communications (ICC), Shanghai, China, 20–24 May 2019. [CrossRef]
32. Park, S.; Suh, Y.; Lee, J. FedPSO: Federated Learning Using Particle Swarm Optimization to Reduce Communication Costs. *Sensors* **2021**, *21*, 600. [CrossRef]
33. Chen, Z.; Chong, K.F.E.; Quek, T.Q.S. Dynamic Attention-based Communication-Efficient Federated Learning. *arXiv* **2021**, arXiv:2108.05765.
34. Larsson, H.; Riaz, H.; Ickin, S. Automated Collaborator Selection for Federated Learning with Multi-Armed Bandit Agents. In Proceedings of the 4th FlexNets Workshop on Flexible Networks Artificial Intelligence Supported Network Flexibility and Agility, Virtual Event, 23 August 2021. [CrossRef]
35. Ji, S.; Pan, S.; Long, G.; Li, X.; Jiang, J.; Huang, Z. Learning Private Neural Language Modeling with Attentive Aggregation. In Proceedings of the 2019 International Joint Conference on Neural Networks (IJCNN), Budapest, Hungary, 14–19 July 2019. [CrossRef]
36. Ribero, M.; Vikalo, H. Communication-Efficient Federated Learning via Optimal Client Sampling. *arXiv* **2020**, arXiv:2007.15197.
37. Konecný, J.; McMahan, H.B.; Yu, F.X.; Richtarik, P.; Suresh, A.T.; Bacon, D. Federated Learning: Strategies for Improving Communication Efficiency. *arXiv* **2016**, arXiv:1610.05492.
38. MacQueen, J.B. Some methods for classification and analysis of multivariate observations. *Proc. Berkley Symp. Math. Stat. Probab.* **1967**, *1*, 281–297.

39. Rousseeuw, P.J. Silhouettes: A Graphical Aid to the Interpretation and Validation of Cluster Analysis. *J. Comput. Appl. Math.* **1987**, *20*, 53–65. [CrossRef]
40. LeCun, Y.; Bottou, L.; Bengio, Y.; Haffner, P. Gradient-based learning applied to document recognition. *Proc. IEEE* **1998**, *86*, 2278–2324. [CrossRef]
41. Xiao, H.; Rasul, K.; Vollgraf, R. Fashion-MNIST: A Novel Image Dataset for Benchmarking Machine Learning Algorithms. *arXiv* **2017**, arXiv:1708.07747.
42. Krizhevsky, A. Learning Multiple Layers of Features from Tiny Images. Available online: https://www.cs.toronto.edu/~kriz/learning-features-2009-TR.pdf (accessed on 18 April 2022).
43. Caldas, S.; Wu, P.; Li, T.; Konecný, J.; McMahan, H.B.; Smith, V.; Talwalkar, A.S. LEAF: A Benchmark for Federated Settings. *arXiv* **2018**, arXiv:1812.01097.
44. LeCun, Y.; Cortes, C. The Mnist Database of Handwritten Digits. Available online: https://www.lri.fr/~marc/Master2/MNIST_doc.pdf (accessed on 18 April 2022).
45. Kang, J.; Xiong, Z.; Niyato, D.; Xie, S.; Zhang, J. Incentive Mechanism for Reliable Federated Learning: A Joint Optimization Approach to Combining Reputation and Contract Theory. *IEEE Internet Things J.* **2019**, *6*, 10700–10714. [CrossRef]
46. Tran, N.H.; Bao, W.; Zomaya, A.; Nguyen, M.N.; Hong, C.S. Federated Learning over Wireless Networks: Optimization Model Design and Analysis. In Proceedings of the IEEE INFOCOM 2019—IEEE Conference on Computer Communications, Paris, France, 29 April 2019–2 May 2019. [CrossRef]
47. Konečný, J.; McMahan, H.B.; Ramage, D.; Richtarik, P. Federated optimization: Distributed machine learning for on-device intelligence. *arXiv* **2016**, arXiv:1610.02527.
48. Zhou, P.; Fang, P.; Hui, P. Loss Tolerant Federated Learning. *arXiv* **2021**, arXiv:2105.03591.

Article

Latency-Aware Semi-Synchronous Client Selection and Model Aggregation for Wireless Federated Learning

Liangkun Yu [1], Xiang Sun [1,*], Rana Albelaihi [1,2] and Chen Yi [3]

1. SECNet Laboratory, Department of Electrical and Computer Engineering, University of New Mexico, Albuquerque, NM 87131, USA; liangkun@unm.edu (L.Y.); ralbelaihi@unm.edu (R.A.)
2. Department of Computer Science, College of Engineering and Information Technology, Onaizah Colleges, Onaizah 56447, Saudi Arabia
3. Chongqing Key Laboratory of Signal and Information Processing, School of Communication and Information Engineering, Chongqing University of Posts and Telecommunications, Chongqing 400065, China; yichen@cqupt.edu.cn
* Correspondence: sunxiang@unm.edu

Abstract: Federated learning (FL) is a collaborative machine-learning (ML) framework particularly suited for ML models requiring numerous training samples, such as Convolutional Neural Networks (CNNs), Recurrent Neural Networks (RNNs), and Random Forest, in the context of various applications, e.g., next-word prediction and eHealth. FL involves various clients participating in the training process by uploading their local models to an FL server in each global iteration. The server aggregates these models to update a global model. The traditional FL process may encounter bottlenecks, known as the straggler problem, where slower clients delay the overall training time. This paper introduces the Latency-awarE Semi-synchronous client Selection and mOdel aggregation for federated learNing (LESSON) method. LESSON allows clients to participate at different frequencies: faster clients contribute more frequently, therefore mitigating the straggler problem and expediting convergence. Moreover, LESSON provides a tunable trade-off between model accuracy and convergence rate by setting varying deadlines. Simulation results show that LESSON outperforms two baseline methods, namely FedAvg and FedCS, in terms of convergence speed and maintains higher model accuracy compared to FedCS.

Keywords: federated learning; client selection; model aggregation; semi-synchronous; IoT

1. Introduction

With the development of the Internet of Things (IoT), numerous smart devices, such as smartphones, smartwatches, and virtual-reality headsets, are widely used to digitize people's daily lives. Traditionally, a huge volume of data generated by these IoT devices is uploaded to and analyzed by a centralized data center that generates high-level knowledge and provides corresponding services to users, thus facilitating their lives [1]. A typical example is smart homes, where various IoT devices, such as smart meters, thermostats, motion detectors, and humidity sensors, are deployed to monitor the status of the smart homes. The data generated by the IoT devices would be uploaded to a centralized data center, which applies a deep reinforcement learning model to intelligently and autonomously control, for example, the smart bulbs and air conditioners in smart homes, to improve the quality of experience and reduce the energy usage of smart homes [2].

On the other hand, sharing data with third-party data centers may raise privacy concerns as data generated by IoT devices may contain personal information, such as users' locations and personal preferences [3]. As a result, various policies have been made, such as General Data Protection Regulation (GDPR) made by the European Union [4], to regulate and hinder data sharing. To fully utilize these personal data while preserving privacy (i.e., without sharing the data), federated learning (FL) is proposed to distributively train machine-learning models by enabling different IoT devices to analyze their data locally without uploading them to a central facility [5]. A typical example of using FL is to train a next-word prediction model, which is used to predict what word comes next based on the existing text information [6]. Basically, as shown in Figure 1, an FL server would first initialize the parameters of the global model and then broadcast the global model to all the clients via wireless networks. Each client would train the received global model based on its local data sets (i.e., their text messages) and upload the updated model to the FL server via wireless networks. The FL server then aggregates the received models from the clients to generate a new global model and then starts a new iteration by broadcasting the new global model to the clients. The iteration continues until the model is converged.

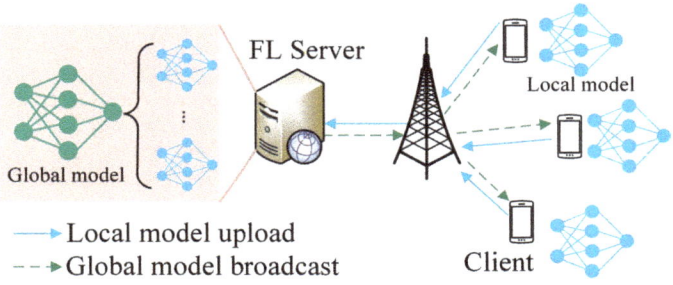

Figure 1. Wireless federated learning.

The traditional FL method can resolve the privacy issue to allow the clients to train the model locally, and it applies the synchronous strategy, where the FL server must wait until it receives the models from all the clients in each global iteration. This may lead to the straggler problem when the configurations of clients are heterogeneous, meaning that they have different computing and communications capabilities. Hence, some stragglers take much longer time to train and upload their models in a global iteration because of their lower computing and communications capabilities, and thus significantly prolong the model training process. To resolve the straggler problem, many client selection methods have been proposed [7–12], which would select the qualified clients that can finish their model training and uploading before a predefined deadline. Normally, client selection and resource allocation are jointly optimized to maximize the number of selected qualified clients. Selecting qualified clients can resolve the straggler problem but may raise other issues. First, the proposed client selection may significantly reduce the number of participating clients, which may slow down the convergence speed [13], thus leading to longer training latency (which equals the sum of the latency for all the global iterations). Second, the proposed client selection may result in the model overfitting issue caused by the reduction of data diversity, i.e., if the FL server only selects the qualified clients to participate in the model training, then the generated model can only fit the data samples in these qualified clients, but not the non-qualified clients. The model overfitting issue would be compounded if the data samples of the qualified clients are not sufficient [14]. The other solution to solve the straggler problem is to apply asynchronous FL, where the FL server does not need to wait until the deadline expires for each global iteration but would update the global model once it receives a local model from a client [15]. However, the asynchronous FL may suffer from (1) the high communications cost since both the FL server and clients will more frequently exchange their models and (2) the stale issue, where some slow clients are training based on an outdated global model, which may lead to slow convergence rate or even global model divergence [16,17].

To solve the slow convergence and model overfitting issues in the synchronous FL while avoiding model divergence in the asynchronous FL, we propose a semi-synchronous FL method, i.e., Latency awarE Semi-synchronous client Selection and mOdel aggregation for federated learNing (LESSON). The basic idea of LESSON is to allow all the clients to participate in the whole learning process with different frequencies. Specifically, the clients are clustered into different tiers based on their model training and uploading latency. The clients in a lower tier (i.e., lower model training and uploading latency) would participate in the learning process more frequently than those in a higher tier (with higher model training and uploading latency). As a result, the straggler problem can be resolved (since the FL server does not need to wait for stragglers in each global iteration), and the model overfitting problem can be fixed (since all the clients join the learning process to provide high data diversity). The main contributions of the paper are summarized as follows.

1. A new semi-synchronous FL algorithm, i.e., LESSON, is introduced. LESSON introduces a latency-aware client clustering technique that groups clients into different tiers based on their computing and uploading latency. LESSON allows all the clients in the system to participate in the training process but at different frequencies, depending on the clients' associated tiers. LESSON is expected to mitigate the straggler problem in synchronous FL and model overfitting in asynchronous FL, thus expediting model convergence.
2. LESSON also features a specialized model aggregation method tailored to client clustering. This method sets the weight and timing for local model aggregation for each client tier.
3. The proposed LESSON algorithm also integrates the dynamic model aggregation and step size adjustment according to client clustering and offers flexibility in balancing model accuracy and convergence speed by adjusting the deadline τ.
4. Extensive experimental evaluations show that LESSON outperforms FedAvg and FedCS in terms of faster convergence and higher model accuracy.

The rest of this paper is organized as follows. The related work is summarized in Section 2. System models are described in Section 3. Section 4 elaborates on the proposed LESSON algorithm, which comprises client clustering and model aggregation. In Section 5, the performance of LESSON is compared with the other two baseline algorithms via extensive simulations, and simulation results are analyzed. Finally, Section 6 concludes this paper.

2. Related Work

Solving the straggler issue is one of the main challenges in synchronous FL. The existing solutions mainly focus on jointly optimizing client selection and resource allocation. Nishio and Yonetani [18] aimed to maximize the number of selected clients that can finish their model training and uploading before a predefined deadline in each global iteration. By assuming that the selected clients must iteratively upload their models to the FL server, they designed FedCS that jointly optimizes the uploading schedule and client selection to achieve the objective. Abdulrahman and Tout [19] designed a similar client selection method FedMCCS. The goal of FedMCCS is to maximize the number of selected clients who can not only finish the model training and uploading before a predefined deadline but also guarantee the resource utilization is less than the threshold to avoid device dropout. Albelaihi et al. [11] proposed a client selection method that tries to achieve the same objective as FedCS, but they argued that the latency of a client in waiting for the wireless channel to be available for model uploading should be considered; otherwise, the selected clients may not upload their local models before the deadline. Yu et al. [20] proposed to dynamically adjust and optimize the trade-off between maximizing the number of selected clients and minimizing the total energy consumption of the selected clients by picking suitable clients and allocating appropriate resources (in terms of CPU frequency and transmission power) in each global iteration. Shi et al. [21] also jointly optimized the client selection and resource allocation for FL. However, the objective is to minimize the overall learning latency (which equals the product of the average latency of one global iteration and the number of global iterations) while achieving a certain model accuracy. They formulated a system model to estimate the number of global iterations given the global model accuracy requirement. All the mentioned client selection methods for synchronous FL can alleviate the straggler problem but may lead to a slow convergence rate and model overfitting issues, as we illustrated previously.

Instead of selecting qualified clients to avoid stragglers, Li et al. [22] proposed to let fast clients train their local models by running more gradient descent iterations in each global iteration. In this way, the fast and slow clients could upload their models at a similar time, but the fast clients may provide better models to fit their local data samples, thus potentially speeding up the model convergence. This method, however, may lead to local model overfitting issues when some fast clients run too many gradient descent iterations over the limited data samples. The overfitted local models would significantly slow down the global model convergence. Wu et al. [23] proposed to perform spilt learning, where a global neural network is divided into two parts. The parameters in the former and latter layers are trained in the clients and the FL server, respectively. As a result, the computational complexity of the clients is reduced, thus potentially reducing the training time and energy consumption of the clients.

Other works aim to design asynchronous FL, where the FL server does not need to wait for the selected clients to upload their local models; instead, once the FL server receives a local model from a client, it would aggregate the received local model to update the global model, and then send the updated global model to the client [24–27]. However, as mentioned before, the fast clients and the FL server must exchange their models more frequently, thus leading to higher communications costs for both the fast clients and FL server [28,29]. Meanwhile, in asynchronous FL, the slower clients may train their local models based on an outdated global model, which results in slow convergence or even leads to model divergence [30,31].

To overcome the drawbacks in synchronous and asynchronous FL, we propose the semi-synchronous FL to allow all the clients to participate in the whole learning process with different frequencies. Although the term "semi-synchronous FL" has been used by the existing works, the definitions are different from what we defined in this paper. For example, Stripelis and Ambite [32] defined semi-synchronous FL as the clients train their local models over different sizes of local data sets, depending on their computing capabilities. The semi-synchronous FL proposed in [33] periodically re-selects a number of clients and follows the same method as asynchronous FL to aggregate and update the global model.

3. System Models
3.1. Federated Learning Preliminary

The idea of FL is to enable distributed clients to cooperatively train a global model such that the global loss function, denoted as $\mathcal{F}(\omega)$, can be minimized. That is,

$$\arg\min_{\omega} \mathcal{F}(\omega) = \arg\min_{\omega} \sum_{i \in \mathcal{I}} \frac{|\mathcal{D}_i|}{|\mathcal{D}|} f_i(\omega), \tag{1}$$

where ω is the set of the parameters for the global model, $\mathcal{I}$ is the set of the selected clients, $|\mathcal{D}|$ is the number of the training data samples of all the clients, $|\mathcal{D}_i|$ is the number of the training data samples at client i (where $\mathcal{D} = \bigcup_{i \in \mathcal{I}} \mathcal{D}_i$), and $f_i(\omega)$ is the local loss function of client i, i.e.,

$$f_i(\omega) = \frac{1}{|\mathcal{D}_i|} \sum_{n \in \mathcal{D}_i} f(\omega, a_{i,n}, b_{i,n}). \tag{2}$$

Here, $(a_{i,n}, b_{i,n})$ is the input-output pair for the nth data sample in user i's data set, and $f(\omega, a_{i,n}, b_{i,n})$ captures the error of the local model (with parameter ω) over $(a_{i,n}, b_{i,n})$.

In each global iteration, FL comprises four steps.

1. Server broadcast: In the k-th global iteration, the FL server broadcasts the global model generated in the previous global iteration, denoted as $\omega^{(k-1)}$, to all the selected clients.

2. Client local training: Each client i trains its local model over its local data set $\mathcal{D}_i$, i.e., $\omega_i^{(k)} = \omega_i^{(k-1)} - \delta \nabla f_i\left(\omega_i^{(k-1)}\right)$, where δ is the learning rate.
3. Client model uploading: After deriving the local model $\omega_i^{(k)}$, client i uploads its local model to the FL server.
4. Server model aggregation: The FL server aggregates the local models from the clients and updates the global model based on, for example, FedAvg [5], i.e., $\omega^{(k)} = \sum_{i \in \mathcal{I}} \frac{|\mathcal{D}_i|}{|\mathcal{D}|} \omega_i^{(k)}$.

The global iteration keeps executed to update the global model $\omega^{(k)}$ until the global model converges.

3.2. Latency Models of a Client

There are four steps in each global iteration for FL, and so the latency of a global iteration equals the sum of the latency among these four steps. The local model training latency in Step (2) and local model uploading latency in Step (3) are different among the clients, depending on their computing and communications capacities. In addition, the global model broadcast latency in Step (1) and model aggression latency in Step (4) are the same for all the clients and are normally negligible as compared to local model training and uploading latency. Thus, we define the latency of client i in a global iteration as follows.

$$t_i = t_i^{comp} + t_i^{upload}, \qquad (3)$$

where t_i^{comp} is the computing latency of client i in training its local model over its local data samples in Step (2), and t_i^{upload} is the uploading latency of client i in uploading its local model to the FL server in Step (3).

3.2.1. Computing Latency

The computing latency of client i in a global iteration can be estimated by [34]

$$t_i^{comp} = \theta \log_2\left(\frac{1}{\epsilon}\right) \frac{C_i |\mathcal{D}_i|}{f_i}, \qquad (4)$$

where θ is a constant determined by the structure of the desired model; $\theta \log_2\left(\frac{1}{\epsilon}\right)$ indicates the estimated number of local iterations to achieve the required training accuracy ϵ; C_i in cycles/sample is the number of CPU cycles required for training one data sample of the local model; $|\mathcal{D}_i|$ is the number of training samples used by client i; f_i in cycles/second is CPU frequency of client i, which is determined by the device hardware.

3.2.2. Uploading Latency

The achievable data rate of client i can be estimated by

$$r_i = b \log_2\left(1 + \frac{pg_i}{N_0}\right), \qquad (5)$$

where b is the amount of bandwidth allocated to each participating client, p is the transmission power of the client, g_i is the channel gain from client i to the BS calculated, and N_0 is the average background noise and inter-cell interference power density. We assume that the size of the local model is s, and so the latency of client i in uploading its local model to the BS is

$$t_i^{upload} = \frac{s}{r_i} = \frac{s}{b \log_2\left(1 + \frac{pg_i}{N_0}\right)}. \qquad (6)$$

4. Latency-awarE Semi-Synchronous Client Selection and mOdel Aggregation for Federated learNing (LESSON)

In contrast to synchronous FL, the proposed LESSON method aims to allow all the clients to participate in the whole learning process while avoiding the straggler problem. The basic idea of LESSON is to cluster the clients into different tiers based on their latency and the deadline. The clients in different tiers would train and upload their local models at different frequencies.

4.1. Latency-Aware Client Clustering

We denote τ as the deadline of a global iteration. The FL server would accept all the models uploaded from the clients before the deadline τ and reject the rest in each global iteration. Hence, we cluster the clients into several tiers, and x_{ij} is used to indicate whether client i is in Tier j (i.e., $x_{ij} = 1$) or not (i.e., $x_{ij} = 0$). Basically, if client i can finish its local model training and uploading before deadline τ, i.e., $t_i \leq \tau$, then client i is in Tier 1, i.e., $x_{i1} = 1$. Similarly, if client i can finish its local model training and uploading between τ and $2 \times \tau$, i.e., $\tau < t_i \leq 2 \times \tau$, then client i is in Tier 2, i.e., $x_{i2} = 1$. The following equation provides a general mathematical expression to cluster client i into a specific tier.

$$x_{ij} = \begin{cases} 1, & \text{if } \tau \times (j-1) < t_i \leq \tau \times j, \\ 0, & \text{otherwise,} \end{cases} \quad (7)$$

where j is the index of tiers.

4.2. Semi-Synchronized Model Aggregation

In each global iteration, clients from different tiers upload their local models, and the FL server can estimate when a client may upload its local model according to its associated tier. Figure 2 provides one example to illustrate the scheduling of the clients from four tiers in LESSON. For example, the clients in Tier 1 are expected to upload their local models in each global iteration, and the clients in Tier 2 are expected to upload their local models in every two global iterations. Denote k as the index of the global iterations, and let y_{jk} be the binary variable to indicate whether the clients in Tier j are expected to upload their local models by the end of kth global iteration, where

$$y_{jk} = \begin{cases} 1, & \text{if } k\%j = 0, \\ 0, & \text{otherwise,} \end{cases} \quad (8)$$

where % is the modulo operation, and so $k\%j = 0$ indicates k is divisible by j. Meanwhile, let z_{ik} be the binary variable to indicate whether client i is expected to upload its local model by the end of kth global iteration ($z_{ik} = 1$) or not ($z_{ik} = 0$), where

$$z_{ik} = x_{ij} y_{jk}. \quad (9)$$

Based on the value of z_{ik}, the FL server would expect which clients will upload their local models in global iteration k, and then aggregate all the received local models based on

$$\omega^{(k)} = \sum_{i \in \mathcal{I}} \frac{|\mathcal{D}_i|}{\sum_{i \in \mathcal{I}} |\mathcal{D}_i| z_{ik}} \omega_i^{(k)} z_{ik}, \quad (10)$$

where $\sum_{i \in \mathcal{I}} |\mathcal{D}_i| z_{ik}$ indicates the total number of the data samples among all the clients, who would upload their local models in global iteration k.

Please note that, in synchronous FL (e.g., FedAvg), each selected client would update its local model $\omega_i^{(k)}$ based on Equation (11) in each global iteration.

$$\omega_i^{(k)} = \omega_i^{(k-1)} - \delta \nabla f_i\left(\omega_i^{(k-1)}\right), \quad (11)$$

where δ is the step size, which is the same for all the selected clients. In LESSON, different clients update their local models in different frequencies, depending on their associated tiers, so it is reasonable to adopt different step sizes for the clients in different tiers [24]. Here, we adjust the step size of a client proportional to its tier (i.e., $\delta \times j$). Thus, when $k\%j = 0$, client i in Tier j would update its local model based on

$$\omega_i^{(k)} = \omega_i^{(k-j)} - j\delta \nabla f_i\left(\omega_i^{(k-j)}\right) \quad (12)$$

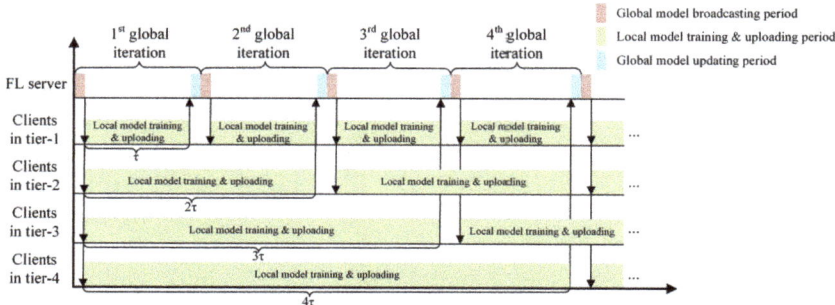

Figure 2. Illustration of client scheduling in LESSON.

4.3. Summary of LESSON

Algorithm 1 provides an overview of the LESSON algorithm. Initially, the FL server estimates the latency of all the clients and clusters the clients into different tiers based on Equation (7), i.e., Steps 1–2 in Algorithm 1. Then, the FL server broadcasts the initial global model $\omega^{(0)}$ to start the collaborative model training process, which unfolds over numerous global iterations.

Within each global iteration k, each client trains and updates its local model $\omega_i^{(k)}$ based on Equation (12). If $z_{ik} = 1$, client i should upload its local model to the FL server by the end of global iteration k. Then, client i would wait until it receives the updated global model $\omega^{(k)}$ from the FL server to start the next round of local model training.

Concurrently, the FL server keeps receiving the local models from the clients in global iteration k. Once the deadline expires, the FL server updates the global model $\omega^{(k)}$ based on Equation (10), and then broadcasts the new global model $\omega^{(k)}$ to the clients, who just uploaded their local models in global iteration k.

Please note that the deadline of a global iteration, i.e., τ, is a very crucial parameter to adjust the performance of LESSON. Specifically, if $\tau \to +\infty$, a single tier is employed, housing all clients. This setup operates akin to the FedAvg. Here, the FL server must patiently await the arrival of local models from all clients during each global iteration.

Conversely, if $\tau \to 0$, LESSON acts as asynchronous FL, where clients with varying latency (i.e., t_i) are distributed across distinct tiers. The FL server will promptly aggregate the local models from the clients with low latency, subsequently updating and broadcasting the global model. This adaptability in τ constitutes one of LESSON's strengths, and we will delve into how different values of τ impact LESSON's performance in Section 5.

Algorithm 1: LESSON algorithm

1. Estimate the latency of all the clients based on Equation (3).
2. Cluster the clients into different tiers based on Equation (7).
3. The FL server initializes the global model $\omega^{(0)}$ and broadcasts to all the clients.
4. Initialize the global iteration index, $k = 1$;
5. **for** *each global iteration k* **do**
6.   Client side:{
7.   **if** $z_{ik} = 1$, *derived with Equation* (9) **then**
8.   Receive the broadcast global model $\omega^{(k)}$ as the local model $\omega_i^{(k-j)}$ with $k_{local} := k_{global} + j$, $\omega^{(k)} \xrightarrow{k:=k+j} \omega_i^{(k-j)}$;
9.   Perform local model training based on Equation (12) over j global iteration;
10.   Upload its local model $\omega_i^{(k)}$ to the FL server;
11.   **end**
12.   }
13.   **FL server side**:{
14.   Receive all the local models uploaded from the clients during kth global iteration, with time length of τ;
15.   Update the global model $\omega^{(k)}$ based on Equation (10);
16.   Broadcast the updated global model $\omega^{(k)}$ to the corresponding clients;
17. $k := k + 1$;
18.   }
19. **end**

5. Simulation

In this section, we conduct extensive simulations to evaluate the performance of LESSON.

5.1. Simulation Setup

5.1.1. Configuration of Clients

We assume that there are 50 clients that are uniformly distributed in a 2 km × 2 km area, which is covered by a BS located at the center of the area. All the clients upload their local models to the FL server via the BS. The pathloss between the BS and client i is calculated based on $128.1 + 37.6 \times d_i$, where d_i is the distance in kilometer between the BS and client i. Then, the channel gain is calculated based on $g_i = 10^{-(128.1+37.6 \times d_i)/10}$ [35]. Meanwhile, the transmission power p_i is set to be 1 Watt for all the clients, and the amount of available bandwidth for each client in uploading its local model is 30 kHz. In addition, each client has around $|\mathcal{D}_i| = 1000$ data samples (i.e., 50,000 combined for all clients) to train its local model. The number of CPU cycles required for training one data sample (i.e., C_i) among clients is randomly selected from a uniform distribution, i.e., $C \sim \mathcal{U}(3,5) \times 10^5$ CPU cycles/sample. The CPU frequency of a client f_i is also randomly selected from a uniform distribution, i.e., $f_i \sim \mathcal{U}(0.8, 3)$ GHz. Other simulation parameters are listed in Table 1.

Figure 3 shows the probability density function of the latency (i.e., t_i) among all the clients in a specific time instance. The median value in the clients' latency is around 10 s, so we initially set up the deadline τ of a global iteration to be 10 s, and we will change the value of τ, later, to see how it affects the performance of LESSON.

Table 1. Simulation parameters.

Parameter	Value
Noise and inter-cell interference (N_0)	-94 dBm
Bandwidth B	30 kHz
Transmission power	0.1 watt
Size of the local model (s)	100 kbit
Number of local iterations ($\theta \log_2(\frac{1}{\epsilon})$)	$1 \times \log_2(\frac{1}{0.05})$
Number of local samples $|\mathcal{D}_i|$	1000
CPU cycles required for training one data sample C_i	$\mathcal{U}(3,5) \times 10^8$
CPU frequency f_i	$\mathcal{U}(0.8,3)$ GHz
Number of local epochs	1
Number of local batch size	20
Non-IID Dirichlet distribution parameter β	$[0.1, 1, 10]$
Client Learning Rate δ_r	0.02

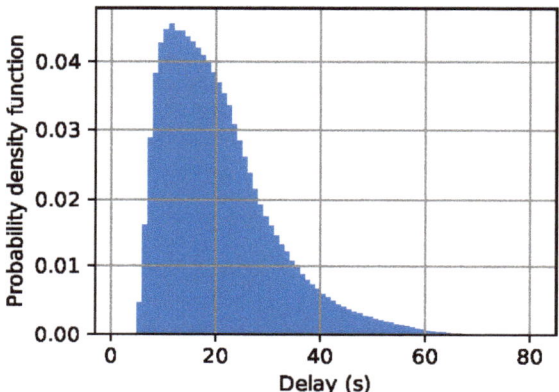

Figure 3. Clients' latency distribution.

5.1.2. Machine-Learning Model and Training Datasets

We will use two benchmark datasets to train the corresponding machine-learning model.

1. CIFAR-10 [36] is an image classification dataset containing 10 labels/classes of images, each of which has 6000 images. Among the 60,000 images, 50,000 are used for model training and 10,000 for model testing.
2. MNIST [37] is a handwritten digit dataset that includes many 28×28 pixel grayscale images of handwritten single digits between 0 and 9. The whole dataset has a training set of 60,000 examples and a test set of 10,000 examples.

We apply the convolutional neural network (CNN) to classify the CIFAR-10 images. The CNN model has four 3×3 convolution layers (where the first layer has 32 channels, and each of the following three layers has 64 channels. Also, only the first two layers are followed with 2×2 max pooling), followed by a dropout layer with rate of 75%, a fully connected 256 units ReLU layer, and a 10-unit SoftMax output layer. There are a total of 1,144,650 parameters in this CNN model.

With respect to MNIST, which is a much simpler image dataset than CIFAR-10, a smaller CNN model has been used. Specifically, the CNN model has two 5×5 convolution layers (where the two layers have 6 and 16 channels, respectively, each of which is followed with a 2×2 max pooling), followed with two fully connected ReLU layers with 120 and 84 units, respectively, and a 10-unit SoftMax output layer. There are a total of 61,706 parameters in this CNN model.

In addition, we partition the MNIST/CIFAR-10 dataset among the 50 clients based on the non-independent and identical distribution (Non-IID), and the probability of having η_m images in label class m at client i is assumed to follow a Dirichlet distribution [38], i.e.,

$$f(\eta_1, \eta_2, \ldots, \eta_M; \beta) = \frac{\Gamma(\beta M)}{\Gamma(\beta)^M} \prod_{m=1}^{M} \eta_m^{\beta-1}, \tag{13}$$

where M is the total number of label classes (i.e., $M = 10$ for both CIFAR-10 and MNIST), $\Gamma()$ is the gamma function ($\Gamma(z) = \int_0^\infty x^{z-1} e^{-x} dx$), and β is the concentration parameter that determines the level of label imbalance. A larger β results in a more balanced data partition among different labels within a client (i.e., much closer to IID) and vice versa. Figure 4 shows how different labels of images are distributed by varying β. In addition, we assume each client would train its CNN model over $|\mathcal{D}_i| = 20$ data samples locally based on stochastic gradient descent (SGD) with base learning rate $\delta = 0.1$ [39] and epoch equal to 1.

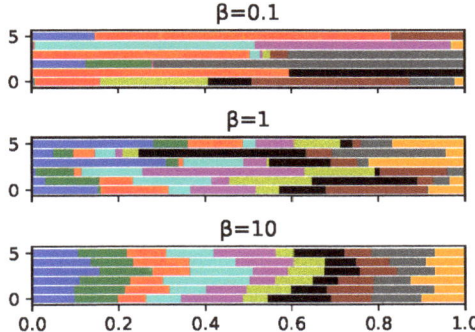

Figure 4. Probability distribution of 10 categories samples for 5 clients with different β.

5.1.3. Baseline Comparison Methods

The performance of LESSON will be compared with the other two baseline client selection algorithms, i.e., FedCS [18] and FedAvg [13]. FedCS only selects the clients that can finish their model uploading before the deadline τ in each global iteration, i.e., only the clients in Tier 1 will be selected to participate in the training process. In FedAvg, all the clients in the network will be selected to participate in the training process for each global iteration, i.e., the FL server will wait until it receives the local models from all the clients and then update the global model for the next global iteration. In addition, the source code of LESSON can be found in https://github.com/fzvincent/FL_AoR/tree/master (accessed on 29 September 2023).

5.2. Simulation Results

Assume that $\beta = 1$ and $\tau = 20$ s. Figure 5 shows the test accuracy of the three algorithms over the global iterations and simulation time for CIFAR-10 and MNIST. From Figure 5a,b, we can find that LESSON and FedAvg have similar test accuracy, i.e., ~70% for CIFAR-10 and ~95% for MNIST. However, the test accuracy achieved by FedCS is lower than LESSON and FedAvg, i.e., ~60% for CIFAR-10 and ~90% for MNIST. This is because FedCS only selects fast clients to participate in the training process, and so the derived global model can only fit the data samples for fast clients, not slow clients, thus reducing the model accuracy. Meanwhile, the convergence rate with respect to the number of global iterations for LESSON and FedAvg is also very similar, which is slightly faster than FedCS. However, by evaluating the convergence rate with respect to the time, as shown in Figure 5c,d, we find out that LESSON is faster than FedAvg. For example, the global model in LESSON has already converged at 20,000 s for MNIST, but the global model in FedAvg is still under-trained. This is because the FL server in FedAvg must wait until the local models from all the clients have been received in each global iteration, and thus, the latency of a global iteration incurred by FedAvg is much higher than that incurred by LESSON. Table 2 shows the average delay of a global iteration incurred by different algorithms, where the average latency of a global iteration incurred by LESSON is 48 s faster than FedAvg. As a result, FedAvg only runs around 588 global iterations at 20,000 s in Figure 5d, respectively, but LESSON runs 2000 global iterations.

Table 2. Average latency per global iteration for different algorithms.

Algorithms	Average Latency of a Global Iteration
FedAvg	68 s
FedCS	20 s
LESSON	20 s

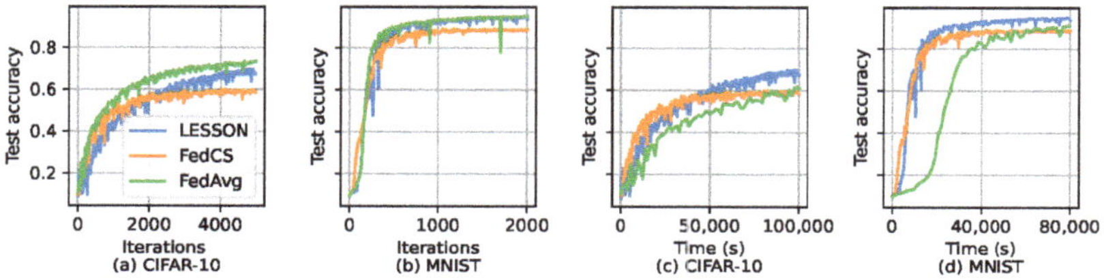

Figure 5. Test accuracy of different algorithms for CIFAR-10 and MNIST with $\beta = 1$, where (**a**) test accuracy vs. the number of global iterations for CIFAR-10, (**b**) test accuracy vs. the number of global iterations for MNIST, (**c**) test accuracy vs. time in CIFAR-10, and (**d**) test accuracy vs. time in MNIST.

We further investigate how the data sample distribution affects the performance of the algorithms based on CIFAR-10. As mentioned before, β is used to change the data sample distribution, i.e., a larger β implies a more balanced data partition among the labels in a client or data sample distribution much closer to IID, and vice versa. Assume $\tau = 20$ seconds, and Figure 6 shows the test accuracy of different algorithms over the number of global iterations by selecting different values of β. From the figures, we can see that if the data sample distribution exhibits non-IID, i.e., $\beta = 0.1$, FedAvg has higher test accuracy than LESSON and FedCS. As β increases, i.e., the data sample distribution is growing closer to IID, the test accuracy gap between FedAvg and LESSON is growing smaller, while the test accuracy of FedCS remains unchanged. On the other hand, Figure 7 shows the test accuracy of different algorithms over time by selecting different values of β. From the figure, we can see that LESSON achieves 2× faster convergence rate than FedAvg under different values of β. Therefore, we conclude that LESSON achieves a faster convergence rate at the cost of slightly reducing the model accuracy, especially when the data distribution exhibits non-IID.

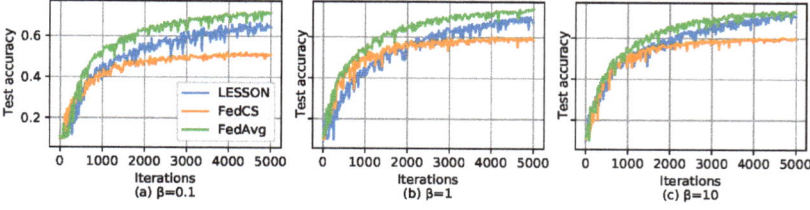

Figure 6. Test accuracy over the number of global iterations for CIFAR-10, where (**a**) $\beta = 0.1$, (**b**) $\beta = 1.0$, and (**c**) $\beta = 10.0$.

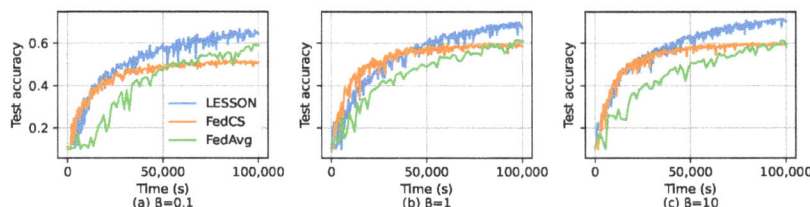

Figure 7. Test accuracy over the time for CIFAR-10, where (**a**) $\beta = 0.1$, (**b**) $\beta = 1.0$, and (**c**) $\beta = 10.0$.

As mentioned in Section 4.3, the deadline of a global iteration, i.e., τ, is a very important parameter to adjust the performance of LESSON. Basically, if $\tau \to +\infty$, LESSON acts as FedAvg, and if $\tau \to 0$, LESSON acts as asynchronous FL. Figure 8 shows the test accuracy of LESSON by having different values of τ and β for CIFAR-10 over global iterations, where we can find that $\tau = 60$ seconds incurs the highest test accuracy for both $\beta = 0.1$ and $\beta = 1$. This is because a larger τ (1) reduces the number of tiers in the system, thus alleviating the performance degradation caused by stale issues, and (2) increases the average number of clients in uploading their local models in a global iteration, which can mitigate the impact caused by non-IID. Also, we can see that the blue curve, i.e., $\tau = 10$ s, is more sensitive to the change in β than the other two curves. This is because as τ reduces, LESSON acts more like asynchronous FL, which has the convergence issue under non-IID. Figure 9 shows the test accuracy of LESSON by having different values of τ and β for CIFAR-10 over time. From Figure 9a, we can find that $\tau = 60$ exhibits the slowest convergence rate with respect to the time because a larger τ implies a longer latency of a global latency, i.e., $\tau = 60$ runs the fewest global iterations than $\tau = 10$ and $\tau = 20$ within a time period. Therefore, we conclude that changing τ can adjust the trade-off between the model accuracy and model convergence rate with respect to time. A large τ can increase the model accuracy but reduce the model convergence rate, and vice versa. Meanwhile, as the data distribution is closer to IID (i.e., as β increases), the difference in the convergence rate among the three algorithms increases, as shown in Figure 9b.

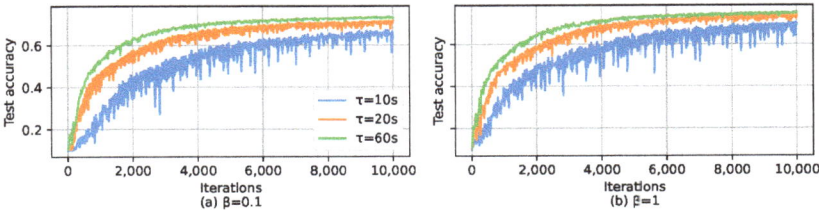

Figure 8. Test accuracy over the number of global iterations for CIFAR-10, where (**a**) $\beta = 0.1$ and (**b**) $\beta = 1.0$.

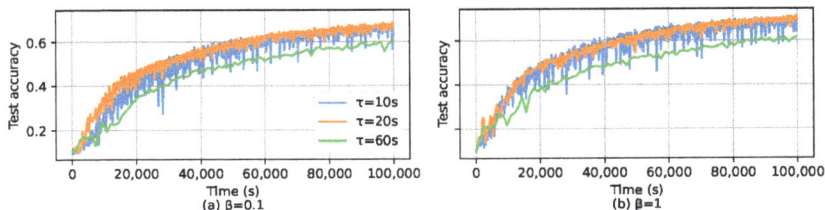

Figure 9. Test accuracy over the time for CIFAR-10, where (**a**) $\beta = 0.1$ and (**b**) $\beta = 1.0$.

The two foundational approaches select clients based on their availability. FedAvg emphasizes the importance of client presence but suffers from delays caused by slow participants, known as stragglers. On the other hand, FedCS prioritizes models that have been recently updated. LESSON integrates the strengths of both approaches: it places stragglers in higher tiers to minimize system disruption and effectively incorporates less up-to-date models to enhance the global model's generalization capability. When dealing with clients who drop out intermittently, FedAvg can experience significant delays, and FedCS does not account for the contributions of clients with unstable connections in the first place. Although LESSON cannot offer guarantees, it provides an opportunity for such disconnected clients to make a partial contribution to the global model.

6. Conclusions

To address challenges related to data diversity and stragglers in synchronous Federated Learning (FL) while also minimizing the risk of model divergence found in asynchronous FL, we introduce LESSON. This novel approach blends semi-synchronous client selection with model aggregation, ensuring the participation of all clients in the FL process, albeit at differing frequencies.

The simulation results show that LESSON and FedAvg have comparable model test accuracy, both of which outperform FedCS at least 10% under different non-IID scenarios. In addition, LESSON reduces the test accuracy by around 5% but accelerates convergence rate at least $2\times$ faster as compared to FedAvg. The adaptability of LESSON is further highlighted through its deadline parameter τ, which allows for adjusting the trade-off between model accuracy and convergence rate, that higher τ can improve model accuracy. Due to the high convergence rate, LESSON can be applied to applications that require quickly deriving a reasonable model adaptive to dynamic environments, such as autonomous drone swarm control [40,41], where actor-critic networks that can be adaptive to be the current wind perturbation should be quickly trained and derived to, for example, avoid collisions.

Future work is poised to delve into the adaptive modification of the τ parameter to augment LESSON's performance. This paper has demonstrated that a lower τ accelerates the model convergence rate, whereas a higher τ achieves a better model accuracy, especially in non-IID data scenarios. As such, dynamically calibrating τ to achieve a resilient and practical FL algorithm is critical but unexplored. In addition, the computing and uploading latency of a client may change over time. If a client moves towards the edge of a base station's coverage area, the uploading latency of this client will be significantly increased. As a result, this client will finally be clustered into a higher tier to train and upload its local model at a lower pace but with a higher learning rate. Yet, how LESSON dynamically adjusts the client clustering based on the updated computing and uploading latency and how the client clustering adjustment affects the performance of LESSON is still unveiled and will be part of our future work.

Author Contributions: Conceptualization, L.Y.; Methodology, L.Y. and X.S.; Software, L.Y.; Investigation, C.Y.; Resources, L.Y.; Writing—original draft, L.Y. and R.A.; Writing—review & editing, X.S., R.A. and C.Y.; Supervision, X.S. and C.Y.; Project administration, X.S.; Funding acquisition, X.S. All authors have read and agreed to the published version of the manuscript.

Funding: This work was supported by the National Science Foundation under Award under grant no. CNS-2323050 and CNS-2148178, where CNS-2148178 is supported in part by funds from federal agency and industry partners as specified in the Resilient & Intelligent NextG Systems (RINGS) program.

Data Availability Statement: Not Applicable, the study does not report any data.

Conflicts of Interest: The authors declare no conflict of interest.

References

1. Sun, X.; Ansari, N. EdgeIoT: Mobile Edge Computing for the Internet of Things. *IEEE Commun. Mag.* **2016**, *54*, 22–29. [CrossRef]
2. Liu, Y.; Yang, C.; Jiang, L.; Xie, S.; Zhang, Y. Intelligent Edge Computing for IoT-Based Energy Management in Smart Cities. *IEEE Netw.* **2019**, *33*, 111–117. [CrossRef]
3. Dhanvijay, M.M.; Patil, S.C. Internet of Things: A survey of enabling technologies in healthcare and its applications. *Comput. Netw.* **2019**, *153*, 113–131. [CrossRef]
4. Goddard, M. The EU General Data Protection Regulation (GDPR): European regulation that has a global impact. *Int. J. Mark. Res.* **2017**, *59*, 703–705. [CrossRef]
5. McMahan, B.; Moore, E.; Ramage, D.; Hampson, S.; y Arcas, B.A. Communication-Efficient Learning of Deep Networks from Decentralized Data. In Proceedings of the 20th International Conference on Artificial Intelligence and Statistics, Lauderdale, FL, USA, 20–22 April 2017; PMLR: Cambridge, MA, USA, 2017; pp. 1273–1282.
6. Hard, A.; Rao, K.; Mathews, R.; Ramaswamy, S.; Beaufays, F.; Augenstein, S.; Eichner, H.; Kiddon, C.; Ramage, D. Federated learning for mobile keyboard prediction. *arXiv* **2018**, arXiv:1811.03604.
7. Imteaj, A.; Amini, M.H. Fedar: Activity and resource-aware federated learning model for distributed mobile robots. In Proceedings of the 2020 19th IEEE International Conference on Machine Learning and Applications (ICMLA), Miami, FL, USA, 14–17 December 2020; pp. 1153–1160.
8. Wu, W.; He, L.; Lin, W.; Mao, R.; Maple, C.; Jarvis, S. SAFA: A semi-asynchronous protocol for fast federated learning with low overhead. *IEEE Trans. Comput.* **2020**, *70*, 655–668. [CrossRef]
9. Reisizadeh, A.; Tziotis, I.; Hassani, H.; Mokhtari, A.; Pedarsani, R. Straggler-resilient federated learning: Leveraging the interplay between statistical accuracy and system heterogeneity. *arXiv* **2020**, arXiv:2012.14453.
10. Xu, Z.; Yang, Z.; Xiong, J.; Yang, J.; Chen, X. Elfish: Resource-aware federated learning on heterogeneous edge devices. *Ratio* **2019**, *2*, r2.
11. Albelaihi, R.; Sun, X.; Craft, W.D.; Yu, L.; Wang, C. Adaptive Participant Selection in Heterogeneous Federated Learning. In Proceedings of the 2021 IEEE Global Communications Conference (GLOBECOM), Madrid, Spain, 7–11 December 2021; pp. 1–6. [CrossRef]
12. Tang, T.; Ali, R.E.; Hashemi, H.; Gangwani, T.; Avestimehr, S.; Annavaram, M. Adaptive Verifiable Coded Computing: Towards Fast, Secure and Private Distributed Machine Learning. In Proceedings of the 2022 IEEE International Parallel and Distributed Processing Symposium (IPDPS), Lyon, France, 30 May–3 June 2022; pp. 628–638. [CrossRef]
13. Wang, J.; Joshi, G. Cooperative SGD: A unified framework for the design and analysis of communication-efficient SGD algorithms. *arXiv* **2018**, arXiv:1808.07576.
14. Shorten, C.; Khoshgoftaar, T.M. A survey on image data augmentation for deep learning. *J. Big Data* **2019**, *6*, 1–48. [CrossRef]
15. Li, L.; Fan, Y.; Lin, K.Y. A survey on federated learning. In Proceedings of the 2020 IEEE 16th International Conference on Control & Automation (ICCA), Singapore, 9–11 October 2020; pp. 791–796.
16. Xu, C.; Qu, Y.; Xiang, Y.; Gao, L. Asynchronous federated learning on heterogeneous devices: A survey. *arXiv* **2021**, arXiv:2109.04269.
17. Damaskinos, G.; Guerraoui, R.; Kermarrec, A.M.; Nitu, V.; Patra, R.; Taiani, F. FLeet: Online Federated Learning via Staleness Awareness and Performance Prediction. In Proceedings of the 21st International Middleware Conference, Delft, The Netherlands, 7–11 December 2020; Association for Computing Machinery: New York, NY, USA, 2020; Middleware '20; pp. 163–177. [CrossRef]
18. Nishio, T.; Yonetani, R. Client Selection for Federated Learning with Heterogeneous Resources in Mobile Edge. In Proceedings of the 2019 IEEE International Conference on Communications (ICC), Shanghai, China, 20–24 May 2019; pp. 1–7. [CrossRef]
19. Abdulrahman, S.; Tout, H.; Mourad, A.; Talhi, C. FedMCCS: Multicriteria Client Selection Model for Optimal IoT Federated Learning. *IEEE Internet Things J.* **2021**, *8*, 4723–4735. [CrossRef]
20. Yu, L.; Albelaihi, R.; Sun, X.; Ansari, N.; Devetsikiotis, M. Jointly Optimizing Client Selection and Resource Management in Wireless Federated Learning for Internet of Things. *IEEE Internet Things J.* **2022**, *9*, 4385–4395. [CrossRef]
21. Shi, W.; Zhou, S.; Niu, Z. Device Scheduling with Fast Convergence for Wireless Federated Learning. In Proceedings of the ICC 2020—2020 IEEE International Conference on Communications (ICC), Dublin, Ireland, 7–11 June 2020; pp. 1–6. [CrossRef]
22. Li, T.; Sahu, A.K.; Zaheer, M.; Sanjabi, M.; Talwalkar, A.; Smith, V. Federated Optimization in Heterogeneous Networks. In Proceedings of the Machine Learning and Systems; Dhillon, I., Papailiopoulos, D., Sze, V., Eds.; 2020; Volume 2, pp. 429–450. Available online: https://proceedings.mlsys.org/paper_files/paper/2020/hash/1f5fe83998a09396ebe6477d9475ba0c-Abstract.html (accessed on 29 September 2023).
23. Wu, D.; Ullah, R.; Harvey, P.; Kilpatrick, P.; Spence, I.; Varghese, B. Fedadapt: Adaptive offloading for iot devices in federated learning. *arXiv* **2021**, arXiv:2107.04271.
24. Chen, Y.; Ning, Y.; Slawski, M.; Rangwala, H. Asynchronous online federated learning for edge devices with non-iid data. In Proceedings of the 2020 IEEE International Conference on Big Data (Big Data), Atlanta, GA, USA, 10–13 December 2020; pp. 15–24.
25. Lu, Y.; Huang, X.; Dai, Y.; Maharjan, S.; Zhang, Y. Differentially private asynchronous federated learning for mobile edge computing in urban informatics. *IEEE Trans. Ind. Inform.* **2019**, *16*, 2134–2143. [CrossRef]
26. Gu, B.; Xu, A.; Huo, Z.; Deng, C.; Huang, H. Privacy-preserving asynchronous federated learning algorithms for multi-party vertically collaborative learning. *arXiv* **2020**, arXiv:2008.06233.

27. Lian, X.; Zhang, W.; Zhang, C.; Liu, J. Asynchronous decentralized parallel stochastic gradient descent. In Proceedings of the International Conference on Machine Learning, Macau, China, 26–28 February 2018; PMLR: Cambridge, MA, USA, 2018; pp. 3043–3052.
28. Chai, Z.; Chen, Y.; Zhao, L.; Cheng, Y.; Rangwala, H. Fedat: A communication-efficient federated learning method with asynchronous tiers under non-iid data. *arXiv* **2020**, arXiv:2010.05958.
29. Feyzmahdavian, H.R.; Aytekin, A.; Johansson, M. A delayed proximal gradient method with linear convergence rate. In Proceedings of the 2014 IEEE International Workshop on Machine Learning for Signal Processing (MLSP), Reims, France, 21–24 September 2014; pp. 1–6.
30. Jiang, J.; Cui, B.; Zhang, C.; Yu, L. Heterogeneity-Aware Distributed Parameter Servers. In Proceedings of the 2017 ACM International Conference on Management of Data, Chicago, IL, USA, 14–19 May 2017; Association for Computing Machinery: New York, NY, USA, 2017; SIGMOD '17; pp. 463–478. [CrossRef]
31. Zhang, W.; Gupta, S.; Lian, X.; Liu, J. Staleness-Aware Async-SGD for Distributed Deep Learning. In Proceedings of the Twenty-Fifth International Joint Conference on Artificial Intelligence, New York, NY, USA, 9–15 July 2016; AAAI Press: Washington, DC, USA, 2016; IJCAI'16; pp. 2350–2356. Available online: https://arxiv.org/abs/1511.05950 (accessed on 29 September 2023).
32. Stripelis, D.; Ambite, J.L. Semi-synchronous federated learning. *arXiv* **2021**, arXiv:2102.02849.
33. Hao, J.; Zhao, Y.; Zhang, J. Time efficient federated learning with semi-asynchronous communication. In Proceedings of the 2020 IEEE 26th International Conference on Parallel and Distributed Systems (ICPADS), Hong Kong, China, 2–4 December 2020; pp. 156–163.
34. Yang, Z.; Chen, M.; Saad, W.; Hong, C.S.; Shikh-Bahaei, M.; Poor, H.V.; Cui, S. Delay Minimization for Federated Learning Over Wireless Communication Networks. *arXiv* **2020**, arXiv:2007.03462.
35. ETSI. Radio Frequency (RF) Requirements for LTE Pico Node B (3GPP TR 36.931 Version 9.0.0 Release 9). 2011, Number ETSI TR 136 931 V9.0.0. LTE; Evolved Universal Terrestrial Radio Access (E-UTRA). Available online: https://www.etsi.org/deliver/etsi_tr/136900_136999/136931/09.00.00_60/tr_136931v090000p.pdf (accessed on 29 September 2023).
36. Krizhevsky, A. Learning Multiple Layers of Features from Tiny Images. 2009. Available online: http://www.cs.utoronto.ca/~kriz/learning-features-2009-TR.pdf (accessed on 29 September 2023).
37. LeCun, Y.; Bottou, L.; Bengio, Y.; Haffner, P. Gradient-based learning applied to document recognition. *Proc. IEEE* **1998**, *86*, 2278–2324. [CrossRef]
38. Li, Q.; Diao, Y.; Chen, Q.; He, B. Federated learning on non-iid data silos: An experimental study. *arXiv* **2021**, arXiv:2102.02079.
39. Kairouz, P.; McMahan, H.B.; Avent, B.; Bellet, A.; Bennis, M.; Bhagoji, A.N.; Bonawitz, K.; Charles, Z.; Cormode, G.; Cummings, R.; et al. Advances and Open Problems in Federated Learning. *Found. Trends Mach. Learn.* **2021**, *14*, 1–210. [CrossRef]
40. Pierre, J.E.; Sun, X.; Fierro, R. Multi-Agent Partial Observable Safe Reinforcement Learning for Counter Uncrewed Aerial Systems. *IEEE Access* **2023**, *11*, 78192–78206. [CrossRef]
41. Salimi, M.; Pasquier, P. Deep Reinforcement Learning for Flocking Control of UAVs in Complex Environments. In Proceedings of the 2021 6th International Conference on Robotics and Automation Engineering (ICRAE), Guangzhou, China, 19–22 November 2021; pp. 344–352. [CrossRef]

Disclaimer/Publisher's Note: The statements, opinions and data contained in all publications are solely those of the individual author(s) and contributor(s) and not of MDPI and/or the editor(s). MDPI and/or the editor(s) disclaim responsibility for any injury to people or property resulting from any ideas, methods, instructions or products referred to in the content.

 *future internet*

Review

Exploring Homomorphic Encryption and Differential Privacy Techniques towards Secure Federated Learning Paradigm

Rezak Aziz [1,*], Soumya Banerjee [1,*], Samia Bouzefrane [1] and Thinh Le Vinh [2]

1. CEDRIC Lab, Cnam, 292 rue Saint Martin, 75003 Paris, France; samia.bouzefrane@lecnam.net
2. Faculty of Information Technology, Ho Chi Minh City University of Technology and Education, Thu Đuc, Ho Chi Minh City, Vietnam; thinhlv@hcmute.edu.vn
* Correspondence: rezak.aziz@lecnam.net (R.A.); soumya.banerjee@lecnam.net (S.B.)

Abstract: The trend of the next generation of the internet has already been scrutinized by top analytics enterprises. According to Gartner investigations, it is predicted that, by 2024, 75% of the global population will have their personal data covered under privacy regulations. This alarming statistic necessitates the orchestration of several security components to address the enormous challenges posed by federated and distributed learning environments. Federated learning (FL) is a promising technique that allows multiple parties to collaboratively train a model without sharing their data. However, even though FL is seen as a privacy-preserving distributed machine learning method, recent works have demonstrated that FL is vulnerable to some privacy attacks. Homomorphic encryption (HE) and differential privacy (DP) are two promising techniques that can be used to address these privacy concerns. HE allows secure computations on encrypted data, while DP provides strong privacy guarantees by adding noise to the data. This paper first presents consistent attacks on privacy in federated learning and then provides an overview of HE and DP techniques for secure federated learning in next-generation internet applications. It discusses the strengths and weaknesses of these techniques in different settings as described in the literature, with a particular focus on the trade-off between privacy and convergence, as well as the computation overheads involved. The objective of this paper is to analyze the challenges associated with each technique and identify potential opportunities and solutions for designing a more robust, privacy-preserving federated learning framework.

Keywords: federated learning; differential privacy; homomorphic encryption; privacy; accuracy

1. Introduction

1.1. Background

The trends of advanced internet applications have had an overwhelming impact, particularly with the introduction of numerous machine learning (ML) algorithms. These algorithms have exhibited immense potential for a wide range of real-world applications. However, the success of these applications relies heavily on the establishment of a trust and secure paradigm. According to Gartner investigations [1], it is predicted that, by 2024, 75% of the global population will have their personal data covered under privacy regulations. Without this foundation trust and security, the future internet and digital economy, with their unlimited potential, will always be underestimated. To address the security concerns in federated environments—including the inherent dilution of the internet among mass usage, common vulnerabilities stemming from the Internet of Things, identity authentication, and significant digital fragmentation—various isolated and separate algorithms have been developed. However, these algorithms have proven insufficient.

The performance of machine learning algorithms depends on access to large amounts of data for training. In traditional machine learning, training is centrally held by one organization that has access to the whole training dataset. In practice, data are often distributed across multiple parties, and sharing it for training purposes is not simple due to privacy policies and regulations like the General Data Protection Regulation [2]. These regulations impose strict rules about how data can be shared and processed between organizations.

Due to these factors, federated learning (FL) has become a hot research topic on machine learning since its emergence on 2016 [3]. This promising technique allows multiple parties to jointly train a global model by only exchanging updates about local models and without the need to share their private datasets. This offers a promising solution to mitigate the potential privacy leakage of sensitive information about individuals. Recent works have demonstrated that FL may not always provide privacy and robustness guarantees [4–14]. While the private data never leaves their owner, the exchanged models are prone to memorization of the private training dataset. Some sensitive information may be inferred from the shared information using some well-known attacks like gradient inversion, reconstruction attacks, membership inference, and property inference attacks.

One way to mitigate this type of attacks is to use privacy preserving techniques like differential privacy (DP) and homomorphic encryption (HE). Differential privacy offers a way to disrupt data while preserving the statistical properties of the data. This allows us to have meaningful analysis and statistics while countering some of previous attacks. On the other hand, homomorphic encryption allows for conducting computation on encrypted data and then decrypting only the result. This allows FL to access the aggregation of gradient without accessing the gradient themselves.

Each technique has its own advantages and limitations. In this paper, we focus on the different works of the literature that use HE and DP techniques in federated learning context. We aim to analyze the advantages and the limitations of each technique taken alone before addressing the combination of the two techniques.

1.2. Motivation

A plethora of research efforts have examined privacy concerns in federated learning. These studies encompassed various aspects and topics including foundational concepts [15–17], identification of threats and corresponding solutions [18–21], exploration of privacy techniques [22,23], and applications within healthcare [24,25], as well as communications and mobile networks [26,27]. The highlights and the key concepts included in these studies are listed in Table 1. While these works offer comprehensive surveys of techniques, they often do not delve into the detailed application of these techniques as evidenced in the literature. Furthermore, with the exception of [22], these studies have largely overlooked the hybrid application of privacy methods where multiple techniques are employed in concert.

Table 1. Comparison with related surveys.

| Ref | Year | Attacks | Defenses | | | Detailed Methods and Strategies |
			DP	HE	Hybrid (DP + HE)	
[17]	2019		✓	✓		
[18]	2020	✓				
[23]	2020		✓	✓		
[24]	2020	✓	✓	✓		
[26]	2020	✓	✓	✓		
[21]	2020	✓	✓	✓		
[20]	2021	✓	✓	✓		✓
[16]	2021	✓	✓	✓		
[22]	2022	✓	✓	✓	✓	
[19]	2023	✓	✓			
[25]	2023		✓	✓	✓	
Ours	2023	✓	✓	✓	✓	✓

The authors of [22] did acknowledge different combinations of techniques in their work, but they did not closely examine the specific methods by which these techniques are employed. In contrast, our paper focuses on the intersection of homomorphic encryption (HE) and differential privacy (DP) within the framework of federated learning. The factors and parameters we take into account while comparing our work with previous studies are the specific attacks and defenses they discuss. Another aspect we consider is how thoroughly they explain their methods and strategies. We delve into the advantages and drawbacks of combining these techniques, as we think that this combination could lead to better privacy-preserving federated learning systems. This would allow us to leverage the unique strengths inherent to each individual technique.

1.3. Contribution

Our paper makes a notable contribution by thoroughly exploring and examining various scholarly sources. The primary scope of this paper revolves around addressing privacy concerns in federated learning. Consequently, certain related issues, such as communications, systems heterogeneity, and statistical heterogeneity, are intentionally excluded from our focus. Within the realm of privacy preservation, our main emphasis lies on exploring and analyzing differential privacy (DP) and homomorphic encryption (HE) techniques. While we acknowledge the existence of other privacy techniques in the literature, such as anonymization, secure multi-party computation, and blockchain, we do not directly delve into them in this paper. By narrowing our focus to DP and HE techniques, we can provide a more detailed and comprehensive analysis of their capabilities and limitations in the context of privacy preservation. This approach allows us to deliver a focused and valuable contribution to the research community and promotes a deeper understanding of the pivotal role these techniques play in ensuring secure and privacy-aware federated learning systems.

The main contributions of this paper are summarized as follows:

1. We scrutinize the array of research addressing privacy-related attacks in federated learning (FL), demonstrating the practicality and real-world relevance of these threats, highlighting their potential implications in distributed learning environments. Our primary focus lies on privacy attacks, where we delve into various techniques that adversaries can employ to compromise the privacy and security of FL systems.
2. We delve into the role of differential privacy (DP) in FL, detailing its deployment across various settings: central differential privacy (CDP), local differential privacy (LDP), and the shuffle model. By providing a comprehensive analysis of these DP deployment settings, we offer insights into the strengths, limitations, and practical implications of each approach.
3. We investigate the application of homomorphic encryption (HE) as a powerful tool to enhance privacy within FL. Our primary focus is on countering privacy attacks and safeguarding sensitive data during the collaborative learning process. Through our investigation, we provide valuable insights into the capabilities and limitations of homomorphic encryption in FL.
4. We examine the body of research that explores the fusion of homomorphic encryption (HE) and differential privacy (DP) in the context of federated learning (FL). Our primary objective is to shed light on the motivations behind such integrations and understand the potential benefits they offer in enhancing privacy and security in distributed learning environments.

The rest of this paper unfolds as follows: Section 2 provides essential background knowledge on HE, DP, and FL. Section 3 delves into various privacy attacks within the FL framework. Section 4 discusses the combination of DP with FL, while Section 5 explores the use of HE for protecting privacy. In Section 6, this paper explores the combined use of HE and DP, emphasizing the potential benefits of this fusion. Section 7 is dedicated to the discussion of the results, offering deeper insight into our findings. Finally, Section 8 presents our conclusions and proposes directions for future research.

2. Preliminaries

The key concepts that we treat in our paper are federated learning, differential privacy, and homomorphic encryption. Here, we give an overview of the different techniques.

2.1. Federated Learning

The term federated learning (FL) was introduced in 2016 by McMahan et al. [3]. FL is a machine learning setting where many clients collaborate to train a centralized ML model. Each client's raw data are stored locally and not exchanged with other parties; only updates needed for immediate aggregation are shared with the central server.

Two main settings are discussed in the literature [16]: the cross-device and the cross-silo. The difference between the two is simple, cross-device is associated with mobiles and IoT devices while cross-silo is associated with organizations like hospitals, banks, etc. In cross-silo, the number of clients is small and they have large computational ability. On the other hand, cross-device considers a huge number of clients with small computation power. Another difference between the two settings is reliability. In cross-silo, the organizations are always available to train, unlike user devices.

FL can also be classified by data partition. We distinguish Horizontal FL, Vertical FL and Hybrid FL. In HFL, the datasets of the clients have the same features space. In VFL, the local datasets have the same individuals, but with different features. The hybrid setting is a combination between HFL and VFL.

A typical federated training process is considered by the algorithm of FedAvg proposed by McMahan et al. [3]. It consists of five steps: The server selects a subset of clients according to some criteria. The selected client downloads the current model weights and a training program from the server. Each client locally computes an update to the model by executing the training program. The server then collects an aggregate of device updates and updates the central model.

2.2. Differential Privacy

Differential privacy is a widely used standard to guarantee privacy in data analysis. The main idea of DP is to consider a thought experiment in which we compare how an algorithm behaves on a dataset D_1 with the way it behaves on a hypothetical dataset D_2, in which one person's record has been removed or added. These two datasets are considered "neighbors" in the dataset space. Hence, we say that an algorithm is differentially private if running the algorithm on two neighboring datasets yields roughly the same distribution of outcomes. In other words, differential privacy ensures that the outcomes of M are approximately the same whether or not the person i joins the dataset. Formally, DP is defined by Dwork et al. in 2006 [28] as follows.

Definition 1. *A randomized function M gives (ϵ, δ)-differential privacy if for all datasets D_1 and D_2 differing on at most one element, and all $S \subset Range(M)$,*

$$Pr[M(D_1) \in S] \leq e^\epsilon \times Pr[M(D_2) \in S] + \delta \quad (1)$$

In the Definition 1, ϵ is a non-negative real number that determines the level of privacy protection provided by the algorithm. A lower value of ϵ corresponds to a stronger privacy guarantee. The value of δ is a small positive real number that represents the probability of any failure of the definition. When δ is set to 0, it is referred to as pure differential privacy.

Three major properties arise directly from this definition: composition, post-processing, and group privacy. These properties are the key to design powerful algorithm from basic mechanisms:

- Composition: offers a way to bound privacy cost of answering multiple queries on the same data.
- Post-processing: ensures that the privacy guarantees of a differential privacy mechanism remain unchanged even if the output is further processed or analyzed.

- Group privacy: this definition can be extended to group privacy by considering two datasets differing on at most k records instead of 1 record.

As stated in the definition, DP is a property of an algorithm M. There are several methods to achieve DP based on adding noise to the input data, the output data, or the intermediate result. The noise can be generated using different mechanisms, the well-known ones are the Laplace mechanism, the Gaussian mechanism, and the exponential mechanism.

Two main settings are discussed in the literature for differential privacy: the centralized DP (CDP) and the local DP (LDP). In CDP, the noise is added by a centralized server that collects first the data then applies the mechanism. In LDP, the noise is added at the client level before collecting the data. LDP offers stronger privacy guarantees, as the noise is added closer to the source of the data. Additionally, a hybrid setting called the shuffle model is also explored in the literature. The shuffle model aims to combine the benefits of both CDP and LDP. In this setting, privacy is enhanced through anonymization achieved by shuffling the data. The noise is added centrally by a shuffler before passing the data to the analyst server, which enables the system to attain the performance advantages of CDP while maintaining the privacy guarantees provided by LDP.

2.3. Homomorphic Encryption

Homomorphic encryption is a cryptographic primitive that allows third parties to perform arithmetic operations on ciphertexts without decrypting them. It provides the same result as encrypting after operating in cleartext messages.

More formally, an encryption scheme is called homomorphic over an operation $*$ if it supports the following property:

$$E(m_1) * E(m_2) = E(m_1 * m_2)$$

where E is the encryption algorithm and m_1, m_2 belong to M the set of all possible messages.

An HE scheme consists of four algorithms [29]: *KeyGen, Enc, Dec*, and *Eval*. *KeyGen* generates a pair (public key, private key) for the asymmetric configuration and a secret key for the symmetric version. *Enc* is the encryption algorithm and *Dec* is the decryption algorithm.

While the three algorithms (*KeyGen, Enc, Dec*) are common to conventional cryptosystems, an additional algorithm is needed for homomorphic encryption schemes, called the *Eval* algorithm. This algorithm is defined as follows:

$$Eval(f, C_1, C_2) = f(m_1, m_2)$$

where $Dec(C_1) = m_1$, $Dec(C_2) = m_2$ and f is a function that can be addition or multiplication.

Based on the number (limited or unlimited) and the type of operation (addition or multiplication), HE is classified into three types of schemes: Partially Homomorphic encryption (PHE), Somewhat Homomorphic Encryption (SWHE), and Fully Homomorphic Encryption (FHE). PHE allows only to perform one type of operation on unlimited way. When the operation is addition, like in the Paillier Scheme [30], we say it is an Additive Homomorphic Encryption (AHE). When it is the multiplication, we say that it is a multiplicative scheme, like in the RSA scheme.

SWHE allows for both operations, but the number of operations is limited. On the other hand, FHE allows making unlimited operations of both types. This type of scheme was possible after the Gentry breakthrough in 2009 [31].

3. Privacy Attacks in FL

While federated learning (FL) is generally regarded as a privacy-preserving technique in machine learning, recent studies have revealed a potential privacy concern (see Figure 1). This concern arises from the fact that, although FL avoids the need to share private client datasets during the learning process, the exchange of gradients in FL can inadvertently disclose sensitive information about the client's private data. This issue is particularly pronounced in FL due to the large number of participants involved and the inherent white-box setting of the FL framework. An insider may exploit the exchanged gradients to perform powerful attacks using passive strategy (one that doesn't influence the learning process) or an active approach (where they actively influence the learning process) such as conducting membership inference or launching a reconstruction attack. In this section, we will see the different attacks on privacy in FL. The goal and the vulnerabilities exploited by the adversary in these attacks are presented in Table 2.

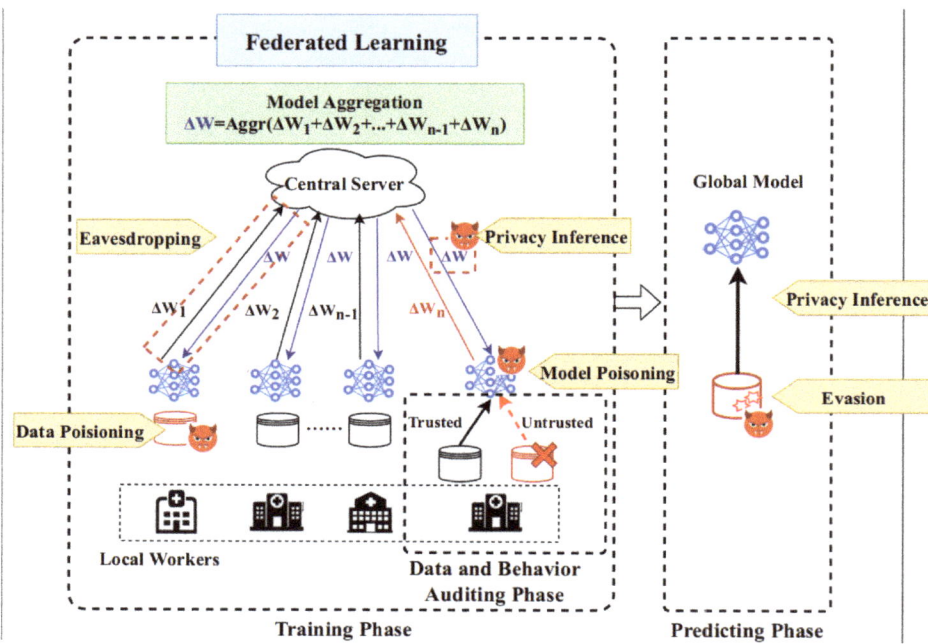

Figure 1. Attacks on the federated learning process [32].

3.1. Membership Inference

Membership inference is a type of attack in machine learning that aims to figure out whether a target data point is used to train a certain ML model. More formally, given x as the target point, M as a trained model, and some external knowledge K, this attack can be defined by the following function

$$A : x, M, K \rightarrow \{False, True\}$$

Here, this function returns *True* if the target x is in the training dataset and *False* otherwise. This attack can be made either in a black-box setting, where the attacker has only access to an API of the model M, or in a white-box setting, where the attacker has access to the whole model.

As we can remark, the attack model A is a binary classifier, and it can be constructed using different ways.

The first membership inference attack against machine learning models was presented by Shokri et al. in 2017 [33]. In this work, they consider a black-box setting and try to exploit the fact that ML models have a different behavior on the data they were trained on and the data that they see for the first time. In other words, they are modeling the membership inference problem as a problem of binary classification and try to train a model that distinguishes members from non-members of the target model. The idea of this work is to train the attack model using a shadow training technique (that was introduced in this work). They construct multiple shadow models that mimic the behavior of the target model, but for which the training set is known and have the same structure. Shokri et al. proposed some methods to generate the shadow training data and then the method used to train the attack model. The proposed attack was evaluated against neural networks using different datasets: CIFAR, Purchases, Locations, Texas hospital stays, MNIST, and UCI Adult. The authors confirm that their results show that models created using MLaaS can leak a lot of information about their training datasets. The assumptions considered by Shokri et al. are considered strong, which reduce the scope of the membership inference attack [34]. This motivated Salem et al. in 2019 [34] to propose relaxations of these assumptions. They showed that relaxing the number of shadow models to one shadow model and assuming that the shadow training data are distributed similarly to target training data produce performances that are similar to those provided by Shokri et al. [33]. Furthermore, considering an attack model that is independent of the training data distribution may also reveal some information, but this is not as efficient as in the previous work.

The two previous works focus on general machine learning (ML) models, but it is important to consider the unique characteristics of federated learning, which may present a larger attack surface [35]. Pustozeova and Mayer in 2020 [35] demonstrated that membership attacks performed by an insider in a sequential federated learning setting are more effective compared to centralized settings. Unlike the work of Shokri et al. [33] that examines black-box attacks, in the federated learning setting, an insider attacker has knowledge of the model's architecture, making the attack more efficient. Additionally, if multiple insider attackers collaborate, the attack can become more sophisticated. Hu et al. [36] further assert that, through Membership Inference Attacks (MIA), adversaries can even infer which participant possesses the data. The authors demonstrate that an honest-but-curious server can estimate the data source without violating federated learning protocols.

In 2019, Nasr et al. [37] introduced a comprehensive Membership Inference Attack (MIA) that targets the privacy vulnerabilities of the stochastic gradient descent (SGD) algorithm within the context of federated learning. Their study focused on the white-box setting, wherein the attacker has access to the model's loss and can compute the gradients of the loss with respect to all parameters using a simple backpropagation algorithm. The authors demonstrated that, in deep neural networks, the distribution of the model's gradients on members can be distinguished from the distribution of non-members. They explained that the initial layers of the neural network tend to contain less individual-specific information, requiring the attacker to devise specific attacks for each layer. The attack model proposed by Nasr et al. consisted of feature extraction components and an encoder component. To extract features from the output of each layer, they employed a fully connected network, incorporating the one-hot encoding of the true label and the loss. For the gradients, a convolutional neural network was utilized. The output from this step was then fed into an FCN encoder, which provided the membership probability of the input. Through experimentation with various datasets such as CIFAR100, Texas100, and Purchase100, the authors demonstrated that even well-generalized models are highly susceptible to white-box membership inference attacks.

Gu et al. in 2022 [38] proposed a membership inference attack named CS-MIA, which utilizes prediction confidence series (PCS) in federated learning. This attack takes advantage of the observation that the prediction confidence on training and testing data exhibit distinct changes over rounds in federated learning. The authors demonstrated that the variations of models across rounds in federated learning can be leveraged to differentiate between members and non-members of the target model. They trained a fully connected network to process the PCS and learn the discrepancies between training and testing data. The researchers designed membership inference methods for both local and global attackers and introduced an active global attack to enhance attack performance. To train the attack model, the authors drew inspiration from the shadow training technique introduced by Shokri et al. [33]. They generated shadow confidence series for member and non-member instances by involving members in a federated learning process. Subsequently, they computed the confidence of the shadow model on both member and non-member instances, using this information to train the attack model. Experimental results highlighted the vulnerability of federated learning privacy to the differences between training and testing confidence series. CS-MIA achieved a membership inference accuracy of over 90% on various benchmark datasets, indicating a significant threat to the privacy of federated learning.

3.2. Class Representatives Inference

The inference of class representatives tries to extract generic class representatives of the global data rather than the real data in the training datasets [39]. This is similar to the concept of model inversion attack, proposed by Fredrikson et al. in 2015 [40]. In the special case where all class members are similar, the result of this attack is similar to the training data. For example, in a facial recognition model, each class corresponds to a single individual, and the output of this attack is similar to any image that represent this person.

In the realm of federated learning, the utilization of Generative Adversarial Networks (GANs) allows the execution of such attacks. Hitaj et al. in 2017 [41] designed such an attack in federated learning using GAN. The attacker, acting as an honest-but-curious client in the federated learning topology, tries to influence the learning process. In their work [41], the attacker locally trains a GAN model capable of generating synthetic samples that look like the samples from the victim's data but that are supposed to belong into a different class. In this way, the victim will work harder to distinguish the fake class from his class and reveal more information about his dataset. The experiment results showed that this attack is effective and generate representative samples of training datasets.

Furthermore, in 2018, Wang et al. [39] expanded the scope of the attack to breach client-level privacy. While acknowledging the effectiveness of the GAN-based attack proposed by Hitaj et al. [41], the authors observed that the adversarial influence of the client could alter the architecture of the shared model. Moreover, they considered a powerful malicious client in their analysis. In order to overcome these limitations, Wang et al. introduced a more practical and inconspicuous attack on the federated learning model, known as mGAN-AI. In contrast to the previous attack, which was conducted by the client, the authors of mGAN-AI assumed the presence of a malicious server. They went a step further in breaching client-level privacy by utilizing a GAN with a multitask discriminator. This discriminator not only performed the task of a standard GAN, but also distinguished the real data distribution of the victim from that of other clients. Through experimental evaluations on datasets such as MNIST and AT&T, the researchers demonstrated that mGAN-AI could reconstruct samples close to the victim's training samples.

3.3. Properties Inference

The properties inference attack was introduced by Ateniese et al. in 2013 [42]. It aims to extract some private statistical information about the training set. This statistical information is unexpected to be shared and might be irrelevant to the main training task. This type of attack violates the intellectual property of the model producer, while it can be used to perform more complex attacks that infer something private about the individuals. According to the findings presented in [42], the adversary can construct a meta-classifier capable of categorizing the target classifier based on the presence or absence of a specific property, denoted as P, that the adversary seeks to infer. In the context of the study, the application considered was the inference of the ethnicity of a population, specifically distinguishing between Indian and non-Indian individuals, utilized in the training process. To accomplish this, shadow classifiers were trained on the same task and using similar datasets as the target classifier, but constructed to possess or lack the property P. The parameters of these shadow classifiers were then employed to train the meta-classifier.

The work presented in [42] focuses on a centralized machine learning (ML) context using Support Vector Machines (SVM) and Hidden Markov Models (HMM). In contrast,

Melis et al. in 2018 [43] were the first to explore the unintended feature leakage within collaborative machine learning and federated learning (FL). They demonstrated that the exchanged updates during the FL process can inadvertently disclose information about the participants' data. By exploiting this leakage, both passive and active property inference attacks can be executed to infer properties that are unrelated to the original task of the model. In this scenario, the adversary is a participant in the process of FL that exploits the periodic updates of the global model to perform the attack. The information leakage that can be exploited are the leakage from the sparse embedding layer, particularly for the non-numerical data such as in Natural Language Processing, and leakage from the gradients. The results suggest that leakage of unintended features exposes FL to powerful inference attacks.

Ganju et al. in 2018 [44] concentrated on inferring global properties of the training data by conducting a white-box attack against Fully Connected Neural Networks (FC-NNs). Their goal was to deduce properties such as the data production environment or the proportion of data belonging to a specific class. Unlike the approach proposed by Ateniese et al. [42], which is not practical for FCNNs, Ganju et al. addressed the challenges posed by FCNNs, particularly the fact that permutations of nodes in each hidden layer can lead to equivalent FCNNs. This property makes it difficult for meta-classifiers. To overcome this challenge, Ganju et al. proposed two strategies: neuron sorting and set-based representation. These strategies enhance the effectiveness of the attack by ensuring better classification performance. The authors compared their results with the work of Ateniese et al. [42] and demonstrated the improved performance of their approaches when applied to FCNNs. The results underscore the challenge posed by FCNNs and highlight the effectiveness of the neuron sorting and set-based representation strategies in addressing this challenge.

Several works have studied models other than Fully Connected Neural Networks (FCNNs) to explore their vulnerability to property inference attacks. Zhou et al. [45] investigated generative models, particularly generative adversarial networks (GANs). Their work proposed a general attack pipeline applicable to both the full black-box and partial black-box settings. This research demonstrated the feasibility of conducting property inference attacks not only on discriminative models but also on generative models, highlighting the effectiveness of such attacks across both model types.

3.4. Training Samples and Labels Inference

Training samples and labels inference, also known as reconstruction attacks, aim to reconstruct the original dataset belonging to a client involved in the federated learning process. These attacks focus on recovering the training samples and their corresponding labels from the aggregated model. By exploiting the information present in the model's parameters or gradients, adversaries attempt to recreate the client's original dataset, potentially compromising the privacy and confidentiality of the client's data.

Zhu et al. [4] in 2019 demonstrated that it is possible to obtain the private training data from the publicly shared gradients. Their method, known as Deep Leakage from Gradient (DLG), utilizes an optimization algorithm to recover pixel-wise accurate information for images and token-wise matching for texts. The attack is performed by generating "dummy" inputs, then by performing the forward–backward pass, they compute dummy gradients from the global model. Instead of updating weights of the dummy model, they update the dummy inputs and labels by minimizing the distance between dummy gradients and real gradients. The results show that they can achieve exact pixel-wise data recovering using just the shared global model and local gradients.

Zhao et al. [5] observed that DLG is unable to extract the ground-truth labels. To address this limitation, they proposed a method called iDLG. They demonstrated that the signs of gradients of the classification loss with respect to correct and wrong labels are opposite. This enables to always extract the ground truth labels.

Geiping et al. [6] in 2020 state that previous works are based on Euclidean cost function with an optimization via L-BFGS. These choices may not be optimal for realistic architectures. The authors propose to use a cost function based on cosine similarity to catch more information about the data. They find that, if we decompose the gradient into its norm magnitude and its direction, then the magnitude captures only information about the state of the training while the direction can carry significant information about the change in prediction when taking a gradient step towards another data point. This approach aims to find images that pursue similar prediction changes, and it was the first work that pushed the boundary towards ImageNet-level gradient inversion.

Yin et al. [46] introduced in 2021 GradInversion to recover the individual images that a client possesses within a batch by optimizing the input data to match the gradients provided by the client. The main challenge is to identify the ground-truth label for each data point in the batch. The main contribution is the introduction of the group consistency regularization term by computing a registered mean image from all candidate images. This allows for the reduction of the variance of the candidates, hence improving the convergence towards the ground truth images.

Jin et al. in 2021 [9] affirmed that existing approaches do not scale well with large-batch data recovery and do not provide a strong theoretical justification on the capability of data recovery. Therefore, they designed CAFE (catastrophic data leakage in vertical federated learning), an advanced data leakage attack with theoretical analysis on the data recovery performance. The proposed algorithm consists of three steps: Recover the gradients of loss with respect to the outputs of the first FC layer, use the recovered gradients as a learned regularizer to improve the performance of the data leakage attack, and then use the updated model parameters to perform the data leakage attack. The experimental results demonstrate that CAFE can recover private data from the shared aggregated gradients while overcoming the batch limitation problem in previous attacks.

Ren et al. in 2022 [7] proposed a generative regression neural network (GRNN) to recover images from the shared gradient in FL. The attack recovers a private training image up to a resolution of 256*256 and a batch size of 256, which surpasses the previous state of the art. The proposed method addresses three major challenges in existing methods: model stability, the feasibility of recovering data from large batch size, and fidelity with high resolution. GRNN consists of a GAN model for generating fake training data and an FCN for generating the corresponding label. A fake gradient is generated given the shared model, and the two generators are optimized by approximating this fake gradient to the true gradient. The extensive experiments conducted by the authors show that their work outperforms DLG in terms of the addressed challenges.

Table 2. Privacy inference attacks against FL.

Ref	Year	Assumption Adversary	Active/Passive	Goal	Exploit
[41]	2017	Client	Active	Class representative inference	Influencing the learning process.
[39]	2018	Server	Active	Class representative inference	Influencing the learning process.
[37]	2019	Client	Active/Passive	Membership inference	Vulnerabilities of the SGD algorithm.
[38]	2022	Client/Server	Passive	Membership inference	Prediction confidence series.
[43]	2018	Client	Passive	Properties inference	Global model updates.
[44]	2018	Client	Passive	Global Properties inference	Shared gradients.
[4]	2019	Server	Passive	Training data inference	Shared gradients.
[5]	2020	Server	Passive	Training data inference	Shared gradients and their signs.
[6]	2020	Server	Passive	Training data inference	Shared Gradients and Cosine similarity.
[46]	2021	Server	Passive	batch data recovery	Gradient inversion.
[9]	2021	Server	Passive	Large batch data recovery	Shared aggregated gradients.
[7]	2022	Server	Passive	Training image recovery	Shared gradients.

4. Federated Learning with Differential Privacy
4.1. Role of DP in FL

As previously stated, DP is a powerful technique that gives strong mathematical guarantees for privacy protection. Differential privacy in the context of FL was explored at the early stages of FL by McMahan et al. in 2017 [47]. DP offers several benefits, including:

1. Protecting individual participant's data: DP achieves this by adding noise to the shared updates, thereby hiding the contributions of each individual in the FL process.
2. Protecting data against membership inference and reconstructions attacks: DP is known to be robust to this type of attacks.
3. Encouraging the user to participate in the learning process: DP provides strong privacy guarantees to the user by offering plausible deniability for them.
4. Facilitating compliance with regulations: DP offers a way for companies to comply with the requirements of various data protection regulations, such as the General Data Protection Regulation (GDPR).

In summary, DP in FL provides multiple advantages, including individual data protection, defense against privacy attacks, enhanced user privacy guarantees, and regulatory compliance support.

4.2. Related Works

The combination of DP with FL is an active research area. The main challenge in this field is the trade-off between privacy and utility. This challenge is addressed using the different setting in DP, including Centralized DP (CDP), Local DP (LDP), and the shuffle model. Table 3 presents the different selected works, presenting the key ideas and the shortcoming.

The use of CDP for federated learning was explored in 2017 by McMahan et al. [47]. They were the first to show that it is possible to train large recurrent language models with CDP. Their proposed algorithm is based on the FedAvg algorithm [3] and the moments' accountant technique [48], which provides tight composition guarantees for the repeated application of the Gaussian mechanism. The authors extended the FedAvg and FedSGD algorithms to provide differential privacy guarantees. Their findings show that achieving DP comes at the cost of increased computation rather than in decreased utility.

At the same time as McMahan et al. [47], Geyer et al. [49] investigated the use of CDP to protect participants' data from other malicious participants while considering the server honest-but-curious. They proposed an algorithm that aims to hide clients' contributions during the training while balancing the trade-off between privacy loss and model performance. The idea is to approximate the averaging of client models with a randomized mechanism. This mechanism involves random subsampling of clients, clipping the updates before transmission to the server, and distorting the clipped updates using a Gaussian mechanism before the aggregation. Experimental results show the feasibility of using CDP in FL; however, the number of clients has a major impact on the accuracy of the model.

In 2019, Choudhury et al. [50] studied the performance of CDP in healthcare applications using real-world electronic health data. They proposed to add noise to the objective function of the model instead of perturbing the data. They show that using differential privacy can lead to a significant loss in model performance for this kind of application.

Hu et al. in 2020 [51] emphasized that the research should focus on the trade-off between privacy loss and accuracy of the model. The authors proposed a privacy-preserving approach for learning personalized models on distributed data. Their approach consists of training a personalized model of each client using their local data but also the shared updates from other clients. They used a Gaussian mechanism to provide (ϵ, δ)-differential privacy guarantees for the shared gradient. The added noise is calibrated using the sensitivity of the updates. Hu et al. considered a threat model with an honest-but-curious server and malicious users. While evaluating their approach, they affirmed that it is robust to device heterogeneity and perturbation of noises, offering a good trade-off between accuracy and privacy.

The use of LDP has also been largely investigated in the context of FL. The motivation is that, contrary to CDP, LDP protects the user's data even from a malicious server and gives more flexibility to the clients to manage their privacy.

Bhowmick et al. in 2019 [52] investigated the use of LDP to defend against reconstruction attacks in FL. In this work, the privacy was provided through two steps. First, the LDP was employed at the client side to protect the private individuals' data. Then, in the server-side computation, the LDP was used to guarantee the privacy preservation of the global model update. This approach aimed to mitigate the reconstruction attacks while maintaining privacy and accuracy.

Liu et al. in 2020 [53] observed that applying LDP is challenging when the dimension of the data is large, as the injected noise is proportional to the number of dimensions. Additionally, a large batch size is needed to obtain acceptable accuracy. To overcome these challenges, the authors proposed a two-stage LDP privatization framework for federated stochastic gradient descent (SGD). In the first stage, they privately select the top k dimensions based on their contribution to the gradients. Their idea behind this stage is that not all the dimensions are equally important. While selecting the Top 1 dimension can be easily accomplished by the exponential mechanism, extending this to select k dimensions is more challenging. For this case, the authors proposed two alternative mechanisms. In the second stage, value perturbation using LDP is applied to ensure privacy while preserving the utility.

Ni et al. in 2021 [54] proposed an adaptive differential privacy federated learning model for medical IoT applications. Specifically, they proposed a DNN (named DPFLAGD-DNN) for adding noise to the model parameters according to the correlation between the model output and the characteristic of the training data. According to the authors, this method reduces the unnecessary noise and improves the accuracy. The process is that each client performs the model training according to the parameters obtained from the server and adaptively adds noise by DPFLAGD-DNN. After that, the noisy parameters are sent back to the server. Considering also the leakage from the down link, the authors proposed to add noise using the same mechanism in the server side before broadcasting the parameters. Experimental results show that the proposed algorithm can achieve high accuracy and may be more practical for medical IoT applications.

Sun et al. in 2021 [55] considers again the DNN in a DPFL setting. They addressed two main challenges, the fixed weight range assumptions in previous work and the privacy degradation due to high dimensionality of DNN. They proposed a new adaptive LDP mechanism according to the weight ranges of different DNN layers. They also proposed a shuffling mechanism for parameters to anonymize the data source. Here, the mechanism of shuffling considers the parameters and not the models. They assume that this is more efficient against side-channel linkage attacks than in the standard method of shuffling models.

The cross-silos setting of FL was considered by Chamikara et al. in 2022 [56]. The authors addressed the challenge of managing the noise and the privacy budget due to high dimensionality of parameter matrices in DNN. The method proposed by Chamikara et al. adds noise to the data input instead of the parameters. By considering a malicious clients and server, the noise is added in a specific manner. First, the clients locally train a conventional neural network (CNN) using their respective data and then use the convolutional module of the CNN to obtain flattened vectors of the input. These flattened vectors are then encoded into binary vectors. After that, the randomized response is applied as a DP mechanism to perturb the vectors before training the local deep neural network (DNN). Finally, the clients send their respective trained local models to the server for training the global model.

Shen et al. in 2023 [57] raised the issue in previous works that consider the same privacy's requirements for all clients. This approach fails to acknowledge that each client in the real world has unique privacy needs. The authors introduced a perturbation algorithm that enables personalized LDP. In other words, each client adjusts its privacy parameter ϵ_i according to the sensitivity of its data. The experimental analysis demonstrated that clients can adjust their privacy parameters while still maintaining high accuracy.

The shuffle model of DP was studied by Girgis et al. in 2021 [58–60]. Their research aimed to address the challenge of poor learning performance in LDP and tried to enhance the trade-off between privacy and utility. To achieve this, they propose to amplify the privacy by self-sampling and shuffling. The main contribution of their work lies on the concept of self-sampling. Contrary to the standard shuffle model where the server knows who the participants are, in this setting, the server does not have knowledge of the participant at each step. This approach avoids the need for coordination in participant selection during the federated process.

Table 3. Privacy-preserving FL using DP.

Ref	Year	DP Type	Key Idea	Trade-offs and Shortcomings
[47]	2017	CDP	Adding Gaussian noise by the server before global aggregation.	Increased computation cost and poor performance in non-IID setting
[49]	2017	CDP	Same as [47], but using subsampling of clients and clipping before sending updates.	The number of clients has a major impact on the accuracy of the model.
[50]	2019	CDP	Adding noise to the objective function instead of the updates.	Poor performance for healthcare applications
[51]	2020	CDP	Training a personalized model for each client using local data and the shared updates from other clients (Protected using DP).	Increased computation and communication cost
[52]	2019	LDP	Protecting local update from server using DP in the client side and protect global updates from clients using DP in the server side.	Increased computation cost
[61]	2020	LDP	Reducing noise injection by selecting the top k important dimension, then applying LDP.	Increased computation cost
[54]	2021	LDP	Adding adaptive noise to the model parameters using a deep neural network.	Increased computation cost
[55]	2021	LDP	Same as [54], but using adaptive range setting for weights and adding a shuffling step to amplify privacy	Increased computation cost
[56]	2022	LDP	Using the randomized response mechanism instead of the Gaussian and Laplacian mechanism.	Increased computation cost
[57]	2023	LDP	Using personalized privacy budget according to clients' requirements	The privacy budget is the same for all attributes.
[60]	2021	Shuffle	Amplifying privacy by self-sampling and shuffling. Real participants are unknown to the server.	Increased system complexity.

4.3. Discussion and Learned Lessons

The use of DP has been widely studied in federated learning using different settings, including CDP, LDP, and the shuffle model. One of the central challenges addressed in these settings is balancing between privacy and model performance.

CDP and LDP consider two primary adversaries: the clients and the aggregation server. CDP offers protection by safeguarding other clients' data from a malicious client while considering a trusted server. However, achieving this trust in practice can be challenging. Using LDP, on the other hand, eliminates the requirement to trust the server as the noise is added at the client level. However, this security comes at a cost to model performance.

The independent generation of noise by different clients in LDP adds substantial noise and requires more data to achieve the same level of accuracy as CDP.

Another issue by CDP and LDP is the anonymity of the clients. The server can track the source of updates, which widens the attack surface. The solution proposed to have the benefits of the two worlds of CDP and LDP while also guaranteeing anonymity is to use the shuffle model. In the shuffle model, the noise is generated by a shuffler, which also conducts the shuffling of updates to preserve the anonymity of the clients. The model can achieve a performance similar to CDP while not relying on a trusted server, as in LDP.

Many solutions have been designed in these different settings, going from designing new suitable mechanisms for DP to proposing alternative definitions of DP in the context of federated learning. It is also important to consider factors such as data distribution (vertical, horizontal, or hybrid) and the setting of FL (cross-device or cross-silo). Additionally, considering the correlation between the different attributes of the data is crucial. In fact, correlation is considered as a threat and may compromise the process of DP.

Furthermore, it is worth noting that DP alone may not counter all possible attacks. As a result, some works proposed to amplify DP by anonymization techniques. Other works also propose to amplify privacy by using other techniques such as secure multiparty computation and homomorphic encryption.

5. Federated Learning with Homomorphic Encryption

5.1. Role of HE in FL

Homomorphic encryption (HE) enables calculations over an encrypted domain, making it a good candidate for collaborative training of joint models in FL. HE can be applied in various ways within the FL framework, as seen in previous works.

One application of HE in FL is to hide client updates from the server. Instead of accessing the client's updates directly, the server will perform the aggregations in the encrypted domain and only access the final result. This approach provides an added security layer against eavesdropping and data breaches. By encrypting the updates, even if an unauthorized person intercepts the data, it will not have access to the raw data or the model updates.

Another way to utilize HE in FL is to collaboratively train the model without the need for intermediate decryption. In this scenario, the server conducts aggregations in the encrypted domain while having no method to decrypt the final result. Only clients having the decryption key can share the model.

HE can have other applications to counter adversarial attacks that do not deal with privacy, or auxiliary attacks that are facilitating privacy attacks, such as poisoning attacks. These attacks aim to compromise the integrity or reliability of the FL process. From security perspectives, to defend the server from model poisoning attacks, researchers have explored various variational measures. One such measure is CosDetect, proposed by Yaldiz et al. in 2023 [62], which employs a cosine similarity-based outlier detection algorithm to address fundamental issues more effectively than existing security solutions. The authors observed that the weight of the last layer pertaining to the local model update could be more sensitive to the local data distribution than other layers. This observation is significant, as it suggests that the last layer of local updates from malicious clients should exhibit outlier characteristics compared to updates from honest clients, making it more meaningful to a privacy attack. However, as this paper does not focus on such attacks, we will not delve deeper into them.

5.2. Related Works

The first-level combination of FL and HE has been initiated by researchers. The main purpose of HE in the context of privacy preserving is to safeguard the leakage of gradients, thereby by enabling secure aggregation during the learning process. Table 4 presents the different selected works, presenting the key ideas and the shortcoming.

Zhang et al. in 2020 [63] introduced BatchCrypt, a solution that reduces encryption and communication overhead when applying HE in cross-silo FL. The authors proposed a batch encryption technique where clients encode a batch of quantized values of gradients to a long integer and encrypt it. The main challenge addressed in their work is finding a feasible batch encryption scheme that allows direct summation of ciphertexts without intermediate decryption. To achieve this, they proposed a novel encoding technique using quantization of gradients. They adopt two complement representations with two sign bits, padding, and advanced scaling to avoid overflow. They also tackle the challenge of unbounded gradient by proposing an efficient analytical model (named dACIQ) for clipping. Compared with the stock FATE, their implementation using FATE shows an acceleration of 81 times and a reduction by 101 times of the traffic overhead.

Fang and Qian in 2021 [64] introduced a multi-party privacy-preserving machine learning framework called PFMLP (private federated multi-layer perceptron). This framework is based on partially homomorphic encryption and federated learning to protect privacy. The main objective is to mitigate membership inference attack. The authors proposed to counter such attack by hiding the shared gradients from the server using HE. In order to reduce the computational overhead of homomorphic encryption, they proposed to use an improved version of the Paillier scheme described by Jost et al. in 2015 [65]. Using this version, they speed up the training by 25–28% compared to the initial version of the Paillier scheme [30]. The authors conducted experimentation on MNIST and fatigue datasets and demonstrated that PFMLP achieves the same accuracy as the standard MLP (multi-layer perceptron) without HE.

Feng and Du in 2021 [66] proposed FLZip, a framework that uses gradients compression before encryption, to address the same challenges as BatchCrypt [63]. The key idea behind FLZip is to reduce the number of gradients to be encrypted by filtering insignificant gradients by introducing a hyperparameter. Then only the sparse significant gradients are encrypted. The lock in this scenario is how to design a feasible compression–encryption scheme that allows direct summation of ciphertexts without decryption. The authors focus on finding a "mergeable" compression scheme that maintains the addition property of HE. To achieve this, they proposed to select top-k significant gradients, encode them using key–value pairs, and then encrypt the values using the Paillier scheme [30]. Comparing their results to BatchCrypt, FLZip achieves a reduction in encryption and decryption operations by 6.4 times and 13.1 times, respectively, and shrinks the network footprints to and from the server by 5.9 times and 12.5 times, respectively, while maintaining model accuracy.

Liu et al. in 2022 [67] addressed the efficiency and the collusion threats in the previous works. For that, they developed a secure aggregation scheme, called doubly homomorphic secure aggregation (DHSA). The solution consists of two protocols: the Homomorphic Model Aggregation protocol (HMA) and the Masking Seed Agreement protocol (MSA). The HMA protocol utilizes a simple masking scheme based on a seed homomorphic random generator to hide the model updates. Then the demasking seed is securely calculated using the MSA protocol, which employs multi-key homomorphic encryption to ensure that the aggregation is only known by the clients. The work was compared to BatchCrypt [63] and the results show a speedup of up to 20 times while obtaining a similar accuracy to non-secure, uncompressed FedAvg.

Shin et al. [68] noticed that previous works do not protect the dataset size of each client. This information can inadvertently reveal sensitive data, such as the number of patients in the local hospital, rare diseases among the regions, etc. They considered a healthcare scenario and proposed a protocol for private federated averaging for the cross-silo setting using partial homomorphic encryption based on the Paillier scheme. In their protocol, each client interacts with a randomly selected neighbor to send the encrypted calculation result, instead of sending them to the server. The final result is then sent to the server for decryption. In this way, the local results of each client remain hidden from other clients and from the server.

Jin et al. in 2023 [69] proposed an HE–FL optimization scheme, named FedML-HE, that minimizes the size of model updates for encrypted computation while preserving privacy guarantees. The work addresses challenges related to communication and computation overhead (e.g., 10× reduction for HE-federated training of ResNet-50 and 40× reduction for BERT). In their approach, an honest-but-curious server aggregates the encrypted gradients from clients before decrypting them. Two techniques are introduced: parameter efficiency and parameter selection. In parameter efficiency, the goal is to reduce the model size through techniques such as model compression and parameter efficient tuning like in FLZip [66]. In parameter selection, the idea is to hide parts of the model instead of encrypting the whole model. The proposed solution was implemented using PALISADE for HE. The experimentation shows that the communication and computation overheads are reduced using the optimization techniques. The effectiveness of the parameter selection defense was also tested against gradient inversion, and the results show that encrypting 42% of the parameters is effective when using random selection mechanism, but using a more robust selection mechanism by selecting more important parameters is more efficient, and it is necessary to just encrypt 10% of the parameters to counter the DLG attack.

Table 4. Privacy-preserving FL using HE.

Ref	Year	Scheme	Key Idea	Trade-offs and Shortcomings
[63]	2020	Additive	Propose a batch additive scheme to reduce communication and computation overhead.	Batchcrypt is not applicable in Vertical FL.
[64]	2021	Additive	Hide shared gradients from from the server to protect against membership inference attack.	Scalability issue, computational and communication overhead
[66]	2021	Additive	Reduce the number of gradients to be encrypted by filtering insignificant gradients.	Scalability issues, computational and communication overhead
[67]	2022	Additive	Use a doubly homomorphic secure aggregation by using homomorphic encryption and masking technique.	Computational and communication overhead
[68]	2022	Additive	Additionally to previous work, protect the dataset size by adding interactions between clients using homomorphic encryption.	Computational and communication overhead
[69]	2023	Additive	Encrypting only a part of the model instead of the whole model. They showed that encrypting just 10% of the model parameter using a robust selection mechanism is efficient to counter DLG attack.	Need for theoretical analysis of the trade-offs among privacy guarantee, system overheads and model performance.

5.3. Discussion and Learned Lessons

The central challenge when using HE in FL is the computation and communication overhead. Unlike DP, which requires reducing the trade-off between privacy and model performance, in HE, the focus is on reducing the trade-off between privacy and computation overhead.

Several techniques have been explored to address this challenge, including batching, gradient compression, masking, parameter efficiency, and parameter selection. Batching techniques aim to encode many values within the same ciphertext while ensuring that the result can be obtained using only one operation on the ciphertext. Gradient compression, on the other hand, tries to compress the ciphertext to reduce the communication overhead. Masking is used as a lightweight technique that hides information using a mask seed, with the demasking seed calculated collaboratively using homomorphic encryption. Parameter efficiency and parameter selection techniques select only the efficient parameters and then encrypt only the most significant updates that may reveal much information about the data, rather than encrypting all the parameters. Previous works affirm that encrypting only the significant parameter is sufficient to counter privacy attacks.

Homomorphic encryption is well suited to counter eavesdropping attacks and the attacks that may exploit the updates coming from the client. It is also a good solution for anonymization, since the server will not access the updates provided by clients. However, the security of HE relies on the chosen scheme and the encryption keys. In addition, if the server accesses the final result, it still has the potential to perform a model inversion attack against the global model.

One drawback of HE is that the only operations possible are the addition and multiplication. Most research focus only on additive homomorphic encryption. Moreover, the computational complexity poses a challenging in terms of term efficiency and performance when applying HE in FL.

6. Combining DP and HE in Federated Learning

6.1. Related Works

Each technique has its own advantages and drawbacks in the context of privacy and security in federated learning. However, by combining these two techniques, we can potentially mitigate the drawbacks of each and achieve more comprehensive privacy protection. Several works have tried to combine these two techniques; Table 5 presents the different selected works, presenting the key ideas and the shortcomings.

Xu et al. in 2019 [70] proposed HybridAlpha, an FL framework that combines additive homomorphic encryption with differential privacy. The goal is to limit inference attacks from a curious aggregator during the process of learning and when using the final model. The system consists of a third-party authority (TPA) that generates the keys and distributes them, as well as an Inference Prevention Module. The module examines requests for private keys for specific vectors that may allow a specific curious aggregator to make an inference-enabling inner product. Hence, after receiving public keys from the TPA, the client will use LDP to protect their model updates from the server and then encrypt them. The server will then accomplish the aggregation before decrypting the data. The experimental results show that HybridAlpha can reduce the training time by 68% and data transfer volume by 92% while having similar privacy guarantees or model performance compared to existing works that use SMC, DP, and HE.

Wang et al. in 2020 [71] proposed two protocols to improve the utility of the data while guaranteeing better privacy. They proposed to build their solution based on the shuffler model proposed in Prochlo [72]. The challenge is to find a mechanism whose utility does not degrade with the evolution of the size of the data. They proposed a mechanism, named Shuffler-Optimal Local Hash (SOLH), and compared it to generalized random response (GRR) and unary encoding (RAPPOR). The results showed that SOLH outperformed GRR when the size of the data was large. However, when analyzing the security of this method, the authors found that collusion attacks may reveal information about the clients even when using DP. Therefore, they proposed a method called "Private Encrypted Oblivious Shuffle" that uses AHE to counter collusion attacks. The method was compared to various methods using shuffling, local hashing, and unary encoding.

Gu et al. in 2021 [73] proposed PRECAD, a framework for FL via crypto-aided differential privacy. This framework achieves differential privacy and uses cryptography against poisoning attacks. The author suggested using two non-colluding servers in an honest-but-curious model. The clients split their updates into two shares and send them to the servers. Additive secret sharing is used to verify the validity of the sharing, mitigating poisoning attacks. The servers then add CDP noise and conduct a secure aggregation step. The goal of this work is to improve the trade-off between privacy and robustness against poisoning attacks, contrary to previous works that try to improve the trade-off between privacy and utility. However, the experimentation also included tests on utility in order to validate the feasibility of the solution.

Sébert et al. in 2022 [74] published a work named "protecting data from all parties" that combines DP and HE in federated learning. In their work, each client applies successive transformations to achieve DP (clipping, noising, and quantization) then encrypt the data using HE before sending them to the server. HE protects the data from the semi-honest server, which performs calculations in an encrypted domain, while DP protects the data from the malicious clients. The challenges raised in this work are the computation cost of HE and the noise generation in DP. To decrease the computation cost, the authors suggest to use fixed-point numbers with a limited number of bits instead of floating-point numbers. They propose a new probabilistic quantization operator called "Poisson quantization" to handle the noise generation in a distributed manner, preventing the server from sharing the noise with other clients. In order to prove the feasibility of this framework, the experimentation was conducted using the FEMNIST dataset, a largely used dataset in previous works on federated learning.

One remarkable work that combines DP with HE is by Roy Chowdhurry et al. in 2020 [75]. The authors proposed crypt-ϵ a framework for executing DP programs. However, the framework is not specifically designed for the context of FL.

Table 5. Privacy preserving FL combining DP and HE

Ref	Year	Key Idea	Trade-offs and Shortcomings
[70]	2019	Add less noise by amplifying privacy by homomorphic encryption	Trade-off between privacy, communication, and computation.
[71]	2020	Amplify privacy with the shuffle model and protect data against collision attacks using Encrypted oblivious shuffle.	Increased system complexity.
[73]	2021	Split the updates into two shares and send them to two non-colluding servers that add CDP and use additive secret sharing to mitigate poisoning attacks and conduct secure aggregation.	Increased system complexity.
[74]	2022	Protect updates from the server using homomorphic encryption and protect global updates from clients using DP	Computational overhead.

6.2. Discussion and Learned Lessons

The combination of DP and HE in FL offers the potential to achieve a more comprehensive approach to privacy and security in federated learning. By leveraging the strengths of each technique, it becomes possible to mitigate their respective drawbacks and achieve enhanced privacy protection. HE can amplify the privacy offered by DP to protect the updates from all the parties, as in Sébert et al. [74]. While HE protects the intermediate updates from the server, DP also ensures the final model remains secure, preventing adversaries from performing model inversion attacks.

This combination is interesting also in terms of model performance. In fact, augmenting DP with HE can allow adding less noise and, by the way, having more utility of the data. The authors of the aforementioned work refer to this approach as crypto-aided differential privacy, emphasizing its potential for balancing between privacy and utility.

HE and DP can effectively mitigate various attacks from curious aggregators and from clients. By encrypting the data and applying differential privacy mechanisms, the privacy of the model updates and inference process can be safeguarded, preventing adversaries from extracting sensitive information. In addition, other attacks like collusion and poisoning attacks can be addressed using the combination of these techniques.

However, it is essential to acknowledge that the combination of DP and HE in FL does come with certain trade-offs and complexities. As the number of participants in the learning process increases, managing these entities can become challenging. Furthermore, the computational overhead associated with HE introduces resource consumption, impacting communication and computation within the system.

In summary, the integration of DP and HE in federated learning holds immense promise in enhancing privacy and security while striking a balance between utility and protection. However, it is crucial to carefully manage the system complexity and consider resource implications to fully harness the potential of this powerful privacy-preserving approach.

7. Discussion

While federated learning (FL) is often recognized as a technique that inherently protects privacy, it can still fall prey to numerous privacy attacks, as discussed in Section 3. The process of exchanging gradient updates across participating nodes in FL might inadvertently lead to potential privacy leaks. These leaks can expose sensitive aspects of the client's private data even without directly sharing the actual training datasets. This vulnerability is amplified due to the large number of participants involved in FL and the transparency of the framework's operations, which could provide ample opportunity for adversaries to launch powerful attacks.

In an effort to mitigate these vulnerabilities, our research highlights the potential of two techniques: differential privacy (DP) and homomorphic encryption (HE). In the academic community, DP is often split into three main categories: central differential privacy (CDP), local differential privacy (LDP), and the shuffle model. CDP is designed to shield raw data from potentially malicious clients, thus preventing unauthorized access. However, LDP goes a step further by also protecting data against adversarial servers. This additional layer of security, though, often comes at the expense of model performance due to the added noise.

This inherent trade-off gave rise to the exploration of the shuffle model, where privacy is fortified through a process of anonymization and shuffling. This technique severs the link between client-side updates and their origin, adding a further layer of privacy. Despite its advantages, the shuffle model requires trusting the shuffler as an 'honest-but-curious' server, which could be a potential point of vulnerability.

Balancing privacy and model performance is one of the major challenges when implementing DP. To ensure privacy, noise is added to the data, which can negatively impact the accuracy of the model. This inevitable trade-off is a critical consideration, prompting our exploration of other potential solutions, such as HE.

HE, though computationally expensive, has emerged as a promising technique. It promotes privacy by allowing only aggregated updates to be shared; thus, the aggregation server does not directly observe individual client updates. This approach minimizes accuracy loss, a crucial advantage. Yet, there are still concerns. For example, adversaries might potentially infer useful information from the final model using model inversion attacks. Further, the security provided by HE relies heavily on the strength of the encryption key and the security of the underlying encryption scheme. Unlike DP, it also does not offer plausible deniability, leaving users potentially exposed.

As outlined in Section 6, depending solely on one technique leaves potential gaps in security coverage. Therefore, an integrated approach, combining DP and HE, might offer a comprehensive solution. This hybrid model attempts to leverage the strengths of both DP and HE, offering accuracy from HE and plausible deniability from DP. However, this integration is far from straightforward. The challenge lies in navigating the trade-off between privacy, accuracy, and computational complexity to create a robust and efficient privacy-preserving FL framework.

In brief, the utilization of DP (differential privacy) and HE (homomorphic encryption) in federated learning can be depicted using Figures 2 and 3. The federated process, utilizing DP and HE, operates through a sequence of two alternating procedures, as depicted in Figures 2 and 3. The sequence kicks off with the server transmitting the global model to the clients. Subsequently, the clients proceed to train a local model and transmit their updates back to the server following the steps illustrated in Figure 2. After that, the server conducts secure aggregation and updates the global model based on the outlined process in Figure 3. These procedures persist until either convergence is reached or the maximum number of iterations is attained.

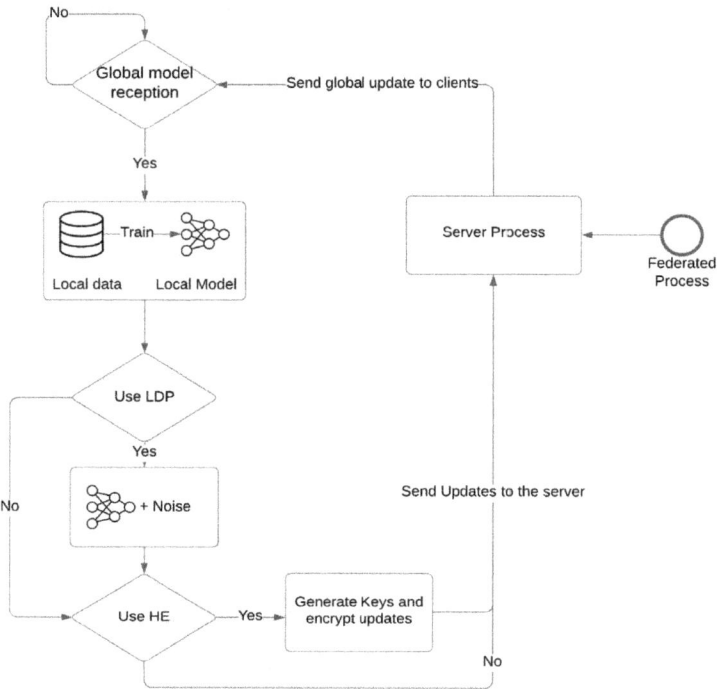

Figure 2. Client process in secure federated learning.

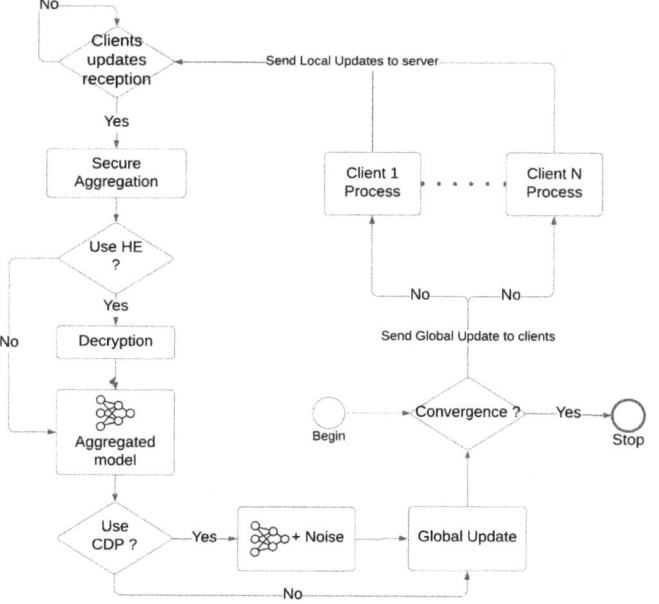

Figure 3. Server process in secure federated learning.

Ongoing Research

Inspired by recent seminal research on secured federated learning, specifically Time-varying Hierarchical Gradient Sparsification [76], we propose a novel homomorphic scheme to insert an additional layer for configuring an encryption mask. We conducted a preliminary overview analysis to determine the immediate impact of this proposed augmentation with HE in a secured federated environment.

It is feasible to reconfigure the encryption matrix for HE before applying the sparsification scheme. Assuming the idea of blind encryption, we propose configuring it through the Paillier modulus, while fetching a random value that is relatively prime to the multiplication modulo. Introducing the concept of relatively prime values can assist in distributing the masking of the matrix autonomously with less dependency on the operator. Similarly, to unmask the encryptor, we will evaluate the Paillier encryption with homomorphic computation. However, we anticipate that this logic may not fully mask the real value. Therefore, one alternative solution could be to generate two random values, ensuring that neither is 0. At the time of preparing this article, we have not investigated the deep-dive impact on the optimization of the double-layered secured matrix for the federated environment. This will be an extension of the present research.

8. Conclusions and Future Works

The core contributions of this study encompass a comprehensive analysis of recent implementations of DP and HE to handle privacy concerns within the context of FL. While FL is commonly perceived as a means of safeguarding privacy, our analysis has brought to light significant vulnerabilities present in various works. We delve into the spectrum of privacy attacks, illuminating their real-world relevance and implications for distributed learning. Furthermore, we offer nuanced insights into DP's deployment settings, HE's potential for safeguarding sensitive data, and the intersection of HE and DP techniques. Our work significantly augments the understanding of privacy strategies in FL and lays the groundwork for future advancements in this evolving landscape.

Regarding DP, the main challenge is striking a balance between privacy and accuracy. Addressing this challenge entails further research into devising more resilient mechanisms that introduce minimal noise while offering heightened privacy assurances. Furthermore, alternative relaxations of DP specifically designed for the FL environment or enhancing DP through auxiliary methods like anonymization, subsampling, or cryptography could offer novel avenues of investigation.

Concerning HE, the central challenge centers on mitigating the trade-off between privacy and computational complexity. Attacking this challenge requires a concerted effort to accelerate HE primitives while identifying algorithmic approaches to reduce the complexity of certain operations, such as division. By improving the efficiency of HE, we can simultaneously uphold privacy principles and mitigate computational overhead.

Furthermore, the combination of HE and DP is also an interesting direction. However, this amalgamation is far from straightforward, necessitating a careful equilibrium between computational complexity, model precision, and privacy considerations. As suggested in the work of Sébert et al. [74], combining these two techniques has the potential to safeguard raw data across all participants in the FL process, thereby showcasing a direction for future exploration.

Author Contributions: Conceptualization, R.A., S.B. (Soumya Banerjee) and S.B. (Samia Bouzefrane); methodology, R.A. and S.B. (Soumya Banerjee); validation, R.A., S.B. (Soumya Banerjee), S.B. (Samia Bouzefrane) and T.L.V.; investigation, R.A.; writing—original draft preparation, R.A., S.B. (Soumya Banerjee) and S.B. (Samia Bouzefrane); writing—review and editing, R.A. and T.L.V.; supervision, S.B. (Samia Bouzefrane). All authors have read and agreed to the published version of the manuscript.

Funding: This research was funded by ROC team attached to CEDRIC Lab, Cnam Paris.

Institutional Review Board Statement: Not Applicable.

Informed Consent Statement: Not Applicable.

Data Availability Statement: Not Applicable.

Conflicts of Interest: The authors declare no conflict of interest.

Abbreviations

The following abbreviations are used in this manuscript:

AHE	Additive Homomorphic Encryption
CDP	Centralized Differential Privacy
CNN	Convolutional Neural Network
DLG	Deep Leakage from Gradients
DNN	Deep Neural Network
DP	Differential Privacy
FC	Fully Connected
FCN	Fully Connected Network
FCNN	Fully connected neural network
FHE	Fully Homomorphic Encryption
FL	Federated Learning
GAN	Generative Adversarial Network
GDPR	General Data Protection Regulation
GRNN	Generative Regression Neural Network
HE	Homomorphic Encryption
HFL	Horizontal Federated Learning
LDP	Local Differential Privacy
MIA	Membership Inference Attack
ML	Machine Learning
PCS	Prediction Confidence series
PHE	Partially Homomorphic Encryption
SGD	Stochastic Gradient Descent
SWHE	Somewhat Homomorphic Encryption
VFL	Vertical Federated Learning

References

1. Gartner. Gartner Identifies Top Five Trends in Privacy Through 2024. Available online: https://www.gartner.com/en/newsroom/press-releases/2022-05-31-gartner-identifies-top-five-trends-in-privacy-through-2024 (accessed on 1 June 2023).
2. European Commission. Regulation (EU) 2016/679 of the European Parliament and of the Council of 27 April 2016 on the protection of natural persons with regard to the processing of personal data and on the free movement of such data, and repealing Directive 95/46/EC (General Data Protection Regulation) (Text with EEA relevance). *Off. J. Eur. Union* **2016**, *4*, 1–88.
3. McMahan, B.; Moore, E.; Ramage, D.; Hampson, S.; Arcas, B.A. Communication-efficient learning of deep networks from decentralized data. In Proceedings of the Artificial Intelligence and Statistics, Lauderdale, FL, USA, 20–22 April 2017; pp. 1273–1282.
4. Zhu, L.; Liu, Z.; Han, S. Deep Leakage from Gradients. In *Proceedings of the Advances in Neural Information Processing Systems*; Wallach, H., Larochelle, H., Beygelzimer, A., d'Alché-Buc, F., Fox, E., Garnett, R., Eds.; Curran Associates, Inc.: Red Hook, NY, USA, 2019; Volume 32.
5. Zhao, B.; Mopuri, K.R.; Bilen, H. idlg: Improved deep leakage from gradients. *arXiv* **2020**, arXiv:2001.02610.
6. Geiping, J.; Bauermeister, H.; Dröge, H.; Moeller, M. Inverting Gradients—How easy is it to break privacy in federated learning? In *Proceedings of the Advances in Neural Information Processing Systems*; Larochelle, H., Ranzato, M., Hadsell, R., Balcan, M., Lin, H., Eds.; Curran Associates, Inc.: Red Hook, NY, USA, 2020; Volume 33, pp. 16937–16947.
7. Ren, H.; Deng, J.; Xie, X. GRNN: Generative Regression Neural Network—A Data Leakage Attack for Federated Learning. *ACM Trans. Intell. Syst. Technol.* **2022**, *13*, 1–24. [CrossRef]
8. Wei, W.; Liu, L.; Loper, M.; Chow, K.H.; Gursoy, M.E.; Truex, S.; Wu, Y. A Framework for Evaluating Client Privacy Leakages in Federated Learning. In *Proceedings of the Computer Security—ESORICS 2020*; Chen, L., Li, N., Liang, K., Schneider, S., Eds.; Springer International Publishing: Cham, Switzerland, 2020; pp. 545–566.
9. Jin, X.; Chen, P.Y.; Hsu, C.Y.; Yu, C.M.; Chen, T. CAFE: Catastrophic Data Leakage in Vertical Federated Learning. In *Proceedings of the Advances in Neural Information Processing Systems*; Ranzato, M., Beygelzimer, A., Dauphin, Y., Liang, P., Vaughan, J.W., Eds.; Curran Associates, Inc.: Red Hook, NY, USA, 2021; Volume 34, pp. 994–1006.

10. Zhang, J.; Zhang, J.; Chen, J.; Yu, S. GAN Enhanced Membership Inference: A Passive Local Attack in Federated Learning. In Proceedings of the ICC 2020—2020 IEEE International Conference on Communications (ICC), Dublin, Ireland, 7–11 June 2020; pp. 1–6. [CrossRef]
11. Mao, Y.; Zhu, X.; Zheng, W.; Yuan, D.; Ma, J. A Novel User Membership Leakage Attack in Collaborative Deep Learning. In Proceedings of the 2019 11th International Conference on Wireless Communications and Signal Processing (WCSP), Shaanxi, China, 23–25 October 2019; pp. 1–6. [CrossRef]
12. Chen, J.; Zhang, J.; Zhao, Y.; Han, H.; Zhu, K.; Chen, B. Beyond Model-Level Membership Privacy Leakage: An Adversarial Approach in Federated Learning. In Proceedings of the 2020 29th International Conference on Computer Communications and Networks (ICCCN), Honolulu, HI, USA, 3–6 August 2020; pp. 1–9. [CrossRef]
13. Wang, L.; Xu, S.; Wang, X.; Zhu, Q. Eavesdrop the composition proportion of training labels in federated learning. *arXiv* **2019**, arXiv:1910.06044.
14. Zhang, W.; Tople, S.; Ohrimenko, O. Leakage of Dataset Properties in Multi-Party Machine Learning. In Proceedings of the 30th USENIX Security Symposium (USENIX Security 21), Vancouver, BC, Canada, 11–13 August 2021; pp. 2687–2704.
15. Li, Q.; Wen, Z.; Wu, Z.; Hu, S.; Wang, N.; Li, Y.; Liu, X.; He, B. A Survey on Federated Learning Systems: Vision, Hype and Reality for Data Privacy and Protection. *IEEE Trans. Knowl. Data Eng.* **2023**, *35*, 3347–3366. [CrossRef]
16. Kairouz, P.; McMahan, H.B.; Avent, B.; Bellet, A.; Bennis, M.; Bhagoji, A.N.; Bonawitz, K.; Charles, Z.; Cormode, G.; Cummings, R.; et al. Advances and Open Problems in Federated Learning. *arXiv* **2021**, arXiv:1912.04977.
17. Yang, Q.; Liu, Y.; Chen, T.; Tong, Y. Federated Machine Learning: Concept and Applications. *ACM Trans. Intell. Syst. Technol.* **2019**, *10*, 1–19. [CrossRef]
18. Lyu, L.; Yu, H.; Yang, Q. Threats to Federated Learning: A Survey. *arXiv* **2020**, arXiv:2003.02133.
19. Rodríguez-Barroso, N.; Jiménez-López, D.; Luzón, M.V.; Herrera, F.; Martínez-Cámara, E. Survey on federated learning threats: Concepts, taxonomy on attacks and defences, experimental study and challenges. *Inf. Fusion* **2023**, *90*, 148–173. [CrossRef]
20. Zhang, K.; Song, X.; Zhang, C.; Yu, S. Challenges and future directions of secure federated learning: A survey. *Front. Comput. Sci.* **2021**, *16*, 165817. [CrossRef]
21. Li, Z.; Sharma, V.; Mohanty, S.P. Preserving Data Privacy via Federated Learning: Challenges and Solutions. *IEEE Consum. Electron. Mag.* **2020**, *9*, 8–16. [CrossRef]
22. Yin, X.; Zhu, Y.; Hu, J. A Comprehensive Survey of Privacy-Preserving Federated Learning: A Taxonomy, Review, and Future Directions. *ACM Comput. Surv.* **2021**, *54*, 1–36. [CrossRef]
23. Li, T.; Sahu, A.K.; Talwalkar, A.; Smith, V. Federated Learning: Challenges, Methods, and Future Directions. *IEEE Signal Process. Mag.* **2020**, *37*, 50–60. [CrossRef]
24. Kaissis, G.A.; Makowski, M.R.; Rückert, D.; Braren, R.F. Secure, privacy-preserving and federated machine learning in medical imaging. *Nat. Mach. Intell.* **2020**, *2*, 305–311. [CrossRef]
25. Gu, X.; Sabrina, F.; Fan, Z.; Sohail, S. A Review of Privacy Enhancement Methods for Federated Learning in Healthcare Systems. *Int. J. Environ. Res. Public Health* **2023**, *20*, 6539. [CrossRef]
26. Lim, W.Y.B.; Luong, N.C.; Hoang, D.T.; Jiao, Y.; Liang, Y.C.; Yang, Q.; Niyato, D.; Miao, C. Federated Learning in Mobile Edge Networks: A Comprehensive Survey. *IEEE Commun. Surv. Tutor.* **2020**, *22*, 2031–2063. [CrossRef]
27. Niknam, S.; Dhillon, H.S.; Reed, J.H. Federated Learning for Wireless Communications: Motivation, Opportunities and Challenges. *arXiv* **2020**, arXiv:1908.06847.
28. Dwork, C.; Kenthapadi, K.; McSherry, F.; Mironov, I.; Naor, M. Our Data, Ourselves: Privacy Via Distributed Noise Generation. In *Proceedings of the Advances in Cryptology—EUROCRYPT 2006*; Vaudenay, S., Ed.; Springer: Berlin/Heidelberg, Germany, 2006; pp. 486–503.
29. Albrecht, M.; Chase, M.; Chen, H.; Ding, J.; Goldwasser, S.; Gorbunov, S.; Halevi, S.; Hoffstein, J.; Laine, K.; Lauter, K.; et al. *Homomorphic Encryption Security Standard*; Technical Report; HomomorphicEncryption.org: Toronto, ON, Canada, 2018.
30. Paillier, P. Public-key cryptosystems based on composite degree residuosity classes. In Proceedings of the Advances in Cryptology—EUROCRYPT'99: International Conference on the Theory and Application of Cryptographic Techniques, Prague, Czech Republic, 2–6 May 1999; pp. 223–238.
31. Gentry, C. Fully Homomorphic Encryption Using Ideal Lattices. In Proceedings of the Forty-First Annual ACM Symposium on Theory of Computing, Bethesda, MD, USA, 31 May–2 June 2009; Association for Computing Machinery: New York, NY, USA; pp. 169–178. [CrossRef]
32. Liu, P.; Xu, X.; Wang, W. Threats, attacks and defenses to federated learning: Issues, taxonomy and perspectives. *Cybersecurity* **2022**, *5*, 4. [CrossRef]
33. Shokri, R.; Stronati, M.; Song, C.; Shmatikov, V. Membership Inference Attacks against Machine Learning Models. *arXiv* **2017**, arXiv:1610.05820.
34. Salem, A.; Zhang, Y.; Humbert, M.; Berrang, P.; Fritz, M.; Backes, M. ML-Leaks: Model and Data Independent Membership Inference Attacks and Defenses on Machine Learning Models. In Proceedings of the 2019 Network and Distributed System Security Symposium, San Diego, CA, USA, 24–27 February 2019. [CrossRef]
35. Pustozerova, A.; Mayer, R. Information Leaks in Federated Learning. In Proceedings of the 2020 Workshop on Decentralized IoT Systems and Security, San Diego, CA, USA, 23 February 2020. [CrossRef]
36. Hu, H.; Salcic, Z.; Sun, L.; Dobbie, G.; Zhang, X. Source Inference Attacks in Federated Learning. *arXiv* **2021**, arXiv:2109.05659.

37. Nasr, M.; Shokri, R.; Houmansadr, A. Comprehensive Privacy Analysis of Deep Learning: Passive and Active White-box Inference Attacks against Centralized and Federated Learning. In Proceedings of the 2019 IEEE Symposium on Security and Privacy (SP), Francisco, CA, USA, 20–22 May 2019; pp. 739–753. [CrossRef]
38. Gu, Y.; Bai, Y.; Xu, S. CS-MIA: Membership inference attack based on prediction confidence series in federated learning. *J. Inf. Secur. Appl.* **2022**, *67*, 103201. [CrossRef]
39. Wang, Z.; Song, M.; Zhang, Z.; Song, Y.; Wang, Q.; Qi, H. Beyond Inferring Class Representatives: User-Level Privacy Leakage From Federated Learning. In Proceedings of the IEEE INFOCOM 2019—IEEE Conference on Computer Communications, Paris, France, 29 April–2 May 2019; pp. 2512–2520. [CrossRef]
40. Fredrikson, M.; Jha, S.; Ristenpart, T. Model Inversion Attacks that Exploit Confidence Information and Basic Countermeasures. In Proceedings of the 22nd ACM SIGSAC Conference on Computer and Communications Security, Denver, CO, USA, 12–16 October 2015; pp. 1322–1333. [CrossRef]
41. Hitaj, B.; Ateniese, G.; Perez-Cruz, F. Deep Models Under the GAN: Information Leakage from Collaborative Deep Learning. In Proceedings of the 2017 ACM SIGSAC Conference on Computer and Communications Security, Dallas, TX, USA, 30 October–3 November 2017; CCS '17, pp. 603–618. [CrossRef]
42. Ateniese, G.; Mancini, L.V.; Spognardi, A.; Villani, A.; Vitali, D.; Felici, G. Hacking Smart Machines with Smarter Ones: How to Extract Meaningful Data from Machine Learning Classifiers. *Int. J. Secur. Netw.* **2015**, *10*, 137–150. [CrossRef]
43. Melis, L.; Song, C.; Cristofaro, E.D.; Shmatikov, V. Exploiting Unintended Feature Leakage in Collaborative Learning. *arXiv* **2018**, arXiv:cs.CR/1805.04049.
44. Ganju, K.; Wang, Q.; Yang, W.; Gunter, C.A.; Borisov, N. Property Inference Attacks on Fully Connected Neural Networks Using Permutation Invariant Representations. In Proceedings of the 2018 ACM SIGSAC Conference on Computer and Communications Security, New York, NY, USA, 15–19 October 2018; Association for Computing Machinery: New York, NY, USA; pp. 619–633. [CrossRef]
45. Zhou, J.; Chen, Y.; Shen, C.; Zhang, Y. Property Inference Attacks Against GANs. *arXiv* **2021**, arXiv:2111.07608.
46. Yin, H.; Mallya, A.; Vahdat, A.; Alvarez, J.M.; Kautz, J.; Molchanov, P. See through Gradients: Image Batch Recovery via GradInversion. In Proceedings of the 2021 IEEE/CVF Conference on Computer Vision and Pattern Recognition (CVPR), Nashville, TN, USA, 19–25 June 2021; pp. 16332–16341. [CrossRef]
47. McMahan, H.B.; Ramage, D.; Talwar, K.; Zhang, L. Learning Differentially Private Language Models Without Losing Accuracy. *arXiv* **2017**, arXiv:1710.06963.
48. Abadi, M.; Chu, A.; Goodfellow, I.; McMahan, H.B.; Mironov, I.; Talwar, K.; Zhang, L. Deep learning with differential privacy. In Proceedings of the 2016 ACM SIGSAC Conference on Computer and Communications Security, Vienna, Austria, 24–28 October 2016; pp. 308–318.
49. Geyer, R.C.; Klein, T.; Nabi, M. Differentially Private Federated Learning: A Client Level Perspective. *arXiv* **2017**, arXiv:1712.07557.
50. Choudhury, O.; Gkoulalas-Divanis, A.; Salonidis, T.; Sylla, I.; Park, Y.; Hsu, G.; Das, A. Differential Privacy-enabled Federated Learning for Sensitive Health Data. *arXiv* **2019**, arXiv:1910.02578.
51. Hu, R.; Guo, Y.; Li, H.; Pei, Q.; Gong, Y. Personalized Federated Learning With Differential Privacy. *IEEE Internet Things J.* **2020**, *7*, 9530–9539. [CrossRef]
52. Bhowmick, A.; Duchi, J.; Freudiger, J.; Kapoor, G.; Rogers, R. Protection Against Reconstruction and Its Applications in Private Federated Learning. *arXiv* **2019**, arXiv:1812.00984.
53. Liu, R.; Cao, Y.; Yoshikawa, M.; Chen, H. FedSel: Federated SGD under Local Differential Privacy with Top-k Dimension Selection. *arXiv* **2020**, arXiv:2003.10637.
54. Ni, L.; Huang, P.; Wei, Y.; Shu, M.; Zhang, J. Federated Learning Model with Adaptive Differential Privacy Protection in Medical IoT. *Wirel. Commun. Mob. Comput.* **2021**, *2021*, 8967819. [CrossRef]
55. Sun, L.; Qian, J.; Chen, X. LDP-FL: Practical Private Aggregation in Federated Learning with Local Differential Privacy. *arXiv* **2021**, arXiv:2007.15789.
56. Chamikara, M.A.P.; Liu, D.; Camtepe, S.; Nepal, S.; Grobler, M.; Bertok, P.; Khalil, I. Local Differential Privacy for Federated Learning. *arXiv* **2022**, arXiv:2202.06053.
57. Shen, X.; Jiang, H.; Chen, Y.; Wang, B.; Gao, L. PLDP-FL: Federated Learning with Personalized Local Differential Privacy. *Entropy* **2023**, *25*, 485. [CrossRef] [PubMed]
58. Girgis, A.; Data, D.; Diggavi, S. Renyi Differential Privacy of The Subsampled Shuffle Model In Distributed Learning. In *Proceedings of the Advances in Neural Information Processing Systems*; Curran Associates, Inc.: Red Hook, NY, USA, 2021; Volume 34, pp. 29181–29192.
59. Girgis, A.M.; Data, D.; Diggavi, S. Differentially Private Federated Learning with Shuffling and Client Self-Sampling. In Proceedings of the 2021 IEEE International Symposium on Information Theory (ISIT), Melbourne, Australia, 12–20 July 2021; pp. 338–343. [CrossRef]
60. Girgis, A.; Data, D.; Diggavi, S.; Kairouz, P.; Suresh, A.T. Shuffled Model of Differential Privacy in Federated Learning. In Proceedings of the 24th International Conference on Artificial Intelligence and Statistics, San Diego, CA, USA, 13–15 April 2021; pp. 2521–2529.

61. Li, Y.; Chang, T.H.; Chi, C.Y. Secure Federated Averaging Algorithm with Differential Privacy. In Proceedings of the 2020 IEEE 30th International Workshop on Machine Learning for Signal Processing (MLSP), Espoo, Finland, 21–24 September 2020; pp. 1–6. [CrossRef]
62. Yaldiz, D.N.; Zhang, T.; Avestimehr, S. Secure Federated Learning against Model Poisoning Attacks via Client Filtering. *arXiv* **2023**, arXiv:2304.00160.
63. Zhang, C.; Li, S.; Xia, J.; Wang, W.; Yan, F.; Liu, Y. BatchCrypt: Efficient Homomorphic Encryption for Cross-Silo Federated Learning. In Proceedings of the 2020 USENIX Conference on Usenix Annual Technical Conference, Boston, MA, USA; 15–17 July 2020; USENIX ATC'20.
64. Fang, H.; Qian, Q. Privacy Preserving Machine Learning with Homomorphic Encryption and Federated Learning. *Future Internet* **2021**, *13*, 94. [CrossRef]
65. Jost, C.; Lam, H.; Maximov, A.; Smeets, B.J.M. Encryption Performance Improvements of the Paillier Cryptosystem. *IACR Cryptol. ePrint Arch.* **2015**, 864. Available online: https://eprint.iacr.org/2015/864 (accessed on 2 June 2023).
66. Feng, X.; Du, H. FLZip: An Efficient and Privacy-Preserving Framework for Cross-Silo Federated Learning. In Proceedings of the 2021 IEEE International Conferences on Internet of Things (iThings) and IEEE Green Computing & Communications (GreenCom) and IEEE Cyber, Physical & Social Computing (CPSCom) and IEEE Smart Data (SmartData) and IEEE Congress on Cybermatics (Cybermatics), Melbourne, Australia, 6–8 December 2021; pp. 209–216. [CrossRef]
67. Liu, Z.; Chen, S.; Ye, J.; Fan, J.; Li, H.; Li, X. DHSA: Efficient doubly homomorphic secure aggregation for cross-silo federated learning. *J. Supercomput.* **2023**, *79*, 2819–2849. [CrossRef]
68. Shin, Y.A.; Noh, G.; Jeong, I.R.; Chun, J.Y. Securing a Local Training Dataset Size in Federated Learning. *IEEE Access* **2022**, *10*, 104135–104143. [CrossRef]
69. Jin, W.; Yao, Y.; Han, S.; Joe-Wong, C.; Ravi, S.; Avestimehr, S.; He, C. FedML-HE: An Efficient Homomorphic-Encryption-Based Privacy-Preserving Federated Learning System. *arXiv* **2023**, arXiv:2303.10837.
70. Xu, R.; Baracaldo, N.; Zhou, Y.; Anwar, A.; Ludwig, H. HybridAlpha: An Efficient Approach for Privacy-Preserving Federated Learning. In Proceedings of the Proceedings of the 12th ACM Workshop on Artificial Intelligence and Security. *arXiv* **2019**, arXiv:1912.05897.
71. Wang, T.; Ding, B.; Xu, M.; Huang, Z.; Hong, C.; Zhou, J.; Li, N.; Jha, S. Improving Utility and Security of the Shuffler-Based Differential Privacy. *Proc. VLDB Endow.* **2020**, *13*, 3545–3558. [CrossRef]
72. Bittau, A.; Erlingsson, Ú.; Maniatis, P.; Mironov, I.; Raghunathan, A.; Lie, D.; Rudominer, M.; Kode, U.; Tinnes, J.; Seefeld, B. Prochlo: Strong Privacy for Analytics in the Crowd. In Proceedings of the 26th Symposium on Operating Systems Principles, Shanghai, China, 28–31 October 2017; SOSP '17, pp. 441–459. [CrossRef]
73. Gu, X.; Li, M.; Xiong, L. PRECAD: Privacy-Preserving and Robust Federated Learning via Crypto-Aided Differential Privacy. *arXiv* **2021**, arXiv:2110.11578.
74. Sébert, A.G.; Sirdey, R.; Stan, O.; Gouy-Pailler, C. Protecting Data from all Parties: Combining FHE and DP in Federated Learning. *arXiv* **2022**, arXiv:2205.04330.
75. Roy Chowdhury, A.; Wang, C.; He, X.; Machanavajjhala, A.; Jha, S. Crypt ϵ: Crypto-Assisted Differential Privacy on Untrusted Servers. In Proceedings of the 2020 ACM SIGMOD International Conference on Management of Data, Portland, OR, USA, 14–19 June 2020; pp. 603–619. [CrossRef]
76. Liu, T.; Wang, Z.; He, H.; Shi, W.; Lin, L.; An, R.; Li, C. Efficient and Secure Federated Learning for Financial Applications. *Appl. Sci.* **2023**, *13*, 5877. [CrossRef]

Disclaimer/Publisher's Note: The statements, opinions and data contained in all publications are solely those of the individual author(s) and contributor(s) and not of MDPI and/or the editor(s). MDPI and/or the editor(s) disclaim responsibility for any injury to people or property resulting from any ideas, methods, instructions or products referred to in the content.

 *future internet*

Article

Secure Data Sharing in Federated Learning through Blockchain-Based Aggregation

Bowen Liu and Qiang Tang *

Luxembourg Institute of Science and Technology (LIST), 5, Avenue des Hauts-Fourneaux, L-4362 Esch-sur-Alzette, Luxembourg
* Correspondence: qiang.tang@list.lu

Abstract: In this paper, we explore the realm of federated learning (FL), a distributed machine learning (ML) paradigm, and propose a novel approach that leverages the robustness of blockchain technology. FL, a concept introduced by Google in 2016, allows multiple entities to collaboratively train an ML model without the need to expose their raw data. However, it faces several challenges, such as privacy concerns and malicious attacks (e.g., data poisoning attacks). Our paper examines the existing EIFFeL framework, a protocol for decentralized real-time messaging in continuous integration and delivery pipelines, and introduces an enhanced scheme that leverages the trustworthy nature of blockchain technology. Our scheme eliminates the need for a central server and any other third party, such as a public bulletin board, thereby mitigating the risks associated with the compromise of such third parties.

Keywords: federated learning; privacy-preserving; blockchain

1. Introduction

With the advancement of big data and artificial intelligence (AI) technologies, the challenge of securely and reliably training machine learning (ML) models on distributed and heterogeneous data sources without compromising privacy and integrity has become increasingly prominent. The term federated learning (FL) was introduced by Google in 2016, at a time when the use and misuse of personal data were gaining global attention. The Cambridge Analytica scandal awakened Facebook users and those of similar platforms to the dangers of sharing personal information online [1]. It also sparked a wider debate on the pervasive tracking of people on the internet, often without their consent. In response, many countries and regions have passed or proposed data privacy laws, such as the General Data Protection Regulation (GDPR) in Europe [2].

FL is a distributed ML paradigm that enables multiple entities to collaboratively train a model from their local data, without exposing their raw data to each other or a central server [3]. This approach stands in contrast to traditional centralized ML techniques, where local datasets are merged into one location. Therefore, FL has the potential to address the prevalent limitations and challenges in the traditional approach, particularly the critical issues of data privacy. The main application of FL is to train models on data that are sensitive, distributed, or heterogeneous, such as personal data on mobile phones or data from different organizations. For example, FL can be used to improve spam filters and recommendation tools without accessing users' emails or preferences. It can also be used to leverage data from sensors and smart devices for various tasks, such as anomaly detection, predictive maintenance, and optimization.

Despite the promises of FL, two main risks persist in the distributed and decentralized nature of the learning process, namely the privacy challenge and model quality. Privacy concerns arise from adversaries attempting to identify sensitive patterns in local updates, potentially compromising the global model [4–6]. Lyu et al. [7] provide a general discussion

Citation: Liu, B.; Tang, Q. Secure Data Sharing in Federated Learning through Blockchain-Based Aggregation. *Future Internet* **2024**, *16*, 133. https://doi.org/10.3390/fi16040133

Academic Editors: Qiang Duan, Zhihui Lu and Paolo Bellavista

Received: 19 February 2024
Revised: 4 April 2024
Accepted: 11 April 2024
Published: 15 April 2024

Copyright: © 2024 by the authors. Licensee MDPI, Basel, Switzerland. This article is an open access article distributed under the terms and conditions of the Creative Commons Attribution (CC BY) license (https://creativecommons.org/licenses/by/4.0/).

about privacy and robustness attacks against FL and provide some direction for mitigating them. The German BSI published a detailed report on specific privacy risks, such as membership inference attacks and model inversion attacks [8]. Simultaneously, in terms of model quality, integrity challenges stem from participants acting maliciously by injecting poisoned or malformed inputs during the FL process, where even a single malicious input can have a significant impact [9,10]. Apart from these risks, there are also other related concerns for FL in practice, and a comprehensive survey on them is provided in [11]. To mitigate these risks, various solutions have been proposed. For example, with secure aggregation, instead of sharing the plaintext local update, only masked updates are transmitted, so that the server can aggregate the global model correctly without the knowledge of individual updates [12,13]. In addition, differential privacy is also widely used, adding noise to the exchanged values to provide additional robustness [14,15]. In the literature, one notable contribution to addressing these challenges is the EIFFeL framework [16]. By leveraging a public bulletin board, EIFFeL aims to preserve the privacy of input data from different clients as well as guarantee the integrity of the inputs from these clients (e.g., the value of inputs should be in proper ranges).

Contribution and Organization

As privacy and integrity are two key challenges hindering the widespread adoption of FL, this paper is dedicated to investigating a rigorous solution to address these challenges. Referring to [11], FL can be categorized into two categories: cross-silo FL and cross-device FL. In this paper, we focus on the cross-silo setting, wherein model training occurs on siloed data belonging to several clients from different organizations. These clients can communicate with third-party servers in a synchronous manner.

Our first contribution involves investigating the architecture and workflow of the EIFFeL framework along with analyzing its security guarantees. To this end, we identify specific areas where the EIFFeL framework exhibits potential risks, such as the compromise of the central server and/or the public bulletin board. We also highlight other efficiency concerns.

Our second contribution involves adapting the EIFFeL framework to leverage the security guarantees of blockchain platforms. To this end, we adapt the operations in the EIFFeL framework so that the functions of both the central server and the public bulletin board can be replaced by a blockchain platform. To address the challenge posed by blockchain's limitation to only perform deterministic operations and the requirement that no direct communication among clients is necessary, we integrate the Burmester-Desmedt group key exchange protocol into our solution, to make sure that the clients can jointly compute the final parameter update without breaching its confidentiality.

Our last contribution involves implementing our solution and shedding some light on the computational complexities. Note that the proposed solution is blockchain platform agnostic, so we omit the implementation details related to the blockchain part. This is earmarked for future work.

It is worth noting that privacy protection for FL is a very challenging task. Even with secure aggregation, some privacy risks may still remain [11]. To address this, differential privacy, particularly local differential privacy, can be applied. Since such measures are used to secure aggregation and can be applied independently, we leave this out in this paper.

The paper consists of the following sections: we present the background and motivation of FL and blockchain in Section 2. In Section 3, we review the design and analysis of the EIFFeL framework. Following this, an enhanced scheme is proposed; its security analysis, along with a demonstration of performance, is presented in Section 4. Finally, we summarize our work in Section 5.

2. Preliminary

2.1. Federated Learning Approach

FL represents a decentralized paradigm that is reshaping traditional ML methods. In this collaborative approach, multiple clients contribute to training a shared model without divulging raw data. Assuming a central server and n clients C_i ($1 \leq i \leq n$), a high-level overview of the FL workflow is summarized in Figure 1; we refer to the relevant handbook for more details, such as [3].

1. Initial phase:
    (a). The central server defines an initial model, m_{init}, which can be chosen based on prior knowledge or domain expertise.
    (b). Each client, C_i, synchronizes the initial model, m_{init}, from the server, and sets its local model to be $m_i = m_{init}$.
2. The following training steps are iterated for a certain number of iterations until a satisfactory model is achieved. Here, each iteration is called an **Epoch**.
    (a). **Local model training**: Each client, C_i, trains its local model using its local dataset, D_i, and obtains a new local model with new parameters, u_i.
    (b). **Model parameter sharing**: Each client, C_i, sends the newly generated model parameters, u_i, to the central server.
    (c). **Model parameter aggregation**: The central server aggregates the model updates received from the clients to produce an aggregate update, $\mathcal{U}$, and sends it back to each client.
    (d). **Model update**: Each client, C_i, resets its local model with the parameters, $\mathcal{U}$.

Figure 1. Federated learning approach.

As we mentioned in Section 1, while FL enhances privacy by not sharing raw data with the central server or other devices, a crucial concern arises: the trustworthiness of the central server. Two major challenges need to be considered: privacy challenge and integrity challenge, as explained in Section 3.

2.2. Blockchain Overview

A blockchain is a chain of blocks; each block contains a list of transactions. These blocks are linked and secured through cryptographic hashes, forming a continuous, unalterable chain. The decentralized nature of a blockchain means that no single entity has control over the entire network, mitigating the risk of a central point of failure. Transactions in a blockchain are grouped into blocks, and each block includes a reference to the previous block, creating a chronological chain of events. Miners, i.e., participants in the network with computational power, play a crucial role in validating and adding transactions to the blockchain. This sequential structure ensures the integrity of the data, as altering information in one block would require changing all subsequent blocks, which is an impractical and computationally infeasible task. For a more comprehensive review, we refer to comprehensive references, such as [17–19]. Irrespective of the variations in blockchain structures, the following properties are anticipated:

- Democracy and decentralized control: In systems utilizing proof of work (PoW) as the consensus mechanism in permissionless scenarios, everyone has the potential to act as a miner, possessing equal privileges to generate and approve blocks for the blockchain. Although variations may exist in different cases, the overarching principle remains: blockchain technology eliminates the need for a singular, fully trusted entity, thereby averting the vulnerability of a single point of failure.
- Integrity and immutability: In the absence of an attacker or a coalition of attackers dominating the consensus process, such as when more than 51% of the computing power in the Bitcoin blockchain is handled by semi-honest miners, it becomes infeasible to modify agreed-upon blocks in the consensus.

- Consistency: Despite potential attacks from robust adversaries, the chain upholds a singular and consistent perspective, as outlined by the aforementioned assumptions. However, it is essential to note that deviations from predefined rules by nodes can lead to the generation of forks, resulting in different perspectives among participants, as observed in scenarios like Ethereum.

These properties enhance auditability and transparency and improve the overall trustworthiness of the system. Some have conceptualized blockchain as a social trust machine (https://www.economist.com/leaders/2015/10/31/the-trust-machine (accessed on 1 April 2024)). The trust users place in blockchain systems predominantly stems from the cryptographic viewpoint that the majority of miners will act as semi-honest participants. The semi-honest assumption essentially asserts that these miners will respect the predetermined protocols, carrying out actions exactly as specified and programmed in the blockchain software. In particular, the assumption rules out the possibility of collusion among miners to disrupt the regular operations of the blockchain.

There is a vast body of literature on utilizing blockchain to address security issues in FL, more information can be found in recent survey papers, such as [20,21].

3. EIFFeL Framework and Security Analysis

The EIFFeL framework [16] presents an innovative FL approach that effectively tackles the challenges of data privacy and integrity. Moving beyond the conventional server–client architecture, as outlined in Section 2.1, EIFFeL incorporates a public bulletin board, which broadcasts intermediary information for secure aggregation and integrity checks. This unique architecture positions all clients as verifiers for each other, with the server playing a collective role. In more detail, secure aggregation enables each client to conceal its parameter update within the aggregated value, by leveraging secret sharing and encryption techniques. The integrity property is ensured through non-interactive proof techniques and the adoption of a public bulletin board. In summary, EIFFeL is designed to tolerate multiple malicious client interventions while ensuring the proper aggregation of model parameters.

3.1. Threat Model

In EIFFeL, it assumes that all honest clients correctly follow the protocol and have properly structured inputs. Two types of malicious adversaries are considered:

- Malicious clients: Multiple malicious clients can arbitrarily deviate from the protocol. They may (1) compromise the aggregate by submitting malformed updates; (2) cause the honest clients to complete an integrity check; (3) violate the privacy of honest clients, which may collude with the server.
- Malicious server: It aims to violate the privacy of clients by trying to recover their raw updates. A malicious server may (1) mark the inputs from honest clients as invalid; (2) mark the inputs from malicious clients as valid, so as to decide which one will be aggregated.

3.2. Scheme Architecture and Workflow

As mentioned previously, EIFFeL consists of a public bulletin board $\mathcal{B}$, a single server $\mathcal{S}$, and n clients, $\mathcal{C}_i$ ($1 \leq i \leq n$). It is designed to tolerate a limited number of malicious $m < \lfloor \frac{n}{3} \rfloor$. A high-level sketch of the interactions among a client and other entities is shown in Figure 2 while a detailed description of the EIFFeL scheme is shown in Figures 3 and 4. Note that, for simplicity, we only show one client in the diagram. The numbering of the iteration steps corresponds to the description in Figure 4. In order to ensure (1) privacy for all honest clients, and (2) input integrity, where the server is motivated to verify if all individual updates are well-formed, all clients function as verifiers for each other, while the server also participates collectively in this role. Verification remains achievable even in the presence of m malicious clients.

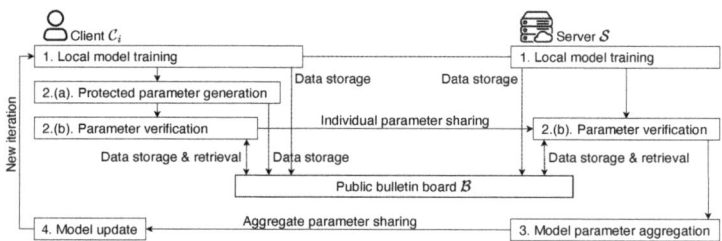

Figure 2. System Architecture of the EIFFeL Scheme.

To achieve the designated security guarantees, EIFFeL relies on several cryptographic building blocks (we omit the detailed definition of algorithms; refer to [16] for the full definitions), with each serving a specific purpose in enhancing the scheme's security:

- Shamir's t-out-of-n secret sharing scheme [22]: This cryptographic method facilitates the distribution of a secret among n participants, and it requires at least t participants (the threshold) to collectively reconstruct the original secret. Two algorithms are defined, $SS.share(\cdot)$ is for generating secret sharing and $SS.recon(\cdot)$ is for reconstructing the secret. Assuming m malicious clients, t is set as $m+1$ in EIFFeL.
- Reed–Solomon error correcting code [23]: It is an error-correcting code used in digital communication and data storage. Reed–Solomon codes add redundant symbols to the original data, allowing the receiver to detect and correct errors during transmission. EIFFeL uses the $[n, m+1, n-m]$ Reed–Solomon error correcting code, where any set of shares containing $m < \lfloor \frac{n}{3} \rfloor$ malicious shares can be used to recover the secret with $robustRecon(\cdot)$.
- Key agreement protocol: It enables two or more parties to agree upon a shared secret key. It involves three algorithms: $KA.param(\cdot)$ is used to generate the parameters, $KA.gen(\cdot)$ is used to generate a public/private key pair, and $KA.agree(\cdot)$ is used to agree on a common secret key.
- Authenticated encryption: A cryptographic process that combines encryption and message authentication to guarantee the integrity and confidentiality of transmitted data. It includes the algorithms of key generation $AE.gen(\cdot)$, encryption $AE.enc(\cdot)$, and decryption $AE.dec(\cdot)$.
- Secret-shared non-interactive proofs (SNIPs) [24]: These are cryptographic protocols that allow multiple parties to jointly prove the truth of a statement without revealing their individual inputs. These proofs are constructed in such a way that the validity of the statement can be verified without requiring interaction between the parties. A public validation predicate $Valid(\cdot)$ is defined to conduct the integrity check.

The EIFFeL framework includes a setup phase and a model training phase. In the model training phase, each training epoch consists of four primary steps, as summarized in Figure 1: (1) local model training, (2) model parameter sharing, (3) model parameter aggregation, and (4) model update. We briefly recap the set and training phases in Figure 3 and Figure 4, respectively, which visually encapsulate the essence of its mechanism.

- Setup:
  - All parties are given the security parameter, k, the number of clients, n, the threshold for malicious clients, m, and a field $\mathbb{F}$ for secret sharing usage. All clients honestly generate $pp \leftarrow KA.gen(k)$, and the server, S, initializes the malicious client list, $C^* = \emptyset$, and lists $Flag[i] = \emptyset$ for clients that have flagged the client, C_i, as malicious.

Figure 3. Setup of EIFFeL scheme.

1. **Local model training**:
   Each client $\mathcal{C}_i$:
   - Generates its key pair $(pk_i, sk_i) \xleftarrow{\$} KA.gen(pp)$ and announces the public key on the public bulletin board $\mathcal{B}$.

   Server $\mathcal{S}$:
   - Publishes the validation predicate $Valid(\cdot)$ on the public bulletin board $\mathcal{B}$.

2. **Model parameter sharing**: The following steps are performed:
   (a). Each client, $\mathcal{C}_i$, generates its protected parameters as follows:

   i. Establishes $n-1$ common secret keys $sk_{i,j} \leftarrow KA.agree(pk_j, sk_i)$ with each of the other clients.

   ii. Generates a proof $\pi_i = (h_i, (a_i, b_i, c_i)), h_i \in \mathbb{F}[X], (a_i, b_i, c_i) \in \mathbb{F}^3, a_i \cdot b_i = c_i$ for the computation $Valid(u_i) = 1$, where $u_i \in \mathbb{F}^d$ is its local update with d dimensions.

   iii. Creates shares of its update u_i for all clients, denoted as $\{(1, u_{i,1}], \cdots, (n, u_{i,n}), \Psi_{u_i}\} \leftarrow SS.share(u, [n], m+1)$.

   iv. Creates shares of its proof π_i for other clients: $\{(1, h_{i,1}], \cdots, (n, h_{i,n}), \Psi_{h_i}\} \leftarrow SS.share(h_i, [n] \setminus i, m+1), \{(1, a_{i,1}], \cdots, (n, a_{i,n}), \Psi_{a_i}\} \leftarrow SS.share(a_i, [n] \setminus i, m+1), \{(1, b_{i,1}], \cdots, (n, b_{i,n}), \Psi_{b_i}\} \leftarrow SS.share(b_i, [n] \setminus i, m-1), \{(1, c_{i,1}], \cdots, (n, c_{i,n}), \Psi_{c_i}\} \leftarrow SS.share(c_i, [n] \setminus i, m+1)$.

   v. Publishes the encrypted proof strings, $\forall \mathcal{C}_j \in \mathcal{C}_{\setminus i}, \overline{(j, u_{j,1})||(j, \pi_{j,1})} \leftarrow AE.enc_{sk_{i,j}}((j, u_{i,j})||(j, \pi_{i,j}))$, $\pi_{i,j} = h_{i,j}||a_{i,j}||b_{i,j}||c_{i,j}$ on the public bulletin board $\mathcal{B}$ with its check strings $(\Psi_{u_i}, \Psi_{\pi_i})$.

   (b). The protected parameters are verified as follows:

   (i) Verifying validity of secret shares:
       Each client $\mathcal{C}_i$:
       (A). Retrieves and decrypts the shares pertaining to it $(i, u_{j,i})||(i, \pi_{j,i}) \leftarrow AE.dec_{pk_{i,j}}(\overline{(i, u_{j,i})||(i, \pi_{j,i})})$.
       (B). Verifies the shares $u_{j,i}(\pi_{j,i})$ using check string $\Psi_{u_i}(\Psi_{\pi_i})$.
       (C). If any share fails to be decrypted or verified, flag its creator on $\mathcal{B}$.

       Server $\mathcal{S}$:
       (A). Upon receiving a report (e.g., $\mathcal{C}_i$ flags $\mathcal{C}_j$), updates $Flag[j] = Flag[j] \cup \mathcal{C}_i$.
       (B). Updates $\mathcal{C}^*$ as follows:
       - If $|Flag[i]| > m$, $\mathcal{C}_i$ is marked as malicious: $\mathcal{C}^* = \mathcal{C}^* \cup \mathcal{C}_i$.
       - If any client, $\mathcal{C}_i$, reported more than m clients, it is considered as malicious: $\mathcal{C}^* = \mathcal{C}^* \cup \mathcal{C}_i$.
       - For a client $\mathcal{C}_i$ that has been reported, but with $|Flag[i]| \leq m$, server $\mathcal{S}$ intervenes for further verification. $\mathcal{S}$ requests the shares (in clear) from $\mathcal{C}_i$ for the clients who flagged it (e.g., $((j, u_{i,j})||(j, \pi_{i,j}))$ generated by $\mathcal{C}_i$ for $\mathcal{C}_j$), and verifies the contents with the relevant check string (e.g., $(\Psi_{u_i}, \Psi_{\pi_i})$). If the verification fails, $\mathcal{C}_i$ is marked as malicious; otherwise, $\mathcal{C}_j$ is instructed to use the released share for its computations.
       (C). Announces the updated $\mathcal{C}^*$ on the public bulletin board $\mathcal{B}$.

   (ii) Generation of proof summaries by the clients:
       Server $\mathcal{S}$:
       - Announces a random number, $r \in \mathbb{F}$, on the public bulletin board, $\mathcal{B}$.

       Each client $\mathcal{C}_i$:
       - Generates a summary, $\sigma_{j,i}$, of the proof string, $\pi_{j,i}$, based on r and SNIP, $\forall \mathcal{C}_j \notin \mathcal{C}^*$, and publishes it on the public bulletin, $\mathcal{B}$.

   (iii) Verification of proof summaries by the server:
       Server $\mathcal{S}$:
       - Collects and verifies all proof summaries from $\mathcal{C} \setminus \mathcal{C}^*$ with $robustRecon(\cdot)$, and updates $\mathcal{C}^*$ based on the result.

   (iv) Each client $\mathcal{C}_i$:
       - If $\mathcal{C}_i \in \mathcal{C}^*$, it can initiate a dispute by transmitting the transcript of the reconstruction of σ_i. If any successful dispute occurs, all clients abort the protocol, since the server, $\mathcal{S}$, is considered malicious by withholding the valid updates.
       - Otherwise, it sends the aggregate $\mathcal{U}_i = \sum_{\mathcal{C}_j \notin \mathcal{C}^*} u_{j,i}$ to the server $\mathcal{S}$.

3. **Model parameter aggregation**: Server $\mathcal{S}$ recovers the final aggregate, $\mathcal{U} \leftarrow robustRecon(\{i, \mathcal{U}_i\}_{\mathcal{C}_j \notin \mathcal{C}^*})$, and sends it to clients.

4. **Model update**: Each client, $\mathcal{C}_i$, resets its local model with the parameters, $\mathcal{U}$.

Figure 4. One iteration/epoch of the EIFFeL scheme.

3.3. Analysis of the EIFFeL Framework

In [16], the authors performed an analysis of the EIFFeL framework and showed that the framework achieves the pre-defined privacy and integrity properties. In the following, we analyze the assumptions made in their analysis and also demonstrate several observations on the design of the framework.

First of all, the existence of the required public bulletin board and the associated assumptions is very tricky. To guarantee the security of EIFFeL, the public bulletin board should offer the following guarantees:

- It should be corrupt-resistant against all entities, including the server, clients, and other attackers. The data should not be changed, deleted, or manipulated by malicious entities in any manner.
- It should be able to validate the identities of clients (and the server) according to some public key infrastructure (PKI). By default, some PKI information should be stored on the bulletin board so that it can validate the identity claims of its users.
- It should be able to establish a secure channel with its users so that the integrity and authenticity of the users' data can be guaranteed during the transmission.

Public bulletin boards have been used in many scenarios [25], and they can certainly play an important role in FL. However, how to achieve the last two guarantees is not trivial. In particular, the involvement of a PKI means that there will be another fully trusted third party. The trust relationship among all the entities in the solution needs to be clarified in order to guarantee that all threats are properly present.

Secondly, there is some ambiguity in remark 1 of reference [16]. It states that EIFFeL prevents the server from "Mark the input of an honest client as invalid and include it in the final aggregate". In fact, the server can manipulate the final aggregate without being noticed, in step 3 of the model parameter aggregation. This is equivalent to invalidating the input of honest clients, as the final aggregate no longer appears to be an aggregation of inputs from all honest clients. This implies that EIFFeL cannot guarantee the integrity of the aggregate in the presence of a malicious server. Note that this observation does not conflict with the desired security properties, i.e., against the server, only privacy is expected. In addition, if the server deviates from the protocol, Lemma 4 from [16] will not hold. This lemma states that "The final aggregate must contain the updates of all honest clients or the protocol is aborted". In fact, the server can maliciously change the aggregate without being detected, as we said before. Although this observation does not show a security flaw in the EIFFeL framework, we regard it as a drawback, and ideally, we should avoid such potential "attacks". This is also motivated by some recent findings (e.g., [26]), which show that failure of integrity (e.g., data poisoning) can lead to privacy breaches.

Thirdly, there are two inefficient designs in the solution. One is about the parameter generation in Step 1 and the key agreement at the beginning of Step 2. During the FL process, all four steps will be iterated hundreds of times in order to reach convergence. According to the description, the key materials need to be repeated in each iteration. This unnecessarily increases the complexity of the solution. These parameters can be set up in the setup phase so that the key materials can be used in all the training iterations (or, epochs). The other involves the usage of authenticated encryption. In the solution, it is assumed that the public bulletin board does not allow any manipulation of the stored data; therefore, the encrypted data in Step 2 will not be manipulated regardless of whether the encryption is authenticated or not. Therefore, standard symmetric encryption will suffice.

Fourthly, the result of the server's operation in Step 2 is confusing. For client C_i, which has been reported but $|Flag[i]| \leq m$, server S intervenes for further verification. S requests the shares (in clear) from C_i for the clients who flagged it (e.g., $((j, u_{i,j})||(j, \pi_{i,j}))$ generated by C_i for C_j), and verifies the contents with the relevant check string (e.g., $(\Psi_{u_i}, \Psi_{\pi_i})$). If the verification fails, C_i is marked as malicious; otherwise, C_j is instructed to use the released share for its computations. The server's operation occurs because either C_i is maliciously flagged C_j or C_j is sent the wrong ciphertext to C_i, on purpose (note that C_j can disclose the right plaintext to make the server's verification pass). However, neither party will be determined as malicious according to the protocol. It is unclear why this is the case.

4. The Enhanced Scheme

In this section, we describe the enhanced scheme that eliminates the need for any third-party server or bulletin board by integrating blockchain technology. It is worth emphasizing that this scheme aims to address the existing privacy and security challenges in the EIFFeL framework, particularly those related to the third-party bulletin board. Certainly, in our design, we attempt to minimize the complexity overhead for all the involved entities.

Our scheme eliminates the need for a central server and any other third party, such as a public bulletin board, thereby mitigating the risks associated with the compromise of such third parties.

Similar to EIFFeL, the enhanced scheme assumes a blockchain platform and multiple (n) clients, and it relies on the same building blocks. In each iteration/epoch, the interactions are shown in Figure 5, where the setup phase is shown in Figure 6 and the numbering of steps corresponds to the description in Figure 7. The overall design of the enhanced scheme is agnostic to any blockchain platform; however, the interaction details between clients and the blockchain (i.e., the smart contracts) may differ in the implementation. To keep the generality and simplicity, we skip the details in our description. The design of smart contracts for the proposed scheme is quite straightforward based on the following fact: when invoking a smart contract, the requester (i.e., a client) can pass the location of necessary input parameters (i.e., where these data are located on the blockchain) so that the smart contract can fetch the data and perform the desired operations in a deterministic manner.

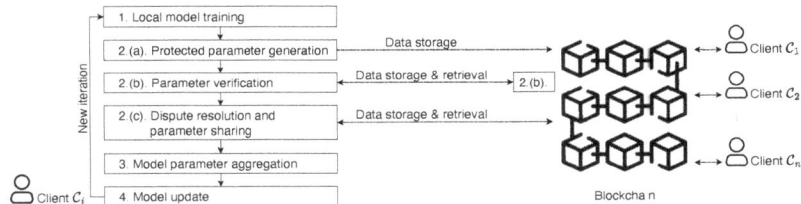

Figure 5. System architecture of enhanced scheme.

To start FL training, the setup phase is depicted in Figure 6, and the training epoch, shown in Figure 7, will be iterated until a satisfactory global model is achieved. By its nature, information stored on a blockchain is not supposed to be updated. In our description in Figure 7, if a piece of information is stored in the blockchain, then it means that a transaction is made to the blockchain to store the information. When we say that a piece of information is updated (e.g., $\mathcal{C}^*$), we simply mean that a new version of this information is stored on the blockchain, and all follow-up computations should be based on this new version of information.

- Setup:
  - Prepare all the necessary smart contracts for the chosen **blockchain**.
  - Generate a security parameter, k, the number of clients, n, the threshold for malicious clients, m, and a filed $\mathbb{F}$ for secret sharing usage. Initialize the malicious client list, $\mathcal{C}^* = \emptyset$, and lists $Flag[i] = \emptyset$ of clients that have flagged the client, $\mathcal{C}_i$, as malicious. A validation predicate, $Valid(\cdot)$, is chosen to guarantee integrity, and a collision-resistant hash function H is chosen. All the parameters are stored on the **blockchain**.
  - A group, $\mathbb{G}$, and its generator, g, are generated for the Burmester-Desmedt group key agreement protocol (Burmester et al., 2005); $\mathbb{G}$ and g are stored on the **blockchain**.
  - Generate $pp \leftarrow KA.gen(k)$ for a two-party key agreement scheme, KA. Based on pp, each client, $\mathcal{C}_i$, generates its key pair $(pk_i, sk_i) \xleftarrow{\$} KA.gen(pp)$ and stores the public key on the **blockchain**. Note that pp is also stored on the **blockchain**. Choose a standard symmetric key encryption scheme, SE (e.g., AES in the counter mode), and store its information on the **blockchain**.
  - Each client, $\mathcal{C}_i$, establishes $n - 1$ common secret keys $sk_{i,j} \leftarrow KA.agree(pk_j, sk_i)$ with every other client. It stores the hash values $H(sk_{i,j}||i||j)$ ($1 \leq j \neq i \leq n$) on the **blockchain**.
  - All clients check the hash values of secret keys generated by others and resolve any mistakes, if there are any. Note that $sk_{i,j}$ can be computed by both clients, $\mathcal{C}_i$ and $\mathcal{C}_j$, so that they can check each other's hash values.

Figure 6. Setup of the Enhanced scheme [27].

1. **Local model training**:
   Each client $\mathcal{C}_i$:
   - Generates its local update, $u_i \in \mathbb{F}^d$, which is a value of d dimensions.

2. **Model parameter sharing**: The following steps are performed:

   (a). Each client, $\mathcal{C}_i$, generates its protected parameters as follows:
      i. Generates a proof $\pi_i = (h_i, (a_i, b_i, c_i)), h_i \in \mathbb{F}[X], (a_i, b_i, c_i) \in \mathbb{F}^3, a_i \cdot b_i = c_i$ for the computation $Valid(u_i) = 1$.
      ii. Creates shares of its update u_i for all clients, denoted as $\{(1, u_{i,1}), \cdots, (n, u_{i,n}), \Psi_{u_i}\} \leftarrow SS.share(u, [n], m+1)$.
      iii. Creates shares of its proof π_i for other clients: $\{(1, h_{i,1}), \cdots, (n, h_{i,n}), \Psi_{h_i}\} \leftarrow SS.share(h_i, [n] \setminus i, m+1)$, $\{(1, a_{i,1}], \cdots, (n, a_{i,n}), \Psi_{a_i}\} \leftarrow SS.share(a_i, [n] \setminus i, m+1)$, $\{(1, b_{i,1}], \cdots, (n, b_{i,n}), \Psi_{b_i}\} \leftarrow SS.share(b_i, [n] \setminus i, m+1)$, $\{(1, c_{i,1}], \cdots, (n, c_{i,n}), \Psi_{c_i}\} \leftarrow SS.share(c_i, [n] \setminus i, m+1)$.
      iv. Publishes the encrypted proof strings $\forall \mathcal{C}_j \in \mathcal{C}_{\setminus i}, \overline{(j, u_{j,1})||(j, \pi_{j,i})} \leftarrow SE.enc_{sk_{i,j}}((j, u_{j,i})||(j, \pi_{i,j}))$, $\pi_{i,j} = h_{i,j} || a_{i,j} || b_{i,j} || c_{i,j}$ with its check strings $(\Psi_{u_i}, \Psi_{\pi_i})$ on the **blockchain**.

   (b). The protected parameters are verified as follows:
      i. Verifies validity of secret shares:
         Each client $\mathcal{C}_i$:
         (A). Retrieves and decrypts the shares pertaining to it: $(i, u_{j,i})||(i, \pi_{j,i}) \leftarrow SE.dec_{pk_{i,j}}(\overline{(i, u_{j,i})||(i, \pi_{j,i})})$.
         (B). Verifies the shares $u_{j,i}(\pi_{j,i})$ using the check string $\Psi_{u_i}(\Psi_{\pi_i})$.
         (C). If any share fails to be decrypted or verified, flag its creator on the **blockchain**.
         Blockchain (via smart contract):
         (A). Upon receiving a report (e.g., $\mathcal{C}_i$ flags $\mathcal{C}_j$), updates $Flag[j] = Flag[j] \cup \mathcal{C}_i$.
         (B). Updates $\mathcal{C}^*$ as follows:
            - If $|Flag[i]| > m$, $\mathcal{C}_i$ is marked as malicious: $\mathcal{C}^* = \mathcal{C}^* \cup \mathcal{C}_i$.
            - If any client, $\mathcal{C}_i$, is reported as more than m clients, it is considered malicious: $\mathcal{C}^* = \mathcal{C}^* \cup \mathcal{C}_i$.
            - For every client $\mathcal{C}_j$ that has been reported, but $|Flag[j]| \leq m$, suppose that $\mathcal{C}_i$ has flagged $\mathcal{C}_j$; perform the following steps:
               (I). Asks $\mathcal{C}_i$ and $\mathcal{C}_j$ to publish $sk_{i,j}$ and $sk_{j,i}$ on the **blockchain**.
               (II). Compares these keys to the hash values from the setup phase; if some of them do not match, then flag the owner and update $\mathcal{C}^*$. Note that these keys should be equal and their hash values should be equal to that stored in the setup phase.
               (III). Uses $sk_{i,j}$ to decrypt the encrypted share from $\mathcal{C}_j$ to $\mathcal{C}_i$, and verifies the result. If everything passes, update $\mathcal{C}^* = \mathcal{C}^* \cup \mathcal{C}_i$; otherwise, update $\mathcal{C}^* = \mathcal{C}^* \cup \mathcal{C}_j$.
      ii. Generation of proof summaries:
         Blockchain (via smart contract):
         - Hash the current data on **the blockchain** to generate a random number $r \in \mathbb{F}$.
         Each client $\mathcal{C}_i$:
         - Generates a summary $\sigma_{j,i}$ of the proof string $\pi_{j,i}$ based on r and SNIP, $\forall \mathcal{C}_j \notin \mathcal{C}^*$, and publishes it on the **blockchain**.
      iii. Verification of proof summaries:
         Blockchain (via smart contract):
         - Collects and verifies all proof summaries from $\mathcal{C} \setminus \mathcal{C}^*$ with $robustRecon(\cdot)$, and updates $\mathcal{C}^*$ based on the result.

   (c). Each client $\mathcal{C}_i$:
      i. If $\mathcal{C}_i \in \mathcal{C}^*$, it can raise a dispute. If any successful dispute occurs, all clients abort the protocol.
      ii. Selects a random number, r_i, and generates the Burmester-Desmedt group key agreement material g^{r_i}, publishes g^{r_i} on the **blockchain**.
      iii. Generates $tk_i = (\frac{g^{r_{i+1}}}{g^{r_{i-1}}})^{r_i}$ and publishes it on the **blockchain**.
      iv. Computes the Burmester-Desmedt group key as $ek_i = (tk_{i-1})^{l \cdot r_i} \cdot (tk_i)^{n-1} \cdots tk_{i-2}$, supposing l clients are participating at this stage; publishes $H(ek_i || i)$ on the **blockchain**.
      v. Checks that all other clients possess the same ephemeral key as ek_i.
      vi. If so, publishes the aggregate $SE.enc_{ek_i}(\mathcal{U}_i)$, where $\mathcal{U}_i = \sum_{\mathcal{C}_j \notin \mathcal{C}^*} u_{j,i}$, on the **blockchain**.

3. **Model parameter aggregation**: Each client, $\mathcal{C}_i$, recovers the final aggregate $\mathcal{U} \leftarrow robustRecon(\{x, \mathcal{U}_x\}_{\mathcal{C}_x \notin \mathcal{C}^*})$, after obtaining all the $\mathcal{U}_x$ after decryption.

4. **Model update**: Each client, $\mathcal{C}_i$, resets its local model with the parameters, $\mathcal{U}$.

Figure 7. Training procedures in one iteration/epoch.

4.1. Security Analysis

Similar to other setup phases in cryptosystems, we assume this phase is performed in a trusted manner. Depending on the precise FL scenario, some trusted entity might be needed to supervise and help carry out this phase. The chosen blockchain platform should be tamper-resistant and will not collude with any entity in the FL system (i.e., none of the clients should be able to collude with the blockchain). For simplicity, we assume there is a secure channel between the blockchain and any client, in the sense that the client will be authenticated for its access to the blockchain, and the communication is protected regarding its integrity. Similar to EIFFeL, we assume that, at most, $m < \lfloor \frac{n}{3} \rfloor$ malicious users are tolerated, and the threshold of Shamir's t-out-of-n secret sharing scheme is also set as $t = m + 1$. We omit attacks with the single purpose of denial of service (DoS). In practice, such attacks can be prevented by additional security mechanisms.

In comparison to the EIFFeL scheme, the major philosophy of the enhanced scheme is to use the blockchain platform to replace both the public bulletin board and the server. To this end, all the actions performed by the blockchain platform are deterministic. Apart from the new setup phase, the following major changes have been made: (1) regarding the fourth comment in Section 3.3, a new verification procedure has been proposed for the blockchain platform to trace the malicious client. (2) Leveraging the blockchain platform, the clients execute a Burmester-Desmedt group key agreement protocol [27] to generate a shared group key. The validity of the key is checked as well. (3) Instead of asking a third party to compute the aggregate, the clients store the encrypted shares under the group key on the blockchain platform, so that they can recover the aggregate locally. In contrast to the EIFFeL scheme, the need for a dedicated server has been eliminated. As a result, the risks following the compromise of the server are also eliminated. By asking the clients to share the credentials and intermediary results on the blockchain platform, the clients can check by themselves the validity of the credentials and results from other users. This is facilitated by making the validation operations deterministic.

It is worth stressing that the enhanced scheme preserves all the privacy and integrity properties of the EIFFeL scheme due to the fact that all the security and integrity mechanisms have been kept in the new scheme.

4.2. Performance Analysis

We implemented the enhanced scheme in Python with several existing libraries, such as NumPy [28] and Cryptography [29] (the source code of the enhanced scheme instantiation is available at https://github.com/MoienBowen/Blockchair.-Federated-Learning (accessed on 1 April 2024)). In the experiment, we used a PC as the simulation platform, with an Intel® Core™i7-4770 CPU @ 3.4 GHz processor with 16 GB RAM.

Dataset. Given our primary focus on 5G security, we selected a dataset tailored to this domain: the 5G-NIDD dataset [30], a robust compilation of network intrusion data specifically designed for 5G wireless networks, containing 1,215,890 records. This dataset was meticulously generated on an operational 5G testbed, part of the 5G test network (5GTN) at the University of Oulu, Finland. It features an extensive range of simulated attack scenarios, offering a valuable dataset for AI/ML model training. Detailed categories and their respective distributions are presented in Table 1.

Setup. Our parameter selection was guided by our goal of 128-bit security. For example, we used the Secp256r1 curve for the Burmester-Desmedt group key agreement protocol [27], AES-CTR for encryption, SHA-256 for hashing, and a 256-bit prime field as $\mathbb{F}$. Moreover, we considered that there were $n = 50, 100, 150$, and 200 clients, tolerating up to $m = \frac{n}{10}$ malicious ones, with $d = 1000$ as the size of the update gradient vector. Each client owned 24,053, 12,156, 8100, and 6075 records, respectively (each category of the dataset was divided equally and randomly into n copies). We omitted the consensus time of the blockchain but this did not affect the representation of the protocol performance.

Table 1. The 5G-NIDD dataset attack categories and distribution.

Category	Number of Records
Benign	477,737
ICMPFlood	1155
HTTPFlood	140,812
SlowrateDos	73,124
SYNFlood	9721
SYNScan	20,043
TCPConnectScan	20,052
UDPFlood	457,340
UDPScan	15,906

Results. In Table 2, we emphasize the runtime of Step 2—model parameter sharing and Step 3—model parameter aggregation, as the performance mainly depends on the number of clients. The values represent the average execution times of single iterations/epochs over 10 runs.

Table 2. Runtime of proposed scheme in ms.

Step	Participant	Runtime (ms)			
		n = 50	100	150	200
2.(a).	Client	491.37	974.21	1477.88	1990.13
	Blockchain	-	-	-	-
2.(b).	Client	1073.43	2106.11	3204.75	4283.49
	Blockchain	995.14	1997.64	3091.71	4107.93
2.(c).	Client	2079.58	4215.38	6314.49	8284.27
	Blockchain	-	-	-	-
3.	Client	171.21	354.14	498.87	637.61
	Blockchain	-	-	-	-

Regarding the blockchain in Step 2, we calculate the computational time on the PC we use. In practice, the computational time will be based on the mining nodes. Moreover, the complexity will also come from the consensus protocol used in the blockchain platform. Obtaining precise running time statistics on chosen blockchain platforms will be looked at in future work.

5. Conclusions

This paper culminates with an in-depth discussion of the enhanced scheme for FL, which harnesses the power of blockchain technology. The scheme eliminates the need for a dedicated server and a public bulletin board in the EIFFeL scheme, thereby reducing the risks associated with the compromise of these entities. The clients share credentials and intermediary results on the blockchain platform, allowing them to verify the validity of credentials and results from other users. This paper provides a performance analysis of the enhanced scheme, demonstrating its efficiency and effectiveness in the realm of FL. This paper shows that blockchain technology can enhance the privacy and integrity of FL and open up new possibilities for collaborative ML in various domains.

There are several directions for future work. Here, we only mention two examples. One is to fully implement the proposed scheme, particularly by selecting a blockchain platform, and encoding the desired operations into smart contracts. This will help us understand the overall complexity of the proposed scheme. The other one is to incorporate the concept of differential privacy to further reduce the privacy risks. To this end, it is interesting to see how privacy enhancement could affect accuracy and other metrics. This will help us understand the precise trade-offs between privacy protection and the performance of FL.

Author Contributions: Conceptualization, Q.T.; formal analysis, B.L. and Q.T.; funding acquisition, B.L. and Q.T.; investigation, B.L. and Q.T.; methodology, B.L. and Q.T.; project administration, Q.T.; software, B.L.; supervision, Q.T.; validation, B.L. and Q.T.; writing—original draft, B.L. and Q.T.; writing—review and editing, B.L. and Q.T. All authors have read and agreed to the published version of the manuscript.

Funding: Bowen Liu and Qiang Tang are supported by the 5G-INSIGHT bi-lateral project (ANR-20-CE25-0015-16), funded by the Luxembourg National Research Fund (FNR) and the French National Research Agency (ANR).

Data Availability Statement: Data are contained within the article.

Conflicts of Interest: The authors declare no conflicts of interest.

References

1. Davies, H. Ted Cruz Using Firm That Harvested Data on Millions of Unwitting Facebook Users. Available online: https://www.theguardian.com/us-news/2015/dec/11/senator-ted-cruz-president-campaign-facebook-user-data (accessed on 4 January 2024).
2. European Parliament; Council of the European Union. Regulation (EU) 2016/679 of the European Parliament and of the Council. Available online: https://data.europa.eu/eli/reg/2016/679/oj (accessed on 4 May 2016).
3. Krishnan, S.; Anand, A.J.; Srinivasan, R.; Kavitha, R.; Suresh, S. *Federated Learning*; CRC Press: Boca Raton, FL, USA, 2024.
4. Boenisch, F.; Dziedzic, A.; Schuster, R.; Shamsabadi, A.S.; Shumailov, I.; Papernot, N. Reconstructing Individual Data Points in Federated Learning Hardened with Differential Privacy and Secure Aggregation. In Proceedings of the 2023 IEEE 8th European Symposium on Security and Privacy (EuroS&P), Delft, The Netherlands, 3–7 July 2023; IEEE Computer Society: Piscataway, NJ, USA, 2023; pp. 241–257.
5. Melis, L.; Song, C.; De Cristofaro, E.; Shmatikov, V. Exploiting unintended feature leakage in collaborative learning. In Proceedings of the 2019 IEEE Symposium on Security and Privacy (SP), San Francisco, CA, USA, 19–23 May 2019; IEEE: Piscataway, NJ, USA, 2019; pp. 691–706.
6. Yin, H.; Mallya, A.; Vahdat, A.; Alvarez, J.M.; Kautz, J.; Molchanov, P. See through gradients: Image batch recovery via gradinversion. In Proceedings of the IEEE/CVF Conference on Computer Vision and Pattern Recognition, Nashville, TN, USA, 20–25 June 2021; pp. 16337–16346.
7. Lyu, L.; Yu, H.; Ma, X.; Chen, C.; Sun, L.; Zhao, J.; Yang, Q.; Yu, P.S. Privacy and Robustness in Federated Learning: Attacks and Defenses. *IEEE Trans. Neural Netw. Learn. Syst.* **2022**, 1–21. [CrossRef] [PubMed]
8. Adilova, L.; Böttinger, K.; Danos, V.; Jacob, S.; Langer, F.; Markert, T.; Poretschkin, M.; Rosenzweig, J.; Schulze, J.P.; Sperl, P. Security of AI-Systems: Fundamentals. Available online: https://doi.org/10.24406/publica-1503 (accessed on 15 March 2024).
9. Blanchard, P.; El Mhamdi, E.M.; Guerraoui, R.; Stainer, J. Machine learning with adversaries: Byzantine tolerant gradient descent. *Adv. Neural Inf. Process. Syst.* **2017**, *30*.
10. Fang, M.; Cao, X.; Jia, J.; Gong, N. Local model poisoning attacks to {Byzantine-Robust} federated learning. In Proceedings of the 29th USENIX security symposium (USENIX Security 20), Boston, MA, USA, 12–14 August 2020; pp. 1605–1622.
11. Kairouz, P.; McMahan, H.B.; Avent, B.; Bellet, A.; Bennis, M.; Bhagoji, A.N.; Bonawitz, K.; Charles, Z.; Cormode, G.; Cummings, R.; et al. Advances and Open Problems in Federated Learning. *Found. Trends Mach. Learn.* **2021**, *14*, 1–210. [CrossRef]
12. Bell, J.H.; Bonawitz, K.A.; Gascón, A.; Lepoint, T.; Raykova, M. Secure single-server aggregation with (poly) logarithmic overhead. In Proceedings of the 2020 ACM SIGSAC Conference on Computer and Communications Security, Virtual, 9–13 November 2020; pp. 1253–1269.
13. Bonawitz, K.; Ivanov, V.; Kreuter, B.; Marcedone, A.; McMahan, H.B.; Patel, S.; Ramage, D.; Segal, A.; Seth, K. Practical secure aggregation for privacy-preserving machine learning. In Proceedings of the 2017 ACM SIGSAC Conference on Computer and Communications Security, Dallas, TX, USA, 30 October–3 November 2017; pp. 1175–1191.
14. Kairouz, P.; Liu, Z.; Steinke, T. The distributed discrete gaussian mechanism for federated learning with secure aggregation. In Proceedings of the International Conference on Machine Learning, PMLR, Virtual, 18–24 July 2021; pp. 5201–5212.
15. Liu, B.; Pejó, B.; Tang, Q. Privacy-Preserving Federated Singular Value Decomposition. *Appl. Sci.* **2023**, *13*, 7373. [CrossRef]
16. Roy Chowdhury, A.; Guo, C.; Jha, S.; van der Maaten, L. Eiffel: Ensuring integrity for federated learning. In Proceedings of the 2022 ACM SIGSAC Conference on Computer and Communications Security, Los Angeles, CA, USA, 7–11 November 2022; pp. 2535–2549.
17. Diedrich, H. *Ethereum: Blockchains, Digital Assets, Smart Contracts, Decentralized Autonomous Organizations*; Wildfire Publishing: Sydney, Australia, 2016.

18. Narayanan, A.; Bonneau, J.; Felten, E.; Miller, A.; Goldfeder, S. *Bitcoin and Cryptocurrency Technologies: A Comprehensive Introduction*; Princeton University Press: Princeton, NJ, USA, 2016.
19. Swan, M. *Blockchain: Blueprint for a New Economy*; O'Reilly Media, Inc.: Sebastopol, CA, USA, 2015.
20. Qammar, A.; Karim, A.; Ning, H.; Ding, J. Securing federated learning with blockchain: A systematic literature review. *Artif. Intell. Rev.* **2023**, *56*, 3951–3985. [CrossRef] [PubMed]
21. Yu, F.; Lin, H.; Wang, X.; Yassine, A.; Hossain, M.S. Blockchain-empowered secure federated learning system: Architecture and applications. *Comput. Commun.* **2022**, *196*, 55–65. [CrossRef]
22. Shamir, A. How to share a secret. *Commun. ACM* **1979**, *22*, 612–613. [CrossRef]
23. Lin, S.; Costello, D.J. *Error Control Coding: Fundamentals and Applications*; Pearson/Prentice Hall: Upper Saddle River, NJ, USA, 2004.
24. Corrigan-Gibbs, H.; Boneh, D. Prio: Private, robust, and scalable computation of aggregate statistics. In Proceedings of the 14th USENIX Symposium on Networked Systems Design and Implementation (NSDI 17), Boston, MA, USA, 27–29 March 2017; pp. 259–282.
25. Suwito, M.H.; Tama, B.A.; Santoso, B.; Dutta, S.; Tan, H.; Ueshige, Y.; Sakurai, K. A Systematic Study of Bulletin Board and Its Application. In Proceedings of the ASIA CCS '22: ACM Asia Conference on Computer and Communications Security, Nagasaki, Japan, 30 May–3 June 2022; Suga, Y., Sakurai, K., Ding, X., Sako, K., Eds.; ACM: New York, NY, USA, 2022; pp. 1213–1215.
26. Tramèr, F.; Shokri, R.; Joaquin, A.S.; Le, H.; Jagielski, M.; Hong, S.; Carlini, N. Truth Serum: Poisoning Machine Learning Models to Reveal Their Secrets. In Proceedings of the 2022 ACM SIGSAC Conference on Computer and Communications Security, CCS 2022, Los Angeles, CA, USA, 7–11 November 2022; Yin, H., Stavrou, A., Cremers, C., Shi, E., Eds.; ACM: New York, NY, USA, 2022; pp. 2779–2792.
27. Burmester, M.; Desmedt, Y. A secure and scalable Group Key Exchange system. *Inf. Process. Lett.* **2005**, *94*, 137–143. [CrossRef]
28. Python Cryptographic Authority. Python Library NumPy. Available online: https://numpy.org/ (accessed on 13 February 2024).
29. Oliphant, T.; Contributors Community. Python Library Cryptography. Available online: https://cryptography.io/en/latest/ (accessed on 13 February 2024).
30. Samarakoon, S.; Siriwardhana, Y.; Porambage, P.; Liyanage, M.; Chang, S.Y.; Kim, J.; Kim, J.; Ylianttila, M. 5G-NIDD: A Comprehensive Network Intrusion Detection Dataset Generated over 5G Wireless Network. *arXiv* **2022**, arXiv:2212.01298.

Disclaimer/Publisher's Note: The statements, opinions and data contained in all publications are solely those of the individual author(s) and contributor(s) and not of MDPI and/or the editor(s). MDPI and/or the editor(s) disclaim responsibility for any injury to people or property resulting from any ideas, methods, instructions or products referred to in the content.

 *future internet*

Article

Multi-Level Split Federated Learning for Large-Scale AIoT System Based on Smart Cities

Hanyue Xu [1,2], Kah Phooi Seng [1,3,4,*], Jeremy Smith [2] and Li Minn Ang [4]

1. School of AI and Advanced Computing, Xi'an Jiaotong-Liverpool University, Suzhou 215000, China; hanyue.xu19@student.xjtlu.edu.cn
2. Department of Electrical Engineering and Electronics, University of Liverpool, Liverpool L69 3GJ, UK; j.s.smith@liverpool.ac.uk
3. School of Computer Science, Queensland University of Technology, Brisbane, QLD 4000, Australia
4. School of Science, Technology and Engineering, University of the Sunshine Coast, Petrie, QLD 4502, Australia; lang@usc.edu.au
* Correspondence: jasmine.seng@xjtlu.edu.cn

Abstract: In the context of smart cities, the integration of artificial intelligence (AI) and the Internet of Things (IoT) has led to the proliferation of AIoT systems, which handle vast amounts of data to enhance urban infrastructure and services. However, the collaborative training of deep learning models within these systems encounters significant challenges, chiefly due to data privacy concerns and dealing with communication latency from large-scale IoT devices. To address these issues, multi-level split federated learning (multi-level SFL) has been proposed, merging the benefits of split learning (SL) and federated learning (FL). This framework introduces a novel multi-level aggregation architecture that reduces communication delays, enhances scalability, and addresses system and statistical heterogeneity inherent in large AIoT systems with non-IID data distributions. The architecture leverages the Message Queuing Telemetry Transport (MQTT) protocol to cluster IoT devices geographically and employs edge and fog computing layers for initial model parameter aggregation. Simulation experiments validate that the multi-level SFL outperforms traditional SFL by improving model accuracy and convergence speed in large-scale, non-IID environments. This paper delineates the proposed architecture, its workflow, and its advantages in enhancing the robustness and scalability of AIoT systems in smart cities while preserving data privacy.

Keywords: federated learning; split learning; split federated learning; artificial intelligent internet of things; edge computing

Citation: Xu, H.; Seng, K.P.; Smith, J.; Ang, L.M. Multi-Level Split Federated Learning for Large-Scale AIoT System Based on Smart Cities. *Future Internet* **2024**, *16*, 82. https://doi.org/10.3390/fi16030082

Academic Editors: Qiang Duan and Zhihui Lu

Received: 30 January 2024
Revised: 21 February 2024
Accepted: 26 February 2024
Published: 28 February 2024

Copyright: © 2024 by the authors. Licensee MDPI, Basel, Switzerland. This article is an open access article distributed under the terms and conditions of the Creative Commons Attribution (CC BY) license (https://creativecommons.org/licenses/by/4.0/).

1. Introduction

With the acceleration of urbanization, smart cities are proposed to utilize various artificial intelligence (AI) technologies or urban infrastructure to integrate artificial intelligence Internet of Things (AIoT) systems, improve resource utilization efficiency, optimize city management and services, and achieve the idea of the Internet of Everything. By analyzing and processing the massive historical and real-time data generated by IoT devices such as sensors, AI technology can make more accurate predictions about future devices and user habits, such as smart grid [1], smart transportation [2], and smart healthcare [3]. On the other hand, hyperscale data connected through IoT can also lay the foundation for deep learning in AI. However, with the continuous development of big data technology, the meaning of the data generated in smart cities for everyone is no longer insignificant information but a digital asset. For example, the user driving habits data of smart vehicles need user authorization to be used for model training and learning of AI technology [4]. Therefore, the need to train deep learning models without aggregating and accessing sensitive raw data on the client side is a major challenge that AIoT systems need to solve for multi-client collaborative learning.

In recent years, the concept of distributed collaboration machine learning (DCML) has been proposed to solve the above challenges, including federated learning [5–7] and split learning [8–10]. Different from traditional centralized machine learning, DCML addresses data privacy challenges by collaborating with multiple IoT devices (clients) to train machine learning or deep learning models in collaboration with a central server, without sharing local data generated by individual IoT devices. In federated learning (FL), the global model is constructed by aggregating the model parameters trained by the local model on each client through the cloud server. In split learning (SL), the deep learning model is split into two parts: the first few layers are trained by the IoT device (client), and the bottom layer is calculated by the central server (cloud), which is mainly used to solve the problem of the limited computing resources of IoT devices. However, the performance of split learning decreases as the number of clients increases, and federated learning is not suitable for IoT devices with limited resources, so they all have limitations in large-scale AIoT systems. Therefore, split federated learning [11–13] is proposed to combine the advantages of SL and FL to make an AIoT system parallel in data and model training, which not only considers the problem of limited client resources but also reduces the influence of the number of clients on the performance of the model. Furthermore, it does not lose the protection of data privacy and the robustness of the model.

Although split federated learning has become a new paradigm for future collaborative learning in AIoT systems, the performance and efficiency of model training are greatly reduced due to the large number of clients contained in large AIoT systems, the different transmission distances of different clients, and the insufficient stability of single cloud center server nodes. During the training process, there may be statistical heterogeneity and system heterogeneity among AIoT devices that have different computing and storage resources, and the generated data are not independent and identically distributed (non-IID). These factors all affect the performance of models trained in a split federated learning framework with only an end-cloud architecture. In addition, it has been found that model aggregation frequency can significantly affect federated learning performance [14]. This inspired us to propose a multi-level split federated learning (multi-level SFL) framework in which the large-scale client model parameters can be initially aggregated at the edge layer, fog layer, or higher levels, compensating for the scalability of traditional SFL in large AIoT systems. Since the parameters of the client can be preliminarily aggregated at multiple levels before being sent to the cloud server, the communication delay between the cloud server and the client is reduced, the processing speed of the central server is improved, and the global model can be trained by receiving the model parameters of the client in a wider range. The current hierarchical federated learning architecture is composed of client–edge–cloud system, which solves the communication efficiency problem of traditional cloud-based federated learning [15]. However, in the scenario of large AIoT systems based on smart cities, it is difficult for hierarchical FL to cover a larger number of IoT devices and be more widely distributed, so this architecture still limits the number of IoT devices that can be accessed. Compared to hierarchical FL, multi-level architectures can receive a wider range of IoT devices and adjust the number of layers of the architecture as the training task or the number of IoT devices changes, thereby enhancing the generalization of federated learning in AIoT systems. The multi-level aggregation architecture also reduces the single point of failure of the cloud server and resolves the problem of the model training being stuck because the client cannot upload the model information in time due to the long transmission distance. The addition of split learning balances the problem of system heterogeneity among clients and enhances the scalability of the system to incorporate more IoT devices for collaborative learning. Allocating only a portion of the network for training on the end devices can reduce the processing load compared to running a full network in multi-level FL. This enables resource-limited IoT devices to participate in collaborative training, enhancing the diversity of trainable tasks and reducing the impact of data silos in resource-limited devices. Compared with traditional split federated learning, our proposed framework can better solve the system and statistical heterogeneity and improve the scalability of large-scale AIoT systems. The main contributions of this paper are as follows:

1. This paper proposes a multi-level split federated learning architecture based on IoT device location model information aggregation. The architecture reduces the communication delay between the client and the cloud server. Compared to hierarchical FL, multi-level SFL improves the scalability of the AIoT system through initial aggregation in multi-level edge nodes before the cloud server's aggregation.
2. The split learning algorithm is added to multi-level federated learning, which reduces the impact of system heterogeneity on client collaborative learning and the possibility of abandonment due to limited client computing resources.
3. We utilize the Message Queuing Telemetry Transport (MQTT) protocol to aggregate geographically located IoT devices by sending topics and assigning the nearest master server for split learning training. The client groups in each region communicate with the primary server through their respective local networks.
4. Simulation experiments on multi-level split federated learning using Docker verify that our proposed framework can effectively improve the model accuracy of collaborative training under large-scale clients. In addition, compared with traditional SFL, multi-level SFL in non-IID scenarios can converge faster and reduce the influence of non-IID data on model accuracy.

The rest of this article is organized as follows. Section 2 reports some work related to the article. Section 3 discusses the proposed multi-level split federated learning architecture and associated workflows. In Section 4, the results of the simulation experiments are presented and analyzed. Finally, Section 5 summarizes the article.

2. Related Works

Our proposed work is concerned with three primary DCML topics: multi-level FL, SL, and SFL. Federated learning is an emerging distributed machine learning paradigm that allows clients to jointly model without sharing data, breaking down data silos. With the deepening of research, systematic heterogeneity and statistical heterogeneity have become obstacles to the development of federated learning [16–19]. Karimireddy et al. [20] proposed that the Scaffold algorithm corrects local model updates by adding variance reduction techniques to local training to approximately correct the drift of local training on the client side. In addition to optimizing model parameter aggregation algorithms, there is a lot of work to solve the above problems through personalization techniques [21]. Xu and Fan [22] proposed FedDK, which utilized knowledge distillation for model parameter transmission, and designed the personalized model for each group by using the missing common knowledge to fill circularly between clients. Traditional federated learning frameworks also lack scalability in large AIoT systems. Guo et al. designed [23] a multi-level federated learning mechanism to improve the efficiency of federated learning in device-heavy edge network scenarios by utilizing reinforcement learning techniques to select IoT devices for collaborative training. Campolo et al. [24] proposed a federated learning framework based on the MQTT protocol and lightweight machine-to-machine semantics (LwM2M) to improve communication efficiency and scalability by optimizing message transmission. Furthermore, Liu et al. [25] proposed a multi-level federated learning framework, MFL, which combines the advantages of edge-based federated learning to achieve a balance between communication cost and computational performance for intelligent traffic flow prediction. Multi-level federated learning can also be combined with personalization techniques to solve the problem of statistical heterogeneity. Wu et al. [26] proposed a framework that combines self-attention personalization techniques with multi-level federated graph learning to further capture features of large received signal strength (RSS) datasets for indoor fingerprint localization.

Split learning (SL) is a distributed learning paradigm for resource-limited devices that has the same data-sharing constraint as FL. The principle is to split the deep learning network: each device retains only one part of the network, while the server computes another part of the network, and the different devices only carry out forward and backpropagation to the local network architecture [27]. SL solves the problem of limited computing resources of edge devices in FL but also increases the communication overhead of the system. Chen et al. [10] proposed a loss-based asynchronous training framework for split learning, which allows the client model parameters to be updated according to the loss, thus reducing the communication frequency of split learning. Moreover, Ayad et al. [28] introduced autoencoders and adaptive threshold mechanisms to track gradients in split learning to reduce the amount of data sent to the client in forward computation and the number of updates in post-feedback communication. Therefore, hybrid split federated learning (SFL) is proposed, which combines the advantages of FL and SL, reduces the communication overhead of split learning, and is suitable for IoT devices with limited resources. In the framework, each client sends its own cutting layer to the master server, which trains the split network and sends the fed server to aggregate the gradient of the split model from each client [29]. Tian et al. [30] split the BERT model according to the calculated load of the embedded layer and transformer layer of the BERT model under the FedBert framework so that it could be deployed on devices with limited resources. Moreover, FedSyL [31], HSFL [32], and ARES [33] frameworks optimized the splitting strategy of deep learning networks, which select the splitting points that can minimize the training cost per round through adaptive analysis based on client computing resources.

Although the above studies have made advances in multi-level federated learning frameworks and split federated learning, they do not take into account collaborative learning in large-scale AIoT system scenarios. Our work greatly improves the scalability of large-scale AIoT systems in collaborative learning by combining the advantages of multi-level federated learning frameworks and the principles of split federated learning.

3. Proposed Framework

In this section, we will introduce multi-level split federated learning in detail, where we group clients according to their geographic distribution and assign corresponding master nodes for model training for split learning, as shown in Figure 1.

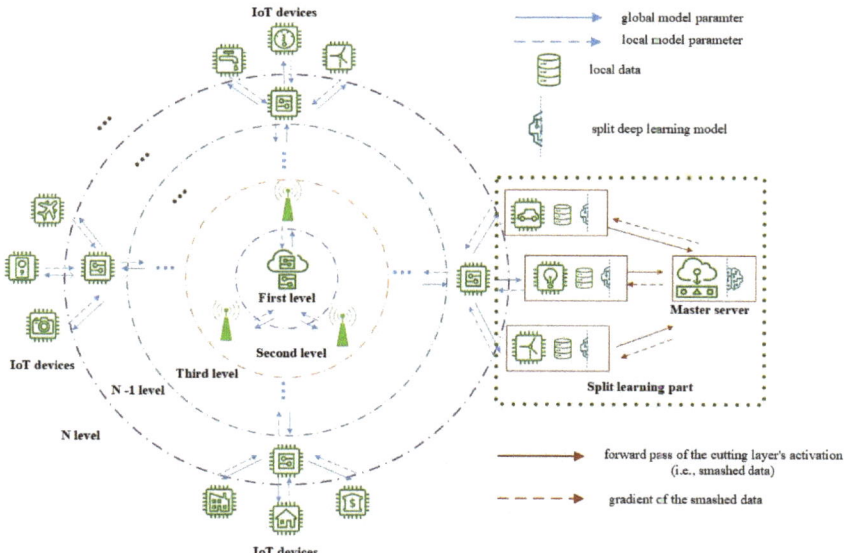

Figure 1. Multi-level split federated learning framework in large-scale AIoT system.

Multi-level split federated learning is designed with a combination of cloud- and edge-based FL and master server-based SL. The cloud server is located in the first level, and the outer level extends to the end device layer of the Nth level, which can contain the $N-2$ level edge servers and fog nodes for the initial aggregation of the local model of the IoT devices. The Nth level is the device layer (end layer), which contains a large number of smart devices and sensors in the smart city, including street lights, sensors, cameras, etc., responsible for sensing the surrounding environment and generating data in real time. The number of levels N of the architecture is determined by the number of IoT devices participating in collaborative training and the area they are located in. As the number of IoT devices increases, the rate at which the cloud server receives model parameters also decreases, increasing the time cost of the computing of the cloud server to some extent. In addition, the larger the range of IoT devices involved in training, the more uneven the transmission distance between different IoT devices, and cloud servers also lead to a reduction in training efficiency. Depending on the number of IoT devices and their geographic location required for different training tasks, the proposed architecture automatically adds adjacent and idle edge nodes or fog or edge nodes with more computing power for hierarchical expansion. Since the infrastructure of most smart cities is fixed, we assume that in this design, the IoT devices will be stable when training collaboratively, and the geographical location will be constant during training time. The IoT nodes in the end layer (Nth level) are composed of heterogeneous resource-constrained devices, the data generated by each IoT node are saved locally and cannot be shared, and each uses its own local data trainer for the local model. Depending on the geographical location of the IoT devices, they are divided into different groups, and each group is assigned the nearest master server, which is the server with high-performance computing resources. All IoT devices in parallel perform forward propagation on their local model and transmit their smashed data to the master server. The master server calculates the forward propagation and backward propagation of the smashed data for each IoT device in its server-side model and sends the gradient to the respective IoT devices to operate backpropagation. The closer the edge nodes of each layer of the multi-level SFL are to the cloud server, the stronger the computing and communication capabilities. For example, edge nodes such as routers and gateways close to IoT devices have stronger computing performance and storage space than IoT devices. Higher-level edge nodes or fog nodes that connect to this level, such as base stations or regional servers, have more computing capabilities than edge nodes closer to IoT devices. Therefore, the highest level (the first level) consists of one cloud server. After the edge nodes of each layer initially aggregate the parameters of the local model of the IoT device through the FedAvg algorithm, the aggregated model parameters are further uploaded to the cloud server for the aggregation of global model parameters. Compared with the traditional SFL architecture, multi-level SFL does not need to wait for all clients to update and upload model parameters to a single cloud server for parameter aggregation, reducing the communication cost of AIoT system collaborative learning and expanding the IoT devices available for training. The detailed workflow of multi-level SFL is as follows.

3.1. MQTT Protocol-Based Message Exchange

Message Queuing Telemetry Transport (MQTT) is a lightweight communication protocol based on the publish/subscribe model, which is built on the TCP/IP protocol and commonly used in Internet of Things systems. The advantage of MQTT is that it provides reliable messaging services for connecting remote devices with limited bandwidth, so it is suitable for low-bandwidth environments consisting of resource-limited end devices. In the multi-level SFL framework, we use the MQTT protocol for message exchange between client nodes and server nodes. The server of MQTT is brokered by VerneMQ. Edge nodes and device nodes find device nodes that split federated learning on the MQTT topic and control the aggregation operation of model parameters. The specific complete topic is shown in Table 1.

Table 1. Topics used in the MQTT protocol.

Message Exchange.	Topic	Details
Device–Edge	client/group	IoT devices are grouped according to the public socket IP they provide, and the corresponding master server is assigned.
	train/start	The grouped IoT devices receive the signal from the edge server to start the model training.
	train/update	When the server needs to receive the local model weight of the IoT device, the IoT device receives the signal from the edge server.
Edge–Edge Edge–Cloud	train/start	The edge server receives the signal from the upper-level server and starts to trigger the model training.
	train/update	At the beginning of each communication turn, the selected clients are notified that their weights will be aggregated.
	client/join	Receive messages when a new IoT device joins a group. The message includes contextual information about the newly joining IoT device, including its status (whether it can participate in training) and its public socket IP.

The MQTT agent publishes the subject client/group, groups IoT devices under the same LAN by receiving the IP of each IoT device, and assigns the master server node under the same LAN. The server nodes on the connected edge of each group connect to the upper-layer edge nodes or cloud servers through the backbone (internet) network. At the beginning of each round of communication, the edge server will randomly aggregate the model parameters of the IoT devices by publishing a list of IDs containing the selected IoT devices to the train/update topic. When an IoT device receives a message published on this topic, it checks if its ID is in the list, and if so, it sends its local model parameters to the edge node; otherwise, it receives the average weight of the model parameters from the edge node. The message exchange between edge nodes at each layer and between edge nodes and cloud servers is similar. However, when the new IoT device node joins the group, it receives the message of the new IoT device through the topic client/join, and groups and evaluates the new IoT devices according to their own information.

To analyze the communication overhead of the proposed framework through MQTT, we assume M represents the number of parameters for the model, D represents the total number of IoT devices, s represents the size of the total samples, q is the size of the smashed layer, E represents the total number of edge nodes in the middle levels, and α represents the proportion of model parameters on the IoT device side. For instance, the model parameters in IoT devices can be expressed as αM, and in the master server, they can be expressed as $(1-\alpha)M$. Multi-level SFL mainly carries out two parts of information transferred through MQTT protocol. The first part is the transfer of information between the IoT device and the master server. The information that the IoT device transfers to the master server is the smash data from the cutting layer of the local model, and the information that the master server transfers to the IoT device is the gradient of the smash data. Therefore, the size of the information transmitted by the split learning section depends on the size of the private data generated by the local IoT device. The total communication overhead in the split learning part can be denoted as $2sq$. The second part of the communication overhead comes from the size of the information transmitted by multi-level federated learning. The information transferred size of FL depends on the number of parameters in the IoT device's local model [34], but since the local model is split, the communication overhead of multi-level FL can be expressed as $2\alpha M(D+E)$. Therefore, the communication overhead of a multi-level SFL can be expressed as $2sq + 2\alpha M(D+E)$. Table 2 shows a comparison of the size of information transferred by the proposed framework over MQTT versus that transferred by traditional federated learning. As can be seen from Table 2, multi-level SFL can reduce the size of information transmitted by the device and improve the transmission efficiency of the framework when training large deep learning models with the same size of training data.

Table 2. Communication overhead of different distributed learning methods.

Method	Comms. per IoT Devices	Total Comms.
FL	$2M$	$2DM$
SL	$(2s/D)q$	$2sq$
Multi-level SFL	$(2s/D)q + 2\alpha M$	$2sq + 2\alpha M(D+E)$

3.2. Split Learning Side

After grouping IoT devices according to their geographic location, each group first performs a split learning algorithm with the assigned master server. The algorithm can be divided into four main computational parts. The IoT device is responsible for performing two parts of the deep learning network computation, namely the forward propagation and backward propagation of the IoT device network. The master server is responsible for calculating the remaining layers and loss calculations. We define a deep learning network as a function f, which contains the network layers that can be represented as $\{l_0, l_1, \ldots, l_K\}$. For the input local data (*local data*), the output of the neural network is

$$l_K(l_{K-1} \ldots (l_0(local\ data))) \to f(local\ data). \tag{1}$$

Let $Loss(output, label)$ represent the last layer to calculate the loss function of the real label and the network output. Δl_i^T represents the backpropagation process at each network layer, so the backpropagation of the entire deep learning network can be expressed as

$$\Delta l_K^T \left(\Delta l_{K-1}^T \ldots \left(\Delta l_i^T \right) \right) \to \Delta f^T. \tag{2}$$

Therefore, the deep network structure can be divided into two parts according to the disassembly layer, assuming that the layer l_n is the cutting layer of the neural network. The network layer retained by the IoT device and the master server node is represented as follows

$$f_c \leftarrow \{l_0, l_1, \ldots, l_n\}, \ n \in N, \tag{3}$$

$$f_m \leftarrow \{l_{n+1}, l_{n+2}, \ldots, l_N\}, \ n \in N. \tag{4}$$

The client sends the activation of the cutting layer generated by the forward propagation of the local network model to the master server for forward propagation of the rest of the network layers. The master server is responsible for calculating the loss of labels and outputs and propagating backward to update the master server's network layer weights. The client smashed data from the forward propagation of the local network model to the main server for forward propagation of the rest of the network Assuming a set of D IoT devices in t time period, the model update of the master server part of the network can be expressed as follows [29]:

$$W_{t+1}^M := W_t^M - \eta \frac{s_D}{s} \sum_{m=1}^{D} \Delta L_m \left(W_t^M; \alpha_t^M \right), \tag{5}$$

where η is the learning rate to train the deep learning model, and s is the size of the total samples. α_t^M represents the activation in master server, and $\Delta L_D(W_t^M; \alpha_t^M)$ denotes the gradient of backpropagation in the master server's network layer.

Algorithm 1 shows the exact algorithm flow of the split learning part. The backpropagation gradient received by the client from the master server is sent to the edge server for aggregation, so Algorithm 1 is only one part of the multi-level SFL, and the entire algorithm will be presented later.

Algorithm 1 Split learning part in multi-level split federated learning

Notations: s is the size of total samples; t is time period; α_t^d is the smashed data of IoT device at t; ΔL_d is the gradient of the loss for IoT device d; Y_d is the true label from IoT device d.
Initialize: for each IoT device $d \in D$ in parallel **do**
$f_d \leftarrow \{l_0, l_1, \ldots, l_n\}$, initialize weight f_d using W_t^d
end for
In master server: $f_m \leftarrow \{l_{n+1}, l_{n+2}, \ldots, l_N\}$, initialize weight f_m using W_t^M

1:   **for** each IoT device in the same group $d \in D$ in parallel **do**
2:     **while** local epoch $e \neq E$ **do**
3:     IoT device received model weight the from cloud server
4:     Forward propagation compute activation (smashed data) on cutting layer $\alpha_t^d \leftarrow f_d(data)$
5:     Send activation α_t^d and local label Y_d to master server
6:     **end while**
7:   **Master server executes:**
8:     Forward propagation with α_t^d on f_m, compute $output \leftarrow f_m\left(\alpha_t^d\right)$
9:     Calculate Loss $L_d \leftarrow lossfunction(output, Y_d)$
10:    Backpropagation on f_m, calculate the gradient $\Delta L_d(W_t^M; \alpha_t^M)$
11:    Send gradient of cutting layer $d\alpha_t^d := \Delta L_d(W_t^M; \alpha_t^M)$ to IoT device for backpropagation
       $f_d \leftarrow backPropagation\left(W_t^d, d\alpha_t^M\right)$
12:   **end for**
13:   Model f_m from master server update $W_{t+1}^M := W_t^M - \eta \frac{s_d}{s} \sum_{m=1}^d \Delta L_m(W_t^M; \alpha_t^M)$

3.3. Multi-Level Federated Learning Workflow

The cloud server publishes topics through the MQTT protocol to match the edge server to the nearest IoT device group. Then, the edge server publishes topics to receive the tasks performed by the IoT device, information about the local model, and information about the respective resources of the IoT device, including computing resources and storage resources. Based on the IoT device information, the edge server will determine whether the IoT device meets the requirements of collaborative training (whether it is idle and has enough computing resources) and send the training task to the cloud server. Depending on the training task, the cloud server randomly initializes the global model parameters and sends them to the IoT device. Each group of IoT devices receives the cutting layer gradient from the master server and backpropagates the local model to update the parameters of the neural network. The next major step is parameter aggregation in the edge server and cloud server, where we use the FedAvg aggregation algorithm.

After the IoT devices in each group update the weights of the local model through the model gradient sent by the master server, they send the model parameters (weights) to the associated edge server. Each edge node is responsible for collecting updated parameters from local IoT devices in its region and using the FedAvg algorithm for weighted averaging to update the weights of the local partial model (initial aggregation). Suppose there are E edge servers; then, the FedAvg algorithm [35] can be expressed as

$$W^e = \sum_{m=1}^{D} \frac{s_m}{s} W_d^e, \quad e \in E. \tag{6}$$

There are two situations when model parameters are sent to an edge server. If the edge device is in the middle layer of the hierarchy, the aggregation of model parameters can be expressed as

$$W^{e_{N-1}}_{t+1} = \frac{\sum_{d_i \in e_{N-1}} S_d W_t^d}{S_D^{e_{N-1}}}, \quad e \in E, \tag{7}$$

where $S_d \epsilon S_D$, S_D denotes the size of the total samples in the IoT device from one group under the e_{N-1}, which is the edge server located in layer $N-1$. The edge node in the middle layer will forward the aggregated average weight to the upper connected edge node to aggregate again. Similarly, the edge server in level $N-2$ executes the aggregation algorithm and can be represented as

$$W^{e_{N-2}}{}_{t+1} = \frac{\sum_{d_i \in e_{N-2}} S_{e_{N-1}} W^d_{e_{N-1},t}}{S^{e_{N-2}}_D}, \ e \in E. \tag{8}$$

If the edge node is at the top of the hierarchy, that is, the cloud server, the weights from the edge nodes of the previous layer are aggregated and weighted and then sent back to the lower level. The cloud server aggregates all the model parameters for each group of IoT devices. The aggregation operation in the server can be expressed as

$$W^C{}_{t+1} = \frac{\sum_{S_{e_2^d} \in S} S_{e_2^d} W^d_{e_2,t}}{S^{e_{N-2}}_D}, \ e \in E. \tag{9}$$

The final average weight is sent from the cloud server back to the edge server and client in the same path as the model parameters were previously uploaded, as shown in Figure 2. After receiving the global parameters, each set of IoT devices updates its local model and forwards the cutting layer activation to the master server for forward propagation and loss calculation. The entire multi-level federation learning begins a new iteration until the model converges. Algorithm 2 illustrates the precise algorithm flow of the multi-level SFL framework and shows the algorithm of the multi-level FL part in detail.

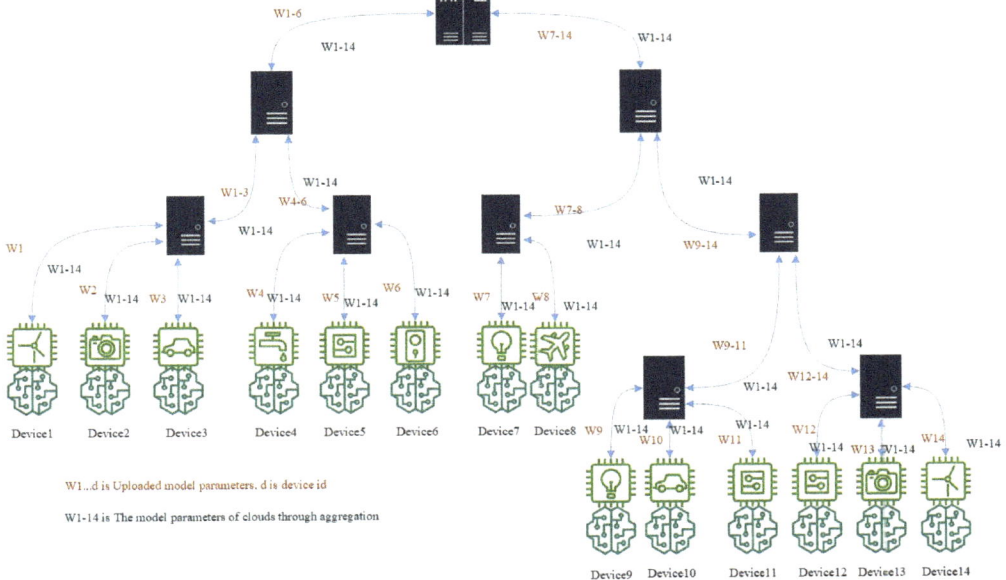

Figure 2. Multi-level federated learning workflow.

Algorithm 2 Multi-level SFL algorithm and multi-level FL workflow
---
Notations: s is the size of total samples; t is time period; E is the number of edge servers in each level.
Initialize: $level = N$; global model in cloud server W^C;

1:   if t = 0 **do**
2:     send W^C to all IoT devices for model weight initialization
3:   **else**
4:     master server and IoT device executes split learning part,
      $f_d \leftarrow backPropagation\left(W_t^d, d\alpha_t^M\right)$
5:     if $level = N - 1$ **do**
6:       **for** each IoT device $S_d \epsilon S_D$ in parallel **do**
7:         Send model weight to edge sever $W_{t+1}^E \leftarrow backPropagation\left(W_t^d, d\alpha_t^M\right)$
8:       **end for**
9:       Aggregate model parameter $W^{e_{N-1}}{}_{t+1} = \frac{\sum_{d_i \in e_{N-1}} S_d W_t^d}{S_D^{e_{N-1}}}$
10:     **end if**
11:     level --;
12:     if $level \neq 1$ **do**
13:       **for** edge server $e \in E$ **do**
14:         Send model weight to upper-level edge sever $W^{e_{N-1}}{}_t \leftarrow W^{e_{N-2}}{}_t$
15:       **end for**
16:       Aggregate model parameter utilized FedAvg algorithm
17:       level --;
18:     **end if**
19:     if $level = 1$ **do**
20:       **for** edge server $e \in E$ **do**
21:         Send model weight to cloud sever
22:       **end for**
23:       Aggregate model parameter from lower-level edge server (all IoT devices model parameter)
      $W^C{}_{t+1} = \frac{\sum_{s_{e_2^d} \in S} S_{e_2^d} W_{e_2,t}^d}{S_D^{e_{N-2}}}$
24:       Send $W^C{}_{t+1}$ to all lower-level edge server and all IoT device as previous upload path
25:     **end if**
26:   **end if**

4. Experiment

In this section, we describe the performance of multi-level split federated learning on different datasets (Fashion MNIST, HAM10000) and different machine learning models (LeNet, ReNet18). The feasibility of our proposed framework is verified by comparing the traditional split federated learning, such as SFLV1, multi-level federated learning, and centralized learning in an independent identically distributed (IID) and balanced dataset, an unbalanced dataset, and a non-independent identically distributed (non-IID) dataset. We also tested the performance of multi-level SFL with a different number of clients and demonstrated that multi-level architecture can reduce the impact of an increasing number of clients on model training accuracy. Since the aim of the experiments is to simulate the real smart cities AIoT system in Docker, the model accuracy and the time cost of training the model will be the evaluation criteria to test the framework we proposed.

4.1. Experiment Setting

The experiment is built on Docker 24.0.7 and API 1.43, using multiple isolated Docker containers to simulate the end devices in the smart city AIoT system, such as cameras, indicators, temperature sensors, etc. Docker compose v2.23.3 is used to manage multiple clusters of Docker containers. To simulate a close-to-real-world scenario, clients have been assumed to be divided into distinct groups based on their region. Due to each region having its own WLAN or PAN, the clients in each group are connected through Docker's bridge network built under different IP addresses (local network). The upper-level nodes of each group, namely edge nodes and fog nodes, are connected to the cloud server through a global network. The MQTT protocol is used for message transfer between nodes at various levels, through the publication and subscription of messages to manage the joining of group nodes, the start and end of model training, and the aggregation of model parameters. We also use Secure Sockets Layer (SSL) sockets to add a secret key to the transmission of model weights in the system, so the sent weights will be hashed together with the key, ensuring the security and privacy of data transmission in the real world. The experiment used SSL single authentication, that is, the client should authenticate the identity of the cloud server, and the server does not need to authenticate the client. Once the authentication is complete and the server and client SSL session is established, the two parties begin an MQTT connection over the secure SSL channel and communicate over the encrypted channel by publishing and subscribing context, as shown in Figure 3.

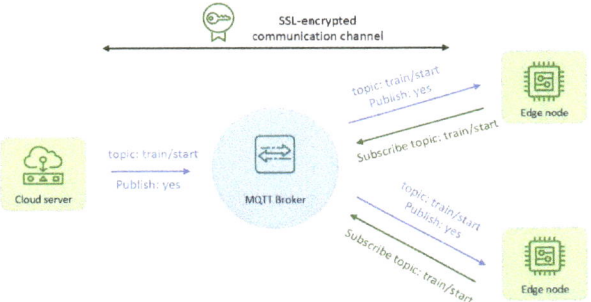

Figure 3. Experiment simulation smart cities MQTT protocol with encrypted SSL.

All programs are written by Python3.6 and TensorFlow1.8 and built on a Windows computer with an NVIDIA GeForce RTX4090 GPU (Santa Clara, CA, USA) and Intel Core i9-12900K CPU (Santa Clara, CA, USA). The NVIDA GeForce RTX4090 is a public version of the card manufactured by NVIDIA, and the device is sourced from the United States. Intel Core i9-12900K CPU is Boxed Intel® Core™ i9-12900K Processor (30M Cache, up to 5.20 GHz) FC-LGA16A, for China. We selected HAM10000 and Fashion MNIST datasets, ResNet18 and LeNet, as machine learning network architectures to train these two datasets, respectively. Both architectures belong to the classical convolutional neural network-type architectures. ResNet18, consisting of 15 convolutional layers and 2 pooling layers, was used to test the proposed framework as a large machine learning task. Moreover, LeNet contains three convolutional layers and 2 pooling layers as machine small learning tasks to test the proposed framework. In addition, the learning rate of both networks is 0.0001.

In all experiments under the split federated setting, the network is split according to the following layer: the third layer of ResNet18 (the BatchNormalization layer) and the second layer of LeNet (the MaxPool layer). Generally, two factors are considered in the selection of the cutting layer of the machine learning model: one is the proportion of computing amount between the end device and the master computing node after the model is split, and the other is the hidden layer feature dimension of the cutting layer. The former is mainly determined by the processing speed, memory size, and power consumption budget of the end device. The latter is mainly determined by the bandwidth of the network connection between the end device and the master server. Since the experiment is set for training on resource-limited IoT devices and the bandwidth of MQTT protocol is much less than other protocols [36], the choice of destratification of the model does not need to consider the size of the feature dimension too much but rather the computing resources of the IoT devices. Therefore, we chose to train on IoT devices at a model layer with less split while ensuring that fragmented data do not compromise the privacy of the source data.

4.2. Experiment Dataset and Simulation

Two public image datasets were used in the experiment: Fashion MNIST [37] and HAM10000 [38], as shown in Table 3. Fashion MNIST is an image dataset that replaces the MNIST handwritten numerals set. It includes front images of 70,000 different products from 10 categories. Fashion MNIST's size, format, and training/test set division are exactly the same as the original MNIST, with a 60,000/10,000 training test data partition, 28×28 gray scale picture. As the MNIST dataset is too simple and the amount of data is small, Fashion MNIST is more consistent with the machine learning tests AIoT system based on smart cities. The HAM10000 dataset consists of 10,015 dermatoscopic images for the classification of pigmented skin lesions. There are seven labels: Akiec, bcc, bkl, df, mel, nv, and vasc. The number of samples in each category of the HAM10000 dataset is not the same, so its sample imbalance is prone to overfitting. We used this dataset to test the performance of multi-level SFL under unbalanced samples. The dataset is divided by the number of clients, each client holds a portion of the dataset, and the label of the dataset is stored in the master server of each client group.

Table 3. Training and testing of dataset.

Dataset	Training Samples	Testing Samples	Image Size
Fashion MNIST [37]	60,000	10,000	28×28
HAM10000 [38]	9013	1002	600×450

In order to simulate the limited computing resources of the IoT device and the sufficient computing resources of the master server used for computing in split learning, part of the model trained in the client is calculated by the CPU, while the other part of the model in the server is calculated by the GPU. Since the cloud server only needs to perform the task of parameter averaging, the cloud server is also simulated by a container in Docker. Cloud server containers publish task topics to edge nodes over the backbone network, and multiple containers simulate different groups of IoT devices receiving task selection datasets from edge nodes. The containers of each group are connected via a local network within the group, but each container trains the local model independently and communicates only when a topic is published for new devices to join. MQTT protocol is simulated by docker-vernemq, and container clusters are deployed by docker-composer. All containers are independent of each other to simulate the condition that data cannot be shared between IoT devices.

4.3. Performance of Multi-Level SFL, FL, and Centralized Learning

Centralized learning and multi-level federated learning serve as benchmarks for testing our proposed multi-level split federated learning. Multi-level federated learning and multi-level split learning are, respectively, tested in the AIoT system of four levels. The end layer is set with 50 nodes, which are divided into two groups according to geographical location, and the edge layer and fog layer are set with 2 nodes, which are, respectively, responsible for aggregating the model weights of the two groups of end nodes. The cloud has one node responsible for performing the FedAvg algorithm to aggregate the model weights of the edge nodes. Table 1 summarizes the accuracy of distributed collaborative learning over 50 global epochs with a batch size of 32 (Fashion MNIST) or 1024 (HAM10000) for each local epoch.

As shown in Table 4, multi-level split federated learning and multi-level federated learning perform well in experimental settings, and there is no significant difference between centralized learning and multi-level federated learning. Although centralized learning on both machine large learning tasks (ResNet18) and small machine learning tasks LeNet) has slightly better convergence results than multi-level split federated learning and federated learning, only a few accuracy losses are negligible. Moreover, we compare multi-level SFL and FL, both of which do not overfit on the HAM10000 and Fashion

MNIST datasets, because multi-level SFL and FL execute the FedAvg algorithm on multiple upper layers, so the client can reduce the number of local model updates. In addition, as shown in Table 4, multi-level SFL performs better than multi-level FL in the HAM10000 dataset. Because the sample size of the HAM10000 dataset is unbalanced and multi-level SFL inherits the properties of SL, machine learning performance is better under the unbalanced dataset.

Table 4. Train and test result in different distributed setting.

Dataset	Architecture	Centralized Learning		Multi-Level FL		Multi-Level SFL	
		Train	Test	Train	Test	Train	Test
HAM10000	ResNet18	74.4%	79.6%	76.9%	77.3%	78.6%	79.4%
Fashion MNIST	LeNet	88.7%	90.2%	86.1%	87.6%	87.9%	88.9%

In Figure 4, the X-axis represents the epoch of training, the Y-axis on the left represents the accuracy of training, and the Y-axis on the right represents the training loss. It can be seen from the experimental results that both multi-level SFL and FL can converge after 50 epochs on the Fashion MNIST dataset, reaching an accuracy of 88.9% and 88.6%. We note that multi-level SFL and FL converge first, while centralized learning begins to converge later, presumably because the dataset each client trains on is too small and the data type is large due to the random allocation of the dataset. Furthermore, the convergence rate of multi-level SFL is faster, and the model began to converge at about 20 epochs. This shows that multi-level SFL can reduce the communication overhead during training.

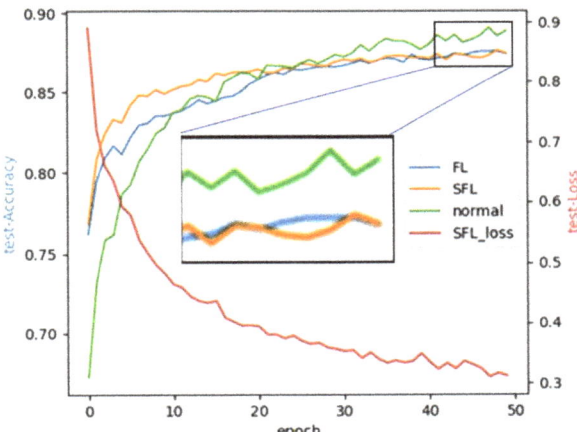

Figure 4. Testing convergence of LeNet on Fashion MNIST under various learning.

4.4. Effect of Different Clients on Performance

In this section, we will analyze the influence of edge client data on model training accuracy. For multi-level SFL, we increase the number of nodes on each tier as well as the number of clients for aggregation of model weights, as shown in Table 5. Considering that the master server running the split model needs to run the split model for each client node, we assume that each client group in different regions is equipped with a master server node, so during the model training and optimization process, we do not consider the transfer time between the master service node and the client node.

Table 5. Number of clients and multi-level nodes for training.

The number of clients	5	10	20	50
The number of edge nodes in edge level	2	2	2	4
The number of fog nodes in fog level	1	1	2	2
The number of cloud servers	1	1	1	1
The number of master servers	2	2	2	4

This section will analyze the impact of the number of LeNet users on Fashion MNIST. Figure 5 shows how the test accuracy and convergence rate vary with the number of epochs when a multi-level SFL is trained on a different number of clients (5, 10, 20, 50 clients). We can see that as the number of clients increases, the convergence speed of multi-level SFL will slow down, but the convergence speed is not obvious, and it is always better than the convergence speed of centralized learning. Moreover, for multi-level SFL, presumably, as the number of clients increases, the model accuracy decreases. For example, when the number of clients reaches 20 and 50, the accuracy of the test is significantly lower than that of the concentrated learning. However, the accuracy of the model trained on 50 clients is slightly higher than the accuracy of the model trained on 20 clients because the edge nodes of the middle layer also increase as the layers of the client are interlayer, so the number of middle-layer nodes of the multi-level SFL helps the SFL reduce the loss of accuracy.

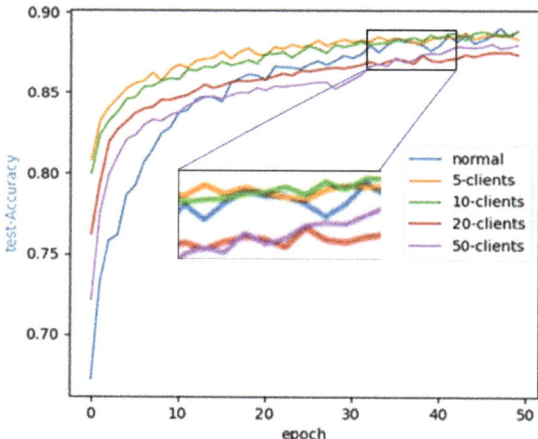

Figure 5. Effect of the number of clients on testing accuracy for LeNet on Fashion MNIST.

Figure 6 shows the time cost required for LeNet to train the Fashion MNIST dataset with a different number of clients. As can be seen from the figure, the training time required for centralized learning is always better than the time cost of training the model under multi-level SFL with different clients. This is because the experiment simulates the MQTT protocol used by the AIoT system to communicate, so the communication time and the time spent waiting for all the clients to train will layer the time cost of the multi-level SFL. The training time of the model decreases first and then increases with the increase in clients. This is because as the number of multi-level SFL clients increases, the amount of data locally decreases accordingly, reaching the minimum time overhead with 20 clients. However, when the number of clients reaches 50, the time overhead for model training starts to rise because the time for cloud servers and nodes in the middle level to publish topics and receive requests under the MQTT protocol starts to increase.

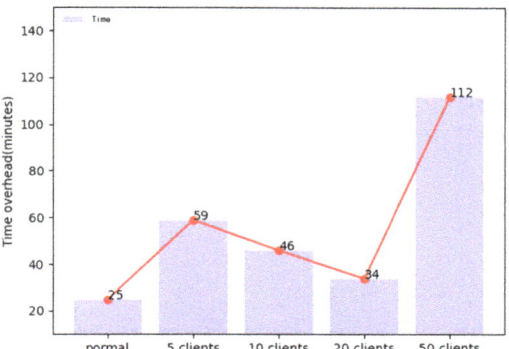

Figure 6. Time required for LeNet model to reach convergence in number of clients.

4.5. Impact of Different Level Layer on the SFL Model Training

Traditional split federated learning architecture, such as SFLV1 and SFLV2 [29], has only two levels: the server executing FedAvg and the clients with the master server. It has only one operation of model parameter aggregation, and when a client is corrupted, the FedAvg server will wait and freeze. Multi-level SFL performs model aggregation operations at multiple levels, and due to the MQTT protocol, nodes performing aggregation operations can communicate with clients by publishing topics, so there is no need to wait for broken nodes. Therefore, we set up two SFL scenarios: traditional SFL (SFLV1) and multi-level SFL, both of which have 20 clients for collaborative learning, and multi-level SFL with 4 edge nodes and 2 fog nodes to perform aggregation of global model weights. In addition, we make the dataset to which each client is assigned non-independent and identically distributed (non-IID). Moreover, the local dataset of the clients is divided according to the label distribution of the sample, which means the sample label distribution on each client is different.

Figure 7 shows the relationship between epochs and model test accuracy by non-IID SFLV1 and multi-level SFL architectures under the MQTT communication protocol. After 50 epochs, multi-level SFL and SFLV1-trained LeNet models can achieve approximately 88% and 86% accuracy, respectively, under non-IID. As can be seen from the figure, in the non-IID scenario, multi-level SFL is superior to traditional SFL, with faster convergence and higher model accuracy. This indicates that non-IID has a negative effect on splitting federated learning, but multi-level SFL can improve this problem. In the federated learning part, compared with traditional split federation learning, multi-level split federation learning can aggregate more clients at the same time for model training, so the model convergence speed will be faster. In the split learning part, since the multi-level SFL performs aggregation operations at each layer, the multi-level SFL clients undergo more local model updates, which alleviates the non-IID problem.

4.6. Comparison of Multi-Level SFL and FL Time Cost

This section compares the time overhead of multi-level SFL and multi-level FL when training large (ResNet18) and small (LeNet) machine learning tasks. Both use a four-level multi-level architecture, and the number of clients is 20. In order to simulate the limited computing resources of the client and the efficient computing resources of the master server, the local training of the client uses the CPU for computing, while the split model trained by the master server uses the GPU for training. We test the impact of multiple levels of SFL on resource-limited clients by the time overhead on model training.

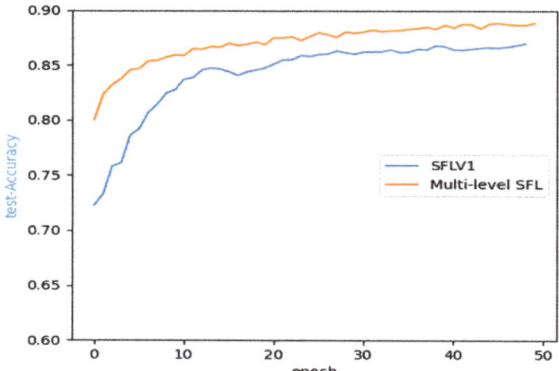

Figure 7. Testing convergence of LeNet on non-IID dataset.

As shown in Figure 8, centralized learning has the lowest time cost for both small and large machine learning tasks, at 25.32 min and 85.57 min, respectively. In the training of small model LeNet, the time cost of multi-level FL is slightly lower than that of multi-level SFL, and the difference in time cost between the two is not obvious. This is because when training the small network LeNet, the computing cost of the two-layer network in the local training of the client is relatively small, and the master server only needs to train the three-layer network, so the impact of split learning on the global training of the AIoT system cannot be reflected. Furthermore, because the master server and client also communicate via the MQTT protocol, multi-level SFL has a partial longer topic release time than multi-level FL. Therefore, in the small network training, multi-level SFL cannot present its advantage. However, on a large network, such as ResNet18, which has 18 layers, 15 of which are computed by the master server, the time cost of multi-level SFL is significantly lower than that of multi-level FL. And because the split learning process of multi-level SFL is run in parallel in the main server, rather than a linear run similar to split learning, the time cost of multi-level learning in large machine learning tasks is lower. The experimental results show that multi-layer SFL is more suitable for clients in AIoT with limited resources than multi-layer FL.

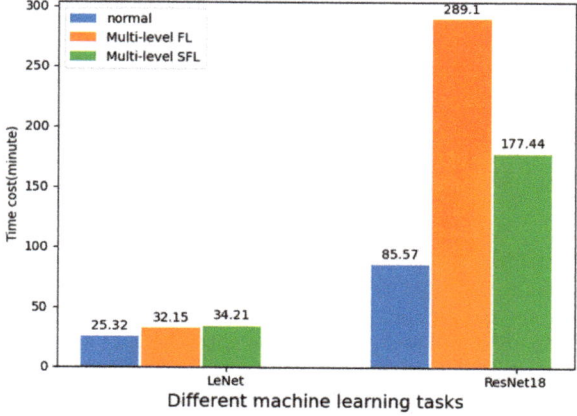

Figure 8. Time cost of multi-level SFL and multi-level FL train different models.

5. Conclusions

In this work, we proposed a novel multi-level split federated learning (SFL) framework for the enhancement of collaborative learning in large-scale AIoT systems. The multi-level SFL framework addresses the connectivity and data processing challenges that occur in a large-scale AIoT system with a multitude of clients. Through multiple levels of aggregation of model parameters, it significantly reduces the communication delay between the cloud server and the clients, enhancing the processing speed and entire performance of the central server. By integrating split learning into the framework, it balances the system heterogeneity among clients and boosts the system's scalability to incorporate more IoT devices for collaborative learning. It also mitigates the single point of failure risk of the central cloud server and ensures continuous model training even in the event of longer transmission distances. The use of the Message Queuing Telemetry Transport (MQTT) protocol and Docker containers in the experimental setup substantiates the practical feasibility of the proposed multi-level SFL framework. The resulting improvements in model accuracy under large-scale clients and faster convergence in non-IID scenarios, as evidenced by the simulation experiments, further validate the effectiveness of the proposed solution. Although our proposed multi-level SFL architecture has shown some advantages in model accuracy, it still has some shortcomings in terms of transmission overhead. For example, we have not further explored the effect of different sized datasets on the size of the information transferred and how to balance the overall communication overhead through MQTT generated by federated learning and split learning. Future work will further study these aspects.

Author Contributions: Conceptualization, H.X., K.P.S. and L.M.A.; methodology, H.X. and K.P.S.; resources, K.P.S.; data curation, H.X., K.P.S. and L.M.A.; writing—original draft preparation, H.X., K.P.S. and J.S.; writing—review and editing, K.P.S., J.S. and L.M.A. All authors have read and agreed to the published version of the manuscript.

Funding: This research received no external funding.

Data Availability Statement: The Fashion MNIST dataset can be found in Kaggle: https://www.kaggle.com/datasets/zalando-research/fashionmnist (accessed on 15 January 2024). The HAM10000 dataset comes from the paper: "The HAM10000 dataset, a large collection of multi-source dermatoscopic images of common pigmented skin lesions", DOI: https://doi.org/10.1038/sdata.2018.161.

Conflicts of Interest: The authors declare no conflicts of interest.

References

1. Su, Z.; Wang, Y.; Luan, T.H.; Zhang, N.; Li, F.; Chen, T.; Cao, H. Secure and Efficient Federated Learning for Smart Grid With Edge-Cloud Collaboration. *IEEE Trans. Ind. Inform.* **2022**, *18*, 1333–1344. [CrossRef]
2. Xu, C.; Qu, Y.; Luan, T.H.; Eklund, P.W.; Xiang, Y.; Gao, L. An Efficient and Reliable Asynchronous Federated Learning Scheme for Smart Public Transportation. *IEEE Trans. Veh. Technol.* **2023**, *72*, 6584–6598. [CrossRef]
3. Lian, Z.; Yang, Q.; Wang, W.; Zeng, Q.; Alazab, M.; Zhao, H.; Su, C. DEEP-FEL: Decentralized, Efficient and Privacy-Enhanced Federated Edge Learning for Healthcare Cyber Physical Systems. *IEEE Trans. Netw. Sci. Eng.* **2022**, *9*, 3558–3569. [CrossRef]
4. Taïk, A.; Mlika, Z.; Cherkaoui, S. Clustered Vehicular Federated Learning: Process and Optimization. *IEEE Trans. Intell. Transp. Syst.* **2022**, *23*, 25371–25383. [CrossRef]
5. Bebortta, S.; Tripathy, S.S.; Basheer, S.; Chowdhary, C.L. FedEHR: A Federated Learning Approach towards the Prediction of Heart Diseases in IoT-Based Electronic Health Records. *Diagnostics* **2023**, *13*, 3166. [CrossRef]
6. Hsu, R.-H.; Wang, Y.-C.; Fan, C.-I.; Sun, B.; Ban, T.; Takahashi, T.; Wu, T.-W.; Kao, S.-W. A Privacy-Preserving Federated Learning System for Android Malware Detection Based on Edge Computing. In Proceedings of the 2020 15th Asia Joint Conference on Information Security (AsiaJCIS), Taipei, Taiwan, 20–21 August 2020; pp. 128–136.
7. Yamamoto, F.; Ozawa, S.; Wang, L. eFL-Boost: Efficient Federated Learning for Gradient Boosting Decision Trees. *IEEE Access* **2022**, *10*, 43954–43963. [CrossRef]
8. Jiang, L.; Wang, Y.; Zheng, W.; Jin, C.; Li, Z.; Teo, S.G. LSTMSPLIT: Effective SPLIT Learning Based LSTM on Sequential Time-Series Data. In Proceedings of the 36th AAAI Conference on Artificial Intelligence, Vancouver, BC, Canada, 28 February–1 March 2022.
9. Hsieh, C.-Y.; Chuang, Y.-C.; Wu, A.-Y. C3-SL: Circular Convolution-Based Batch-Wise Compression for Communication-Efficient Split Learning. In Proceedings of the 2022 IEEE 32nd International Workshop on Machine Learning for Signal Processing (MLSP), Xi'an, China, 22–25 August 2022.

10. Chen, X.; Li, J.; Chakrabarti, C. Communication and Computation Reduction for Split Learning Using Asynchronous Training. In Proceedings of the 2021 IEEE Workshop on Signal Processing Systems (SiPS), Coimbra, Portugal, 19–21 October 2021; pp. 76–81.
11. Abedi, A.; Khan, S.S. FedSL: Federated Split Learning on Distributed Sequential Data in Recurrent Neural Networks. *Multimed. Tools Appl.* **2023**. [CrossRef]
12. Wu, Y.; Kang, Y.; Luo, J.; He, Y.; Yang, Q. FedCG: Leverage Conditional GAN for Protecting Privacy and Maintaining Competitive Performance in Federated Learning. *arXiv* **2022**, arXiv:2111.08211.
13. Zhang, Z.; Pinto, A.; Turina, V.; Esposito, F.; Matta, I. Privacy and Efficiency of Communications in Federated Split Learning. *IEEE Trans. Big Data* **2023**, *9*, 1380–1391. [CrossRef]
14. Deng, Y.; Lyu, F.; Ren, J.; Zhang, Y.; Zhou, Y.; Zhang, Y.; Yang, Y. SHARE: Shaping Data Distribution at Edge for Communication-Efficient Hierarchical Federated Learning. In Proceedings of the 2021 IEEE 41st International Conference on Distributed Computing Systems (ICDCS), Washington, DC, USA, 7–10 July 2021; pp. 24–34.
15. Liu, L.; Zhang, J.; Song, S.H.; Letaief, K.B. Client-Edge-Cloud Hierarchical Federated Learning. In Proceedings of the ICC 2020—2020 IEEE International Conference on Communications (ICC), Dublin, Ireland, 7–11 June 2020; pp. 1–6.
16. Mansour, Y.; Mohri, M.; Ro, J.; Suresh, A.T. Three Approaches for Personalization with Applications to Federated Learning. *arXiv* **2020**, arXiv:2002.10619.
17. Hao, M.; Li, H.; Luo, X.; Xu, G.; Yang, H.; Liu, S. Efficient and Privacy-Enhanced Federated Learning for Industrial Artificial Intelligence. *IEEE Trans. Ind. Inform.* **2020**, *16*, 6532–6542. [CrossRef]
18. Wang, H.; Kaplan, Z.; Niu, D.; Li, B. Optimizing Federated Learning on Non-IID Data with Reinforcement Learning. In Proceedings of the IEEE INFOCOM 2020—IEEE Conference on Computer Communications, Toronto, ON, Canada, 6–9 July 2020; pp. 1698–1707.
19. Guo, J.; Ho, I.W.-H.; Hou, Y.; Li, Z. FedPos: A Federated Transfer Learning Framework for CSI-Based Wi-Fi Indoor Posi-tioning. *IEEE Syst. J.* **2023**, *17*, 4579–4590. [CrossRef]
20. Karimireddy, S.P.; Kale, S.; Mohri, M.; Reddi, S.J.; Stich, S.U.; Suresh, A.T. SCAFFOLD: Stochastic Controlled Averaging for Federated Learning. In Proceedings of the 37th International Conference on Machine Learning, PMLR, Online, 13–18 July 2020; Volume 119, pp. 5132–5143.
21. Tan, A.Z.; Yu, H.; Cui, L.; Yang, Q. Towards Personalized Federated Learning. *IEEE Trans. Neural Netw. Learn. Syst.* **2023**, *34*, 9587–9603. [CrossRef]
22. Xu, Y.; Fan, H. FedDK: Improving Cyclic Knowledge Distillation for Personalized Healthcare Federated Learning. *IEEE Access* **2023**, *11*, 72409–72417. [CrossRef]
23. Guo, S.; Xiang, B.; Chen, L.; Yang, H.; Yu, D. Multi-Level Federated Learning Mechanism with Reinforcement Learning Optimizing in Smart City. In *Proceedings of the Artificial Intelligence and Security*; Sun, X., Zhang, X., Xia, Z., Bertino, E., Eds.; Springer International Publishing: Cham, Switzerland, 2022; pp. 441–454.
24. Campolo, C.; Genovese, G.; Singh, G.; Molinaro, A. Scalable and Interoperable Edge-Based Federated Learning in IoT Contexts. *Comput. Netw.* **2023**, *223*, 109576. [CrossRef]
25. Liu, L.; Tian, Y.; Chakraborty, C.; Feng, J.; Pei, Q.; Zhen, L.; Yu, K. Multilevel Federated Learning-Based Intelligent Traffic Flow Forecasting for Transportation Network Management. *IEEE Trans. Netw. Serv. Manag.* **2023**, *20*, 1446–1458. [CrossRef]
26. Wu, Z.; Wu, X.; Long, Y. Multi-Level Federated Graph Learning and Self-Attention Based Personalized Wi-Fi Indoor Fingerprint Localization. *IEEE Commun. Lett.* **2022**, *26*, 1794–1798. [CrossRef]
27. Thapa, C.; Chamikara, M.A.P.; Camtepe, S.A. Advancements of Federated Learning Towards Privacy Preservation: From Federated Learning to Split Learning. In *Federated Learning Systems: Towards Next-Generation*; Rehman, M.H.U., Gaber, M.M., Eds.; Studies in Computational Intelligence; Springer International Publishing: Cham, Switzerland, 2021; pp. 79–109. ISBN 978-3-030-70604-3.
28. Ayad, A.; Renner, M.; Schmeink, A. Improving the Communication and Computation Efficiency of Split Learning for IoT Applications. In Proceedings of the 2021 IEEE Global Communications Conference (GLOBECOM), Madrid, Spain, 7–11 December 2021; pp. 01–06.
29. Thapa, C.; Chamikara, M.A.P.; Camtepe, S.; Sun, L. SplitFed: When Federated Learning Meets Split Learning. *Proc. AAAI Conf. Artif. Intell.* **2022**, *36*, 8485–8493. [CrossRef]
30. Tian, Y.; Wan, Y.; Lyu, L.; Yao, D.; Jin, H.; Sun, L. FedBERT: When Federated Learning Meets Pre-Training. *ACM Trans. Intell. Syst. Technol.* **2022**, *13*, 66:1–66:26. [CrossRef]
31. Jiang, H.; Liu, M.; Sun, S.; Wang, Y.; Guo, X. FedSyL: Computation-Efficient Federated Synergy Learning on Heterogeneous IoT Devices. In Proceedings of the 2022 IEEE/ACM 30th International Symposium on Quality of Service (IWQoS), Oslo, Norway, 10–12 June 2022; pp. 1–10.
32. Deng, R.; Du, X.; Lu, Z.; Duan, Q.; Huang, S.-C.; Wu, J. HSFL: Efficient and Privacy-Preserving Offloading for Split and Federated Learning in IoT Services. In Proceedings of the 2023 IEEE International Conference on Web Services (ICWS), Chicago, IL, USA, 2–8 July 2023; pp. 658–668.
33. Samikwa, E.; Maio, A.D.; Braun, T. ARES: Adaptive Resource-Aware Split Learning for Internet of Things. *Comput. Netw.* **2022**, *218*, 109380. [CrossRef]

34. Gao, Y.; Kim, M.; Abuadbba, S.; Kim, Y.; Thapa, C.; Kim, K.; Camtep, S.A.; Kim, H.; Nepal, S. End-to-End Evaluation of Federated Learning and Split Learning for Internet of Things. In Proceedings of the 2020 International Symposium on Reliable Distributed Systems (SRDS), Shanghai, China, 21–24 September 2020; pp. 91–100.
35. McMahan, B.; Moore, E.; Ramage, D.; Hampson, S.; y Arcas, B.A. Communication-Efficient Learning of Deep Networks from Decentralized Data. In Proceedings of the 20th International Conference on Artificial Intelligence and Statistics, PMLR, Fort Lauderdale, FL, USA, 20–22 April 2017; pp. 1273–1282.
36. Shahri, E.; Pedreiras, P.; Almeida, L. Extending MQTT with Real-Time Communication Services Based on SDN. *Sensors* **2022**, *22*, 3162. [CrossRef] [PubMed]
37. Lecun, Y.; Bottou, L.; Bengio, Y.; Haffner, P. Gradient-Based Learning Applied to Document Recognition. *Proc. IEEE* **1998**, *86*, 2278–2324. [CrossRef]
38. Tschandl, P.; Rosendahl, C.; Kittler, H. The HAM10000 Dataset, a Large Collection of Multi-Source Dermatoscopic Images of Common Pigmented Skin Lesions. *Sci. Data* **2018**, *5*, 180161. [CrossRef] [PubMed]

Disclaimer/Publisher's Note: The statements, opinions and data contained in all publications are solely those of the individual author(s) and contributor(s) and not of MDPI and/or the editor(s). MDPI and/or the editor(s) disclaim responsibility for any injury to people or property resulting from any ideas, methods, instructions or products referred to in the content.

 *future internet*

Article

A Lightweight Neural Network Model for Disease Risk Prediction in Edge Intelligent Computing Architecture

Feng Zhou [1], Shijing Hu [1,*], Xin Du [1], Xiaoli Wan [2] and Jie Wu [1]

[1] School of Computer Science, Fudan University, Shanghai 200438, China; 19110240047@fudan.edu.cn (F.Z.); xdu20@fudan.edu.cn (X.D.); jwu@fudan.edu.cn (J.W.)
[2] Information Center, Zhejiang International Business Group, Hangzhou 310000, China; wanxl@zibchina.com
* Correspondence: sjhu21@m.fudan.edu.cn

Abstract: In the current field of disease risk prediction research, there are many methods of using servers for centralized computing to train and infer prediction models. However, this centralized computing method increases storage space, the load on network bandwidth, and the computing pressure on the central server. In this article, we design an image preprocessing method and propose a lightweight neural network model called Linge (Lightweight Neural Network Models for the Edge). We propose a distributed intelligent edge computing technology based on the federated learning algorithm for disease risk prediction. The intelligent edge computing method we proposed for disease risk prediction directly performs prediction model training and inference at the edge without increasing storage space. It also reduces the load on network bandwidth and reduces the computing pressure on the server. The lightweight neural network model we designed has only 7.63 MB of parameters and only takes up 155.28 MB of memory. In the experiment with the Linge model compared with the EfficientNetV2 model, the accuracy and precision increased by 2%, the recall rate increased by 1%, the specificity increased by 4%. the F1 score increased by 3%, and the AUC (Area Under the Curve) value increased by 2%.

Keywords: federated learning; edge computing; deep learning; image classification; disease risk prediction

Citation: Zhou, F.; Hu, S.; Du, X.; Wan, X.; Wu, J. A Lightweight Neural Network Model for Disease Risk Prediction in Edge Intelligent Computing Architecture. *Future Internet* **2024**, *16*, 75. https://doi.org/10.3390/fi16030075

Academic Editor: Symeon Papavassiliou

Received: 22 January 2024
Revised: 13 February 2024
Accepted: 17 February 2024
Published: 26 February 2024

Copyright: © 2024 by the authors. Licensee MDPI, Basel, Switzerland. This article is an open access article distributed under the terms and conditions of the Creative Commons Attribution (CC BY) license (https:// creativecommons.org/licenses/by/ 4.0/).

1. Introduction

Current research on disease risk prediction mainly uses physiological indicators and risk factors to predict disease risk [1], images to predict disease risk [2], and audio to predict disease risk [3]. These studies have achieved good results. In these studies, the risk of diabetes was predicted with 99.8% accuracy, the risk of Parkinson's disease was predicted with 98% accuracy, and the risk of laryngeal air cyst was predicted with 98.5% accuracy. Some researchers use the prediction of mean arterial blood pressure in patients with sepsis to assist in treating septic shock [4].

The current application scenarios of disease risk prediction models mainly include hospitals, health management centers, insurance institutions, and elderly care institutions. Hospitals use disease risk prediction models to assist doctors in providing medical services to patients. The health management center uses disease risk prediction models to predict health risks for users and develops health intervention plans based on health analysis reports. Insurance institutions use disease risk prediction models to assist staff in making business risk judgments. Elderly care institutions use disease risk prediction models to periodically provide disease risk predictions to the elderly, improving their health status and reducing the pressure on public health services.

Although the application scenarios of disease risk prediction models are diverse, according to our research, these application scenarios also have standard rules. When designing and implementing disease risk prediction models using centralized computing methods, these application scenarios must go through model design, sample processing, model training, and optimization. In the sample processing stage, when different institutions or enterprises use centralized computing methods, they will summarize the data of each branch unit. This method increases the overhead of data storage space and brings hidden dangers to data transmission security and integrity. In the model training and optimization phase, different institutions or enterprises use central server calculations when using centralized computing methods. This method increases the burden on the central server and wastes edge server resources. The usage of our proposed distributed intelligent edge computing technology for disease risk prediction is shown in Figure 1.

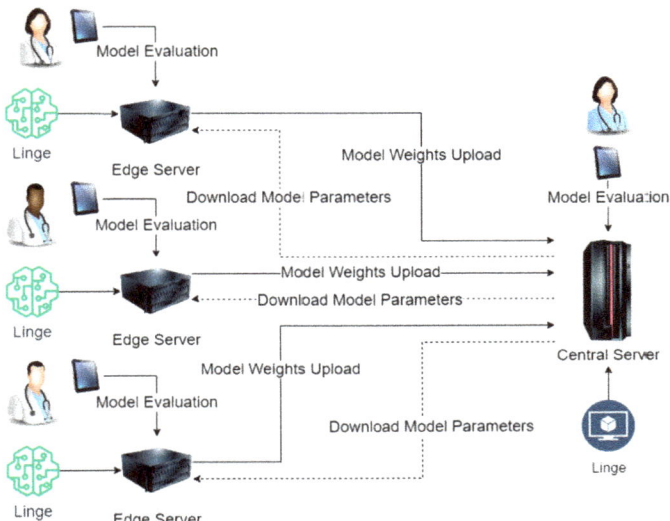

Figure 1. Implementation Process of Distributed Intelligent Edge Computing Approach for Disease Risk Prediction.

As shown in Figure 1, the lightweight neural network model Linge (Lightweight Neural Network Models for the Edge) we designed will be deployed on the enterprise or institution's central server and each branch unit's edge servers. The prediction model's training and inference are completed on each branch unit's edge servers. The prediction model on the edge server of each branch unit will upload the model weights output to the central server after training and download the latest model parameters from the central server. During the inference process of the prediction model, disease risk prediction experts evaluate and correct the inference results of the model on the central server and each edge server. Using this distributed intelligent edge computing method to train disease risk prediction models does not increase data storage space, completely eliminates hidden dangers in data transmission security and data transmission integrity, and does not increase computing pressure on the central server.

The research goal of this article is to achieve effective prediction of disease risk in diverse disease risk prediction application scenarios based on federated learning algorithms, edge computing, the MRI (Magnetic Resonance Imaging) image preprocessing method designed in this article, and lightweight neural network models. In this article's research on effective disease risk prediction, the main work carried out is as follows:

- To further improve the quality of the data set, reduce the cost of feature extraction by the model, and improve the model's accuracy, we designed an MRI image preprocessing method.
- For the configuration attributes of the edge server, we designed a new lightweight neural network model based on the lightweight attention mechanism.

- For diverse application scenarios, we propose a distributed intelligent edge computing technology for disease risk prediction based on federated learning algorithms, edge computing, the MRI image preprocessing method designed in this article, and lightweight neural network models.

The introductory section of this article describes the background of our research. The related work section describes the current research status. The Preliminaries section describes related techniques. The model design and implementation section describes the designed image preprocessing method, lightweight neural network model, and distributed intelligent edge computing technology for disease risk prediction. The experimental results analysis and conclusion sections describe the experiments during the research process of this article, summarize the research results, and discuss future research.

2. Related Works

Many current disease risk prediction studies are based on federated learning or edge computing. For example, to achieve accurate heart disease prediction on the medical Internet of Things platform, Y. Pan et al. proposed a multilayer perceptron model based on a convolutional neural network to help doctors effectively diagnose heart disease patients on the cloud platform [5]. This model achieved an accuracy of 94.9% in experiments. To perform training tasks on wearable devices [6], Yeting Guo et al. proposed a federated edge learning system for efficient privacy-preserving mobile healthcare based on federated learning. S. Hakak et al. proposed a conceptual framework for leveraging edge computing to support healthcare analytics based on user-generated data [7]. This framework can be extended to develop distributed disease management systems based on personal health data.

To solve the problems of network congestion and low response speed that occur when implementing clinical decision support systems using traditional methods [8], Z. Xue et al. proposed a technology that integrates mobile edge computing and software-defined networks. D. Gupta et al. proposed an anomaly detection model based on federated learning to solve the anomaly detection problem in centralized healthcare ecosystems [9], which often suffer from severe response time delays and high-performance overhead. To reduce the cost of data transmission to the cloud in the healthcare Internet of Things [10], W. Y. B. Lim et al. proposed a dynamic contract design based on federated learning and edge computing architecture for innovative medical applications. Since the urban digital twin system relies on long-term collected data to make appropriate decisions to solve the limitations when major infectious disease emergencies occur [11], J. Pang et al. proposed a framework that integrates the urban digital twin system with federated learning. V. Gomathy et al., based on edge computing methods and linear regression [12], studied polluted air and mortality caused by COVID-19 (Corona Virus Disease 2019) and concluded that in areas with air pollution, the mortality caused by COVID-19 is 77% higher. D. Y. Zhang et al. proposed a new federated learning framework to solve the class imbalance problem in abnormal health detection [13]. This framework achieves an F1 score of 0.816 in driver drowsiness detection applications.

Q. Wu et al. proposed a new cloud edge-based federated learning framework for home health monitoring [14]. This framework learns a global model shared in the cloud from multiple homes at the network's edge and achieves data privacy protection by saving user data locally. This framework achieved an accuracy of 95.87% in experiments. D. C. Nguyen et al. proposed a new blockchain-based framework to implement COVID-19 detection using generative adversarial networks in edge cloud computing [15]. This framework implements the joint design of federated learning and GAN (Generative Adversarial Networks) in a distributed medical network with edge cloud computing. This framework achieved an accuracy of 97.5% in experiments.

To solve the problem of high latency in the healthcare system due to its reliance on central servers [16], V. Hayyolalam et al. used edge computing to move computing and storage resources closer to end users. This method utilizes a metaheuristic-based feature selection method of the Black Widow Optimization (BWO) algorithm to detect heart disease in patients. Experimental results show that they achieved an accuracy of 90.11%. To improve the confidence of the prediction model [17], Linardos et al. proposed a simulated federated learning research method on cardiovascular diseases based on CNN (Convolutional Neural Networks). To realize human motion recognition based on federated learning through wearable devices in intelligent medical systems [18], Arikumar KS et al. proposed a federated learning-based human motion recognition method based on bidirectional long short-term memory (BiLSTM). The accuracy of this method in experiments reached 99.67%. To protect the data privacy of healthcare applications that rely on the Internet of Things [19], H. Elayan et al. proposed a deep federated learning framework for healthcare data monitoring and analysis using IoT devices. This framework achieved an accuracy of 84.8% and an AUC (Area Under the Curve) of 97% in experiments on detecting skin diseases.

To solve the privacy and security issues during interactions caused by potential patient data leakage in the healthcare Internet of Things [20], Z. Lian et al. proposed a decentralized, efficient, and privacy-enhanced federated edge learning system based on convolutional neural networks. This system achieved an accuracy of 87% in experiments on the skin cancer data set. B. T. H. Dang et al. proposed a collaboration framework [21]. This framework is used to train convolutional neural network-based heart disease prediction models. This framework uses federated learning to implement model training using distributed data stored individually on multiple machines. This framework uses the MIT-BIH arrhythmia data set to train the model. In experiments, this framework achieved an accuracy of 98.92%, a recall of 97.41%, a precision of 99.23%, and an F1 score of 98.02%.

To solve the security and privacy issues of the medical Internet of Things under edge intelligent computing [22], R. Wang et al. proposed a privacy protection scheme for federated learning under edge computing. Xiaomin Ouyang et al. proposed an end-to-end system integrating multimodal sensors and federated learning algorithms to achieve digital biomarker detection of multidimensional Alzheimer's disease in natural living environments [23]. The system achieved an accuracy of 95% in experiments detecting digital biomarkers and an average accuracy of 87.5% in experiments identifying Alzheimer's disease. L. Zhang et al. proposed a privacy-preserving federated learning method based on homomorphic encryption and deep neural network (DNN) for the Internet of Things healthcare system [24]. This method achieved an accuracy of 76.9% in experiments using the HAM10000 data set.

As can be seen from the above description and Table 1, current research based on machine learning, federated learning, and edge computing has achieved good results. For example, the accuracy of predicting the risk of cardiovascular disease reaches 99.67%, the accuracy of predicting the risk of skin cancer reaches 87%, and the accuracy of predicting the risk of heart disease reaches 98.92%. However, in the above studies, the neural network model parameters used are too large when predicting disease risk. In the application scenarios of federated learning and edge computing, they are limited by hardware resource requirements and are challenging to promote widely. The lightweight neural network model designed in this article has only 7.63 MB of parameters and only occupies 155.28 MB of memory. In the experiment, the accuracy of stroke risk prediction was 96%, the precision rate was 95%, the recall rate was 93%, the specificity was 95%, the F1 score was 98%, and the AUC was 97%. This experimental result shows that the distributed intelligent edge computing technology proposed in this article for disease risk prediction can provide practical support for disease risk prediction.

Table 1. Related Research Statistics.

Researcher	Research Objectives	Basic Algorithm	Accuracy
Q. Wu et al. [14]	Health Monitoring	CNN	95.87%
D. C. Nguyen et al. [15]	COVID-19	GAN	97.5%
Linardos et al. [17]	Cardiovascular Diseases	BiLSTM	99.67%
Z. Lian et al. [20]	Skin Cancer	CNN	87%
B. T. H. Dang et al. [21]	Heart Disease	CNN	98.92%

3. Preliminaries

The data sets used in the experiments of this article are the publicly available "Acute Ischemic Stroke MRI" data set and subject data, which are all image data. Therefore, when designing the lightweight neural network model structure, this article refers to the lightweight attention mechanism and the structure of the EfficientNetV2 network model.

3.1. Channel Attention Mechanism

SENET is the champion model of ImageNet 2017 [25]. SENET is used in the core MBConv module and Fused-MBConv module of the EfficientNetV2 network model to improve network performance. The SENET module structure is shown in Figure 2.

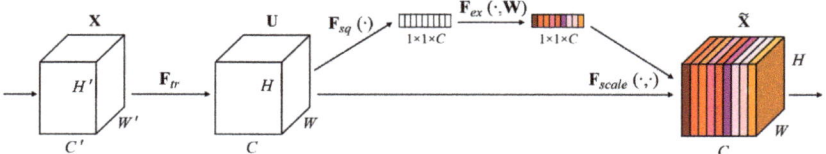

Figure 2. The SENET module structure [25].

In Figure 2, given an input X with a feature channel number of C', a feature with a feature channel number of C is obtained after a series of convolution and other transformations [25].

ECA-Net (Efficient Channel Attention Network) is an attention model used for computer vision tasks [26], designed to enhance the ability of neural networks to model image features. The overall structure of the ECA-Net module is shown in Figure 3 below.

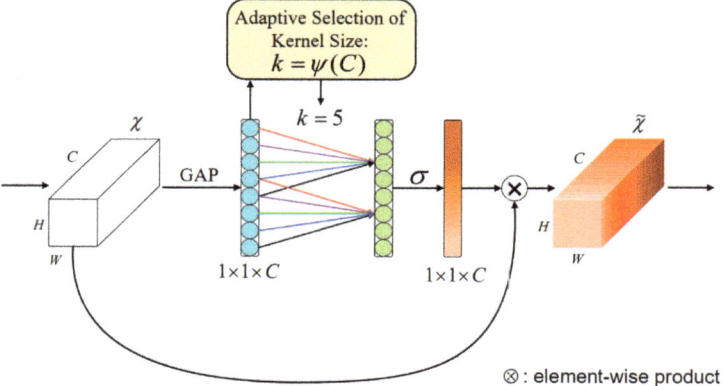

Figure 3. The ECA-Net module structure [26].

Figure 3 gives the aggregated features obtained through Global Average Pooling GAP (Global Average Pooling) [26]. ECA-Net generates channel weights by performing fast one-dimensional convolutions of size k, with a convolution kernel size k representing the coverage of local cross-channel interactions, where k is adaptively determined by the mapping of the channel dimension C. After global average pooling without reducing the dimensionality, ECA-Net captures local cross-channel interactive information by using each channel and its adjacent channels. This method ensures model efficiency and computational effect.

3.2. Lightweight Neural Network

Berkeley and Stanford researchers proposed that the parameters of the SqueezeNet network model are only 1/50 of Alexnet [27], but it achieves similar effects to Alexnet on ImageNet. Due to too few parameters, SqueezeNet is less effective in expressing complex problems. Google researchers proposed the MobileNet network model using depthwise separable convolutions [28]. MobileNetV2 optimizes the model structure based on MobileNet, which not only improves the performance of the network model but also reduces the calculation amount of the model. MNasNet integrates the inverted residual block designed based on MobileNetV2 as a building block into NAS [29]. Since MNasNet performs very well in block search but needs to be more comprehensive in the search of each layer width, MobileNetV3 uses MNasNet to search blocks [30]. For a series of models using the same building block, refer to the coefficients in MobileNet and MobileNetV2 and quickly obtain models of different sizes by directly increasing the width, depth, and resolution [31]. However, balancing the relationship between width, depth, and resolution has become vital.

To balance the relationship between width, depth, and resolution, the EfficientNet network model came into being [32]. However, this network model consumes much video memory when the input image is large. In addition, the EfficientNet network model has a significant overhead in reading and writing data. To further improve the EfficientNet network model, the EfficientNetV2 network model was born, which combines training-aware NAS and scaling [33].

4. Model Design and Implementation

This section introduces the MRI image sample preprocessing method, lightweight neural network model, distributed intelligent edge computing technology implementation, and model algorithm for disease risk prediction designed in this article.

4.1. MRI Image Sample Preprocessing Method

MRI (Magnetic Resonance Imaging) images provide doctors with clear, high-resolution images of the internal tissues and organs of the body. These images can reveal abnormal structures and help doctors accurately diagnose and develop treatment plans. To further improve the accuracy and reliability of the model, we designed a method to preprocess MRI image samples. The specific process is summarized as shown in Figure 4.

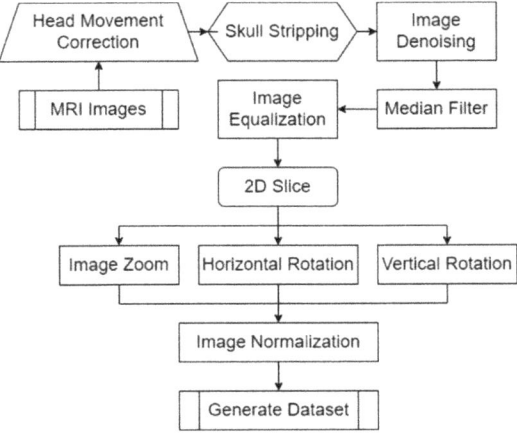

Figure 4. MRI image sample preprocessing method flow.

Since each MRI image is not entirely aligned, the MRI image sample preprocessing method we designed is shown in Figure 4. The image is first corrected for head motion. Since MRI images contain some non-brain structures (such as skulls), we delete non-brain structures in the images to avoid increasing the computational load and improving model efficiency. To further improve the training efficiency of the model, we denoise the image and use median filtering to denoise the spatial domain of the image. To extract more detailed features in the image, we equalize the image. Since MRI images are three-dimensional data, the model designed in this article inputs two-dimensional images. Therefore, in the MRI image sample preprocessing method we designed, only the coronal, sagittal, and transverse planes in the MRI images are extracted. To prevent the model from overfitting and improve the generalization ability of the model, we scale and rotate the MRI images. Finally, the MRI image sample preprocessing method we designed normalizes the data by traversing each pixel in the MRI image matrix. The normalization operation formula is summarized in Formula (1) during the processing process.

$$\hat{I} = \log 10(I) / \log 10(\max(I)) \tag{1}$$

I in Formula (1) represents the original image, $\hat{I}$ represents the normalized image, $\log 10(I)$ represents the logarithmic transformation function with base 10, and $\max(I)$ represents the maximum value in the image data.

4.2. Lightweight Neural Network Model

To improve the feature extraction capability and robustness of the model and focus more on the information of practical feature areas in the image, this article designed the EMBConv module and EFused-MBConv module concerning the EfficientNetV2 model structure. The structures of the EMBConv module and EFused-MBConv module are shown in Figure 5.

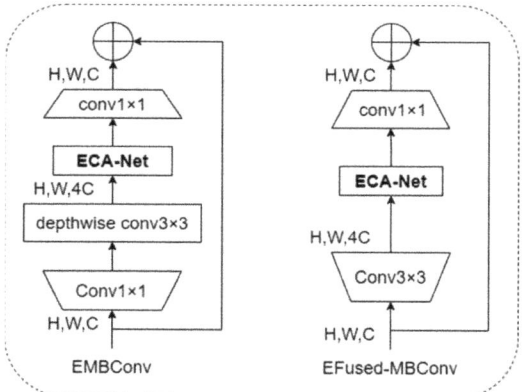

Figure 5. Structure of EMBConv module and EFused-MBConv module.

As shown in Figure 5, this article integrates the lightweight attention mechanism into the EMBConv module and EFused-MBCon module in the lightweight neural network model structure. The EfficientNetv2-S network model is the lightest model among the EfficientNetv2 network models. However, problems like large computational workload, long training time, and giant model space during training still need to be solved. Considering the application scenarios of distributed intelligent edge computing for disease risk prediction to allow model training and inference to be completed at the edge, this article refers to the backbone network structure of the EfficientNetv2-S network model and designs the Linge model. Because EMB-Conv has a smaller expansion ratio than EFused-MBConv, more minor expansion has less memory access overhead. Therefore, in the structure of the lightweight neural network model Linge designed in this article, EFused-MBConv is used in the Stage1 and Stage2 stages, and the EMBConv module is used in the Stage3, Stage4, Stage5, and Stage6 stages. This adjustment increases the size of the model's receptive field, reduces the depth and complexity of the model, and further improves the lightweight of the model. The structure of the new lightweight neural network model is shown in Table 2.

Table 2. Linge network model structure.

Stage	Operator	Stride	#Channels	#Layers
0	Conv3x3	2	24	1
1	EFused-MBConv1, k3x3	1	24	2
2	EFused-MBConv4, k3x3	2	48	4
3	EMBConv4, k3x3	2	64	4
4	EMBConv4, k3x3, ECA0.25	2	128	6
5	EMBConv6, k3x3, ECA0.25	1	160	9
6	EMBConv6, k3x3, ECA0.25	2	256	15
7	Conv1x1 & Pooling & FC	-	1280	1

Table 2, ECA0.25 indicates that the number of nodes in the first fully connected layer in the ECA module is 1/4 of the number of feature matrix channels input to the EMBConv module. The new lightweight neural network model reduces memory access overhead and improves feature extraction capabilities and model robustness.

4.3. Implementation of Distributed Intelligent Edge Computing Technology for Disease Risk Prediction

The implementation process of the distributed intelligent edge computing technology proposed in this article for disease risk prediction is summarized as shown in Figure 6.

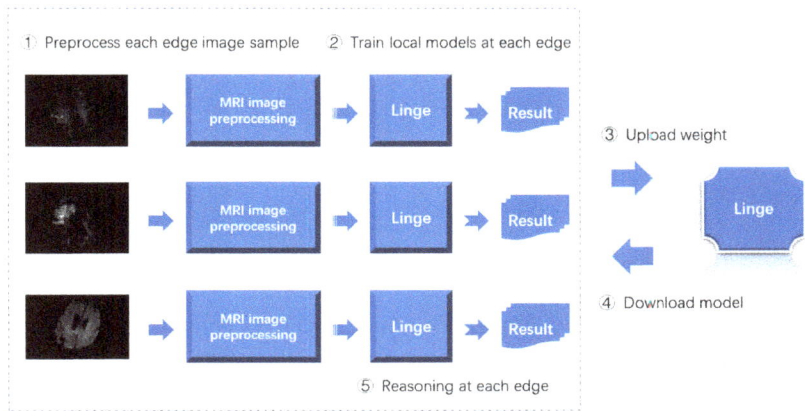

Figure 6. Implementation process of distributed intelligent edge computing technology for disease risk prediction.

As shown in Figure 6, when implementing distributed intelligent edge computing technology for disease risk prediction, the image samples at each edge are first processed using the MRI image preprocessing method designed in this article. Secondly, the preprocessed image samples train the lightweight neural network model designed in this article. Then, upload the model weights obtained by training to the central server. Then, each edge end downloads the most complete model. Finally, the inference is completed by each edge end.

The model training, verification, and testing of distributed intelligent edge computing technology for disease risk prediction uses public MRI image data sets. To verify the versatility of the distributed intelligent edge computing technology proposed in this article for disease risk prediction, this article uses the subject's MRI image data set to verify the designed prediction model. Experimental results show that the distributed intelligent edge computing technology proposed in this article for disease risk prediction has good versatility.

4.4. Model Algorithm

The algorithm process of the distributed intelligent edge computing technology proposed in this article for disease risk prediction is summarized as follows:

In Algorithm 1, $\{I_1, I_2, \ldots, I_n\}$ represents the "Acute Ischemic Stroke MRI" data set published on Kaggle. T represents the training sample data, V represents the verification sample data, S represents the test sample data, and epoch represents the number of training iterations.

Algorithm 1: Algorithms for intelligent edge computing technology

Input: $\{I_1, I_2, \ldots, I_n\}$
Output: Disease Risk Prediction Model

1. $T, V, S \leftarrow$ use the image feature preprocessing method designed in this article to preprocess $\{I_1, I_2, \ldots, I_n\}$
2. for $n = 0$ to epoch do
3.   Training a predictive model using Linge network
4.   Evaluate training effectiveness
5.   Model parameter optimization
6.   if the evaluation indicators are qualified:
7.   Output prediction model
8.   break
9.   else:
10. $n = n + 1$
11. Output the model with the highest evaluation
12. The edge side uploads model weights to the central server
13. The edge downloads the model from the central server and performs inference on the edge.

In Algorithm 1, each edge end uses the image preprocessing method to first preprocess the data set published on Kaggle. Then, the preprocessed samples were used to train the lightweight neural network model designed in this article. Secondly, each edge end uploads the model weight to the central server. The edge then downloads the central server model. Finally, the edge side completes the inference.

5. Experimental Results and Analysis

This section describes the sample data, evaluation metrics, experimental environment, prediction results, model performance indicator comparison, and model optimization comparison used in the experimental process of the proposed distributed intelligent edge computing technology for disease risk prediction. The federated learning framework we used in the experiment is TensorFlow Federated, and the deep learning framework is Tensorflow-GPU 2.6.0.

5.1. Sample Data

The data set used in this article is the "Acute Ischemic Stroke MRI" data set publicly available on Kaggle. The Neurology Department of Turgut Özal University Medical College Hospital collected this brain image data set. The Ethics Committee of the Faculty of Medicine of Turgut Özal University approved this study [34].

The sample data in Table 3 use MRI images of patients with acute ischemic infarction who were admitted to the hospital in 2021. This data set consists of ischemic acute infarction and standard images. To further verify the model's generalization ability, we used subject data from a nursing home to test the model further [34].

Table 3. Related Research Statistics [34].

Diffusion MRIs	Male	Female	Total	Male Age	Female Age	Number of MRIs
Ischemic Acute Infarction	33	44	77	73.36 ± 13.52	70.39 = 15.17	1002
Healthy	21	16	37	68.9 ± 8.72	71.43 = 16.39	1008

5.2. Evaluation Metrics

The indicators used to evaluate the prediction model in this article are accuracy, precision, recall, specificity, F1 score, and AUC value.

$$Accuracy = \frac{TP + TN}{TP + TN + FP + FN} \times 100\% \quad (2)$$

$$Precision = \frac{TP}{TP + FP} \times 100\% \quad (3)$$

$$Recall = \frac{TP}{TP + FN} \times 100\% \quad (4)$$

$$Specificity = \frac{TN}{TP + FN} \times 100\% \quad (5)$$

$$F1 = \frac{2TP}{2TP + FP + FN} \times 100\% \quad (6)$$

In Formulas (2)–(6), TP means that the correct prediction is a positive example; that is, the prediction is a positive example and the prediction result is correct [1]. In Formulas (2)–(6), TP means that the correct prediction is a positive example, and TN means that the correct prediction is a counterexample. FP means that the wrong prediction is a positive example. For example, FN indicates that the wrong prediction is a counterexample [2,3].

5.3. Experimental Environment

When conducting experiments in this article, four machines were used, one of which was used as the central server and three as edge servers. The topology diagram is shown in Figure 7.

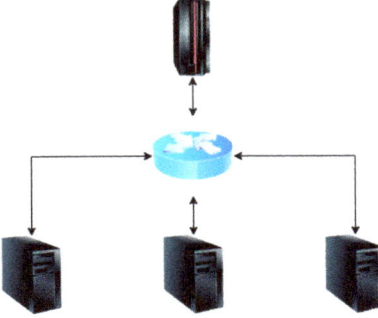

Figure 7. Experimental environment topology diagram.

As shown in Figure 7, in the hardware configuration of the central server during the experiment, the CPU is i7-13700F, the memory is 32 GB, the SSD is 3 TB, and the graphics card is RTX4060Ti. In the hardware configuration of the edge server during the experiment, the CPU is i5-13400F, the memory is 16 GB, the SSD is 1 TB, and the graphics card is RTX3060Ti. The operating systems of both the central and edge servers use the Ubuntu 20.04 LTS Server.

5.4. Prediction Results

In image classification prediction research, standard lightweight neural network models include LeViT, EfficientNetV2, MobileViTv2, EdgeViTs, EdgeNeXt, and AFFNet. Lightweight neural network models such as LeViT, EfficientNetV2, MobileViTv2, EdgeViTs, EdgeNeXt, and AFFNet are relatively common lightweight neural network models that achieve SOTA performance. Therefore, in order to understand the experimental effect of the lightweight neural network model proposed in this article, we conducted comparative experiments with network models such as LeViT, EfficientNetV2, MobileViTv2, EdgeViTs, EdgeNeXt, and AFFNet. The "Acute Ischemic Stroke MRI" data set published on Kaggle is used in experiments in papers published by researchers such as B. Tasci. Therefore, we chose to use this data set in the experiment, divided the training set, verification set, and test set according to the ratio of 8:1:1, and applied it to the comparative experiments of all models. When conducting experiments, we used all Adam optimizers; the batch_size settings were all 16, and the learning_rate settings were all 0.0001. The results of the experiment are shown in Table 4.

Table 4. Comparison of experimental results of various network models on public data sets.

Basic Algorithm	Accuracy	Precision	Recall	Specificity	F1	AUC
LeViT [35]	0.84	0.83	0.81	0.79	0.85	0.92
EfficientNetV2 [33]	0.94	0.93	0.92	0.91	0.95	0.95
MobileViTv2 [36]	0.86	0.84	0.85	0.83	0.87	0.93
EdgeViTs [37]	0.87	0.85	0.88	0.86	0.91	0.92
EdgeNeXt [38]	0.89	0.87	0.90	0.88	0.93	0.91
AFFNet [39]	0.93	0.92	0.91	0.89	0.94	0.96
Linge	0.96	0.95	0.93	0.95	0.98	0.97

Table 4 shows the experimental results on the public data set "Acute Ischemic Stroke MRI" introduced in this article. As seen from Table 4, in the experiment using public data sets to compare various network models, the EdgeNeXt and AFFNet network models achieved better experimental results. The lightweight neural network model proposed in this article has the best experimental results. When conducting comparative experiments, we accepted 350 MRI image data from two categories (with and without stroke risk, 175 images, respectively) provided by a medical institution. We organized them into a subject data set. This subject data set is used as a test data set for further testing of the model. To gain an in-depth understanding of the comparative experimental effects, we further tested each network model using the subject data set. The experimental results are shown in Table 5.

Table 5. Comparison of experimental results of various network models on the subject data set.

Basic Algorithm	Accuracy	Precision	Recall	Specificity	F1	AUC
LeViT [35]	0.83	0.82	0.77	0.78	0.81	0.93
EfficientNetV2 [33]	0.95	0.94	0.91	0.93	0.92	0.94
MobileViTv2 [36]	0.85	0.87	0.80	0.81	0.83	0.94
EdgeViTs [37]	0.88	0.89	0.85	0.83	0.84	0.93
EdgeNeXt [38]	0.90	0.91	0.87	0.89	0.86	0.92
AFFNet [39]	0.92	0.93	0.89	0.91	0.90	0.95
Linge	0.97	0.96	0.94	0.96	0.97	0.95

As shown in Table 5, in the experiment using the subject data set to compare various network models, the EdgeNeXt and AFFNet network models achieved better experimental results. The lightweight neural network model proposed in this article has the best experimental results.

This experiment shows that the lightweight neural network model proposed in this article can effectively support our proposed intelligent edge computing method for disease risk prediction.

5.5. Model Performance Indicator Comparison

To gain an in-depth understanding of the various performance effects of the lightweight neural network we proposed, this article conducted comparative experiments using lightweight neural network models LeViT, EfficientNetV2, MobileViTv2, EdgeViTs, EdgeNeXt, and AFFNet. The experimental comparison results are shown in Table 6.

Table 6. Comparison of model performance indicators with experimental results.

Basic Algorithm	Parameter Quantity/MB	Number of Operations/G	Memory Capacity Occupied/MB
LeViT [35]	11.93	11.97	192.97
EfficientNetV2 [33]	11.78	11.39	188.85
MobileViTv2 [36]	11.25	11.26	186.78
EdgeViTs [37]	10.27	10.86	185.63
EdgeNeXt [38]	9.55	9.98	170.35
AFFNet [39]	8.98	6.59	160.79
Linge	7.63	5.91	155.28

Table 6 shows that the proposed lightweight neural network's performance effects are significantly better than the lightweight neural network models LeViT, EfficientNetV2, MobileViTv2, EdgeViTs, EdgeNeXt, and AFFNet. Model performance index comparison experimental results show that the lightweight neural network model we proposed has the lowest number of parameters, the smallest number of operations, and the smallest occupied memory capacity compared to the above six models, and the model's overall performance is the best.

To further understand the timing performance of our proposed model, we used the Android platform to conduct comparative experiments on the inference time of the Linge model and lightweight neural network models such as LeViT, EfficientNetV2, MobileViTv2, EdgeViTs, EdgeNeXt, and AFFNet. The comparative experimental results are shown in Table 7.

Table 7. Model timing performance comparison experimental results.

Basic Algorithm	Inference Time (Seconds)/Photo
LeViT [35]	5.38
EfficientNetV2 [33]	4.89
MobileViTv2 [36]	4.61
EdgeViTs [37]	4.57
EdgeNeXt [38]	4.15
AFFNet [39]	3.93
Linge	3.26

Among the hardware platforms used in our inference speed performance comparison experiments, the operating system is Android 11, the display chip is Mali G52 2EE, the CPU is Allwinner A133, the running memory is 4 GB, and the memory capacity is 64 GB. As shown in Table 7, the proposed model has the fastest inference speed on the same hardware platform.

5.6. Model Optimization Comparison

To improve the performance of the Linge network model we proposed, this article adjusted the Linge network model's relevant parameters in training the prediction model using the "Acute Ischemic Stroke MRI" data set published on Kaggle. The experimental comparison results before and after adjusting the Linge network model parameters are shown in Figure 8.

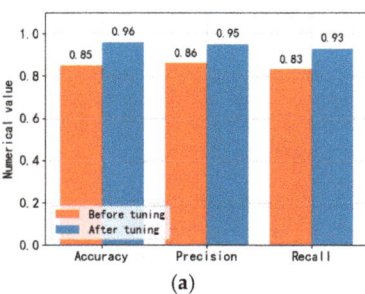
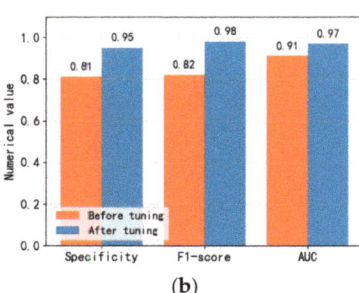

Figure 8. Comparison of accuracy, precision, recall, specificity, F1 score and AUC values before and after adjustment of Linge model parameters. (**a**): Comparison of accuracy, precision and recall. (**b**): Comparison of specificity, F1 score and AUC value.

In optimizing model parameters in this article, we mainly adjusted the learning rate, batch size, epochs, activation function, optimization algorithm, and Dropout ratio and conducted related ablation experiments. When conducting ablation experiments, our evaluation metrics are accuracy, precision, recall, specificity, F1 score, and AUC value. To obtain the optimal step size updated in each iteration, we conducted comparative experiments on learning_rate and finally set the learning rate to 0.0001. To obtain the optimal number of samples used to update parameters in each iteration, we conducted comparative experiments on the batch size and set the batch size to 16. During the model training process, we found that the LOSS of the model began to converge at epochs 6300. In the comparative experiment of activation functions, we found that when using the SiLU activation function, the evaluation indicators of the model are relatively the highest. In the comparative experiment of optimization algorithms, we found that when using the Adam optimizer, the evaluation indicators of the model are relatively the highest. In the Dropout proportion comparison experiment, we found that when the random deactivation is set to 0.78, the evaluation indicators of the model are relatively the highest. Figure 8 shows that various evaluation indicators of the prediction model have improved to a certain extent after adjusting relevant parameters.

This section describes in detail the experimental process of our proposed distributed intelligent edge computing technology for disease risk prediction from sample data, evaluation indicators, prediction results, model performance indicators, and model optimization.

6. Conclusions

To meet the diverse application scenarios of disease risk prediction, we propose distributed intelligent edge computing technology for disease risk prediction. To reduce the computing pressure on edge and central servers, we propose a lightweight neural network model. The Linge network model parameter size is only 7.63 MB, and the memory only takes up 155.28 MB. In experiments on stroke risk prediction, the Linge network model achieved an accuracy of 96%, a precision of 95%, a recall of 93%, a specificity of 95%, an F1 score of 98%, and an AUC of 97%. According to the characteristics of MRI images, we further designed an MRI image preprocessing method to improve the model's confidence and generalization ability. The data set used in the experiments of this article is the "Acute Ischemic Stroke MRI" data set publicly available on Kaggle. To verify the distributed intelligent edge computing technology for disease risk prediction proposed in this article, we conducted verification experiments using subject MRI data. The verification experiment results show that our proposed distributed intelligent edge computing technology for disease risk prediction can be well applied to diverse business scenarios. In future research, we will collect and organize training samples covering more diseases to improve the prediction range of the model.

Author Contributions: F.Z. and S.H. wrote the main manuscript text. X.D. and X.W. provided the idea. J.W. prepared the data and figures. All authors reviewed the manuscript. All authors have read and agreed to the published version of the manuscript.

Funding: The work of this paper is supported by the National Key Research and Development Program of China (2019YFB1405000), and the National Natural Science Foundation of China under Grant (Nos. 61873309, 92046024, 92146002).

Data Availability Statement: The "Acute Ischemic Stroke MRI" data set is from https://www.kaggle.com/datasets/buraktaci/mri-stroke (accessed on 15 October 2023).

Acknowledgments: Thanks to Peijie Wang, attending TCM physician at Ningbo Hospital of Traditional Chinese Medicine, Zhejiang University of Chinese Medicine, for his medical guidance and cooperation.

Conflicts of Interest: The authors declare no conflicts of interest.

References

1. Zhou, F.; Hu, S.; Du, X.; Wan, X.; Lu, Z.; Wu, J. Lidom: A Disease Risk Prediction Model Based on LightGBM Applied to Nursing Homes. *Electronics* **2023**, *12*, 1009. [CrossRef]
2. Zhou, F.; Hu, S.; Wan, X.; Lu, Z.; Wu, J. Diplin: A Disease Risk Prediction Model Based on EfficientNetV2 and Transfer Learning Applied to Nursing Homes. *Electronics* **2023**, *12*, 2581. [CrossRef]
3. Zhou, F.; Hu, S.; Wan, X.; Lu, Z.; Wu, J. Risevi: A Disease Risk Prediction Model Based on Vision Transformer Applied to Nursing Homes. *Electronics* **2023**, *12*, 3206. [CrossRef]
4. Tang, Y.; Brown, S.M.; Sorensen, J.; Harley, J.B. Physiology-Informed Real-Time Mean Arterial Blood Pressure Learning and Prediction for Septic Patients Receiving Norepinephrine. *IEEE Trans. Biomed. Eng.* **2021**, *68*, 181–191. [CrossRef]
5. Pan, Y.; Fu, M.; Cheng, B.; Tao, X.; Guo, J. Enhanced Deep Learning Assisted Convolutional Neural Network for Heart Disease Prediction on the Internet of Medical Things Platform. *IEEE Access* **2020**, *8*, 189503–189512. [CrossRef]
6. Guo, Y.; Liu, F.; Cai, Z.; Chen, L.; Xiao, N. FEEL: A Federated Edge Learning System for Efficient and Privacy-Preserving Mobile Healthcare. In Proceedings of the 49th International Conference on Parallel Processing (ICPP '20), Edmonton, AB, Canada, 17–20 August 2020; Association for Computing Machinery: New York, NY, USA, 2020; Article 9. pp. 1–11. [CrossRef]
7. Hakak, S.; Ray, S.; Khan, W.Z.; Scheme, E. A Framework for Edge-Assisted Healthcare Data Analytics using Federated Learning. In Proceedings of the 2020 IEEE International Conference on Big Data (Big Data), Atlanta, GA, USA, 10–13 December 2020; pp. 3423–3427. [CrossRef]
8. Xue, Z.; Zhou, P.; Xu, Z.; Wang, X.; Xie, Y.; Ding, X.; Wen, S. A Resource-Constrained and Privacy-Preserving Edge-Computing-Enabled Clinical Decision System: A Federated Reinforcement Learning Approach. *IEEE Internet Things J.* **2021**, *8*, 9122–9138. [CrossRef]
9. Gupta, D.; Kayode, O.; Bhatt, S.; Gupta, M.; Tosun, A.S. Hierarchical Federated Learning based Anomaly Detection using Digital Twins for Smart Healthcare. In Proceedings of the 2021 IEEE 7th International Conference on Collaboration and Internet Computing (CIC), Atlanta, GA, USA, 13–15 December 2021; pp. 16–25. [CrossRef]
10. Lim, W.Y.B.; Garg, S.; Xiong, Z.; Niyato, D.; Leung, C.; Miao, C.; Guizani, M. Dynamic Contract Design for Federated Learning in Smart Healthcare Applications. *IEEE Internet Things J.* **2021**, *8*, 16853–16862. [CrossRef]
11. Pang, J.; Huang, Y.; Xie, Z.; Li, J.; Cai, Z. Collaborative city digital twin for the COVID-19 pandemic: A federated learning solution. *Tsinghua Sci. Technol.* **2021**, *26*, 759–771. [CrossRef]
12. Gomathy, V.; Janarthanan, K.; Al-Turjman, F.; Sitharthan, R.; Rajesh, M.; Vengatesan, K.; Reshma, T.P. Investigating the Spread of Coronavirus Disease via Edge-AI and Air Pollution Correlation. *ACM Trans. Internet Technol.* **2021**, *21*, 105. [CrossRef]
13. Zhang, D.Y.; Kou, Z.; Wang, D. FedSens: A Federated Learning Approach for Smart Health Sensing with Class Imbalance in Resource Constrained Edge Computing. In Proceedings of the IEEE INFOCOM 2021—IEEE Conference on Computer Communications, Vancouver, BC, Canada, 10–13 May 2021; pp. 1–10. [CrossRef]
14. Wu, Q.; Chen, X.; Zhou, Z.; Zhang, J. FedHome: Cloud-Edge Based Personalized Federated Learning for In-Home Health Monitoring. *IEEE Trans. Mob. Comput.* **2022**, *21*, 2818–2832. [CrossRef]
15. Nguyen, D.C.; Ding, M.; Pathirana, P.N.; Seneviratne, A.; Zomaya, A.Y. Federated Learning for COVID-19 Detection With Generative Adversarial Networks in Edge Cloud Computing. *IEEE Internet Things J.* **2022**, *9*, 10257–10271. [CrossRef]

16. Hayyolalam, V.; Otoum, S.; Özkasap, Ö. A Hybrid Edge-assisted Machine Learning Approach for Detecting Heart Disease. In Proceedings of the ICC 2022—IEEE International Conference on Communications, Seoul, Republic of Korea, 16–20 May 2022; pp. 2966–2971. [CrossRef]
17. Linardos, A.; Kushibar, K.; Walsh, S.; Gkontra, P.; Lekadir, K. Federated learning for multi-center imaging diagnostics: A simulation study in cardiovascular disease. *Sci. Rep.* **2022**, *12*, 3551. [CrossRef]
18. Arikumar, K.S.; Prathiba, S.B.; Alazab, M.; Gadekallu, T.R.; Pandya, S.; Khan, J.M.; Moorthy, R.S. FL-PMI: Federated Learning-Based Person Movement Identification through Wearable Devices in Smart Healthcare Systems. *Sensors* **2022**, *22*, 1377. [CrossRef]
19. Elayan, H.; Aloqaily, M.; Guizani, M. Sustainability of Healthcare Data Analysis IoT-Based Systems Using Deep Federated Learning. *IEEE Internet Things J.* **2022**, *9*, 7338–7346. [CrossRef]
20. Lian, Z.; Yang, Q.; Wang, W.; Zeng, Q.; Alazab, M.; Zhao, H.; Su, C. DEEP-FEL: Decentralized, Efficient and Privacy-Enhanced Federated Edge Learning for Healthcare Cyber Physical Systems. *IEEE Trans. Netw. Sci. Eng.* **2022**, *9*, 3558–3569. [CrossRef]
21. Dang, B.T.H.; Luan, P.H.; Ngan, V.D.T.; Trong, N.T.; Duy, P.T.; Pham, V.-H. TrustFedHealth: Federated Learning with Homomorphic Encryption and Blockchain for Heart Disease Prediction in the Smart Healthcare. In Proceedings of the 2023 International Conference on Advanced Technologies for Communications (ATC), Da Nang, Vietnam, 19–21 October 2023; pp. 178–183. [CrossRef]
22. Wang, R.; Lai, J.; Zhang, Z.; Li, X.; Vijayakumar, P.; Karuppiah, M. Privacy-Preserving Federated Learning for Internet of Medical Things Under Edge Computing. *IEEE J. Biomed. Health Inform.* **2023**, *27*, 854–865. [CrossRef] [PubMed]
23. Ouyang, X. Design and Deployment of Multi-Modal Federated Learning Systems for Alzheimer's Disease Monitoring. In Proceedings of the 21st Annual International Conference on Mobile Systems, Applications and Services (MobiSys '23), Helsinki, Finland, 20–22 June 2023; Association for Computing Machinery: New York, NY, USA, 2023; pp. 612–614. [CrossRef]
24. Zhang, J.; Xu, J.; Vijayakumar, P.; Sharma, P.K.; Ghosh, U. Homomorphic Encryption-Based Privacy-Preserving Federated Learning in IoT-Enabled Healthcare System. *IEEE Trans. Netw. Sci. Eng.* **2023**, *10*, 2864–2880. [CrossRef]
25. Hu, J.; Shen, L.; Sun, G. Squeeze-and-Excitation Networks. In Proceedings of the 2018 IEEE/CVF Conference on Computer Vision and Pattern Recognition, Salt Lake City, UT, USA, 18–23 June 2018; pp. 7132–7141. [CrossRef]
26. Wang, Q.; Wu, B.; Zhu, P.; Li, P.; Zuo, W.; Hu, Q. ECA-Net: Efficient Channel Attention for Deep Convolutional Neural Networks. *arXiv* **2020**, arXiv:1910.03151.
27. Iandola, F.N.; Han, S.; Moskewicz, M.W.; Ashraf, K.; Dally, W.J.; Keutzer, K. SqueezeNet: AlexNet-level accuracy with 50x fewer parameters and <0.5 MB model size. *arXiv* **2016**, arXiv:1602.07360.
28. Howard, A.G.; Zhu, M.; Chen, B.; Kalenichenko, D.; Wang, W.; Weyand, T.; Andreetto, M.; Adam, H. MobileNets: Efficient Convolutional Neural Networks for Mobile Vision Applications. *arXiv* **2017**, arXiv:1704.04861.
29. Tan, M.; Chen, B.; Pang, R.; Vasudevan, V.; Sandler, M.; Howard, A.; Le, Q.V. MnasNet: Platform-Aware Neural Architecture Search for Mobile. *arXiv* **2019**, arXiv:1807.11626.
30. Sandler, M.; Howard, A.; Zhu, M.; Zhmoginov, A.; Chen, L.-C. MobileNetV2: Inverted Residuals and Linear Bottlenecks. *arXiv* **2019**, arXiv:1801.04381.
31. Howard, A.; Sandler, M.; Chu, G.; Chen, L.-C.; Chen, B.; Tan, M.; Wang, W.; Zhu, Y.; Pang, R.; Vasudevan, V.; et al. Searching for MobileNetV3. *arXiv* **2019**, arXiv:1905.02244.
32. Tan, M.; Le, Q.V. EfficientNet: Rethinking Model Scaling for Convolutional Neural Networks. *arXiv* **2020**, arXiv:1905.11946.
33. Tan, M.; Le, Q.V. EfficientNetV2: Smaller Models and Faster Training. *arXiv* **2021**, arXiv:2104.00298.
34. Tasci, B.; Tasci, I. Deep feature extraction based brain image classification model using preprocessed images: PDRNet. *Biomed. Signal Process. Control* **2022**, *78*, 103948. [CrossRef]
35. Graham, B.; El-Nouby, A.; Touvron, H.; Stock, P.; Joulin, A.; Jégou, H.; Douze, M. LeViT: A Vision Transformer in ConvNet's Clothing for Faster Inference. *arXiv* **2021**, arXiv:2104.01136.
36. Mehta, S.; Rastegari, M. Separable Self-attention for Mobile Vision Transformers. *arXiv* **2022**, arXiv:2206.02680.
37. Pan, J.; Bulat, A.; Tan, F.; Zhu, X.; Dudziak, L.; Li, H.; Tzimiropoulos, G.; Martinez, B. EdgeViTs: Competing Light-weight CNNs on Mobile Devices with Vision Transformers. *arXiv* **2022**, arXiv:2205.03436.
38. Maaz, M.; Shaker, A.; Cholakkal, H.; Khan, S.; Zamir, S.W.; Anwer, R.M.; Khan, F.S. EdgeNeXt: Efficiently Amalgamated CNN-Transformer Architecture for Mobile Vision Applications. *arXiv* **2022**, arXiv:2206.10589.
39. Huang, Z.; Zhang, Z.; Lan, C.; Zha, Z.-J.; Lu, Y.; Guo, B. Adaptive Frequency Filters As Efficient Global Token Mixers. *arXiv* **2023**, arXiv:2307.14008.

Disclaimer/Publisher's Note: The statements, opinions and data contained in all publications are solely those of the individual author(s) and contributor(s) and not of MDPI and/or the editor(s). MDPI and/or the editor(s) disclaim responsibility for any injury to people or property resulting from any ideas, methods, instructions or products referred to in the content.

Article

UP-SDCG: A Method of Sensitive Data Classification for Collaborative Edge Computing in Financial Cloud Environment

Lijun Zu [1,2,3], Wenyu Qi [4], Hongyi Li [1], Xiaohua Men [3], Zhihui Lu [1,2,*], Jiawei Ye [1] and Liang Zhang [4]

1. School of Computer Science, Fudan University, Shanghai 200433, China; zulijun@unionpay.com (L.Z.); 22210240089@m.fudan.edu.cn (H.L.); jwye@fudan.edu.cn (J.Y.)
2. Institute of Financial Technology, Fudan University, Shanghai 200433, China
3. China UnionPay Co., Ltd., Shanghai 201210, China; menxiaohua@unionpay.com
4. Huawei Technologies Co., Ltd., Nanjing 210012, China; qiwenyu1@huawei.com (W.Q.); zhangliang1@huawei.com (L.Z.)
* Correspondence: lzh@fudan.edu.cn

Abstract: The digital transformation of banks has led to a paradigm shift, promoting the open sharing of data and services with third-party providers through APIs, SDKs, and other technological means. While data sharing brings personalized, convenient, and enriched services to users, it also introduces security risks, including sensitive data leakage and misuse, highlighting the importance of data classification and grading as the foundational pillar of security. This paper presents a cloud-edge collaborative banking data open application scenario, focusing on the critical need for an accurate and automated sensitive data classification and categorization method. The regulatory outpost module addresses this requirement, aiming to enhance the precision and efficiency of data classification. Firstly, regulatory policies impose strict requirements concerning data protection. Secondly, the sheer volume of business and the complexity of the work situation make it impractical to rely on manual experts, as they incur high labor costs and are unable to guarantee significant accuracy. Therefore, we propose a scheme UP-SDCG for automatically classifying and grading financially sensitive structured data. We developed a financial data hierarchical classification library. Additionally, we employed library augmentation technology and implemented a synonym discrimination model. We conducted an experimental analysis using simulation datasets, where UP-SDCG achieved precision surpassing 95%, outperforming the other three comparison models. Moreover, we performed real-world testing in financial institutions, achieving good detection results in customer data, supervision, and additional in personally sensitive information, aligning with application goals. Our ongoing work will extend the model's capabilities to encompass unstructured data classification and grading, broadening the scope of application.

Keywords: sensitive data; classification and grading; augmentation; synonym mining; financial scenarios

1. Introduction

With the advent of the big data era, data have been recognized as essential production factors. To promote the data factor market, ensuring data security is a fundamental requirement. In this context, sensitive data pertain to information that, if disclosed or compromised, has the potential to inflict significant harm upon individuals or society. Sensitive data encompass personal privacy information, such as names, phone numbers, bank account numbers, ID numbers, addresses, passwords, email addresses, educational backgrounds, and medical records. Additionally, this includes enterprise data that are not suitable for public disclosure, such as the company's operational details, IP address lists, and network structure.

Effectively addressing the diverse and constantly evolving compliance requirements poses a formidable challenge. As the digital transformation gains momentum, numerous

countries' laws and regulations, coupled with security requirements stipulated by industry organizations (e.g., PCI DSS [1], SOX [2], HIPAA, GDPR [3], CCPA [4], etc.), underscore the importance of identifying and classifying sensitive data as the initial step in data protection. Enterprises are confronted with the task of streamlining their compliance workflows by leveraging simplified technology environments and pre-built templates. This necessitates understanding the precise locations of their data and determining whether additional safeguards are necessary. It also involves identifying both structured and unstructured sensitive data, both locally and in the cloud, that fall under regulatory scrutiny. Subsequently, these data must be categorized and cataloged for ongoing vulnerability monitoring.

In recent years, the financial industry has witnessed a rapid acceleration of the open banking model, where data applications are shared between banks and third-party service providers. More than 30 countries and regions worldwide have already adopted or are in the process of adopting this model [5]. Open banking offers numerous advantages, including enhanced customer experiences, the creation of new revenue streams, and the establishment of sustainable service models in markets with limited access to traditional banking services [5]. However, open banking also presents significant challenges, particularly concerning data security. The shared data encompass user identity information, financial transaction details, property, and other sensitive information. This extensive data sharing deepens the risk of data leakage and misuse [6].

To enhance the security of open banking data, we propose a sensitive data processing technique in a cloud-edge collaborative environment, as depicted in Figure 1. Firstly, financial institutions in the central cloud of a bank need to conduct a comprehensive assessment of their data assets to create a visual map of sensitive data before sharing with external parties. Secondly, the data application side (third-party organizations) deploys a regulatory outpost on the edge to ensure the security and compliance of open banking data. The Regulatory Sentinel is an independent software system designed to monitor every step of data operations performed by the application side, including storage, retrieval, and sharing. It also incorporates sensitive data identification, anonymization, watermarking, and records all user data operations for log auditing, leakage detection, data flow mapping, and situational awareness of data security [7].

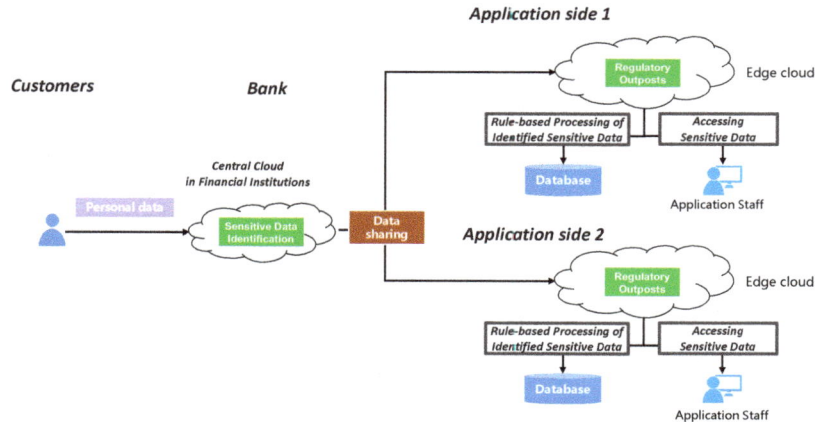

Figure 1. Cloud-Edge collaborative framework for sensitive data processing.

From the description of the regulatory outpost, it is evident that it deeply integrates into the data processing workflow of the application side, leveraging the characteristics of edge-based data processing. To avoid compromising the overall data processing experience and incurring significant costs for the application side, the deployment of the Regulatory Sentinel should meet the following requirements:

1. Elastic scalability of resources: As data processing by the application side requires computational resources, which fluctuate with varying data volumes, the deployment should allow for elastic scalability of resources to minimize investment costs for the application side.
2. Low bandwidth utilization cost and reduced data processing latency: The data traffic accessed by the application side needs to pass through the regulatory outpost. It is crucial to ensure low bandwidth utilization costs and reduced data processing latency to minimize any impact on the application side's user experience.
3. Ensuring data compliance: In the context of open banking, the application side tends to locally store open banking data, necessitating compliance checks on these data to prevent potential leaks. As shown in Figure 2, a way is given for the application side to perform operations such as data desensitization and watermarking locally to enhance data security, in which data classification and grading is the basis.

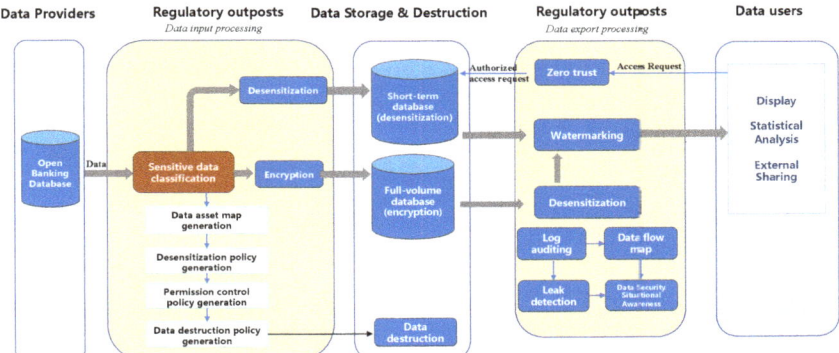

Figure 2. Data processing workflow in regulatory outposts within edge cloud scenarios. We conducted a comprehensive study on various security issues within open banking and proposed a data security framework. In this paper, our primary focus is on the issue of classifying sensitive data. Security measures such as watermarking are addressed in other works [7].

Hence, the automated classification and grading of sensitive data in the financial sector are garnering increasing attention. Firstly, financial institutions should conduct a comprehensive assessment of their own data landscape to achieve a visualized map of sensitive data assets before engaging in data sharing. Secondly, for third-party service providers collaborating with financial institutions, it is imperative that they enhance their data security management capabilities in accordance with government regulatory requirements and contractual agreements with financial institutions, which include encrypting sensitive data during storage or implementing data anonymization techniques, with the prerequisite being the prompt identification and classification of sensitive data transmitted during the collaboration process.

From the aforementioned scenario, the automated classification and categorization of sensitive data in the financial domain is a fundamental capability of the technology platform. Currently, the financial industry employs two primary methods for data classification and grading. One involves manual classification, which spans multiple departments, leading to a lengthy and inefficient process, and it lacks reusability, posing limitations on its scalability and adaptability. Another relies on automated classification and grading based on pattern matching, utilizing internally constructed data dictionaries. However, this approach suffers from low accuracy rates, especially when dealing with incomplete data dictionaries.

Building upon the aforementioned challenges, we present a data classification and grading framework to the financial industry which adheres to the relevant industry standards. Our framework encompasses both structured and unstructured data classification and grading. For structured data, we introduce a novel sensitive data classification and grading algorithm named UP-SDCG, leveraging self-enrichment and broadening techniques. Additionally, we enhance the financial data hierarchical classification by employing an augmentation model to expand keywords and lexicons, which significantly boosts the accuracy and recall of data classification and grading. Furthermore, we incorporate a synonym discrimination model to further expand the keywords and dictionaries in the industry data hierarchical classification library, resulting in improved accuracy and recall of data classification and grading. In our future work, we aim to further develop a scheme for classifying and grading unstructured sensitive data. This scheme will also support the coarse-grained classification of document data containing sensitive information. Additionally, we will propose a fine-grained classification approach to identify the types of sensitive data and their corresponding levels within the document.

Our research makes the following contributions:

- We propose a financial data classification and grading framework and a self-enlarging structured sensitive data classification and grading algorithm named UP-SDCG, with a synonym discrimination model innovatively introduced to further expand keywords and lexicons.
- Testing on real-world financial industry data, UP-SDCG outperforms existing public cloud algorithms in terms of accuracy and recall for sensitive data classification and grading.
- We further propose unstructured sensitive data classification and grading design scheme and scenario analysis.

2. Related Work

When it comes to data classification and grading, distinct approaches are employed to classify and grade various data structures. Data can be categorized into two main types based on their structure: structured and unstructured. Structured data are typically stored within databases, encompassing data types and field designations. This structured nature aids in effective data classification and grading, demanding meticulous categorization. Moreover, this process necessitates classifying and grading outcomes for individual columns. Conversely, unstructured data commonly appear in formats such as logs and documents, encompassing contextual semantics. Leveraging Natural Language Processing (NLP) methods facilitate semantic analysis, unveiling concealed sensitive information within the document. Within this context, the classification granularity can vary between broad and detailed. Broad classification involves furnishing classification results for the entire document, while fine-grained classification mandates identifying specific sensitive data types contained within the document alongside their corresponding levels.

2.1. Structured Sensitive Data Classification

Guan X. et al. [8] conducted a comprehensive investigation into the classification approach for structured sensitive data in the realm of electric power. They introduced a hierarchical identification technique, which initially identifies attributes within the database as sensitive data and subsequently categorizes them based on the specific characteristics of the sensitive information. Furthermore, different levels of sensitivity are assigned to these attributes in accordance with the varying permissions of the involved users. On the other hand, Rajkamal M. et al. [9] focused on safeguarding data stored in the cloud by extracting sensitive data components and post-encryption using Attribute-Based Encryption (ABE), and proposed a classification technique based on fuzzy rule analysis to effectively categorize attributes within structured data. In the healthcare domain, Ray S. et al. [10] combined domain experts and expert systems to assign sensitivity scores to attributes, enabling the identification of sensitive data through techniques such as random sampling and multiple scanning, eliminating the need for data cleansing before identification.

However, the standalone accuracy of rule-based sensitive data classification methods presents limitations due to the dynamic nature of industry attributes and linguistic context, leading to instances where the algorithm may miss identifying the sensitive data. Mouza C. et al. [11] devised a strategy that involves semantically designating which concepts constitute sensitive information, thereby ascertaining sensitive content within structured data. Subsequently, the attributes in the database that semantically correspond to these concepts are retrieved. While this algorithm exhibits robust performance on smaller datasets, its scalability to larger datasets is a challenge. In response to the limitations of individual sensitive attribute detection, Tong Y. [12] introduced correlation rules to identify interconnected sensitive attributes. Similarly, Xiao Y. [13] proposed determining the correlation among sensitive attributes in structured data through a multidimensional bucket grouping technique, which enables the establishment of sensitive categories and levels based on attribute correlations.

Chong P. [14] employed machine learning techniques, including Bert models and regular expressions, for real-time active identification, classification, and validation of sensitive data. Similarly, Silva P. [15] harnessed NLP tools (NLTK, Stanford, and CoreNLP) to identify and validate personally identifiable information within datasets. Recent advancements have embraced deep learning-based NER models, showcasing their potential in automatic feature discovery for enhanced classification or detection [16]. Furthermore, Park J. et al [17] introduced NER techniques for structured data, constructing the Text Generation Module (TG Module) and Named Entity Recognition Module (NER Module) to generate sentences and recognize entities, respectively. While the application of AI models has indeed enhanced the accuracy of sensitive data recognition to a certain extent, the models often lack domain-specific knowledge at their inception. For instance, they may overlook the recognition of synonyms, leading to suboptimal performance in real-world engineering applications.

2.2. Unstructured Sensitive Data Classification

Jiang H. et al. [18] explored the use of text categorization methods, employing TF-IDF for feature extraction and initially evaluated Bayesian, KNN, and SVM classifiers for the classification of medically sensitive data. Adam Považane [19] employed document classification based on data confidentiality, comparing the performance of commonly used text classification algorithms across resume, legal document, and court report datasets. Notably, both Huimin Jiang's and Považane's studies limited test data classification to binary sensitive and non-sensitive categories. In contrast, Yang R. et al. [20] presented a sophisticated label distribution learning classification approach that aimed to categorize power data into six main categories and twenty-three subcategories but lacked specific experimental outcomes. Additionally, Gambarelli G. et al. [21] focused on personal information in their study of sensitive data. Their model consisted of three stages: SPeDaC1 for sentence classification as sensitive or non-sensitive, SPeDaC2 for multi-class sentence categorization, and SPeDaC3 for detailed labeling with 61 distinct personal data categories. It is important to highlight that empirical findings indicated reduced effectiveness in the model's fine-grained classification performance.

Dias M. et al. [22] endeavored to extract and categorize unstructured Portuguese text containing sensitive data. They constructed a named entity recognition module to identify sensitive information, such as personal names, locations, emails, and credit card numbers, within the text. In contrast, García-Pablos A. [23] introduced a deep learning model, BERT, to identify and categorize sensitive data in Spanish clinical text, aiming to recognize various types of sensitive information, including dates, hospital names, ages, times, doctors, genders, kinships, locations, patients, and occupations. However, there exists potential for further refinement and enhancement of the observed experimental outcomes.

2.3. Data Classification and Grading Framework

In the realm of data classification and grading, scholars typically commence their endeavors by establishing policies to ensure data compliance, which serves as a foundational step in constructing programs and frameworks for data classification and grading. For instance, Aldeco-Perez et al. introduced a compliance analysis framework based on data source and data usage, aligned with the UK Data Protection Act [24,25]. Their approach focuses on averting the misuse of personal sensitive data and evaluating the propriety of its utilization. However, they overlooked the potential risk stemming from the exposure of personal sensitive data under unforeseen circumstances. Subsequently, Yang M presented the Gen-DT scheme [26], which leverages legal statutes to establish an external knowledge base. They employed a generalization-enhanced decision tree algorithm to categorize data into regulatory and non-regulatory types. Nonetheless, this scheme solely dichotomizes data without specifying the sensitive classification and corresponding levels within regulatory data, which poses an inconvenience for implementing distinct protective measures for varying levels of sensitive data. Addressing the challenge of information extraction from regulations, Elluri L constructed a knowledge graph by automatically extracting information from GDPR and PCI DSS [27,28]. Building upon this, Yang M. [29] introduced the GENONTO framework, which autonomously extracts data classification and grading information from enacted regulations to construct a knowledge base. These frameworks expedite the extraction of classification and grading data from regulatory guidelines, facilitating their application in our module following calibration. Expanding beyond compliance considerations, academics have introduced additional metrics to optimize classification and grading outcomes. For instance, Wang J. et al. [30] introduced data value evaluation indicators to enhance data grading results within the context of classification criteria. This optimization was assessed within the new energy automobile industry.

3. Methodology

3.1. Data Classification Framework

Our proposed framework for sensitive data classification and grading consists of four key modules, as illustrated in Figure 3. These modules are the preprocessing module, the classification and grading module, the result presentation module, and the comprehensive analysis module.

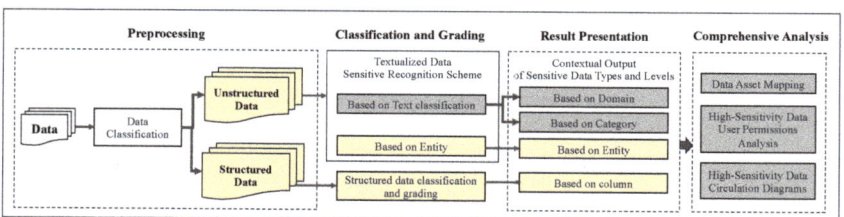

Figure 3. Data classification framework. The highlighted module in the figure is the main focus of this work.

The preprocessing module is responsible for classifying data into two categories: structured data and unstructured data. Depending on the data type, the classification and grading module applies different processes. For structured data, we designed a specialized model called the structured sensitive data classification and grading model (UP-SDCG). On the other hand, for unstructured data, we devised both coarse-grained and fine-grained data classification and grading schemes. The coarse-grained approach is based on text classification, while the fine-grained approach relies on entity recognition. The result presentation module displays unstructured data with details such as the Category, Type and Entity Type of the text, presented with granularity ranging from coarse to fine. For structured data, the module inputs the classification and grading results for each column. Finally, in the comprehensive analysis module, we utilized the obtained classification and grading results to build data asset maps and other capabilities that provide users with a deeper understanding of the data landscape.

In the following sections, we present our proposed model, UP-SDCG, which focuses on the classification and grading of structured sensitive data.

3.2. Structured Data Classification Framework

Figure 4 illustrates the components of the structured data classification and grading framework, comprising three main modules: the hierarchical classification library building module, the keyword augmentation module, and the data classification and grading module. The hierarchical classification library building module is responsible for building industry-specific data classification and grading libraries, which are designed based on industry compliance standards. The keyword augmentation module leverages NLP technology to expand the keywords present in the industry data hierarchical classification library. Additionally, it trains the synonym discrimination model to enhance the library's capabilities. Lastly, the data classification and grading module utilizes the keywords, rules, dictionaries, and synonymous discriminative models from the hierarchical classification library. These components collectively enable the module to classify and grade structured data. The resulting output includes sensitive data types and their respective grades organized by columns.

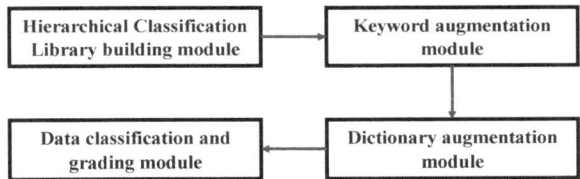

Figure 4. Structured data classification framework.

3.2.1. Library Building Module

To construct UP-SDCG's data classification hierarchy for the financial industry, we followed the guidelines outlined in the Financial Data Security Classification Guidelines (JR/T 0197-2022) [31]. This library encompasses the standard data commonly found in financial institutions, which can be categorized into four Level 1 subcategories, thirteen Level 2 subcategories, seventy-one Level 3 subcategories, and two hundred and seventy-nine Level 4 subcategories.

To extract entity names from the content, including names, genders, nationalities, and so on, we utilized pattern-matching technology. Subsequently, the sensitivity level is based on the identified entity. These entities are categorized into three groups based on expert knowledge and experience: strong rule entities, weak rule entities, and irregular entities.

- Strong Rule Entities: These entities are characterized by explicit and well-defined rules, resulting in minimal recognition errors, including Chinese ID numbers and Chinese cell phone numbers.
- Weak Rule Entities: These entities, including passwords and balances, exhibit some identifiable patterns, but regular expressions alone cannot guarantee complete matching.
- Irregular Entities: Unlike strong and weak rule entities, irregular entities lack discernible patterns or rules, making their identification particularly challenging.

We employed distinct recognition methods tailored to various entity types, as illustrated in Table 1.

Table 1. Entity recognition methods for structured data.

Entity Type	Structured Recognition Method
Strong Rule Entities	Regular Expression
Weak Rule Entities	Keyword + Regular Expression
Irregular Entities	Keyword + Dictionary

Based on the identification concepts outlined above, we developed the financial data hierarchical classification library for UP-SDCG. The structure of this library is presented in Table 2.

Table 2. Illustrative examples of UP-SDCG financial data hierarchical classification library.

Entity Name	Sensitivity Level	Entity Type	Keywords	Features
Name	3	Irregular Entity	Name	Name
Gender	3	Weak Rule Entities	Gender	Gender (Broad)
Gender	3	Strong Rule Entities	-	Gender (Narrow)
Nationality	3	Irregular Entity	Nationality	Country Name
ID Effective Date	3	Weak Rule Entities	ID Effective Date	Date
Enrollment Date	2	Weak Rule Entities	Enrollment Date	Date
Personal Income	3	Weak Rule Entities	Personal Income	Amount
Deposit	2	Weak Rule Entities	Deposit	Amount

We constructed the feature library by extracting content characteristics of entities, including information such as birthdays, the effective date of documents, the expiration date of documents, the date of enrollment, and other entities represented in date format. Similarly, personal income, deposit, credit card cash withdrawal amount, product amount, and other entities are represented in amount format. Additionally, we categorized presentation forms such as name, gender, country, date, and amount to form the comprehensive "Feature Library". This Feature Library comprises three distinct modules: Feature Name, Regular Expression, and Dictionary. The Feature Name within the Feature Library is associated with the features found in the Financial Data Hierarchical Classification Library. For further clarity, please refer to the structure of the Feature Library presented in Table 3.

Table 3. Illustrative examples of UP-SDCG Features Library.

Feature Name	Regular Expression	Dictionary
Name	-	Chinese Name
Gender (Broad)	$Male\|\|Female\|\|0\|\|1\|\|2$	-
Gender (Narrow)	$Male\|\|Female$	-
Country Name	-	Country Name
Date	$\backslash d\{4\}year(1[0-2]\|\|[1-9]\|0[1-9])day$	-
	$\backslash d\{4\}(1[0-2]\|\|[1-9]\|0[1-9])day$	-
Amount	$^\wedge(-\|\backslash+)?([1-9]\backslash d\{0,9\}\|0)(\backslash.\backslash d\{1,10\})?$	-

3.2.2. Keyword Augmentation Module

In the design of the identification scheme, we observed that entity identification heavily relies on keywords. However, the lack of uniformity in data dictionaries across different departments and enterprises, as well as the reliance on manual labeling, presented challenges in achieving comprehensive keyword coverage. For instance, when referring to the income situation of an entity, keywords such as "monthly salary", "salary," "wage," "income," "treatment," and "remuneration" may be involved. Therefore, we proposed a keyword augmentation framework with a synonym discrimination model.

- Keyword Augmentation Framework

Keyword augmentation relies on the fundamental concept of synonym mining, which can be broadly categorized into two main types: knowledge-based augmentation and pattern-based augmentation.

As illustrated in Figure 5, knowledge-based augmentation primarily relies on four types of knowledge bases:

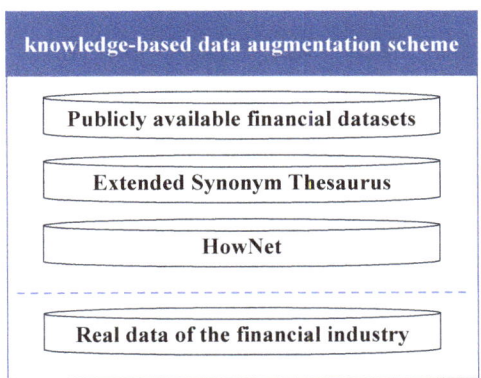

Figure 5. Knowledge-based keyword augmentation.

(1) Publicly available financial datasets: We used publicly accessible financial structured data to accumulate keywords. For example, we extracted statistics provided by the China Banking and Insurance Regulatory Commission;
(2) Extended Synonym Thesaurus: Considering the uniqueness of Chinese synonyms, we employed the Synonym Thesaurus [32] compiled by Mei J. et al. [33] at the Harbin Institute of Technology Information Retrieval Laboratory as the foundation to construct the Extended Synonym Thesaurus. This extended version encompasses nearly 70,000 entries organized in a hierarchical tree-like structure, utilizing a five-level encoding pattern to classify the entries into five tiers: major category, intermediate category, minor category, word group, and atomic word group. Each atomic word group includes one or more synonymous words;
(3) HowNet [34]: KnowNet utilizes tree-like sense-principal graphs and net-like sense-principal graphs to describe lexical properties;
(4) Real data of the financial industry: We incorporated real information from the financial industry, specifically the banking industry interface.

The central concept behind pattern-based keyword augmentation lies in bootstrapping. Bootstrapping is a statistical estimation method that involves inferring the distributional properties of the aggregate by resampling the observed information. The idea of implementing relationship extraction based on semi-supervised learning bootstrapping methods was proposed in Snowball [35]. We introduced this approach to the domain of keyword synonym mining, which comprises the following four sub-steps, as shown in Figure 6.

(1) Preparing the seed word set: This step involves collecting a set of high-quality alias word pairs for the current keyword;
(2) Mining the occurrence patterns: We analyzed the occurrence patterns of both the native names and aliases in a corpus constructed from Wikipedia and the Baidu Encyclopedia. These patterns encompass instances like "X, also known as Y." Furthermore, we utilized the seed word set to facilitate the identification of these patterns;
(3) Generating pattern sets: Based on the identified occurrence patterns, we generated sets of patterns that can be used for further analysis;

(4) Mining synonym pairs: Using the pattern sets, we extracted pairs of synonyms from the corpus. This step expands the range of synonymous terms associated with the designated keyword and facilitates a more comprehensive understanding of its semantic variations.

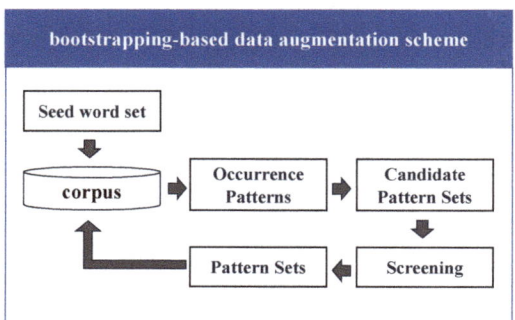

Figure 6. Pattern-based keyword augmentation.

- Synonym Discrimination Model

We developed a synonymy discrimination model classifier to determine whether a word can be added to a certain keyword collection. The construction process is as follows:

(1) We extracted keyword sets $\{S_1, S_2, \ldots, S_n\}$ from the existing UP-SDCG Financial Data Hierarchical Classification Library. Each keyword set S_i consists of several words with similar meanings;
(2) For each keyword set S_i, we employed knowledge-based and pattern-based keyword expansion techniques to extract the top five similarity words $\{t_{i1}, t_{i2}, \ldots, t_{i5}\}$. These similarity words are used to construct the keyword candidate set;
(3) We labeled the candidate words in the keyword candidate set. Words belonging to this keyword set were labeled as 1, while those not belonging to it were labeled as 0. Candidate keywords labeled as 1 were then expanded into the keyword set, resulting in the expanded keyword set. To train the classifier, we generated a collection of keyword training set-instance pairs from the pattern-based augmented keyword set. For each keyword set S_i, we randomly retained an instance $t_{pos} \in S_i$ and constructed a positive set of instance samples (S_i, t_{pos}) where the label y_{pos} was 1. For each positive sample (S_i, t_{pos}), we generated a negative sample (S_i, t_{neg}) by randomly selecting a negative instance t_{neg} where the label y_{neg} was 0. Following the research [36] experimental analysis, for each positive instance sample, we constructed five negative instance samples as shown in Table 4.

Table 4. Training data and labeling.

Candidate Keywords	Keywords Set	Label
t_{11}	S_1	0
t_{12}	S_1	1
...	...	...
t_{i1}	S_i	1
t_{i2}	S_i	1
...	...	...
t_{n4}	S_n	0
t_{n5}	S_n	0

(4) Next, we constructed the keyword set-candidate word classifier. We set the keyword set as S_i, the candidate word as t_{ij}, and the corresponding label as y_{ij}. We followed work [36] for similar candidate word discrimination through scores. First, we used $q(*)$ to quantify the degree of set similarity:

$$q(S_i) = g(\sum_{i=1}^{m} f_1(x_i)) \quad (1)$$

where $S_i = t_1, t_2, \ldots, t_m$ was put into the embedding layer to obtain the embedding vector $f_1(S_i) = x_1, x_2, \ldots, x_m$ and after that the original score representation was obtained and $g(*)$ represents the post-transformer, we then used a fully connected neural network with three hidden layers to transform the obtained vectors into scores. Then, we computed the difference between the set S_i and the set $S_i \cup \{t_{ij}\}$, and transformed it into a probability to determine the similarity between t_{ij} and keyword in S_i:

$$P(t_{ij} \in S_i) = \phi(q(S_i \cup t_{ij}) - q(S_i)) \quad (2)$$

where $\phi(*)$ is the sigmoid function. The model was optimized by minimizing the loss function:

$$loss(t_{ij}) = \begin{cases} -\log(max(1 - P(t_{ij} \in S_i), \alpha)) & \text{if } y_{ij} = 0 \\ -\log(max(P(t_{ij} \in S_i), \alpha)) & \text{if } y_{ij} = 1 \end{cases} \quad (3)$$

$$loss = \sum_{i=1}^{n} \sum_{j=1}^{5} loss(t_{ij}) \quad (4)$$

where t_{ij} belongs to S_i while y_{ij} equals to 1, and y_{ij} is 0 when t_{ij} does not belong to S_i. We set the parameter α to 10^{-5} to prevent the loss function from yielding infinite values.

By employing the aforementioned method, we optimized using an Adam optimizer with an initial learning rate of 0.001 and set the dropout to 0.5.

3.2.3. Dictionary Augmentation Module

In the Financial Data Hierarchical Classification Library of UP-SDCG, the detection of certain entities using regular expressions presents challenges. To address this issue, we need to construct specific dictionaries for entities such as names, app names, car brands, and others. Unlike keywords, the words within these dictionaries do not have exact semantic matches but tend to appear within similar contextual structures. Leveraging this characteristic, we propose a word2vec-based augmentation scheme, illustrated in Figure 7, to enhance the detection capabilities.

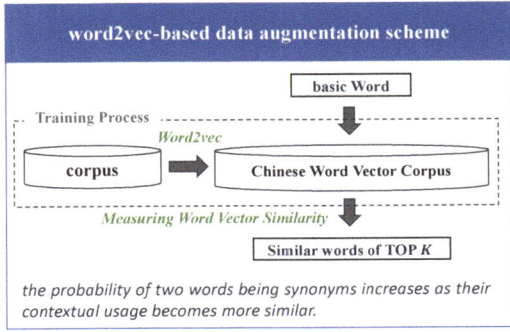

Figure 7. Word2vec-based dictionary augmentation scheme.

Word2vec [37] is a word embedding technique introduced by Google, which aims to represent abstract words as vectors in the real number domain. The method comprises two architectures: Continuous Bag of Words (CBOW) and Skip-gram. CBOW predicts the current word based on its context, whereas Skip-gram predicts the context given the current word. To enhance training efficiency, Word2vec introduces two training algorithms: Hierarchical Softmax and Negative Sampling. Word2vec's ability to capture synonymy between words proves advantageous in dictionary construction. In our study, we utilized word2vec to train a Chinese word vector library specifically tailored to the financial domain. By combining publicly available Chinese word vectors from the industry, we constructed a dictionary using word vector similarity. The process is as follows:

(1) Utilize open-source pre-trained word vectors, such as Tencent AI Lab Embedding Corpus for Chinese Words and Phrases [38], Stanford GloVe Embeddings [39], fastText word vectors [40];
(2) Load the Embedding model with the selected pre-trained word vectors and fine-tune it using the financial corpus, which includes financial reports, financial news messages, etc.;
(3) Subsequently, extract similar words from the fine-tuned word vectors using cosine distance to calculate the distance between words and construct the dictionary.

3.2.4. Data Classification and Grading Module

In this module, we present the fundamental principle of quantifying information quantity. Specifically, in structured data, when column A and column B have an equal number of rows and pertain to the same type of sensitive data, the difference $\in$ in the information they provide falls within a certain range [41]. This can be formulated as follows:

$$|H(A) - H(B)| \leqslant \in \quad (5)$$

Here, we introduce $H(*)$ as a measure function to quantify the amount of information provided by each column of data.

$$H(X) = -\sum_{x \in A} P(x) \log P(x) \quad (6)$$

In Equation (6), $0 \leq P(x) \leq 1$, $\sum_{x \in A} P(x) = 1$ and $P(x)$ represent the probability of occurrence for each discrete piece of information.

To apply the basic principle of information quantity quantization, we computed the average amount of information provided by each subclass $\{S_1, S_2, \ldots, S_n\}$ in the data dictionary. This was achieved by defining the equation as follows:

$$S_i = k_{ij}{}_{i=1}^{m_1} \quad (7)$$

where k_{ij} represents a single keyword and m_i (where $m_i \geq 1$) denotes the number of keywords in subclass S_i.

To proceed, we identified columns in the dataset with k_{ij} as the field name and extracted 100 rows from each column to form $c_{ijk}{}_{k=1}^{r_i}$. Subsequently, we calculated the number of discrete information elements q and information entropy H in each class.

$$q_i = \frac{1}{m_i} \sum_{j=1}^{m_i} \left(\frac{1}{r_i} \sum_{k=1}^{r_i} |c_{ijk}| \right) \quad (8)$$

$$H_i = \frac{1}{m_i} \sum_{j=1}^{m_i} \left(\frac{1}{r_i} \sum_{k=1}^{r_i} H(c_{ijk}) \right) \quad (9)$$

The process of automatically classifying and grading structured data based on synonym discrimination and information quantification, as illustrated in Figure 8, involves the following steps:

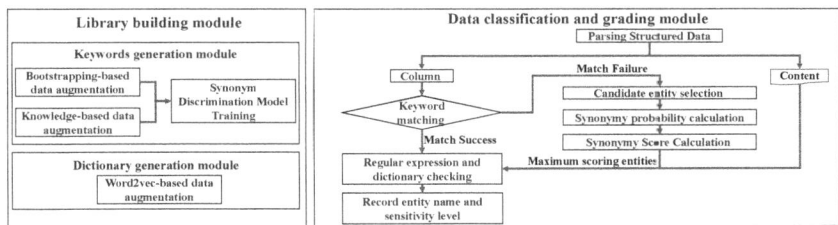

Figure 8. Structured data classification and grading process.

(1) Parsing: Structure the data into two parts: field names and data content;
(2) Field name identification: Utilize the keywords from the financial data hierarchical classification library to match the field names. If a corresponding field name is found, proceed to step 6; otherwise, move to step 3;
(3) Candidate entity selection: Randomly select 100 rows of data (denoted as d_i for $i = 1, 2, \ldots, 100$) and identify the data types, such as numeric value, English character, Chinese character, mixed character and date. Consider entities with the same data type from the Financial Data Hierarchical Classification Library as candidate entities;
(4) Synonym probability calculation: Apply the synonym discriminant model to determine if the field name is synonymous with the keyword set of the candidate entity. Input the candidate entity's keyword set S_i and the field name s into the synonym discriminant model, resulting in the probability $P(s \in S_i)$ that the field name belongs to the keyword set. Iteratively traverse all candidate entities to obtain:

$$\{P(s \in S_1), P(s \in S_2), \ldots, P(s \in S_i)\} \tag{10}$$

(5) Synonym score calculation: Calculate the number of discrete information q and information entropy $H(d)$ of the data:

$$Score = \theta_1 P(s \in S_i) - \theta_2 |q - q_i| - \theta_3 |H(d) - H_i| \tag{11}$$

$$\theta_1 + \theta_2 + \theta_3 = 1 \tag{12}$$

where θ_i represents the weight share of each index. The entity belonging to the keyword set with the highest score becomes the classification result, and step (6) is executed;
(6) Calibration: Perform stratified sampling of the corresponding content of the field name. Apply sensitive rules belonging to the keywords that match successfully in the feature library under its regular items and dictionaries for secondary detection of the sampling results. Recognition is considered successful if the matching rate exceeds the set threshold; otherwise, it is considered a recognition failure;
(7) Output: Output the corresponding entity name and sensitivity level from the Financial Data Hierarchical Classification Library if the recognition is successful. If the recognition fails, output NULL.

4. Experiments

The experiment was divided into two parts. Firstly, we organized a batch of simulation test data tailored to the data characteristics of financial institutions. Using this dataset, we compared the performance of our proposed algorithm with that of existing public algorithms. Secondly, we conducted a verification of the practical effectiveness of our algorithm using real business system data from financial institutions.

We present an automatic classification and grading program written in C++ (with 5000 lines of codes) and tested using financial data. The experiments were conducted on a Windows host with an Intel Core i7-8700 CPU @ 3.20 GHz 3.19 GHz processor. The synonym determination module in this paper was trained using Python 3.

4.1. Evaluation Metrics

This experiment evaluates the data classification and grading model using Precision, Recall, and F1-score. Precision, also known as recall, represents the probability of correct classification results among all the samples classified by the model, and it is calculated as follows:

$$Precision = \frac{TP}{TP + FP} \qquad (13)$$

where TP is the number of samples with correct classification and grading and FP is the number of samples with errors in classification or grading.

Recall represents the probability of correctly classifying and grading the samples that are actually required to be classified and graded from the original sample. It is expressed as:

$$Recall = \frac{TP}{TP + FN} \qquad (14)$$

where FN represents the number of samples that are not classified and graded.

The F1-score considers both Precision and Recall, facilitating their simultaneous maximization and balance. The F1-score is mathematically represented as follows:

$$F1 = \frac{2 \times Precision \times Recall}{Precision + Recall} \qquad (15)$$

4.2. Comparative Analysis

4.2.1. Datasets

The simulation dataset comprises three primary categories: personnel, projects, and contracts. Table 5 provides an overview of the experimental data, presenting relevant details for each category.

Table 5. Overview of simulation data.

Dataset	Row Number	Column Number	Sensitive Columns	Non-Sensitive Columns	Sensitive Type
Personnel Information	22,618	111	19	92	Name, gender, phone number, email address, company name
Project Information	23,208	301	31	270	Information about departments and personnel involved in the project
Contract Information	6351	37	15	22	Contract payment information

- Personnel information: The personnel dataset consists of 111 variables (columns) and 22,618 data points, encompassing details such as the employee's name, gender, work number, cell phone number, email, department, and position.
- Project information: The project dataset contains basic information about the bank's projects, comprising 301 variables and 23,208 data points. This dataset includes information pertaining to project personnel, departments, project budgets, and other relevant factors. It is noteworthy that the dataset contains a substantial amount of missing values.
- Contract information: The contract dataset has 37 variables and 6351 data points that relate to basic contract information as well as supplier information.

In the simulation dataset, the sensitive information in each column was identified through expert auditing, and the distribution of sensitive information in this dataset is illustrated in Figure 9. Among the various data columns, the contract data contained the highest proportion of sensitive information, accounting for over 40% of the dataset. On the other hand, the project data exhibited a relatively smaller percentage of sensitive data, mainly due to a significant number of missing values present in the data.

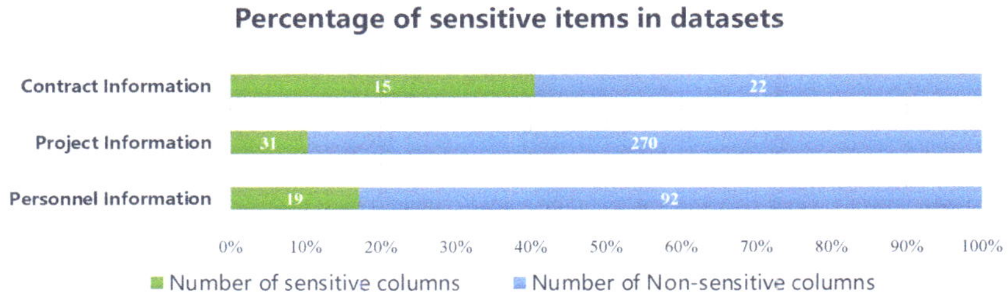

Percentage of sensitive items in datasets

Category	Number of sensitive columns	Number of Non-sensitive columns
Contract Information	15	22
Project Information	31	270
Personnel Information	19	92

Figure 9. Statistical analysis of sensitive data distribution in simulation dataset.

4.2.2. Experimental Results

Using the test dataset, we conducted a comprehensive comparison of UP-SDCG with the existing sensitive data recognition models commonly employed in the industry. In the subsequent sections, we elaborate on the specifics of the comparison model and present the results of our experiments.

- DSC sensitive data identification model(Alibaba): Including 210 detection rules, the financial classification template in the DSC sensitive data identification model is constructed with reference to the industry standard Financial Data Security Data Security Classification Guide;
- DSGC Sensitive Data Identification Model (Tencent): Use the built-in general classification and grading standard template for identification, which contains 41 detection rules;
- GoDLP (Bytedance): ByteDance's open source tool for sensitive data identification in 2022, which can support structured data and unstructured data identification, with 36 built-in detection rules.

UP-SDCG exhibited exceptional accuracy, surpassing all other three comparison models with a remarkable accuracy rate of over 95% on all three datasets, as depicted in Figure 10. Notably, the DSC achieved high accuracy in recognizing personnel information, boasting a perfect 100% accuracy rate for both personnel information and project information. However, its performance in detecting contract dates was subpar, attributed to the complexity of contract data that often contain various types of date information, such as contract start and end dates. DSC's limitations lie in its inability to correctly classify the granularity of the date categories, resulting in insufficient delineation ability.

In contrast, our model demonstrated fine-grained category classification through the utilization of keyword augmentation techniques, leading to a significant improvement in recognition accuracy. By effectively recognizing and classifying sensitive data, including numerical information like employees' work numbers and identity IDs, our model outperformed DSGC, which has a high misclassification rate for such data. Furthermore, while GoDLP achieved a higher accuracy rate by adhering to stricter rules, it recognized fewer sensitive data instances.

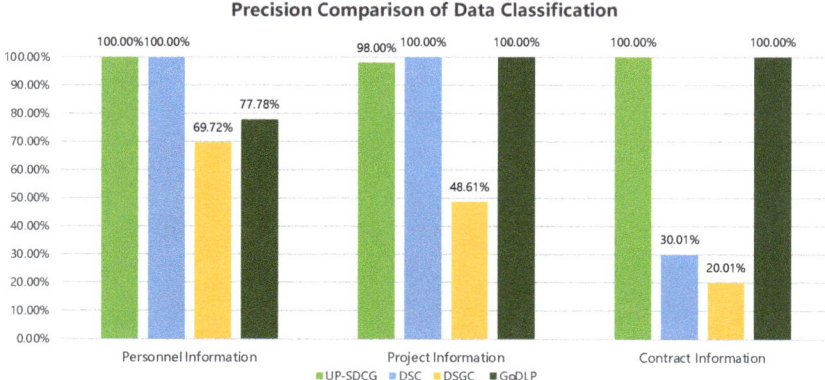

Figure 10. Comparison of precision in data grading and classification models.

UP-SDCG demonstrated a remarkable recall rate of over 94% across all test sets, resulting in fewer omissions, as depicted in Figure 11. By formulating more than 1100 detection rules based on industry standards, UP-SDCG covered a broader range of sensitive data compared to other three comparison models. As a result, its recall rate exhibited significant improvement. A comparison with models DSGC and GoDLP, which utilize generic sensitive data recognition templates revealed the limitations of current generic data classification and grading models in the financial domain. This highlights the crucial role played by domain-specific detection rules in achieving accurate recognition within the financial context.

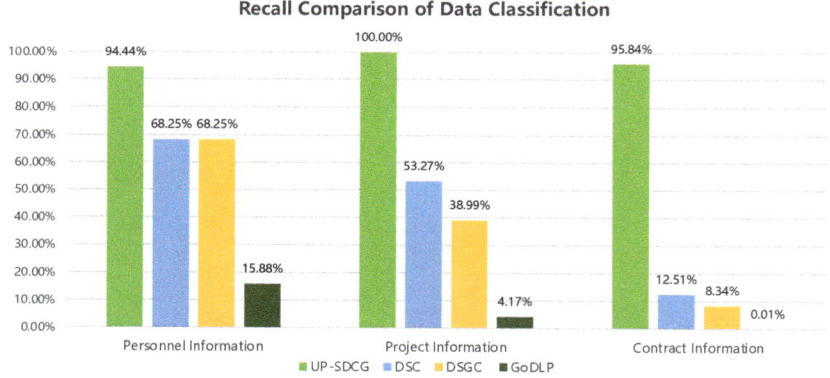

Figure 11. Comparison of recall in data grading and classification models.

By considering both false alarms and leakage cases, we demonstrate the superior performance of UP-SDCG over existing industry models, as illustrated in Figure 12. Specifically, when compared to DSC, which also leverages financial hierarchical classification template recognition and detection based on industry standards, our model achieves a lower leakage rate due to its comprehensive detection rules. Additionally, we incorporated keyword augmentation and expansion techniques, enabling fine-grained and accurate hierarchical classification, thus effectively mitigating false alarm situations. Furthermore, a comparison with generalized sensitive data hierarchical classification models, such as

DSGC and GoDLP, further underscores the advantages of our financial data recognition hierarchical classification rule base construction.

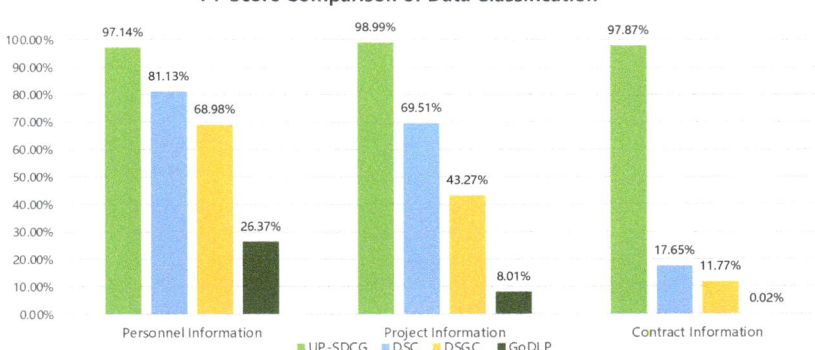

Figure 12. Comparison of F1-score in data grading and classification models.

The comprehensive results of this experiment are presented in Table 6, revealing significant advantages of our method over existing industry models across the three types of test data. Our approach excels in terms of Precision, Recall, and F1-score, which are the three key evaluation metrics used for performance assessment.

Table 6. Performance metrics of different models on various datasets.

Dataset	UP-SDCG			DSC			DSGC			GoDLP		
	Precision	Recall	F1	Precision	Recall	F1	Precision	Recall	F1	Precision	Recall	F1
Personnel Information	100.00%	94.44%	97.14%	100.00%	68.25%	81.13%	69.72%	68.25%	68.98%	77.78%	15.88%	26.37%
Project Information	98.00%	100.00%	98.99%	100.00%	53.27%	69.51%	48.61%	38.99%	43.27%	100.00%	4.17%	8.01%
Contract Information	100.00%	95.84%	97.87%	30.01%	12.51%	17.65%	20.01%	8.34%	11.77%	100.00%	0.01%	0.02%

4.3. Practical Validation

4.3.1. Dataset

The dataset utilized in this study comprises real business data from financial institutions. The experiments were conducted within a secure inner loop environment. The dataset encompasses four major categories, namely customer information, service data, operation management, and financial supervision. A comprehensive overview of the experimental data is presented in Table 7.

Table 7. Overview of the business dataset.

Dataset	Row Number	Sensitive Columns	Non-Sensitive Columns	Sensitive Type
Customer Information	73	12	61	Personal information, such as name, certificate number, income, address, phone number, account password, etc.
Service Data	23,208	103	78	Loans, insurance, bonds, cross-border business, etc.
Operation Management	13	0	13	Personal and financial information
Financial Supervision	3	0	3	Risky assets and capital adequacy

- Customer information: The customer dataset comprises 73 variables, encompassing a wide range of data including customer names, ID numbers, income details, addresses, phone numbers, and account passwords.

- Service data: The service dataset, encompassing information on loans, insurance, bonds, and cross-border transactions, comprises a total of 103 variables.
- Operation management: The Operation management dataset has 13 variables related to personal information as well as company financial information.
- Financial supervision: The financial supervision dataset has three variables related to information on regulatory indicators.

4.3.2. Experimental Results

Our model demonstrated exceptional performance, achieving over 90% precision, recall, and F1-score across all four types of test data, as presented in Table 8. The false alarm and omission cases primarily arose from the following two factors:

- Ambiguous content representation: The data content pertaining to real-world business scenarios lacked clarity, which leads to certain omissions and false alarms in our analysis;
- Data quality challenges: In real business scenarios, we encounter issues such as typos, missing characters, and other irregularities, which contributed to certain omissions in our data processing.

Table 8. Experimental effects of classification and grading.

Dataset	Precison	Recall	F1-Score
Customer Information	100.00%	98.36%	99.17%
Service data	96.05%	93.59%	94.81%
Operation management	91.67%	92.31%	91.99%
Financial Supervision	100.00%	100.00%	100.00%

UP-SDCG demonstrated greater effectiveness in detecting customer information and service data, suggesting that it currently outperforms other models for identifying personal sensitive information. However, when it comes to financial data related to business operations and management, its performance slightly lagged due to the inherent uncertainty in the data structure. Nevertheless, UP-SDCG still achieved precision, recall, and F1-scores surpassing 90%.

4.4. Performance Analysis

We sought to understand the factors influencing the time consumption of UP-SDCG. To investigate this, we analyzed six key variables, specifically row count, column count, sensitive column count, non-sensitive column count, sensitive data percentage, and the computational time taken by the test dataset. These variables are detailed in Table 9.

Table 9. Time consumption examples of the UP-SDCG Model on partial datasets.

Dataset	Rows	Columns	Sensitive Columns	Non-Sensitive Columns	Sensitive Ratio	Time (s)
Personnel Information1	9	50	6	44	0.120	6.351
Personnel Information2	11,280	25	6	19	0.240	5.597
Personnel Information3	11,329	36	8	28	0.222	4.825
Contract Information1	4372	9	3	6	0.333	2.025
Contract Information2	1979	28	12	16	0.429	4.269
Project Information1	20,206	151	10	141	0.066	49.493
Project Information2	3002	150	28	122	0.187	29.860
Bank Data1.csv	48	132	111	21	0.841	6.675
...	...	...	...	...	...	...

Initially, we utilized the Pearson correlation coefficient to quantify the linear relationship between variables. The Pearson correlation coefficient is computed using the following formula:

$$\rho_{X,Y} = \frac{cov(X,Y)}{\sigma_X \sigma_Y} = \frac{E[(X - \mu_X)(Y - \mu_Y)]}{\sigma_X \sigma_Y} \tag{16}$$

The resulting correlation values for pairwise variables are computed and presented in Table 10.

Table 10. Pairwise variable correlations.

	Rows	Columns	Sensitive Columns	Non-Sensitive Columns	Sensitive Ratio	Time (s)
Rows	1.000	−0.305	−0.193	−0.235	0.576	−0.008
Columns	−0.305	1.000	0.537	0.834	−0.268	0.779
Sensitive Columns	−0.194	0.537	1.000	−0.017	0.429	−0.032
Non-sensitive Columns	−0.235	0.834	−0.017	1.000	−0.598	0.944
Sensitive Ratio	0.576	−0.268	0.429	−0.598	1.000	−0.421
Time(s)	−0.008	0.779	−0.032	0.944	−0.421	1.000

The strength of the correlation between variables can be determined by the magnitude of the correlation coefficient ρ. When $|\rho| > 0.8$, it signifies a strong correlation, while $0.5 \leq |\rho| < 0.8$ indicates a moderate correlation. For $|\rho|$ values falling within $0.3 \leq |\rho| < 0.5$, the correlation is considered weak, and if $|\rho| < 0.3$, the variables are essentially uncorrelated. Analyzing Table 10, we observe that model execution time exhibits a strong correlation with the number of non-sensitive columns, a moderate correlation with the number of data columns, a weak correlation with the percentage of data sensitivity, and a negligible correlation with the number of data rows and sensitive columns. Although both the count of non-sensitive columns and the number of data columns influence the model's runtime, their correlation coefficient stands at 0.83449, signifying a strong linear correlation. In this context, either one of these factors could be selected for analysis. However, it is important to note that the Pearson correlation coefficient solely addresses linear correlations between variables. Our comprehensive analysis is extended further in Figure 13.

Upon analyzing Figure 13, it became evident that a curvilinear relationship exists between the model's elapsed time and the data sensitivity ratio, represented by the equation $y = \frac{1}{x}$. Consequently, we performed the reciprocal of the sensitivity ratio to derive the column $\frac{1}{sensitivity\_ratio}$. Subsequently, we recalculated Pearson's correlation coefficient with the elapsed time, yielding the results presented in the updated Table 11:

Table 11. Model execution time and correlation coefficients with various variables.

	Rows	Columns	Sensitive Columns	Non-Sensitive Columns	Sensitive Ratio
Time (s)	−0.00756	0.77861	−0.03227	0.94370	−0.80537

$$Time = a + b \cdot insensitivity\_column + \frac{c}{sensitivity\_ratio} \tag{17}$$

Through fitting the execution time, we obtained the fitted equation:

$$Time = -0.578811 + 0.263136 \cdot insensitivity\_column + 0.419442/sensitivity\_ratio \tag{18}$$

The *R-squared* value of this fitted equation is 0.895, and the *p*-value is 3.02×10^{-48}, indicating a favorable fit.

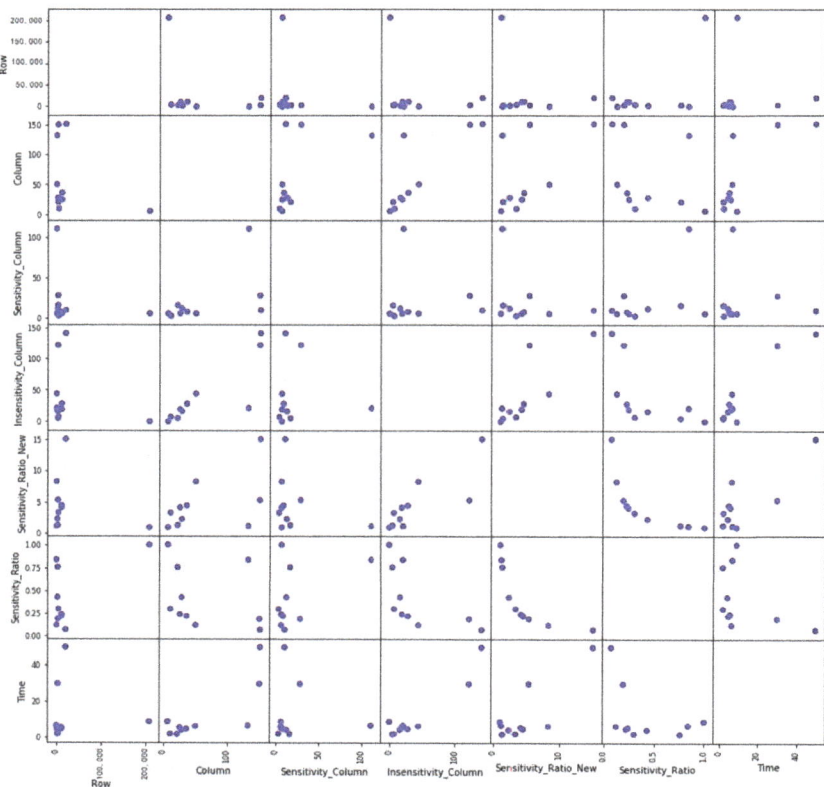

Figure 13. Scatter plots of pairwise variables.

5. Conclusions

Data security is an important basic condition for financial institutions to build a data-based ecology, and how to accurately identify massive data for classification and grading control has become a key issue. Under the overall framework of financial sensitive data classification and grading research work, we propose a self-enlarging and broadening financial sensitive data classification and grading method (UP-SDCG), which combines the traditional recognition technology with NLP technology, effectively solves the problem of low accuracy rate of the traditional recognition technology. The experimental results show that it has a significant advantage of effect compared with other publicly available platform algorithms, and also has been validated in real financial institutions. The results have also been verified in real financial institution business scenarios. Compared to existing classification and grading frameworks, our approach offers a finer granularity, enabling more precise implementation of protective measures tailored to various data types and levels, which significantly mitigates the risk of high-sensitivity data leakage. Our subsequent work will focus on the research of Unstructured Financial Data Classification and Graded Recognition (UP-UDCG), mainly realizing the two major functions of data classification and grading based on text classification and data classification and grading based on entities, and essential research methodology can be referred to in Appendix A. By deploying the sensitive data classification algorithm at the regulatory outposts, we aspire for our work to contribute to enhancing data security in open banking.

Author Contributions: Conceptualization, L.Z. (Lijun Zu); Methodology, L.Z. (Lijun Zu), W.Q. and H.L.; Software, W.Q.; Validation, H.L. and X.M.; Resources, L.Z. (Lijun Zu) and X.M.; Data curation, W.Q.; Writing—original draft, L.Z. (Lijun Zu), W.Q. and H.L.; Writing—review & editing, Z.L.; Supervision, Z.L., J.Y. and L.Z. (Liang Zhang). All authors have read and agreed to the published version of the manuscript.

Funding: This work was supported by National Key Research and Development Program of China (Grant 2021YFC3300600).

Data Availability Statement: The data can be shared up on request. The data are not publicly available due to the sensitivity and confidentiality of financial industry data.

Conflicts of Interest: Author Xiaohua Men was employed by Unionpay Co., Ltd. Her position is engineer. Author Liang Zhang employed by Huawei Technologies Co., Ltd His position is senior engineer. Author Wenyu Qi was employed by Huawei Technologies Co., Ltd. Her position is engineer. The remaining authors declare that the research was conducted in the absence of any commercial or financial relationships that could be construed as a potential conflict of interest.

Appendix A. Unstructured Data Classification and Grading Framework

The framework for unstructured data classification and grading comprises two modules: text-based data classification and grading, and entity-based data classification and grading. The text-based module determines the domain and type of the text, while the entity-based module identifies specific entities embedded within the text. As depicted in Figure A1, the framework provides information on the domain of the text, the involved text type (such as diplomas, CVs, insurance policies, etc.), and the sensitive entities present in the text (e.g., ID card numbers, email addresses, cell phone numbers, etc.).

FileName	MD5	Domain	Type	Sensitivity level	Level 1 Sensitive Entity Category	Level 2 Sensitive Entity Category	Level 3 Sensitive Entity Category	Level 4 Sensitive Entity Category
Diploma.pdf	4C1B1AF08F0A06EB	Academic	diploma	4	...	...	Email, cell phone, name	...
Transcript.pdf	9E3CBA4BD8F987CD	Academic		3	...	Province, city	...	...
AttendanceRecord.doc	84ABD7194DD3D07D	Academic		2	...	...	Email, cell phone, name	...
1213.pdf	ED33D2B8CC1BD034	Medical	policy	4	...	...	Email, cell phone, name	...

Entity ☐   Text classification ☐

Figure A1. Example of classification and grading of unstructured data.

Appendix A.1. Data Classification Based on Text Classification

Various classification algorithms can be chosen depending on the specific context or scene. We provide an overview of common text classification algorithms, along with their respective applicable scenarios, advantages, and disadvantages, as shown in Table A1.

Table A1. Applications and Pros/Cons of Common Text Classification Algorithms.

Text Classification Algorithm	Suitable Scenarios	Advantages	Disadvantages
FastText	Large sample sizes, multiple categories, tasks with limited semantic understanding	Fast, low computational requirements	Limited semantic understanding
CNN	Tasks requiring some semantic understanding	Captures more, broader, and finer text features	Long training time
Self-Attention	Tasks requiring some semantic understanding	Captures more, broader, and finer text features, long-term dependencies within the text	Long training time
Traditional Machine Learning	Short texts (e.g., messages, microblogs, comments) with less than 150 words	Fast training	Unable to handle long texts
BERT	Limited labeled data scenarios	High accuracy	Long training and prediction time

Appendix A.2. Data Classification Based on Entity

Entity-based unstructured data classification and grading builds upon the principles of structured data classification and grading, employing keywords and patterns to detect sensitive entities. While structured data utilizes a "keyword+dictionary" approach for identifying irregular entities, this method is not suitable for unstructured data. Therefore, we adopt the Named Entity Recognition (NER) model to handle irregular entities. The specific identification process is illustrated in Figure A2.

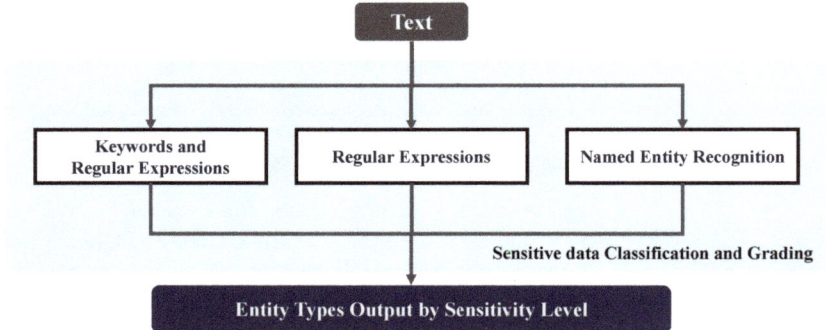

Figure A2. Unstructured Data Classification and Grading Process.

Likewise, the selection of NER models can be tailored to specific scenarios. We provide an overview of various NER models along with their respective applicable scenarios, highlighting their individual strengths and limitations, as shown in Table A2.

Table A2. Applicability and Pros/Cons of Common NER Models.

Model	Application Scenarios	Advantages	Disadvantages
BiLSTM + CRF	Large sample data, multiple label categories	Simple model structure, fast training speed	Moderate entity extraction performance
StructBert	Insufficient annotated data	Good entity extraction	Lower overall performance
StructBert + CRF	Small data scenarios	Good entity extraction performance	Lower overall performance

Appendix B. Unstructured Data Classification and Grading Framework

In the module for constructing hierarchical classification libraries, industry experts have the capability to create data hierarchical classification libraries that align with compliance standards and requirements. Table A3 presents the data security compliance standards applicable to China's core industries. This allows for a systematic and structured approach to organizing and managing data in accordance with industry-specific regulations.

Table A3. Data Security Compliance Standards in Key Chinese Industries.

Industry	Compliance Standard	Regulatory Authority
General	"Guidelines for Cybersecurity Standard Practice—Network Data Classification and Grading"	National Information Security Standardization Technical Committee
Industrial	"Guidelines for Industrial Data Classification and Grading"	Ministry of Industry and Information Technology (MIIT) of China

Table A3. *Cont.*

Industry	Compliance Standard	Regulatory Authority
Financial	"Financial Data Security—Data Classification and Grading Guidelines"	People's Bank of China (PBOC)
Financial	"Technical Specifications for Personal Financial Information Protection"	People's Bank of China (PBOC)
Financial	"Guidelines for Securities and Futures Industry Data Classification and Grading"	China Securities Regulatory Commission (CSRC)
Telecommunication	"Method for Data Classification and Grading of Basic Telecommunication Enterprises"	Ministry of Industry and Information Technology (MIIT) of China
Telecommunication	"Guidelines for Identifying Important Data in Basic Telecommunication Enterprises"	Ministry of Industry and Information Technology (MIIT) of China
Medical	"Information Security Technology—Healthcare Data Security Guidelines"	China National Information Security Standardization Technical Committee
Automotive	"Regulations on Automotive Data Security Management"	Ministry of Industry and Information Technology (MIIT) of China

References

1. Seaman, J. *PCI DSS: An Integrated Data Security Standard Guide*; Apress: Berkeley, CA, USA, 2020.
2. George, G. The Public Company Accounting Reform and Investor Protection Act of 2002: Any implications for Australia? *Aust. J. Corp. Law* **2002**, *14*, 286–295.
3. General Data Protection Regulation. General Data Protection Regulation (GDPR)—Final Text Neatly Arranged. Available online: https://gdpr.verasafe.com/ (accessed on 13 March 2024).
4. Pardau, S.L. The California consumer privacy act: Towards a European-style privacy regime in the United States. *J. Technol. Law Policy* **2018**, *23*, 68.
5. Brodsky, L.; Oakes, L. *Data Sharing and open Banking*; McKinsey & Company: Chicago, IL, USA, 2017; p. 1105.
6. Yuan, J. Practice and Thoughts on Information Security Protection of Open Banks under the New Financial Situation; Financial Electronification: 2021. Available online: https://www.secrss.com/articles/35541 (accessed on 13 March 2024).
7. Zu, L.; Li, H.; Zhang, L.; Lu, Z.; Ye, J.; Zhao, X.; Hu, S. E-SAWM: A Semantic Analysis-Based ODF Watermarking Algorithm for Edge Cloud Scenarios. *Future Internet* **2023**, *15*, 283. [CrossRef]
8. Guan, X.; Zhou, C.; Cao, W. Research on Classification Method of Sensitive Structural Data of Electric Power. In Proceedings of the 2022 IEEE 12th International Conference on Electronics Information and Emergency Communication (ICEIEC), Beijing, China, 15–17 July 2022; pp. 268–271.
9. Rajkamal, M.; Sumathi, M.; Vijayaraj, N.; Prabu, S.; Uganya, G. Sensitive data identification and protection in a structured and unstructured data in cloud based storage. *Ann. Rom. Soc. Cell Biol.* **2021**, *25*, 1157–1166.
10. Ray, S.; Mishra, K.N.; Dutta, S. Sensitive data identification and security assurance in cloud and IoT based networks. *Int. J. Comput. Netw. Inf. Secur. IJCNIS* **2022**, *14*, 11–27. [CrossRef]
11. Mouza, C.; Métais, E.; Lammari, N.; Akoka, J.; Aubonnet, T.; Comyn-Wattiau, I.; Fadili, H.; Cherfi, S.S.S. Towards an automatic detection of sensitive information in a database. In Proceedings of the 2010 Second International Conference on Advances in Databases, Knowledge, and Data Applications, Menuires, France, 11–16 April 2010; pp. 247–252.
12. Yi, T.; Shi, M. Privacy protection method for multiple sensitive attributes based on strong rule. *Math. Probl. Eng.* **2015**, *2015*, 464731. [CrossRef]
13. Xiao, Y.; Li, H. Privacy preserving data publishing for multiple sensitive attributes based on security level. *Information* **2020**, *11*, 166. [CrossRef]
14. Chong, P. Deep Learning Based Sensitive Data Detection. In Proceedings of the 2022 19th International Computer Conference on Wavelet Active Media Technology and Information Processing (ICCWAMTIP), Chengdu, China, 16–18 December 2022; pp. 1–6.
15. Silva, P.; Gonçalves, C.; Godinho, C.; Antunes, N.; Curado, M. Using nlp and machine learning to detect data privacy violations. In Proceedings of the IEEE INFOCOM 2020—IEEE Conference on Computer Communications Workshops (INFOCOM WKSHPS), Toronto, ON, Canada, 6–9 July 2020; pp. 972–977.
16. Ma, J.; Zhang, J.; Xiao, L.; Chen, K.; Wu, J. Classification of power quality disturbances via deep learning. *IETE Tech. Rev.* **2017**, *34*, 408–415. [CrossRef]
17. Park, J.s.; Kim, G.w.; Lee, D.h. Sensitive data identification in structured data through genner model based on text generation and ner. In Proceedings of the 2020 International Conference on Computing, Networks and Internet of Things, Sanya, China, 24–26 April 2020; pp. 36–40.
18. Jiang, H.; Chen, C.; Wu, S.; Guo, Y. Classification of Medical Sensitive Data based on Text Classification. In Proceedings of the 2019 IEEE International Conference on Consumer Electronics-Taiwan (ICCE-TW), Yilan, Taiwan, 20–22 May 2019; pp. 1–2.
19. Považanec, A. Comparison of Machine Learning Methods for Sensitive Data Identification. Undergraduate Thesis, Masaryk University, Brno, Czech Republic, 2020.

20. Yang, R.; Gao, X.; Gao, P. Research on intelligent recognition and tracking technology of sensitive data for electric power big data. In Proceedings of the 2021 13th International Conference on Measuring Technology and Mechatronics Automation (ICMTMA), Beihai, China, 16–17 January 2021; pp. 229–234.
21. Gambarelli, G.; Gangemi, A.; Tripodi, R. Is Your Model Sensitive? SPeDaC: A New Benchmark for Detecting and Classifying Sensitive Personal Data. *arXiv* **2022**, arXiv:2208.06216.
22. Dias, M.; Boné, J.; Ferreira, J.C.; Ribeiro, R.; Maia, R. Named entity recognition for sensitive data discovery in Portuguese. *Appl. Sci.* **2020**, *10*, 2303.
23. García-Pablos, A.; Perez, N.; Cuadros, M. Sensitive data detection and classification in Spanish clinical text: Experiments with BERT. *arXiv* **2020**, arXiv:2003.03106.
24. Aldeco-Pérez, R.; Moreau, L. A provenance-based compliance framework. In Proceedings of the Future Internet Symposium, Berlin, Germany, 20–22 September 2010; pp. 128–137.
25. Aldeco Perez, R.; Moreau, L. Provenance-based auditing of private data use. In Proceedings of the Visions of Computer Science—BCS International Academic Conference (VOCS), London, UK, 22–24 September 2008.
26. Yang, M.; Tan, L.; Chen, X.; Luo, Y.; Xu, Z.; Lan, X. Laws and regulations tell how to classify your data: A case study on higher education. *Inf. Process. Manag.* **2023**, *60*, 103240. [CrossRef]
27. Elluri, L.; Nagar, A.; Joshi, K.P. An integrated knowledge graph to automate gdpr and pci dss compliance. In Proceedings of the 2018 IEEE International Conference on Big Data (Big Data), Shanghai, China, 15–17 January 2018; pp. 1266–1271.
28. Elluri, L.; Joshi, K.P. A knowledge representation of cloud data controls for EU GDPR compliance. In Proceedings of the 2018 IEEE World Congress on Services (SERVICES), San Francisco, CA, USA, 2–7 July 2018; pp. 45–46.
29. Yang, M.; Chen, X.; Tan, L.; Lan, X.; Luo, Y. Listen carefully to experts when you classify data: A generic data classification ontology encoded from regulations. *Inf. Process. Manag.* **2023**, *60*, 103186.
30. Wang, J.; Wang, L.; Gao, S.; Tian, M.; Li, Y.; Xiao, K. Research on Data Classification and Grading Method Based on After sales Energy Replenishment Scenarios. In Proceedings of the 2022 2nd International Conference on Big Data, Artificial Intelligence and Risk Management (ICBAR), Xi'an, China, 25–27 November 2022; pp. 11–15.
31. JR/T 0197-2022; Financial Data Security—Guidelines for Data Security Classification. Technical Report. People's Bank of China: Beijing, China, 2020.
32. Quan, Y.; Yuquan, S. Research on Semantic Similarity Calculation Based on the Depth of "Synonymous Treebank". *J. Comput. Eng. Appl.* **2020**, *56*, 48–54.
33. Mei, J.; Zhu, Y.; Gao, Y.; Yin, H. *Synonym Word Forest*; Shanghai Dictionary Press: Shanghai, China, 1983.
34. Dong, Z.; Dong, Q. HowNet—A hybrid language and knowledge resource. In Proceedings of the International Conference on Natural Language Processing and Knowledge Engineering, Beijing, China, 26–29 October 2003; pp. 820–824.
35. Agichtein, E.; Gravano, L. Snowball: Extracting relations from large plain-text collections. In Proceedings of the Proceedings of the Fifth ACM Conference on Digital Libraries, San Antonio, TX, USA, 2–7 June 2000; pp. 85–94.
36. Shen, J.; Lyu, R.; Ren, X.; Vanni, M.; Sadler, B.; Han, J. Mining entity synonyms with efficient neural set generation. In Proceedings of the AAAI Conference on Artificial Intelligence, Honolulu, HI, USA, 27 January–1 February 2019; Volume 33, pp. 249–256.
37. Mikolov, T.; Chen, K.; Corrado, G.; Dean, J. Efficient estimation of word representations in vector space. *arXiv* **2013**, arXiv:1301.3781.
38. Song, Y.; Shi, S.; Li, J.; Zhang, H. Directional skip-gram: Explicitly distinguishing left and right context for word embeddings. In Proceedings of the 2018 Conference of the North American Chapter of the Association for Computational Linguistics: Human Language Technologies, New Orleans, LA, USA, 1–6 June 2018; Volume 2 (Short Papers), pp. 175–180.
39. Pennington, J.; Socher, R.; Manning, C.D. Glove: Global vectors for word representation. In Proceedings of the 2014 Conference on Empirical Methods in Natural Language Processing (EMNLP), Doha, Qatar, 25–29 October 2014; pp. 1532–1543.
40. Bojanowski, P.; Grave, E.; Joulin, A.; Mikolov, T. Enriching word vectors with subword information. *Trans. Assoc. Comput. Linguist.* **2017**, *5*, 135–146. [CrossRef]
41. He, W. Intelligent Recognition Algorithm and Adaptive Protection Model for Sensitive Data. Master's Thesis, Guizhou University, Guiyang, China, 2020.

Disclaimer/Publisher's Note: The statements, opinions and data contained in all publications are solely those of the individual author(s) and contributor(s) and not of MDPI and/or the editor(s). MDPI and/or the editor(s) disclaim responsibility for any injury to people or property resulting from any ideas, methods, instructions or products referred to in the content.

Article

E-SAWM: A Semantic Analysis-Based ODF Watermarking Algorithm for Edge Cloud Scenarios

Lijun Zu [1,2,3], Hongyi Li [1], Liang Zhang [4,*], Zhihui Lu [1,3], Jiawei Ye [1,*], Xiaoxia Zhao [2] and Shijing Hu [1]

[1] School of Computer Science, Fudan University, Shanghai 200433, China; zulijun@unionpay.com (L.Z.); 22210240089@m.fudan.edu.cn (H.L.); lzh@fudan.edu.cn (Z.L.); sjhu21@m.fudan.edu.cn (S.H.)
[2] China UnionPay Co., Ltd., Shanghai 201210, China; zhaoxiaoxia@unionpay.com
[3] Institute of Financial Technology, Fudan University, Shanghai 200433, China
[4] Huawei Technologies Co., Ltd., Nanjing 210012, China
* Correspondence: zhangliang1@huawei.com (L.Z.); jwye@fudan.edu.cn (J.Y.)

Abstract: With the growing demand for data sharing file formats in financial applications driven by open banking, the use of the OFD (open fixed-layout document) format has become widespread. However, ensuring data security, traceability, and accountability poses significant challenges. To address these concerns, we propose E-SAWM, a dynamic watermarking service framework designed for edge cloud scenarios. This framework incorporates dynamic watermark information at the edge, allowing for precise tracking of data leakage throughout the data-sharing process. By utilizing semantic analysis, E-SAWM generates highly realistic pseudostatements that exploit the structural characteristics of documents within OFD files. These pseudostatements are strategically distributed to embed redundant bits into the structural documents, ensuring that the watermark remains resistant to removal or complete destruction. Experimental results demonstrate that our algorithm has a minimal impact on the original file size, with the watermarked text occupying less than 15%, indicating a high capacity for carrying the watermark. Additionally, compared to existing explicit watermarking schemes for OFD files based on annotation structure, our proposed watermarking scheme is suitable for the technical requirements of complex dynamic watermarking in edge cloud scenario deployment. It effectively overcomes vulnerabilities associated with easy deletion and tampering, providing high concealment and robustness.

Keywords: edge cloud; OFD files; semantic analysis; dynamic watermarking

1. Introduction

In the dynamic landscape of the digital economy, commercial banks face the challenge of sharing a significant amount of financial data with clients' designated digital applications in electronic file format [1]. As a novel file format, the open fixed-layout document (OFD) format has gained popularity within the financial industry [2]. It offers unique advantages for various financial processes, including electronic receipts and financial statements, which are in increased demand, leveraging the capabilities of the OFD format in the domain of financial management.

In addition to the advantages of data sharing, the prevention of data leakage has emerged as a growing concern [3]. Currently, most banks rely on contractual agreements to enforce compliance and security measures during the transmission and utilization of data by application parties, lacking sufficient technical support. In cases of data leakage within the application scenario, banks encounter difficulties in promptly and accurately assigning responsibility to the relevant application parties, resulting in detrimental consequences for customers, banks, and the overall financial system. Given the increasing openness of the scenario ecosystem, relying solely on contractual agreements becomes increasingly challenging for banking institutions to mitigate risks associated with data sharing. It is imperative to incorporate additional technical support to fortify data security measures and enable effective prevention and monitoring of data security risks. The integration of watermarks in OFD files plays a crucial role in ensuring timely traceability and accountability following instances of data leakage. Currently, there is a lack of a comprehensive security framework in the financial industry that effectively addresses the challenges of data leakage prevention and tracking during the transmission and processing of financial data between cloud edges. This issue becomes particularly evident in the context of the OFD file format landscape, where the technology is still in its early stages of application. Furthermore, there is a dearth of dynamic watermarking algorithms that possess high transparency, concealment, robustness, and the capacity to carry substantial financial antileakage tracking information.

Banking and financial institutions heavily rely on data centers to facilitate financial services in conjunction with cloud-based scenarios. Within this service framework, the banking system is responsible for processing the entire collection of the bank's financial documents in the OFD format before transmitting them to the service scenario side for subsequent business processing. Ensuring the security of financial data during this processing stage is of utmost importance. We present E-SAWM, an implicit watermarking service framework for OFD files based on semantic analysis in an edge cloud computing scenario. Scenario-side edge cloud computing, an extension of the banking institution-side cloud computing center, is positioned closer to the user scenarios. In financial data-sharing scenarios, deploying data protection edge services on the scenario side enables accelerated and secure data processing. By leveraging the close proximity of edge computing to the data and utilizing its real-time capabilities, the scenario side allows for the application of more advanced security algorithms to meet diverse and higher-level financial data protection requirements, ensuring enhanced data security processing.

In this paper, we propose an OFD implicit watermarking framework, E-SAWM, based on semantic analysis in edge cloud scenarios. To ensure the security of embedded watermarks, we leverage the inherent semantic properties of the internal structured files of OFD. By using semantic analysis techniques, we generate highly authentic pseudostatements that closely resemble genuine content. These pseudostatements are then distributed efficiently and seamlessly integrated into the redundant bits of the OFD structured files. The proposed method offers the following significant advantages:

1. Transparency: E-SAWM ensures zero interference with the structure and display of the OFD file, preserving its original integrity;
2. Concealment: E-SAWM utilizes transformations and realistic pseudosentences to effectively conceal the watermark, impeding detection by potential attackers;
3. Robustness: E-SAWM employs distributed embedding of the watermark across multiple structural files and selects distributed redundant bits within the same file. This approach enhances the robustness of the watermark and hinders attackers from destroying the watermark information in the OFD file;
4. High capacity: E-SAWM supports unlimited watermark information in terms of length and quantity, enabling the embedding of a substantial amount of watermark data.

The rest of this paper is structured as follows. In Section 2, we present an overview of the related work in this field. Section 3 introduces the architecture of the open bank data service based on edge cloud and presents the OFD implicit watermarking algorithm scheme that relies on semantic analysis. In Section 4, we present the experimental results and analyze the outcomes in the context of real-world scenarios in the financial industry. Finally, in Section 5, we conclude the paper and provide an outlook for future research in this domain.

2. Related Work

2.1. Application of Edge Computing in the Domain of Financial Data Protection

Since 2015, edge cloud computing has emerged as a prominent technology, positioned on the Gartner technology maturity curve and experiencing rapid industrialization and growth. Edge computing represents a distributed computing paradigm that positions primary processing and data storage at the edge nodes of the network. According to the Edge Computing Industry Alliance [4], it is an open platform integrating network, computing, storage, and application core capabilities at the edge of the network, in close proximity to the data source. This setup enables the provision of intelligent edge services to meet crucial requirements for industrial digitization, including agile connectivity, real-time services, data optimization, application intelligence, and security and privacy protection. International standards organization ETSI [5] defines edge computing as the provisioning of IT service environments and computing capabilities at the network edge, aiming to reduce latency in network operations and service delivery, ultimately enhancing the user experience. Infrastructure for edge cloud computing encompasses various elements, such as distributed IDCs, carrier communication network edge infrastructure, and edge devices like edge-side client nodes, along with their corresponding network environments.

Serving as an extension of cloud computing, edge cloud computing provides localized computing capabilities and excels in small-scale, real-time intelligent analytics [6]. These inherent characteristics make it highly suitable for smart applications, where it can effectively support small-scale smart analytics and deliver localized services. In terms of network resources, edge cloud computing assumes the responsibility for data in close proximity to the information source. By facilitating local storage and processing of data, it eliminates the need to upload all data to the cloud [7]. Consequently, this technology significantly reduces the network burden and substantially improves the efficiency of network bandwidth utilization. In application scenarios that prioritize data security, especially in sectors such as finance, edge clouds offer enhanced compliance with stringent security requirements. By enabling the storage and processing of sensitive data locally, edge clouds effectively mitigate the heightened risks of data leakage associated with placing such critical information in uncontrollable cloud environments.

In the evolving landscape of the financial industry, there is a paradigm shift toward open banking, often referred to as banking 4.0. Departing from the traditional customer-centric approach, open banking places emphasis on user centricity and advocates for data sharing facilitated by technical channels such as APIs and SDKs. Its primary goal is to foster deeper collaboration and forge stronger business connections between banks and third-party institutions, which enables the seamless integration of financial services into customers' daily lives and production scenarios. The overarching objective is to optimize the allocation of financial resources, enhance service efficiency, and cultivate mutually beneficial partnerships among multiple stakeholders. An illustrative example of this paradigm shift is evident in bank card electronic payment systems, where the deployment of secure and encrypted POS machines at the edge enables convenient electronic payments [8].

Extensive research has been conducted to address the security challenges in edge cloud environments. M. Ati et al. [9] proposed an enhanced cloud security solution to enhance data protection against attacks. Similarly, L. Chen et al. [10] proposed a heterogeneous endpoint access authentication mechanism for a three-tier system ("cloud-edge-end") in edge computing scenarios, which aimed to support a large number of endpoint authentication requests while ensuring the privacy of endpoint devices. Building upon this, Z. Song et al. [11] introduced a novel attribute-based proxy re-encryption approach (COAB-PRE) that enables data privacy, controlled delegation, bilateral access control, and distributed access control capabilities for data sharing in cloud edge computing. On the other hand, G. Cui et al. [6] developed a data integrity checking and corruption location scheme known as ICL-EDI, which focuses on efficient data integrity checking and corruption location specifically for edge data. Additionally, Z. Wang et al. [12] introduced a flexible time-ordered threshold ring signature scheme based on blockchain technology to secure collected data in edge computing scenarios, ensuring a secure and tamper-resistant environment. However, to the best of our knowledge, the existing research has not extensively addressed the topic of leakage tracking techniques for sensitive data in edge computing scenarios.

2.2. Edge Cloud-Based Financial Regulatory Outpost Technology

The open sharing of data brings inherent risks to personal privacy data leakage. In the financial industry, it is crucial to ensure compliance with regulations such as the Data Security Law and the Personal Information Protection Law while conducting business operations. To tackle this challenge, we propose the deployment of regulatory outpost at the edge of the data application side, with a specific focus on third-party institutions, which aims to enhance the security and compliance of open banking data within the application side of the ecosystem.

Regulatory outpost is a standalone software system designed to monitor data operations on the application side, aiming to prevent data violations and mitigate the risk of data leakage. The system offers comprehensive monitoring capabilities throughout different stages of the application's data operations, including data storage, reading, and sharing, as well as intermediate processing tasks, such as sensitive data identification, desensitization, and watermarking. In addition, the regulatory outpost maintains meticulous records of all user data operation logs, facilitating log audits, leak detection, and generation of data flow maps and enabling situational awareness regarding data security.

In light of the above considerations, regulatory outpost operates at the edge side of data processing and plays a significant role in the data processing process. To ensure optimal efficiency and cost-effectiveness, the deployment of regulatory outposts should satisfy the following requirements in the context of data operations:

1. Elastic and scalable resource allocation: Data processing applications necessitate computational resources, but the overall data volume tends to vary. For instance, during certain periods, the data volume processed by the application side may increase, requiring more CPU performance, memory, hard disk space, and network throughput capacity. Conversely, when the processing data volume decreases, these hardware resources remain underutilized, leading to wastage. Therefore, it is essential for regulatory outposts to support the elastic scaling of resources to minimize input costs associated with data processing operations;
2. Low bandwidth consumption cost and data processing latency: The application's data traffic is directed through the regulatory outpost, which can lead to increased bandwidth consumption costs and higher network latency, especially if the outpost is deployed in a remote location like another city. The current backbone network, which is responsible for interconnecting cities, incurs higher egress bandwidth prices, and its latency is relatively higher compared to the metropolitan area network and local area network. To minimize the impact on the application experience, it is essential to maintain low bandwidth utilization costs and minimize data processing latency;
3. Data compliance: Due to concerns about open banking data leakage, the application side tends to prefer localized storage of open banking data to the greatest extent possible, which enables the application side to more conveniently monitor the adequacy of security devices and the effectiveness of security management protocols.

Edge clouds provide significant advantages due to their proximity to data endpoints, including cost savings in network bandwidth, low latency in data processing, and improved data security. Moreover, they offer the scalability, elasticity, and resource-sharing benefits commonly associated with centralized cloud computing. Hence, deploying regulatory outposts in the edge cloud is a logical decision. Figure 1 showcases an example deployment scenario.

The regulatory outpost consists of two components: "regulatory outpost—data input processing" and "regulatory outpost—data export processing". The specific data processing work flow is illustrated in Figure 2.

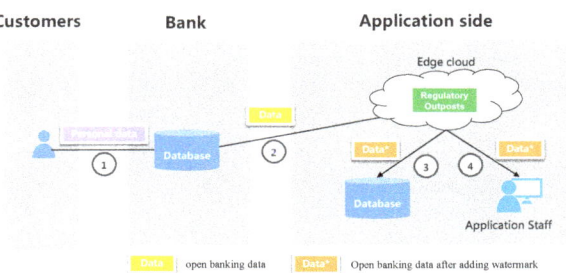

Figure 1. Deployment of Regulatory Outposts on Edge Clouds.

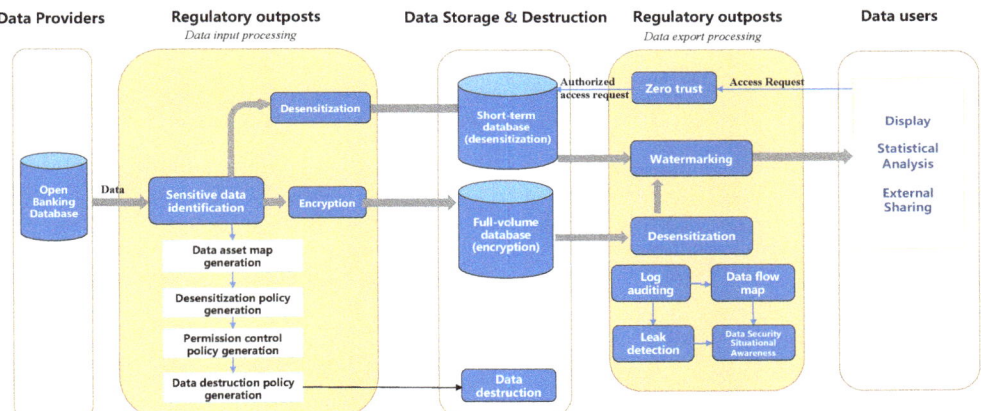

Figure 2. Data processing work flow in regulatory outposts within edge cloud scenarios. Components of the regulatory outpost data process: (1) Data provider: a bank or transit platform responsible for data processing and forwarding. (2) Data storage and destruction: a database provided by the application, subject to audit by regulatory outposts. (3) Data user: terminal equipment or other business systems accessing the database for tasks such as data display, statistical analysis, and external sharing.

2.2.1. Regulatory Outpost—Data Input Processing

This component automatically identifies sensitive data on among inflowing data and generates a data asset map, data desensitization policy, a permission control policy for the zero trust module, and a data destruction policy based on the identified sensitive data. To cater to the frequent viewing of short-term data such as logs by application-side users, a two-tier data storage approach is employed. The desensitized data are saved in a short-term database, while a full-volume database retains all the data. In cases in which the data contain highly confidential information, they are encrypted prior to being written into the full-volume database.

2.2.2. Regulatory Outpost—Data Export Processing

In the data access scenario, the zero trust module of the regulatory outpost plays a critical role in verifying access privileges for data users. When accessing data from a short-term database, open banking data are transmitted to the data user after incorporating watermark information, such as the data user's identity, data release date, and usage details. However, if the data are retrieved from the full-volume database, they must undergo desensitization based on the desensitization policy before the inclusion of watermark information and subsequent transmission to the data user. To ensure accountability, the log auditing module captures and logs all data operations for auditing purposes. The audit results are then utilized to generate data flow maps, detect instances of data leakage, and provide valuable insights into data security situational awareness. These insights facilitate the identification of existing data security risks and offer suggestions for improvement measures.

2.3. Document Watermarking Techniques

The file is a prominent data format used for data sharing. In the process of sharing files from the cloud (bank side) to the edge cloud (application side), it becomes crucial to monitor potential data leakage at each step. This concern is particularly relevant for the edge side, where the development of a watermarking algorithm that possesses high levels of transparency, concealment, robustness, and capacity has become a subject of significant academic interest.

Electronic document formats can be categorized into two types: streaming documents and versioned documents. Streaming documents, such as Word and TXT files, support editing, and their display may vary depending on the operating system and reader version. On the other hand, versioned documents have a fixed layout that remains consistent across different operating systems and readers.

OFD is an innovative electronic document format that conforms to the "GB/T 33190-2016 Electronic Document Storage and Exchange Format—Layout Documents" standard [13]. OFD was specifically developed to fulfill the demands of effectively managing and controlling layout documents while ensuring their long-term preservation. By offering a dependable and standardized format, OFD facilitates the maintenance of consistent layouts and supports the preservation of electronic documents. Our work primarily concentrates on the watermarking technology for OFD files, which serves as the prevalent file format utilized in the financial sector.

The OFD file format adopts XML (Extensible Markup Language) to define document layout, employing a "container + document" structure to store and describe data. The content of a document is represented by multiple files contained within a zip package, as illustrated in Figure 3. A detailed analysis and explanation of the internal structure components of an OFD file are provided in Table 1.

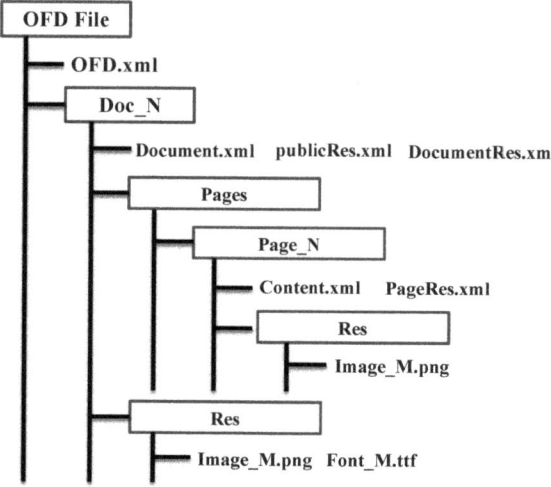

Figure 3. Structure of OFD.

Table 1. Internal Structural file description of OFD.

FLIE/FOLDER	Description
OFD.xml	OFD file main entry file; describes the basic OFD file information
Doc_N	The Nth document folder
Document.xml	Doc_N folder description file, including information about subfiles and subfolders contained under Doc_N
Page_N	The Nth page folder
Content.xml	Content description on page N
PageRes.xml	Resource description on page N
Res	Resource folder
PublicRes.xml	Document public resources index
DocumentRes.xml	Document own resource index
Image_M.png/Font_M.ttf	Resource files

In the realm of layout document formats, OFD and PDF are widely utilized. Watermarking techniques for layout documents can be categorized into several methods:

1. Syntax- or semantics-based approaches: leveraging natural language processing techniques to replace equivalent information, perform morphological conversions, and adjust statement structures to facilitate watermark embedding [6,14];
2. Format-based approaches encompass techniques such as line shift coding, word shift coding, space coding, modification of character colors, and adjustment of glyph structures [15];
3. Document structure-based approaches leverage PDF structures like PageObject, imageObject, and cross-reference tables, enabling the embedding of watermarks while preserving the original explicit location [16].

The field of PDF watermarking has reached a relatively mature stage of development. However, watermarking algorithms that rely on syntax and format modifications may alter the original text content, which conflicts with the requirement of preserving the originality of digital products. Consequently, watermarking algorithms based on the document structure are commonly employed to add watermarks to PDF files. ZHONG Zheng-yan et al. [17] presented a novel method for watermarking PDF documents, which involves embedding watermarks based on the redundant identifier found at the end of the PDF cross-reference table. By leveraging this technique, the original text content and display of the PDF remain unaltered, thereby achieving complete transparency when viewed using PDF readers. Kijun Han et al. [18] added watermarks based on the PageObject structure within the PDF structure, which offers resistance against attacks such as adding or deleting text to manipulate the page content. By utilizing these document structure-based watermarking techniques, PDF files can be effectively watermarked without compromising the original content and maintaining transparency and integrity in PDF readers.

The field of watermarking in the context of OFD has received limited attention in both academia and industry. In academia, there is a noticeable dearth of research studies and published papers specifically dedicated to OFD watermarking. On the industry front, existing OFD watermarking techniques primarily rely on explicit watermarks, which are implemented based on the following principles:

The watermark text content, along with relevant information such as position, transparency, size, and color, is defined within the annotation structure file named Annotation.xml. This file is an integral part of the internal structure of the OFD file and is typically located in the Annots/Page_n folder. The details of watermark addition are depicted in Figures 4 and 5.

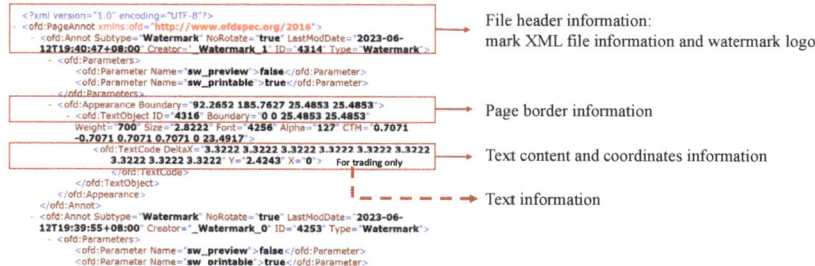

Figure 4. OFD annotation file contents for watermarking.

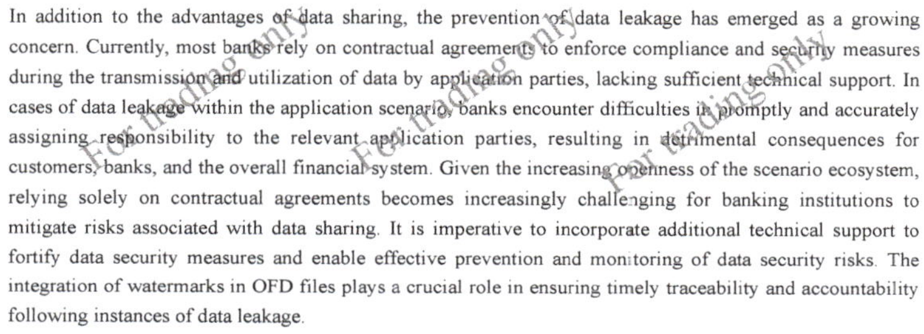

In addition to the advantages of data sharing, the prevention of data leakage has emerged as a growing concern. Currently, most banks rely on contractual agreements to enforce compliance and security measures during the transmission and utilization of data by application parties, lacking sufficient technical support. In cases of data leakage within the application scenario, banks encounter difficulties in promptly and accurately assigning responsibility to the relevant application parties, resulting in detrimental consequences for customers, banks, and the overall financial system. Given the increasing openness of the scenario ecosystem, relying solely on contractual agreements becomes increasingly challenging for banking institutions to mitigate risks associated with data sharing. It is imperative to incorporate additional technical support to fortify data security measures and enable effective prevention and monitoring of data security risks. The integration of watermarks in OFD files plays a crucial role in ensuring timely traceability and accountability following instances of data leakage.

Figure 5. Illustration of OFD page with added explicit watermark.

Although the structure of the watermark may seem clear and straightforward, it is susceptible to various attacks. Adversaries have the ability to manipulate the Annotation.xml folder, leading to vulnerabilities in the watermark's integrity, decryption, and identification, with potential for malicious removal. Consequently, the task of tracing compromised data becomes significantly challenging.

3. Model and Algorithm

3.1. Dynamic Watermarking Implementation

In compliance with regulatory requirements, data users in open banking must possess data traceability capabilities to effectively trace and determine data leakage incidents. Watermarking is a widely used technical approach to trace and assign responsibility in such scenarios.

Based on the aforementioned service architecture, an effective approach for tracking data and mitigating the risk of data leakage involves leveraging the data proximity processing capabilities of the edge cloud, which requires the utilization of the edge cloud's computing power to implement data leakage tracking technology. Furthermore, it is essential to employ a highly efficient and flexible watermarking algorithm on the edge cloud side to support the tracking of financially sensitive data. Specifically, in the context of OFD file applications, the edge cloud watermarking service facilitates the dynamic addition of timely watermarks after file processing on the edge cloud to ensure effective tracking in the event of data leakage.

Data watermarking in the financial industry encompasses two main approaches: static watermarking and dynamic watermarking. Static watermarking involves adding a large number of watermarks to the data during the pre-preparation phase, which is done once and remains unchanged. On the other hand, dynamic watermarking is performed in real time during the data access process, including data querying, accessing, real-time exchange, and dynamic release. This approach ensures that the watermarks are dynamic and updated in real time.

Unlike static watermarking, which can be pre-processed in batches on the central cloud without real-time requirements, dynamic watermarking is primarily deployed in the edge cloud to meet the demands of real-time data processing. Specifically, in financial business scenarios, where sensitive data need to be accessed by various platforms via API interfaces, the bank's data documents are appended with a unified static watermark before being shared. Upon reaching the third-party application, a dynamic watermark is added by the "regulatory outpost" based on the application's information and document content. Subsequently, the watermark information is dynamically replaced at each stage of data usage, ensuring accurate tracking of any potential data file leakage. The following examples provide a step-by-step illustration of the watermarking process:

1. Adding watermarks during data reception by the application-side database, as depicted in Figure 6. As the application side receives open banking data from a bank, a dynamic watermark is added, either explicitly or implicitly, while the data traverses a supervisory outpost situated in the edge cloud. This watermarking enables traceability in the event of an open banking data breach, allowing for identification of the breaching application side. The standard format typically follows: "Received Data from XXX Bank by XX Organization on xx/xx/xxxx (date). Purpose: XXXX".;
2. Adding watermarks during the download of data from the database by application-side employees, as shown in Figure 7. Whenever an application-side employee retrieves data from the application-side database, a dynamic watermark, typically implicit in nature, is embedded. This watermark serves the purpose of identifying the individual responsible for any data leakage when tracing its origin in the context of open banking. The format commonly follows "On xx/xx/xxxx (date), employee xxx downloaded open banking data from the database. Purpose: XXXX". Remarkably, the newly added watermark can coexist with the original watermark;
3. Adding watermarks when sharing data with external entities on the application side, as shown in Figure 8. In some cases, the application side needs to desensitize the open banking data, then share it with a partner, such as in the need for business cooperation. Hence, it is necessary to add a watermark to identify the specific partner when the leakage is traced. Typically, the format is "On xx/xx/xxxx (date), xxxx shared open banking data with the collaborator, xxxx. Purpose: XXXX".

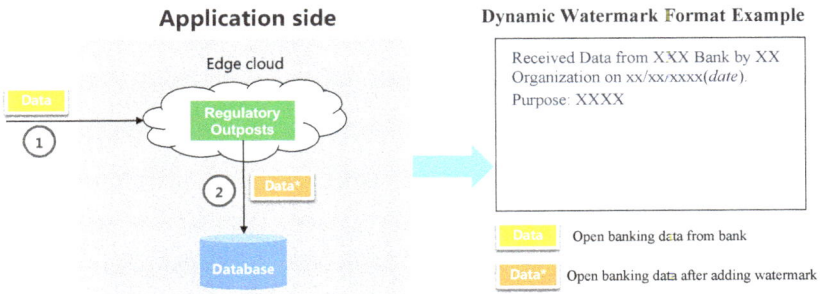

Figure 6. Adding watermark to data received from banking applications database.

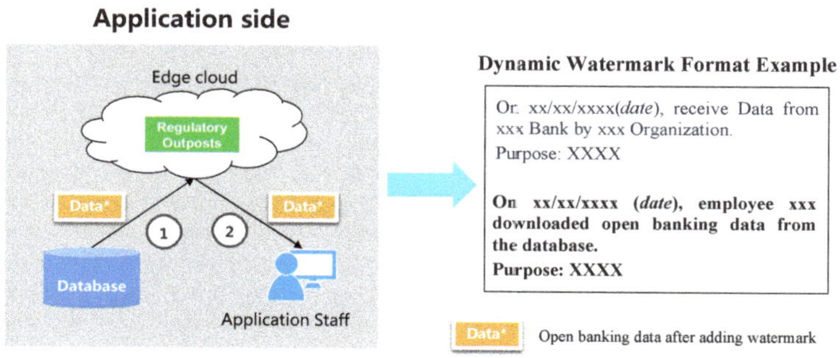

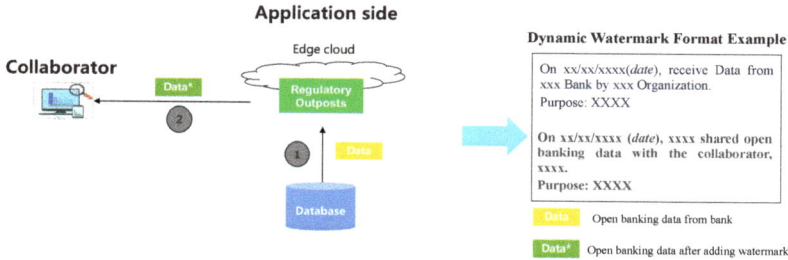

Figure 7. Adding watermark when application-side employees download data from the database.

Figure 8. Adding watermark when the application side shares externally.

3.2. Dynamic Watermarking Algorithm for OFD

To address the aforementioned scenario, we propose E-SAWM, a watermarking algorithm based on semantic analysis. At the file level, we incorporate a watermark into the key structural file, Content.xml of OFD. This integration renders the entire OFD page corrupted if the attacker deletes the content.xml file. At the content level, we leverage semantic analysis of the structural statements within Content.xml to generate highly realistic pseudo structural statements. These pseudo structural statements, carrying the watermark, are distributed and embedded within each Content.xml file. This distributed embedding approach ensures that the watermark remains concealed, making it challenging for attackers to identify its existence, location, and content. Furthermore, E-SAWM exhibits robustness against attempts to destroy or tamper with the watermark fields.

3.2.1. Semantic Analysis Model

In the realm of natural language processing, computers often face challenges when dealing with complex text systems. Consequently, the conversion of "words" into a form that computers can easily handle has emerged as a pressing concern. To tackle this challenge, word2vec has introduced the concept of mapping "words" to real number vectors, known as word embedding, resulting in word vectors. The Word2Vec model encompasses two primary variants: Skip-Gram and CBOW (Continuous Bag-of-Words). Intuitively, Skip-Gram predicts the context given an input word, whereas CBOW predicts the input word based on the context [19].

- Skip-Gram model

In the skip-gram model, every word is associated with two d-dimensional vectors, which are utilized to calculate conditional probabilities. Specifically, for a word indexed as i in the lexicon, the two vectors are represented by $v_i \in \mathbb{R}^d$ and $u_i \in \mathbb{R}^d$ when it functions as a central word and a contextual word, respectively. When provided with a central word (w_c) (indexed as c in the dictionary), the conditional probability of generating any context word (w_o) (indexed as o in the dictionary) can be modeled through a softmax operation on the dot product of the vectors as follows:

$$P(w_o \mid w_c) = \frac{\exp(u_o^T v_c)}{\sum_{i \in v} \exp(u_i^T v_c)} \tag{1}$$

where the set of word table indexes is $V = 0, 1, ..., |V| - 1$. Given a text sequence of length T, where the words at time step t are denoted as $w^{(t)}$, assume that the context words are generated independently given any central word. For a context window (m), the likelihood function of the jump meta model is the probability of generating all context words given any central word:

$$\prod_{t=1}^{T} \prod_{-m \leq j \leq m, j \neq 0} \log P(w^{(t+j)} | w^{(t)}) \tag{2}$$

- CBOW model

CBOW is a variation of the skip-word model, with the main distinction being that CBOW assumes that the central word is generated based on the surrounding contextual words within the text sequence.

In CBOW, the inclusion of multiple context words is considered. To calculate the conditional probabilities, the context word vectors are averaged. Let $v_i \in \mathbb{R}^d$ and $u_i \in \mathbb{R}^d$ represent the vectors corresponding to the context words and central words, respectively, for any word at index i in the dictionary. The conditional probability of generating a central word (w_c) (indexed by c in the word list) given the context words ($w_{o1}, ..., w_o2m$) (indexed by $o_1, ..., o_2m$ in the word list) can be represented using the following equation:

$$P(w_c | w_{o1}, ..., w_{o2m}) = \frac{\exp\left(\frac{1}{2m} u_c^T (v_{o1} + ... + v_{o2m})\right)}{\sum_{i \in v} \exp\left(\frac{1}{2m} u_i^T (v_{o1} + ... + v_{o2m})\right)} \tag{3}$$

Let $W_o = w_o 1, ..., w_o 2m$, $\bar{v}_o = \frac{v_{o1} + ... + v_{o2m}}{2m}$; then, the above equation can be simplified as

$$P(w_c | W_o) = \frac{\exp(u_c^T \bar{v}_o)}{\sum_{i \in V} \exp(u_i^T \bar{v}_o)} \tag{4}$$

Considering a text sequence of length T, where the words at time step t are represented as $w^{(t)}$ and employing a context window of size m, the likelihood function of the CBOW expresses the probability of generating all central words given their respective context words:

$$\prod_{t=1}^{T} P(w^{(t)} | w^{(t-m)}, ..., w^{(t-1)}, w^{(t+1)}, ..., w^{(t+m)}) \tag{5}$$

- Word-embedding model comparison

Assuming a text corpus with V words and a window size of K, the CBOW model predicts approximately $O(V)$, which is equivalent to the number of words in the corpus. In contrast, Skip-gram performs more predictions than CBOW. In Skip-gram, each word is predicted once using surrounding words when it serves as the central word, resulting in a time complexity of $O(KV)$.

While CBOW trains faster than Skip-gram, the latter produces superior word vector representations. When dealing with a corpus containing many low-frequency words,

Skip-gram provides better word vectors for these words but requires more training time. Conversely, CBOW is more efficient in such cases. The choice between the models depends on specific requirements. For higher prediction accuracy and lower training efficiency, the Skip-gram model is preferred. Conversely, the CBOW model can be chosen [20].

3.2.2. OFD Watermarking Algorithm Based on Semantic Analysis

Word2vec is a widely utilized concept across various domains. Tomas Mikolov introduced doc2vec, an algorithm that enables the representation of sentences or short texts as vectors by considering sentences of different lengths as training samples [21]. In the field of biology, Asgari and Mofrad proposed BioVec for the analysis of biological sequence word vectors [22].

For OFD, the structural documents consist of statements that adhere to specific rules. Here, we use the term "structural statements" to refer to the structural information present in OFD files. By treating these statements as natural languages, it becomes possible to generate a context specific to each structural document. Consequently, we devised a sophisticated watermark-embedding algorithm by leveraging semantic analysis. In the case of contextual datasets, the process involves mapping word separation to word vectors distributed in a high-dimensional space using word2vec. This mapping enables the evaluation of word similarity. When dealing with known contexts, we utilize the word2vec model to transform them, resulting in k words that closely resemble the original context words. Subsequently, these words are distributedly embedded within the original structural document, serving as watermark carriers. Our approach capitalizes on semantic analysis to develop a highly covert watermark-embedding algorithm.

The algorithm follows the flow depicted in Figure 9 and is divided into four main modules:

1. Semantic analysis model trainingConstruct a pseudo structural library based on the original structural library of OFD. Gather n instances of context data from structured documents in OFD format. Utilizing these context data, along with the pseudo structure body library, generate n' instances of the context dataset with pseudo structure bodies. These contextual datasets are then trained separately using the CBOW model and the Skip-gram model to develop the semantic analysis model. When conducting semantic analysis on an OFD-structured document, the context is initially extracted. For a context dataset containing a higher frequency of low-frequency structural bodies, the Skip-gram model is preferred for semantic analysis due to its improved performance and efficiency. On the other hand, for the contextual dataset containing a higher frequency of high-frequency structures, CBOW is used for semantic analysis.

Assume that m structural files with embeddable watermarks are extracted for an OFD file that requires watermark addition. V_i structural keywords are extracted from file F_i, and the training window size is K. In such cases, the time complexity for training using the CBOW model can be calculated as follows:

$$T_{CBOW} = V_0 + V_1 + \cdots + V_{m-1} = O(\sum_{i=0}^{m-1} V_i) \quad (6)$$

The time complexity for training using the Skip-gram model is as follows:

$$T_{\text{skip-gram}} = K \cdot V_0 + K \cdot V_1 + \ldots + K \cdot V_{m-1} = O(K \sum_{i=0}^{m-1} V_i) \quad (7)$$

Based on the size of the text words, we set the threshold (τ) to select the model with the best training effect for calculation:

$$\text{model} = \begin{cases} \text{skip-gram}, & \sum_{i=0}^{m-1} V_i < \tau \\ \text{CBOW}, & \sum_{i=0}^{m-1} V_i < \tau \end{cases} \quad (8)$$

As mentioned in Section 3.2.1, the Skip-gram model exhibited higher accuracy compared to the CBOW model in our experiments. In particular, when the time consumed is similar, the Skip-gram model outperforms CBOW. In our work, this occurred when τ had a value of 1000.

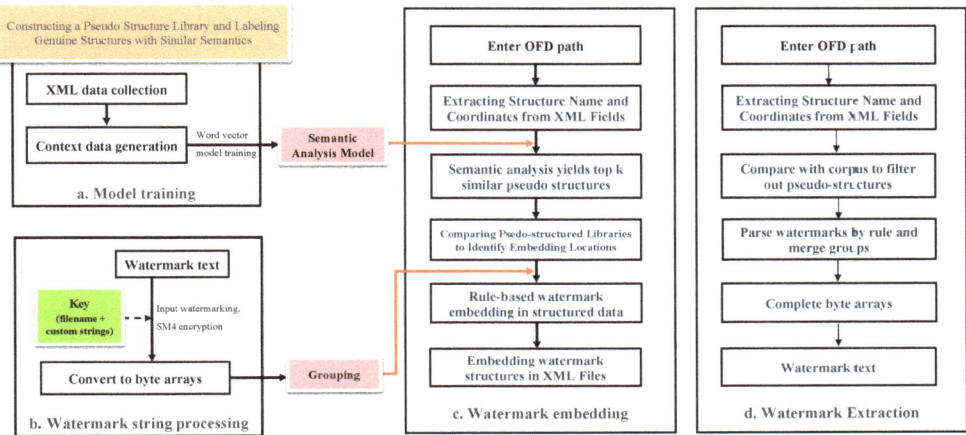

Figure 9. Overview of E-SAWM.

2. Watermark content processing. Encrypt the watermark text (*originalInfo*) using the SM4 algorithm with a key derived from the combination of the file name (*fileName*) of the watermarked file, and a custom string (*myString*) provided by the adder. This encryption process is represented by Equation (9).

$$SecretWatarmarkMessage = SM4((fileNameomyString)\ originalInfo) \quad (9)$$

Subsequently, convert the encrypted watermark message into a byte array and perform grouping on the byte array;

3. Watermark embedding. For each structural file within the target OFD file, conduct structure extraction. Combine these structures as contexts in their original order. Utilize the semantic analysis model trained in step 1 to perform semantic analysis, then obtain pseudo structures with the top K similarity. Insert these pseudo structures into the structural files of the OFD, and embed the watermark grouping acquired in step 2 into each pseudo structure;

4. Watermark Extraction. Extract structure names and contents from all structural files within the OFD file intended for watermarking, which is compared with the corpus, and filter out any pseudo structures. Based on the grouping information within the structure, combine byte array groups associated with the same watermark. This process results in a complete byte array, which is then parsed into a string and further parsed using a key. Finally, the complete watermark is obtained.

4. Experiments

To evaluate the effectiveness of our proposed OFD watermarking algorithm that utilizes semantic analysis, we performed various attack tests, including a robustness test, steganography, and watermark capacity detection [17,23]. Additionally, we compare our findings with the results obtained by existing OFD watermarking algorithms commonly employed in the industry.

4.1. Steganography

One of the fundamental requirements of an invisible watermark is its imperceptibility. The embedded watermark in the OFD document must remain completely hidden, ensuring that no noticeable alterations are made to the visible display interface of the document. Moreover, users should be unable to detect the presence of the watermark, making it challenging for attackers to identify its location or develop cracking methods.

The most common watermarking algorithm employed in the industry is categorized as an explicit watermarking algorithm, relying on annotated files. When a highly transparent watermark is added, it becomes difficult to visually discern the watermark with the naked eye. Nevertheless, it is still possible to identify the watermark by converting the OFD page into an image and adjusting the image's contrast. In contrast, a low-transparency watermark is clearly visible to the naked eye. To the best of our knowledge, there is no existing research on watermarking of OFD files. While some studies have focused on watermarking PDF files using syntax- and format-based algorithms, these approaches tend to alter the original text content, which may not comply with the originality requirements for digital products.

We propose an experiment to test the steganographic potential of E-SAWM. Figure 10 shows the comparison effect of OFD document watermarking. The two documents appear indistinguishable to the naked eye, and even after converting OFD pages to images, the watermark information remains hidden. In comparison to traditional watermarking algorithms that rely on annotated documents, the proposed OFD watermarking algorithm based on semantic analysis exhibits robust steganography capabilities.

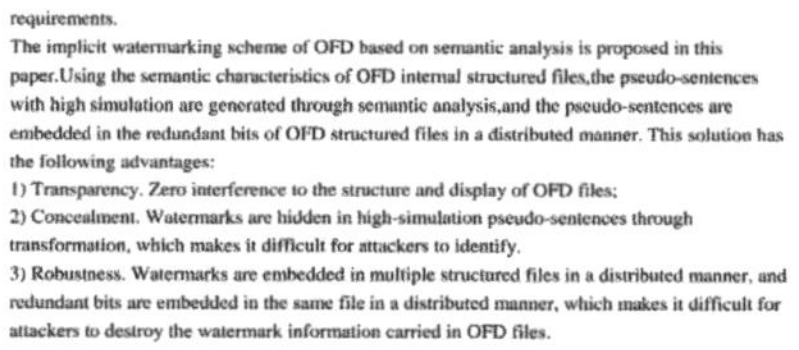

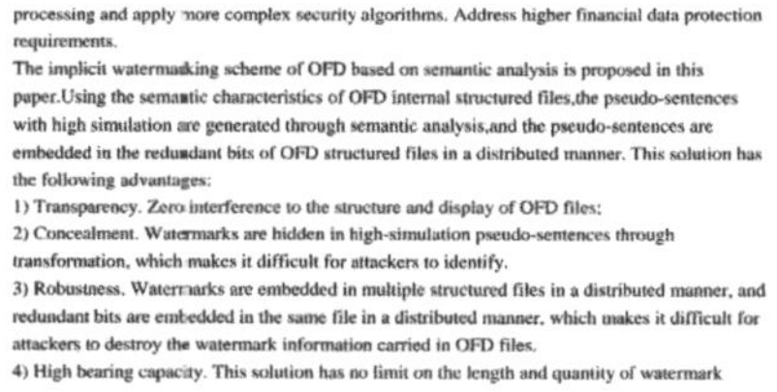

Figure 10. Visual comparison of watermark effects. (**a**) OFD page before adding watermark. (**b**) OFD page after adding watermark.

4.2. Robustness

We provide users with various editing options to test the algorithm's robustness. Robustness testing is conducted following the approach outlined in reference [18]. These options include highlighting, underlining, strikethrough, wavy lines, handwritten scribbles, and text overlay. Users can apply these edits to randomly selected locations within the watermarked OFD file.

The visual appearance of the watermark information in the industry's OFD watermarking algorithm, which is based on an annotation structure, can be influenced by attacks like highlighting and underlining, but it does not compromise integrity.

We conducted robustness testing on E-SAWM. Figure 11 illustrates an example of an attack, while Table 2 presents the results of watermark extraction. E-SAWM introduces the integration of semantically similar pseudo structures into structured files. Notably, any structural changes that may arise in the original file when incorporating features like highlighting or underlining have no impact on the pseudo structural content. Consequently, the results show that our OFD watermarking algorithm demonstrates effective resistance against the attacks listed in the table, achieving a 100% success rate in watermark extraction for OFD files under each attack type.

In addition to the convenience of data sharing, more attention is paid to the data leakage prevention capability.

According to our research, most banks use contract agreements to restrict the compliance and security of applications during data transmission and use. However, technical tools are still lacking. Once data leakage occurs on the scenario side, it is difficult for banks to hold relevant applications accountable in a timely and accurate manner. It has a negative impact on customers, banks and the financial system as a whole. With the continuous opening

display of OFD files:

2) Concealment. Watermarks are hidden in high-simulation pseudo-sentences through transformation, which makes it difficult for attackers to identify.

3) Robustness. Watermarks are embedded in multiple structured files in a distributed manner, and redundant bits are embedded in the same file in a distributed manner, which makes it difficult for attackers to destroy the watermark information carried in OFD files.

4) High bearing capacity. This solution has no limit on the

Figure 11. Example of each post-attack OFD page. Please note that in the visual representation presented: Colorful lines symbolize distinct attack methods, with yellow representing "highlight", blue indicating "Wavy line", a green line representing "underline", and red signifying "Strikethrough". Green font signifies "Handwritten graffiti", while gray font indicates "Text overlay".

Table 2. Extraction success rate of watermarks following each attack.

Attack Type	Example of Attack Content	Watermark Extraction Success Rate
Highlight	Left Column—Line 1 Right Column—Lines 2–5	100%
Underline	Left Column—Line 2 Right Column—Lines 2–3	100%
Strikethrough	Left Column—Line 5 Right Column—Lines 2–3	100%
Wavy line	Left Column—Line 6 Right Column—Line 4	100%
Handwritten graffiti	Right Column—Lines 2	100%
Text overlay	Full Page	100%

4.3. Watermark Capacity

Watermark capacity refers to the proportion of the watermark information size to the size of the document being watermarked. It can be calculated as follows:

$$WatermarkCapacity = \frac{watermark\ data\ bits}{OFD\ file\ bits} \quad (10)$$

By utilizing a watermark algorithm with a higher watermark capacity, the document can be embedded more effectively within the watermark information. This capability enables the handling of diverse document lengths and multilevel watermarks, facilitating the transmission of larger amounts of information in practical applications.

In the annotation structure-based watermarking algorithm, the process of adding a watermark involves appending both annotation structure information and the watermark content itself to the corresponding Annot.xml file of the target watermark page. Conversely, E-SAWM converts and encrypts the watermark information into multiple groups (referred to as k groups). These k groups, along with their corresponding encrypted watermark characters, are then added to the Content.xml file of the designated watermark page. Compared to the annotation structure-based algorithm, our algorithm enriches the original OFD file with additional information during the watermarking process.

To assess whether the increased information can be accommodated within the acceptable carrying range, we conducted a watermarking capacity test. For this evaluation, we randomly selected twenty OFD files of various sizes as samples. Additionally, we generated twenty watermarks with different information contents. Each watermark was individually matched with a corresponding file and embedded using the watermark algorithm. To measure the impact of watermarking on document size, we calculated the rate of change in the OFD file size by comparing its size before and after the watermark-embedding process, as shown in Figure 12.

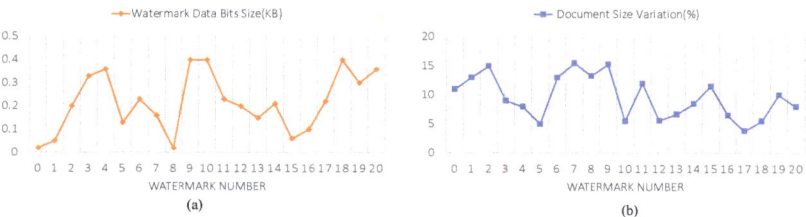

Figure 12. Watermark capacity tests. (**a**) Watermark data size in various OFD Files. (**b**) Variation of the corresponding OFD files before and after watermark embedding.

The experiments demonstrate that when embedding watermarks of various sizes into each sample OFD document, the document size experiences minimal fluctuations, which suggests that E-SAWM effectively handles the embedding of high-capacity watermark information without significantly impacting the document size. Moreover, it showcases the algorithm's ability to accommodate a substantial amount of watermark information.

5. Conclusions

With the rapid development of the Internet, ensuring data security has become a critical concern within the financial industry. Tracing leaked data plays a crucial role in safeguarding data integrity. The growing use of OFD documents, particularly in electronic tax returns and statements, emphasizes their importance in the financial sector.

We propose an innovative OFD watermarking framework, E-SAWM, in the edge cloud scenario that utilizes semantic analysis to incorporate implicit watermarks into OFD documents. By encrypting watermarking information into highly simulated structural statements and securely embedding them within the structural components of OFD files, E-SAWM provides a robust solution. Experimental evaluations confirm the effectiveness of the algorithm, demonstrating its high concealment, strong robustness, and substantial watermarking capacity. Consequently, the proposed algorithm enhances data security in the financial industry. Overall, our research contributes to the advancement of data security measures in the financial domain, addressing the pressing need for traceability and protection against data leakage in an era of rapid technological advancements.

Author Contributions: Conceptualization, L.Z. (Lijun Zu), H.L. and L.Z. (Liang Zhang); Methodology, L.Z. (Lijun Zu) and J.Y.; Software, L.Z. (Liang Zhang); Validation, L.Z. (Lijun Zu) and H.L.; Formal Analysis, L.Z. (Lijun Zu) and H.L.; Investigation, L.Z. (Lijun Zu) and X.Z.; Resources, L.Z. (Liang Zhang) and X.Z.; Data Curation, X.Z.; Writing—Original Draft Preparation, L.Z. (Lijun Zu) and L.Z.; Writing—Review and Editing, L.Z. (Lijun Zu) and H.L.; Visualization, H.L.; Supervision, Z.L.(Lijun Zu) and S.H.; Funding Acquisition, J.Y. All authors have read and agreed to the published version of the manuscript.

Funding: This research was funded by the National Key Research and Development Program of China (grant number 2021YFC3300600) and National Natural Science Foundation of China under Grant (No. 61873309, No. 92046024, No. 92146002) and Shanghai Science and Technology Project under Grant (No. 22510761000).

Institutional Review Board Statement: Not applicable.

Informed Consent Statement: Not applicable.

Data Availability Statement: Not applicable.

Conflicts of Interest: The authors declare no conflict of interest.

References

1. Premchand, A.; Choudhry, A. Open banking & APIs for Transformation in Banking. In Proceedings of the 2018 International Conference on Communication, Computing and Internet of Things (IC3IoT), Chennai, India, 15–17 February 2018; pp. 25–29.
2. Longlei, H.; Peiliang, Z.; Hua, J. Research and implementation of format document OFD electronic seal module. *Inf. Technol.* **2016**, *40*, 76–80.
3. Kassab, M.; Laplante, P. Trust considerations in open banking. *IT Prof.* **2022**, *24*, 70–73. [CrossRef]
4. Hong, X.; Wang, Y. Edge computing technology: Development and countermeasures. *Strateg. Study Chin. Acad. Eng.* **2018**, *20*, 20–26. [CrossRef]
5. Giust, F.; Costa-Perez, X.; Reznik, A. Multi-access edge computing: An overview of ETSI MEC ISG. *IEEE Tech Focus* **2017**, *1*, 4.
6. Cui, G.; He, Q.; Li, B.; Xia, X.; Chen, F.; Jin, H.; Xiang, Y.; Yang, Y. Efficient verification of edge data integrity in edge computing environment. *IEEE Trans. Serv. Comput.* **2021**, *15*, 3233–3244. [CrossRef]
7. Gu, L.; Zhang, W.; Wang, Z.; Zeng, D.; Jin, H. Service Management and Energy Scheduling Toward Low-Carbon Edge Computing. *IEEE Trans. Sustain. Comput.* **2022**, *8*, 109–119. [CrossRef]
8. Zhang, Z.; Avazov, N.; Liu, J.; Khoussainov, B.; Li, X.; Gai, K.; Zhu, L. WiPOS: A POS terminal password inference system based on wireless signals. *IEEE Internet Things J.* **2020**, *7*, 7506–7516. [CrossRef]
9. Ati, M.; Al Bostami, R. Protection of Data in Edge and Cloud Computing. In Proceedings of the 2022 IEEE International Conference on Computing (ICOCO), Sabah, Malaysia, 14–16 November 2022; pp. 169–173.
10. Chen, L.; Liu, Z.; Wang, Z. Research on heterogeneous terminal security access technology in edge computing scenario. In Proceedings of the 2019 11th International Conference on Measuring Technology and Mechatronics Automation (ICMTMA), Qiqihar, China, 28–29 April 2019; pp. 472–476.
11. Song, C.; Ma, H.; Zhang, R.; Xu, W.; Li, J. Everything Under Control: Secure Data Sharing Mechanism for Cloud-Edge Computing. *IEEE Trans. Inf. Forensics Secur.* **2023**, *18*, 2234–2249. [CrossRef]
12. Wang, Z.; Fan, J. Flexible threshold ring signature in chronological order for privacy protection in edge computing. *IEEE Trans. Cloud Comput.* **2020**, *10*, 1253–1261. [CrossRef]
13. GB/T 33190; 2016 Electronic Files Storage and Exchange Formats—Fixed Layout Documents. China National Standardization Management Committee: Beijing, China, 2016.
14. Yu, Z.; Ting, L.; Yihen, C.; Shiqi, Z.; Sheng, L. Natural Languagetext Watermarking. *J. Chin. Inf. Process.* **2005**, *19*, 57–63.
15. Wang, X.; Jin, Y. A high-capacity text watermarking method based on geometric micro-distortion. In Proceedings of the 2022 26th International Conference on Pattern Recognition (ICPR), Montreal, QC, Canada, 21–25 August 2022; pp. 1749–1755.
16. Zhao, W.; Guan, H.; Huang, Y.; Zhang, S. Research on Double Watermarking Algorithm Based on PDF Document Structure. In Proceedings of the 2020 International Conference on Culture-oriented Science & Technology (ICCST), Beijing, China, 28–31 October 2020; pp. 298–303.
17. Zhengyan, Z.; Yanhui, G.; Guoai, X. Digital watermarking algorithm based on structure of PDF document. *Comput. Appl.* **2012**, *32*, 2776–2778.
18. Khadam, U.; Iqbal, M.M.; Habib, M.A.; Han, K. A Watermarking Technique Based on File Page Objects for PDF. In Proceedings of the 2019 IEEE Pacific Rim Conference on Communications, Computers and Signal Processing (PACRIM), Victoria, BC, Canada, 21–23 August 2019; pp. 1–5.
19. Mikolov, T.; Chen, K.; Corrado, G.; Dean, J. Efficient estimation of word representations in vector space. *arXiv* **2013**, arXiv:1301.3781.
20. Mikolov, T.; Sutskever, I.; Chen, K.; Corrado, G.S.; Dean, J. Distributed representations of words and phrases and their compositionality. *Adv. Neural Inf. Process. Syst.* **2013**, *26*, 1–9.
21. Asgari, E.; Mofrad, M.R. Continuous distributed representation of biological sequences for deep proteomics and genomics. *PLoS ONE* **2015**, *10*, e0141287. [CrossRef] [PubMed]
22. Le, Q.; Mikolov, T. Distributed representations of sentences and documents. In Proceedings of the International Conference on Machine Learning, Beijing, China, 21–26 June 2014; pp. 1188–1196.
23. Hao, Y.; Chuang, L.; Feng, Q.; Rong, D. A Survey of Digital Watermarking. *Comput. Res. Dev.* **2005**, *42*, 1093–1099.

Disclaimer/Publisher's Note: The statements, opinions and data contained in all publications are solely those of the individual author(s) and contributor(s) and not of MDPI and/or the editor(s). MDPI and/or the editor(s) disclaim responsibility for any injury to people or property resulting from any ideas, methods, instructions or products referred to in the content.

Review

Federated Learning for Intrusion Detection Systems in Internet of Vehicles: A General Taxonomy, Applications, and Future Directions

Jadil Alsamiri and Khalid Alsubhi *

Faculty of Computing and Information Technology, King Abdulaziz University, Jeddah 21589, Saudi Arabia; jalsamiri@stu.kau.edu.sa
* Correspondence: kalsubhi@kau.edu.sa

Abstract: In recent years, the Internet of Vehicles (IoV) has garnered significant attention from researchers and automotive industry professionals due to its expanding range of applications and services aimed at enhancing road safety and driver/passenger comfort. However, the massive amount of data spread across this network makes securing it challenging. The IoV network generates, collects, and processes vast amounts of valuable and sensitive data that intruders can manipulate. An intrusion detection system (IDS) is the most typical method to protect such networks. An IDS monitors activity on the road to detect any sign of a security threat and generates an alert if a security anomaly is detected. Applying machine learning methods to large datasets helps detect anomalies, which can be utilized to discover potential intrusions. However, traditional centralized learning algorithms require gathering data from end devices and centralizing it for training on a single device. Vehicle makers and owners may not readily share the sensitive data necessary for training the models. Granting a single device access to enormous volumes of personal information raises significant privacy concerns, as any system-related problems could result in massive data leaks. To alleviate these problems, more secure options, such as Federated Learning (FL), must be explored. A decentralized machine learning technique, FL allows model training on client devices while maintaining user data privacy. Although FL for IDS has made significant progress, to our knowledge, there has been no comprehensive survey specifically dedicated to exploring the applications of FL for IDS in the IoV environment, similar to successful systems research in deep learning. To address this gap, we undertake a well-organized literature review on IDSs based on FL in an IoV environment. We introduce a general taxonomy to describe the FL systems to ensure a coherent structure and guide future research. Additionally, we identify the relevant state of the art in FL-based intrusion detection within the IoV domain, covering the years from FL's inception in 2016 through 2023. Finally, we identify challenges and future research directions based on the existing literature.

Keywords: Federated Learning (FL); intrusion detection systems (IDS); Internet of Vehicles (IoV); deep learning; machine learning

Citation: Alsamiri, J.; Alsubhi, K. Federated Learning Based Intrusion Detection Systems in Internet of Vehicles: A Literature Survey. *Future Internet* 2023, 15, 403. https://doi.org/10.3390/fi15120403

Academic Editors: Qiang Duan and Zhihui Lu

Received: 30 October 2023
Revised: 9 December 2023
Accepted: 12 December 2023
Published: 14 December 2023

Copyright: © 2023 by the authors. Licensee MDPI, Basel, Switzerland. This article is an open access article distributed under the terms and conditions of the Creative Commons Attribution (CC BY) license (https://creativecommons.org/licenses/by/4.0/).

1. Introduction

The rapid expansion of the Internet of Things (IoT) has led to a number of novel applications, such as smart cities, smart grids, and the Internet of Vehicles (IoV). When these smart objects take the form of interconnected vehicles over the internet, the IoT becomes the IoV. Significant interest in IoV technologies has emerged due to substantial advancements in the smart automobile industry. IoV networks are integrated and open network systems that connect vehicles, human intelligence, neighboring environments, and public networks. These networks aim to increase road safety, reduce human error-related accidents, and mitigate congestion. This is accomplished by continuously monitoring traffic congestion. However, despite the numerous benefits offered by the IoV, several issues must be addressed to safeguard the lives of all road users. The IoV is vulnerable to cyberattacks, which threaten its stability, robustness, and can lead to vehicle unavailability and traffic accidents. Since communication in these networks requires the involvement of multiple components, they are susceptible to a broad array of attacks. Thus, ensuring their security requires advanced intrusion detection systems (IDSs) that can address potential cyberattacks. IDSs excel at identifying anomalies and attacks in the network's data during communications between vehicles and various devices. Given that the IoV is a relatively new network paradigm, new and ever-evolving attacks against it continue to emerge. The IoV network creates a huge amount of data very quickly, especially when there are cyberattacks. The accuracy of machine learning and deep learning approaches makes them a preferred choice in this high-stakes environment [1]. Nevertheless, the need to store and transmit data to a centralized server may compromise privacy and security. In contrast, Federated Learning (FL), a decentralized learning approach that protects privacy, trains models locally before sending only the parameters to the centralized server. Even though FL for IDS development has made significant progress, a comprehensive survey specifically exploring the applications of FL for IDS in the IoV environment has yet to be conducted. To the best of our knowledge, a gap exists in the availability of a study that comprehensively assesses current IDSs based on FL for IoV, similar to the successful systems research conducted in deep learning.

To address this gap, the key contributions of our survey can be summarized as follows:

- We offer a generic taxonomy for describing FL systems (FLSs) to ensure a coherent structure and guide future research.
- We undertake a well-organized literature review on IDSs based on FL in an IoV environment. This review identifies the latest advancements in FL-based intrusion detection within the IoV domain, covering the years from FL's inception in 2016 to 2023.
- Furthermore, we highlight several challenges and potential future directions based on the existing literature.

The remainder of the paper is organized as follows. Section 2 explores the background within this domain, covering IoV, FLSs, and IDSs. Section 3 aims to provide a thorough overview of FL research within the context of IDSs in IoV environments. Finally, we conclude the paper by describing open research challenges and outlining possible future research directions in Section 4. For increased clarity and understanding, abbreviations section summarizes the abbreviations used in this manuscript.

2. Background

2.1. An Overview of Internet of Vehicles

Transportation has become a significant challenge in many countries due to population growth. Often, the transportation system itself is outdated, making upgrading a costly and daunting task. By 2035, the number of vehicles around the globe is estimated to reach two billion. This substantial number will strain existing transportation systems and most likely result in more accidents and traffic jams. Therefore, changes must be made in the transportation system's framework to adjust to emerging prerequisites of new vehicles, travelers, and drivers [2]. Technological advancements have motivated the enhancement of a wide array of gadgets to be used in various fields, including IoT. Additionally, the Internet is helping societies develop much faster, and people in developed societies, in turn, are seeking a better way of life [3]. A few of these technologies have resulted in the further advancement of IoV, a field commonly considered an extension of IoT. IoT is a universal network of interconnected smart devices equipped with embedded hardware and software for environmental sensing and data exchange, with the capability to act on that information. Therefore, including vehicles as devices makes IoV a field with applications in intelligent transportation, crash prevention, and smart cities [4]. IoV networks require software applications to monitor vehicle movements and provide security against malicious attacks. These systems function through interactions with various components, including vehicle communication with roads, roadside units, and sensors [5]. IoV brings together two cutting-edge dreams—the network and intelligent vehicles—while centering around the objects (e.g., humans, vehicles, systems) to create a perceptive system that relies on information technology and communication features to assist authorities in huge urban territories and entire countries [3]. IoV enables extensive communication between vehicles in various forms, including vehicle-to-vehicle, vehicle-to-road, vehicle-to-human, vehicle-to-infrastructure, and vehicle-to-sensor connections through wireless communication technologies [6]. Additionally, human-to-human interaction occurs in IoV. Generally, though, the human component is gaining importance as the services develop. In their research, Rim et al. [7] view IoV as a worldwide network with three integrated subnets: the intravehicle network, the intervehicle network, and the vehicular mobile internet. By contrast, Garg et al. [3] define IoV from the angle of integration of on-board sensors and communication technologies. These researchers view IoV as intelligent vehicles with advanced devices that utilize modern communication and networking technology to provide vehicles with complex environment sensors, intelligent decision making, and control functions.

2.1.1. Benefits of Internet of Vehicles

IoV has the potential to transform the transportation industry's landscape, making travel safer, more efficient, and friendlier to the environment. The IoV provides several opportunities for improvement and numerous benefits, including the following [3]:

- Lower costs: Improved traffic control results in lower costs, including insurance premiums and operational costs.
- Time efficiency: Traffic is meticulously monitored, examining the time people spend on the road.
- Reduced risk of fatalities: Examining the transportation environment can reduce accidents, such as by helping drivers navigate traffic [8].
- Smart cities development: Smart cities are more organized due to the services they provide, including enhanced navigation and real-time traffic.
- Greenhouse effect reduction: This limits harm to the world.
- Emergency response: IoV can autonomously notify emergency services in the case of an accident, potentially diminishing reaction times and saving human lives.
- Autonomous driving: IoV is an essential part of the development of autonomous and semi-autonomous vehicles, both of which can lower the number of accidents resulting from human mistakes and enhance general road safety.
- Traffic documentation: Filming traffic accidents using services such as pics-on-wheels allows any vehicle on the road to act as a witness to any accident. Among other outcomes, this encourages people to maintain decorum on the road.

In general, IoV offers the potential for safer, more intelligent, and more efficient mobility for individuals and society as a whole.

2.1.2. **Internet of Vehicles' Characteristics and Challenges**

This section elaborates on the characteristics of IoV and discusses various challenges that IoV faces. Compared to other types of networks, IoV networks are distinguished by several qualities. IoV is an evolution of traditional vehicular ad hoc networks (VANETs) and shares many characteristics with VANETs, including dynamic topology, fluctuating network density, high vehicular mobility, and network obstacles [2]. However, IoV networks possess the following additional attributes:

- Scalability: Compared to traditional VANETs, IoV networks have the capacity to incorporate a significantly larger number of interconnected vehicles, ranging from hundreds to thousands. Furthermore, IoV has the potential to significantly augment the number of interlinked gadgets to a magnitude of millions, depending on the utilized application.

- Multiple wireless access methods: The IoV platform supports several types of wireless access methods, including WLANs, WiMAX, cellular wireless, and satellite communications.
- Extended network communication: IoV enables a broader range of communication options than conventional VANETs, characterized by their restricted communication capabilities. IoV facilitates vehicle-to-smart object connection, including devices such as smartphones and tablets.
- Cloud computing: Unlike VANETs, the activities in IoV mostly rely on cloud computing services.
- Predictable mobility: Vehicular networks differ significantly from other ad-hoc network types because vehicles often move quickly and in any direction. Vehicles are predictable in their movement due to the topography, roadway layout, use of signal-received traffic lights, and consideration of other moving vehicles' distance. Therefore, vehicles are predicted to possess integrated GPS systems to ascertain information on their movement.
- Highly dynamic topology: A vehicle network's topology exhibits a high degree of dynamism, characterized by intermittent and rapid changes. Hence, the intricate network topology dynamics must be thoroughly analyzed to advance the IoV environment. IoV encompasses a collection of vehicles that exhibit regular variations in both their velocity and trajectory. As a result, the configuration of the moving vehicles' topology likewise undergoes alteration. Therefore, IoV supports a highly dynamic topology, and the routing protocols are designed to consider this [9].

The IoV encounters a multitude of issues that require thorough investigation to enhance communication dependability, robustness, and steadiness, including the following:

- Fault tolerance: Because the IoV design is built on cloud connections, some vehicles could malfunction; nevertheless, these failures should not influence the functioning of the remainder of the network.
- Latency: The term "latency" refers to the amount of time that passes while a packet is transferred through a network. Latency must be reduced as much as possible in some mission-critical applications, such as accident warnings, to ensure that messages are transmitted quickly.
- Network compatibility: To develop applications and protocols for IoV, researchers must consider the numerous access technologies supported by IoV. This ensures that the networks they create are compatible and allows IoV to function with the various access technologies available today.
- Security: The data shared over the IoV network is sensitive and private, which is especially important given that users can access the internet. As a result, the process of protecting these networks is an essential undertaking and a prerequisite for the implementation of IoV.
- Connectivity: The rapid movement of vehicles can result in frequent fluctuations in network architecture, impacting connectivity. As a result, a significant portion of the rate at which nodes arrive and leave can be influenced. The need to contend with such a restriction depletes an essential amount of communication overhead. Thus, nodes must often choose a trustworthy route to ensure that data is delivered to specific destinations to function correctly. The vehicles must be continuously linked to one another.

2.1.3. IoV Network Requirements and Generic Architecture

The Internet of Vehicles (IoV) is a transformative advancement in the realm of vehicular communications, merging traditional vehicular networks with cutting-edge information and communication technologies. This integration not only expands vehicular capabilities but also introduces intricate challenges and requirements in security, privacy, and functionality. Understanding the architecture and requirements of IoV networks is pivotal for developing sophisticated solutions like Federated Learning (FL)-based Intrusion Detection Systems (IDS). In this subsection we provide a summary analysis of the essential security, privacy, and functional requirements of IoV networks, alongside a detailed description of a generic IoV network architecture. Figure 1 shows the essential IoV network requirements.

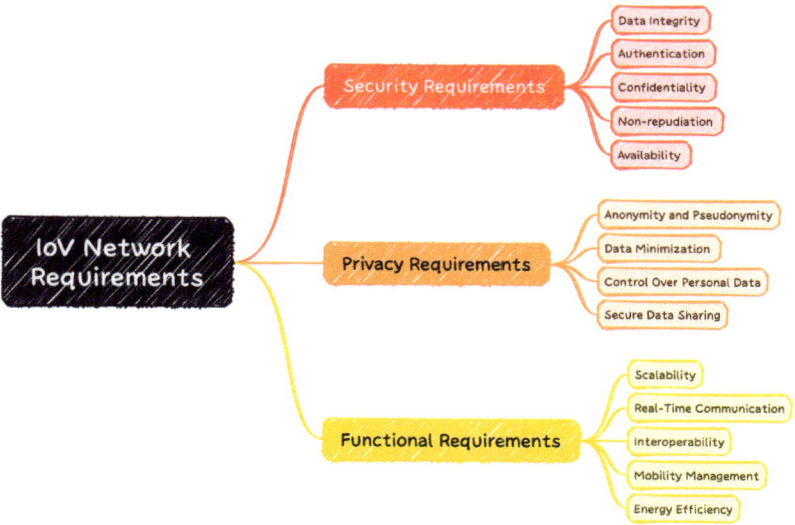

Figure 1. IoV Network Requirements.

Security Requirements in IoV Networks

Security within Internet of Vehicles (IoV) networks is uniquely complex, given the dynamic and mobile nature of vehicular communications [10]. Here, data integrity must go beyond standard concerns—it is critical for safe vehicular operation as vehicles rely on accurate, real-time shared information for essential functions. Any unauthorized data manipulation can lead to immediate safety risks. Authentication in IoV networks is also more challenging than in static networks. It is not just about securing data, but about reliably verifying the rapidly changing participants in the network—vehicles, road infrastructure, and other connected entities—to prevent malicious activities [11]. The confidentiality of data in IoV systems carries additional weight. Protecting user privacy, like location and travel habits, is not only about privacy rights but also about safeguarding against potential threats that could exploit this sensitive data for harmful purposes. Non-repudiation, while important in many digital systems, takes on heightened significance in IoV. Here, it is crucial for legal and liability reasons, ensuring that a vehicle or network component cannot deny its actions, especially in incident analysis and forensic investigations following accidents or security breaches. Lastly, the aspect of continuous availability in IoV networks is paramount. The challenge is to maintain seamless service in a mobile, high-speed environment, where Denial of Service (DoS) attacks or other disruptions not only compromise data but can directly impact physical safety and traffic efficiency.

Privacy Requirements in IoV Networks

Privacy concerns in Internet of Vehicles (IoV) networks are especially pronounced due to the continuous and detailed data generation by vehicles. Protecting user identities and sensitive data here goes beyond typical privacy considerations. Users in an IoV context should have options for anonymity or pseudonymity [3], crucial for preventing the real-time tracking of their vehicles, which could lead to physical tracking in the real world.

The principle of data minimization becomes even more critical in IoV environments. Here, the vast amount of data generated by vehicles, including location, travel routes, and driving patterns, must be carefully managed. Collecting only the necessary data for intended functionalities not only preserves privacy but also reduces the risk of data breaches with potentially severe real-world consequences. User control over data in IoV networks is vital. Given the diverse sources of data collection and dissemination in IoV—from traffic management systems to third-party service providers—users must have clear and manageable controls over who accesses their data and for what purpose. This aspect is particularly challenging in IoV due to the interconnected nature of vehicular networks and the range of stakeholders involved [12]. Moreover, when data sharing is necessary for the functionality of IoV services, its execution requires robust security measures. It is essential to ensure that sensitive information, such as real-time location or travel behavior, is accessible only to authorized entities [4]. This protection is crucial in preventing the potential misuse of data, which could lead to privacy infringements or even safety hazards.

Functional Requirements in IoV Networks

The functionality of Internet of Vehicles (IoV) networks is not just about enabling vehicular communication; it is about doing so in a way that meets the unique demands of a highly mobile and rapidly evolving vehicular environment. Scalability is more than a feature here; it is a necessity. The IoV network must seamlessly integrate an ever-growing number of vehicles and infrastructure elements, each adding to the complexity and volume of data exchange [13]. Real-time communication in IoV networks is about more than just speed; it is about life-critical decisions. Low latency is indispensable for enabling timely reactions in dynamic driving scenarios, where milliseconds can mean the difference between safety and danger. Interoperability in IoV extends beyond standard tech compatibility. It involves harmonizing a myriad of vehicle models, diverse infrastructural technologies, and varied network protocols to ensure uninterrupted communication, a task that is significantly more complex given the varying standards and technologies in the automotive sector. Effective mobility management in IoV is not just about maintaining network connections; it is about doing so in a context where vehicles are constantly moving at high speeds, often transitioning between different network zones, which requires sophisticated handover mechanisms and robust connectivity management [14]. Furthermore, optimizing energy usage, especially in the realm of electric vehicles, goes beyond conventional energy management concerns. In IoV, this is critical for the sustainable operation of not just individual vehicles, but the entire network, impacting everything from data transmission efficiency to the overall environmental footprint of the vehicular ecosystem.

Generic Architecture of IoV Networks

The Internet of Vehicles (IoV) is an advanced network architecture that integrates vehicular technology with information and communication systems to enhance road safety, traffic efficiency, and driving experiences. The core components of IoV architecture include [15]:

- Vehicles: The primary entities in IoV are the vehicles themselves, equipped with sensors, communication modules, and computing capabilities. These vehicles can collect and share a vast array of data, including speed, location, traffic conditions, and environmental data.
- Roadside Units (RSUs): These are fixed infrastructural components placed alongside roads. RSUs facilitate communication between vehicles and the broader network infrastructure, acting as access points for data transmission and reception [5].
- Central Servers: Central servers provide backend support for data processing, storage, and advanced computational tasks. They play a critical role in managing the overall network, including traffic control, data aggregation, and system updates.
- Communication Network: This includes both Vehicle-to-Vehicle (V2V) and Vehicle-to-Infrastructure (V2I) communications, enabled through technologies like Dedicated Short Range Communications (DSRC) and cellular networks. The network ensures seamless and continuous connectivity within the IoV.

- Traffic Management Center (TMC): The TMC acts as the control hub for traffic management, receiving data from various sources and making decisions to optimize traffic flow, reduce congestion, and enhance road safety [5].
- Cloud and Edge Computing Resources: Cloud computing provides vast storage and processing capabilities, essential for handling the large volumes of data generated in IoV. Edge computing, on the other hand, offers localized processing at the network edge, enabling real-time data processing and decision-making.

This architecture fosters an interconnected environment essential for various applications, including IDS. The architecture's distributed nature, real-time communication capabilities, and integration of advanced computing technologies are vital for implementing effective FL-based IDS.

2.1.4. Security in Internet of Vehicles

IoV technologies are developing rapidly, and a number of industries investing in these technologies are in a race to launch state-of-the-art self-driving vehicles. These rapid advancements in IoV result in security issues that threaten not only the industry but consumers as well [8]. The challenge lies in preventing security breaches and privacy violations in IoV, making it less susceptible to cyberattacks [3].

Cyberattacks in Internet of Vehicles Networks

Vehicular sensor networks comprise a variety of vehicle sensors used to monitor and measure various physical parameters associated with the vehicle and the environment in which it is located. These sensors contribute to a more comfortable driving experience and smoother driving operations. Table 1 lists some of the most frequently employed smart vehicle sensors. Each of these sensors is built using cutting-edge electronic components and communication systems. Due to their limited available resources, implementing sophisticated and reliable security algorithms on these sensors directly is impractical. Consequently, these sensors are susceptible to various cyberattacks [16].

IoVs are susceptible to several types of attacks and threats, including the following:

- The flow of bogus information: Attackers use fake information to make users believe in a false environment.
- Message injection attack: Attackers send seemingly legitimate messages to gain access to one or more entities, which they can also utilize to send out malicious messages [16].
- Replay attack: Attackers iterate messages to gain unlawful access to the network's services and resources [17].
- Cookie theft attack: Resembling the previous attack, attackers use a copy of the cookies they stole to reach the network's resources.
- Sybil attack: Attackers create fabricated vehicles around the vehicle they are targeting and generate a signal jam, compelling the target to use an alternate path. To do this, they use a countless number of fake IDs for a single node to create the appearance of multiple nodes [18].
- Man-in-middle attack: Attackers insert themselves between two communicating entities. In this type of attack, which can be active or passive, the attackers can receive messages from one entity and send them to the other [16].
- Denial-of-service and distributed denial-of-service attacks: Attackers attempt to disrupt the network's efficiency by flooding the target channel with messages that exceed its handling capacity. This is carried out to use the network's limited resources illegally [10].
- Dissimulation of GPS attack: Attackers intercept and modulate GPS signals before the intended receiver receives them. This type of attack can endanger the lives of the people in the target vehicle as they are given the wrong directions.
- Impersonation attack: As the name implies, attackers impersonate the identity of a legitimate user on the network to spoof unsuspecting vehicles on the network with messages that are not only fictitious but dangerous.

- Masquerading attack: Again, as the name implies, attackers masquerade as authorized users. Unlike the previous attack, attackers copy the legitimate ID of one of the network's nodes and can create two different senders using the same identity.
- Wormhole attack: Attacker nodes fake incorrect information about the distance from the target node, aiming to obtain every message sent from the receiver to flow through it. Deadlocks are typically created by these types of attacks [17].
- Eavesdropping attack: Attackers passively listen to the communication on the network. They become a part of the network, aiming to secretly obtain confidential, sensitive data and use it unlawfully.

Table 1. Common sensors in vehicle sensor networks.

Sensor	Use of Sensors in Vehicles
Camera	Identifies traffic signs, enhances night vision, adapts to the light system, determines the likelihood of being involved in a collision, detects lanes, records emergencies, and provides parking aid.
GPS	Tracks location, provides path direction, minimizes fuel costs, lowers operational costs, helps with theft recovery and in an emergency.
Ultrasonic sensors	Include parking assist systems, which monitor the immediate surroundings of the vehicle and measure distance to obstacles.
LiDAR	Ensures safe navigation by detecting objects and estimating distances.
Radar	Detects obstacles or pedestrians, deploys automatic emergency braking, and enables blind-spot monitoring, lane-keeping assistance, and parking assistance in autonomous mode.
Inertial sensors	Provide data concerning the rate of acceleration and the current direction of the vehicle, includes automotive safety systems like airbag and anti-skidding protection.
Tire pressure monitoring system	Monitors tire air pressure and alerts the driver when it falls dangerously low.

2.2. An Overview of Federated Learning

As the risk of a data breach grows increasingly significant, many governments are enacting legislation to protect their citizens' data. Because of a breach that occurred in 2016 involving the personal information of 600,000 drivers, Uber was forced to pay USD 148 million to resolve the investigation [19]. In response to these situations, Google introduced the notion of FL to facilitate on-device learning while ensuring the preservation of data privacy. FL enables collaborative learning among devices without necessitating data sharing with a centralized server. In other words, machine learning and deep learning may be trained across various devices and servers using decentralized data thanks to the capabilities of the technology [20]. This process can be repeated multiple times. This section provides an overview of FL, introducing the concept and highlighting its potential applications and benefits in several domains.

2.2.1. Definition of Federated Learning

FL facilitates the collaborative training of a machine learning model by many parties without the need for the direct exchange of their respective local data. The subject matter encompasses a range of methodologies derived from various fields of research, including distributed systems, machine learning, and privacy. Building on the definitions of FL provided by previous studies [19,21,22] we propose the following definition for FL. In an FL framework, numerous entities work together to train machine learning models without the need to share their raw data. The result of the process is a machine learning model for each entity involved (which may be identical or distinct). A crucial restriction of a practical FLS is that the performance of the model acquired through FL should surpass that of a model obtained through local training when evaluated using a designated measure, such as test accuracy, using the same model architecture. FLSs include the following aspects:

- Data privacy: An FLS tackles the issue of data privacy by enabling individual entities to maintain their data locally, hence avoiding the need to share it with a centralized server. This is especially crucial when handling private or sensitive data [23].
- Collaborative training: Models are trained collaboratively within the FLS. Based on its local data, each party or device independently computes updates to the model and shares them with other participants or a central server.
- Aggregated model: By combining the model updates from each participant, the central server creates an enhanced global model that gains from everyone's combined expertise. The participants then receive a copy of this combined model.
- Iterative process: The iterative nature of the FLS entails the incorporation of several training rounds. During each iteration, individuals involved in the process update their respective local models and then contribute to the overall global model. The aforementioned iterative procedure persists until the global model reaches a satisfactory performance level.
- Customized models: The FLS enables the customization of models to cater to each participant's specific needs and requirements. Participants may have models customized to their individual needs, depending on the distribution of data and local requirements.

2.2.2. Components of a Federated Learning Framework

In today's data-driven world, the conventional centralized approach to ML—in which data from multiple sources is pooled on a single server for training—is encountering obstacles, particularly regarding privacy and efficiency. This technique collects data from various sources and then stores it on a server. FL has emerged as a potential solution, enabling decentralized training while ensuring that data is kept on its original device, thereby reducing the overhead associated with data transfer [24]. This section discusses the fundamental elements that comprise an FL framework.

- Client devices: These are edge devices, including smartphones, tablets, IoT devices, and even personal computers; they can store and process data locally and oversee local model training.
- Central server: This entity serves as the primary aggregation point in the FL structure. The central server is responsible for communicating with client devices, collecting model updates, and disseminating the global model back to the clients [21].
- Local models: Each client device is equipped with its own version of the ML model, which is trained using the local data available on that device.
- Global model: This model aggregates all the local models stored on the client devices and is hosted on the central server.
- Communication protocol: The primary objective of the communication protocol is to establish reliable and effective communication between the client devices and the central server while ensuring the security of the data sent. It is responsible for overseeing the transmission of updates to the model and the distribution of the global model.
- Aggregation algorithm: The algorithm is implemented on the central server, integrating the model updates received from all client devices to enhance the global model.
- Privacy mechanisms: During model aggregation and communication, additional layers of data security can be added by integrating various techniques, such as differential privacy and Secure Multiparty Computation (SMPC).

By gaining a comprehensive understanding of the fundamental components of FL, one can develop a deeper appreciation for the complexities and possibilities that FL offers in addressing contemporary challenges within the field of data science. The significance of such decentralized techniques is expected to continue expanding as the digital ecosystem evolves, making FL a cornerstone in the future of ML.

2.2.3. Typical Federated Training Process

The FL process begins with each device developing a localized model using its own dataset. After completing local training, the device transmits model changes—specifically weights and gradients—to a central server, rather than sending raw data [16]. This approach ensures that confidential information remains in its original location, effectively mitigating various privacy risks commonly associated with traditional data centralization [25]. The model updates from all participating devices are consolidated on the central server to create an enhanced global model that incorporates insights derived from all the decentralized data sources. This aggregated model is then distributed to all devices, allowing them to leverage the collective intelligence of the entire network. The iterative process involves local training, model update transmission, aggregation, and global model dissemination, with each iteration progressively improving the accuracy and resilience of the global model [21]. By employing this innovative methodology, FL addresses the challenges related to data privacy and ML efficiency, effectively utilizing a wide range of authentic data sources from the real world while safeguarding the security of individual data [26].

2.2.4. Federated Learning Systems Taxonomy

FLSs facilitate cooperative model training while upholding the principles of data privacy and security. This approach is especially suitable for situations where data is distributed across multiple sources, and the parties involved are hesitant to share their data in a centralized manner. Many new FLSs have emerged since the creation of FL in 2016. There are a general taxonomy describing the difference of FLS is was presented in [19] and also replicated in [27]. Even though their taxonomy was very helpful for many researchers, it had several limitations that need to be addressed. Firstly, the taxonomy primarily focuses on the most prevalent and widely adopted Federated Learning scenarios, and as such, does not encompass all possible scenarios. Secondly, there might be gaps in terms of the different types of data distributions, models, and algorithms presented, indicating that the taxonomy might not be exhaustive. Thirdly, the taxonomy does not delve deeply into the specifics of each category, which could lead to overlooking certain nuances. Lastly, it is worth noting that the taxonomy is a reflection of the state of Federated Learning in 2021 and may require updates.

As the domain progresses, we present a general taxonomy describing the differences between these FLSs in this section. We use the taxonomy to clarify the distinctions between different FLSs, which can be categorized according to their essential features and characteristics. This multidimensional classification considers the most significant components of FLSs, such as data sources, privacy, model aggregation techniques, learning models, scalability, and network topology. Given the prevalent system abstractions and foundational components employed in various FLSs, we can classify these systems based on six key aspects: data distribution, model management, privacy method, communication architecture, FL algorithms, optimization techniques, use cases, and applications. Figure 2 shows this taxonomy of FLSs.

Data Distribution

When discussing the taxonomy of FLSs, the term "data distribution" refers to the process by which various participants or nodes in an FL environment are given different portions of the data. It affects the effectiveness and level of privacy maintained during the learning process, making it an essential component of FL.

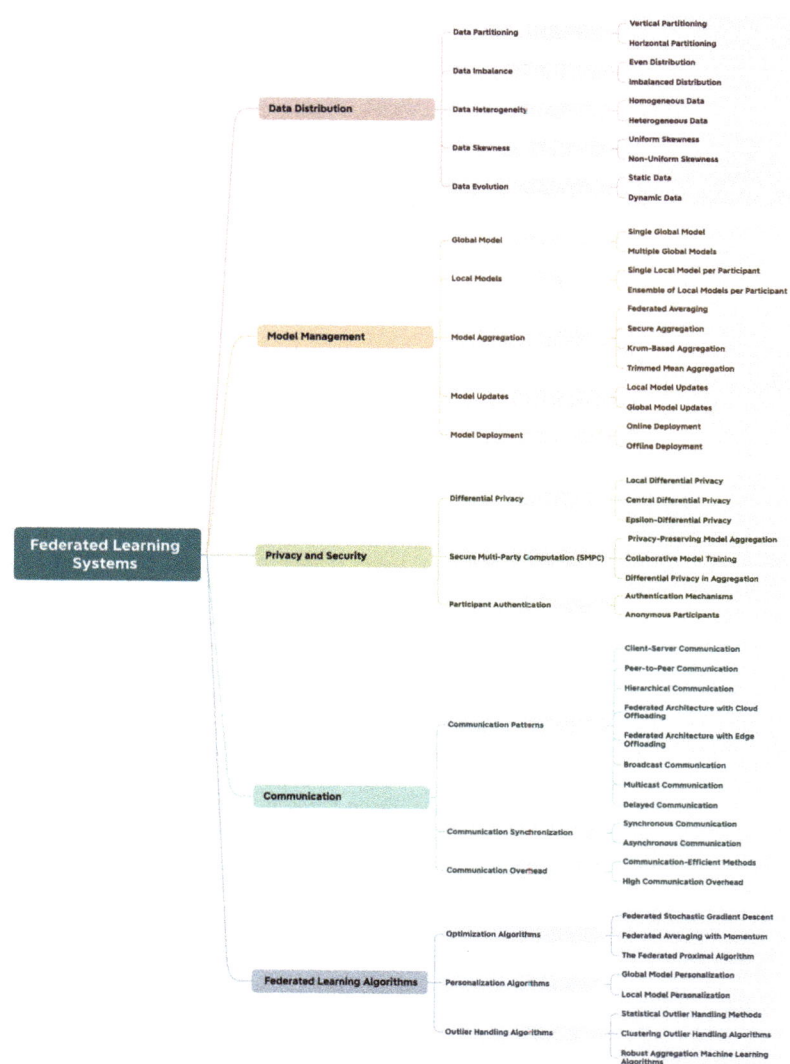

Figure 2. Taxonomy of Federated Learning systems (FLSs).

The following list reviews important factors regarding the distribution of data within this taxonomy:

- Data partitioning: The concept of data partitioning describes how data is allocated or divided among entities. Generally, FLSs can be divided into two categories, vertical and horizontal FLSs, depending on how the data are spread over the sample and feature spaces. The vertical partitioning strategy involves allocating distinct aspects or attributes of the dataset to various participants. For instance, a given participant may possess data pertaining to age and gender, whereas another participant may possess data on income and location. By contrast, in horizontal partitioning, participants have access to distinct sections of the data instances. A slice of the dataset with the same attributes belongs to each participant. For example, one member might have customer

data for a particular location, whereas another participant might have customer data for a different location.
- Data imbalance: The notion of data imbalance holds significant importance within the taxonomy of FLSs as it relates to the uneven allocation of data among the participants or nodes within the system. An imbalanced data distribution can have a substantial impact on the performance, fairness, and effectiveness of FL models [28]. Generally, FLSs can be categorized into systems with an even distribution and those with an imbalanced distribution. In even distribution, data can be distributed among participants to ensure an equitable allocation, thereby resulting in each participant possessing a proportionate share of the data. This methodology is commonly employed in situations with a reasonably equal distribution of data among participants and without substantial disparities in the quantity or significance of the data. In contrast, in imbalanced distribution, participants' data are not dispersed equally, resulting in some participants having noticeably more data than others. Managing data imbalance is a crucial factor to consider, as it might impact the FL process's performance and fairness.
- Data heterogeneity: A vital component of the FLS taxonomy is data heterogeneity, which describes the variation in the kinds, forms, and quality of data among nodes or participants in an FLS [29]. The FL context offers different opportunities and problems when dealing with heterogeneous data. Homogeneous data refers to particular instances of FL where the data possessed by participants exhibits a considerable degree of similarity concerning data type, format, and quality. The utilization of homogeneous data in the FL process facilitates the training of models by enabling a more streamlined approach since the consistency of the data allows for easier training. Homogeneous situations can facilitate model aggregation, sharing updates, and making assumptions about data features. On the other hand, heterogeneous data relates to scenarios when the data obtained from diverse participants exhibit notable variations in terms of data kinds, formats, and quality. Heterogeneity can manifest in myriad ways, such as disparities in feature representations, variations in data preparation techniques, and discrepancies in data-gathering methodologies. Data heterogeneity arises for a variety of reasons, such as the utilization of disparate technologies, the involvement of many companies, and the integration of data from sources that possess separate data schemas. The issue of data heterogeneity is highly significant in the FL context, as it has notable implications for the capacity to develop a valuable global model from varied data sources while ensuring data privacy and model performance. The efficient management of data heterogeneity and adaptation to accommodate the different attributes of individual participants' data are crucial considerations in developing effective FLSs.
- Data skewness: The concept of data skewness holds significant relevance within the FLS taxonomy, as it specifically refers to the uneven distribution of data across the participants or nodes in an FLS. Skewness pertains to the extent of asymmetry or lopsidedness in the distribution of data [30]. The comprehension of data skewness is essential due to its potential impact on the performance, fairness, and convergence of models in the FL context. In certain instances of FL, the distribution of data among participants may exhibit a uniform skew. This implies that each participant's data are subject to a comparable degree of skewness. Uniform skewness is observed when participants show identical patterns of data distribution despite potential variations in the quantity of data. By contrast, non-uniform skewness is observed when the skewness of the data distribution across different participants varies. Certain participants may have heavily skewed data distributions, while others may have more evenly balanced ones. Dealing with non-uniform skewness can pose difficulties as it necessitates accepting diverse levels of skewness in the data distribution. The presence of data skewness in FL gives rise to several challenges, including training imbalance, model bias, concerns over privacy, and increased communication overhead. Weighted

aggregation approaches can be utilized in FLSs to address the issue of data skewness and reduce its impact. These strategies involve allocating varying weights to participants based on the degree of skewness in their data distribution. Participants who possess more highly skewed data may be assigned lower weights in order to prevent their data from exerting an excessive impact on the overall model.

- Data evolution: The evolution of data in FLS taxonomy pertains to the temporal modifications that transpire within the datasets maintained by participants. These modifications can have noteworthy consequences in terms of the efficiency and precision of FL models. In certain FL situations, the data remain static throughout the FL process, resulting in a simplified training procedure. Static data are typically seen in situations where the underlying data exhibits few changes, as in the case of historical datasets or reference databases. Notably, dynamic data have the potential to change over time. Consequently, participants may find it necessary to update their respective local datasets regularly.

Model Management

Another critical component of the FLS taxonomy is model management, which refers to the approaches and techniques used to manage the machine learning models within an FL framework. It includes several aspects of model deployment, customization, aggregation, initialization, and updates in FL environments. The following elements are essential in understanding model management within the FLS taxonomy:

- Global model: In an FL environment, the global model represents the machine learning model trained and updated collectively by all participating devices or nodes. Without consolidating the data, the global model captures the common knowledge derived from the decentralized data sources. Most FL situations have a single global model that all participants work together to enhance. Meanwhile, some global models may be employed in other specialized applications, each tailored to a particular task, set of features, or user group. The central focus of FL is the global model, encapsulating collective intelligence from various data sources while safeguarding data privacy and promoting decentralization. The successful management of the global model is crucial, involving appropriate initialization, secure updates, and precise evaluation.
- Local model: The term "local model" refers to individual machine learning models maintained and updated by each participating device or node in the network. These local models are trained using local data accessible on each individual device, and the raw data is not shared with a centralized server throughout this process. Each participant may have their own unique local model, which they are responsible for maintaining. During the training, participants do not discuss their models, nor do they exchange raw data or model parameters with one another. As an alternative, each participant may maintain their own local ensemble of models, allowing for a variety of perspectives and levels of competence. The ensemble may include models that use various algorithmic approaches, architectural layouts, or hyperparameter settings. More reliable and accurate results can sometimes be achieved by combining the predictions of different models. Local models are essential to the FL process because they enable individuals to contribute to the collective intelligence without compromising the privacy of their personal information. Effective local model management is crucial for the success of FLSs across various domains and applications. This management must include secure training, customization, and evaluation.
- Model aggregation: A key component of model management in the FLS taxonomy is model aggregation, which describes the procedure for combining local model updates from many collaborators to produce a current global model. This procedure is essential to FL because it guarantees the integration of all participants' aggregate knowledge without centralizing their raw data [31]. FLSs use various standard methods for aggregating models. Federated averaging is the most widely used model aggregation technique for FL. After using their own data to train their local model, all participants

transmit the updated model—gradients—to a central server. A new global model is produced by averaging these modifications. Since no raw data is transferred, privacy is guaranteed [32]. This approach's efficiency and simplicity enable quick adjustments to the global model. Another popular FL model aggregation method is secure aggregation. This technique combines model updates while protecting the privacy of individual modifications. It uses cryptographic techniques, such as SMPC, to aggregate data without disclosing the unprocessed changes. It is appropriate for sensitive applications since it offers a high degree of privacy and secrecy. Additionally, it safeguards the integrity of the aggregation process from malevolent attempts. Krum-based aggregation, the third aggregation technique, is designed to stave off Byzantine attacks. This aggregation approach entails sorting the updates from participants according to their impact. The update with the smallest cumulative distance to the k-nearest updates is selected for aggregation [33]. Because it is robust against updates that differ significantly from one another, it can be used in adversarial environments. Trimmed mean aggregation, a popular variation of federated averaging, removes a predetermined proportion of extreme updates before averaging. After sorting the participant updates, the updates with the largest variances from the mean are eliminated. By using this method, the aggregation process becomes more resilient to updates that contain outliers. Participants in the weighted aggregation technique are given varying weights according to the caliber or applicability of their updates. During aggregation, higher weights are assigned to participants who provide more accurate or diverse updates, increasing their contributions' effect on the global model. This allows for the prioritization of more trustworthy or pertinent updates, enhancing the global model's overall quality. In FL, model aggregation is a crucial stage since it establishes the quality and efficacy of the final global model. The best aggregation technique is determined by specific application needs, such as privacy concerns, resilience against adversarial attacks, communication limitations, and required model quality. Effective model aggregation approaches enable FLSs to create precise, reliable, and privacy-preserving global models.

- Model updates: Model updates pertain to modifications made to machine learning models during the FL process. Implementing these updates is paramount in improving the models' overall performance, accuracy, and generalization capabilities. On the one hand, local model updates can be employed in scenarios where players train their own local models using their respective datasets, resulting in model updates derived from their individual training procedures. Local updates are computed via methodologies such as stochastic gradient descent (SGD) or its variations, such as federated averaging. The updates are contingent upon the data on individual participants' devices, enabling models to catch localized patterns. On the other hand, in global model updates, changes are computed by aggregating information from the local models of all participants. Global updates are produced by combining the local model updates contributed by several participants. These updates indicate the cumulative understanding of the FL network as a whole. Model updates play a vital role in the FL context, as they enable the integration of the collective intelligence derived from various data sources into one cohesive and improved model. The success of FLSs in many domains and applications heavily relies on the efficient administration of model updates, encompassing privacy protection, security, and adaptability.

- Model deployment: Model deployment in FLSs includes the steps required to make the trained machine learning model accessible and functional for generating predictions or providing services to end-users or applications. However, model deployment in FL exhibits notable differences from conventional machine learning model deployment, mostly stemming from the decentralized and privacy-preserving characteristics inherent in the FL methodology. The strategic process of deploying models in FLSs involves striking a compromise between real-time adaptation and safeguarding user privacy and data security. FL involves the collaborative training of models on dispersed devices while preserving the confidentiality of sensitive data within local servers [26]. Following the completion of training, models can be deployed in both online and offline environments. The process of online deployment in FLSs entails the seamless and immediate incorporation of model changes originating from distributed devices. This facilitates the prompt reaction to evolving data patterns and user behaviors in real time. This methodology enables rapid model aggregation, maintaining the pertinence and precision of forecasts in dynamic settings. By employing strategies such as the integration of real-time noise injection to ensure privacy and the implementation of continuous monitoring, the online deployment of the model ensures its ability to promptly adapt to developing trends. Feedback loops facilitate the collection of user interactions in real time, enabling prompt modifications and refinements. Utilizing adaptive learning rates and personalization settings guarantees customized experiences for individual users. Online deployment generally ensures that FL models offer timely, accurate, customized predictions while protecting user privacy. This makes it crucial for applications that require swift and exact answers to real-time data streams. Conversely, offline deployment in FLSs encompasses using pretrained models on novel data without necessitating real-time adaptation. After the FL model completes the training and aggregation process by incorporating updates from devices involved in the process, it can be implemented offline for many applications. Offline deployment is especially advantageous in situations when immediate adjustment is not critical and regular updates are satisfactory. In this particular situation, the model that has undergone training is implemented on servers or edge devices, enabling it to provide predictions or services by leveraging its accumulated knowledge. This deployment strategy demonstrates efficacy when employed in applications characterized by consistent data patterns and when privacy-preserving methodologies have been included during the training phase. Although offline deployment may not possess the immediate responsiveness of online deployment, it offers the advantage of ensuring consistency and accuracy in predictions. This characteristic renders offline deployment well-suited for numerous FL applications. Table 2 provides a comparison of online and offline model deployment in FLSs.

Table 2. Comparison between online and offline model deployment in Federated Learning systems.

Adaptability	Online deployment is well-suited for dynamic environments subject to rapid change, as it enables instant adaptation to new data. In contrast, offline deployment ensures consistency but may not adapt as rapidly to new circumstances.
Privacy	Both deployment strategies prioritize privacy during the training period. However, online deployment guarantees real-time privacy maintenance while updating the model, offering enhanced privacy for continuous interactions.
Resource usage	Online deployment requires consistent and instantaneous information exchange, as well as the availability of computational resources to implement model revisions promptly. In contrast, offline deployment reduces the need for continuous communication, enhancing resource efficiency.
Use cases	Online deployment is highly advantageous in scenarios where real-time adjustments and customized responses are crucial. Offline deployment is a suitable option for applications requiring periodic model updates and consistent forecasts, particularly in situations where continuous communication may not be practical or essential.

The selection of online or offline deployment in FLSs is contingent upon the particular use case, data patterns, privacy stipulations, and the necessity for real-time adaption. Each option presents distinct advantages, enabling organizations and developers to customize their strategy according to the application's specific requirements.

Privacy and Security

Privacy and security are of utmost importance in the taxonomy of FLSs. The preservation of data privacy, secrecy, and security is critical due to the involvement of various sources. The following key elements pertain to privacy and security within FLSs:

- Differential privacy: Differential privacy is a core principle within the field of privacy-preserving data analysis, such as in FL. Differential privacy techniques ensure that the presence or absence of a particular data point does not materially affect the output by adding noise to the computations made on the data [34]. Even when combined with or applied to updates to machine learning models, it safeguards the privacy of individual data pieces. Differential privacy is used in FLSs to protect participant data privacy while enabling group participation in machine learning model training [35]. The following are the fundamental types of differential privacy inside FLSs:
    - Local differential privacy (LDP): When using LDP, noise is applied locally to individual data points on the users' devices before transferring the perturbed data to the central server. This ensures that raw data are never transmitted outside users' devices, offering a higher level of privacy but making it more difficult to aggregate the data [35].
    - Central differential privacy (CDP): In the CDP technique, noise is added to the aggregated statistics or model parameters in a centralized location. This helps to ensure that no participant's data are made public. It is appropriate for situations in which a reliable central server compiles the updates contributed by participants without disclosing their private data [35].
    - Epsilon-differential privacy (ϵ-differential privacy): The level of privacy can be quantified using a parameter known as epsilon. A lower value for epsilon indicates a greater degree of discretion and confidentiality. A balance must be struck between personal privacy and practicality. Lower values result in increased privacy but could also lead to a less accurate global model.

In FLSs, differential privacy is crucial to guaranteeing that users can provide data for model training without risking their privacy. Ensuring the security of sensitive information while maintaining accuracy in models is a critical component of privacy-preserving machine learning in collaborative settings. Table 3 provides a comparison summary between these three standard differential privacy techniques.

- Secure multiparty computation: SMPC is a cryptographic methodology that facilitates collaborative computation of a function by numerous entities while ensuring the privacy of their inputs. Within the realm of FLSs, SMPC assumes a pivotal role in upholding privacy and security. The integration of SMPC inside the FLS taxonomy can be elucidated as follows:
    - Privacy-preserving model aggregation: SMPC guarantees participants' ability to safely submit their model updates or gradients to collectively construct a global model while ensuring that no individual party can access the specific contributions made by others. The integration of collective intelligence from multiple participants while maintaining individual privacy is of utmost importance in the FL context.
    - Collaborative model training: The SMPC technique facilitates the cooperative training of machine learning models, allowing participants to cooperatively compute model parameters without sharing their raw data. Collaborative efforts among participants can be employed to enhance the model's accuracy while maintaining the privacy and confidentiality of their respective datasets.
    - Differential privacy in aggregation: The combination of SMPC and differential privacy approaches allows for the introduction of noise into aggregated results, hence offering a robust privacy assurance. The utilization of the aggregated model guarantees that the determination of the contribution made by any particular

participant remains computationally infeasible, thus upholding the preservation of individual privacy [35].

Table 3. Comparison summary between three common differential privacy techniques.

	Local Differential Privacy	Central Differential Privacy	Epsilon-Differential Privacy
Privacy level	Ensures robust individual privacy by ensuring raw data remains exclusively on the participants' devices.	Provides privacy at an aggregate level, ensuring that individual data is not directly exposed in any circumstance.	Adjusting epsilon allows for custom privacy levels, offering flexibility.
Aggregation complexity	Aggregating locally perturbed data while maintaining privacy is complex.	Since noise addition happens centrally, aggregation is simpler.	The aggregation complexity is determined by the particular implementation and the noise-adding mechanism.
Centralization	Completely decentralized, with no centralized entity participating in the processing of data.	The addition of noise necessitates the use of a reliable centralized server, resulting in centralization.	The centralization level depends on the noise-adding mechanism.
Flexibility	High privacy but increased noise levels may reduce usability.	A balanced approach with group-level privacy.	Flexible, enabling privacy levels to be changed in accordance with application needs.
Challenges	Aggregation complexity. Increased noise.	Central trust. Potential central attack.	Utility trade-off.

The utilization of SMPC-based aggregation plays a crucial role in the FL context, as it enables participants to collectively improve the accuracy of a global model while simultaneously ensuring the protection of their data's privacy. FLSs can utilize safe multiparty computation techniques to use the combined information from various remote sources effectively. This approach ensures that security, privacy, and integrity are maintained during the collaborative learning process.

- Participant authentication: Participant authentication is an essential component within the taxonomy of FLSs, as it verifies the identity and legitimacy of entities involved in the collaborative learning process. Participant authentication can be conducted using authentication mechanisms, or participants can remain anonymous through anonymous participant techniques. Authentication systems are an essential feature of FLSs. They ensure that all participants and entities interacting with the system have their identities checked and are granted the appropriate permissions. Within the FLS taxonomy, the following authentication mechanisms are used:
    - User credentials authentication: In this mechanism, participants must provide their usernames and passwords to verify their identities. This fundamental mechanism is used extensively despite the fact that, if not adequately secured, it is susceptible to password-based attacks.
    - Biometric authentication: The authenticity of the participants is determined by using distinctive biological characteristics, such as fingerprints or facial recognition. Because copying biometric data is so complex, this technique provides a very high level of security.
    - Token-based authentication: Participants authenticate subsequent requests with tokens, which are typically generated once an initial login has been completed successfully. It improves security by minimizing the amount of sensitive credentials that must be transmitted regularly.
    - Certificate-based authentication: Participants show digital certificates signed by a reliable certificate authority to authenticate themselves. This improves security by guaranteeing that a reliable third party confirms participants' identities.

- Multi-factor authentication: In order to gain access, participants are required to furnish a variety of authentication methods, including a password and a verification number transmitted to their mobile device. The implementation of various proofs of identification enhances the level of security.
- oAuth and OpenID connect: The use of secure authentication and authorization protocols is prevalent in web-based FLSs. The system offers standardized and secure authentication techniques, effectively integrating them with a wide range of applications and services.
- Device-based authentication: The authentication of participants' devices is contingent upon the utilization of distinct device identifiers or certificates linked to the hardware. Implementing device authorization in the FLS bolsters security measures by only allowing access to authorized devices.
- Role-based access control: Participants are allocated distinct roles and permissions in accordance with their respective tasks inside the FLS. Implementing access controls guarantees that participants possess suitable levels of access, hence mitigating the risk of unauthorized activities and access to data.
- Continuous authentication: The activities and behaviors of participants are continuously watched to identify any anomalies, ensuring that authenticated users maintain their authentication status. Including this feature enhances security measures by rapidly detecting and addressing any questionable behavior.
- Symmetric encryption: In FLS, symmetric encryption plays a crucial role in maintaining data confidentiality and integrity. This method, utilizing the same key for both encryption and decryption, is particularly efficient for the large volumes of data typical in FLS. It ensures that sensitive information remains secure during transmission, as only model updates or insights are shared across the network, not the raw training data. This encryption method not only protects the data from potential eavesdroppers but also maintains their integrity, making any unauthorized alterations easily detectable. While symmetric encryption is central to preserving data privacy and consistency in FLS, it is typically complemented by other security measures, such as secure key management protocols, to provide a comprehensive security framework. The efficiency and effectiveness of symmetric encryption in these systems highlight its indispensability in the secure and efficient operation of FLS.

The specific requirements of a particular FLS determine the most suitable authentication approach, taking into account aspects such as security, usability, scalability, and management complexity. These techniques can frequently be combined to achieve an efficient balance between security and usability. Table 4 provides a comparison of the main authentication mechanisms within FLSs.

- Anonymous participants: When discussing FLSs, the term anonymous participants refers to the practice of protecting the participants' right to privacy and maintaining the confidentiality of their data and identities. Ensuring that users can participate in FLSs while maintaining anonymity is essential for protecting their data privacy. This objective is accomplished by using a variety of strategies and approaches. In FLSs, the following methods are frequently used by participants who wish to remain anonymous:
    - Participant identity concealment: The concealment of participants' identities is a crucial measure in the FL process, as it guarantees the protection of their personal information from being disclosed. The preservation of user privacy fosters engagement from individuals and businesses who are apprehensive about the potential risks associated with data disclosure.
    - Data anonymization: In the context of FL, personal data undergo anonymization procedures prior to engagement, guaranteeing that even in the event of unauthorized access, the data cannot be directly associated with identifiable individuals.

Methods such as differential privacy, k-anonymity, and data perturbation can be employed to achieve data anonymization
- Pseudonymization: During the FL process, participants are not required to reveal their true identities and instead employ pseudonyms or temporary IDs. The utilization of this technology affords a level of anonymity, making it more challenging to trace particular data contributions to specific individuals.
- Blockchain-based identity management: The utilization of blockchain technology facilitates the management of participants' identities and transactions in a decentralized and tamper-proof manner. The elimination of a central authority and the provision of transparent and safe identity management contribute to the enhancement of security and privacy.

The emphasis on preserving participant anonymity is pivotal for building trust, encouraging engagement, and safeguarding privacy within FLSs. FLSs align with regulatory frameworks like the General Data Protection Regulation, which prioritize principles such as user permission and the anonymization of personal data. By taking these factors into account, FL platforms have the potential to establish a secure, privacy-preserving environment for collaborative machine learning initiatives.

Table 4. Comparison of the main authentication mechanisms within Federated Learning systems.

Authentication Mechanisms	Strengths	Weaknesses
User credentials authentication	Simple, widely understood and used.	Vulnerable to password-based attacks if weak passwords are used.
Biometric authentication	Highly secure, unique to individuals, eliminates the need for passwords.	Hardware requirements (e.g., fingerprint scanners), potential false positives/negatives.
Token-based authentication	Reduces reliance on passwords, enhances security for multiple requests.	Requires secure token storage and transmission mechanisms.
Certificate-based authentication	Strong security, verified by certificate authorities.	Complex certificate management, reliance on a trusted certificate authority.
Multi-factor authentication	Adds an extra layer of security, even if one factor is compromised.	User inconvenience, requires additional verification steps.
OAuth and OpenID Connect	Widely adopted, standardized, secure token-based authentication.	Requires integration and understanding of protocols.
Device-based suthentication	Ensures device authenticity, useful for Internet of Things devices.	Complex device management, potential security vulnerabilities.
Role-based access control	Granular control over user permissions, scalable for large systems.	Initial setup complexity, requires ongoing management.
Continuous authentication	Provides real-time security monitoring, identifies and responds to anomalies.	Requires sophisticated monitoring tools, potential false positive/negative issues.

Communication

Another vital element of FLSs is communication, which involves the exchange of data between the central server and participants, including devices, clients, or edge nodes. Effective and safe communication is necessary for FLSs to function well. The following provides an analysis of the various components related to communication within the taxonomy of FLSs.

- Communication patterns: Communication patterns in FLSs concern how participants, including diverse devices or entities, interact with one another and the central server during the collaborative learning procedure. These patterns play a crucial role in facilitating the effective and secure transmission of data and updates to models. In FLSs, the following communication patterns are considered to be the most common:

- Client–server communication: In this communication pattern, the participants' devices establish direct contact with a central server, through which they transmit their changes and receive aggregated model parameters. It is frequently observed in situations where participants possess restricted computational capabilities and depend on a central server to aggregate models.
- Peer-to-peer communication: In this setting, users directly communicate with one another, facilitating the exchange of model updates or aggregated information without needing a central server to mediate the process. Utilizing decentralized environments is advantageous as it allows players to establish direct connections, minimizing latency and decreasing reliance on a central server.
- Hierarchical communication: In this pattern, participants are systematically grouped into hierarchical structures, wherein updates are initially consolidated at lower levels before being transmitted to higher levels for additional consolidation. This approach exhibits scalability, particularly in the context of massive federated networks, enabling effective aggregation at several hierarchical levels [36].
- Federated architecture with cloud offloading: Participants carry out the preliminary computations at their respective locations and then send the more intensive computations (such as aggregation) to a central server hosted in the cloud. It allows devices with limited resources to take part by offloading complicated activities and distributing computation evenly between on-premise and remote resources.
- Federated architecture with edge offloading: The process resembles cloud offloading, but its computations are offloaded to edge devices situated within the local network. This approach diminishes latency and decreases dependence on a remote cloud server. This technology is well-suited to use cases requiring real-time responses and minimal delay, frequently seen in IoT and edge computing environments.
- Broadcast communication: The central server disseminates model updates to all participants concurrently, maintaining consistency across all devices. The broadcasting of updates, particularly when all participants require identical model parameters, conserves bandwidth and reduces time consumption.
- Multicast communication: Model updates are distributed to distinct groups of participants, enabling selective broadcasting based on the degree to which two sets of data are comparable. When multiple groups of people work on similar activities, this pattern is helpful because it allows for the more efficient use of network resources.
- Delayed communication: Participants gather updates on their local machines and deliver them in batches at regular intervals, thus decreasing the time spent communicating with the centralized server. This reduces the overhead of transmission and the delay, particularly in situations when real-time updates are not essential.

The selection of a communication pattern substantially influences the effectiveness, scalability, and responsiveness of FLSs, rendering it a critical element in their design and execution. Every communication pattern possesses distinct advantages and trade-offs, making them appropriate for specific use scenarios. The selection of a particular pattern is contingent upon various aspects, including but not limited to the configuration of the network, the capabilities of the participants involved, the need for real-time features, and the need to maintain anonymity. A combination of these patterns is frequently utilized to achieve an ideal balance of various components.

- Communication synchronization: In FLSs, "communication synchronization" refers to the process of coordinating and aligning the various communication activities that take place among the participating devices or nodes. It ensures that the processes of aggregation, exchanging data, and updating models happen in a structured and synchronized way. The devices must be synchronized correctly in order to maintain the reliability and precision of the collaborative model being trained across distributed devices. Communication in FLSs can be either synchronous or asynchronous [37].
- Synchronous communication: This type of communication involves individuals sending real-time updates on a predetermined timetable to the central server or other

participants. Everybody synchronizes their communication so that aggregations and model updates happen simultaneously. This synchronous method creates an FLS with a coordinated and organized workflow. Synchronous communication is necessary for applications in autonomous vehicles because it ensures that the vehicle's model can adjust in real time to the constantly shifting conditions of the road and its surroundings. To take full advantage of the benefits of synchronous communication in FLSs, it is vital to properly manage network latency and bandwidth usage.

- Asynchronous communication: This type of communication involves devices or nodes functioning autonomously without the requirement of precise time synchronization. In contrast to synchronous communication, which involves coordinating updates in rounds or at predetermined intervals, asynchronous communication enables participants to individually transmit their updates to the central server or other nodes according to their unique schedules [38]. Asynchronous communication, for instance, makes it easier for research institutes located in several time zones to collaborate, enabling scientists to share their discoveries without being constrained by synchronized communication periods. To fully utilize asynchronous communication's advantages in FLSs, its associated problems must be addressed.

The selection of one of these two approaches is contingent upon the particular demands and limitations of the FLS and the attributes of the involved devices or nodes. Table 5 provides a summary of the comparison between asynchronous and synchronous communication in the context of FLSs.

- Communication overhead: Within the context of FL, the term "communication overhead" refers to the additional data transmission and processing resources necessary for participants to exchange model updates, gradients, and other information while the collaborative learning process is being carried out [39]. The effective management of communication overhead is essential because it directly affects the bandwidth of the network, the latency, and the overall effectiveness of the FLS. In FLSs, a number of different techniques have been established to reduce the amount of communication overhead. Table 6 presents a comprehensive summary of several prominent methodologies.

Table 5. Comparison between asynchronous and synchronous communication in FLSs.

	Synchronous Communication	Asynchronous Communication
Communication Timing	Participants communicate according to a predefined schedule or specific synchronization points.	Participants communicate independently, sending updates whenever they have new data or model improvements to contribute.
Flexibility	Less flexible as participants are bound to fixed communication schedules, potentially causing delays for some participants.	Highly flexible, allowing participants to operate at their own pace, accommodating varying network conditions and device availability.
Dependency on central control	Often requires central control to coordinate communication, ensuring all participants adhere to the predefined schedule.	Reduces dependency on central control, enabling decentralized decision-making and autonomous operation of participants.
Latency	Lower latency as updates are synchronized, allowing rapid model adjustments and real-time responses to changing data patterns.	Potentially higher latency due to the lack of synchronization, especially if updates from critical participants are delayed.

Table 5. Cont.

	Synchronous Communication	Asynchronous Communication
Communication overhead	More predictable communication patterns, potentially reducing overall communication overhead.	Can lead to higher communication overhead due to the lack of synchronization, efficient data compression and differential updates are essential to manage this.
Adaptability to dynamic environments	Might struggle to adapt to dynamic environments where network conditions or participant availability fluctuate.	More adaptable to dynamic environments, allowing participants to contribute whenever they can, ensuring continuous collaboration.
Fault tolerance	Susceptible to disruptions if a participant fails to communicate at a scheduled time, potentially affecting the entire synchronization process.	More fault-tolerant as one participant's failure does not disrupt the entire system. Other participants can continue to contribute independently.
Privacy and security	Easier to implement security protocols and encryption as communication occurs at predictable times.	Requires robust encryption and security measures to ensure the safety of data transmitted independently by participants.

Each of the strategies mentioned above are designed to target distinct facets of communication overhead in the context of FL. Frequently, these methodologies are synthesized in practical contexts to attain maximum communication efficacy while concurrently upholding the principles of data confidentiality, model precision, and system promptness. The selection of methodologies is contingent upon the particular application scenario, prevailing network circumstances, and attributes of the involved devices. On the other hand, the presence of significant communication overhead in FLSs can be attributed to several variables. These variables include the utilization of large model sizes, frequent updates, non-selective participant communication, high data dimensionality, non-localized computing, and excessive reliance on encryption or privacy measures. The transmission of machine learning models across distant devices can result in massive data transmission and consume significant network resources, particularly when these models are sizable or updated often. The practice of non-selective communication further exacerbates the issue because all participants send updates without considering their relevance. In addition, many gradients must be transmitted for high-dimensional data, resulting in an additional increase in communication volume. When computations are concentrated in a central location, participants must send unprocessed data, resulting in inefficiencies. Furthermore, an excessive focus on encryption and privacy protocols can increase the quantity of data, thus intensifying the difficulties associated with communication. The presence of inefficient communication protocols can exacerbate these concerns. To address the issue of high communication overhead, techniques such as model compression, intelligent participant selection, dimensionality reduction, localized computation, and the judicious application of encryption methods must be strategically implemented. This ensures a balance between the protection of data and the effectiveness of communication.

Federated Learning Algorithms

FL algorithms are yet another essential component of FLSs. These algorithms make it possible to train collaborative models without transferring raw data between devices and a central server. This helps protect users' privacy while reducing the amount of communication overhead required. The following is a list of essential uses of FL algorithms.

Table 6. An overview of some of key communication-efficient methods.

Methods	Description	Advantages	Considerations
Differential updates	Instead of transmitting the entire model, participants compute and transmit only the changes (gradients) in their local model parameters.	Significantly reduces the amount of data transmitted, especially when only small parts of the model have changed.	Efficient algorithms are needed to calculate and transmit the differentials accurately.
Model compression	Techniques like quantization, where model parameters are represented with fewer bits, and pruning, where insignificant model weights are removed, reduce the model size before transmission.	Reduces the amount of data that must be transmitted, reducing bandwidth and computational overhead.	Balancing compression levels to maintain model accuracy is crucial.
Decentralized optimization	Algorithms like federated averaging allow model updates to be computed locally and averaged among participants, reducing the need to transmit raw data or gradients.	Minimizes communication overhead by performing local computations and transmitting only the aggregated model updates.	Requires careful coordination to ensure accurate aggregation.
Smart sampling and client selection	Algorithms that intelligently select a subset of clients for participation, reducing the total number of updates transmitted.	Reduces the communication overhead by selecting a representative subset of clients, optimizing the use of bandwidth.	Requires algorithms that balance randomness and representation to avoid biased sampling.
Edge computing	Computation and updates are performed locally on edge devices, reducing the need for frequent communication with a central server.	Minimizes communication by allowing edge devices to handle computations and updates, reducing latency and bandwidth usage.	Ensuring that edge devices have sufficient computational resources and storage capacity is essential.
Adaptive communication	Dynamic communication frequency and volume adjustment based on network conditions, participant capabilities, and system requirements.	Optimizes communication overhead in real time, ensuring efficient use of resources.	Requires continuous monitoring and adaptation, potentially introducing computational overhead.
Cryptography and encryption	Secure communication protocols use encryption techniques to protect data during transmission.	Ensures data privacy and security, allowing sensitive information to be transmitted securely.	Introduces computational overhead for encryption and decryption processes.

- Optimization algorithms: Optimization algorithms have a crucial function in FLSs, providing the aggregation of information from various devices and enabling the construction of accurate and efficient machine learning models. These algorithms have been specifically developed to achieve a harmonious equilibrium between the collaborative aspects of FL and the imperative requirements of privacy preservation and computational efficiency [21]. Federated optimization techniques commonly prioritize minimizing a global objective function by integrating local updates obtained from individual devices. Several examples of prominent optimization algorithms employed in FLSs are mentioned below:
    - Federated SGD: This is a pivotal algorithm that has revolutionized the framework of collaborative machine learning in decentralized environments, particularly in the context of Federated Learning Systems (FLSs). This algorithm offers a

nuanced approach to model training, diverging from traditional methods that necessitate the transmission of raw data to a central repository.

At the heart of Federated SGD lies the principle of gradient computation at the local device level. Each participating device in the network utilizes its local data to calculate gradients, which represent the partial derivatives of the loss function with respect to the model parameters. This local computation not only preserves the privacy of user data by avoiding raw data transmission but also significantly reduces the volume of data that needs to be communicated across the network. This aspect of Federated SGD is particularly advantageous in scenarios where network bandwidth is limited.

* Privacy preservation and data integration. The privacy-preserving nature of Federated SGD is one of its standout features. By enabling local gradient computation, the algorithm ensures that sensitive data remains within the confines of the originating device. These locally computed gradients, encapsulating the necessary information for model updates, are then securely transmitted to a central server [40]. On the server, an aggregation process takes place, where these gradients from multiple devices are combined to update the global model. This approach not only safeguards individual data confidentiality but also facilitates the integration of heterogeneous datasets into a unified model. By aggregating diverse local updates, Federated SGD harnesses the collective intelligence embedded in disparate data sources, enhancing the robustness and relevance of the global model.
* Bandwidth optimization and application versatility The reduction in data transmission volume inherent to Federated SGD addresses the challenges posed by restricted bandwidth environments. In traditional centralized learning models, the transmission of large volumes of raw data can be a significant bottleneck, consuming substantial network resources. Federated SGD elegantly circumvents this issue by transmitting only essential gradient information, thereby optimizing bandwidth usage. This optimization is crucial for ensuring the scalability and efficiency of FLSs, particularly when deployed in bandwidth-constrained settings. Furthermore, the versatility of Federated SGD extends its applicability across a broad spectrum of domains. From healthcare to finance, and from mobile computing to Internet of Things (IoT) applications, this methodology proves instrumental in diverse fields by facilitating effective model training across various scenarios while maintaining data privacy and minimizing risk.

- Federated Averaging with Momentum (FedAvgM): represents a significant enhancement over the traditional Federated Averaging (FedAvg) algorithm, primarily used in Federated Learning Systems (FLSs). This advanced algorithm introduces a momentum component to the model updates, enhancing the overall efficiency and accuracy of the learning process. FedAvgM not only leverages the collaborative capabilities inherent in Federated Learning but also introduces the stability and efficiency offered by momentum-based optimization. This results in a more robust and responsive learning algorithm capable of adapting to the nuanced requirements of distributed learning scenarios.

The central innovation in FedAvgM lies in the incorporation of a velocity component, or momentum, into the model updates. This momentum term allows the algorithm to 'remember' and integrate a portion of the previous update into the current one.

* Enhanced convergence and optimization: By maintaining its previous trajectory through the velocity term, FedAvgM accelerates the convergence process. This momentum-driven approach is particularly beneficial in scenarios with non-IID data distributions or significant data volatility, where traditional FedAvg might struggle with slow or unstable convergence.

* Application in diverse scenarios: FedAvgM demonstrates remarkable effectiveness in a variety of distributed environments. Its ability to facilitate rapid and steady knowledge acquisition across distributed devices makes it an ideal choice for FLSs dealing with complex data landscapes. The algorithm effectively balances the need for accurate and efficient model training while maintaining user privacy and data security. In summary, Federated Averaging with Momentum elevates the traditional Federated Learning approach by introducing a dynamic and adaptive component that significantly enhances model training effectiveness. Its ability to handle complex data distributions and volatile environments, while ensuring rapid convergence and optimization, marks it as a valuable tool in the realm of Federated Learning. The inclusion of momentum in the federated averaging with momentum optimization algorithm enhances the traditional federated averaging approach in FLSs. This modification introduces a velocity component into model updates, enabling the algorithm to maintain its previous trajectory while accelerating, resulting in faster convergence and improved optimization. It facilitates rapid and steady knowledge acquisition across distributed devices, particularly in scenarios involving non-identically distributed (non-IID) data or significant volatility. Federated averaging with momentum demonstrates remarkable effectiveness in achieving accurate and efficient model training while safeguarding user privacy and data security. It combines the collaborative capabilities of FL with the stability offered by momentum-based optimization.
- The Federated Proximal Algorithm: The Federated Proximal Algorithm represents an advanced iteration in the evolution of FL algorithms, tailored to address the challenges posed by non-IID (independently and identically distributed) data across a network of devices. This algorithm is particularly relevant in scenarios where the data distribution varies significantly among the participating nodes, a common occurrence in real-world applications. The Federated Proximal Algorithm is built upon the foundation of the standard Federated Learning framework but introduces a crucial modification in the optimization process. The key innovation lies in the incorporation of a proximal term to the optimization objective. This term essentially acts as a regularizer that encourages the local models to not deviate significantly from the global model. The mathematical formulation of this algorithm involves adding a proximal term to the local loss function, typically represented as a squared Euclidean distance between the local and global model parameters.
    * Addressing non-IID data challenges: In standard Federated Learning setups, the assumption is often that the data across devices is identically distributed. However, in many practical situations, this assumption does not hold, leading to significant challenges in model convergence and performance. The Federated Proximal Algorithm mitigates these issues by ensuring that local model updates remain 'proximal' to the global model. This approach effectively handles the statistical heterogeneity of data, ensuring more stable and consistent model training across diverse data distributions.
    * Optimization process in Federated Proximal Algorithm: During the training process, each participating device computes its local model update by optimizing the modified loss function, which includes the proximal term. Once the local updates are computed, they are sent to a central server where a global aggregation occurs. The server updates the global model by averaging these updates, similar to standard Federated Learning, but with the added nuance provided by the proximal regularization.
    * Advantages and practical applications: The incorporation of the proximal term offers several advantages. Primarily, it enhances model performance

in non-IID data scenarios, which are prevalent in many real-world applications such as healthcare, finance, and mobile services [41]. Additionally, by controlling the extent of deviation of local models from the global model, the Federated Proximal Algorithm promotes more uniform learning across the network, leading to improved overall model accuracy and convergence rates. In summary, the Federated Proximal Algorithm represents a significant advancement in the field of Federated Learning, offering a robust solution to the challenges posed by non-IID data distributions. Its ability to ensure consistent and efficient learning across a decentralized network of devices makes it a valuable tool in the arsenal of Federated Learning algorithms.

The optimization algorithms utilized in FLSs undergo continuous development to effectively address the challenges posed by diverse and privacy-sensitive data. The use of these algorithms ensures the efficient generation of precise global models in FL while protecting user privacy. As a result, these algorithms play a critical role in advancing collaborative and privacy-preserving machine learning methodologies.

- Personalization algorithms: Personalization algorithms within FLSs play a crucial role in customizing user experiences while preserving data privacy. These algorithms facilitate the development of personalized models for users while ensuring the decentralization of their sensitive data. Personalization algorithms utilize data from local interactions and activities on user devices to discern trends and preferences. FL enables the integration of these insights into the global model while upholding user privacy. This practice ensures that recommendations, services, or materials provided to consumers are highly relevant and engaging, aligning with their preferences and needs [42]. FL empowers organizations and service providers to deliver personalized experiences on a large scale, simultaneously enhancing user satisfaction and safeguarding their privacy and data security. Personalization algorithms can be applied to tailor both global and local models within FLSs.

  – Global model personalization in Federated Learning Systems: Global model personalization within Federated Learning Systems (FLSs) is a sophisticated approach that aims to adapt a universally trained model to meet the specific needs and preferences of individual users or user groups. This concept is particularly vital in ensuring that the one-size-fits-all model can be effectively tailored to diverse user contexts while preserving privacy and data security. Global model personalization involves the adaptation of a shared global model, initially trained across multiple devices or data sources, to better align with the unique characteristics, behaviors, or preferences of individual users or specific segments [43]. This adaptation is crucial in FLSs, where a single global model is collaboratively trained but needs to be relevant and effective for each participant in the system. Techniques for global model personalization:

    * Client-side personalization: This involves adjusting the global model on the client's device using local data. Techniques such as model fine-tuning, where the model is slightly adjusted using the user's data, or layer retraining, where specific layers of the model are retrained, are commonly used.
    * User embeddings: Incorporating user embeddings into the model is another effective method. User embeddings are vector representations that capture the unique characteristics of each user. These embeddings can be integrated into the global model to ensure that the model's outputs are personalized for each user.
    * Transfer learning: Leveraging transfer learning, where a model trained on one task is adapted for another related task, can also be employed for personalization. This is particularly useful when the global model is trained on a broad dataset but needs to be adapted for specific user scenarios.

* Meta-learning: Meta-learning, or learning to learn, is a technique where the model is trained to quickly adapt to new tasks or data. In the context of personalization, meta-learning can enable the global model to rapidly adjust to individual user data.

Challenges in global model personalization:

* Data diversity and quality: Ensuring that the global model can effectively personalize across a wide range of diverse user data is a significant challenge.
* Resource limitations: The computational and storage limitations of client devices must be considered, especially when personalization involves additional model training on the device.
* Privacy concerns: Maintaining user privacy during the personalization process, especially when user-specific data are used for model adjustments, is crucial.

Global model personalization in FLSs represents a key strategy in making Federated Learning models more user-centric and effective. By adapting the shared global model to align with individual users' unique tastes and features, FLSs can provide customized and relevant experiences to users, enhancing the overall utility and acceptance of these systems.

- Local model personalization in Federated Learning Systems: Local model personalization in Federated Learning Systems (FLSs) addresses the challenge of customizing machine learning models at an individual level, using data that reside on a user's device. This approach is crucial in FLSs, where maintaining data privacy and catering to specific user needs are paramount.

Local model personalization revolves around adapting a federated model to fit individual user profiles based on their unique data. Unlike global model personalization, which modifies a shared model to suit general user characteristics, local personalization focuses on leveraging data available on each user's device to create a model that reflects their specific preferences, behaviors, and usage patterns.

Techniques for local model personalization:

* On-device training: This involves adjusting the federated model directly on the user's device. The model is fine-tuned with the user's local data, ensuring that the personalized model captures individual preferences and behaviors.
* Data augmentation: Enhancing the local training process with data augmentation techniques can improve the model's ability to learn from a limited amount of user data. This might include generating synthetic data points based on the user's existing data to provide a more comprehensive training dataset.
* Layer customization: In some cases, only specific layers of the neural network are personalized, while others remain shared across all users. This approach can be particularly effective in scenarios where certain aspects of the model need to be user-specific, while others can benefit from broader, global training.
* User feedback integration: Incorporating user feedback directly into the training process allows the model to adapt dynamically to changing user preferences and behaviors. This can be achieved through techniques like reinforcement learning, where the model learns and adapts based on user interactions.

Challenges in local model personalization:

* Resource constraints: Personalizing models on individual devices requires computational and storage resources, which might be limited, especially in mobile or IoT devices.

* Data quality and diversity: The quality and diversity of local data can significantly impact the effectiveness of personalization. Ensuring that the model can handle a variety of data types and qualities is essential.
* Privacy preservation: Even though the data do not leave the device, ensuring that the personalization process itself does not compromise user privacy is crucial.

Advancements in lightweight machine learning models, efficient on-device training algorithms, and privacy-preserving techniques will be key to enhancing local model personalization. Research into optimizing these elements can lead to more effective and user-friendly personalized experiences in FLSs.

Local model personalization in FLSs represents a critical step towards creating more user-centric and efficient learning models. By leveraging local data to tailor models to individual user needs, FLSs can provide more relevant, accurate, and privacy-preserving services. This personalized approach not only enhances user experience but also drives the effectiveness and adaptability of learning models in diverse real-world scenarios.

- Outlier handling algorithms: Handling outliers is a crucial aspect of data analysis and statistical modeling. Outliers are data points that significantly deviate from the majority [44]. Algorithms within FLSs play a vital role in maintaining the precision and reliability of machine learning models, especially when dealing with noisy or aberrant data points. These methods focus on detecting and managing outliers, which are data examples that deviate substantially from the established norm. The presence of outliers within a dataset can introduce bias during the model training process, potentially compromising the accuracy of subsequent predictions. The management of outliers is of utmost importance in FL, which involves utilizing data from various heterogeneous sources. Once outliers are identified, they can be addressed through data cleaning, imputation, or robust model training techniques. FLSs enhance the performance and utility of models across numerous applications and user scenarios by successfully managing outliers, ensuring data quality and model reliability. Various techniques for detecting outliers, including statistical methods, clustering algorithms, and robust machine learning models, are utilized to find abnormal data points.
    - Statistical outlier handling methods: Statistical techniques are essential tools for addressing outliers within FLSs, offering a quantitative framework for detecting and effectively handling anomalies in data. Methods such as the Z-score, interquartile range, or Tukey's fences are commonly used to identify outliers by quantifying their deviation from the dataset's mean or median. Through the application of statistical metrics, FLSs can pinpoint data points that significantly deviate from the established norm, signifying their potential classification as outliers. Once identified, these outliers can be managed using techniques such as data imputation, transformation, or exclusion to prevent them from unduly affecting the collaborative model training process. Methods for controlling statistical outliers offer a systematic and objective approach to preserving the integrity of data utilized in FL, thereby enhancing the precision and reliability of the resulting machine learning models.
    - Clustering outlier handling algorithms: Clustering algorithms are efficient tools for managing outliers in FLSs, especially when dealing with diverse and heterogeneous data sources. These methods facilitate the clustering of data points that exhibit similarities, allowing the detection and analysis of patterns inherent in the data. Outliers, characterized by significant deviation from the norm, frequently show unusual clustering patterns, making their identification more straightforward. FLSs can effectively detect outlier clusters using clustering algorithms such as k-means, hierarchical clustering, or DBSCAN. Clustering techniques aid in handling outliers within FLSs, providing a data-driven and adaptable approach.

This ensures the robust and accurate collaborative training of models, regardless of the diversity of data sources and patterns.
- Robust aggregation machine learning algorithms: Robust aggregation algorithms play an essential part in FLSs by effectively managing outliers, particularly in scenarios with noisy or inconsistent data originating from multiple sources. These algorithms are designed to minimize the impact of outliers on the aggregation process, ensuring that inaccurate or deceptive data points do not significantly distort the overall model. The use of robust aggregation strategies helps mitigate the influence of outliers during the model aggregation phase. Techniques like the trimmed mean, median-based aggregation, or methods derived from robust statistics are effective in achieving this objective. FLSs can thus maintain the integrity of the shared model, even when confronted with outliers, by reducing the significance of extreme or incorrect updates originating from individual devices. Robust aggregation algorithms are of utmost importance in enhancing the robustness of FL models. These algorithms guarantee that the resulting model accurately captures the collective intelligence of the devices involved, even in scenarios where the data are contaminated with noise or anomalies.

In summary, statistical techniques offer a straightforward and comprehensible approach, albeit potentially lacking in their ability to handle intricate data distributions effectively. Clustering algorithms can uncover subtle patterns within datasets but may be sensitive to parameters and initialization. Robust aggregation methods have been purposefully developed to address the presence of outliers during the process of model aggregation in FLSs, thereby guaranteeing the creation of a more dependable and resilient global model. Table 7 is a comparison table of some common techniques for outlier detection in FLS, including statistical methods, clustering algorithms, and robust machine learning models. The selection of an outlier handling method frequently relies on the data characteristics and the specific requirements of the FLS.

Table 7. A comparison table of some common techniques for outlier detection in FLS.

Technique	Approach to Outlier Detection	Advantages	Disadvantages	Typical Applications
Statistical methods	Use statistical metrics (like Z-score, IQR) to identify data points that deviate significantly from the norm.	Simple to implement; effective for univariate data.	Can be less effective with complex, high-dimensional data.	Data with a well-defined statistical distribution.
Clustering algorithms	Group similar data points together; outliers are points that fall outside clusters.	Effective in identifying groups and anomalies in multi-dimensional space.	May misclassify outliers as a separate cluster, requires determination of the number of clusters.	Multi-dimensional data with distinguishable clusters.
Isolation forest	Isolates anomalies by randomly selecting features and splitting values; outliers are easier to isolate.	Efficient for high-dimensional datasets; low linear time complexity.	Random forest mechanism may lead to inconsistent results.	Large datasets with many features.
Autoencoders (NN)	Neural networks trained to reconstruct input data; outliers are data with high reconstruction error.	Effective in capturing complex, nonlinear relationships in data.	Requires substantial data for training; computationally intensive.	Complex datasets with intricate patterns.

Table 7. Cont.

Technique	Approach to Outlier Detection	Advantages	Disadvantages	Typical Applications
Robust ML Models	Models that are less sensitive to outliers, like Random Cut Forest or models with regularization.	Can handle outliers while performing the primary learning task.	May require careful tuning; could ignore subtle but important anomalies.	Scenarios where model robustness is crucial.

This taxonomy offers a structured framework for comprehending and classifying the primary distinctions and factors that must be considered when dealing with FLSs. Depending on the specific use case and context, FL implementations may vary significantly along these dimensions. Understanding these variations is essential for the proper development and deployment of FL solutions.

2.3. An Overview of Intrusion Detection Systems

The IDS is a vital cybersecurity tool specifically developed to observe and evaluate network traffic to identify any malicious activity or breaches of established policies. The system functions as a diligent protector, continuously monitoring the network environment for atypical patterns or behaviors that could signify a security breach or unauthorized entry [45]. Upon detecting suspicious activity, the IDS provides alerts or notifications, facilitating IT professionals' rapid investigation of and response to security issues. In the realm of network security, IDSs assume a pivotal role by enhancing the overall protection of computer networks. These systems enable enterprises to promptly identify and counteract potential cybersecurity threats, thereby fortifying the security of sensitive data and upholding the integrity of computer systems.

2.3.1. Types of Intrusion Detection Systems

IDSs can be classified based on their focus areas, deployment strategies, and detection techniques. The two primary types of IDS are the host intrusion detection system (HIDS) and the network intrusion detection system (NIDS) [45].

- HIDS: A HIDS is a critical cybersecurity component that focuses on monitoring and protecting specific hosts or devices within a network. It operates directly on endpoints such as servers, workstations, or other devices, analyzing local activities and configurations. HIDS identifies signs of malicious actions by comparing observed activity to predefined security regulations or baselines [46]. These activities may include unauthorized access attempts, file alterations, and unusual processes. HIDS employs methods like log analysis, file integrity verification, and real-time system monitoring to detect potential security issues. If suspicious actions are detected, HIDS generates notifications, alerting administrators to investigate and take appropriate actions to protect individual devices and their stored data. HIDS is particularly useful in environments where safeguarding specific hosts from internal and external threats is paramount.

- NIDS: NIDS is a cybersecurity solution that monitors and analyzes network traffic for indicators of malicious activity or potential security concerns. Unlike host-based systems, NIDS operates at the network level, analyzing data packets as they traverse the network. NIDS is strategically placed at critical points throughout the network, passively observing and analyzing all incoming and outgoing traffic in real time. It generates alerts when it detects suspicious trends, allowing security teams to promptly investigate and respond to potential security incidents. NIDS is especially beneficial for securing large and complex networks

2.3.2. Intrusion Detection Approaches

In the field of cybersecurity, IDSs utilize a range of methodologies to detect and counteract potential security breaches. The primary IDS approaches include the following:

- Signature-based detection: An essential component of an IDS involves comparing known attack patterns, often referred to as signatures, with incoming network traffic or system actions. If there is a match between the observed data and a saved signature, the IDS generates an alert indicating a potential security breach. This method efficiently recognizes well-known attacks that have been documented in the past, including various forms of malware, viruses, and infiltration attempts. However, its most significant limitation is its inability to identify novel or zero-day attacks. These types of security threats exploit vulnerabilities unknown to security professionals. Despite this limitation, signaturebased detection remains a vital part of any comprehensive security strategy. When used as one component of a layered security approach, it can be combined with other detection approaches, such as anomaly-based detection.
- Anomaly-based detection: IDSs use this sophisticated method to identify anomalous patterns or behaviors within the network traffic or system operations. Anomaly-based detection establishes a baseline of normal behavior by examining historical data to create a reference point, rather than relying on pre-defined attack signatures. It identifies any behavior that deviates from this baseline, such as unexpected patterns of network traffic or actions that are atypical for the system, as a potential security threat. ML algorithms are frequently utilized to analyze large datasets, detecting subtle variations that may indicate a security breach. Because it is highly effective at identifying entirely new types of attacks, anomaly-based detection is an essential component of contemporary cybersecurity methods. However, it requires accurate baselines and ongoing tuning to minimize false positives and negatives, maximizing the likelihood of identifying serious threats while reducing interference with legitimate network operations.

2.3.3. Internet of Vehicle Intrusion Detection

Within the dynamic and constantly changing domain of the IoV, IDSs play a vital role as digital protectors, safeguarding the resilience of interconnected vehicular networks against an increasingly diverse range of cyberattacks. Fundamentally, an IDS in an IoV setting entails a multifaceted approach that involves behavioral analysis, signature-based detection, and anomaly-based detection. Behavioral analysis is a fundamental aspect that involves careful observation and a comprehensive understanding of the complex patterns exhibited by vehicle behavior and network connections [47]. By effectively distinguishing between typical and atypical behaviors, the system can immediately detect deviations, therefore flagging possible intrusions or harmful operations. Simultaneously, signature-based detection functions as the initial layer of protection. This approach entails comparing incoming data with an extensive database of identified attack patterns. When a match occurs, it initiates an alert, facilitating prompt remedial action. Anomaly-based detection, a more advanced technique, creates baselines of typical behavior. When anomalies—such as atypical data traffic or unauthorized system access—are identified, alerts are sent, facilitating proactive measures to address potential security risks [48].

Furthermore, within the context of the IoV, ensuring the security of vehicle-to-everything communication is critical. Establishing robust cryptographic protocols is necessary to safeguard the complex communication network between vehicles and outside entities. These protocols play a crucial role in guaranteeing the secrecy, integrity, and validity of the data being communicated. Incorporating physical and cybersecurity measures provides an enhanced level of safeguarding. The detection systems for physical tampering serve to notify the IDS of potential threats, facilitating proactive cybersecurity measures [6]. By harnessing the capabilities of machine learning-based detection, IDSs can dynamically adjust and evolve. Machine learning algorithms, specifically deep learning models, can analyze extensive datasets obtained from car sensors and network interactions. This enables the detection of subtle patterns that can serve as indicators of cyber risks, including those previously unidentified.

Significantly, the implementation of real-time threat response mechanisms dramatically enhances the effectiveness of IDSs in IoV. Real-time notifications, activated by irregularities or suspected breaches, are received by individuals inside the vehicle, managers overseeing the fleet, and centralized monitoring systems. These notifications prompt swift and targeted actions, including measures such as network segment isolation and emergency protocol activation. These actions effectively contain threats and safeguard the overall integrity of the network. The IDSs employed in the IoV encompass a complex integration of several components, including behavioral analysis, pattern identification, cryptographic techniques, machine learning capabilities, and instantaneous reactions. These technologies ensure secure data transmission inside the IoV and protect the safety, privacy, and trust of all individuals connected to this complex vehicular network. In doing so, they strengthen the fundamental basis upon which the future of transportation technology relies.

3. State of the Art

In this section, we present a well-organized literature review on IDSs based on FL in the IoV environment. This review aims to identify the latest advancements in FL-based intrusion detection within the IoV domain, covering the years from FL's inception in 2016 to 2023.

3.1. Intrusion Detection Systems Based on Federated Learning

The emergence of IDSs that utilize FL represents a significant advancement in cybersecurity. This innovative technique ensures the security of networked environments while upholding data privacy [26]. Unlike conventional IDSs that depend on centralized data analysis, FL-based IDSs operate on a decentralized principle. Within this innovative framework, each device independently generates localized ML models by leveraging their own data inputs. These models are subsequently improved through a collaborative learning process, where devices communicate changes to the models rather than exchanging raw data [49]. Ongoing research efforts continuously enhance this approach, leading to the emergence of FL-based IDSs as a potential future in the pursuit of secure and privacy-conscious network defense mechanisms [46].

Motivation to Adapt Federated Learning in Intrusion Detection Systems

The incorporation of FL into IDSs is driven by the significant demand for heightened security and privacy in our increasingly interconnected society. Despite the notable advancements made by ML and DL in the field of IDSs, various limitations associated with these technologies must be acknowledged, particularly concerning data privacy and communication efficiency. FL addresses these challenges by facilitating localized model training without compromising the privacy of raw data, thereby safeguarding individual privacy while promoting collaborative learning.

FL facilitates decentralized, real-time threat detection in contexts such as the IoT or IoV, where various geographically scattered devices generate data. The IDS's capacity to adapt to local contexts allows it to detect and recognize distinct threats peculiar to individual environments. The motivations for implementing FL in IDSs revolve around several essential elements, including the following [45]:

- Privacy preservation: FL enables collaborative model training while ensuring the privacy of sensitive raw data. Data privacy is of utmost importance in contexts where it holds significant value, such as the healthcare, finance, or government sectors. FL guarantees the protection of individual privacy by maintaining data locally and exchanging model updates. This approach aligns with legal and ethical requirements around privacy.
- Data efficiency: Data efficiency is a significant concern in conventional centralized systems, as transmitting substantial amounts of raw data to a central server may prove

unfeasible. This is particularly true when there are constraints on available bandwidth or communication costs are high. FL addresses this issue by focusing on lowering the volume of data transferred. Specifically, only updates to the model are exchanged, resulting in a substantial reduction in communication overhead.
- Adaptability and customization: The adaptability and customization of FL models allow for their adaptation to specific local settings. In the IDS field, various contexts may encounter distinct and specific threats. FL permits individual devices to customize their intrusion detection models based on their unique threat landscapes, ensuring precision in identifying potential threats.
- Continuous learning: Continuous learning is essential in the security field as threats perpetually evolve. FL permits the ongoing updating of models as new data become accessible. The capacity to adapt in real time ensures that IDSs remain effective in the face of developing threats, providing a significant advantage in dynamic situations.
- Robustness and fault tolerance: The inherent robustness of FL systems is based on their ability to withstand and recover from faults. In the event of a device failure or offline status, the system can maintain operation by utilizing the remaining functional devices [37]. The maintenance of fault tolerance is of the utmost importance in guaranteeing uninterrupted intrusion detection capabilities inside diverse and large-scale networks.
- Decentralization and edge computing: The utilization of FL facilitates decentralized learning, which aligns with edge computing principles, wherein data processing occurs in close proximity to its origin. In scenarios like IoT or IoV, where devices are dispersed geographically, FL enables localized learning, ensuring prompt reactions to potential risks without dependence on a central server.

These elements make FL a compelling and viable approach for enhancing the efficacy and confidentiality aspects of IDSs in diverse settings.

3.2. Related Surveys

A few reviews have focused on the topic of FL-based IDSs. Table 8 succinctly outlines the primary differentiators between our work and the previously conducted surveys. For instance, ref. [45] offers a comprehensive survey of FL-based IDS approaches and discusses the difficulties and challenges of using these methods. This review also outlines potential future directions for FL in IDS. Meanwhile, the authors of [27] focus on the current scientific progress of FL applications in attack detection problems for IoT and explore these applications. The extensive review presented in [50] draws from an analysis of 39 research papers published from 2018 to March 2022, with a specific focus on the IoT. The analysis examined evaluation variables related to IoT, particularly concerning FL, and identified and dis-cussed prospects and unresolved issues pertaining to FL-based IoT. The authors of [25] also provided an overview and comparison of six studies that use FL to enhance IDS effectiveness for IoT. In the absence of specific datasets for assessing FL, the authors emphasized data partitioning modeling among clients. Additionally, they investigated the modeling of bias in the test data to assess its impact on the effectiveness of the ML model. The authors of [51] discussed the implementation of FL-based IDSs in various domains and highlighted distinctions between different architectural configurations. Their structured literature analysis offers a reference architecture that can be used as a set of principles for comparing and designing FL-based IDS. Despite significant progress in FL for IDS development, a comprehensive survey exploring FL for IDS applications within the context of IoV is conspicuously lacking. To the best of our knowledge, no survey has thoroughly evaluated existing IDSs based on FL for IoV. In this direction, we present an organized literature analysis that examines recent developments in IDSs based on FL in an IoV environment. The review covers the years from 2016 (when FL was first introduced) to 2023. We conducted our search using the terms "federated learning", "intrusion detection", and "internet of vehicles".

Table 8. Summary of related surveys on Federated Learning-based IDS.

Survey Title	Year	Main Focus	Key Contributions	IDS	IoV
Survey [45]	2021	FL-based IDS	Discussion on the role of FL in intrusion detection - Comprehensive review of ML/DL/FL in intrusion detection - Highlighting open research challenges	✓	X
Survey [27]	2022	FL in IDS within (IoT) domain	Understanding of federated learning, privacy preservation, and anomaly detection in network systems, with a particular focus on applications in IoT and related domains.	✓	X
Survey [25]	2022	FL-based IDS	- Review of FL system architectures - Review of Evaluation Datasets - Comparative analysis of proposed systems Open challenges and future directions	✓	X
Survey [50]	2022	FL-based IoT	Organizing and reviewing FL-based IoT domains - Creating a taxonomy to organize various aspects of FL-based IoT Providing some research questions about the FL-based IoT area and answering them Reviewing evaluation factors Focusing on open issues and future research challenges	X	X
Survey [51]	2022	FL-based IDS	Review of FL application in attack detection and mitigation Proposal of a reference architecture Establishment of a taxonomy Identification of open issues and research directions	✓	X
Our Survey	2023	FL-based IDS in IoV environment	Offer of a generic taxonomy for describing FL systems A well-organized literature review on IDSs based on FL in an IoV environment. Highlighting challenges and potential future directions based on the existing literature.	✓	✓

Note: In this table, ✓: indicates that the survey discussed the relevant aspect of Federated Learning (FL) or Intrusion Detection Systems (IDS), while X signifies that the aspect was not discussed in the survey.

3.3. Comparative Analysis of Federated Learning-Based Intrusion Detection Systems for Internet of Vehicles

In the rapidly evolving landscape of cybersecurity within IoV, FL has emerged as a transformative paradigm, promising enhanced security and privacy preservation. As the IoV ecosystem expands, robust IDSs become essential to safeguard vehicles, passengers, and the underlying network infrastructure from ever-evolving cyber threats. This section offers an extensive analysis of the relevant literature in the field of IDS based on FL, specifically tailored to the intricacies of IoV. This comparative survey aims to extract significant insights by examining the unique techniques, strategies, and structures of recent studies. These insights are crucial for understanding the current state of IDS solutions based on FL in IoV and provide valuable guidance for future research. We employed a range of criteria to evaluate and differentiate the related works in the domain of FL-based IDSs within the framework of IoV. We formulated the following research questions for our review:

- What kinds of FL designs are used for IDS?
- What ML model architectures are employed in the proposed solutions?
- Which datasets are utilized for evaluating the proposed solutions?
- What types of attacks can be identified by the proposed solutions?
- Which measures do the authors employ to validate their proposed solutions?
- Which communication patterns are utilized in the solutions they offer?
- Do the proposed solutions operate in synchronous or asynchronous mode?
- Which aggregation model do the proposed solutions utilize?
- Which optimization algorithms do the proposed solutions utilize?
- Are the proposed solutions designed to support real-time processing?
- Are the proposed solutions designed to support imbalanced data distribution?
- What is the impact of the implemented solutions on overhead costs?

Based on the formulated questions, we considered the following criteria during our review of the papers to organize the information in a structured manner that allowed for easy comparison and understanding:

- Year of publication;
- Datasets used;
- Attacks detected;
- ML models;
- Communication patterns;
- Communication synchronization;
- Evaluation metrics;
- Model aggregation algorithms;
- Optimization algorithms;
- Real-time considerations;
- Data distribution;
- Communication overhead.

While FL-based IDSs for IoV are the primary focus of this paper, we did not conduct any experiments on the reviewed approaches to evaluate them. The study aimed to highlight open difficulties and research directions by considering the described factors. Table 9 provides a summary of the comparison's results.

Table 9. Comparative Analysis of Federated Learning-based intrusion detection systems for IoV.

Ref.\Year	Dataset	Attacks Detected	ML Model	Communication Patterns	Communication Synchronization	Evaluation Metrics	Model Aggregation	Optimization Algorithms	Real-Time Processing	Data Imbalance	Overhead
[52], 2022	The attack-free dataset of CAN messages published by the HCR Lab of Korea University	-Spoofing -Replay -Drop -Denial-of-Service (DoS)	Convolutional Long Short-Term Memory (ConvLSTM) model	Client-server mode	Synchronous mode	-FPR, TPR -Accuracy -Precision -Recall -F1-score	Secure MultiParty Computation	The Federated Proximal Algorithm	Real-time processing	Imbalanced data distribution.	Reduces the overhead
[53], 2021	VeReMi dataset	-Constant attack -Constant offset attack -Random attack -Eventual stop attack.	Long Short-Term Memory (LSTM) neural network.	Client-server mode	Synchronous mode	-Precision -Recall -Accuracy	Federated Averaging Algorithm (FedAvg)	Federated Stochastic Gradient Descent (Federated SGD)	Batch processing	Imbalanced data distribution.	Reduces the overhead
[54], 2022	Simulated dataset	Black hole attack	Random Forest 1-dimensional CNN (1 D CNN) 1-dimensional RNN (1-D RNN)	Client-server mode	Synchronous mode	-Precision -Recall -F1-score	Weighted aggregation model	–	Batch processing	–	–
[55], 2023	VeReMi dataset	-Constant attack -Constant offset attack -Random attack -Eventual stop attack.	Deep neural networks	Federated Arch. with edge offloading	–	-Accuracy -Consensus time -Incentive mechanisms	Federated Averaging Algorithm (FedAvg)	Federated Stochastic Gradient Descent (Federated SGD)	–	–	Reduces the overhead
[56], 2023	The simulated Sybil attack dataset	Sybil attack	–	Client-server mode	Synchronous mode	Accuracy Number of global aggregations	Weighted aggregation model	Fuzzy logic-based technique	Batch processing	–	Reduces the overhead
[16], 2022	Car Hacking dataset	-Flooding -Spoofing -Replay -Fuzzing	Gated Recurrent Unit (GRU) with a Random Forest (RF)-based ensembler unit.	Client-server mode	asynchronous mode	-Accuracy -Precision -Recall -F1 score	Federated Averaging Algorithm (FedAvg)	Adam optimizer	Batch processing	–	–
[57], 2021	CAN-Intrusion dataset (OTIDS)	-DoS attack -Fuzzy attack -Spoofing attack	Random Forest	Client-server mode	–	-Accuracy -Precision -Recall	–	–	Batch processing	–	–
[58], 2022	Car Hacking dataset	-DoS attack -Fuzzy attack -Spoofing attack	Multilayer Perceptron (MLP) model	Client-server mode	–	-Accuracy -Loss -AUC score -Time Cost	Federated Averaging Algorithm (FedAvg)	Stochastic Gradient Descent (SGD) optimizer	Real-time processing	–	–

Table 9. Cont.

Ref.\Year	Dataset	Attacks Detected	ML Model	Communication Patterns	Communication Synchronization	Evaluation Metrics	Model Aggregation	Optimization Algorithms	Real-Time Processing	Data Imbalance	Overhead
[59], 2022	Practical dataset	-Spoofing attacks -Replay attacks -Drop attacks -DoS attacks	Long Short-Term Memory (LSTM) neural network.	Client–server mode	–	-The detection accuracy	–	–	Real-time processing	–	–
[60], 2023	Car Hacking dataset	-DoS attack -Fuzzy attack -Spoofing attack	Convolutional Neural Network (CNN)	Client–server mode	–	-Accuracy -Recall -Precision -F1-score	Federated Averaging Algorithm (FedAvg)	Bayesian Optimization (BO)	Real-time processing	Imbalanced data distribution.	Reduces the overhead
[47], 2023	NSL-KDD dataset	-DoS attack -Probe attack -R2L (Remote to Local) -U2R (User to Root)	Memory-Augmented Autoencoder Model	Client–server mode	Synchronous mode	-Accuracy -Precision -Recall -F1 score	Weighted Aggregation Model	Adam optimizer	Batch processing	Imbalanced data distribution.	–
[61], 2023	VeReMi Extension dataset	-Constant attack -Constant offset attack -Random attack -Random offset attack -Eventual stop attack.	Long Short-Term Memory (LSTM) neural network.	–	–	-F1-scores	–	–	–	–	–
[62], 2023	The dataset [RAKGZ20]	-SYN flood attack -UDP flood attack	The deep autoencoder method	Federated Arch. with edge offloading	–	-F1-Score -The false positive rate (FPR)	Federated Averaging Algorithm (FedAvg)	Federated Averaging Algorithm (FedAvg)	–	–	–
[63], 2022	CAN-Intrusion dataset (OTIDS)	-DoS attack -Fuzzy attack -Impersonation attack	Statistical Adversarial Detector	–	–	-Maximum Mean Discrepancy (MMD) -Energy distance (ED)	–	–	Batch processing	–	–
[64], 2023	The CIC-IDS 2017 dataset	DoS attack, web attacks, port scan, bot, brute force attacks	A Cat Boost model	Client–server mode	–	Precision, recall, Kappa score, accuracy	The Bagging Classifier technique	The grid search method	–	Imbalanced data distribution	–

3.4. Analysis and Discussion

The analysis of the research papers aided us in formulating the following conclusions:

- Dataset: The selection of a dataset is a crucial aspect when evaluating the effectiveness and resilience of proposed solutions in the field of IDS based on FL within the context of IoV. Given the dynamic and complex nature of IoV, it is imperative to use datasets that can accurately depict real-world vehicular communication scenarios, encompassing both normal and malicious activities. These datasets play a fundamental role in training and evaluating IDS models, enabling them to effectively identify threats within the IoV environment. The following describes the datasets utilized in the provided papers to assess the efficacy of various IDS solutions. Three of the papers, namely [52,57,63], employed the CAN-intrusion dataset (OTIDS), which was sourced from the Hacking and Countermeasure Research Lab at Korea University. This dataset provides a comprehensive representation of intrusion scenarios within in-vehicle networks, making it suitable for assessing IDSs specifically designed for vehicular contexts. By contrast, refs. [53,55,61] employed the VeReMi dataset for their experimental analysis. The publicly accessible VeReMi dataset was explicitly developed for analyzing mechanisms to detect misbehavior in VANETs. The authors of [16,58,60] employed the Car-Hacking dataset derived from the "Car Hacking: Attack & Defense Challenge" competition held in 2020. Additionally, some papers used simulated datasets, such as [54], where a simulated dataset was employed to evaluate the effectiveness of their proposed approach in vehicle-to-vehicle and ve-hicle-to-infrastructure scenarios. The authors of [56] employed a simulated attack dataset consisting of simulated Sybil attack flows and normal traffic flows in their experimental analysis. Meanwhile, the simulations in [59] were conducted using the authors' proprietary dataset. Although the NSL-KDD and CIC-IDS 2017 datasets are not dedicated to IoVs and are primarily general intrusion detection datasets, the authors of [47,64] conducted their experiments on these datasets to evaluate the performance of their proposed methods. Finally, ref. [62] utilized the [RAKGZ20] dataset to evaluate the authors' proposed solutions. These datasets collectively offer a comprehensive view of various intrusion detection scenarios, particularly within automotive networks.
- Attacks detected: Within the domain of FL-based IDSs for IoV, numerous research papers have put forth methodologies to identify a diverse range of cyber threats. DoS attacks [47,52,57–60,63] and constant attacks [53,55,61] are the most frequently discussed types of attacks in the literature. In addition, some authors emphasized specific attacks, such as the Sybil assault [56] and the black hole attack [54]. Several papers also explored detecting advanced attacks in in-vehicle networks, including adversarial attacks like fuzzy attacks [16,57,58,60,63], flooding attacks [16,62], and spoofing attacks [16,52,58–60]. These studies highlighted the diverse and persistent nature of cyber threats in the IoV environment, underscoring the critical need for robust IDS solutions. IDSs based on FL in IoV not only demonstrate the adaptability and robustness of FL techniques but also illustrate the essential role these techniques play in protecting the future of connected vehicular systems against a wide array of cyberattacks.
- ML models: Researchers have turned to more powerful ML models to construct resilient FL-based IDSs capable of addressing challenges posed by vehicular networks. These models, tailored to meet the unique requirements of vehicular communication, offer promising ways to detect and mitigate potential attacks. To improve detection capacities and ensure vehicular safety, numerous ML models based on FL in IoV have been implemented in the field of IDS. The following summarizes the ML models utilized in the proposed solutions across the reviewed papers.
    - Long short-term memory (LSTM): This architecture of recurrent neural networks is prominently featured in articles [16,52,53,59,61]. One notable advantage of this approach is its proficiency in identifying patterns over different time intervals, making it well-suited for analyzing time-series data such as network traffic.

- Deep convolutional neural network (DCNN): Papers such as [55,60] utilized DCNNs to effectively handle structured grid data, including images or time-series data. These DCNNs possess the capability to automatically and adaptively learn spatial hierarchies.
- Support vector machine (SVM): ref. [60] utilized SVM, a supervised ML approach applicable to both classification and regression tasks.
- Statistical adversarial detector: As explicitly stated in [63], this approach employs statistical techniques to identify adversarial examples.
- Random forest: refs. [54,57] employed the random forest algorithm, an ensemble learning technique. This algorithm constructs numerous decision trees during the training phase and determines the class output by selecting the mode of the classes for classification.

The utilization of a wide array of ML models in the articles highlights the intricate and multifaceted characteristics of intrusion detection in IoV. Researchers have used diverse techniques, such as recurrent networks like LSTM, capable of capturing temporal relationships, and ensemble methods like random forest, which provide robustness. These approaches enhance the security and dependability of vehicular networks.

- Communication patterns: Most of the articles we reviewed provided solutions formulated according to the client–server mode of operation, as exemplified by [47,54,58,60,64], among others. In this mode, clients engage in the process of training their models on a local level without sharing raw data. Subsequently, the model updates are transmitted to the server, the central entity responsible for aggregating them. This procedure guarantees the protection of data privacy and minimizes the necessity of data centralization. Meanwhile, some papers adopted a federated architecture with an edge-offloading technique [55,62]. As mentioned above, this approach diminishes latency and reduces dependence on a remote cloud server. As discussed in the publications mentioned above, the client–server mode of operation emphasizes the shifting paradigm of decentralized data processing in IoV. FL-based IDSs not only protect users' data privacy but also pave the way for more effective and scalable security solutions in rapidly developing vehicular networks. These systems enable vehicles to train models locally, with central servers aggregating the training results.
- Communication synchronization: The communication synchronization mode, whether synchronous or asynchronous, significantly impacts the efficiency and effectiveness of the FL process. Ref. [52] discussed the operational characteristics of synchronous FL, which involves a single launch point and a single aggregate point for the global model. In this model, the beginning of each iteration occurs concurrently for all clients, and the federated aggregation process is performed without establishing a predetermined objective for the learning rounds. In [53], the authors presented a synchronous FL approach, and ref. [54] introduced a conventional synchronous FL protocol. This protocol is considered appropriate for a wide range of FL scenarios, including those involving bottlenecks. On the other hand, ref. [16] preferred an asynchronous mode, which can provide greater flexibility in dynamic settings and effectively handle frequent model changes and bottlenecks. This strategy enables increased adaptability in the learning process, accommodating partial updates from clients that may impact convergence performance. Nevertheless, not all research explicitly addressed this matter. Most of the publications did not specify their operational mode concerning synchronization. The variations mentioned above highlight the varied approaches that researchers have utilized to enhance the effectiveness of IDSs within the rapidly changing environment of IoV. In summary, while synchronous FL was a prevalent technique in the suggested solutions, some studies acknowledged the advantages of asynchronous methods, particularly in environments characterized by frequent updates and potential bottlenecks.
- Evaluation metrics: In most of the papers that were reviewed, the evaluation of the efficacy of FL-based IDS systems relied on ML measures that assess the effectiveness

of the analytic model. These metrics include accuracy, precision, recall, and F-measure. A limited number of research publications examined the effects of FL. In particular, ref. [55] discussed the consensus time, which is impacted by the quantity of FL workers and the number of created blocks. The study additionally assessed the effectiveness of the FL-enabled edge node by manipulating the reward and accuracy of the local model. This evaluation considered various elements, including the reward, energy consumption, and processing overhead. Moreover, the researchers did not overlook the significance of accuracy as a fundamental measure for evaluating the efficacy of their proposed solution. The paper also addressed the issues associated with recruiting FL workers, highlighting the possibility of bias and imbalance when selection is primarily predicated on reputation. The authors proposed various strategies to address these difficulties, such as including randomization in the selection procedure. In addition, in [56], the authors considered the "number of global aggregations (NGA)" as an evaluation metric. They presented information regarding the number of global aggregations performed in the proposed system and other state-of-the-art baseline frameworks. Their research demonstrated how many global aggregations are necessary for different numbers of communication rounds (R) to achieve the desired level of accuracy. The FLEMDS framework proposed in the study necessitates a reduced number of global aggregations in comparison to the baseline frameworks to attain a comparable level of accuracy.

- Aggregation model: In the domain of distributed ML, the combination of data or model updates from several nodes holds significant importance in determining the overall performance and efficiency of the system. The aggregation process has been extensively explored in contemporary research, with numerous novel approaches and models offered in recent research papers. These aggregation models aim to successfully harness the collective intelligence of all participating nodes while simultaneously overcoming problems such as data heterogeneity, communication overheads, and adversarial threats.

The examined literature suggested a range of aggregation models to improve the effectiveness and precision of distributed systems, particularly in the domain of FL. One of the most common aggregation models used in the reviewed papers is the federated averaging method, where local model updates are averaged to produce a global model [16,53,55,58,60,62]. This approach is simple yet impactful, particularly in situations involving non-identically and independently distributed (non-IID) data [32]. An alternative methodology uses weighted federated averaging, as described in several papers [47,54,56]. This technique involves assigning varying weights to local models, considering factors such as the quantity of data samples or the quality of the model. Secure aggregation is another widely employed model aggregation technique in the field of FL, as observed in [52]. In this technique, various cryptographic techniques, including SMPC, are employed to consolidate data while preserving the confidentiality of the unprocessed updates. The authors of [64] used the Bagging Classifier technique as aggregation model in their developed solution. This technique aggregates the predictions of multiple models to produce a single, more accurate model. The resulting supermodel, created by the central server, exhibits better robustness than the individual edge device models.

Each aggregation method provides specific benefits designed to address the challenges and requirements of dispersed learning settings. The models described above are at the forefront of current research, each tackling distinct issues. As technology advances and increasingly intricate situations arise, these models are expected to continue to develop, facilitating the implementation of more resilient and effective distributed learning systems. The ongoing investigation and advancement of aggregation models serve as evidence of the dynamic characteristics of ML research and its dedication to optimizing the utilization of distributed nodes' collective intelligence.

- Optimization algorithms: The utilization of FL in IDSs presents a new and innovative method for addressing the issues related to data privacy and effective model training in IoV. Advanced algorithms play a pivotal role in optimizing FL models. For instance, the federated proximal algorithm has been used to fine-tune model parameters, ensuring optimal performance in detecting intrusions [52]. Similarly, some studies have adopted federated stochastic gradient descent (federated SGD) to optimize the parameters of the proposed IDS models [53,55,58]. Furthermore, some papers utilized other optimization techniques, such as the Adam optimizer [16,47], a fuzzy logic-based technique [56], Bayesian optimization (BO) [60], and the federated averaging (FedAvg) algorithm [62]. The authors of [64] used the grid search method for hyperparameter tuning as an optimization algorithm in their solution. This method is employed to optimize the Cat Boost model, a gradient boosting algorithm that utilizes decision trees as the classifier model for edge devices. The grid search technique exhaustively searches over a specified set of hyperparameters to improve the model's accuracy.

  The integration of optimization approaches, combined with the decentralized nature of FL, holds the potential to deliver resilient and effective IDSs for the IoV environment. Decentralizing the learning process and applying complex optimization algorithms not only enhances detection capabilities but also ensures that modern concerns regarding privacy and efficiency within the IoV landscape are effectively addressed. This represents a significant advancement for the industry. The ongoing expansion and development of IoV necessitate the use of innovative strategies to ensure the protection and security of our networked automotive environment.

- Real-time processing: A critical aspect of FL-based IDSs is their ability to process data in real time, ensuring timely detection and response to potential threats. Our review found several papers that proposed IDSs designed for real-time operation [52,58–60]. For instance, refs. [52,53,58] highlighted the significance of real-time processing for IDSs, especially when dealing with vehicular networks. In addition, ref. [60] introduced ImageFed IDS, a system designed for real-time inference. It employs a lightweight image-based feature extraction for CAN packets, making it suitable for real-time applications. On the other hand, some papers supported a batch processing approach rather than real-time processing [16,47,56]. Some papers did not explicitly mention whether their proposed solutions are designed for real-time or batch processing. Nevertheless, all the papers emphasized the importance of real-time processing in IDSs for IoV, with various solutions and methodologies proposed to achieve this objective. The operational significance of IDSs for vehicle networks increases as these networks undergo continuous evolution and encounter a diverse range of cyber threats. The research presented in these papers offers solutions and approaches that contribute to the development of a more secure and responsive IoV environment by emphasizing the significance of real-time processing.

- Data distribution: While imbalanced data distribution is a significant concern in ML and AI research, most of the research papers we reviewed did not address this aspect. We only identified five articles, namely [47,52,53,60,64], that specifically addressed the issues and implications associated with imbalances in data distribution in FL scenarios. They stressed the importance of dealing with this problem to achieve robust and stable model performance. The authors of [52] emphasized that in real FL contexts, the data distributed across many nodes or devices may exhibit non-IID characteristics. These characteristics sometimes arise due to an imbalanced distribution of data, wherein certain data classes may be overrepresented in one node while being underrepresented in another. To overcome this difficulty, the study suggested an IDS that uses FL to help handle imbalanced data distribution. The authors of [53] examined the vulnerability of models to adversarial attacks, particularly when confronted with data imbalance. The presence of an imbalance in vulnerability can be exploited by adversarial examples, resulting in the misclassification of benign data. The authors presented various techniques for identifying these adversarial examples, indirectly addressing the difficulties associated with data imbalance. From another perspective, the authors of [60] showed that data distribution among vehicles in FL scenarios, particularly in the context of IoV, might exhibit a significant imbalance. This imbalance can potentially impact the overall performance of the global model. The paper introduced various methodologies aimed at alleviating the repercussions of this imbalance, thereby ensuring the robustness of the FL framework. The issues presented by imbalanced data distribution were also addressed in [47]. The authors highlighted the potential emergence of unexpected attack behaviors in the context of IoV development. The absence of comprehensive analysis and systematic gathering of various attack behaviors has resulted in an imbalanced distribution of sample data categories within intrusion detection for IoV. Consequently, this disparity leads to diminished accuracy in detection. The authors proposed an intrusion detection approach integrating FL and a memory-augmented autoencoder (FL-MAAE) to tackle this issue. They have considered the problem posed by imbalanced data distribution in their produced solution, hence ensuring the continued effectiveness of the model. Lastly, the proposed framework in [64] employs the Synthetic Minority Over-sampling Technique (SMOTE) to tackle the issue of class imbalance in the dataset. This approach of oversampling minority classes helps to create a more balanced dataset, which in turn allows for a more accurate and representative evaluation of the classification models. Addressing data imbalance is critical for guaranteeing the resilience and dependability of ML models, particularly in distributed learning scenarios such as FL.

- The overhead: One of the primary issues frequently encountered in the domain of IDSs based on FL is the significant overhead associated with these systems. The effectiveness and responsiveness of IDSs in IoV contexts can be significantly affected by overhead, including computing, communication, and storage expenses. Addressing this overhead is crucial to ensure the seamless operation of these systems without compromising their primary function of identifying and mitigating threats. Several of the reviewed papers examined the issue of overhead, which holds significant importance in the field of distributed systems and FL [52,53,55–57,60]. In [52], the term "overhead" refers to the complexity of the algorithms offered, and the authors stressed how important it is to reduce this complexity as much as possible to ensure efficient operations. In addition, ref. [53] discussed overhead in the context of communication costs, emphasizing the relevance of minimizing overhead to improve system performance. Overhead was explored in relation to the computing expenses of the proposed approaches in [55], which emphasized the necessity of striking a balance between accuracy and computational efficiency in the methods offered. The research presented in [56] investigated the overhead caused by the consensus process in blockchains and suggested that using a lightweight consensus method can reduce overhead and increase scalability. The topic of overhead was discussed in the context of data transmission in [57], which emphasized the significance of effective data-sharing systems to reduce overhead. Lastly, ref. [60] provided a comparative analysis of various solutions. This research suggested that FL approaches often incur less overhead than alternative distributed learning modes. The study also discussed processing overhead in the context of incentive mechanisms for FL. Taken together, these papers highlight the importance of properly managing overhead costs to guarantee the efficiency, scalability, and effectiveness of distributed and federated information systems.

Upon reviewing the collection of work relevant to IDSs based on FL in IoV, it becomes apparent that the realm of security within vehicular networks is experiencing a significant and fundamental change. FL has emerged as a promising solution for effectively addressing the intertwined issues of safeguarding data privacy and enhancing threat detection efficiency. In conclusion, Table 10 presents a comparative analysis of the advantages and drawbacks of each one of these proposed solutions that we discussed.

Table 10. Comparative analysis of FL-based IDS for IoV: advantages and drawbacks.

Ref	Advantages	Drawbacks
[56]	Three-level model aggregation. Fuzzy Logic-Based FL Vehicle Selection (FLBFLVS). Reduced latency.	Complex system architecture.
[52]	Reduced model size and convergence time. High detection accuracy (over 95%)	Complexity of implementation. Scalability concerns.
[53]	Privacy preservation. Reduction in communication overhead. Handling position falsification attacks.	Complexity in implementation. Challenges in federated averaging. Experimental limitations.
[54]	Trust estimator integration. Effective learning with fewer rounds. Improved network performance	Challenges in synchronization and model aggregation. Need for regular updates and maintenance.
[55]	Blockchain integration for trust. Smart contract use. Efficient consensus protocol. High performance.	Resource intensity. Challenges in worker selection and bias. Scalability in real-world deployment.
[16]	High accuracy in cyberattack detection. Reduced communication overhead. Resource efficiency.	Complex implementation.
[57]	Blockchain integration. Decomposition using Fourier transform. High performance.	Complex system architecture. Resource intensiveness. Challenges in blockchain integration.
[58]	High accuracy (up to 98.45%). Low-complexity structure. Adaptability.	Dependency on local data quality.
[59]	High detection accuracy (beyond 90%).	-
[60]	High performance metrics (with an average 99.54% F1-score and 99.87% accuracy, alongside low detection latency). Lightweight feature extraction.	-
[47]	Robust to imbalanced data. Effective in detecting unknown attacks.	The evaluation is conducted used the NSL-KDD dataset, which is not dedicated to IoVs and is primarily an intrusion detection dataset.
[61]	High accuracy in threat detection.	Complexity in tradeoffs between utility and privacy.
[62]	Zero-day attack detection. High detection rates. Multi-access Edge Computing (MEC) assistance.	Complexity in implementation and management
[63]	Adversarial attack detection. Blockchain integration. High detection accuracy Lightweight feature extraction.	Computational overhead. Limitations in detecting certain adversarial attacks.
[64]	Robust to imbalanced Data. Handling class imbalance.	The evaluation is conducted used the CIC-IDS 2017, dataset which is not dedicated to IoVs and is primarily an intrusion detection dataset.

4. Discussion of Challenges and Future Research Directions

IoV is anticipated to experience significant growth in the coming decade, emerging as a prominent paradigm movement. This projection suggests that IoV will receive substantial attention and witness considerable advancements across several sectors and industries. The integration of FL into IDSs within IoV scenarios presents a significant opportunity to bolster the security of interconnected vehicles in this dynamic environment. The primary objective of incorporating collaborative intelligence concepts and technologies into the domain of

IoV is to facilitate the integration of data and resources from a vast array of vehicles, users, infrastructure, and networks. This integration aims to enhance the reliability, connectivity, and ease of management, control, and operation of IoV systems. Nevertheless, this novel methodology also presents a series of challenges that necessitate meticulous consideration to guarantee the efficiency and security of these systems. These constraints arise from the heterogeneous characteristics of vehicle data, constrained network resources, the persistent risk of adversarial assaults, strict regulatory obligations, and the imperative to uphold the security of FL models. The ability to effectively deal with these intricacies is crucial to fully harness the capabilities of FL-enabled IDSs in IoV scenarios. This will establish a resilient, secure, and privacy-conscious vehicular network. Drawing upon the literature analysis, this section aims to elucidate some of the main challenges we found and possible future research directions for investigating the development of IDSs empowered by FL within the IoV context. Figure 3 summarizes the challenges and future research directions in FL-enabled IDS IoV.

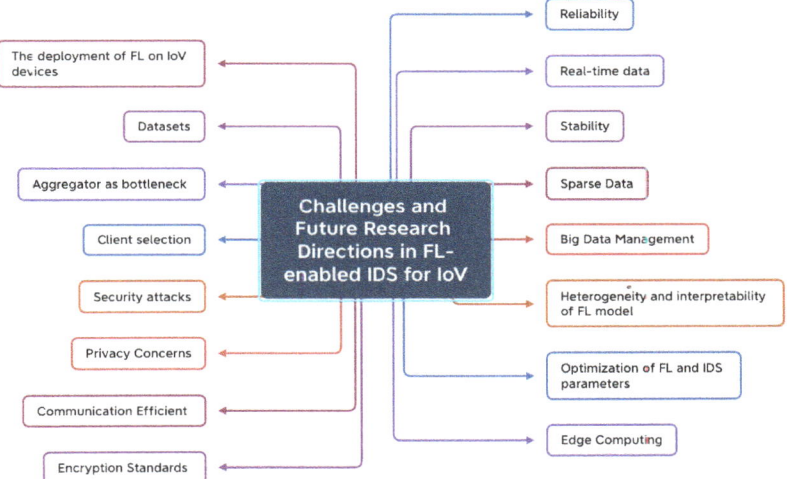

Figure 3. Challenges and future research directions in FL-enabled IDS for IoV.

Here, we cover some of the primary challenges and future research directions associated with developing FL-enabled IDSs in IoV scenarios.

- The deployment of Federated Learning on Internet of Vehicles devices: Deploying an FL-enabled IDS architecture on real IoV devices presents many challenges. One notable obstacle involves the presence of resource constraints since IoV devices frequently have restricted processing capabilities and memory capacities, making the efficient execution of intricate FL algorithms difficult. This challenge can be exacerbated when employing deep learning techniques, as they often require more computational resources than traditional ML [65]. To overcome these restrictions, a prevailing approach involves the implementation of intermediate nodes positioned at the network edge. These nodes serve as clients for FL, receiving data from end devices. Real-time processing poses an additional challenge in the context of IDSs in IoV. These IDSs need to effectively evaluate incoming data and promptly identify any instances of intrusion, requiring the implementation of algorithms that strike a delicate balance between accuracy and processing speed. Consequently, more work is needed to examine the real-world constraints of FL-enabled IDS techniques in IoV contexts to ensure optimal levels of security and efficiency.
- Limitations of existing FL-enabled IDS datasets for IoV: The current datasets available for FL-enabled IDSs in the context of IoV exhibit various limitations. The issue of

data diversity presents a notable obstacle as datasets may lack a comprehensive representation of the wide range of real-world scenarios and driving conditions, resulting in the development of biased models. Data imbalance is a significant issue that warrants attention, as specific categories of security threats may be inadequately represented in the dataset, posing challenges for the FL-enabled IDS to detect these less frequent intrusions accurately and efficiently. Data quality is essential, as any inaccuracies or noise present in the data can significantly impact the learning process, potentially leading to the development of intrusion detection models that are less reliable and potentially misleading. Furthermore, the issue of data privacy poses a significant constraint in the context of IoV. The data generated by IoV systems frequently encompass confidential personal and vehicular details, thereby presenting a formidable obstacle in creating extensive datasets that simultaneously safeguard users' privacy. The concern regarding the scalability of current datasets becomes particularly significant as IoV networks experience rapid expansion. These constraints must be acknowledged and addressed to create resilient IDSs that effectively capture the complicated nature of actual IoV settings while upholding user privacy and data integrity.

- Aggregator as a bottleneck: In the context of IoV scenarios involving FL-enabled IDS, the aggregator frequently becomes a bottleneck despite being a central component. The processing capacity of the aggregator can be overwhelmed by the sheer volume of incoming information if data from multiple vehicles are sent to the aggregator for model training and updating [65]. The influx of data, especially in extensive IoV networks, has the potential to result in delays when it comes to aggregating and updating FL models. Furthermore, given the real-time nature of intrusion detection in vehicle contexts, introducing any delay at the aggregator level can impede prompt responses to security threats. The challenge of balancing the requirement for comprehensive model updates with the practical constraints of aggregators is of utmost importance. This necessitates using innovative approaches in distributed computing, efficient algorithms, and optimized communication protocols. These measures are necessary to address the bottleneck and ensure the smooth operation of FL-enabled IDSs in IoV scenarios.

- Client selection: Identifying suitable clients for FL-enabled IDSs in the IoV context presents a significant challenge. During each training iteration, the coordinator can choose a specific subset of devices to engage as FL clients in the training procedure. The environments in which IoV operates exhibit a high degree of dynamism, characterized by the continuous movement of vehicles within and beyond the network coverage area. The dynamic nature of the environment poses difficulties in maintaining a consistent group of clients who actively participate in the training of FL models. For instance, specific devices may not be accessible during a particular round due to mobility issues or disruptions in connectivity. In addition, the criteria for selection need to consider factors such as the device's current state, its battery life, its computational and networking capabilities, and even the precision of the ML technique. The client selection process can significantly impact the accuracy achieved and, consequently, the detection of potential security breaches within the framework of an IDS approach. Striking a balance in the client selection process, where a diverse, accurate, and current dataset is maintained, necessitates the utilization of advanced algorithms and real-time decision-making to manage the ever-changing pool of participating vehicles effectively. Addressing this challenge is essential to maintain the integrity and accuracy of FL-enabled IDSs in IoV scenarios. Therefore, future strategies for devising an efficient client selection process in IoV systems must consider the dynamic nature of device conditions throughout each training iteration.

- Security attacks: In the context of FL-enabled IDSs in IoV scenarios, security attacks pose a severe threat. Attackers can exploit vulnerabilities inherent in the FL architecture [66]. These exploits can manifest as various types of attacks, including data poisoning [24], where adversaries inject deceptive data into the training process to manipulate the IDS model [45]. Model inversion attacks can also occur, in which attackers attempt to deduce confidential data from the trained model. In addition, the confidentiality and integrity of data might be compromised by eavesdropping attacks that specifically target the communication channels established between vehicles and the central server. To address these security concerns, robust security measures are essential, including strong encryption, secure communication protocols, anomaly detection techniques, and continuous monitoring. Preserving security in FL-enabled IDSs within IoV scenarios is of utmost importance for protecting against a diverse range of potential cyberattacks and maintaining the efficiency of IDSs in interconnected vehicular networks.

- Privacy concerns: Privacy considerations emerge as a significant challenge in the context of FL-enabled IDSs in IoV scenarios. Although the primary purpose of FL is to address the privacy concerns associated with centralized learning methods, FL may still inadvertently disclose information from the training data of individual clients. FL relies on data provided by individual vehicles for the purpose of training models, raising issues concerning user privacy and data confidentiality. Within IoV, vehicles can generate substantial quantities of sensitive data, including location information, driving behavior, and recordings of communication. The central issue revolves around the need to effectively utilize this data for training IDS models while safeguarding the privacy of both vehicle owners and occupants. As a result, there has been a notable surge of interest has occurred in implementing privacy-preserving methodologies in the field of FL [23]. These methodologies include differential privacy techniques, SMPC, and homomorphic encryption. However, using these advanced approaches often entails a trade-off in terms of precision and effectiveness, potentially compromising the IDS's ability to identify attacks. Deploying these advanced methods is necessary to strike a balance between the need for effective intrusion detection, strict privacy requirements, and meeting user expectations. Further research is required to find the optimal balance between privacy and performance to develop efficient IDS methodologies.

- Communication efficiency: Implementing FL-enabled IDSs within IoV introduces a significant challenge in terms of communication efficiency. In IoV scenarios, where vehicles are in constant motion, transmitting substantial amounts of data to train FL models on a central server can strain network bandwidth and result in significant communication overhead. This challenge is further exacerbated by the need for real-time intrusion detection, where rapid responses are crucial. Optimizing communication protocols and data transmission techniques is essential to alleviate the network's burden while ensuring the timely delivery of relevant data to the central server for model updates. Future research in this field is oriented towards developing sophisticated communication-efficient techniques tailored specifically for IoV scenarios. Approaches such as model quantization, edge computing, and strategic data sampling can be leveraged to minimize the volume of transferred data, thereby enhancing communication efficiency. Balancing the requirement for extensive data exchange with the constraints imposed by network bandwidth is essential for the effective implementation of FL-enabled IDSs in dynamic and bandwidth-limited IoV environments. Research efforts also focus on exploring 5G and beyond-5G technologies, which hold the potential to provide increased bandwidth and reduced latency. These advancements can significantly transform the communication landscape of FL-enabled IDSs in IoV.

- Encryption standards: Encryption standards play a significant and multifaceted role in the context of FL-enabled IDSs within IoV. Ensuring the security and privacy of sensitive vehicular data during the transmission process is of paramount importance. The main challenge lies in adopting encryption standards that combine robustness and efficiency to effectively manage the substantial volumes of data transmitted between vehicles and central servers. Moreover, within the FL framework, which entails collaborative model training on various devices, selecting encryption methods that can protect data while preserving the integrity of the collaborative learning process is a complex task [67]. Future advancements in this field primarily focus on developing encryption techniques that successfully reconcile the requirements of security, efficiency, and the necessity for collaborative learning. Research efforts aim to establish standardized encryption protocols tailored specifically for IoV settings. These protocols are intended to ensure data security and integrity while facilitating seamless model updates and promoting collaborative learning within a broad spectrum of vehicular networks.

- Edge computing: Incorporating edge computing into FL-enabled IDSs within IoV introduces both challenges and potential solutions. While local data processing on devices has the potential to alleviate network bandwidth demands, it also brings about issues related to resource limitations and data diversity. IoV devices, often constrained in terms of available resources, face difficulties when attempting to execute computationally intensive FL algorithms on the device itself. Furthermore, ensuring consistency and accuracy in updating models across various vehicles with different hardware configurations and data formats presents a significant challenge. Future research in this domain seeks to enhance the effectiveness of edge computing methodologies, facilitating efficient local data processing and collaborative learning while mitigating the variations in device capabilities. Leveraging edge computing, IDSs empowered by FL in IoV can realize benefits such as reduced communication overhead and improved real-time intrusion detection capabilities [68]. This, in turn, contributes to the establishment of more secure and responsive vehicular networks

- Optimization of Federated Learning and intrusion detection system parameters: FL predominantly relies on deep learning models that involve a diverse set of trainable parameters, which the user can configure. Additionally, IDSs are highly sensitive to these parameters. The next research avenue in FL-enabled IDSs for IoV involves optimizing FL and IDS parameters, as this directly impacts performance and training effectiveness [45]. Given the dynamic and diverse nature of IoV environments, it becomes imperative to identify the most suitable parameters for FL algorithms. This includes determining appropriate learning rates, aggregation methods, and local model parameters. In addition, customizing these parameters for specific intrusion detection tasks and diverse vehicular datasets can significantly improve the performance and accuracy of FL-enabled IDSs [51]. Future research should explore these factors in greater depth, utilizing methodologies such as hyperparameter tuning and adaptive learning algorithms [51]. By optimizing these parameters, researchers can finely tailor FL-enabled IDSs to suit specific IoV scenarios. This optimization process ensures effective collaboration, precise intrusion detection, and minimized communication overhead, ultimately paving the way for the development of more robust and responsive vehicular security systems.

- Heterogeneity and interpretability of the Federated Learning model: In the realm of FL-enabled IDSs for IoV, the heterogeneity and interpretability of FL models are of paramount importance. Heterogeneity stems from the distinct characteristics of vehicular data and the varying capabilities of different vehicles and their sensors. Coordinating multiple models for effective collaboration, especially in real-time intrusion detection, introduces a high degree of complexity. Moreover, prioritizing the interpretability of these models is crucial, as it enables a comprehensive understanding of the rationale behind intrusion alerts. This understanding is valuable for both developers and end-users. Future research endeavors are geared towards developing approaches that harmonize these diverse models, ensuring their seamless integration to enhance intrusion detection accuracy Simultaneously, researchers are dedicated to enhancing the interpretability of FL models through methodologies like explainable AI, which provides insights into the decision-making processes of these models. By effectively addressing these challenges, FL-enabled IDSs in IoV can achieve a state of equilibrium that encompasses various data sources, model interpretability, and efficient intrusion detection. This, in turn, fosters confidence and comprehension among stakeholders in vehicular security.

- Big data management: Effective management of big data poses a significant challenge within the context of FL-enabled IDSs in IoV. The sheer volume, velocity, and diversity of data generated by vehicles require robust storage, processing, and analysis capabilities [69]. The integration of FL-enabled IDSs necessitates the use of extensive data for training and model updates. Efficiently handling this vast amount of data is paramount. The complexity lies in maintaining timely data collection, aggregation, and storage while preserving real-time intrusion detection capabilities, particularly when considering the limited resources of vehicle networks. Future studies will concentrate on creating distributed and scalable storage systems, better data processing algorithms, and advanced data analytics methods. By addressing big data management challenges, FL-enabled IDSs in IoV can harness the wealth of vehicular data efficiently, enhancing the precision and agility of IDSs in dynamic and networked vehicular environments.

- Sparse data: Vehicle data, especially regarding specific types of security threats, can be sparse and unevenly distributed across vehicles. Data sparsity may lead to biased models, as they might not adequately capture certain types of intrusions. Consequently, this limitation can hinder the overall effectiveness of the IDS. Addressing the issue of sparse data requires innovative methodologies, such as data augmentation, imputation approaches, or customized algorithms designed to handle incomplete datasets effectively [70]. Future research efforts aim to develop algorithms that can successfully enable FL models to learn from limited and irregular data. By effectively tackling the issue of sparse data, FL-enabled IDSs in IoV can enhance their precision, ensuring a more comprehensive and nuanced understanding of various intrusion patterns across different vehicular scenarios.

- Stability: Stability is a significant challenge within the context of FL-enabled IDSs in IoV. The inherent instability of the FL process is introduced by the dynamic nature of vehicular networks, characterized by the continuous changes in the composition and positions of vehicles. This variability can potentially disrupt the FL environment, affecting the consistency and accuracy of the IDS models. Maintaining stability requires the implementation of robust systems to address fluctuations in participation rates, network disconnections, and intermittent data availability [69]. Future research aims to develop algorithms that can adapt dynamically to changes in the network, ensuring the stability of FL models, even when confronted with evolving IoV scenarios. By addressing this challenge, FL-enabled IDSs in IoV can consistently perform at a high level, providing reliable capabilities for detecting unauthorized access despite the everchanging characteristics of vehicular networks.

- Reliability: Applications related to intelligent transportation and unmanned aerial vehicle detection demand a high level of reliability due to their safety-critical nature. Failures in meeting reliability standards can lead to severe consequences, including significant loss of life and property. Achieving reliability in the context of intrusion detection within a diverse and dynamic vehicle network presents significant challenges. Maintaining constant and accurate IDS performance is complicated by factors such as network latency, fluctuations in data quality, and the reliability of data transfer from individual vehicles. To ensure reliability, robust FL algorithms are needed to manage data discrepancies, adapt to changing network conditions, and effectively integrate data from diverse vehicles. Moreover, the timely and accurate deployment of intrusion detection solutions depends on the reliability of model updates and communication protocols. Future research aims to enhance the reliability of IDSs in IoV by refining FL algorithms, improving data preprocessing methods, and optimizing communica-

tion protocols. This will ultimately ensure the consistent and reliable operation of FL-enabled IDSs across diverse IoV environments.
- Real-time data: In the context of vehicle environments, responding promptly to security threats is crucial for ensuring passenger safety and network security. Swift and effective intrusion detection relies on processing the substantial volume of real-time data provided by vehicles. The primary challenge lies in developing FL algorithms capable of handling this increased data volume efficiently, with a focus on enabling timely anomaly or intrusion identification. Moreover, optimizing communication protocols to efficiently transmit relevant real-time data to central servers for model updates is of paramount importance. Future research in this area is directed towards creating FL models that combine lightweight characteristics with high-performance capabilities. This involves exploring the use of edge computing for local real-time analysis and improving communication protocols to facilitate seamless and swift sharing of real-time data [68]. By effectively addressing this challenge, the utilization of FL-enabled IDSs in IoV can offer immediate responses to security threats, thereby enhancing the overall safety and security of vehicular networks.

5. Conclusions

When we consider the extensive landscape of IDSs supported by FL in the context of IoV, it becomes abundantly clear that we are on the threshold of a revolutionary era in the field of vehicular network security. This realization is supported by the fact that IoV is the foundation upon which IDSs are constructed. IoV requires a security paradigm that is both resilient and adaptable due to its vast network of interconnected devices and vehicles. With its decentralized approach, Federated Learning has emerged as a beacon, offering a harmonious balance between data privacy and collaborative intelligence. It addresses the growing concerns about data privacy in our hyper-connected world by enabling vehicles to train models locally, ensuring that sensitive data are always retained on the device, thus solving this problem. The aggregation of these local models at a central location produces IDSs that are more accurate and capable of adapting to changing threat land-scapes, while simultaneously tapping into the collective wisdom of the entire network. However, challenges persist, as is expected with any emerging technology. Further research should take into account issues such as scalability, real-time processing demands, and maintaining model correctness across a wide range of vehicle nodes. In this paper, we conducted a well-organized literature review on IDSs based on FL within an IoV environment. We identified the relevant state of the art in FL-based IDSs within the IoV domain, covering the years from FL's inception in 2016 through 2023. Additionally, we introduced a general taxonomy to describe the FL systems, ensuring a coherent structure to guide future research. Finally, drawing upon the literature analysis, we elucidated some of the main challenges and potential directions for future studies in developing IDSs empowered by FL within the IoV context. In conclusion, as IoV continues to rapidly evolve, the interdependence between FL and IDSs will play a crucial role in establishing a vehicular ecosystem that is both secure and resilient, all while also safeguarding privacy.

Author Contributions: J.A.: Conceptualization, Methodology, Analysis, Writing—Original Draft Preparation, Visualization,Validation; K.A.: Supervision, Writing—Review & Editing, Investigation. All authors have read and agreed to the published version of the manuscript.

Funding: This research work was funded by Institutional Fund Projects under grant no. (IFPDP-269-22). Therefore, the authors gratefully acknowledge technical and financial support from Ministry of Education and Deanship of Scientific Research (DSR), King Abdulaziz University (KAU), Jeddah, Saudi Arabia.

Data Availability Statement: Data are contained within the article.

Conflicts of Interest: The authors declare no conflict of interest.

Abbreviations

The following abbreviations are used in this manuscript:

IoV	Internet of Vehicles
IDS	Intrusion Detection System
FL	Federated Learning
IoT	Internet of Things
SMPC	Secure MultiParty Computation
SGD	Stochastic Gradient Descent
DP	Differential Privacy
LDP	Local Differential Privacy
CDP	Central Differential Privacy
non-IID	non-Independent and Identically Distributed
HIDS	Host Intrusion Detection System
NIDS	Network Intrusion Detection System
ML	Machine Learning
DL	Deep Learning
VANETs	Vehicular Ad-hoc Networks
V2V	Vehicle-to-Vehicle
V2I	Vehicle-to-Infrastructure
DoS	Denial-of-Service
LSTM	Long Short-Term Memory
DCNN	Deep Convolutional Neural Network
SVM	Support Vector Machine
RF	Random Forest
FedAvg	Federated Averaging Algorithm
BO	Bayesian Optimization
MLP	Multilayer Perceptron
R2L	Remote to Local
U2R	User to Root
FPR	The False Positive Rate
MMD	Maximum Mean Discrepancy
ED	Energy Distance
NGA	Number Of Global Aggregations
R	Numbers Of Communication Rounds
FL-MAAE	Federated Learning Memory-Augmented Autoencoder
SMC	Secure-Multiparty Computation
UAV	Unmanned Aerial Vehicle

References

1. Alladi, T.; Kohli, V.; Chamola, V.; Yu, F.R. Securing the internet of vehicles: A deep learning-based classification framework. *IEEE Netw. Lett.* **2021**, *3*, 94–97. [CrossRef]
2. Ji, B.; Zhang, X.; Mumtaz, S.; Han, C.; Li, C.; Wen, H.; Wang, D. Survey on the internet of vehicles: Network architectures and applications. *IEEE Commun. Stand. Mag.* **2020**, *4*, 34–41. [CrossRef]
3. Garg, T.; Kagalwalla, N.; Churi, P.; Pawar, A.; Deshmukh, S. A survey on security and privacy issues in IoV. *Int. J. Electr. Comput. Eng.* **2020**, *5*, 2088–8708. [CrossRef]
4. Zavvos, E.; Gerding, E.H.; Yazdanpanah, V.; Maple, C.; Stein, S. Privacy and Trust in the Internet of Vehicles. *IEEE Trans. Intell. Transp. Syst.* **2021**, *23*, 10126–10141. [CrossRef]
5. Bevish Jinila, Y.; Merlin Sheeba, G.; Prayla Shyry, S. PPSA: Privacy preserved and secured architecture for internet of vehicles. *Wirel. Pers. Commun.* **2021**, *118*, 3271–3288. [CrossRef]
6. Peng, R.; Li, W.; Yang, T.; Huafeng, K. An internet of vehicles intrusion detection system based on a convolutional neural network. In Proceedings of the 2019 IEEE Intl Conferences on Parallel & Distributed Processing with Applications, Big Data & Cloud Computing, Sustainable Computing & Communications, Social Computing & Networking (ISPA/BDCloud/SocialCom/SustainCom), Xiamen, China, 16–18 December 2019; pp. 1595–1599.
7. Gasmi, R.; Aliouat, M. Vehicular ad hoc networks versus internet of vehicles-a comparative view. In Proceedings of the 2019 International Conference on Networking and Advanced Systems (ICNAS), Annaba, Algeria, 26–27 June 2019; pp. 1–6.
8. Indu, S.K. Internet of Vehicles (IoV): Evolution, Architecture, Security Issues and Trust Aspects. *Int. J. Recent Technol. Eng. (IJRTE)* **2019**, *7*, 260–280.

9. Fu, W.; Xin, X.; Guo, P.; Zhou, Z. A practical intrusion detection system for Internet of vehicles. *China Commun.* **2016**, *13*, 263–275. [CrossRef]
10. Sherazi, H.H.R.; Iqbal, R.; Ahmad, F.; Khan, Z.A.; Chaudary, M.H. DDoS attack detection: A key enabler for sustainable communication in internet of vehicles. *Sustain. Comput. Inform. Syst.* **2019**, *23*, 13–20. [CrossRef]
11. Bagga, P.; Das, A.K.; Wazid, M.; Rodrigues, J.J.; Park, Y. Authentication protocols in internet of vehicles: Taxonomy, analysis, and challenges. *IEEE Access* **2020**, *8*, 54314–54344. [CrossRef]
12. Osibo, B.K.; Zhang, C.; Xia, C.; Zhao, G.; Jin, Z. Security and privacy in 5G internet of vehicles (IoV) environment. *J. Internet Things* **2021**, *3*, 77. [CrossRef]
13. Abbasi, S.; Rahmani, A.M.; Balador, A.; Sahafi, A. Internet of Vehicles: Architecture, services, and applications. *Int. J. Commun. Syst.* **2020**, *34*, e4793. [CrossRef]
14. El Madani, S.; Motahhir, S.; El Ghzizal, A. Internet of vehicles: Concept, process, security aspects and solutions. *Multimed. Tools Appl.* **2022**, *81*, 16563–16587. [CrossRef]
15. Seth, I.; Guleria, K.; Panda, S.N.; Anand, D.; Alsubhi, K.; Aljahdali, H.M.; Singh, A. A taxonomy and analysis on Internet of Vehicles: Architectures, protocols, and challenges. *Wirel. Commun. Mob. Comput.* **2022**, *2022*, 9232784. [CrossRef]
16. Driss, M.; Almomani, I.; e Huma, Z.; Ahmad, J. A federated learning framework for cyberattack detection in vehicular sensor networks. *Complex Intell. Syst.* **2022**, *8*, 4221–4235. [CrossRef]
17. Sharma, N.; Chauhan, N.; Chand, N. Security challenges in Internet of Vehicles (IoV) environment. In Proceedings of the 2018 First International Conference on Secure Cyber Computing and Communication (ICSCCC), Jalandhar, India, 15–17 December 2018; pp. 203–207.
18. Hu, Q.; Fan, X.; Shan, A.; Wang, Z. Sybil attack detection method based on timestamp-chain in Internet of vehicles. In Proceedings of the 2021 IEEE International Conference on Smart Internet of Things (SmartIoT), Jeju, Republic of Korea, 13–15 August 2021; pp. 174–178.
19. Li, Q.; Wen, Z.; Wu, Z.; Hu, S.; Wang, N.; Li, Y.; Liu, X.; He, B. A survey on federated learning systems: Vision, hype and reality for data privacy and protection. *IEEE Trans. Knowl. Data Eng.* **2021**, *35*, 3347–3366. [CrossRef]
20. Konečný, J.; McMahan, H.B.; Yu, F.X.; Richtárik, P.; Suresh, A.T.; Bacon, D. Federated learning: Strategies for improving communication efficiency. *arXiv* **2016**, arXiv:1610.05492.
21. Kairouz, P.; McMahan, H.B.; Avent, B.; Bellet, A.; Bennis, M.; Bhagoji, A.N.; Bonawitz, K.; Charles, Z.; Cormode, G.; Cummings, R.; et al. Advances and open problems in federated learning. *Found. Trends Mach. Learn.* **2021**, *14*, 1–210. [CrossRef]
22. Qiang, Y.; Liu, Y.; Chen, T.; Tong, Y. Federated machine learning: Concept and applications. *ACM Trans. Intell. Syst. Technol. (TIST)* **2019**, *10*, 1–19.
23. Ruzafa-Alcázar, P.; Fernández-Saura, P.; Mármol-Campos, E.; González-Vidal, A.; Hernández-Ramos, J.L.; Bernal-Bernabe, J.; Skarmeta, A.F. Intrusion detection based on privacy-preserving federated learning for the industrial IoT. *IEEE Trans. Ind. Inform.* **2021**, *19*, 1145–1154. [CrossRef]
24. Shejwalkar, V.V. Quantifying and Enhancing the Security of Federated Learning. 2023. Available online: https://www.cics.umass.edu/event/20230426/quantifying-and-strengthening-security-federated-learning (accessed on 6 September 2023).
25. Fedorchenko, E.; Novikova, E.; Shulepov, A. Comparative review of the intrusion detection systems based on federated learning: Advantages and open challenges. *Algorithms* **2022**, *15*, 247. [CrossRef]
26. Alazab, M.; RM, S.P.; Parimala, M.; Maddikunta, P.K.R.; Gadekallu, T.R.; Pham, Q.V. Federated learning for cybersecurity: Concepts, challenges, and future directions. *IEEE Trans. Ind. Inform.* **2021**, *18*, 3501–3509. [CrossRef]
27. Belenguer, A.; Navaridas, J.; Pascual, J.A. A review of federated learning in intrusion detection systems for iot. *arXiv* **2022**, arXiv:2204.12443.
28. Sattler, F.; Wiedemann, S.; Müller, K.L.; Samek, W. Robust and communication-efficient federated learning from non-iid data. *IEEE Trans. Neural Netw. Learn. Syst.* **2019**, *31*, 3400–3413. [CrossRef] [PubMed]
29. Aledhari, M.; Razzak, R.; Parizi, R.M.; Saeed, F. Federated learning: A survey on enabling technologies, protocols, and applications. *IEEE Access* **2020**, *8*, 140699–140725. [CrossRef] [PubMed]
30. Sittijuk, P.; Tamee, K. Performance measurement of federated learning on imbalanced data. In Proceedings of the 2021 18th International Joint Conference on Computer Science and Software Engineering (JCSSE), Virtual, 30 June–3 July 2021; pp. 1–6.
31. Moshawrab, M.; Adda, M.; Bouzouane, A.; Ibrahim, H.; Raad, A. Reviewing Federated Learning Aggregation Algorithms; Strategies, Contributions, Limitations and Future Perspectives. *Electronics* **2023**, *12*, 2287. [CrossRef]
32. Li, T.; Sahu, A.K.; Zaheer, M.; Sanjabi, M.; Talwalkar, A.; Smith, V. Federated optimization in heterogeneous networks. *Proc. Mach. Learn. Syst.* **2020**, *2*, 429–450.
33. Prakash, S.; Avestimehr, A.S. Mitigating byzantine attacks in federated learning. *arXiv* **2020**, arXiv:2010.07541.
34. Rodríguez-Barroso, N.; Jiménez-López, D.; Luzón, M.V.; Herrera, F.; Martínez-Cámara, E. Survey on federated learning threats: Concepts, taxonomy on attacks and defences, experimental study and challenges. *Inf. Fusion* **2023**, *90*, 148–173. [CrossRef]
35. El Ouadrhiri, A.; Abdelhadi, A. Differential privacy for deep and federated learning: A survey. *IEEE Access* **2022**, *10*, 22359–22380. [CrossRef]
36. Liu, J.; Huang, J.; Zhou, Y.; Li, X.; Ji, S.; Xiong, H.; Dou, D. From distributed machine learning to federated learning: A survey. *Knowl. Inf. Syst.* **2022**, *64*, 885–917. [CrossRef]

37. Li, T.; Sahu, A.K.; Talwalkar, A.; Smith, V. Federated learning: Challenges, methods, and future directions. *IEEE Signal Process. Mag.* **2020**, *37*, 50–60. [CrossRef]
38. Mammen, P.M. Federated learning: Opportunities and challenges. *arXiv* **2021**, arXiv:2101.05428.
39. Huang, C.; Huang, J.; Liu, X. Cross-silo federated learning: Challenges and opportunities. *arXiv* **2022**, arXiv:2206.12949.
40. Wang, S.; Tuor, T.; Salonidis, T.; Leung, K.K.; Makaya, C.; He, T.; Chan, K. Adaptive federated learning in resource constrained edge computing systems. *IEEE J. Sel. Areas Commun.* **2019**, *37*, 1205–1221. [CrossRef]
41. Kholod, I.; Yanaki, E.; Fomichev, D.; Shalugin, E.; Novikova, E.; Filippov, E.; Nordlund, M. Open-source federated learning frameworks for IoT: A comparative review and analysis. *Sensors* **2020**, *21*, 167. [CrossRef] [PubMed]
42. Jamali-Rad, H.; Abdizadeh, M.; Singh, A. Federated learning with taskonomy for non-IID data. *IEEE Trans. Neural Netw. Learn. Syst.* **2022**, *34*, 8719–8730. [CrossRef] [PubMed]
43. Tan, A.Z.; Yu, H.; Cui, L.; Yang, Q. Towards personalized federated learning. *IEEE Trans. Neural Netw. Learn. Syst.* **2022**, *34*, 9587–9603. [CrossRef] [PubMed]
44. Huong, T.T.; Bac, T.P.; Ha, K.N.; Hoang, N.V.; Hoang, N.X.; Hung, N.T.; Tran, K.P. Federated learning-based explainable anomaly detection for industrial control systems. *IEEE Access* **2022**, *10*, 53854–53872. [CrossRef]
45. Agrawal, S.; Sarkar, S.; Aouedi, O.; Yenduri, G.; Piamrat, K.; Alazab, M.; Bhattacharya, S.; Maddikunta, P.K.R.; Gadekallu, T.R. Federated learning for intrusion detection system: Concepts, challenges and future directions. *Comput. Commun.* **2022**, *195*, 346–361. [CrossRef]
46. Rashid, M.M.; Khan, S.U.; Eusufzai, F.; Redwan, M.A.; Sabuj, S.R.; Elsharief, M. A Federated Learning-Based Approach for Improving Intrusion Detection in Industrial Internet of Things Networks. *Network* **2023**, *3*, 158–179. [CrossRef]
47. Xing, L.; Wang, K.; Wu, H.; Ma, H.; Zhang, X. FL-MAAE: An Intrusion Detection Method for the Internet of Vehicles Based on Federated Learning and Memory-Augmented Autoencoder. *Electronics* **2023**, *12*, 2284. [CrossRef]
48. Amanullah, M.A.; Loke, S.W.; Chhetri, M.B.; Doss, R. A Taxonomy and Analysis of Misbehaviour Detection in Cooperative Intelligent Transport Systems: A Systematic Review. *ACM Comput. Surv.* **2023**, *56*, 1–38. [CrossRef]
49. Rani, P.; Sharma, C.; Ramesh, J.V.N.; Verma, S.; Sharma, R.; Alkhayyat, A.; Kumar, S. Federated Learning-Based Misbehaviour Detection for the 5G-Enabled Internet of Vehicles. *IEEE Trans. Consum. Electron.* **2023**. [CrossRef]
50. Hosseinzadeh, M.; Hemmati, A.; Rahmani, A.M. Federated learning-based IoT: A systematic literature review. *Int. J. Commun. Syst.* **2022**, *35*, e5185. [CrossRef]
51. Lavaur, L.; Pahl, M.-O.; Busnel, Y.; Autrel, F. The evolution of federated learning-based intrusion detection and mitigation: A survey. *IEEE Trans. Netw. Serv. Manag.* **2022**, *19*, 2309–2332. [CrossRef]
52. Yang, J.; Hu, J.; Yu, T. Federated AI-enabled in-vehicle network intrusion detection for internet of vehicles. *Electronics* **2022**, *11*, 3658. [CrossRef]
53. Uprety, A.; Rawat, D.B.; Li, J. Privacy preserving misbehavior detection in IoV using federated machine learning. In Proceedings of the 2021 IEEE 18th Annual Consumer Communications & Networking Conference (CCNC), Las Vegas, NV, USA, 9–12 January 2021; pp. 1–6.
54. Hbaieb, A.; Ayed, S.; Chaari, L. Federated learning based IDS approach for the IoV. In Proceedings of the 17th International Conference on Availability, Reliability and Security, Vienna, Austria, 23–26 August 2022; pp. 1–6.
55. Boualouache, A.; Brik, B.; Senouci, S.-M.; Engel, T. On-Demand Security Framework for 5GB Vehicular Networks. *IEEE Internet Things Mag.* **2023**, *6*, 26–31. [CrossRef]
56. Vinita, L.J.; Vetriselvi, V. Federated Learning-based Misbehaviour detection on an emergency message dissemination scenario for the 6G-enabled Internet of Vehicles. *Hoc Netw.* **2023**, *144*, 103153. [CrossRef]
57. Aliyu, I.; Feliciano, M.C.; Van Engelenburg, S.; Kim, D.O.; Lim, C.G. A Blockchain-Based Federated Forest for SDN-Enabled In-Vehicle Network Intrusion Detection System. *IEEE Access* **2021**, *9*, 102593–102608. [CrossRef]
58. Zainudin, A.; Akter, R.; Kim, D.-S.; Lee, J.-M. FedIoV: A Federated Learning-Assisted Intrusion Messages Detection in Internet of Vehicles. 2022; pp. 305–306. Available online: https://www.dbpia.co.kr/Journal/articleDetail?nodeId=NODE11197063 (accessed on 6 October 2023).
59. Yu, T.; Hua, G.; Wang, H.; Yang, J.; Hu, J. Federated-lstm based network intrusion detection method for intelligent connected vehicles. In Proceedings of the ICC 2022-IEEE International Conference on Communications, Seoul, Republic of Korea, 16–20 May 2022; pp. 4324–4329.
60. Taslimasa, H.; Dadkhah, S.; Neto, E.C.P.; Xiong, P.; Iqbal, S.; Ray, S.; Ghorbani, A.A. ImageFed: Practical Privacy Preserving Intrusion Detection System for In-Vehicle CAN Bus Protocol. In Proceedings of the 2023 IEEE 9th Intl Conference on Big Data Security on Cloud (BigDataSecurity), IEEE Intl Conference on High Performance and Smart Computing, (HPSC) and IEEE Intl Conference on Intelligent Data and Security (IDS), New York, NY, USA, 6–8 May 2023; pp. 122–129.
61. Xu, Q.; Zhang, L.; Ou, D.; Yu, W. Secure Intrusion Detection by Differentially Private Federated Learning for Inter-Vehicle Networks. *Transp. Res. Rec.* **2023**, *2677*, 421–437. [CrossRef]
62. Korba, A.A.; Boualouache, A.; Brik, B.; Rahal, R.; Ghamri-Doudane, Y.; Senouci, S.M. Federated Learning for Zero-Day Attack Detection in 5G and Beyond V2X Networks. In AlgoTel 2023-25èmes Rencontres Francophones sur les Aspects Algorithmiques des Télécommunications. 2023. Available online: https://hal.science/hal-04087452/ (accessed on 22 September 2023).
63. Aliyu, I.; Engelenburg, S.V.; Mu'Azu, M.B.; Kim, J.; Lim, C.G. Statistical Detection of Adversarial Examples in Blockchain-Based Federated Forest In-Vehicle Network Intrusion Detection Systems. *IEEE Access* **2022**, *10*, 109366–109384. [CrossRef]

64. Sebastian, A. Enhancing Intrusion Detection in Internet of Vehicles Through Federated Learning. *arXiv* **2023**, arXiv:2311.13800.
65. Campos, E.M.; Saura, P.F.; González-Vidal, A.; Hernández-Ramos, J.L.; Bernabé, J.B ; Baldini, G.; Skarmeta, A. Evaluating Federated Learning for intrusion detection in Internet of Things: Review and challenges. *Comput. Netw.* **2022**, *203*, 108661. [CrossRef]
66. Billah, M.; Mehedi, S.T.; Anwar, A.; Rahman, Z.; Islam, R. A systematic literature review on blockchain enabled federated learning framework for internet of vehicles. *arXiv* **2022**, arXiv:2203.05192.
67. Duy, P.T.; Hao, H.N.; Chu, H.M.; Pham, V.H. A Secure and Privacy Preserving Federated Learning Approach for IoT Intrusion Detection System. In Proceedings of the Network and System Security: 15th International Conference, NSS 2021, Tianjin, China, 23 October 2021; Springer International Publishing: Berlin/Heidelberg, Germany, 2021; pp. 353–368.
68. Duan, Q.; Huang, J.; Hu, S.; Deng, R.; Lu, Z.; Yu, S. Combining Federated Learning and Edge Computing Toward Ubiquitous Intelligence in 6G Network: Challenges, Recent Advances, and Future Directions. *IEEE Commun. Surv. Tutor.* **2023**, *25*, 2892–2950. [CrossRef]
69. Danba, S.; Bao, J.; Han, G.; Guleng, S.; Wu, C. Toward collaborative intelligence in IoV systems: Recent advances and open issues. *Sensors* **2022**, *22*, 6995. [CrossRef]
70. Thonglek, K.; Takahashi, K.; Ichikawa, K.; Nakasan, C.; Leelaprute, P.; Iida, H. Sparse communication for federated learning. In Proceedings of the 2022 IEEE 6th International Conference on Fog and Edge Computing (ICFEC), Messina, Italy, 16–19 May 2022; pp. 1–8.

Disclaimer/Publisher's Note: The statements, opinions and data contained in all publications are solely those of the individual author(s) and contributor(s) and not of MDPI and/or the editor(s). MDPI and/or the editor(s) disclaim responsibility for any injury to people or property resulting from any ideas, methods, instructions or products referred to in the content.

MDPI AG
Grosspeteranlage 5
4052 Basel
Switzerland
Tel.: +41 61 683 77 34

Future Internet Editorial Office
E-mail: futureinternet@mdpi.com
www.mdpi.com/journal/futureinternet

Disclaimer/Publisher's Note: The title and front matter of this reprint are at the discretion of the Guest Editors. The publisher is not responsible for their content or any associated concerns. The statements, opinions and data contained in all individual articles are solely those of the individual Editors and contributors and not of MDPI. MDPI disclaims responsibility for any injury to people or property resulting from any ideas, methods, instructions or products referred to in the content.

www.ingramcontent.com/pod-product-compliance
Lightning Source LLC
LaVergne TN
LVHW070148100526
838202LV00015B/1912